THOMSON

OURSE TECHNOLOGY

ofessional ■ Trade ■ Reference

D0690319

inspired
3D SHORT FILM PRODUCTION

by
Jeremy Cantor
Pepe Valencia

Foreword by
BILL KROYER
Animation Director,
ACADEMY AWARD® nominee

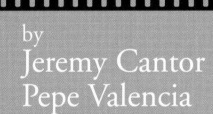

emier
ess

Series Editors
Michael Ford and Kyle Clark

SVP, Thomson Course Technology PTR: Andy Shafran

Publisher: Stacy L. Hiquet

Senior Marketing Manager: Sarah O'Donnell

Marketing Manager: Heather Hurley

Manager of Editorial Services: Heather Talbot

Senior Acquisitions Editor: Kevin Harreld

Senior Editor: Mark Garvey

Associate Marketing Managers: Kristin Eisenzopf and Sarah Dubois

Project Editor/Copy Editor: Cathleen D. Snyder

Technical Reviewer: Mike Ford

Thomson Course Technology PTR Market Coordinator: Amanda Weaver

Interior Layout Tech: Bill Hartman

Cover Designer: Mike Tanamachi

Indexer: Kelly Talbot

Proofreader: Kim V. Benbow

ISBN: 1-59200-117-3

Library of Congress Catalog Card Number: 2003112929

Printed in the United States of America

06 07 08 BU 10 9 8 7 6 5 4 3

THOMSON

COURSE TECHNOLOGY

Professional ■ Trade ■ Reference

Thomson Course Technology PTR, a division of Thomson Course Technology

25 Thomson Place ■ Boston, MA 02210 ■ http://www.courseptr.com

To my lovely wife, Tanya, for her
inspiration, support, and patience
—JC

To Cristina, my beautiful wife,
and Nilo, my beloved son
—PV

Foreword

As a short-films Oscar nominee and a member of the Executive Board of the Short Films/Animation Branch of the Motion Picture Academy, I'm often invited to festivals and panels related to short films. At one such panel in the heart of Hollywood, I was asked a straightforward question: Why bother to make a short film if there's no chance of making money on it?

Good question, if the only thing that's important to you is making money. Is anything else important to you in your life? How about fun? Creativity? Imagination? Emotions? How about *art*?

I think the animated film is just about the greatest art form yet devised. I can back that with the following argument: Animation uses and expands upon almost every other art form, including drawing, painting, sculpture, acting, dance, photography, and cinematography, as well as architectural, costume, and set design, to name a few. But most significantly, animation allows all of these art forms and the very world they exist in to be completely created by the artist.

The definition of the word "animation" contains perhaps the art form's greatest allure. The word means "to give life to." Jeremy Cantor and Pepe Valencia describe it in this book as the magic moment. When the character you have created moves, speaks, and appears to think, feel, and be alive, you will experience a feeling that is magical. It is, well…God-like. It is the feeling that has kept a lot of us hooked on the art form from the day our first pencil test talked back at us from the screen.

Pencil test—ah, the good old days when animation was hand-drawn. This book describes a production process that could be, if you so choose, pencil-free. Although techniques constantly evolve, story and characters will always be the heart of the medium. That's why the short film is not some junior brother to the feature film. It's not a stepping stone to something bigger.

At the Motion Picture Academy, we are passionate about the principle that the short film is as vital and powerful as any form of filmmaking. Some ideas should be stated in three minutes; that's the right length for that idea.

The average Hollywood feature film screenplay has 17,000 words, and 99 percent of them are deservedly forgettable. It took only 224 words to express the most eloquent and poetic vision of democracy ever written (the Gettysburg Address), and people have been comforted and inspired for 2,000 years by the 114 words of the Twenty-Third Psalm.

Truly, in art, size does not matter.

Find the right story to tell, tell it well, and you can entertain people. You can change minds. You can change the world.

Incidentally, for the fellow in Hollywood who asked the question at the panel, you can make *some* money. There are festival awards, TV rights, and film compilations that get theatrical distribution. A lot of filmmakers sell their films as DVDs directly over the Internet. These days, because no business is booming faster than CG animation, a good animated short film is almost a guarantee of a job offer from the studios.

And yes, the short film can be a stepping stone to feature films, and has been the direct path for the likes of John Lasseter (*Tin Toy* to *Toy Story*), Nick Park (*Wallace & Gromit* to *Chicken Run*), Chris Wedge (*Bunny* to *Ice Age*), and yours truly (*Technological Threat* to *FernGully: The Last Rainforest*)!

Success is wonderful, audience response is a thrill, and critical acclaim is nice, but please take my advice: Don't make a film for those reasons. Make it because you have something to say, a vision that no one else in the world alive now or evermore will see exactly as you see it.

As Jeremy and Pepe teach you in this book, the tools are available as never before to bring your vision to life. That is the magic moment. Give life to a work of art and it's a great feeling, a special feeling, a feeling that money can't buy. Do your best, have fun, and enjoy what you have made. That's the best kind of success, the kind no one can take from you.

Good Luck. Now get started!

—Bill Kroyer

About Bill Kroyer

Bill Kroyer is an award-winning director of animation and computer graphics commercials, short films, movie titles, and theatrical films. Trained in classic hand-drawn animation at the Disney Studio, Bill was one of the first animators to make the leap to computer animation as Computer Image Choreographer on Disney's groundbreaking 1982 feature, *TRON*. Founding his own company, Kroyer Films, Inc., Bill and his wife Susan pioneered the technique of combining hand-drawn animation with computer animation. Bill was director of such projects as his Academy Award-nominated short film, *Technological Threat* (see Figure I.1), and the theatrical animated feature film, *FernGully, The Last Rainforest.* He is currently Senior Animation Director at Rhythm & Hues Studios in Los Angeles, where he recently served as Animation Director on Fox Studio's feature, *Garfield*, and Warner Bros.' summer hit, *Scooby-Doo*. He supervised animation on the photo-real CG animals in Warner Bros.' *Cats and Dogs* and the dinosaurs in Universal Pictures' *The Flintstones in Viva Rock Vegas*, and he has directed commercials for Novell, AT&T, and the Coca-Cola Polar Bears. Bill's animation has won awards at festivals all over the world. He serves on the Executive Board of the Animation Branch of the Academy of Motion Picture Arts and Sciences.

Figure I.1
Bill Kroyer's Oscar-nominated short, *Technological Threat*

Acknowledgments

First of all, I'd like to thank the (more than 135) CG artists and filmmakers who graciously contributed screenshots, production artwork, documents, and videos to this endeavor. The incredible collection of imagery we were able to assemble is nothing short of amazing. Special thanks to Tonya Noerr and Morgan Kelly for their excellent case study chapters. Thanks to Kevin Johnson, Sande Scoredos, and Jim McCampbell for their insightful interviews. And Bill Kroyer deserves special recognition for miraculously agreeing to write such a perfectly appropriate and inspirational foreword on such short notice.

I would also like to thank our project editor, Cathleen Snyder, and our acquisitions editor, Kevin Harreld, for pushing just hard enough.

Thanks also to my family for their eternal support, and especially to Mom, Dad, Janice, and Mike for not pulling any punches when they read and critiqued my early chapters.

Thanks, of course, to my wife, Tanya, for her love and understanding.

Thanks also to my students at CalArts, for unwittingly serving as guinea pigs for many of the ideas and lessons presented in this book.

Thanks to my partner, Pepe, for his unwavering energy and enthusiasm.

And finally, I'd like to thank Mike Ford and Kyle Clark for thinking of me in the first place.

—JC

I continue to feel immensely blessed for having known and worked with Jeremy Cantor. My heartfelt thanks to Isaac Kerlow for his expertise and motivating words. Deep thanks to Hun Chung (Diego), who contributed immeasurably with his tireless spirit and extraordinary enthusiasm. Special thanks also to Alex Sokoloff, my "best man" as always, for being receptive, responsive, and wonderfully real.

Also, I would like to express gratitude to my colleagues at Imageworks, especially to Ivo Horvat, Luis Labrador, Sergio Garcia Abad, and Dan Ziegler for their help.

Warm thanks to Ivo Kos for always being there when I need him.

I would also like to thank Didier Levy, Raquel Morales, Ferran Piquer, Rafael Castelblanco, Sebastian Sylvan, Marcos Fajardo, and all my old theater company pals for their friendship.

Many ideas in this book grew from teaching relationships at CalArts, from past and present students who regularly fed me with energy, wit, and intellect. I also benefited greatly from working with the Director of the Computer Animation Labs, Michael Scroggins—thanks for your humor and talent during our night classes.

Much love to my extended family, Antonio Rodriguez and Pina, Franco, Diego, Tata, and Laura Capitanio.

Finally, I want to thank my family—my mother, Magdalena, who has taught me since I was kid to believe, and my sisters, Rocio and Mari Cruz, for their love and encouragement across the sea and across all worlds.

—PV

About the Authors

Jeremy Cantor, Animation Supervisor at Sony Pictures Imageworks, has been working far too many hours a week as a character/creature animator and supervisor in the feature film industry for the past decade or so at both Imageworks and Tippett Studio in Berkeley, California. His film credits include *Harry Potter, Evolution, Hollowman, My Favorite Martian*, and *Starship Troopers*. Before entering the movie biz, he spent several years doing all manner of art and animation at varying levels of seniority in the video game industry, which included directing the animation on the award-winning digital "petz" project, *Catz*. Prior to that, he paid the rent as a freelance illustrator and storyboard artist. Jeremy has had two short films featured in touring animation festivals, and his latest CG short, *Squaring Off*, is featured in the DVD collection, "North America's Best Animated Shorts." In addition to his current part-time stint teaching CG character animation at the California Institute of the Arts in Valencia, Jeremy has also taught classes and presented lectures at venues such as The Art Academy of Los Angeles, Massachusetts Institute of Technology, Gnomon School of Visual Effects, The American Film Institute, The Academy of Art College in San Francisco, and various SIGGRAPH and ASIFA events. Jeremy recently completed his duties as the Art and Animation Director for Full Spectrum Warrior, a console-based training simulation project for the U.S. Army, on which he was responsible for all visual assets and animation-related tools programming. Currently, he is supervising the animation on Wes Craven's upcoming werewolf film, *Cursed*. For more information, go to http://www.zayatz.com.

Pepe Valencia has been at Sony Pictures Imageworks since 1996. In addition to working as an animation supervisor on the feature film *Peter Pan*, his credits include *Early Bloomer, Charlie's Angels: Full Throttle, Stuart Little 2, Harry Potter and the Sorcerer's Stone, Stuart Little, Hollowman, Godzilla*, and *Starship Troopers*. Before joining Sony, he worked at Cinesite as a Technical Director on *Space Jam* and previously spent five years at a number of smaller production houses in New York and Madrid. His work has been shown at SIGGRAPH '90, Imagina '92, Art Futura '92, and Cannes '94. He served as a jury member for the 2001 ASIFA Annie Awards in the Short Animated Films competition and has written articles for Cinevideo 20 and Campaña. He has lectured at the Reina Sofia Art Center, the Universidad Complutense de Madrid, and Virtuality 2003 in Torino. Pepe co-created a DVD detailing the art of previsualization for Alias/Wavefront. He has taught Maya master classes in Seoul and San Diego and animation classes at the Gnomon School of Visual Effects. Pepe studied computer animation at Pratt Institute and has a breadth of experience in the visual and dramatic arts, including five years with the Spanish theater company T.E.C. Pepe currently teaches the Digital Short Workshop at California Institute of the Arts. For more information, go to his Web page at http://www.pepe3d.com.

Contents at a Glance

Contents

Contents

xvii

Introduction

Everybody loves a good story. Whether listening, viewing, reading, writing, telling, or showing, most of us regularly find ourselves participating in the storytelling process as an entertaining, educational, and time-honored pastime.

As audience members, we spend a fair amount of our daily lives watching movies and TV shows; reading books; and listening to our friends, teachers, students, and loved ones spin yarns about their past experiences and future plans.

> "Begin at the beginning, and go on till you come to the end: then stop."
> *Alice in Wonderland*

As storytellers, we often weave imaginative and dramatic tales of near fact or outright fiction in the interest of entertaining or inspiring others, and occasionally we use our narrative creativity to bend the truth to get ourselves out of trouble. We recount our weekend festivities to our coworkers on Monday mornings. We invent excuses for late homework assignments. We create elaborate rationalizations for running stop signs. We read, augment, and modify fairy tales for our children at bedtime.

Stories can be recited, written, or performed. And ever since the earliest man scrawled images of his hunting triumphs on his cavern walls, *visual* storytelling has been a popular and effective tool for narrative expression (see Figure I.2).

If one agrees that a picture is worth a thousand words, then a motion picture running at 24 (or 30) frames per second must be perhaps the most effective storytelling instrument available. The medium of animation expands upon cinema's storytelling potential even further by widening the opportunities for invention, exaggeration, fantasy, and style variation because, in animation, anything is possible.

Animated shorts are more popular than ever these days. And with the ever-increasing availability of 3D CG tools, the home PC, rather than the pencil, is becoming the preferred tool for creating this art form.

3D animated shorts are premiering before feature films, introducing video games, headlining festivals, and winning awards all over the world. And as CG hardware and software tools are continuing to increase in power and decrease in price, digital desktop filmmakers are finding a new, powerfully efficient, and extremely flexible medium for bringing their story ideas to life.

Figure I.2
Stories can be recited, written, performed, or told through pictures.

When you, the artist, student, hobbyist, or professional, originally decided to become a contributor to the world of filmmaking or computer graphics, you were likely manifesting a desire to tell stories. And while many artists, animators, and technicians are content to spend their careers contributing their skills to large, collaborative film projects for which their individual shot assignments are mere subsets of someone else's cinematic vision, we are assuming that you have stories of your own to tell.

If that assumption is correct, then this book is for you. We hope to provide you, the budding desktop filmmaker, with the necessary inspiration, examples, and pipeline suggestions to help you turn your story ideas into reality through the medium of the 3D animated CG short.

Structure of This Book

Inspired 3D Short Film Production is broken up into four areas, each one dealing with a different phase of a typical production cycle.

- **Development.** This covers the initial planning stages, including story development, character design, art direction, and storyboarding.
- **Pre-production.** This is where the digital elements that will be included in your film are planned, created, and assembled. This section includes chapters on schedules and budgets, dialogue, 2D and 3D animatics, CG modeling, texturing, and character setup.
- **Shot production.** This focuses on your actual production pipeline, from animation to lighting, rendering, FX, and compositing.
- **Post-production.** This deals with the wrap-up phase, which includes audio, final editing, titles, and marketing.

This book will walk you through the process of creating a 3D animated short by breaking down the steps along one possible digital pipeline into individual chapters in which the concepts and techniques of the topic are discussed and demonstrated by way of general theories, examples, suggested exercises, case studies, and occasional interviews with short-film directors and various industry specialists. Each chapter will cover a different aspect of the short film creation process, from early development to post-production (see Figure I.3).

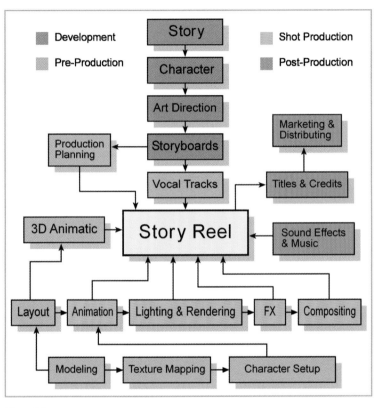

Inspired 3D Short Film Production pipeline

In our suggested production pipeline, you begin with a story, character designs, and preliminary look-development to determine the overall visual style of your film. Then storyboard panels are drawn so you can start working out the structure and pacing of your story in visual terms, including basic shot staging and continuity issues. Once you are confident that your story will work as a film, you will plan your production with regard to equipment, staffing, budgets, and schedules to ensure a smooth and successful filmmaking experience.

The next step is to introduce the concept of an editorial department, where you will use a piece of non-linear editing software to initiate the production of a story reel, which will act as an evolving template upon which your film will grow. This story reel begins as a 2D *animatic*—a filmstrip of storyboard images; held for story-appropriate durations; and synched to any necessary temporary or final dialogue, narration, sound effects, or music tracks. Then your story reel will be upgraded to a 3D animatic, where you will replace your held storyboard images with rough CG layout versions of your shots, which add dimensionality, basic positioning and movement of scene elements, and camera direction.

The next step is to model, texture, and rig your digital objects and characters so you can officially enter the shot-production stage. Then animation begins, where you refine the movements of your digital objects; breathe life into your character puppets through body language, facial expressions, and lip-synching; and replace the basic shot layouts in your story reel with final animation passes. You will also add any necessary effects animation and then light, render, and possibly composite each shot until you can insert final imagery into your story reel. Then you add sound effects, music, titles, and credits, and finally you are ready to duplicate, distribute, and market your film so that the world can experience your completed cinematic masterpiece.

Because the topic of each individual chapter in this book warrants an entire volume dedicated to its particular subject, *Inspired 3D Short Film Production* will be wide rather than deep. The chapters will offer general overviews rather than comprehensive or software-specific discussions on each topic; therefore, we will assume that you possess a reasonable level of proficiency with a piece of CG software, such as Maya or 3D Studio MAX, and a non-linear editing package, such as Adobe Premiere or Final Cut Pro.

Keep in mind that the order of the chapters in this book represents just one possible development pipeline and should not be considered the only way to structure your production. For instance, we have chosen to discuss music toward the end of the production process. However, you might choose to use a piece of music as the driving force for the flow of your narrative. You might prefer to begin your story development process by drawing thumbnails instead of actually writing out a script. You might want to forego storyboarding and pre-visualization completely and just make up your camera direction and transitions as you go along.

Furthermore, the size and skills of your team can significantly affect the way you structure your production. If you are working alone, you might want to complete your shots sequentially. If you are working with a crew, you might find it advantageous to distribute individual sequences or characters to different team members. If your crew is made up of artists with specialized skills, you'll schedule your production very differently than you would if you had a team of generalists.

Consider our pipeline examples, but then do what works best for you.

Are You Ready?

Before embarking on this time-consuming, potentially arduous, sometimes frustrating, but extremely rewarding journey, you need to ask yourself whether you are truly ready and willing to do what it takes to create a unique, high-quality, and entertaining CG short.

Realize that you will need to make sacrifices to accomplish this mission successfully. You might have to turn down social invitations, postpone vacations, and possibly lose a lot of sleep if you hope to see the finish line of your production within a reasonable amount of time. You will need to balance your film-making schedule with your other responsibilities, such as work, family, friends, school, and chores.

And just how long will this journey last? Unfortunately, there is no easy answer to this question. It will depend on your project complexity, team size, equipment, skills, tenacity, and the number of hours per week you will be able to dedicate to it. One thing you can be assured of, however, is the fact that the film you are planning will very likely take longer than you initially expect. The trick is going to be efficiency and economy. If you start with a well thought out production plan, strive to keep your cinematic elements simple and stylized, and continuously seek shortcuts, you will see your idea come to cinematic life within a reasonable time schedule.

Aim for nothing less than cinematic excellence and expect a few headaches along the way. But keep in mind that the rewards awaiting you at the end of this journey will almost certainly justify the means.

Regretfully, animated shorts do not get the same degree of exposure as their feature length counterparts, therefore, most of their titles are not exactly household names. If we mention *Shrek* or *Snow White*, you will undoubtedly make an immediate visual connection. However, if we illustrate a point about story structure using *Mickey's Buddy* as an example, a similar level of familiarity cannot be assumed. Since many of the animated shorts exemplified in this book do not have the benefit of world-wide distribution and large marketing campaigns, we have included a complete film list in Appendix A, which provides information as to where each short can be viewed, or at least presented in greater detail. Those titles marked with a pair of asterisks can also be found on the DVD included with this book (see Appendix E)

chapter 1
Getting Started

Creating a short animated film can be artistically as well as financially rewarding. A successful short can lead to festival screenings, awards, cash prizes, and perhaps most importantly, job offers.

In the professional world, film artists and animators rarely have the opportunity to contribute significantly to the creative areas of the filmmaking process. Rather, most of their working hours are spent lending their talents to the realization of someone else's creative vision, which can indeed be quite satisfying and sometimes rather lucrative. However, developing your own CG (*computer-generated*) short film in the comfort of your own home or dorm room represents a unique opportunity for complete creative control over your artistic vision.

Producing an animated short might also help you decide what you want to be when you "grow up" and enter the CG workplace. Many animation studios and visual effects companies prefer to pigeonhole their artists into specific categories of their digital pipelines. The desktop filmmaker, on the other hand, gets to be screenwriter, producer, director, visual effects supervisor, art director, modeler, animator, cinematographer, lighting technician, compositor, musical director, Foley artist, voice actor, and editor (see Figure 1.1). This represents a rare opportunity to try out any and all of these possible future job descriptions and decide which ones to pursue further. Also, the more you know about each of the individual disciplines of a production pipeline, the better you'll be able to communicate and collaborate with your intra-departmental teammates.

Many film and animation employers greatly appreciate storytellers. Employees with at least a fundamental understanding of story elements and structure are that much more likely to see the "big picture" when working on films, video games, TV shows, or commercials.

Finishing a short film also demonstrates that you have the patience and determination to see a project through to completion. The ability to finish is often the very thing that separates successful and employable creative individuals from the starving artists of the world.

A completed short film is an impressive accomplishment. Even if it never achieves a substantial degree of recognition or critical acclaim, it will forever represent a significant milestone in your career progression. Years after your film is completed, you'll be able to look back and marvel at its primitive qualities as it becomes a barometer for how far you've grown as an artist and storyteller.

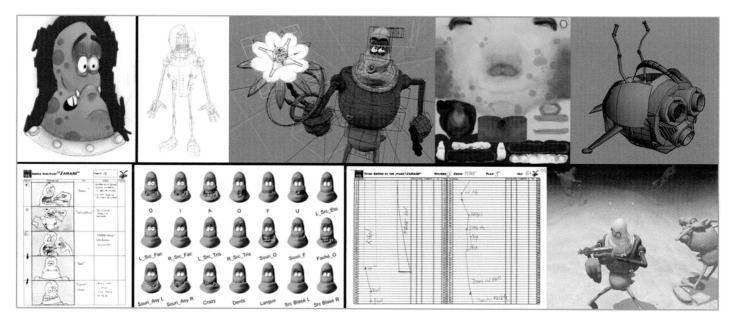

Figure 1.1
The desktop filmmaker gets to occupy many (if not all) of the production roles of his or her pipeline.

And, of course, a completed animated short can make a great demo reel for the beginner or an excellent supplement to a working professional's ever-evolving cinematic portfolio.

What Is a Short?

The Academy of Motion Picture Arts and Sciences defines a short film as being less than 40 minutes in length. With regard to a short animated film, we prefer to set the bar at about 15 minutes. However, for you, the individual or small team, we recommend a maximum of about six-and-a-half minutes (the length of a typical Bugs Bunny cartoon), and we strongly suggest that you aim for something in the three- to four-minute range (the length of an average pop song).

While producing a short animated film can indeed be an enjoyable and rewarding experience, many students and hobbyists don't initially realize the amount of work that goes into one; they often attempt to create films that are simply too long and too complex for their budget, schedule, and skills. Try to keep yours to a manageable length and a reasonable level of complexity.

It is important to realize that a short film is not just a compressed feature. A short is not created by simply taking all the story beats of a feature and then delivering them more quickly. Rather, shorts generally need to be simpler, more linear, and extremely efficient. Feature films often contain lengthy establishing shots, deep development of multiple characters, elaborate sets, and intricate plot structures. A short, on the other hand, usually contains a single or a small number of characters that are developed more quickly, often by way of descriptive design and one or two quick, defining actions. Settings must be established succinctly. The action must get up and running as soon as possible. And complex narrative devices such as subplots, intricate twists, multiple endings, and lengthy soliloquies must be kept to a minimum.

What Is a Good Short?

It is not enough to make just any short film. Rather, your goal must be to make a *good* short film. A good CG short must be

- ◆ Entertaining
- ◆ Accessible
- ◆ Original
- ◆ Memorable

Your film will be *entertaining* if you successfully capture and maintain your audience's attention. This is achieved through interesting and dramatic plot structure, story pacing, character development, style, and appeal. These elements must be delivered with an effective combination of anticipation and uncertainty. Each scene and plot beat must have a purpose and move the story along by continuing, punctuating, or explaining a previous scene or by introducing, announcing, or anticipating a subsequent scene without giving anything away prematurely.

Accessibility will be realized if your audience is willing and able to follow your narrative flow. To connect your viewers to your film, the characters and events of your story must be believable and at least somewhat related to familiar reality. But keep in mind that while realism is optional, believability is imperative. The progression of your story beats must also be easy to follow—or if they are intentionally confusing, you must offer some degree of explanation. In a fantasy or a comedy, outlandish scenarios and characters need not be explained, but the story must flow with immediate or eventual clarity.

Originality is achieved by introducing unique story, character, or design elements, and your film will be memorable if it inspires an intellectual response, emotional reaction, or some degree of aesthetic appreciation from your viewers. In other words, it must make your audience think, feel, or admire. At least one of these three experiences must be delivered or your film will be routine and forgettable.

Balancing these four elements can sometimes be tricky. Your film must be unique enough to be entertaining and memorable, but it must contain enough familiar ingredients to be accessible. Something about your plot, punch line, character design, or art direction must be new and interesting; otherwise, there will be no reason for anyone to watch or remember your film. However, be wary of trying to make all of these ingredients completely extraordinary or pushing any one of them too far into abstract fantasyland—doing so will run you the risk of losing believability and accessibility.

You absolutely must give your audience something new, but try not to reinvent every wheel.

Perhaps the best way to strike this delicate but necessary balance is to add a few unique ingredients to an otherwise familiar whole (see Figure 1.2). For instance, you might try building a standard story structure around an original character (*Recycle Bein'*). Or you could place a generic character in a unique setting (*Framed*). Parody a well-known film or scene with new characters (*Pump Action*). Display the ordinary world through the eyes of extraordinary characters (*Das Rad*). Start with a familiar scenario but then introduce a new twist (*Ritteschlag*) or a unique, unexpected punch line (*Snookles*). Tell an existing story with a new and captivating visual style (*L'Enfant de la Haute Mer*). Or deliver a familiar message in a unique setting (*Bert*).

Figure 1.2
These films are entertaining and memorable due to appropriate mixes of familiarity and originality.

And maintain originality by avoiding overused cinematic devices such as the frozen-action, spinning-camera effect made popular in the *Matrix* films. Such formerly unique visual conventions have become clichés and should only be used if you can think of a particularly new and original way to display or satirize them.

Milestones Related to CG Shorts

In every creative discipline, it is a good idea to know something about the history of your medium. The following sections provide a chronological account of significant milestones in CG shorts, features, and television commercials, and a description of how the last 30 years of experimentation have made possible the stunning level of technical and aesthetic excellence we have today.

The Early Days

3D computer graphics had their humble beginnings in the late 1970s when schools such as the University of Utah and companies such as R/Greenberg began experimenting with this new form of imagery. This was an exploratory time when points and vectors were being manipulated to simulate form and dimension, although nothing resembling realism or narrative structure would be seen for several years to come. 1973 ushered in the first SIGGRAPH conference, which would become one of the world's most significant showcases for technical and aesthetic achievement in CG imagery.

The Eighties

In 1981, the art form began to take flight when Robert Abel and Associates treated viewers to the very first three-dimensional CG television commercial, *Glider.* That same year, Information International, Inc. dazzled the world with *Adam Powers, the Juggler*, introducing the possibility of creating somewhat realistic humans with CG technology (see Figure 1.3).

The early 1980s also brought us *TRON,* which introduced the feature film world to an exciting, surreal, and new visual technique.

And then came John Lasseter, who paired up with Alvy Ray Smith at Lucasfilm to create *The Adventures of André & Wally B.* This film contained a small semblance of story elements, thus qualifying it as the first true CG short and foreshadowing Lasseter's future contributions to the medium.

Robert Abel and Associates pushed the CG character envelope even further that year by creating the TV commercial, *Brilliance*, which featured a female robot with lifelike movement achieved through rudimentary rotoscoping techniques.

Figure 1.3
Even in the earliest days of CG imagery, the creation of believable characters was a worthy and formidable goal, as seen here in *Adam Powers.*

Picking up where *TRON* left off, 1984's *The Last Starfighter* became the first feature film with realistic 3D CG elements in the form of alien starships. The days of using miniature physical spaceship models as an effective visual effect were now officially numbered.

TAARNA Studios, Inc. brought subtle human movement and emotional content to a CG character for the first time in 1985 with their moody *Tony de Peltrie.* It was beginning to look like it might actually be possible to create believable characters with the bulky, cold, room-sized electronic machines of the day. But not just yet.

Also in 1985, a new rendering technique known as *ray tracing* was popularized in the fantastical *Quest: A Long Ray's Journey into Light*. And CG dinosaurs appeared for the first (but certainly not the last) time in *Chromosaurus* from Pacific Data Images, one of the oldest, yet still thriving, CG studios in the world.

1. Getting Started

CG characters were slowly but surely coming to life; however, the feature film world had not yet participated in their evolution. That all changed when Lucasfilm brought a stained-glass window to menacing, bipedal activity in 1985's *Young Sherlock Holmes.*

Music videos jumped into the CG character fray the next year with "Money for Nothing" from Dire Straits (see Figure 1.4). These characters were indeed dimensional and appealing, but their movements were basic and unrealistic so audiences still did not see digitally animated characters as being alive like their cel-drawn counterparts. Because of this, the traditional animation world did not consider CG to be a true character animation technique, and most of the viewing public still saw the art form as little more than a technical novelty.

But everything changed in 1986 when John Lasseter brought believable character movement to a pair of otherwise inanimate desk lamps in *Luxo Jr.* The significance of this little film to the world of CG animation was unparalleled. For the first time, it was demonstrated that audiences could believe and care about CG characters. And the fact that Lasseter achieved this illusion of life without the benefit of dialogue or facial expressions proved beyond a shadow of a doubt that if skillfully handled, 3D CG was indeed a viable character animation technique. An Oscar nomination further validated the significance of this short experiment. Lasseter's next film, produced in 1987 at the newly created Pixar, was *Red's Dream,* which further advanced the use of lighting, rendering, and weather effects to create mood.

By this point, it was no longer about bouncing silver balls, teakettles, and spaceships. Living, emoting characters were now the key elements.

Symbolics applied flocking and herding algorithms to the background characters in their surreal love story, *Stanley and Stella in "Breaking the Ice."*

Not content with just being known as one of the *TRON* guys, Bill Kroyer combined CG and hand-drawn computer characters in his amusing short film, *Technological Threat* (see Figure 1.5). This

Figure 1.4
In the mid-1980s, 3D characters began appearing in music videos.

Figure 1.5
Bill Kroyer's multi-dimensional *Technology Threat*

1. Getting Started

short proved that not only could CG characters stand on their own as believable animated characters, but they could successfully share the stage with traditional cartoon characters as long as the fundamental principles of animation were applied effectively and consistently in both mediums.

Pixar scored another big point for the world of CG animation when 1988's *Tin Toy* became the first 3D film to win an Oscar for Best Animated Short.

The 1980s were drawing to a close, but not before ILM would create the first somewhat realistic CG creatures for a feature film in James Cameron's *The Abyss*.

CG techniques such as particle animation, motion capture, instancing, and inverse kinematics would reach stunning new visual heights in 1989, as seen in short films such as Karl Sims' *Particle Dreams*, Kleiser/Walczak's *Don't Touch Me*, J. Amanatides and D. Mitchell's *Megacycles*, and Michael Girard's *Eurhythmy* (see Figure 1.6). Traditional animation principles such as squash and stretch were also pushed to new limits in films such as *Locomotion* from PDI. And Pixar's *Knick Knack* represented a fitting conclusion to this groundbreaking decade because it would be their last short before attempting an all-CG feature.

Figure 1.6
The 1980s was a decade of major technical achievement in digital imagery, when signature CG techniques like *particle animation* and *inverse kinematics* were developed and explored in films such as *Particle Dreams* by Karl Sims (©1988) and *Eurhythmy* by Michael Girard and Susan Amkraut.

The Nineties

In 1990, MIT joined the world of narrative CG shorts with their science fiction comedy, *Grinning Evil Death*, which featured a creature whose motion was mostly achieved through programming (see Figure 1.7).

1991 saw the world's first all-CG television series with Fantome's *Geometric Fables*. That same year, James Cameron pushed the feature film VFX envelope even further with realistic CG motion on a human character in *Terminator II: Judgment Day*.

But despite all the technical advances and animation study going on, most CG characters, whether realistic, abstract, or cartoony, still had that ultra-dimensional, synthetic look. Then, in 1992, Pacific Data Images brought a bit more creativity to CG art direction with stylized rendering methodology designed to simulate more traditional art techniques in their painterly and fantastical *Gas Planet*. But before PDI could upgrade the shiny, metallic look of their 1985 dinosaurs from *Chromosaurus*, Steven Spielberg and Dennis Muren brought CG imagery to dizzying new heights in 1993 with *Jurassic Park*, featuring the first truly realistic CG film creatures. Stop motion characters as visual effects were now a thing of the past.

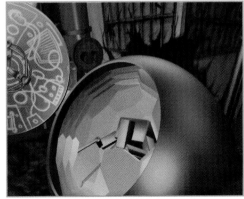

Figure 1.7
Grinning Evil Death

1994 brought the first half-hour, all-CG television shows: Mainframe's *Reboot* and Fantome's *Insektors*, with CG insect characters pre-dating *A Bug's Life* by four years. Also in 1994, Karl Sims experimented with artificial intelligence algorithms applied to simple, geometric creatures that miraculously invented their own motion cycles and competitions in his remarkably abstract but disturbingly real, *Evolved Virtual Creatures* (see Figure 1.8).

Cartoon-style CG animation continued its traditional appeal in Pixar's Listerine commercials and in feature films such the Tex Avery-inspired *The Mask*.

In 1995, Pixar broke ground once again with the world's first all-CG feature film, *Toy Story*. The critical and box office success of this film removed all doubt as to the validity and appeal of CG character animation, as audiences found themselves captivated by such imagery for 81 straight minutes. It was a feat that many thought was not possible, and the world of animated features would never be the same.

Continuing their aesthetic experimentation, PDI successfully translated the personality and movement of 2D animated cartoon characters into the three-dimensional CG world with their surreal but effective segment in the 1995 *Simpsons* Halloween special.

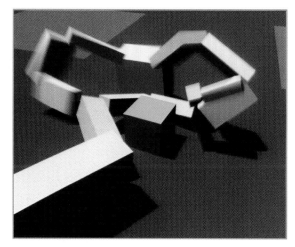

Figure 1.8
Rudimentary artificial intelligence was captivating and concerning viewers in the mid-1990s. Image from *Evolved Virtual Features* by Karl Sims (©1994).

The first CG main character in an otherwise live action feature film was brought to life in 1996's *Dragonheart*.

In 1998, PDI created the world's second all-CG feature with *Antz*, while Pixar experimented with advances in CG cloth and facial animation with Jan Pinkava's Oscar-winning *Geri's Game*.

Nelvana's children's TV show, *Rolie Polie Olie*, demonstrated the notion of elegant simplicity in design and execution. The ongoing popularity of this show continues to prove the appeal of such artistic direction. On the other side of the complexity spectrum, Blue Sky's Chris Wedge pushed mood lighting and fur techniques to new heights with his Oscar-winning short, *Bunny*. And the first title role for a CG character in a live action film was seen in 1998, with Sony's *Stuart Little*.

By the latter half of the 1990s, personal computers and CG software had become powerful and affordable enough for students and hobbyists to begin competing against large studios in the creation of refined and entertaining animated shorts. A new breed of independent animated filmmaker had been born.

2000 and Beyond

With the new millennium, it seemed that most of the technical breakthroughs in CG had been reached. It was possible to create almost anything with this medium—from realistic humans and perfectly lifelike spaceships, to proper hair and fur behavior, to simple and appealing cartoon characters. The technique had all but completely matured, so it was time to get back to filmmaking fundamentals. And while CG imagery continues to evolve, dazzling the world with new technological milestones is no longer a worthy goal for digital filmmakers. Perfection in story, character development, and art direction are now the holy grails of the industry, and audiences are proving this by voting with their feet. The varying successes of feature films such as *Monsters, Inc.*, *Final Fantasy*, *Jimmy Neutron*, *Shrek*, *Ice Age*, and *Finding Nemo* are proving that it's no longer about flawless technique—rather, it's all about strong story elements.

Utilizing the medium of the CG animated short for showing off new particle system algorithms and lighting techniques is no longer acceptable, either. The award-winning shorts of the twenty-first century, such as Jason Wen's *f8*, Tomek Baginski's *The Cathedral*, Ralph Eggleston's *For the Birds*, Sam Chen's *Eternal Gaze*, and Supinfocom's *Le Deserteur*, and *Tim Tom*, are further examples of the fact that audiences and critics are no longer impressed by a filmmaker's ability to manipulate software. Rather, CG shorts of today achieve popularity, critical acclaim, memorable entertainment value, and festival honors through the implementation of unique and compelling story elements and art direction (see Figure 1.9).

Figure 1.9
Technical achievements no longer engage audiences. Today, captivating imagery and strong story elements are the necessary ingredients for success in short CG films.

> The world of animated shorts has always been the proving ground for techni-
> cal and aesthetic advances in CG imagery. Keep this tradition alive and stand
> out from the crowd in this age of powerful PCs and Internet distribution by
> telling interesting and entertaining stories with unique visual styles. Always
> remember that technique is secondary to story.

What Kind of Short Do You Want to Make?

Now that we've recounted a partial history of CG shorts, it's time for you to think about the type of film you want to create. There are a number of issues to consider.

◆ **How long should it be?** You might want to try delivering a quick gag in a minute or less, such as Jamie McCarter's *Point 08*, or perhaps a longer, three-act plot structure with a sig-nificant character arc, such as Wojtek Wawszcyk's seven-minute *Mouse* (see Figure 1.10).

◆ **How complex should it be?** The size of your team, the limits of your budget, the tightness of your schedule, and the power of your tools will dictate the scope of your production. Elegant simplicity, as seen in films such as Moonsung Lee's *Bert*, is always a recommended goal.

Figure 1.10
An entertaining gag can be successfully delivered in less than a minute, while more complex stories may require several minutes or more.

◆ **Will narrative elements be present?** Do you want to tell an actual story, such as the tense and moody *f8*, or would you prefer a fine arts piece that will merely dazzle your audience with unique and captivating imagery set to music, such as *Garden of the Metal*?

◆ **What will be the visual style of your short?** Should it be realistic, cartoony, or abstract? A futuristic world or a historical period piece? Dark and somber or bright and happy (see Figure 1.11)? Full color or perhaps glorious black and white?

◆ **What kind of audience reaction do you hope to generate?** Laughter? Tears? Fear? Disgust? Awe? Confusion? Inspiration? Education?

◆ **Will your film be didactic?** Do you want to deliver a message, like *Passing Moments* from Don Phillips, Jr., or simply entertain, like the action-packed *Killer Bean* series from Jeff Lew (see Figure 1.12)?

Figure 1.11
What kind of mood will you want the visual style of your film to inspire?

◆ **What do you want the overall tone to be?** Should it be warm and cute, like an episode of *Rolie Polie Olie*, or sick and twisted, like a segment of *Celebrity Death Match*? Perhaps you might enjoy juxtaposing cuteness with horror in the tradition of *Itchy and Scratchy* or *Happy Tree Friends*.

◆ **How many characters will your short contain?** One is certainly the simplest, but your story idea might require several.

Figure 1.12
Didactic or just plain fun?

◆ **Will your film need dialogue?**

Remember that silence is very often golden. As proof, take a look at all of the animated shorts from Pixar. There are a number of advantages to making a short without vocals: Such films tend to have an easier time gaining universal appeal because there are no language barriers, and words can sometimes restrict a film's symbolic or interpretive qualities. Also, silent films are much simpler to produce because strong voice talent is hard to find, and lip-synching can be a tedious process. By all means, use dialogue in your short if you so desire, but make sure your writing is solid, your actors have appealing voices and strong delivery skills, and you have the time and skills to create the necessary models and deformers for lip-synch animation.

◆ **Will your short have a music track?** If so, will it be a background score that simply enhances the mood, as in Keith Lango's *Lunch*, or perhaps a Top 40 hit that actually dictates the action, as in Victor Navone's *Alien Song* (see Figure 1.13)?

◆ **What is the ultimate goal for your piece?** Is it just a personal learning experience that you'll never show to anyone, or do you yearn to see your creativity on the big screen? Will you simply use your short for your demo reel, or do you hope to enter festivals and ultimately win an Academy Award? If you are simply looking to create a piece for your demo reel, make sure you choose a subject matter and style that will effectively demonstrate your skills. If you want universal appeal, make sure your film is original and entertaining, and carefully consider the use of gratuitous sex, violence, or bathroom humor.

Of course, you don't necessarily need to have all of this worked out before you start. Leaving a few details undetermined can often keep the production process fresh. But never forget the advantages of planning ahead.

Still images from the animation "Alien Song"

©1999 Victor Navone

Figure 1.13
Music can add to (or actually dictate) the action of an animated short.

What Will You Need to Create Your Short?

To create your short, you'll need imagination, story sense, time, determination, production skills, a quiet place to work, and unfortunately, a bit of potentially expensive hardware and software. At the bare minimum you will need a decent computer, a good graphics card, a fair amount of hard drive space, a piece of CG animation software, and some kind of audio creation and implementation tools. Depending on the sound requirements, art direction, and proposed complexity of your film, you might also need items such as a scanner, digital camera or camcorder, 2D painting software, a digital pen tablet, multimedia editing software, access to the Internet, and perhaps a few teammates. Consider your available time, budget, and resources, and plan your production accordingly.

The Six Laws of Animated Short Film Production

Although we strive to rarely use the words "should," "must," or "always," we hereby submit the following list of laws, which we feel should never be ignored. And don't worry about memorizing them right now. We will repeat these mantras so often throughout this book that you will have no choice but to remember them.

Inspired Law #1: Story Elements Are More Important Than Production Elements

Story elements include plot, character, setting, pacing, and structure. Production elements include design, modeling, animation, lighting, camera direction, compositing, and sound effects. Unless you are making a non-narrative fine arts piece, strong story elements are absolutely essential to a successful animated short. A compelling and entertaining story can be successfully told with stick figures (see Figure 1.14). However, a weak plot with forgettable characters cannot be saved by even the most stylish design, masterful animation, or effective lighting. Yes, a number of films have found commercial success by hiding plot holes and logic errors behind dazzling special effects and expensive marketing campaigns; however, we hope your intention is to create quality rather than mere spectacle. Ideally, you want to deliver a solid plot and compelling characters *with* captivating visuals and sound. However, always remember that production elements exist to support story elements, not the other way around.

Inspired Law #2: Don't Bite Off More Than You Can Chew, and Always Think Ahead

Economy and efficiency are your friends. Less is very often more (see Figure 1.15). Keep the elements of your film simple enough to produce within a reasonable schedule and budget. Remember that while you will have the creative advantage of occupying many (or perhaps all) of the roles in your production pipeline, this can also be a daunting responsibility. Even the shortest CG film can end up being much more complicated than you might initially expect, especially if you are working alone (see Figure 1.16). However, if you keep your film fairly short, simple, and stylized with only a few characters and limited or absent dialogue, you will be that much more likely to finish without burning yourself out. Also remember that the cost of revisions progressively increases as production continues. The earlier you catch problems, the less expensive they will be to repair.

Figure 1.14
A successful and entertaining story can be told effectively with even the simplest of visual ingredients. Image from *Rejected* by Bitter Films/Don Hertzfeldt (©2000).

Figure 1.15
Films such as *Bert, Squaring Off, Framed, Values, Lunch,* and *Toilet* are fine examples of what can be accomplished in a relatively short amount of time when a lone filmmaker avoids dialogue and applies the concept of elegant simplicity to his design and production elements.

The creation of a CG short is a cumulative process. Each production phase will impact the complexity of successive phases. Don't let the pre-production artist in you make life difficult for the post-production artist you will eventually become. As the saying goes, work locally but think globally. Don't try to be everywhere at once, but think about the whole forest when you design each tree.

Figure 1.16
Sony Imageworks' *The Chubb Chubbs* contains a large number of characters, detailed models and textures, advanced character rigging, multiple light setups, dialogue and lip-synching, particle effects, intricate camera movement, and song licensing. This represents the opposite end of the spectrum, and you should only attempt such cinematic complexity if you have a huge budget, a lengthy production cycle, and a large team of specialists.

Furthermore, as you write your scenes, design your environments, and model your characters, think ahead and continually ask yourself whether you have the time, tools, and skills to effectively deliver what you are proposing. If you design a space monster with 17 arms, nine tentacles, and three tails, will you be able to successfully rig and animate him? If you want to make a comedy, do you have the necessary understanding of humor to make an audience laugh? If you are making a documentary, do you know enough about the subject to successfully educate your viewers? At every stage of your production, constantly ask yourself what you can leave out. Don't make your film incomplete, but strive to avoid unnecessary characters, scenes, or details.

Inspired Law #3: Show Some Originality

New and high-quality CG shorts are being produced at an impressive rate these days. As we were working on the chapters of this book, it seemed that nearly every week we would find several new CG shorts worthy of mention and praise on school Web sites, online film festivals, "links" pages, and demo reels. The power of today's digital equipment and the availability of quality books, schoolteachers, college curricula, and Internet distribution centers means it is easier than ever for individuals or small teams to develop and display their story ideas as entertaining and visually captivating CG films.

The good news about all this is that a large variety of great shorts are currently available for study and inspiration, and new ones crop up all the time. The bad news is that the competition for festival acceptance, awards, and job offers is now quite fierce. To stand out in this crowd, your short must display a significant degree of originality in its storyline, character design, and/or art direction. If you create a film with a familiar story structure, an obvious ending, generic characters, and an all-too-common visual style, the resulting cinematic experience will be a waste of your time as well as your audience's. Even a personal learning experience that you never intend to show anyone should contain some element of originality. Who knows, you might change your mind someday and decide to share it with the rest of the world.

Inspired Law #4: You Must Like Your Film Elements or Nobody Else Will

Creating a CG short film can be a long, arduous, and sometimes even tedious process. It takes a great deal of stamina to make it through to completion, especially near the end. It is always easy to stay excited and motivated in the early stages of production when everything is fresh and interesting, but you'll only be able to muscle through the often difficult and sometimes monotonous final stages if you are particularly fond of the elements of your film. Something about your short must provide you with extreme creative satisfaction and inspiration or you will lose interest halfway through production. Furthermore, if you are not personally interested in or excited by your characters, your art direction, the quality of your animation, your music, your punch line, or the subtlety of your central message, you can't expect anybody else to be, either. If any of these elements seems weak, fix it. If you can recognize components of your film that need work, so will your audience. New-age psychologists say, "If you don't like yourself, why would anyone else?" The same is true for your creations. Trying to pass off weak elements in the hopes that nobody else will notice them is like handing a disgusting food item to a friend and saying, "This tastes awful! Want some?" Make sure you are creating a film that *you* would want to see.

Inspired Law #5: Save Often and Back Up Regularly

Files get overwritten. CPUs lock up. Hard drives crash. These are the hard facts of life that every computer user should expect and fear. Hours, days, or even months of work can be lost when such technical glitches rear their ugly heads. Protect yourself from disaster by saving your work continuously and making regular backups. Consider storing copies of your most important files offsite, like at your Mom's house or somewhere in cyberspace. There is no such thing as being too paranoid or careful when it comes to guarding against technological mishaps.

Inspired Law #6: There Are No Rules

Every apparent "rule" in this or almost any other book should be interpreted as a principle, tendency, or mere suggestion. Trusting your instincts and doing what feels right is very often much more effective than following rules and formulas. Rules should be learned and understood, but then bent, broken, or ignored as appropriate to fit the demands of your unique creative vision—but remember not to break rules arbitrarily just to be different.

All lists are incomplete. All statements are interpretive. All conclusions are subjective. And while all rules indeed have exceptions, these six laws, of course, are virtually absolute!

Considering Your Audience

If your intention is for others to see your work, it is a good idea to consider your future audience to some degree as you develop your film. This does not mean your creativity should be dictated or restricted by a need to please others, but it is certainly okay to be somewhat influenced by the desire for your intended audience to enjoy, understand, remember, and recommend your work.

Do you have a target audience in mind? If you want to produce a film for children, you'll probably want to avoid blood and guts. However, if you want to use your film as a demo reel to apply for a job at a video game company that specializes in gratuitously violent entertainment, go ahead and pull out the big guns. If you want to submit your film to *Spike and Mike's Sick and Twisted Festival of Animation*, a bit of bathroom humor might be in order.

Take a moment to think about where you ultimately hope to see your film displayed. If your goal is the Internet film-festival circuit, realize that shorts distributed in this arena need to be rendered at small image resolutions for the sake of download speed. Therefore, films with lush and complex landscapes, such as *The Cathedral* (see Figure 1.17) are not really appropriate for Web distribution because they require large-screen formats to be fully appreciated. Also, if you hope to win a Best Animated Short Oscar, be forewarned that initial display on the Internet will disqualify your film from being nominated. Look at http://www.oscars.org/74academyawards/rules/rule19.html for the Academy's eligibility rules.

If your ultimate goal is the Electronic Theater at SIGGRAPH, be aware that the judges for this festival usually prefer more refined, visually captivating imagery, such as Jason Wen's *f8*, rather than films with beautiful animation applied to hardware-rendered stick

Figure 1.17
The small image format of most Internet film festivals would not be sufficient for the visual magnificence of a film like Tomek Baginski's *The Cathedral*.

figures, which would be more appropriate for an animation-specific demo reel. If you are creating a short film that will act as your demo reel, make sure you come up with a story and a style that will offer you opportunities to show off your strengths and career objectives.

If you want to be an art director, create a story that will feature unique and compelling worlds with opportunities to creatively explore color, light, shadow, and perhaps weather effects, such as Thelvin Cabezas' *Poor Bogo*. If you want to be a character animator, make sure you create a story that will display a significant amount of acting performances, not just walk cycles and fight scenes (see Figure 1.18). If you want to use your short to help get you a job in a game company or a smaller film studio, create a film that will demonstrate a breadth of different skill sets, such as *El Arquero* or *For the Birds*.

Also consider the audience reaction you hope to achieve. If you want to make people laugh, your film should obviously contain at least one punch line. If your goal is to simply impress your colleagues with your unique visual style or technical proficiency in lighting and animation, consider a fine arts piece in which nar-

Figure 1.18
A film such as Leonid Larionov's *The Butterfly*, which displays amusing and believable animation but extreme simplicity in all other visual aspects, might not captivate SIGGRAPH judges, but it would make an excellent demo reel piece for someone seeking a job as a character animator.

rative elements are not required. If you want to scare people, make a horror film. If you want to educate your viewers, make a documentary. If you want to deliver a political or social message, create a clear but subtle metaphor.

As you develop your film, it is sometimes a good idea to get a bit of external feedback on your creative vision, especially if you are less than confident about the effectiveness or clarity of a particular element of your production. If you're not sure whether your characters are appealing, show your drawings to a select group of friends and see what they think. If you're concerned that your social statement might be too heavy-handed, tell your story to a couple of people before beginning production. If they feel like they've just attended a sermon, consider applying a more subtle approach.

When you show your work to others, remember that all reactions can be helpful—even negative ones. Obviously, if everyone thinks your work is brilliant, they might indeed be correct. However, if someone truly dislikes an element of your film and can offer constructive criticism rather than a mere insult, take their opinions seriously and consider their validity. Negative response is often more educational than positive reactions. The worst possible reaction is indifference. If your film is received this way, you definitely need to go back and do some serious reworking.

Of course, it is often desirable to keep the development of your film a closely guarded secret and wait until completion before premiering your unique and captivating visual style and creativity. This is indeed a completely acceptable methodology; however, if you choose to work this way, make sure you develop the ability to critique your own work objectively. The ability to do so is perhaps the most powerful production tool an artist can possess—especially in CG, where a good deal of trial and error often takes place. Try setting your script aside for a while and then reading and evaluating it as if someone else had written it. Look at your character design sketches in a mirror for a fresh point of view. Play your scenes backward to find animation problems. Render your scenes as silhouettes so you can more easily focus on posing and composition issues. Watch your scenes cut together rather than individually to check for clarity, continuity, and effective pacing.

> Be true to your own particular vision and don't let yourself be influenced too significantly by your future audience, but at least acknowledge their existence on occasion.

You Can Do It

To sustain the necessary stamina required to see your production through to completion, you must not only keep things simple and truly like the elements of your film; you must also maintain a reasonable degree of inspiration and confidence.

During your production process, there might be times when you find yourself faced with seemingly impossible problems to conquer. Perhaps you can't figure out a decent ending for your story. Perhaps you can't seem to make your character designs appealing. Maybe you just can't get a particular animation to look quite right no matter how hard you try.

If you truly believe in your film, trust that the answers will eventually come to you. Often it is a good idea to leave something as is and then come back to it later. Such temporary detachment can be an extremely effective problem-solving tool. And if you find yourself losing the inspiration you had when you first began, take a break and watch some of your favorite animated shorts (also see Appendix A to find out where the films exemplified in this book can be viewed). This is often a very good way to regain motivation and momentum.

Remind yourself why you started your film in the first place and allow yourself a few mistakes along the way. Everybody makes them, and accepting the fact that it's okay for you to do so on occasion might relieve some of the pressure. Mistakes are perhaps the most effective learning opportunities available. Make them often, but learn from the experience of correcting them and try not to make the same mistake twice.

Sometimes it can be intimidating to see the high level of craft and creativity displayed in many of the better CG short films out there. You might wonder whether you have the skills and tenacity to create a comparable masterpiece of your own. If you find yourself losing confidence when you look at your competition, remember that many memorable CG shorts, from the Oscar-nominated *Luxo Jr.* to the Oscar-nominated *The Cathedral*, were produced by very small teams of individuals just like yourself, and these future award-winning filmmakers struggled through many of the same creative, technical, and confidence-diminishing issues that you will face. Despite the challenges, these filmmakers tasted success, and you can too.

So gather your creative juices, tell yourself that you're just as talented and determined as anyone else out there, and let's get started....

1. Getting Started

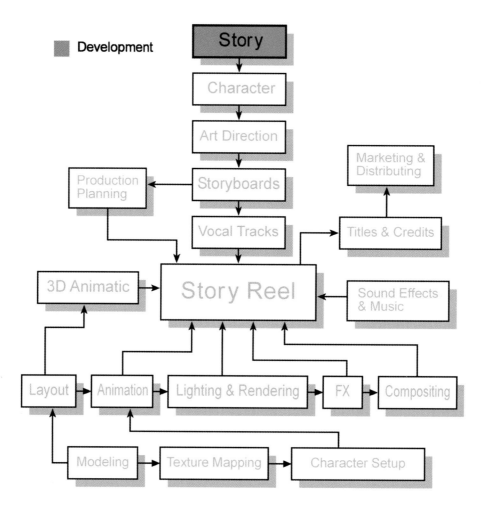

Development

Story

Character

Art Direction

Storyboards

Production Planning

Vocal Tracks

Marketing & Distributing

Titles & Credits

3D Animatic

Story Reel

Sound Effects & Music

Layout

Animation

Lighting & Rendering

FX

Compositing

Modeling

Texture Mapping

Character Setup

chapter 2
Story

A good story is the foundation of nearly every successful animated short. Strong story ingredients are essential if you expect your audience to enjoy, remember, and recommend your film. Simply dazzling your viewers with compelling visuals is sufficient if you are creating a fine arts piece in which narrative elements are intentionally absent. However, trying to hide weak story ingredients behind captivating visuals is a recipe for, at best, mediocrity. Strive for a higher standard and ground your film in a foundation of strong story elements before entering the production phase. Remember that your goal is to capture and maintain an audience's attention and you won't accomplish this mission by telling just any story. You must tell a *good* story.

We understand you're eager to grab your mouse and start animating, but before you do, it is important to understand some basic storytelling concepts. Remember, even the strongest presentation cannot save a poorly formed story idea.

Defining Story

The simplest definition of the word "story" is the telling or retelling of an incident or event. Stories virtually always involve something physical, mental, or spiritual that changes over time, such as a location, a possession, or an attitude. For example:

- ◆ A journey is completed.
- ◆ A problem is solved.
- ◆ An item is acquired or retrieved.
- ◆ A decision is made.
- ◆ An opinion is reversed.

Once upon a time, <u>something happened</u> to <u>someone</u>, and he decided he would pursue a <u>goal</u>. So he devised a <u>plan of action</u>, and even though there were <u>forces trying to stop him</u>, he moved forward because there was <u>a lot at stake</u>. And just as things seemed as <u>bad as they could get</u>, he learned an <u>important lesson</u>, and when <u>offered the prize</u> he had sought so strenuously, he had to <u>decide whether or not to take it</u>, and in making that decision he <u>satisfied a need</u> that had been created by <u>something in his past.</u>

Gary Provost

19

Most of the time these changes go from one extreme to the other. A good situation or person becomes bad. A fool becomes a genius. A tranquil setting erupts into chaos. Life becomes death. Often, these changes come full circle. Rags to riches to rags. Boy gets girl…boy loses girl…boy regains girl.

> A short story is one that delivers narrative progression with economy and efficiency.

Theme

Most stories contain a central theme—the main idea of the story. If you tell someone you are writing a book or making a film, he or she will likely ask what it's about (see Figure 2.1). If you can answer with a single word, such as "revenge," "love," "victory," "escape," "growth," "karma," or "redemption," or a short phrase such as "seize the day" or "blood is thicker than water," then you have a strong grasp of your story's central theme. To maintain a consistent vision as you assemble the elements of your film, it is often a good idea to identify this theme. In the words of Vernon Hardapple to Grady Tripp in *Wonder Boys*, "If you didn't know what it was about, then why were you writing it?"

Figure 2.1
Even if your goal is to simply deliver a quick punch line, your story should be about something. However, don't give yourself writer's block by thinking you absolutely must have a theme worked out before you begin writing. Almost every story will have a central theme, but often it won't reveal itself until much (if not all) of your script is fully written. Also keep in mind that your theme doesn't have to be especially profound. Entertainment, action, and humor are perfectly acceptable themes for short animated films.

> Exercise: Select a few of your favorite stories and see whether you can identify each of the central themes with a single word or a short phrase. For example, the central theme of *The Wizard of Oz* might be, "Home is where the heart is." The central themes of the short film *Values* might be "priorities" or perhaps "approval." Then again, the theme might very well be "values."

Balancing Realism with Imagination

Another important concept to keep in mind is that stories must be at least somewhat related to familiar reality to engage an audience, but abstract and creative enough to entertain. And striking this balance successfully is sometimes tricky. If your story is too close to normal reality, it runs the risk of being dull. On the other hand, if it is too bizarre you might not find an audience. Shorts like *For the Birds*, *Bert*, and *Early Bloomer* achieve such a balance by mixing imaginative characters with familiar social themes (see Figure 2.2).

Figure 2.2
Moonsung Lee's *Bert* is both accessible and memorable because it successfully combines a familiar theme with imaginative design and art direction.

The Three Main Components of a Story

Effectively communicating a story generally requires three basic elements.

◆ Plot

◆ Characters

◆ Setting

Plot is the flow of events contained in your story. Keep in mind that a single event doesn't quite qualify as a story. At least two are generally required, and they must be related somehow, usually by way of cause and effect. "I walked down the street" is not a plot, but "I walked down the street and…" will qualify as a plot once you complete the sentence with another event or a punch line that brings about some form of change ("…and into her life.").

Characters are the living beings who respond to or motivate the events of the story, and setting is the location and era where those events take place. Setting might also indicate specifics, such as season, time of day, and weather conditions.

Any one of these three elements can be the catalyst for a story idea; however, a premise won't progress very far unless at least one of the other two ingredients is added.

Two out of Three Ain't Always Bad

A plot and a setting without characters can occasionally qualify as a story; however, unless the action is centered around a major event like the creation of the universe, it is unlikely that such a tale will be especially memorable or interesting. Audiences yearn to relate, and a film with no characters will have an extremely difficult time establishing such a connection.

Pairing a character and a plot without a setting rarely makes much sense unless you're creating some sort of abstract metaphorical scenario. Settings don't have to be particularly complex, but at least some indication of space or time is generally required to capture and hold a viewer's attention (see Figure 2.3).

Character and setting, however, can combine in compelling ways without the need for much in the way of plot progression. Feature films such as *The Big Chill* and Pixar's CG short, *Geri's Game*, are *character-driven* stories (in which the plot is contained within the evolving personalities, actions, and relationships of the characters), as opposed to *event-driven* stories, such as *Independence Day* and *The Cathedral* (in which the plots are centered on external events and the characters mainly respond, rather than motivate). Most stories are moved along by both character and event, but one is generally the dominant driving force of the other.

Figure 2.3
Where am I?

Starting with an Event

A story premise often begins with an event. If this event is particularly remarkable, like an alien spaceship landing in your backyard, the situation will have obvious narrative possibilities. If the event motivates a subsequent incident or a punch line, you have a series of connected events, which qualifies as a plot. And for an event to create a significant degree of narrative potential, it must contain some kind of conflict. "My dog, Butch, ate his dinner last night" is not a very interesting start. However, "Butch ate *my* dinner last night" creates the expectation of subsequent events, reactions, or consequences, which qualifies the scenario as a potentially interesting story premise. One way of determining whether your story premise has possibilities is by presenting it to someone and gauging his or her reaction. Telling a co-worker that Butch ate *his own* dinner last night will probably not generate much of a response. On the other hand, mentioning that Butch ate *your* dinner last night will undoubtedly result in a question or two. More than likely, you'll be asked what happened next or how you reacted. This request for additional information is a good indication that your dog story premise has legs.

Starting with a Character

Perhaps you've designed an interesting main character and would like to build a story around him or her. If this character is particularly unique, such as a giant, invisible, flying tiger shark, an associated story premise can sometimes seem to write itself because your character's goals and desires will likely be rather obvious (see Figure 2.4). However, many successful stories begin with a more realistic (and perhaps generic or unremarkable) main character, such as your average dog, Butch.

Regardless of whether your character is generic or unique, a simple way of starting to build a story premise around him is to provide a goal—something he either wants or needs, such as food, shelter, money, or love. The process by which your character attempts to accomplish this goal must

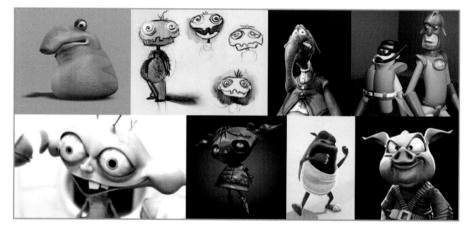

Figure 2.4
Imaginative characters like these should certainly inspire a few story ideas.

ultimately change his locale, health, personality, possessions, opinion, or status through some form of conflict. Conflicts, of course, come in many shapes and sizes. There are external conflicts, such as races to win, villains to defeat, lovers to entice, masters' dinners to eat, and banks to rob. There are also internal conflicts, such as difficult decisions to make, character flaws to adjust, and fears to overcome. Physical conflicts can be very exciting, such as when the protagonist struggles with success versus failure. Moral conflicts can be equally compelling, when the protagonist constantly considers, "Should I or shouldn't I?"

Another effective method of building a story idea around a character is by asking yourself a few questions about the character. Who is he? Where did he come from? Where is he now? What's his motivation? What does he want or need? Who is his greatest enemy? What is his biggest fear? Why didn't Butch just eat his own stupid dinner? Answering such questions can often lead directly to a story idea. Perhaps your character's heritage can inspire some potential plot points if he comes from an interesting place, such as Neptune's third moon. Perhaps your character wants success, respect, affection, a better job, or a bigger house.

Once you've established some idea of your character's identity and given him something to need or desire, the details of a subsequent plot can start to develop as you think of interesting ways for him to accomplish his goals. Of course, a few complications along the way, such as flat tires or guard dogs, are generally necessary for your character's journey to be compelling in the narrative sense.

Still another easy way of building a story idea around a character is by introducing additional characters who will have some kind of relationship with your protagonist. Shorts such as *Luxo Jr.* and *Snookles* are not stories until the second character appears.

One common relationship structure is the notion of two dogs and one bone. This dynamic can take on many forms (for example, two racers and one trophy, or two boys and one girl). Furthermore, both "dogs" don't necessarily need to be characters. One can be a thief and the other a safe, where the cash inside represents the bone. The existence of additional characters often brings about a conflict situation, usually because there are not enough "bones" to go around or because the town is too small for both people (see Figure 2.5).

A story's central conflict could even result from a simple disagreement. Lenny wants sushi but Jenny wants pizza. Or conflicts can arise simply by having one of the characters say no to the other when a request is made, such as "Will you marry me?"

A character with a worthy goal and an associated plan is perhaps the simplest, although certainly not the only, formula for a story premise. Adding a setting, a reason why your character can't achieve his goal immediately, a few complications along his path, and a satisfying conclusion will turn this simple set of ingredients into a fully formed narrative.

Figure 2.5
Two characters and not enough space for both will very likely result in a conflict situation.

Often, a newly introduced second character will intentionally cause the protagonist's conflict. Or a third might cause a struggle between the other two. Perhaps your neighbor's cat, Fluffy, was the one who actually ate your dinner, but she cleverly ran away just in time for you to come home and blame it on Butch. Adding Fluffy to the mix thickens the plot significantly. Now there are two potential conflicts: You versus Butch, who will earn sympathy from the audience if he is wrongly punished, and Butch versus Fluffy, who *should* pay dearly for her frame job.

Of course, rather than opposing each other, all of the main characters might work together toward a common goal, such as a World Series pennant. However, such stories are rarely interesting unless the teammates are forced to conquer a few internal or external problems along the way.

2. Story

23

Starting with a Setting

If your idea begins with a setting, such as an alien landscape or a crowded office on Wall Street, a story will not develop unless you introduce at least one (human or otherwise) character to the scenario and give him something to accomplish. Of course, the setting itself can dictate what your character needs to do. If your story begins at the bottom of a well, your character will probably want to climb out. If the setting is your kitchen and an empty dog bowl, Butch might be compelled to seek his dinner elsewhere, such as the dining room table. Another common method of expanding a setting into a story is by introducing elements that disrupt the status quo, such as a tornado (*Twister*), some ghostly invaders (*Poltergeist*), or a virus (*Outbreak*), thus motivating a need or desire to stop, reverse, or eject the disruption. Of course, if a time limit is involved, the situation becomes that much more dramatic (*Terminator II: Judgment Day*).

Conflict

With very few exceptions, all stories—even the shortest of shorts—contain a setting, a protagonist, a goal, a subsequent action, and an associated conflict. After all, while most of us strive for happy lives with minimal stress, such scenarios make for lousy stories. In the narrative world, happiness and tranquility equal boredom, while conflict equals drama. If only herbivorous beasts and benevolent scientists populated *Jurassic Park*, it might've made for an interesting scenario, but there would've been no story. Furthermore, a story's central conflict must be powerful enough to bring about a change in the protagonist or require him to expend a reasonable amount of energy or thought for its potential resolution. Nobody will be particularly engaged by the story of a burglar who merely encounters a few trivial distractions while robbing a downtown bank. Rather, the complications must be significant and challenging, and the opposing forces must have reasonably equal chances of emerging victorious to create any sense of drama or suspense. There must be moments when it appears that the hero will fail.

One opponent often appears to be the weaker of the two, but the underdog typically summons a degree of tenacity, patience, or ingenuity that makes up for his apparent disadvantages, thereby equalizing his chances (*A Bug's Life*). A completely mismatched tennis game is rarely interesting to watch or play because the ending is too predictable. However, if one player is faster but the other is more powerful, it might be anyone's game. The protagonist and his opposing force don't have to be equal in any particular way, but the outcome of their final confrontation must not be obvious before the fact.

Scholars have suggested that there are three basic types of conflicts (see Figure 2.6).

◆ Man (protagonist) versus man (antagonist)
◆ Man (protagonist) versus nature
◆ Man (protagonist) versus himself

Man versus man examples:

◆ A friendly opponent (*Squaring Off*)
◆ A sadistic villain (*Pump Action*)
◆ A negligent driver (*Point 08*)

Note: As soon as the English language is updated to include a non-gender-specific pronoun, we will be happy to use it in all of our future writings. But for now, please excuse our convenient, grammatically proper, yet politically incorrect use of the words "man" and "him," which are meant to imply either gender.

Figure 2.6
Man versus man, man versus nature, and man versus himself

- A disapproving parent (*Values*)
- An angry loved one (*Polygon Family*)
- A snotty clique (*Early Bloomer*)

Man versus nature examples:

- An annoying insect (*Moosin' Around*)
- Hungry predators (*La Mort de Tau*)
- Nature calling and no place to go (*Fluffy*)
- The irreversible and unstoppable march of time (*OCCASIO*)

Man versus himself examples:

- Curing or being embarrassed by a dysfunctional behavior pattern (*Monkey Pit*)
- Making a difficult decision (*Locomotion*)
- Wrestling with a metaphorical extension of one's self (*Virgil and Maurice*)
- Overcoming a fear (*Passing Moments*)
- Literally man versus himself (*Geri's Game*)

Of course, in most man-versus-man or man-versus-nature stories, the protagonist is often overcoming something within himself while addressing the external conflict (*Comics Trip*). The man-versus-himself theme has a consistent habit of finding its way into all types of conflict-oriented storylines.

Pick a few of your favorite novels, short stories, television shows, commercials, plays, feature films, or animated shorts. Then, for each one, try to identify the basic plot structure, the main characters, their goals, the details of the setting, and the nature of the story's central conflict.

As an example, the central plot of *Star Wars* is a combination of the rescue of the Princess and the destruction of the Death Star. The main characters are Luke, who yearns to be a pilot; Leia, who wants to save her people; Han, who's just in it for the money; and the villain, Darth Vader, who wants it all. The setting is a long time ago in a galaxy far, far away. The central, global conflict is the Alliance versus the Federation, while a number of sub-conflicts abound, including the ultimate struggle between the positive and negative sides of The Force.

Pixar's Oscar-winning short, *For the Birds,* has a simple plot involving an odd newcomer seeking acceptance from a group of snobbish resisters. The central character is the large, clumsy bird. His goal is to join the other birds. The setting is a telephone line. The conflict is the territoriality of the smaller birds.

Fine Arts Films

Conflict is generally regarded as a necessary element of storytelling; however, a number of compelling animated shorts contain no conflict whatsoever because they were not intended to tell stories at all. An animated short film author sometimes foregoes story completely and decides instead to captivate his audience with interesting imagery and movement alone. 1982's *Tango* is one such film, which was so visually compelling it earned an Oscar. These fine arts pieces are often memorable (and sometimes even considered classics) because their imagery is particularly unique or they demonstrate a significant technical achievement.

In the early 1980s, when CG was in its infancy, films such as *Quest: A Long Ray's Journey into Light* and *Chromosaurus* captivated audiences because their imagery was previously unimagined. Computer scientists were impressed by the technical breakthroughs. Artists were introduced to a new visual medium with infinite possibilities. And the general public was witnessing the birth of the next big thing in cinematic imagery. In those days, simply presenting something previously unseen was all that was required to produce a "classic." However, now that CG has been around for a couple of decades, technical breakthroughs are few and far between. Audiences are rarely wowed by technical accomplishments anymore because they've pretty much seen it all by now.

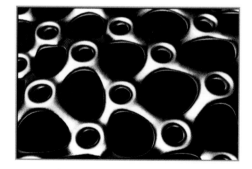

Fortunately, however, while technical milestones are temporary and finite, unique visual style has infinite possibilities. One can still captivate an audience with the absence of story elements if the imagery is significantly unique or compelling (see Figure 2.7). Furthermore, all this talk about story should not deter you from creating a fine arts piece if that is your desire. Just keep in mind that although such pieces qualify as films, they don't qualify as stories in the true sense of the word.

Figure 2.7
Only fine arts films can be without conflict because story elements are intentionally absent.

Where to Get Story Ideas

Story ideas are everywhere. Some will just pop into your head without any invitation whatsoever. Others need to be laboriously crafted through diligent experimentation and a seemingly endless succession of edits and rewrites. One thing to remember, though, is that there is no such thing as a completely unique and original idea. Every concept is at least partially influenced by something that came before. What makes an idea new and interesting are the ways in which those influences are altered and recombined. So don't be too obsessed with the notion of creating something altogether visionary and totally unique in every way. It is quite sufficient to simply put one or two new spins on a familiar premise that has worked successfully in the past.

Here are a handful of ideas and exercises you might try to jumpstart your narrative creativity.

1. **Directly adapt an existing story.** Aesop's fables, folk songs, and cultural myths make for excellent short scripts because they are time-tested and usually copyright-free. Many such stories have been continuously told and retold in new locales, eras, mediums, and styles. How many versions of *The Tortoise and the Hare* have you seen? Surely there's room for one more. William McCrate's student film *Jabberwocky* is a recent adaptation example.

2. **Alter an existing story.** Take a fairy tale or a nursery rhyme and change the ending. Watch a short film that you haven't seen before. Pause halfway through and decide how you would best conclude the story. Then, if the film doesn't end your way, keep your new ending and alter the beginning just enough that the result is a whole new story that is uniquely your own. Try replacing a human character from an existing story with an animal. *Duck Dodgers in the 24 and 1/2 Century* represents such a swap. Take the metaphorical title from an existing story and weave a new tale based on its lit-eral meaning, such as *Cat on a Hot Tin Roof* or *To Kill a Mockingbird*. Tell a familiar story from an alternative point of view, as in the Hamlet-inspired feature film, *Rosencrantz and Guildenstern are Dead*. Try replacing a single word in an existing title to come up with a new twist on a familiar theme: *The Emperor's New Clones* or perhaps *Malice in Wonderland*. Adult-film directors use this technique in many of their titles; however, decorum restricts us from mentioning any specific examples here!

3. **Parody an existing story, documentary, TV commercial, or movie trailer.** Phil McNally's *Pump Action* humorously parodies Quentin Tarantino's *Reservoir Dogs*. Nick Park's Oscar-winning short from 1990, *Creature Comforts*, is a great example of a "mockumentary" (see Figure 2.8).

Figure 2.8
Phil McNally's *Pump Action* parodies Quentin Tarantino's *Reservoir Dogs* in a most imaginative manner, while Nick Park's stop-motion classic, *Creature Comforts*, is an example of a mockumentary.

4. **Create a film based on a song that tells a story.** You might choose Julie Brown's hysterical *The Homecoming Queen's Got a Gun*, for example, or the futuristic *Red Barchetta* by Rush. Of course, if you hope to broadcast your film in public, you'll need permission to use such modern recordings, so it's often preferable to stick with old folk songs or nursery rhymes. You could also invent a narrative that follows the mood and progression of an instrumental piece, such as *El Arquero* by Raphael Perkins (see Figure 2.9). Listen to your favorite Vivaldi concerto or George Winston piano solo. Close your eyes and see whether any images, characters, events, or settings reveal themselves to you.

5. **Draw upon a personal experience.** It's a sure bet that a few interesting or amusing events have occurred in your life. What was your biggest victory? What scared you to the core? Have you ever conquered a fear? Do you have the self-esteem to put your most embarrassing moment up on the screen for the whole world to see? If it's funny, you might want to consider doing so. Personal experience plus a dash of imagination is often regarded as the fundamental formula for fiction writing.

Figure 2.9
Using the beats of a classical music piece to dictate the action timing of a story can be an interesting way to develop a premise, as demonstrated in *El Arquero* from Raphael Perkins.

6. **Use the stream of consciousness method.** Just start writing or talking and see what develops. Begin with the familiar "Once upon a time," or simply invent a first line off the top of your head and then make it up as you go along. Try an especially outlandish first sentence such as, "Jim was quite startled when his doctor told him he was pregnant." You might be surprised at where your imagination can take such a seemingly ludicrous beginning.

7. **Create a character in your mind or on paper and ask yourself a few questions about him (see Figure 2.10).** Where was he born? What's his favorite color? Does he have a family? Who is his nemesis? Is he a villain? If so, how and why did he end up on the wrong side of the law? Then, once you've established some biographical information, give your character a goal. After all, everybody wants or needs something. What's missing from your character's life? Does he need something material? Does he want something elusive? Then consider the ways in which he might try to achieve his goals. If Billy wants a BB gun for Christmas, how might he convince his parents to get him one? How can Frank get his boss fired? How can Benny the burglar steal the Mona Lisa? How will the zebra get his missing stripes back? Also, the type of character you create often demands a story that fits with his particular personality or attributes. A superhero probably needs a powerful nemesis or a global catastrophe to prevent. An arrogant intellectual might need a lesson in humility. A meek introvert should probably find himself in an underdog situation in which he must perform above and beyond his insecurities.

Figure 2.10
What's my story?

8. **Create two characters and introduce a single item they both desire.** This might be a doughnut, a woman, or a bowling trophy. Or give one character an opinion about something that the other vehemently opposes. It can be as trivial as deciding which movie to see. Or perhaps have one character physically, emotionally, or mentally attack the other. The assault can be warranted or completely unmotivated. Just be sure to make the counterattack sufficiently conflict-inducing. A simple surrender or agreement won't result in much dramatic content.

9. **Think of a single word and explore its meanings, connotations, and narrative potential.** Does the word *fanatic* lead to any story ideas? How about *volcano, assassin, toothbrush, shark, hungry, dictator, rabies,* or *connoisseur?*

10. **Write a series of words on tiny pieces of paper.** Start with nouns, verbs, and adjectives, and then mix them up in a hat and randomly pick out two or three. Put them together and see if the combination sparks any ideas. "Enormous bunny" or "purple dancing pickles" might have some narrative potential. Try one hat with characters (eagle, dad, vampire, St. Bernard, policeman) and another with desires (bigger house, better job, more money, spiritual peace of mind, pepperoni pizza), then pick one from each.

11. **Begin with a title that sounds appealing, interesting, conflict-inducing, or simply combines a few words that don't normally go together.** How about *The Caveman's New Cadillac* or *The Piano Juggler?* Don't worry if it sounds silly; you can always change it later.

12. **Start with a conflict of some kind.** A hungry dog has eaten his master's dinner. Two girls love the same boy. A thief wants the Hope Diamond. The ship is sinking. Next think of an appropriate climax, which will be the most significant and intense collision between the opposing forces. Then decide on the resolution. Who wins? Who loses? What is the prize and was it worth the struggle?

13. **Begin at the end.** Think of an interesting or exciting conclusion or resolution, such as the Death Star exploding, a miraculous come-from-behind race victory, a happy couple limping off into the sunset, or a prince returning home with the recovered magic amulet. Then, once you have a satisfying destination, figure out how your plot and characters got there.

14. **Hold a brainstorming meeting with yourself or include a few select friends.** Remove all self-imposed restrictions by making a rule that for the first 10 minutes no idea can be dismissed or criticized. Every thought, no matter how ridiculous or technically impossible, must be fully explored with reckless abandon. Impose limits on your creativity only after it has been given a chance to wander around at the farthest limits of your imagination—not before.

15. **If you have a particular opinion about a social issue or a gripe about something your government is doing, see if you can come up with an interesting way of expressing your point of view.** You might want to make a statement about a major issue, such as global warming, or just call attention to a minor but recurring inconvenience in your life, such as compact parking spaces. Jamie McCarter's animated short, *Point 08* (see Figure 2.11) for instance, reminds us not to drink and drive. Sometimes a direct approach is best, but often a metaphor is in order.

Figure 2.11
Social comments can make for compelling stories as long as their messages are clear and subtle or particularly humorous, as in Jamie McCarter's *Point 08.*

2. Story

Ray Bradbury contended that the best stories are metaphors because they can have different meanings for different people and are therefore more universal. One common method of making a statement is to introduce characters who oppose or ignore your point of view and make them suffer for their negligence or ignorance. A fine example is 1989's Oscar-winning animated short, *Balance*, which punishes its characters for not sharing. Just remember to be clear but subtle. In *The Uses of Enchantment*, Bruno Bettelheim warns that we must never tell a child the moral of a story. This robs the child of the opportunity to find his own interpretation and truly learn from the experience. The same is true for adults.

16. **Tell your favorite joke, limerick, or humorous top 10 list with visuals.** How many ways might you cinematically answer the question, "Why did the chicken cross the road?" The single-beat gag or punch-line series is a very common structure for animated shorts.

17. **Make a movie out of a particularly intriguing (and preferably narrative) dream you had recently.** Your subconscious is very likely more creative than your conscious mind. Keep a notebook next to your bed to record your dreams as soon as you wake up in the morning. If you don't get them down on paper quickly, they'll fade.

18. **Employ the immersion technique, where you watch a multitude of short films and then relax somewhere and see whether your subconscious recombines them in new and interesting ways.** Remember—taking from one source is called stealing, but taking from multiple sources is called research.

19. **Check the newspaper, a magazine, or a history textbook.** True stories are very often stranger than fiction, especially if you twist, exaggerate, or satirize them. The online parody newspaper, *The Onion*, contains an endless array of short stories that satirize actual news reports, such as *Loved Ones Recall Local Man's Cowardly Battle with Cancer*.

20. **Play the "what if" game.** Just start thinking of odd scenarios that begin with those two little words. What if cows could fly? What if my TV's remote control worked on the real world? What if two suns came up tomorrow morning? The important "rule" of this game is to not dismiss any seemingly silly or impossible ideas too early. If J.K. Rowling had thought, "What if a school for wizards existed?" but then decided the idea was too outlandish, a significant literary and cinematic phenomenon known as Harry Potter would be missing from today's popular culture.

21. **Walk down the street, ride the subway, or sit in a coffee shop and observe people as they come and go.** Pick someone out and invent a story about him, based on appearance, behavior, and conversation—but try not to stare. Or perform the same exercise on a zoo animal, where it's probably okay to stare.

22. **Perform acting-class improvisation exercises.** Be a tree. Pick up a coffee cup and think of something obvious or perhaps out of the ordinary to do with it. Imagine yourself as your favorite animal and then get into character and consider what motivates you while inside this new skin.

23. **Give yourself a technical or creative assignment and then try to expand it into a story.** You might want to experiment with low mood lighting for a particular setting. Where might such a scenario exist? Who might occupy such a place? Try a typical animation exercise, such as the popular lifting a heavy object, and see whether you can add a subsequent and original punch line.

24. **Carry around a notebook or preferably a handheld voice recorder.** Ideas have an obnoxious habit of cropping up while a future filmmaker is sitting in traffic, which is not always the best place to grab a pen and start writing.

Beginnings

A strong beginning is essential for audience engagement. You'll need something to grab your viewer's attention so that he feels compelled to watch the rest of your film. There are many ways to hook an audience. Here are just a few:

1. **Introduce a compelling protagonist with some unique character traits.** How about a child with X-ray vision, a dog with six legs, or a man with 17-inch fingernails?

2. **Introduce a character who has an obvious and significant problem.** A fine example is Victor Vinyals' *Top Gum* (see Figure 2.12). How about a frustrated businessman in a broken-down car on the freeway during rush hour, a visiting alien watching his mother ship leave without him, or a castaway on a deserted island?

3. **Establish a tranquil setting and then impose a major disruption.** CG short examples include *AP2000,* which involves a family of fleas, happily frolicking on a dog's back until the dreaded bug spray invades (see Figure 2.13); and *Bert,* where a mother radish is picking children out of the ground, only to find an odd one in the litter.

4. **Introduce a character and then provide him with a self-imposed or externally beckoning goal.** Perhaps a knight who hears the cries of a kidnapped princess or a dorky bird that decides to try and join an apparently exclusive clique (*For the Birds*). Then provide a reason why the goal is not immediately or easily attainable, such as a child reading a party invitation, lamenting the fact that he is grounded, or a snowman that wants to join the other toys on the shelf, but first needs to escape from the prison of his snow globe (*Knick Knack*).

Figure 2.12
Introducing a character with an obvious problem is an effective method of introducing a story or setting up a punch line.

Figure 2.13
Imposing a significant disruption on an otherwise tranquil setting is an excellent way to start an action story.

5. **Start in the middle of an action, when your protagonist is engaged in a performance or is perhaps attempting to conquer or escape from some type of problem or antagonist.** Think about an odd creature performing a singing audition (*Pot Belly Pete*), a small girl carefully crossing a balance beam (*Funambule*), or a late husband attempting to sneak into his house without waking his wife (see Figure 2.14).

6. **Reveal an interesting setting with a unique visual style, preferably with an associated character or characters.** For example, think about a child sharing an island with a large and fantastical factory (*Sarah*); three odd, one-legged creatures on a strange and windy planet, feeding from a bizarre plant (*Gas Planet*); or a pair of otherwise inanimate objects who view their surroundings in a very different manner from the way we humans see the world (*Das Rad*).

© TV Asahi · POLYGON PICTURES · exa · IPA

Figure 2.14
It is a good idea to cut to the chase by starting a story in the middle of an action, such as when the tardy husband from *Polygon Family* attempts to sneak into his house undetected.

Endings

And now for the hard part…. Once you have an interesting story idea and a compelling beginning, you'll need an equally memorable conclusion. After all, a strong ending is often the very thing that distinguishes a good story from a bad one.

Unfortunately, strong endings are often more difficult to write than strong beginnings. This claim can be supported by a quick review of many recent feature films. How many times have you enjoyed the setup and action of a movie, only to be disappointed by a lame, anticlimactic, or predictable ending? Plenty, we imagine. On the other hand, it might be difficult to think of too many films that have weak beginnings but great endings. Beginnings are typically easier because they are, by definition, incomplete. An ending, on the other hand, carries the daunting responsibility of successfully bringing together and concluding something significant about all that has preceded it. A beginning is often a question, whereas the ending needs to provide some kind of answer, even if it is interpretive, inconclusive, or inspires a new beginning.

Furthermore, additional pressure exists because good endings are often considered more important than good beginnings. The resolution of your story is what your audience will ultimately leave with, and the quality of your ending will dictate their level of satisfaction and desire to recommend your work.

Examples of films with great endings include *The Sixth Sense, In the Company of Men, Raising Arizona,* and the animated shorts, *Balance, Geri's Game, The Wrong Trousers, Early Bloomer, Cane-Toad,* and *Das Rad*.

Some story ideas actually begin with an interesting ending or an amusing punch line. If your story premise consists of an especially engaging conclusion, consider yourself lucky. After all, it is much easier to draw a map when you know your destination. But in many cases, a story premise will be a strong setup that begs for an equally successful conclusion. Unfortunately, there are no simple formulas for creating good endings. If such formulas existed, weak film endings would surely be less common.

However, there are a few things you can keep in mind that might keep you from creating a disappointing story conclusion.

1. **Make sure your story actually has an ending.** Unless poignant existentialism is your intent and you have the skills to pull it off effectively, a film that simply stops or fades away without any kind of resolution is rarely well received. The most obvious and often most satisfying way to end a story is by allowing the protagonist to resolve the central conflict, preferably in an interesting or unique manner. Of course, sometimes it's more interesting if the conflict defeats the hero. Keep in mind that an ending doesn't have to tie up all loose ends. It is often desirable to leave at least one unanswered question for the audience to ponder and discuss. An ending that sets up a new beginning is sometimes interesting and amusing. In Pixar's *Knick Knack*, the snowman seemingly resolves one conflict, only to find himself in virtually the same pickle in the end.

2. **Deliver the anticipated scene.** In a sufficiently efficient narrative film, every scene is a step along the pathway toward a climax or conclusion and this anticipated scene must be displayed rather than merely described or glazed over. After your brave knight suffers through a series of trials and tribulations on his quest to rescue the princess, you cannot simply cut to a future scene where he tells his mates at the pub how he defeated the dragon. The fight scene that your audience had been waiting for must be shown. Unless of course the bragging knight was lying!

3. **Don't be too obvious or derivative.** Look and ask around to make sure your ending hasn't been seen too many times. This can lead to predictability and disappointment. The climax or ending of your film must contain a surprise of some kind, although it doesn't necessarily need to be sudden, explosive, or even profound. Just make sure it is not identical to your audience's expectations or their memories of other film conclusions.

4. **Decide on the final reaction you want from your audience and then end your story appropriately.** If you want them to go away smiling, deliver an amusing punch line (*Cane-Toad*) or have your characters live happily ever after (*Bert*). If you want your audience to be saddened by your film, punctuate it with a tragic loss (*Le Deserteur*) or an unfulfilled desire (*Red's Dream*). If you want your audience to feel that justice has been served, let the good guys win (*For the Birds*). If you want your viewers to draw their own conclusions, give them an ambiguous resolution where your protagonist's outcome is both better and worse than it was when the story began. He ultimately gained, but lost something in the process (*The Big Snit*).

5. **Don't beat your audience over the head with a lesson or a moral.** It should be decipherable yet sufficiently subtle and never actually spoken. The short film, *Balance*, for instance, concludes with a perfectly clear and artfully delivered message.

6. **Make your ending climactic in that it results in a significant change in your protagonist's life situation.** In an adventure or suspense film, your final climax should be the most exciting or intense moment of your story. Build up to it and then serve it with a bang. *The Cathedral*, *Grinning Evil Death*, and *Dronez* are fine examples (see Figure 2.15).

7. **Think about the central conflict of your story and the most obvious or effective way to bring about its resolution.** Then consider

Figure 2.15
Climactic endings are often appreciated in adventure tales.

concluding your story with a variation of what is expected or perhaps even the exact opposite (*Pings* or *Getting Started*). Similarly, you might want to begin with an extremely familiar and seemingly predictable setup, but then offer something unique or unexpected at the end (*Passing Moments*, *SOS*, or *Snookles*). There are two obvious ways to end a story—the way the audience hopes for and the way the audience dreads. If you are going for suspense or high drama, make the dreaded ending more likely, then satisfy the audience with the happy one. Or perhaps create tragedy by doing the opposite.

8. **If your story ends with a remarkable triumph of some kind, make sure it is logical and believable, rather than the result of a fortunate coincidence, a convenient miracle, or an unexplained burst of genius or strength.** Such convenient interventions are known as *deus ex machina* ("god from the machine") and should be avoided at all costs unless parody is your intention.

9. **Brainstorm a full spectrum of possible conclusions—from automatic through obvious, common, interesting, unusual, outrageous, and completely absurd.** Try to think of one of each and see whether a satisfying ending exists somewhere between the extremes.

10. **Avoid cop-out endings.** Thank-goodness-it-was-only-a-dream is a far too common story cliché, and it should be avoided unless you can think of an especially unique or amusing spin on it. Similarly, try to steer clear of overused comedic devices, such as randomly dropping a heavy object on your protagonist in the hopes of creating a surprise ending. Doing so generally sends the message that instead of trying to actually finish your film, you simply abandoned it. Victor Navone managed to get away with this maneuver in his short, *Alien Song*, but only because his hero was ironically singing "I Will Survive" (see Figure 2.16).

11. **Detach.** If you've figured out most of your story but you can't come up with a decent conclusion, set your script aside for a while and then come back and read it later, pretending it was written by someone else. As you read, consider how easy it is to tell where the story is heading. If the expected conclusion is satisfying, use it. If it seems too obvious, you might still be able to use it successfully if you go back and make the setup less predictable.

Figure 2.16
Victor Navone's *Alien Song* successfully employs an otherwise overused comedic story-ending device by choosing a song with lyrics that make the conclusion appropriate and amusing.

12. **Know what your story is truly about (its theme) and then make sure your ending delivers your message effectively.** If the theme of your story is "seize the day," then your protagonist must triumph somehow. If your theme is laughter, then your story should end with an effective punch line.

Remember, just because your short will most likely have a beginning, a middle, and an end, it doesn't mean you have to write your story in that order.

Storytelling

Okay, so you've successfully jogged your creative juices and now you have an interesting story premise with a killer ending that's just waiting to be told. The next step is to decide the best way to communicate your idea as a narrative. We've defined plot, character, setting, and conflict as the individual ingredients of a story. However, just as the ingredients of a pie must be combined in the correct proportions, baked at the proper temperature and duration, and served with just enough whipped cream before the result qualifies as a flavorful dessert item, the basic ingredients of your story must also be assembled and delivered properly if you want to successfully engage your audience. The tools for this delivery are as follows:

- Genre.
- Structure.
- Pacing.
- Productions elements, such as camera direction, animation, and lighting. (However, we are distinguishing these from actual story elements, so they will be discussed a bit later.)

Basic story elements might catch an audience's attention, but the nature and quality of your storytelling delivery devices will determine the level of their immersion in your story and ultimately how much they care about its outcome. Even the most ludicrous-sounding plot structure can result in a successful film if the storytelling elements are strong enough. The features *Grosse Point Blanke* and *Donnie Darko* have a number of rather outlandish and unbelievable story beats; however, they are delivered with such unique style and excellent pacing that the audience is too busy being entertained to notice.

Genre

Genre refers to the type or classification of your story, most often determined by setting and style (see Figure 2.17). Video stores typically use genre as a method of sorting their films into various categories, which include

- **Drama.** This genre typically contains realistic depictions of character-based events, as in the animated shorts *Values* and *Geri's Game*. Conflict is essential here, although it doesn't necessarily need to be the violent kind. Films that exaggerate dramatic content for the purpose of emotional response are known as *melodramas*.
- **Comedy.** There are subtle, smirk-inducing films, such as Aardman Animation's *The Deadline*, and broad, all-out-laugh-riot farces, such as *Polygon Family*. A common form of comedy is the *parody*, in which an existing property is satirized, such as

Figure 2.17
Common story genres include drama (*Values*), comedy (*Run, Dragon, Run!!!*, and *Fishman*), fantasy (*Guernica*), crime capers (*Tom the Cat*), and science fiction (*f8*).

35

in *Creature Comforts* and *Fishman*. The fundamental components of comedy are timing, exaggeration, and surprise, and the element that generally separates comedy from drama is that nobody ever really gets hurt. Another common comedic device is ridicule, where a particularly worthy person or institution is appropriately and mercilessly targeted. Comedy is often considered the hardest genre to write and deliver successfully because humor is so subjective and there are no definitive formulas for effectively generating a laugh. Only attempt humor if you have the right source material and the skills to pull it off.

◆ **Suspense.** The protagonist's sense of safety has been (or is about to be) violated. The key ingredients are anticipation and uncertainty with regard to impending danger. Perhaps the most effective way to build suspense is by revealing the impending danger to the audience before the protagonist knows it is coming. Alfred Hitchcock mastered this genre in films such as *Rear Window* and *North by Northwest,* and the animated short *The Wrong Trousers* contains some particularly suspenseful moments.

◆ **Science fiction and fantasy.** Science fiction refers to speculative subjects that have some connection to possibly existent or future technologies. Common themes are robots (*AI*), interplanetary adventures (*Star Trek*), alien invasions (*Lilo & Stitch*), and time travel (*Back to the Future*). Short animated film examples include *f8*, *Grinning Evil Death*, and *The Snowman*. Fantasy, on the other hand, addresses fictional subjects that defy scientific explanation, such as alternate worlds (*Lord of the Rings*), mythological creatures (*Jason and the Argonauts*), or the supernatural (*It's a Wonderful Life*). Short examples include *Within an Endless Sky* and *Ritterschlag*.

◆ **Horror.** This genre is often described as the combination of suspense plus some kind of monstrous or semi-human element. Paul Berry's stop-motion short, *The Sandman*, and *Silhouette*, from Amber Rudolph and Tonya Noerr, are fine examples. Scenes are suspenseful when danger looms, but horrific when the danger actually arrives and the victim is (at least temporarily) unable to defend against it successfully.

◆ **Romance.** In this genre, love is formed or rekindled after a few complications. *When Harry Met Sally* and *My Big Fat Greek Wedding* are popular examples, as is the CG animated short, *Love Tricycle*.

◆ **Black comedy.** Poignant jokes are applied to a not-so-funny subject, such as death, as in films like *To Die For*, *Heathers*, and the animated short, *The Crossing Guard*.

◆ **Crime capers, police stories, and courtroom dramas.** In these stories, justice is (sometimes) served in films such as *Ocean's 11*, *Heat*, and the short, *Tom the Cat*.

◆ **Action adventure.** These are exciting tales of battle, defense, rescue, pursuit, thievery, or escape where the stakes are high, the danger is extreme, the pace is urgent, and the rewards are great. *The Road Warrior*, *Black Hawk Down,* and Jeff Lew's *Killer Bean 2* are fine examples. Westerns fall into this category as well.

◆ **Mystery.** The audience is intentionally confused by a puzzle of some sort, which is (usually) solved or explained at or near the end, in films such as *Young Sherlock Holmes*, *Memento*, and the short, *Bunny*.

◆ **Sports films.** In such stories, we are often presented with an underdog who ultimately prevails because he has heart (*The Tortoise and the Hare*) and perhaps a name that implies determination, such as Rocky.

◆ **Tragedy.** A particularly likeable protagonist dies or suffers significantly in the end, often after accomplishing a selfless or heroic deed. Shakespeare's *Romeo and Juliet* is an especially memorable example.

◆ **Documentaries and biographies.** These are factual and often historical accounts of real-world events or people, such as *Crumb* or *Bowling for Columbine* (which, incidentally, is not a sports film). Short CG documentaries usually demonstrate breakthroughs in lighting, particle, or physics simulation technology and can regularly be seen at venues such as SIGGRAPH's annual Electronic Theater.

◆ **Musicals.** *The Wizard of Oz*, *Chicago*, and the animated segments of Disney's *Fantasia* are all good examples.

Of course, many films combine more than one genre into a single narrative. *Little Shop of Horrors* is a musical-comedy-horror-romance. And the animated short *Creature Comforts* is a comedy-fantasy-parody-documentary.

Genres can usually be distinguished by their intended audience reaction. Good dramas make us relate to and care about the protagonist. Successful comedies make us smirk or laugh. Black comedies make us laugh when perhaps we shouldn't. Suspense films make us squirm, while horror films make us scream. Science fiction and fantasy provide us with a sense of awe. A good romance makes us smile and want to be in love, while tragedies often make us cry. Action adventures put us on the edge of our seat. Sports films make us cheer. Police and courtroom dramas give us a sense of justice (or perhaps the lack thereof). Mysteries make us think. Documentaries make us feel educated. And musicals inspire us to dance.

> If you have your story premise worked out, you've probably already decided on an appropriate genre. But if not, ask yourself what kind of response you want from your audience. Answering this question is often a good way to choose a genre.

Structure

Structure refers to the logical and dramatic ways in which you assemble the plot points and character progressions of your story. In other words, it is the compelling roadmap by which the story travels from setup to resolution.

The purpose of studying story structure is not to force you to fold your creative vision into any standard formula, but to assist you in your ability to analyze and critique your own work. If something doesn't seem to be working in your story, you might be able to find the answer by studying typical time-tested structures, which might provide clues as to where your story went awry.

The Ever-Popular Three-Act Story Structure

The most standard story assembly, described in texts as old as Aristotle's *Poetics*, is the three-act structure—a beginning, a middle, and an end. Although a number of modern scholars make it a point to debunk the validity of the three-act story structure, it is difficult to ignore its significance, popularity, and time-tested effectiveness. The first act establishes the characters and the goal or conflict. For example, you come home from a long day at the office, looking forward to enjoying your wife's famous fettuccini alfredo, only to discover that that your dog, Butch, has already eaten your dinner! The second act involves the main action of the conflict and the climax. For example, you chase Butch around the house and yard, eventually tackling him, and just as you raise your fist to deliver punishment, you notice the neighbor's cat, Fluffy, sitting on your back porch, licking alfredo sauce from her paws. The third act, which is usually the shortest, contains the resolution. The sun sets on a tranquil evening as you and Butch sit in the backyard and share a nice, juicy, barbecued Fluffy-burger.

There are plenty of feature-length stories that contain five or more distinct acts, while many short stories have only one or two. However, the three-act structure is certainly the most common. Occasionally, an act is intentionally left out for dramatic effect. For instance, sometimes a story starts off in the middle of the second act, and the first act exists only as a back-story, revealed during the action by way of flashbacks or conversation. Your story might begin in the middle of a chase where the pursuer yells, "Hey, you stupid mutt! This is the last time you'll eat my dinner!" With this single line of dialogue, the relationship between the characters as well as the reason for the chase are revealed without actually requiring a setup. Act One indeed existed, but it is not contained within the bookends of the actual narrative. Remember this timesaving technique when you are working on your short-form script. The third act is sometimes partially left out to let the audience decide on the ultimate story resolution. These are sometimes referred to as *existential endings*. A third act indeed exists in these films, but the story is left with a significant loose end. Examples include *The Graduate* (What will Ben and Elaine do now?), *The Color of Money* (Will Eddie beat Vince?), and the CG short *Passing Moments* (Will the two train passengers ever cross paths again?).

The Instigating Incident and the Climax

Rarely do individual acts gradually segue into one another. Rather, a clear and significant event usually takes place to announce the arrival of the subsequent act. Once the scenario is established in Act One, the second act generally begins with an *instigating incident* that sets the plot in motion and compels the protagonist to act or respond, perhaps after an initial refusal. The instigating incident generally comes in one of three forms:

◆ An action performed or a decision made *by* the protagonist. ("I think I'll steal somebody's wallet today.")

◆ An occurrence that happens *to* the protagonist. ("Hey, someone just stole my wallet!")

◆ A significant event that the protagonist witnesses or learns of. ("I just heard that someone stole my brother's wallet!")

The incident that ushers in the third act is the *climax* of Act Two (perhaps the capture of the pickpocket). In *Die Hard*, the setting and characters are well established in Act One. The second act officially begins when the terrorists take over the party, and Act Three starts after the roof explodes.

Even the shortest animated film will still contain a beginning, an instigated middle action, and an ending climax. This can be thought of as a compressed but complete three-act structure. For instance, the first short act of the 42-second *Alien Song* establishes Blit sitting on a chair under a spotlight. The instigating incident is the music starting. The main action of Act Two is the performance. The climax is the falling object. And the short third act is the subsequent silence.

> Exercise: Watch or recall a few of your favorite features or shorts and then try to identify the instigating incident that introduces Act Two and the climax that announces the arrival of Act Three.

Remember that Act One grabs the audience's attention, while the memory of Act Three is what they ultimately take home from the experience. This is not to imply that a second act is less important than its siblings, but if you successfully hook your audience with your first act and you have a unique and captivating climax and resolution worked out, figuring out the necessary action and beats of Act Two is very often the easy part.

Messing around with Story Structure

Some clever filmmakers get away with severely altering and reassembling the basic three-act structure. *Pulp Fiction* and *Go* bounce around between different places and times telling multiple stories, each with their own individual (yet related) three-act structure. *The Usual Suspects* begins after the second act, and the pieces leading up to it are told in flashback. The trip to India episode of *Seinfeld*, as well as the feature film, *Memento*, actually turn formal structure completely upside down and tell their stories in reverse. These severe structure rearrangements are often difficult to accomplish in a very short film because such intricacies require a fair amount of time to develop and ultimately connect.

Sometimes plot points are delivered in small pieces, and the complete structure is not revealed until the very end. This structure is sometimes referred to as a *slowly unraveling puzzle*, in which the audience is given bits and pieces along the way, but the entire story doesn't come together completely until the final piece is supplied, usually at the very end. Then the viewer often needs to spend some time putting the pieces together in his head before completely understanding the plot he's just witnessed. Atom Egoyan's *Exotica* and David Lynch's *Mulholland Drive* fall into this category. This structure generally requires the extended length of a feature film or that of a longer short to be accomplished effectively.

The Hero's Journey

No discussion on narrative structure would be complete without addressing Joseph Campbell's theories on the subject, in which he argued that every great story follows at least some variation of a rather formulaic series of events he called *the hero's journey*. The beats of this journey have been rearranged and modified by many scholars since Campbell first introduced them in his 1949 book, *The Hero with a Thousand Faces*. Here is a generalized description of the journey.

◆ **Act One.** You are introduced to the seemingly unremarkable protagonist in his unremarkable home world. A call to adventure is given, and the protagonist initially refuses until a mentor appears to provide an appropriate dose of philosophy, motivation, and perhaps some new weaponry or skills, whereupon the future hero begins his journey into a new and treacherous world.

◆ **Act Two.** Some early but significant conflicts are met, as well as a few new characters who either join or attempt to thwart the journey. The final destination is eventually reached, where the supreme obstacle or villain is conquered, the stolen gem is retrieved, or the princess is rescued.

◆ **Act Three.** The traveler(s) head home along a somewhat dangerous path with the bested villain often in hot pursuit. The hero (usually) makes it back to his home world, delivering the goods, experiencing some kind of physical or spiritual resurrection, and restoring order and happiness as he becomes known as the master of two worlds.

Most hero's journeys contain some element of loss. For instance, the protagonist might initially lose something or someone dear to him, thus motivating the journey. Or a teammate might get killed along the way. Or the protagonist himself might die just after completing his quest, thereby becoming the ultimate hero who has sacrificed his own life for the good of others.

Many feature films follow some variation, subset, or rearranged version of the hero's journey formula, while some films, including *Star Wars*, *Saving Private Ryan*, and *The Wizard of Oz*, actually follow the structure practically beat-for-beat. A multitude of short animated films are constructed around a compressed version of this formula, including *Knick Knack*, *f8*, *Comics Trip*, *Recycle Bein'*, *Pom Pom*, and *Grinning Evil Death* (see Figure 2.18).

It is no big mystery why hero stories are so popular and memorable. Much of our daily lives are spent solving problems and resolving conflicts. What should I get my wife for her birthday? How can I avoid road rage? How will I survive my impending IRS audit? Solving problems requires some degree of heroic effort, even if it is particularly minor in scope, risk, or complication. Conquering dilemmas gives us a sense of accomplishment and the confidence to continue operating in the real world. Witnessing film characters performing even the most minor of heroic deeds gives us inspiration and sometimes

Figure 2.18
Comics Trip, *Pom Pom*, and *Recycle Bein'* are simplified versions of the hero's journey.

specific techniques that we can apply to our own lives. Creating some form or subset of a hero's journey is certainly not mandatory, but it is definitely worth considering as a time-tested and potentially successful narrative structure for your film.

A common variation on the hero's journey is the *lose/learn/win scenario,* where the protagonist is initially bested by the villain, but then embarks on a journey of self discovery, often with the help of a mentor to give guidance or some new weaponry and training, which arms him to return and defeat his enemy. Examples are easy to find and include *The Odyssey*, *The Count of Monte Cristo*, *The Karate Kid*, *Rocky III*, and virtually every Hong Kong Kung Fu feature.

The *relationship arc* is a familiar variation on the lose/learn/win theme, where boy meets girl; boy loses girl; boy grows up a bit and after some kind of heroic deed, altruistic act, uncharacteristically mature behavior, trophy-winning performance, perfectly timed speech, or just plain, old-fashioned patience and determination, boy finally wins back girl. *When Harry Met Sally*, *As Good as It Gets*, and *Shrek* are recent examples.

> It is essential to keep in mind that standard story structures should be considered flexible frameworks rather than restrictive formulas. Learn and understand story structure, but then bend and break the rules to suit your particular creative vision. Just remember that no matter how closely you follow or how far you stray from standard story structure rules, the flow of your story must remain logical, cohesive, and interesting. Stories are only successful if audiences can follow and enjoy them.

Pacing

Pacing refers to the timing of your story point delivery. Effective pacing will keep the mind of your audience occupied for the duration of your story. Have you ever noticed that a lethargic school teacher with a monotonous voice can make even the most exciting historical event sound as boring as nails rusting, while an exuberant and captivating lecturer can keep you on the edge of your seat while describing his uneventful trip to the laundromat? The difference is often due to an innate sense of story pacing. Each beat of your script should move your story along by making your audience want to know what will happen next without actually letting them know before it happens. Anticipation plus uncertainty equals story movement.

Pacing is an extremely important narrative component to study because bad pacing can easily confuse or bore your viewers. If your scenes fly by too quickly, your audience might miss an important piece of information and lose their connection to your story. If a scene significantly slows the action, there needs to be a valid reason for it, such as building suspense, establishing mood, or creating anticipation. Make sure your scenes are long enough to clearly deliver their plot points, but short enough to move the story along at a reasonable pace. Use quick shots during action sequences and slower shots when you want to give the audience time to think.

A story's *arc of intensity* is an important pacing element to consider. Does your story start off gently, build to a climax, and then rapidly return to tranquility? Or does it start off with an explosive action sequence, then mellow out for a while before exploding again at the end? If you plotted most feature films into an intensity graph, you'd see many hills and valleys, while short films generally have simpler arcs. Your film's arc of intensity doesn't necessarily have to rise continuously to be dramatic and entertaining. It can start high and then gradually diminish, or perhaps go up and down like a roller coaster. Just make sure it is not altogether flat. Study classical music pieces and rock songs for potentially interesting intensity arcs (see Figure 2.19).

The Short Story

Short stories are everywhere. Examples include segmented Saturday morning cartoons, narrative music videos, comic books, live action or animated short films, 22-minute sitcoms, children's picture books, multi-paneled comic strips, video game opening sequences, narrative television commercials, story poems, jokes, and songs. These are all formats to examine with regard to short-form storytelling ingredients and structure.

Long-Form versus Short-Form Stories

So far, many of the story concept examples we've been providing fall under the category of the long-form narrative, which includes novels and feature films. The most obvious distinction between these and the short-form story is, of course, length. According to the Academy of Motion Picture Arts and Sciences, a short film is less than 40 minutes in length. As we mentioned before, most short animated films are less than 15 minutes long. We recommend a maximum of about seven minutes, but we suggest you aim for three or four minutes, especially if you are working alone.

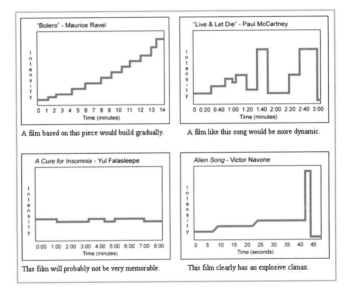

Figure 2.19
Examine the arc of intensity of existing songs and short films.

2. Story

Length, however, is not the only distinction between short- and long-form narratives. The concepts we've discussed in this chapter regarding plot, character, setting, conflict, genre, and style apply similarly to both formats; but the main differences lie in complexity, structure, and pacing. The trick is focus, economy, and efficiency.

> A short story is not just a long story that gets told more quickly. Long-format stories can include large numbers of characters; lengthy establishing shots; multiple acts; complex character development; and often a few twists, false endings, and complicated sub-plots. Depending on your target length, there usually isn't time to include such devices and structures in the short form.

Variations on Long-Form Story Structures

Many popular full-length story structures are simply not appropriate for a short story. However, variations on long-form structures are often quite effective. For instance, you might be able to fit most of the story beats of the hero's journey into a 15- or 30-minute short; however, anything less will require significant pruning of the complete formula. Omitting selected beats or just using a small section are appropriate ways to successfully compress the hero's journey, as in the student films, *AP2000*, *Recycle Bein'*, and *Sarah* from Supinfocom.

Likewise, formal tragedies are rarely advisable for the short form because they generally require a significant length of time for the audience to fully embrace the protagonist in order to be sufficiently saddened by his demise. Ten minutes or more might give you enough time to do so effectively (*f8* or *La Morte de Tau*); however, within the recommended timeframe of four minutes or less, a tragic twist at the end is usually best served as a less severe (and perhaps sudden) comedic moment, such as the punch lines of *Snookles* and *SOS* (see Figure 2.20).

Figure 2.20
Tragedies are best served in the short form as sudden, disastrous, and often comedic final story moments.

Significantly rearranging the normal narrative flow of a story is also rather difficult to pull off in the short form. Films such as *Pulp Fiction* require a lot of screen time to tell the individual stories and then demonstrate how they all fit together. It's usually best to stick with a single, rather linear storyline with only one or a small number of characters. *On the Sunny Side of the Street* and *Tom the Cat* are rare short examples that play with standard narrative structure by telling the same short story twice, from two alternative points of view.

The slowly unraveling puzzle structure is yet another long form example that doesn't quite work in the shortest forms because it requires the pieces to be delivered slowly so viewers can sufficiently incorporate them into their evolving understanding of the story. However, a popular and appropriate short story variation on this theme is something we like to call the *surprise scenario reveal*, in which a single, significant puzzle piece is dropped in at the end, often revealing what the otherwise vague or unremarkable story was really about. Examples include *Bunny*, *Funambule*, and *Oblivious* (see Figure 2.21). This structure can be effectively realized in as little as 30 seconds.

Figure 2.21
The *surprise reveal* is an effective short-form version of the *slowly unraveling puzzle* structure, which is more appropriate for longer films.

Typical Short Story Types and Structures

Just as a multitude of standard long-form story structures exist, some typical short-form structures seem to crop up repeatedly. Of course, short stories can be structured in any number of ways, and you should certainly feel free to assemble your plot points in any manner you choose. Always remember that lists and examples are offered as guidelines, not commands or formulas. But there are quite a few tried and true structures you might want to consider just to be on the safe side.

The Gag

Mainly because of its limited length requirements and therefore less expensive production cycles, the gag is probably the most common short animated film structure. Virtually all shorts of less than a minute fall into this category, which has several forms.

- **Single beat.** This is a quick joke—a simple setup and then a surprise twist or comedic beat. Random violence on a cute character is a common theme (see Figure 2.22). Short animated film examples include *Snookles*, *Alien Song*, *Squaring Off*, and of course, *Bambi Meets Godzilla*. One advantage of this type of story is that it can often be told in as few as 30 seconds. Many amusing television commercials successfully prove this point.

- **Series.** This is a montage of quickly delivered punch lines. Bill Plympton specializes in this structure, which he demonstrates in films such as *How to Kiss*.

- **Surprise reveal.** The audience is unsure of the scenario of the piece (or is intentionally misled) until its true identity is revealed at the end. An example is Alex Whitney's *Oblivious*, in which an alien landscape turns out to be something else entirely. Keep in mind that even though it falls under the gag category, the surprise reveal is often more poignant than funny, as in films such as Chris Wedge's *Bunny*. It can also be tragic, as in the Oscar-nominated *Cathedral*, or merely explanatory, as in *Anniversary* or *Sprout*.

Figure 2.22
The short gag, in which something unexpected usually occurs, is a very popular short animated film genre.

The Booty

In this structure, the protagonist wants something (perhaps money, food, or a girl) and usually suffers through a series of often overly complicated, botched attempts before successfully capturing the object of his desire. Of course, sometimes he ultimately fails. If the object of the protagonist's affection is a moving target, a chase is often involved. Keep in mind that the goal must be worthy and not easily or immediately attainable. Examples include *Fat Cat on a Diet*, *Knick Knack*, *Lunch*, *Egg Cola*, and every Wile E. Coyote cartoon (see Figure 2.23).

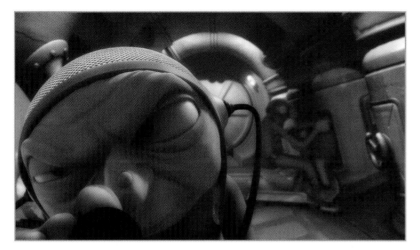

Figure 2.23
An overly complicated attempt at reaching an object of desire represents the popular short film structure we like to call *the booty*.

Figure 2.24
A short animated film can provide the clever filmmaker with a great forum for delivering a message or a moral as long as it is presented with subtlety and clarity. Humor and unique abstraction are especially appropriate styles for this genre.

The Moral

This structure uses allegory or direct finger pointing as a vehicle for making a political or social statement. Often, characters who oppose or ignore the author's agenda ultimately suffer consequences or cause others to suffer because of their negligence, as in *Balance* (don't be greedy), *Point 08* (don't drink and drive), and *One by Two* (selfishness leads to loneliness). In some cases, the character(s) learn an important lesson by eventually adopting the author's view or ultimately realizing the folly of their previously misguided opposition, as in *The Big Snit* (don't miss the forest for the trees). Other short films that practically scream, "and the moral is," include *For the Birds* (he who laughs last, laughs best), *Bert* (don't judge people just because they are different), *Passing Moments* (he who hesitates is lost), *Values* (be supportive of your children's dreams), and *Le Processus* (don't be a lemming—see Figure 2.24). Always remember that messages are best served with an appropriate combination of clarity and subtlety.

The Villain

In this structure, an enemy is at hand and must be conquered or evaded. Many villain stories contain several of the following types of actions, but some contain only one.

◆ **The stronghold—defend!** This action is when the villain is attempting to enter and disturb or destroy the protagonist's happy home, as in *The Three Little Pigs*.

◆ **The invasion—eject!** In this action, an unwanted element (such as a monster, villain, or mother-in-law) has entered the picture, disturbing the hero's happy home, and must be removed, destroyed, or successfully evaded. Sometimes the protagonist does not prevail. Occasionally, the initially unwanted element is ultimately accepted. Invasion examples include *The Wrong Trousers*, *The Cat Came Back*, *Grinning Evil Death*, *Tin Toy*, *AP2000*, and *Technological Threat*.

◆ **The chase—evade!** The hero finds himself dangerously vulnerable, often in open terrain, where he is pursued by the menacing villain. *Sarah* is a fine example. Keep in mind that a straightforward chase scene is not usually a very interesting story. Even if it has a resolution in which the hero either escapes or gets caught, it is still not much of a story unless there is a particularly intriguing setup, the hero comes up with an especially clever escape, or he somehow turns the tables on his pursuer.

◆ **The battle—engage!** The hero partakes in direct physical or mental conflict with his antagonist, as in films such as *Puppet*, *Silhouette*, *Polygon Family*, and every episode of *Celebrity Death Match* (see Figure 2.25).

The Pickle

In this structure, the protagonist finds himself in a predicament (often caused by his own negligence or poor judgment) which he must solve or escape from. In many cases, a beat-the-clock scenario is involved. *The Sorcerer's Apprentice* is a classic example. Others include *Top Gum*, *Locomotion*, and *Coffee Love* (see Figure 2.26).

The Parody

This structure is a parody of a documentary, television commercial, or any other existing property. *Creature Comforts* and *Fishman* are fine examples.

I Wish...

In this structure, the protagonist yearns for (or remembers) a happier or more exciting time or situation. Examples in shorts include *Comics Trip*, *Le Deserteur*, and *Red's Dream* from Pixar (see Figure 2.27).

Figure 2.25
In the popular villain at large scenario, something or someone nefarious or simply unwanted must be evaded, ejected, defended against, or defeated.

Figure 2.26
Well, this is a fine pickle I've gotten myself into!

Figure 2.27
A character dreaming of a better, happier, safer, or more interesting time or place can make for a poignant and entertaining animated short.

The Rescue

In this structure, someone (or a group of characters) shows up and saves the day. *Bunkie & Booboo* and *La Morte de Tau* are two examples. If a character rescues himself, the story either falls under the escape or pickle category.

The Journey

There are two types of journey structures.

- **External.** This type of journey involves an expedition, often in the hopes of finding a better place to live. *Horses on Mars* is a fine example.
- **Internal.** This is a journey of self-discovery or growth. Often an actual geographical quest is the backdrop. PDI's classic *Locomotion* contains a quickly realized internal journey.

Fine Arts

This structure consists of a non-narrative series of imagery and movement, almost always set to music. This is not a true "story"; however, if the imagery is significantly unique or interesting, it can be an extremely engaging and memorable piece. Examples include *Garden of the Metal* and *Au Petit Mort* (see Figure 2.28).

Figure 2.28
Animated shorts with unique and captivating imagery in motion and an intentional absence of significant story elements are known as fine arts films, such as *Au Petite Mort* from Little Fluffy Clouds.

If you are planning to write a short story of more narrative complexity than a single-beat gag, a simple monologue, or a fine arts piece, make sure your plot elements are clear, significant, interesting, and well structured. The setup must spark the audience's interest. The protagonist's goal must be worthy and difficult to achieve to make success triumphant or failure tragic. The main opposing force must be powerful enough to make the challenge interesting. The occasional roadblocks along the journey must be more than simply trivial distractions; otherwise, they won't contribute anything to the action. The ending must be satisfying and logical, and at least some element of your story must be particularly unique or there won't be any reason for anyone to watch your film (and thus there will be no reason for you to enter the production phase).

Keeping It Short

Strive to keep your film as short as possible without compromising flow and clarity. The shorter your story, the simpler it will be to produce as a film and the easier it will be to keep your audience engaged. Here are a few thoughts to keep in mind while developing your story that should help keep things short and sweet.

- **Give yourself a target length and structure your story based on a general idea of your available schedule and budget.** For instance, if you have limited time and money, a single-beat gag, surprise scenario reveal, or fine arts film is a safe bet because such structures can be effectively delivered in less than a minute. A six-minute film can probably contain a fairly full hero's journey, relationship arc, or perhaps even a plot twist or two. A 15-minute film will afford you enough screen time for more complex story structures.

◆ **Hit the ground running.** It is often a good idea to cut to the chase as soon as possible. Start your story in the midst of an action and explain (or don't explain) later. In a feature film, the audience expects to be interested and entertained for 90 minutes or more. After the first several minutes, the viewers will begin asking questions about the story. Who are these people? What are the era and locale? Where is this story going? Is this supposed to be funny or scary? If these questions are not sufficiently addressed, confusion or boredom will set in. In a short story, however, it's all over by the time the audience starts asking such questions. Therefore, the short story writer has a decided advantage because it is often quite acceptable to leave out exposition and simply deliver compelling action with a climax or a punch line. This is especially true with animated shorts, in which the audience can expect to be taken into a fantastical or perhaps abstract world without any real explanation (see Figure 2.29). If you write a short animation script about a chimpanzee police officer, you can pretty much expect that your audience will buy into this scenario for at least a few minutes before they start questioning the reality of the situation. This grace period offers you an excellent opportunity to explore the farthest reaches of your imagination without worrying too much about having to explain everything.

Figure 2.29
Audiences will graciously accept bizarre, unexplained, abstract, surreal, exaggerated, or fantastical scenarios and characters in a short animated film.

2. Story

◆ **Constantly ask yourself what you can leave out.** Your short story should be like a marble sculpture, where you remove everything that is not crucial to the work of art you plan to deliver. Trace through your story and apply the word "why" to every scene, action, character, and line of dialogue. Ask yourself, "Why is this element in my film?" Every component of your story needs to be a step along the path to the climax or punch line. Each scene needs to bring about a change or a movement that directly leads to your story's conclusion or the exploration of its central theme, contributes to setting a mood, or provides necessary information about a character or a current event. If a scene does not satisfy one of these conditions, it should probably be cut (see Figure 2.30). If you have an early scene that establishes the setting of your story, ask yourself whether revealing the locale or era of your story is absolutely necessary. Sometimes it is indeed important for creating a mood, but your story might be just as effective if the setting is vague or not initially established. If you've written a particularly creative or exciting scene and you're certain that it will look really cool on the screen but it contributes nothing to your story's narrative flow, cut it. Is every minor character in your story absolutely required? Can two be combined as one? If a line of dialogue is redundant to an action, get rid of it.

Figure 2.30
Constantly ask yourself, "Why is this scene or character in my film?" If you don't have a satisfactory answer, cut it.

◆ **Once you've established the necessity of every scene, analyze each one for economy and efficiency.** Is every scene as succinct as possible? Is there a faster way to deliver a particular story point or characterize your protagonist?

◆ **Can important plot points be simply referred to in previous or subsequent scenes or acts, rather than actually being played out?** Not every beat of your story necessarily needs to be shown. Often a line or two of dialogue can replace a missing scene, especially if that scene falls under the category of back-story. Sometimes it is desirable to leave out a lengthy first act where the characters and conflicts are established and jump right into the action. With some clear visuals or a couple of lines of dialogue, it's usually pretty easy to bring the audience up to speed.

◆ **Exaggerate.** Because a short story delivers less information than a full-length narrative, it is often necessary to exaggerate its elements in the interest of clarity and efficiency. You must deliver more with less and do so in a limited timeframe. Character traits usually need to be more obvious, indicative, and perhaps rather stereotypical. Conflicts should be magnified where the forces of antagonism are often exaggerated. The stakes should be higher, the crises more extreme, the villains more direct, and the odds against the hero succeeding quite significant. The more exaggerated your story elements, the less time it will take to describe or develop them.

◆ **Consider using text or voiceover narration at the beginning or end of your short to complete the story (but not to reveal a moral), rather than trying to contain too many events within the scope of the film itself.** After all, even though most stories have a complete narrative structure unto themselves, no story exists on an island. Something always came before and something always happens after. Even in a four-hour movie, an author must decide where in the context of a larger story his sub-story will take place. If you feel that your audience requires some additional information with regard to events outside the scope of your actual film for it to stand on its own, text and narration can be effective shortcuts for creating such narrative totality.

◆ **Keep plot twists and digressions to a minimum.** Fairly simple, somewhat linear plots without significant sub-plots are generally recommended.

◆ **Once your story is fully formed in your head or on paper, try to summarize it in a single paragraph as if you were writing the descriptive text for the back of your film's future DVD case.** If it takes more than a few sentences to describe the gist of your story, it might be too long or too complex and you should see what you can do to increase its narrative efficiency.

Think of it this way: Suppose you have a complicated story to tell someone. You'll recite it one way if you have a few hours at your disposal. But imagine you're on a 15-minute coffee break with a coworker instead—or even a three-minute break, for that matter. How will you compress the story to fit into each of these shortened time periods? Certainly not by simply talking faster. Rather, you'll likely leave out extraneous details, avoid sidetracks, and trust that your listener can fill in a few gaps with his own innate sense of continuity.

Exercise: Think of an event in which you participated recently—a soccer game, a trip to France, an exciting night on the town, a first date, or a long and complicated day at the office. Then time yourself telling different versions of the story to a mirror or to a friend. First try to tell the story in 15 minutes. Then tell the same story in seven minutes, then three, then one, and then 30 seconds. Consider the ways in which you compressed and omitted certain details while keeping the story complete in each different time period. If you've written or imagined a script for your short film, apply this same exercise and see just how short you can possibly make your film without losing clarity and continuity. Remember, in general, the shorter your film, the smaller your budget and the simpler your production cycle.

You're Making a Movie, After All

As you develop the individual beats of your story, remember to think cinematically (see Figure 2.31). It is not enough for the scenes of your story to seem strong on paper; they must ultimately look and sound compelling on the screen as well. If you have a scene with dialogue, consider the body language of your characters as well as the delivery and tone of their voices, not just the words themselves. If you are writing an action sequence, think about the camera angles you will use and the pacing of the individual shots.

Also, as you are developing your story, constantly ask yourself whether you have the time, skills, and tools to effectively produce each scene in your chosen visual format. If a scene requires a large number of characters and an epic landscape with lots of weather effects, you might want to consider simplifying or omitting it. In other words, continuously remind yourself not to bite off more than you can chew.

Figure 2.31
Remember, you are not creating a piece of literature; rather, you are planning a film, which is primarily a visual medium. Therefore, always think cinematically while you are developing your story beats.

2. Story

Storytelling Pitfalls That Can Ruin a Good Short Film

Writing a good story is not easy; many things can go wrong. Here are a few pitfalls to try and avoid when constructing your short narrative.

◆ **Too long.** We recommend keeping your short to three or four minutes or less. It is difficult enough to capture an audience in the first place, and the longer your story is, the harder it gets to maintain their attention. If you can't describe the gist of your story in a single sentence, it's probably too long.

◆ **Logic errors, unbelievable coincidences, and plot holes.** Nothing breaks the immersive quality of a story like a glaring mistake in logic, believability, or plot progression. Feature films such as *Godzilla*, *The Last Boy Scout*, and *Hollowman* have so many logic flaws that it's difficult to maintain believability as their plots unfold. The entire premise of Gus Van Zant's *Finding Forrester* is based on an extremely convenient coincidence, which is a perfectly acceptable device in a comedy or a fantasy film, but can be quite distracting in a supposedly realistic drama. Make sure your story beats make sense before you begin production.

◆ **Inconsistent internal logic.** Most animated films ask you to suspend your disbelief to some degree. In doing so, a world is created with its own (possibly altered) rules of physics, gravity, and injury immunity. Once the rules of this world have been established, they must not be broken without an acceptable explanation. If you are creating a haunted house film with ghosts that pass through walls, it doesn't make sense to allow your protagonist to successfully punch one of these otherwise intangible beings. You should feel free (and absolutely encouraged) to bend the rules of reality to suit your storytelling needs. Just remember to consistently stay within the lines of the logic boundaries you've drawn—or at least have a very good reason for straying outside of them.

◆ **Too slow.** There is no more effective way to permanently lose an audience than to bore them. This is why pacing is such an important storytelling device and should be given thorough attention when writing and editing your film. Audiences will sometimes (temporarily) forgive logic errors and plot holes in the hopes that they will be eventually be explained or resolved, but once a viewer falls asleep you may never get them back.

◆ **Style inconsistencies and inappropriate genre juxtapositions.** A slapstick joke, such as a pratfall, in the middle of a poignant, cerebral comedy can irreparably damage the overall style of the piece and break the audience's connection to the story.

◆ **Inconsistent character behavior.** Your audience must be able to relate to your main characters or at least find them interesting to maintain their attention. If a character acts in a way that is inconsistent with his normal or expected behavior, he must have sufficient motivation to do so. Your characters need to be true to themselves and not display uncharacteristic behavior without an acceptable explanation. If Santa Claus commits murder, he had better be a villain in disguise or exist within the context of a particularly dark black comedy.

◆ **Too preachy or too clever.** When you are producing a moral piece, strive for subtle clarity. Try not to be too heavy-handed with your message. Audiences usually don't like to come away from a film experience with the feeling that they've just attended a lecture or a political rally. Be subtle with your message, but don't be so subtle that your film loses clarity. If you construct an intricate puzzle that comes off as a contest to see which audience members are smart enough to get your point, you'll surely lose a lot of them. David Lynch's *Mullholland Drive* is often criticized thusly, while the world of modern poetry is littered with unnecessarily intricate vocabulary and abstract metaphors masquerading as cleverness. Short animated films that deliver their moral or message with a successful combination of clarity and subtlety include *Bert*, *Passing Moments*, *For the Birds*, *Early Bloomer*, *Balance*, and *Values*.

◆ **Manipulative.** In a realistic or serious film, it is generally not considered good narrative form to *tell* an audience how to feel with tear-jerking cinematic tricks or all too obvious villain-identifying clues. And while shamefully manipulative features such as *Philadelphia* and *I Am Sam* tend to be commercially successful, we suggest that you try to hold yourself to a higher standard of dramatic subtlety. Films such as *What's Eating Gilbert Grape* and *You Can Count On Me,* as well as the shorts *Within an Endless Sky, Mouse,* and *Le Processus* invite the audience members to respond naturally because the emotional content is delivered with subtlety and moral ambiguity.

◆ **Not funny.** Be honest with yourself. If you can't tell a joke or write funny material, don't try to make a comedy. Nothing is more embarrassing to a storyteller than a joke that fails. Study the comedic elements of short films by such directors as Peter Lord, Nick Park, Bill Plympton, Cordell Barker, Richard Condie, Chuck Jones, and Bob Hertzfeldt.

◆ **Predictable.** If your film has a punch line, try not to give it away before the fact, and don't give your story a title that reveals the surprise ending. Imagine the loss of effectiveness if *The Empire Strikes Back* had been called *I Am Your Father, Luke.* Furthermore, if you've established a particularly familiar setup, make sure it leads somewhere other than the obvious or expected conclusion. If your audience thinks they know where your story is heading and you prove them right, they will surely come away disappointed.

◆ **Too derivative.** It is perfectly acceptable to reference or vary a story that has been told before, but there is a fine line between paying homage and ripping off. Be wary of crossing that line. If the audience has seen it all before, you won't hold their interest very long.

◆ **No third act.** Although not all film audiences prefer happy endings, most viewers expect some kind of resolution. Conflicts generally need to be resolved, journeys are preferably completed, problems like to be solved, and punch lines need to be clear and complete.

> If you find you're having trouble with the structure and flow of your story, consider working with note cards. Write out each scene or story beat on a separate card and then lay them out on the floor or pin them to a wall and try out various rearrangements until you find the most effective and dramatic narrative flow.

Titles

You can invent your film's title at any stage of production. Perhaps a great title idea is what set your creative storytelling juices flowing in the first place. If not, it's likely that an appropriate one will reveal itself to you as your production develops. Or, you might choose to wait until your script or film is completed before you think up an appropriate title. Either way, here is a list of some common title types that might help spark your imagination.

◆ **The name(s) of the protagonist(s).** Feature films include *Jimmy Neutron, Shrek,* and *Bonnie and Clyde.* Shorts include *Bert, Luxo Jr., Sarah, Snookles, Fishman,* and *Fluffy.*

◆ **The protagonist's profession, hobby, or life situation.** Feature films include *The Godfather, The Graduate, Taxi Driver,* and *Blade Runner.* Shorts include *The Crossing Guard, El Arquero,* and *The Sorcerer's Apprentice.*

◆ **The villain(s) or a supporting character.** Feature films include *Jaws, The Wizard of Oz, Goldfinger,* and *Alien.* Shorts include *The Sandman* and *The Chubb Chubbs.*

◆ **The setting (place, time, or both).** Feature films include *Jurassic Park*, *Casablanca*, *1941*, *Ice Age*, and *2001: A Space Odyssey*. Shorts include *The Cathedral*, *Garden of the Metal*, *Gas Planet*, *Within an Endless Sky*, and *Iceland*.

◆ **A significant story object.** Feature films include *The Maltese Falcon*, *Titanic*, and *Rear Window*. Shorts include *Egg Cola*, *The Snowman*, and *The Wrong Trousers* (see Figure 2.32).

◆ **The protagonist's name plus an associated object, setting, profession, or action.** Feature films include *Lawrence of Arabia*, *Harry Potter and the Sorcerer's Stone*, and *Schindler's List*. Shorts include *Geri's Game*, *Fat Cat on a Diet*, *Red's Dream*, *Horses on Mars*, and *Henry's Garden*.

◆ **The main plot.** Feature films include *The Empire Strikes Back*, *Home Alone*, and *How the Grinch Stole Christmas*. Shorts include *The Cat Came Back*, *La Mort de Tau*, *Lunch*, and *The Deadline*.

◆ **The central theme of the story.** Feature films include *It's a Wonderful Life*, *Love Story*, and *The Way We Were*. Shorts include *Values*, *Balance*, *Getting Started*, and *Passing Moments*.

Figure 2.32
A significant story object like *The Wrong Trousers* can serve as an appropriate short film title.

◆ **A metaphor, cliché, or a double or hidden meaning.**
(Be careful not to give away the punch line or spoon-feed the message to your audience!) Feature films include *Independence Day*, *Gone with the Wind*, *To Kill a Mockingbird*, and *A Clockwork Orange*. Shorts include *A Close Shave*, *Squaring Off*, *For the Birds*, *The Invisible Man in Blind Love*, *Point 08*, *Comics Trip*, *Top Gum*, *The Baby Changing Station*, *Cat Ciao*, and *Framed*.

If you're still stuck for a good title, try thinking of a few words or sentences that describe a significant event or plot point in your film and then consult a thesaurus for alternative words that effectively provide the same information.

Format

If you plan to create your CG short all by yourself or with a very small team of collaborators, you can generally get away with recording your story in whatever medium or format you choose. It might exist entirely in your head, on a series of paper napkins, as a sequence of rough thumbnail drawings, or as an audio recording on a portable tape deck. As long as the story is easily accessible to you and your potential team members, it is generally not necessary to follow proper screenplay structure. However, if you are planning to assemble a large team or you expect to pitch your story to a production company or your boss someday to secure funding, it might be appropriate to write out your story in standard screenplay format. Because this book is aimed at the small team or individual, we will forego any discussion on this matter and instead simply direct you to Appendix B, "Suggested Reading," where you will find a number of excellent books on the subject.

Tell Your Story to Others

During every phase of your short film production, it is often a good idea (and usually quite educational) to consider showing the status of your piece to someone else for feedback, especially if you have any doubts about the strength or clarity of your narrative elements (see Figure 2.33). If you're not sure whether your story makes sense or is too predictable, tell it to a friend and see what he thinks. If the response is boredom, you might want to do some editing. If the response is confusion, analyze the clarity of each plot beat and consider the fact that your story might be a bit too abstract. If you're not sure whether your story has already been told in exactly the same way, ask around.

And be selective about your critics. If you seek feedback from everyone you know, your work could become collaboration, and you'll risk losing sight of your initial artistic vision. The desire to avoid being the victim of plagiarism or to deliver a surprise ending often makes it tempting and desirable to keep your ideas to yourself. These are valid concerns, but don't always expect that you'll be the best judge of your own work.

Keep in mind that oddly enough, negative feedback is often more helpful than compliments as long as the criticisms are constructive rather than merely insulting. Remember that the worst possible reaction is indifference. If most of your critics love your piece, you're probably on the right track. If they think it stinks, most of them should be able to tell you why, and you can then choose to review and perhaps repair the sources of their complaints. If you get no reaction whatsoever you've delivered mediocrity, which is the ultimate sin for an artist. Even a bad story is better than a mediocre story because at least the bad one will get a reaction.

Objective Self-Criticism

If you truly want to keep your idea hidden from external scrutiny until your film is completed, you need to develop the ability to critique your own work as objectively as possible (see Figure 2.34). One way to accomplish this is to give yourself some distance. Set your story aside for a few days and then, when you review it, try to pretend that someone else wrote it. Apply the same critical eye you would use on another writer's work. Ask yourself tough questions about the piece.

◆ Is it paced well?

◆ Are there any plot holes or logic errors?

◆ Are the story beats clear, and does each action contribute directly or indirectly to the central theme, premise, or message of the story?

Figure 2.33
Telling your story to a select audience and gauging their response can often provide you with an opportunity to fix any glaring errors in logic, structure, or pacing before you enter the production phase.

Figure 2.34
Objective self-criticism is perhaps the most effective production tool a filmmaker can possess.

◆ Is the ending sufficiently satisfying?

◆ If it's supposed to be funny, is it?

◆ How many acts does it contain?

◆ If it has three acts, can you identify the instigating incident that ushers in the second act and the climax that brings about the third?

◆ What is the protagonist's goal? Is it worthy of a story?

◆ What is the central obstacle? Is it sufficiently challenging?

And while this might seem like an obvious point, if you're not interested or entertained by your story, nobody else will like it either. Be brutally honest with yourself. If your story has problems, go back and fix them. Don't let yourself believe that your viewers might miss or forgive your errors. Even a child will notice a glaring logic hole or a weak ending.

A Few Examples

Now that we've discussed the elements of storytelling, let's analyze a few examples of CG shorts that contain good stories that are well told.

Figure 2.35
Dan Bransfield's *Fishman*

Dan Bransfield's *Fishman* is a hilarious parody that effectively combines originality with familiarity (see Figure 2.35). The story opens in the midst of an action, where a pair of bumbling superheroes, loosely based on Batman and Robin, fail to accomplish their intended mission after getting caught up in the frustrating and all-too-familiar task of trying to parallel park their oversized car. The humor succeeds mainly because the "hero" arrogantly believes himself to be a successful and observant crime fighter, while his actions tell a very different story. Poking fun at arrogant stupidity is a very popular and effective form of comedy. The ridiculous costumes and exaggerated vehicle design also contribute to the humor of this film. At only two minutes and 19 seconds in length, this film moves along at a solid pace, with suitable music adding to its overall appeal. The style is an interesting and amusing contrast between the dark, film-noir look of a 1930s gangster drama and the silly and overly colorful designs of the main characters and their fish-mobile.

Figure 2.36
Wilhelm Landt and Joachim Bub's *On the Sunny Side of the Street*

On the Sunny Side of the Street, by Wilhelm Landt and Joachim Bub, tells a very simple and straightforward story but achieves appeal and originality with its style and structure (see Figure 2.36). The style is that of an early twentieth-century silent film, using black and white imagery, old-fashioned clothing and props, simulated film projection imperfections, and suitably nostalgic music. The structure of this film is interesting because it tells the same story twice from two different points of view, and then combines these alternate perspectives together at the end. This relatively uncommon structuring helps to make this otherwise straightforward story into something quite original.

Jason Wen's *f8* is a 12-minute science fiction tale that combines a gritty visual style with appropriate pacing, interesting camera angles, and somber music to form a tense and cautionary tone with an air of impending doom (see Figure 2.37). The story gracefully comments on the perils of technology gone astray and the loss of individuality and humanity. The central theme is somewhat familiar to science fiction fans, but the delivery and details are especially unique and interesting.

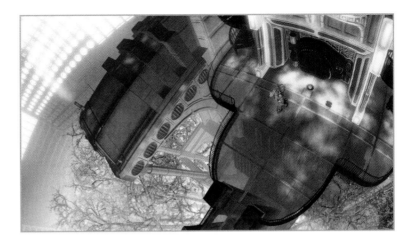

Figure 2.37
Jason Wen's *f8*

Summary

While the commercial success of many blockbuster films might suggest otherwise, strong story elements are more important than strong production elements. A story can be defined as a series of interconnected or related events, which, through conflict, significantly change a scenario or a character. A short story is one that delivers such events with economy and efficiency. The four basic story ingredients are plot, character, setting, and conflict. A character in a setting with a worthy goal, a reason why it can't be immediately achieved, and a subsequent plan with complications is an extremely common formula for a story premise. The way a story is told is equally (if not more) important than the story elements themselves. A good story that is poorly told will be as ineffective as a badly delivered joke. Storytelling tools include genre, structure, and pacing. Remember that a short story is not just a long-form story told more quickly. Rather, you must apply significant differences in structure and pacing. Economy and efficiency are the keys. Linear plots with a single or few characters are recommended. When constructing your short script, think cinematically and apply the word "why" to each scene, character, and action, making sure every element in your story is there for a reason. Remember that all rules of story construction and delivery can be bent and broken as long as you do so creatively, not just because you simply want to appear clever or different. In Chapter 3, "Character Development and Design," we will discuss characters, which are typically used to channel the events and emotional impact of a story to an audience.

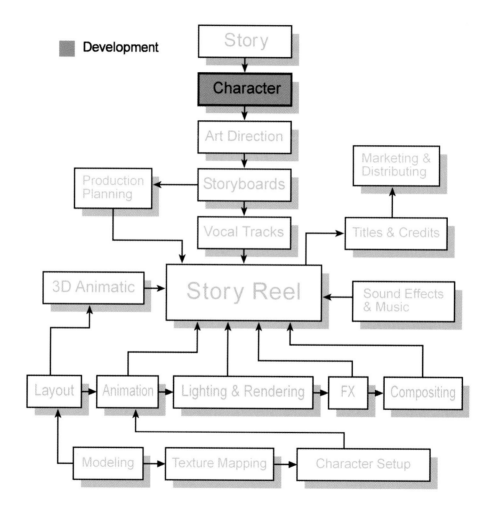

chapter 3
Character Development and Design

M any scholars agree that a story's ability to attract and hold an audience is more a result of strong character development than strong plot progression. It can easily be argued that all memorable films contain memorable characters. Where would *The Godfather* be without Don Corleone? Or *The Wizard of Oz* without the Scarecrow? A *memorable* character is believable, relatable, and interesting. And a *well-developed* character will successfully channel the emotional impact of the events of your story to your audience.

"What is your name?
What is your quest?
What is your favorite color?"
Monty Python and the Holy Grail

It has been said that there are only a few basic storylines. However, an infinite number of variations exist through the introduction of new characters with unique points of views into this otherwise finite group of plots and scenarios.

Some short films of the fine arts or especially abstract variety, such as Hitoshi Akayamo's *Garden of the Metal*, don't require any actual characters in order to provide an audience with engaging entertainment value. However, if your intention is to create an animated short that tells a story, you'll likely need at least one living, breathing, thinking protagonist. Audiences expect to *identify* with or at least be *interested* in the main characters of the films they enjoy. One or both of these character-audience connections is crucial to an engaging character-based narrative. If the viewer sees recognizable features of your main character and can relate to his attitude and behavior, this connection will be well established. However, relatable character traits are not always absolutely necessary. Your protagonist might look and behave in ways that are entirely misunderstood or completely alien to your viewers, but if he or she is sufficiently interesting, your audience will still feel compelled to watch the story unfold. Concern, curiosity, or preferably both is what you ultimately want from your viewers.

Furthermore, it is not necessarily important, nor even desirable, for your audience members to actually *like* all of your characters. When creating a villain, of course, you often want your audience to fear, dislike, or distrust him. Such characters that we love to hate include Darth Vader, The Grinch, Vic Vinyl from Phil McNally's *Pump Action,* and Raf Anzovin's puppet master (see Figure 3.1). Remember that in order to connect your audience to your characters, sympathy is optional but empathy and interest are essential.

Live action films have a decided advantage over animated films when it comes to creating audience-character connections. Assuming that the main characters are human, audiences will automatically identify with the cast members of a live action film because they can safely presume certain shared attributes

Figure 3.1
A villain should inspire an appropriate negative reaction from your audience.

Figure 3.2
Even anthropomorphic, abstract, cartoony, or fantastical characters should have a few familiar human attributes, needs, desires, and behaviors.

and motivations. When creating animated film characters, however, this connection cannot merely be assumed; it must be effectively constructed through design, behavior, and/or dialogue. No matter how realistic your attempt, all animated characters stray from absolute realism by some degree. And most, in fact, are significantly different from their live human or non-human counterparts. Regardless of the species and abstraction level of your main characters, you must establish a connection between them and your audience. To do this effectively, you must give your characters some familiar or identifiably human attributes and goals (see Figure 3.2). Buzz Lightyear is a toy, Stuart Little is a mouse, and Shrek is a monster. However, all of these non-human characters have familiar and relatable traits and desires. Buzz wants identity and respect, Stuart wants to belong to a nice family, and Shrek just wants to be left alone.

Character Styles

The characters in your short film can be humans, animals, anthropomorphized toys or vehicles, vegetables, minerals, spiritual entities, or aliens—or they can defy any standard classification whatsoever. You might choose to make them highly realistic, stylized, idealized, exaggerated, caricature, abstract, or symbolic (see Figures 3.3 through 3.7).

Figure 3.3
Semi-real, cartoony, and abstract humans

Figure 3.4
Realistic, cartoony, and abstract animals

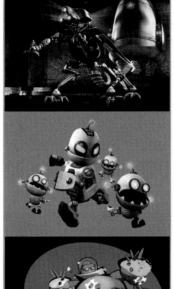

Figure 3.5
Realistic, cartoony, and abstract monsters

Figure 3.6
Realistic and cartoony robots

Figure 3.7
Realistic and cartoony minerals and vegetables

Table 3.1 shows a handy matrix used to classify 3D story characters by genre and style.

Most narrative characters can find an appropriate spot in Table 3.1. Some characters, of course, are hybrids, combining elements from two or more genres. Jimmy Neutron's best friend, Goddard, is a robot dog, and Stuart Little can be considered a hybrid because he looks like a mouse but walks, talks, and dresses like a human (see Figure 3.8). Although mixing genres in a single character can be quite interesting, mixing styles rarely leads to appealing results. Introducing

Figure 3.8
A character can be a design hybrid, like a robot-alien-insect, or an anomaly hybrid, like Stuart Little, whose appearance is that of a mouse, but whose behavior, posture, dialogue, and dress code are that of a human.

59

Table 3.1 Genre/Style Chart

Genre/Style	Real or Semi-Real	Abstract or Cartoony
Human	Aki from *Final Fantasy* The baby from *Tin Toy* The old man from *Geri's Game* The girl from *Respire*	Woody from *Toy Story* *Major Damage* The blue boy from Keith Lango's *Lunch* The couple from *Polygon Family*
Animal	The protagonist from PDI's *Bunny* Falcon from *Stuart Little 2* The prehistoric beasts from *Dinosaur*	Scrat from *Ice Age* Our feathered friends from *For the Birds* Cubicle from *Squaring Off* The *Antz* The tadpoles from *Early Bloomer*
Aliens, monsters, and mythological creatures	The bugs from *Starship Troopers* Draco from *Dragonheart* Gollum from *The Lord of the Rings*	Shrek Sulley and Wazowski from *Monsters, Inc.* The *Chubb Chubbs* The dragon from *Top Gum*
Machines and robots	*Luxo Jr.* *The Iron Giant* The robot from *Dronez*	B.E.N. from *Treasure Planet* Clank from the game *Ratchet & Clank*
Food, minerals, and other inanimate objects	*Horses on Mars* The leaf from *Alma* The carpet from Disney's *Aladdin* *Bunkee & Booboo* The hero from *Coffee Love*	The California Raisins *Killer Bean* Archibald Asparagus from *Veggie Tales* The characters in *Bert* Hew and Kew from *Das Rad*
Too abstract to classify	*Rolie Polie Olie*	The 7-Up "Dot" *Poor Bogo*

abstract or cartoony elements into an otherwise realistic character design generally looks more odd than creative (see Figure 3.9). An exception might be when the opposing elements are particularly stylized, as in the mixing of cartoony heads and more realistic bodies in many Japanese Anime films. Furthermore, the line that separates semi-real from abstract is sometimes a bit blurry. The original video game version of Lara Croft is certainly idealized, but should she be considered semi-real, or are her proportions so exaggerated that she should fall under the category of a cartoon?

Consider the advantages and disadvantages of different character styles, as discussed in Table 3.2.

Be sure that the style of your character works with the genre of your film (see Figure 3.10). Imagine the loss of effectiveness if the characters in dark, poignant morality pieces, such as *f8* or *Balance*, were cute, goofy bunnies with enormous eyeballs and yellow polka-dotted bowties. Similarly, if you plan to drop anvils on life-like human characters without causing any real or permanent damage, you run the risk of confusing your audience with inconsistent internal logic. Cartoon physics generally works best on cartoon characters. Sometimes it is indeed appropriate and quite fun to apply cartoon logic to human characters; however, such rule breaking is usually only acceptable if your piece is a particularly wacky comedy in the style of *The Three Stooges* or Hiroshi Chida's *Polygon Family*.

Figure 3.9
Mixing realistic and cartoony styles within the same character will tend to look odd, rather than uniquely imaginative.

Character Types

Every character in your story will ultimately fall under one of the following classifications, listed in order of story importance:

1. Protagonist
2. Partners, sidekicks, antagonists, and objects of desire
3. Supporting roles
4. Minor characters
5. Extras

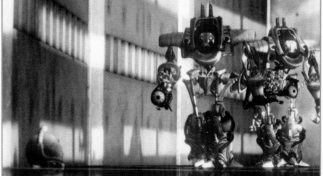

Figure 3.10
In general, the style of your characters should feel appropriate to the genre of your film. A dark, tragic science fiction tale such as *f8* works well with fairly realistic robotic villains.

The most important (or perhaps the only) character in your story is called the *protagonist*. However, assuming your story has multiple characters, the protagonist doesn't necessarily have to be the first one you invent or introduce. It might be desirable to start with your antagonist. After all, he is the one who will very likely create your story's central conflict. Sometimes it is easier to create a hero when his source of antagonism has already been established. Similarly, you might invent an interesting or amusing character who turns out to be more appropriate as a sidekick or a vice president. His particular attributes might even help determine those of his boss.

Table 3.2 Pros and Cons of Character Styles

Style	Pros	Cons
Realistic characters, especially humans	Immediate relatability. Easy to find and study reference material.	Your audience will expect subtle, realistic movement, which is the most difficult form of animation.
Slightly caricatured characters	Close connection with reality, therefore relatively direct relatability. A bit more creative license allowed when it comes to exaggerating behavior and stylizing animation.	Sometimes difficult to find just the right balance between realism and imagination when developing nearly lifelike characters. If the behavior of such a character is too realistic, perhaps there was no good reason to exaggerate him in the first place. If you exaggerate him too much, his behavior and movement will run the risk of being inconsistent with his design.
Cartoon characters	The greatest opportunities for creativity and exaggeration. You can and should feel encouraged to invent your own rules of proportions, symmetry, physics, gravity, and timing; your audience won't expect perfect realism and subtlety from your animations.	Creating unique and appealing cartoon characters is not as simple as it looks. Too much exaggeration can lose all connection with reality. Not enough might just look freakish. It is also sometimes difficult to maintain audience connection with such characters because their designs will stray significantly from real life. Therefore, you must make their behavior sufficiently identifiable and expressive.
Abstract characters	Anything goes. Feel free to break every rule of realism in the book.	Such characters will have the most difficult time establishing an immediate connection with your viewers. Believable movement and behavior will be crucial.

Character Type 1: The Protagonist

The main character in a story is the protagonist (or hero). Although the word "hero" generally implies an individual who is willing to sacrifice for the good of others, we are using the term a bit more loosely to simply refer to any character who strives to overcome a dilemma or a conflict. The protagonist is the person who most directly interacts with the story's central conflict, journey, or punch line, and he is the character the audience is expected to follow, identify with, or care about the most. With very few exceptions, every story has a single main character. Even in buddy films, one partner is always a bit more dominant than the other. In *Monsters, Inc.* and the short *Das Rad,* Sulley and the smaller rock, Kew, respectively, are slightly more dominant if only because their character arcs are more significant (see Figure 3.11). While ensemble films like *Crimes and Misdemeanors*, *Magnolia*, and Supinfocom's *Tom the Cat* have multiple and seemingly equal protagonists, these movies are collections of individual stories, and each one indeed has a single main character.

Figure 3.11
Even in buddy films, one of the two partners nearly always has a more significant character arc, thus qualifying him as the singular protagonist.

Protagonists are rarely perfect or all-powerful. Most have a flaw or two—an Achilles heel, a significant fear, or an obsession of some sort. This is generally necessary to establish believability because, after all, nobody's perfect. Furthermore, protagonists are not always heroes. If a protagonist's flaws dominate his personality, he becomes an antihero. The audience still sympathizes or empathizes with him; however, society would label him as an outlaw or at least a social misfit. Wile E. Coyote is one of the all-time great animated antiheroes. We empathize with his hunger and sympathize with his stupidity, but he is, after all, the villain. Other examples include Leon from *The Professional*, Robin Hood, and Shrek. Thieves often make for interesting antiheroes because they have needs and desires just like the rest of us and they come in a variety of types, including pickpockets, cat burglars, complex heist leaders, crooked politicians, or corporate swindlers. Also, protagonist film thieves usually don't intentionally cause physical harm to their victims, so they are easier to like. The best way to turn a criminal into a sympathetic protagonist is by making *his* enemies even bigger scoundrels (*Payback*, *Ocean's 11*, and Supinfocom's *AP2000*).

There are many other types of heroes as well—unwilling heroes, who are compelled or forced into action despite their fears, laziness, or better judgement (Dorothy or Luke Skywalker); unsung heroes, who remain somewhat anonymous while others gain from their deeds (Aaron Altman from *Broadcast News*); tragic heroes, who suffer significantly for their triumphs (Maximus from *Gladiator* and Alberto Giacometti from *Eternal Gaze*); catalyst heroes, who don't necessarily change or grow themselves, but instead improve the lives of those around them (Monty Brogan from *25th Hour*); superheroes, who have powers or skills beyond those of mere mortals (Spiderman or Major Damage); and underdogs, who beat the odds (Rocky or Supinfocom's *Sarah*) (see Figure 3.12).

Figure 3.12
There are many types of heroes. Alberto Giacometti is portrayed as a tragic hero in Sam Chen's award-winning *Eternal Gaze*. Another common hero type is the underdog, exemplified by the little girl in Supinfocom's *Sarah*.

3. Character Development and Design

Character Type 2: Nearly Equal Partners, Antagonists, and Objects of Desire

Many short films require only a single character. Such simplicity has obvious time, budget, and technical advantages to the individual filmmaker or the small team. However, a second character of nearly equal importance to the protagonist is very often necessary.

This category represents the second most significant character in a story—assuming, of course, that more than one exists. Such number twos generally fall into one of the following three classifications:

◆ Partner, buddy, or teammate

◆ Antagonist

◆ Object of desire

The Partner, Buddy, or Teammate

This character, often only slightly less significant than the protagonist himself, directly contributes to the resolution of the story's central conflict. Laurel had Hardy; Riggs had Murtaugh (*Lethal Weapon*); and Dan Bransfield's Fishman has his patient sidekick (see Figure 3.13). Rarely are a protagonist and his partner of exactly equal significance. The protagonist virtually always has either a bit more screen time or a more significant character arc. And it is almost an absolute rule that the buddy must have a remarkably distinct personality from that of the protagonist. Lennie and George (*Of Mice and Men*), Cates and Hammond (*48 Hours*), and Lilo and Stitch are almost complete opposites; however, they generally share a common goal. One is often the straight man to the other, more comedic role (Martin and Lewis, Shrek and Donkey). If you create two main characters who have basically the same traits and personalities, consider the possibility of simplifying your story by combining them into a single character. A protagonist might also have a group of teammates, each with nearly equivalent significance, such as the Marx Brothers or the members of *Ocean's 11*. Furthermore, the teammates are not always there by choice, nor do they necessarily agree with the protagonist (*Saving Private Ryan*). Regardless of the number or willingness of the partners, they are always at least slightly less dominant than the protagonist.

Figure 3.13
The second most significant character in a film is often the sidekick, like Fishman's trusty partner, shown here.

The Antagonist

More often than not, the second most important character in a story is the antagonist—an opposing force that might be human, animal, monster, or machine. A story's antagonist can also be a non-character element like time or Mother Nature. Antagonists might be full-blown villains who create the central conflict by stealing the gem, kidnapping the princess, or threatening the planet, or they might be mere opponents who compete against the protagonist for a trophy, a dog biscuit, a love interest, or a courtroom judgment. The element that generally distinguishes a villain from a mere opponent is that a villain usually hopes to harm or destroy the protagonist, while an opponent simply wants to win the prize or reach the finish line sooner.

Remember that just as heroes are usually not flawless, villains are usually not all bad. Often they are quite generous and loving to their families, partners, henchmen, or pets. It is often desirable to give your villains some sympathetic qualities so your audience will accept their motivations, and it is not a bad idea to create a villain whom your audience will partially envy, even if they'd rather not admit it. Despite our associated fear or disgust, most of us would probably love to be as brilliant as Hannibal Lecter or as powerful as Saruman.

Opposing forces must be powerful or evil enough to represent a significant and interesting challenge for the protagonist (see Figure 3.14). If a tennis ace plays against an extremely inferior opponent, the game won't be very exciting. Similarly, if your villain is easily defeated, your story won't be especially climactic or memorable. The more powerful the antagonist, the greater the triumph.

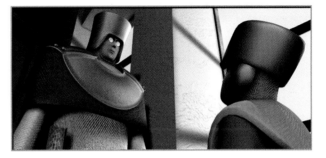

Many villains are obvious bad guys and can easily be identified as such because they display fangs, exposed weaponry, angry dispositions, or especially nasty behavior. However, many of the most sinister villains are demons hiding behind seemingly benevolent or even philanthropic guises. Examples of such wolves in sheep's clothing are Norman Osborn (aka the Green Goblin) and The T1000 from *Terminator 2: Judgement Day*.

Figure 3.14
The force of antagonism must be sufficiently threatening.

It is usually undesirable to have multiple villains in the same story unless they are partners in crime, teams of outlaws, or one is a non-human element, such as a sinking ship mixed with a villainous fiancé (*Titanic*). And unless they are simply psychotic like Norman Bates or sadistic like Vic Vinyl from Phil McNally's *Pump Action*, villains must have logical motivations for their evil deeds. In a short film, however, it is not always necessary to provide this information to your audience. In fact, often you simply won't have time to do so. However, it is usually a good idea for you to know where your bad guys are coming from, even if you don't let your audience in on the secret.

Common human villainous motivations are greed (Big Al from *Toy Story*), power (Dr. Evil in the *Austin Powers* movies), revenge (*Cape Fear*), jealousy (*Fatal Attraction*), and prejudice (*Mississippi Burning*). Common animal and monster motivations are hunger (*Jaws*), territoriality (*For the Birds*), and species preservation (*Alien*).

Remember that most villains see themselves as heroes. Even the most sinister antagonists often believe they are in the right. Badness and goodness are relative—they depend on your point of view and the comparative maliciousness of each opposing force.

The Object of Desire

The third category for character number two is the person waiting on the other side of the conflict—the kidnapped princess, the injured father trapped in a mineshaft, or the elusive love interest (see Figure 3.15). The protagonist must reach, obtain, entice, or rescue this character in order for them to live happily ever after.

Figure 3.15
The elusive love interest

Character Type 3: Supporting Roles

Very often, stories will contain secondary characters who assist or impede the conflict resolution, but not at the same level of significance as the partner or the villain. The archetypal mentor is one such character, as are the seven dwarves, the trusted canine companion, the wacky neighbor, or the enemy's henchman. If your main character is a villain, his victims can probably be appropriately classified as supporting roles. If one of them happens to escape or perhaps defeat your villainous main character, the former victim might indeed graduate to the role of a full-fledged antagonist, even though he will probably be seen as the good guy.

Character Type 4: Minor Characters

Sometimes a few additional characters crop up to sell weaponry, offer brief advice, guard the castle gates, or serve cocktails. These minor roles usually have limited screen time and only marginally assist or temporarily impede the plot's progression or the protagonist's quest. Often they appear to simply give the hero an opportunity to demonstrate a character trait as a result of their interaction.

Character Type 5: Extras

Characters who merely exist as background noise or perhaps as minor obstacles are often included for realism and detail. Extras typically do not speak or directly interact with the main characters.

Character Development

Before, during, or after the creation of your story you'll need to spend some time deciding on the specifics of your protagonists, antagonists, supporting players, and background extras with regard to their physical attributes, personalities, motivations, relationships, and arcs. Demonstrating these characteristics and their progressions to your audience is known as *character development*.

> Keep in mind that protagonists and secondary characters do not necessarily remain static in their classifications. Villains can become partners (my dog, Butch). Partners can turn out to be villains (Denzel Washington in *Training Day*). Mentors might become partners (*The Wedding Planner*). Heroes can fall (Anakin Skywalker), and villains sometimes heroically save the day (Darth Vader).

Character Resumes

Before you can successfully describe a character to an audience, it is often helpful to create a resume or biography for him that will indicate physical, historical, social, and psychological specifics. It is generally a good idea for you to know your characters intimately, even if you won't have the time to deeply develop them within the timeframe of your short film. You can easily assemble a character resume by applying the method-acting technique and asking yourself a few questions about the character. A good place to start is by asking, "What is his dominant character trait?" Everybody has one. Perhaps it's shyness, greed, generosity, musical talent, stubbornness, pacifism, obesity, arrogance, fashion sense, or schizophrenia. Selecting a single dominant trait will help guide your character's design and behavior. Other questions will help to round out the details:

◆ Where did he come from?

◆ How old is he?

◆ What does he look like? Is he exceptionally tall? Dangerously skinny?

- Do people generally like him? Does he have many friends? Enemies?
- Do you want your audience to like, despise, or fear him?
- What does he need or desire? What skills does he possess that will help him achieve his goals?
- What is his biggest fear? Does he have an Achilles heel?
- What, if anything, does he do for a living? Is he good at what he does?
- What is his addiction? Alcohol? Coffee? Chocolate?
- Is he married? Does he have kids?
- How does he see himself? Is it different than the way his friends or enemies see him?
- What are his favorite song, color, and ice cream flavor?

While it is certainly not necessary to complicate your task by answering all of these questions, if you wrap your own head around the most significant attributes, history, and motivations of your character, it will be that much easier to deliver this information to your viewers. And the more you know about your characters, the easier time you'll have appending scenes to your story or some-day producing a sequel.

When describing a character, use specifics such as Persian rather than cat or crotchety instead of old. If your film is going to have multiple characters, indicate their relationships in their resumes. Also take some time to think about the specifics of your characters' environments. Do they exist in a tranquil forest or a dangerous battlefield? An isolated desert island or a heavily populated big city? A housing project near the train station or a penthouse apartment in Beverly Hills? Where a character lives or operates can significantly influence the specifics of his design and personality.

Because you will ultimately be delivering a film, which is primarily a visual medium, a sketch or a render with a few typed or handwritten notes can make an excellent alternative to a formal resume made up of descriptive text (see Figure 3.16).

RESUME FOR MY DOG, BUTCH
- **Breed:** Black Labrador.
- **Color:** Black. (Duh!)
- **Age:** Seven (or 49 in dog years).
- **Size:** 28 inches at the shoulder blades.
- **Weight:** 75 pounds.
- **Where did he come from?** Not sure. He just showed up at my door one day.
- **Favorite food:** Fluffy-burgers and apparently my wife's fettuccini alfredo.
- **Favorite movie:** *Man's Best Friend*.
- **Least favorite animated short:** *The Cat Came Back*.
- **Favorite hobby:** Beach Frisbee.
- **Biggest fear:** Spiders.
- **Favorite place to sleep:** In front of the refrigerator.
- **Other:** Generally suspicious of strangers but loves kids. Often dreams about being a member of the fire department. Wishes we would give him Evian instead of tap water.

Although creating a resume or a bio for your characters is recommended, it is certainly not required. You might choose to keep your piece rather abstract and metaphorical, where a generic character with little or no underlying biographical attributes will be most appropriate. Or perhaps you've designed an especially unique flying dragon and you don't really care about his history or why he is menacing the townspeople and eating all the cows in the village. Perhaps you just want to deliver some exciting flying sequences punctuated with a fierce and explosive confrontation against a powerful and equally one-dimensional wizard.

In a feature film, character history and motivation are important elements for audience connection; however, a short only needs to maintain an audience's attention for a few minutes. Therefore, it is perfectly reasonable to leave out such biographical information and simply deliver a protagonist with a cool look and some exciting mannerisms. By the time your audience starts wondering about where your protagonist came from and why he's behaving with such menacing ferocity, your film will be over. Just remember that if you choose to leave out character history and motivation, the design and behavior of your characters or the significant events of your story will need to be particularly unique and compelling to keep your audience engaged.

Simplicity and Exaggeration

When creating your characters, try to keep them fairly simple in both design and personality. A short animated film is no place for complex characters with lengthy biographies and introspective soliloquies. Choose a few major character traits and explore them sufficiently. Don't arbitrarily add details under the mistaken belief that more is necessarily better. The most important attributes will be the ones that directly relate to your character's behavior within the scope of your actual film. Details can round out characters, but too many can make it difficult to decide how they will react to the events or other characters in your story. Also realize that if you give a character an extreme trait such as a limp or a missing arm, your audience might be distracted from your story while waiting for this abnormality to be explained. Only include such details if they directly or indirectly relate to your story (see Figure 3.17).

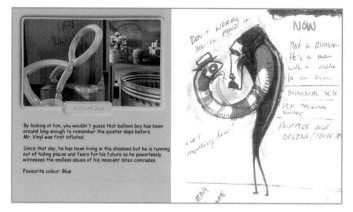

Figure 3.16
A render or drawing with some descriptive notes and questions can work quite well as a character resume.

Keep in mind that because a short film needs to deliver more in a smaller timeframe, it is often a good idea to exaggerate your characters' most significant traits. If your protagonist is fat, make him obese. If your villain is muscular, make him enormous. If a character is allergic to peanuts, make him deathly allergic. Exaggeration not only increases the clarity of your characterizations, but also allows for a bit more margin of error when it comes to modeling and animation. Audiences will generally forgive the bending of physics rules when they are applied to an exaggerated or caricatured character (see Figure 3.18).

Figure 3.17
It is often tempting to arbitrarily add details in the interest of making your characters unique or interesting. However, such elements should only be included if they are important to your story or to the reaction you want to inspire from your viewers.

Figure 3.18
It is often a good idea to exaggerate a character's dominant trait. A bumbling thief should be particularly dorky and clumsy, like this fellow from *Egg Cola*.

Character Development Tools

A filmmaker has four basic tools for developing characters:

◆ Names

◆ Words (text, narration, and speech)

◆ Design

◆ Behavior

Names can be descriptive, connotative, ironic, or completely generic. Words, while often left out completely, can be used to help establish nationality, history, personality, goals, back-stories, and future outcomes. Design will indicate physical attributes, species, profession, social status, and perhaps a few personality traits. Behavior, which is ultimately the most effective method of characterization, will demonstrate personality, attitude, and motivation.

Character Development Tool 1: Names

Long-form writers have the advantage of time; their characters can be slowly and deeply developed through behavior. The short-story author, however, must rely on a few shortcuts to effectively develop characters within the limited timeframe. Names can be particularly effective in this capacity.

Although it is very common and perfectly acceptable to give your characters completely generic names, such as Butch, Sarah, or Sally Burton, you can use more descriptive monikers as handy shortcuts for describing or implying a few important bits of information about your characters. For instance, names can be used to indicate species, profession, or nationality, as in Roger Rabbit; Mr. Potato Head; Krusty the Clown; Luxo Jr.; or Marvin the Martian and his trusty companion, K-9.

A name might also demonstrate an unmistakable character trait, as in Dr. Evil, Dopey, Speedy Gonzales, Bill the Butcher, or Poor Bogo.

Other names contain more suggestive words, allowing them to remain a bit more interpretive or ironic. For instance, Jimmy Neutron is probably smarter than your average schoolboy; Han Solo is presumably something of a loner; Donnie Darko probably doesn't smile a lot; Augustus Gloop likely has a weight problem; Sprout is undoubtedly very young; and oddly enough, a character named Curly is usually bald.

Still other names imply certain personality traits simply because they are associated with particularly famous or infamous historical figures or celebrities, such as Amadeus, Madonna, or Shaquille. The name Arnold was once reserved for bookworms; however, ever since Mr. Schwarzenegger arrived on the scene, that particular handle now inspires images of squared-off chins and oversized biceps. An episode of *Hill Street Blues* once featured a character named Vic Hitler who couldn't understand why his standup comedy career was not more successful. And while it is certainly acceptable to give a particularly adorable little bunny the name Killer, doing so might distract your audience because they will likely spend a fair amount of time wondering whether this name foreshadows some future event or is simply ironic.

You might want to design the look of your characters before giving them names. Often, if you look at a character drawing, a name that feels right will just pop out at you (see Figure 3.19).

Of course, it is often desirable to forego naming your characters at all. In many films, especially short ones, the design, actions, and dialogue of the characters are more than sufficient as narrative tools, and names are simply not required. Vagueness can sometimes be a powerful narrative device because it often allows for a bit more audience interpretation.

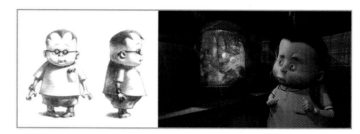

Figure 3.19
This poor kid is definitely a Hubert.

Character Development Tool 2: Text, Narration, and Speech

The limited timeframe of a short film is often insufficient for complete and effective character development through behavior. Displaying text or providing voiceover narration at the beginning of a movie is a timesaving technique you can use to add biographical information and details to the otherwise incomplete character development contained within the scope of the film itself. An advantage of this technique is that it provides the filmmaker the opportunity to open his story in the midst of an action without the need for any actual on-screen setup. Examples include the *Star Wars* films, *The Road Warrior*, and Eric Anderson's *Horses on Mars*.

Similarly, adding a few text lines or a bit of narration at the end of a film can be an effective way of punctuating the piece by providing a bit of information regarding the ultimate outcomes of the characters. This convention is very often used in documentaries, such as *Dogtown and Z-Boys*, films that are based on true stories, such as *Remember the Titans*, and comedies, such as *Animal House*.

You might also choose to intersperse your film with dialogue cards to either simulate the style of early silent films or avoid the time-consuming task of lip-synching.

With regard to actual monologues and dialogues, the pitch, tone, volume, style, accent, vocabulary, and content of a character's words can indicate or imply personality, nationality, status, intelligence, motivation, and goals. Conversations between characters will further define these identity specifics and reveal the nature of their relationships (see Figure 3.20). When Jerry Seinfeld contemptuously greets his neighbor with a sarcastic, "Hello, Newman," we are immediately informed of the fact that these two individuals definitely know one another but probably wish otherwise. Dialogue is one of the strongest devices available for character development (see Chapter 9, "Vocal Tracks").

Figure 3.20
The ways in which people and other creatures interact with one another help to characterize them.

Character Development Tool 3: Design

Sometimes it is preferable to tell a story with completely generic and unremarkable-looking characters that have no distinguishable features whatsoever (see Figure 3.21). Certain metaphorical narratives, such as *Balance*, are often best told with such characters so audience members might have an easier time folding their own points of view into the story. If your desire is to tell a story with generic characters, you will need to connect the audience to them through behavior or dialogue. However, since the short-story format often does not afford the author enough time to effectively develop a character through a lengthy series of indicative actions and conversations, it is generally a good idea to demonstrate at least partially your character personalities and motivations through design.

Definitive versus Interpretive Visual Cues

Before you begin designing a character, ask yourself how important his or her look will be in effectively telling your story. This will help you determine what kinds of painfully clear or vaguely interpretive visual elements your character designs should include. If you want your audience to immediately recognize or understand certain important character traits at first glance, design your characters accordingly with specific and unmistakable visual elements, such as professional uniforms, bloody fangs, wheelchairs, or enormous muscles. However, if you want your characters to be a bit more vague and interpretive, keep such indicative visual clues to a minimum. Giving high heels to a female character or a mustache to a man is certainly a valid element of design, but it doesn't speak to the owners' personalities, attitudes, or goals. Putting those same high heels on the man with the mustache, however, is a much stronger design convention and implies quite a bit about the character's personality and attitude (see Figure 3.22).

Appeal

A well-designed character should have appeal, but keep in mind that the word "appealing" does not necessarily mean "attractive." Rather, in terms of design, it simply means "interesting to look at." And of course, appeal is highly subjective (see Figure 3.23).

Figure 3.21
Generic characters can work just fine in animated shorts as long as their behavior or dialogue is sufficiently interesting.

Figure 3.22
Otherwise generic visual cues, such as mustaches and high heels, can become quite descriptive when combined in a single character.

Figure 3.23
Appeal is in the eye of the beholder.

Indicative Design

A character will also be considered well designed if his visual cues tell the audience something about him. Even if that message is, "I am completely generic and unremarkable," some thought needs to go into the look of that particular character to deliver such a message successfully. Character design can effectively reveal physical attributes (such as strength, gender, age, or race), mental and emotional attributes (such as shyness, intelligence, or courage), and biographical information (such as nationality, religion, or profession) (see Figure 3.24). Motivation and goals are more difficult to imply through design and usually require behavior and dialogue to be demonstrated effectively.

A good character design should also invoke some kind of initial reaction or expectation from your audience (see Figure 3.25). You might want your viewers to immediately feel sympathy for one of your characters, so give him sad eyes, ragged clothing, and a pair of crutches. Or perhaps your audience should be fearful or disgusted at first glance, in which case you should deliver angry brows, sharp weapons, menacing horns and fangs, or huge scars. You might prefer your audience to be confused; therefore, inconsistent visual elements might be in order, such as a tattoo of a peace sign on a soldier's forehead. Or you might want to make a character's design elements more generic and vague so your viewers are forced to wonder about the details of his past, present, and future.

It is sometimes advantageous for a character's design to actually contradict his true nature. For instance, while it is often desirable for the look of a villain to inspire immediate hatred or mistrust from your audience, occasionally the most interesting and dangerous antagonists appear quite harmless until their surprisingly malicious true intentions are revealed.

In general, you simply want to avoid the possibility of your audience reacting to your characters with complete indifference. Some visual cues, even if they are subtle, vague, intentionally confusing, interpretive, or altogether generic, should be included in your character designs to capture at least some degree of audience attention from the start.

Figure 3.24
Character design can imply more than just physical attributes, such as age, species, or gender. Personality, nationality, religion, or profession can also be indicated clearly with the right visual cues.

Figure 3.25
Well-designed characters will often create an immediate audience response. Do these characters inspire sympathy, empathy, suspicion, laughter, or fear?

3. Character Development and Design

Faces

The most distinguishable and expressive part of a character is usually his face. Size, shape, placement, orientation, symmetry, and relative proportions of facial features will generate appeal (or lack thereof) and indicate species, realism level, age, gender, personality, and most importantly, emotion. You can choose to create faceless characters for your film, but keep in mind that doing so will force you to completely rely on body language, animation, and behavior to deliver information regarding personality and emotion.

Facial features can be absent, sparse, highly detailed, cartoony, abstract, or photo-real. Play around with facial feature specifics when designing your characters. Try large eyes and a small mouth, small eyes and no mouth, one large eye and one small eye, a large mouth but only one eye, a huge nose and tiny ears, and so on. Draw many versions of the same character's face with subtle changes in size, placement, and relative proportions of features to find just the right indication of personality and emotion. Try a variety of different facial expressions to see the range of emotions you'll be able to deliver. Scan one of your character sketches into the computer and play around with a digital paint or morph program that will allow you to warp head shapes and feature sizes and see whether anything interesting and unique results. Examine the facial features of existing film characters who emote effectively and apply your discoveries to your own designs (see Figure 3.26).

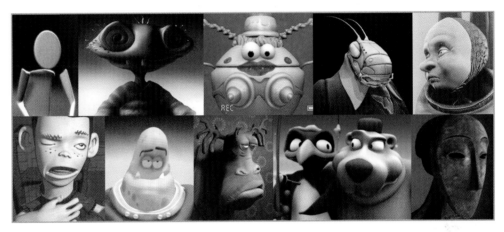

Figure 3.26
Facial features come in a wide variety of shapes, sizes, styles, and proportions.

Hands

Generally speaking, next to facial features the second most expressive parts of a character are his hands, so don't neglect them in your design phase. If a character has no facial features whatsoever, hands (or paws or claws) will often become the primary tools for expressing personality, desire, and emotion. Hands can be mere stubs or simple mittens, or they can contain three, four, five, or perhaps even more fingers (see Figure 3.27). If you expect to rely on hand shapes, poses, and movements to deliver necessary information about a character, make sure you design them appropriately. Give your character enough fingers to get the job done, but realize that a full set of four-plus-thumb is rarely necessary unless you are going for a high level of realism. Fewer fingers will be easier to model, set up, and animate; however, if you don't have enough fingers it might limit the expressiveness of the poses you will be able to create. For instance, you can't make a peace sign with a mitten.

Keep It Simple and Think Ahead

Details will round out a character and often add interest or unique qualities, especially when it comes to realism (see Figure 3.28). However, be careful of overdoing it. Loading up a character with too many obvious visual cues can turn him into a cliché or a confusing mess of unnecessary details (see Figure 3.29). Be efficient and economical with your design elements. A healthy balance between clarity and subtlety is always a desirable goal, and elegant simplicity in design is usually quite appealing (see Figure 3.30). Also remember that it is not necessary to display or demonstrate a particular design element or character trait unless it is important to the story.

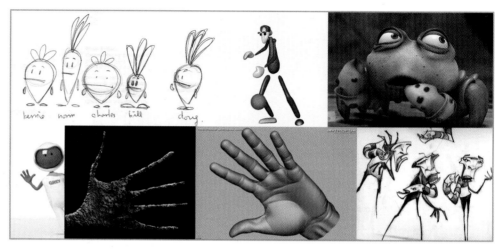

Figure 3.27
An expressive hand can be a stump, a mitten, a claw, a four-finger collection, a full five-finger set, or something else entirely!

Arbitrarily adding details is the same as blindly adding more ingredients to a soup. Less is very often more.

Always think ahead as you design your characters. Only create characters that you or your teammates will be able to model, rig, and animate efficiently (see Figures 3.31 and 3.32). If you give your protagonist a tail, your audience will expect it to swing and

Figure 3.28
Details are important visual characterization tools.

Figure 3.29
More isn't always better. Over-designing a character with too many visual cues and unnecessary details can turn him into a cliché and a modeler's nightmare.

Figure 3.30
Elegant simplicity is often quite appealing.

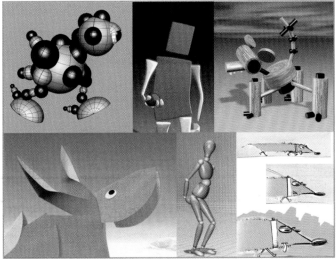

Figure 3.32
Simple characters like these will be relatively easy to build and quite interactive when it comes time to animate them.

sway convincingly, and doing so will require more animation time. If you give your protagonist a huge belly, you're going to have to add appropriate deformers and controls to your character setup to make it squash and stretch properly. A character with a huge head and short arms might not be able to scratch his nose. Short legs and large feet make it difficult to create walk cycles.

Constantly consider how your designs will affect the future stages of your pipeline and consider the possibility of leaving out unnecessary anatomical details. For instance, if you are creating a film with no dialogue, perhaps your characters don't need mouths. If your characters are cartoony or abstract, you can perhaps get away with omitting necks, shoulder joints, or even arms and legs, leaving hands and feet connected to a torso by mere implication (see Figure 3.33). If a certain character will only ever be seen from a distance, don't bother to include very small anatomy or clothing details.

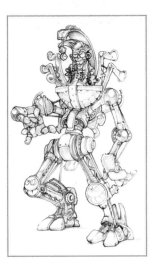

Figure 3.31
This is a great character design, but will you or your teammates have the time and skills to model, rig, and animate such a creature efficiently?

Figure 3.33
In a cartoony or abstract character, you can save yourself a lot of future modeling and rigging time by leaving out anatomical details, such as necks and joints or even arms and legs. Your viewers' innate sense of closure and basic knowledge of anatomy will allow them to visually accept such omissions.

Of course, we are not suggesting that you compromise your designs based on the limits of your current skills. After all, the development cycle of your film should be a learning experience, and it is definitely a good idea to give yourself a few technical and aesthetic challenges along the way. Just realize that character elements such as hair, feathers, loose clothing, and multiple limbs will require additional work down the line (see Figure 3.34). Robots, toys, mannequins, and insects are certainly easier to work with than other more organic creatures, but your story might require more complex characters. If so, consider ways to stylize them that will reduce your future workload. Try using two-dimensional, cartoon-style eyes that float in space (see Figure 3.35). A six-legged spider might look just as convincing as one with the proper eight. A tucked-in shirt will be easier to manage than one that flaps in the breeze. A ponytail will be easier to animate than long, flowing locks. Three fingers will take 25 percent less time to animate than four, and mittens are simpler than gloves. Design your characters to your liking, but think ahead and strive to avoid unnecessary production complications.

Also during the design phase, consider how the physical details of your characters will ultimately affect the style in which you animate them. If you create a robot, is he six inches tall or six stories high (see Figure 3.36)? Is he made of heavy, solid steel or hollow, nearly weightless aluminum cans? Knowing such specifics will be extremely important at the animation stage of your production.

Art Skills

Always remember to think in three dimensions, even if you are designing in two. If you envision your characters

Figure 3.34
This character from Kirill Spiridonov is both unique and appealing, but if you design such a creature be aware that your viewers will expect to see his hair move appropriately. Will you have the time, tools, and skills to accomplish this successfully?

Figure 3.35
Stylizing features such as eyes will make life easier for you during your production phase.

Figure 3.36
Is this creature two inches tall or two stories high? Knowing such details will be important when you start animating.

Figure 3.37
Construction drawings of your characters will help you visualize their forms and apply proper perspective and foreshortening in your drawings.

as combinations of basic shapes (cubes, spheres, cylinders, cones, and so on), it will be that much easier to design them as the three-dimensional characters they will ultimately become. Make a few construction drawings of your characters that show the simplicity of their underlying forms (see Figure 3.37).

This will not only help you understand dimension and form, which will really come in handy at the modeling stage, but it will also assist you when you draw your characters in different poses from various camera angles.

If you choose to design your characters using traditional media, you'll need some basic drawing or sculpting skills. Keep in mind that you don't have to become another Michelangelo to design characters effectively. Many great designers are not necessarily great illustrators; however, if you are not comfortable with your chosen medium, the process of designing characters can feel like a chore rather than a fun and rewarding experience. Indeed, it takes many years to master figure drawing or cartooning, but it actually doesn't take that long to learn enough of the basics to get by. If you're looking for some good books on these subjects, review a few of our recommendations in Appendix B. Although it wouldn't be feasible for us to offer any comprehensive drawing lessons within the scope of this text, here are a few tips that might help you expedite the learning process:

1. **Attend figure-drawing classes as often as possible.** The more you know about the form and structure of real humans, the better you'll be able to effectively create unique exaggerations or abstractions. Always think in three dimensions as you draw. Imagine your piece of paper is actually a box and you are sculpting the model rather than creating a two-dimensional drawing (see Figure 3.38). Try drawing the figure as a collection of simple geometric shapes to more effectively understand volume and perspective. Draw a variety of different poses at different speeds. Do many quick sketches to capture overall lines of action, as well as long sittings where you can really study the details. Challenge yourself by choosing difficult poses, especially those with plenty of foreshortening. Flat, straight-on poses are much easier to draw, but they don't provide you with an opportunity to further your understanding of posing and three-dimensional space. Imagine yourself in the model's pose and try to feel the balance of forces acting upon him or her. Try caricaturing the figure as you draw. This will force you to identify the most meaningful and expressive details of the model. Focus on faces and hands. If figure-drawing classes are not available to you, practice drawing toys, action figures, stuffed animals, and sculptures from many different angles. Working from photographs is less than ideal. Because your creations will ultimately be three-dimensional, your sources should be as well.

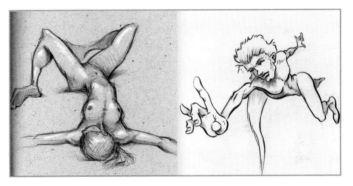

Figure 3.38
Think of your paper as a box and imagine that you are sculpting rather than drawing when you work from live models. Visualizing the human form in this manner will greatly increase your ability to design three-dimensional characters.

2. **Study anatomy.** The most important anatomical elements to study as a character designer are bones and muscles. Unless you are actually designing a skeleton, try to learn about bones in groups rather than individually. Understand the overall shape of the entire ribcage, rather than the specifics of each rib (see Figure 3.39). Gain a cursory understanding of where the major bones fit together and their approximate rotation limits. Also, learn which bones can be seen protruding through the skin. With regard to muscles, it's more important to understand how they work than exactly what each one looks like. Realize that muscles can only pull; they cannot push. Every major muscle causes a joint to bend, and all muscles have opposing counterparts that generate the opposite joint motion—biceps versus triceps, quadrilaterals versus hamstrings. Remember that muscles expand when they operate, but depending on the pose, most of them are usually in their relaxed states. Study the differences between bipeds, quadrupeds, fish, and birds. With all species, a global knowledge of overall bone groups,

muscle systems, and proportions is more important than minutiae. Learn, for instance, that the hind legs of quadrupeds do not have two knees. Rather, four-legged animals walk on the balls of each rear foot, where the lengthened ankle only appears to be a second backward-facing knee (see Figure 3.40).

3. **With regard to proportions, trust your innate knowledge of the human form as well as your eye for appeal.** Don't allow yourself to get caught up in the overly academic proportion rules found in many art books. For instance, the "fact" that the human body is approximately six heads tall is hardly a consistent reality, and this "rule" will only help when you're drawing an adult human standing straight up from a centered camera angle. Once you apply a low-angle POV, a bit of foreshortening, or an age difference, such rules go right out the window. Indeed, understand the existence of this tendency, but realize that it is not a hard and fast rule and trust your instincts. Doing so will make it easier for you to design unique characters and draw odd poses from various camera angles. Remember: If it looks right, it is right (see Figure 3.41).

4. **Understand perspective.** Although there are dozens of very thick volumes available describing all of the rules and details of this subject, the notion of perspective really just comes down to two basic concepts. Objects, dimensions, and relative distances appear smaller as they move away from you, and objects in the foreground tend to obscure objects behind them. All of the specific details of one-, two-, and three-point perspective are actually variations on these two simple concepts. Of course, if you design your characters with sculpture or CG modeling tools, you'll get proper perspective for free.

5. **Learn about color theory.** Color theory is best learned by noticing interesting and appealing color combinations in the real world and then recording your findings in a continuously growing library of quick color sketches you can reference when you are designing your characters and textures.

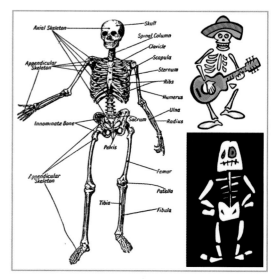

Figure 3.39
When learning anatomy, simplify your education by studying bones in groups, rather than individually.

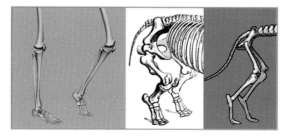

Figure 3.40
Contrary to what some people think, quadrupeds do not have two knees in each rear leg. Rather, they have extended ankles and stand on the balls of their feet.

Figure 3.41
The notion of correct proportions can be rather subjective. If it looks right, it is right.

If you really hate drawing or sculpting or you feel that you simply don't have the ability to effectively put your imagination down on paper or clay, consider collaborating with a friend who has the time and the appropriate skills.

Visual Elements of Effective Character Design

A character designer has a number of visual devices at his disposal, which can be used to effectively indicate or imply a character's physical attributes, personality traits, biographical information, and goals with descriptive clarity or interpretive subtlety. They are as follows:

- ◆ Basic design elements
- ◆ Biological and anatomical specifics
- ◆ Color
- ◆ Posture and facial expressions
- ◆ Style, grooming, and condition
- ◆ Clothing and accessories
- ◆ Exaggeration

Basic Design Elements

If you work out the design of your character with pencil and paper, consider the connotative values of different types of lines and shapes. Horizontals tend to imply tranquility. Vertical lines tend to imply rigidity or balance. Curved lines imply gentleness, while hard angles imply danger or stubbornness. And jagged, erratic lines imply energy, confusion, or imbalance. A cuddly and sympathetic little bear cub will work well with mostly curved shapes, but his angry, battle-worn, man-eating grandfather might be a bit more angular. Try balancing straights against curves for interesting variety. A few simple lines in a circle can not only indicate a face, but also demonstrate a surprisingly large range of emotions depending on their lengths and angles (see Figure 3.42). Appropriately-placed lines can also indicate proportions and attitude (see Figure 3.43).

Basic overall shapes can also have connotative qualities. A V-shaped head might belong to a character with an abnormally large brain, while an A-shaped head looks more Neanderthal (see Figure 3.44). Similarly, someone with a V-shaped body might not necessarily be stronger than someone with a body shaped like an A, but he can most certainly outrun him (see Figure 3.45).

Figure 3.42
Simply varying eyebrow and mouth shapes can create a wide variety of facial expressions.

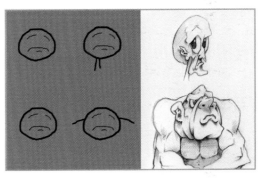

Figure 3.43
The simple placement of a pair of vertical or horizontal lines can drastically change the overall proportions and attitude of otherwise identical characters.

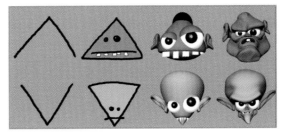

Figure 3.44
These very different characters are based on the same basic shape turned upside down.

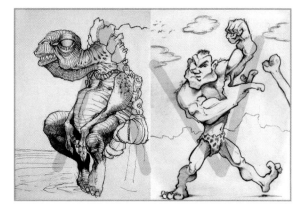

Figure 3.45
Using those same two overall shapes for bodies may suggest the difference between sloth and strength.

Figure 3.46
A character's silhouette will reveal his overall shape construction, which can immediately indicate whether he is warm and friendly or perhaps sharp and dangerous.

Figure 3.47
Asymmetrical eye sizes can be interesting in cartoon characters.

Try drawing your characters in silhouette to better analyze the appeal and visual connotations of their overall shapes (see Figure 3.46).

Symmetry is often considered a necessary component of beauty, but introducing variety in elements such as individual eye sizes can make for some rather interesting character designs (see Figure 3.47).

Introducing extreme contrasts is another basic design strategy that can lead to appealing results, especially when applied to cartoon characters. Think about angular chins with rounded cheeks, huge eyes and a small mouth, or legs so thin they couldn't possibly support the weight of your character's enormous head (see Figure 3.48).

Remember that even subtle variations in basic lines, angles, and shapes can result in drastic changes in mood and personality.

Biological and Anatomical Specifics

Fur, teeth, number of legs, skin color, fur texture, ear shape, and tails can indicate species, while details such as hair length, eye color, nose length, and body proportions can imply age, gender, nationality, and certain personality traits. Exaggerated physical attributes, such as huge ears, ultra-thin limbs, missing necks, or squared-off chins, can also imply intelligence, strength, and self-esteem. Shape and curve specifics such as bowed legs or pigeon toes also contribute to characterization. Interesting proportion contrasts, such as a large tummy and a small head or very long legs and a tiny torso, will also add to a character's interest and appeal. Except in the cases of injury, birth defects, or mutations, all members of our animal kingdom contain an even number of arms and legs, so try 1, 3, or 5 if you want to suggest an alien race.

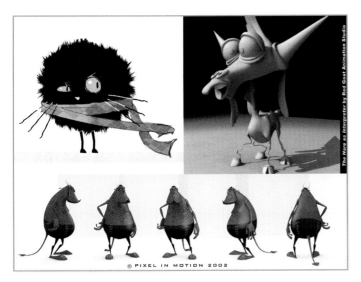

Figure 3.48
Extreme design contrasts, such as huge heads or hands and skinny legs or arms, can be particularly appealing in cartoon characters.

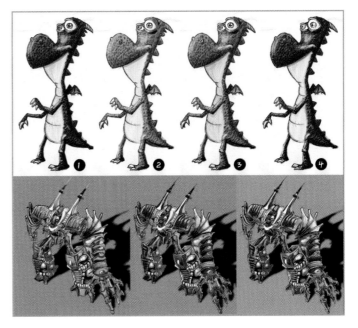

Figure 3.49
Try different color schemes in your character drawings.

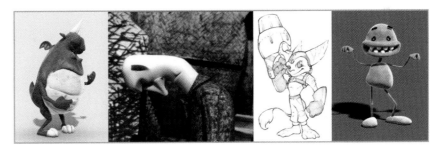

Figure 3.50
Posture will help indicate a character's physical condition, emotional state, personality, or attitude.

Color

Unless your film is going to be black and white, experiment with different color schemes and combinations when designing your characters (see Figure 3.49). Changing a bear from brown to white will result in the suggestion of a different homeland. Making a human character bright green might imply that he is not from this planet. A black top hat might belong to a magician or a nineteenth-century president, while that same hat in orange or purple might belong to a clown or a pimp.

Posture and Facial Expressions

Chest out, shoulders back, and a smirk might imply confidence, while an arched back, drooping shoulders, and upturned eyebrows might suggest meekness or depression (see Figure 3.50). A limp will certainly imply an injury of some kind. Hands on hips and pursed lips might suggest femininity. A character who grins all the time might just be eternally happy, but be careful—he could be hiding something quite sinister

instead. Pay attention to spine and leg curvature. A cat with a con-
cave spine might be old, hungry, or perhaps a bit proud. That
same cat with a convex spine might be stealthy and ready to attack
or perhaps extremely agitated. Similarly, the overall posture curve
of a character will indicate a lot about his personality, condition,
or emotional state. Curved postures are natural and dynamic and
will imply confidence, age, and condition, depending on the overall shape and direction of the arc (see Figure 3.51). An extremely
rigid posture might indicate a missing sense of humor or a creepy
disposition. Recall the first time Hannibal Lecter appeared in
Silence of the Lambs. His calm but abnormally symmetric and
vertical posture was certainly less than reassuring. The way a character sits can also indicate attitude. Crossed arms and crossed legs
send a very different message than knees apart and outstretched
arms. When designing your characters, draw them in a variety of different poses to
discover and suggest mood and personality.

Figure 3.51
The overall posture curve of a character will help imply confidence or perhaps the lack thereof.

Style, Grooming, and Condition

Hairstyles, mustaches, beards, sideburns, ponytails, baldness, lipstick, eye shadow,
and nail polish can indicate attitude, age, social status, and gender (see Figure 3.52).
The condition of these elements will also say a lot about a character. Someone with
torn clothes, unkempt hair, broken fingernails, and dirt all over their face might very
well be homeless. Then again, this person might simply be following the latest fashion
trend. Or he might be wandering away from a recent auto accident or alien abduction.

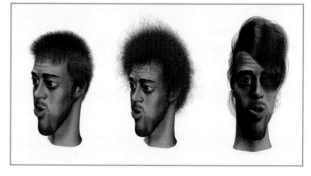

Figure 3.52
Grooming specifics, such as hairstyles, can help add personality to your
characters.

Clothing and Accessories

Type, color, style, and condition of clothing and accessories can imply personality,
nationality, age, gender, and wealth (see Figure 3.53). Someone dressed all in black
might be a funeral director, a cat burglar, or perhaps a deep, introspective poet you couldn't possibly understand. Psychedelic colors imply a free spirit,
while browns and grays often belong to more conservative types. A computer nerd might pull his pants up much too high, while a wannabe rap star might
wear them a bit too low. Untucked shirts and untied shoes might imply laziness, haste, or a casual nature. Hats, scarves, cigarettes, corncob pipes, walking
sticks, backpacks, glasses, bowties, snow boots, weapons, pocket protectors, roller skates, jewelry, tattoos, and uniforms can also indicate personality as
well as profession.

Exaggeration

Different levels of exaggeration can indicate extremes in traits, such as strength, confidence, femininity, and malevolence. A superhero will appear especially super if his biceps are larger than his head. In general, the larger the teeth, the scarier the shark. Keep in mind, however, that extreme exaggeration can cause the opposite effect. A vampire with 12-inch fangs, a huge cape, giant bat wings, glowing red eyes, foot-long fingernails, and enormous, pointed ears will actually be more amusing than a subtler version—not more frightening (see Figure 3.54).

With effective use of the aforementioned tools, the look of your character can directly indicate or merely imply a great deal of information to your audience and quickly establish empathy, familiarity, or interest. Once you've successfully established such a connection between your characters and your audience, your viewers will follow your characters' actions and outcomes with interest. Ask yourself what you hope the design of your characters will indicate to your audience.

Figure 3.53
Clothing choices will help indicate character specifics, such as age, gender, and personality.

- ◆ Do you want your viewers to like your protagonist?
- ◆ Should they immediately fear your villain or should they be unaware of his secret agenda?
- ◆ Should they think your protagonist is strong and courageous or nervous and cowardly?
- ◆ Male or female?
- ◆ Straight or gay?
- ◆ Old or young?
- ◆ Rich or poor?
- ◆ Terrestrial or alien?
- ◆ Animal, mineral, or vegetable?

Play around with some of these design elements and see what kind of information your character can exhibit through visual cues alone. However, keep in mind that most visual design cues can be interpreted in many ways depending on the nationality, culture, history, experience, and opinions of your viewers. Snakes will attract some viewers but

Figure 3.54
Be wary of over-exaggeration. If large fangs are scary, extra large fangs aren't necessarily more so. If you exaggerate scary elements too much, they may become comical.

3. Character Development and Design

83

scare others. Horn-rimmed glasses might remind one person of his favorite aunt but bring up painful memories of a strict and abusive third-grade teacher to someone else.

Designing Multiple Characters

When you are designing partners, teams, or groups, it is generally a good idea to include a fair amount of variety unless you are creating a swarm of killer robot spiders (where it might be more appropriate to make them all exactly alike). Contrasting shapes, sizes, and styles can often make for interesting visual and relationship dynamics (see Figure 3.55). The short, stout man with the tall, thin wife is a familiar combination. The seven dwarves are all approximately the same size, but each has his own style, look, and of course, personality.

Character Design Progression

It is often perfectly acceptable and sometimes even crucial to your narrative to alter a character's physical attributes over time. Examples include overall size increase or decrease, black eyes, smeared makeup, a new crew cut, a torn shirt, an uncharacteristic wardrobe, improved posture, or a shaved beard and mustache. Making such a change can contribute to the indication of a character's development, growth, or decline over the course of your story. If Sammy the Slob shows up in an expensive and well-pressed Armani suit, it might not necessarily indicate any particular change in his attitude or personality, but it will likely indicate that something significant has occurred (or is about to occur) in his life. Perhaps he won the lottery, finally got a real job, or is about to meet his girlfriend's parents for the first time.

Model Sheets

It is always a good idea to create formal model sheets of your characters, especially if you are working with a team. Since you will be designing three-dimensional characters, an effective model sheet will show each of them from several different angles (see Figure 3.56). A variety of poses and facial expressions as well as head and hand close-ups, silhouettes, translucent drawings showing the basic underlying forms, and a few descriptive notes are also important details to include. Character design should be a fun, exploratory process, so draw a lot. Filling up a page or two with a series of small blitz drawings of your character in many different poses and actions is also an excellent way to get to know your character and provide this information to your teammates.

Figure 3.55
It is usually a good idea to vary proportions between partners or teammates.

Figure 3.56
A model sheet showing your character from a variety of different angles will greatly assist you in the future modeling stage.

When you design characters using pencil or brush, it is important to realize that although 2D elements such as line quality and paint strokes will deliver style and appeal to drawings and paintings, they do not translate into 3D. By all means, include such artistic details in your two-dimensional artwork, but pay particular attention to volume, color, shape, proportion, posture, and texture. A poor character design might become a better drawing if you add interesting, calligraphic lines and cross-hatched shading patterns, but doing so will not help the digital sculptor you will eventually become (see Figure 3.57). Always think in terms of three-dimensional space and movement when you are designing your characters.

Character Development Tool 4: Behavior

No matter how effectively you design a character, his true nature will ultimately be defined by his actions, reactions, and interactions. As the comedian Bill Maher once suggested, "You are what you do." In most short films, there simply isn't enough time to fully develop a character this way. Therefore, you must apply shortcuts to successfully characterize through behavior. Exaggerated mannerisms are often quite effective in this capacity. A man who strokes his chin, a girl who twirls her hair, or a cat that limps will be immediately identifiable every time he or she is displayed on screen. In Moonsung Lee's *Bert*, the small vegetable characters trip and fall often. This recurring mannerism helps to identify them as children. Often, providing a character with one or two quick initial actions or gestures is sufficient to tell the audience all they really need to know about a character's personality and goals (see Figure 3.58). In *The Wrong Trousers*, Gromit (the dog) reads a birthday card at the breakfast table and dismisses it with a roll of his eyes. This quick, singular action indicates that he is not only more intelligent than your average illiterate canine, but perhaps a bit less childish as well. Within a few seconds of seeing this character for the first time, viewers have all the information they need to decide whether they'll identify with (or at least be interested in) this character.

Figure 3.57
A nice, detailed drawing does not necessarily always make for a good CG character design image. Make sure you focus on dimensional specifics, such as shape, volume, and proportions, rather than line calligraphy and shading when you create your characters on paper.

Figure 3.58
Deep characterization through behavior is next to impossible in the limited timeframe of most shorts. Therefore, one or two indicative actions in the beginning of a film can be an excellent shortcut for defining a character's personality, motivations, and attitude.

Choices

Behavior is made up of actions and choices. How your character dictates or responds to the events and other characters of your story will define his personality. Is he confident or meek? Intelligent or mentally challenged? Selfish or altruistic? Stubborn or flexible? Serious or comedic? If he decides to kill someone, he will be seen as a villain. If he decides to kick a dog, he will be seen as a really horrible villain. If chooses to run from danger, he is either a coward or rather practical. If he chooses to face a threat head-on, he is either brave or stupid. Keep in mind that in order for a character's decisions to inform an audience of his nature and personality, his choices must not be obvious or trivial. You'll learn nothing about a character who simply chooses pleasure over pain or wealth over poverty. Rather, a character will define who he really is based on the *difficult* choices he makes—for instance, wealth-plus-misery versus poverty-plus-happiness. Choosing between two negatives might shed some light on a character as well. In Martin Scorcese's *Casino*, a pair of cheaters is caught with their dishonest winnings. One gets his hand smashed by a hammer. The other is given a choice: The money and the hammer or no money and the door. The latter might seem like the obvious choice to most people, but a particularly greedy masochist might take the former. Choosing between a pair of positive scenarios can also be rather difficult. Two dates for the prom sounds like an ideal situation, but the ultimate decision will leave at least one member of the equation somewhat disappointed.

Character Arcs

A series of actions, reactions, choices, and interactions will ultimately bring about a change in your protagonist's physical, geographical, social, or mental status. For your story to be particularly interesting, it helps if this change goes from one extreme to another or perhaps comes full circle back to the original status. Examples include

- Life to death
- Rich to poor
- Naïve to wise
- Indifferent to in love
- Drunk to sober
- Desert island to the civilized world
- Male to female
- Rags to riches to rags
- Loner to social butterfly, then outcast again

> Probably the most effective situation in which you can fully develop a character is by showing how he attempts to solve the main conflict of your story. This is where the men are separated from the boys, the strong are separated from the weak, the cunning are separated from the foolish, and often the living are separated from the dead. No choices are more telling than those made under pressure.

Such a change in a character's status is known as a *character arc*. The central plot of many stories is actually contained within the physical or mental arc of the protagonist, rather than through a series of external events. More often than not, plots and character arcs intertwine to form a narrative whole.

For a character to arc, he must have some degree of free will and the capacity to act upon his desires and goals. A paralyzed man who dreams of Olympic gold will not initiate much of a story unless he makes a miraculous recovery, lives vicariously through another, or has his story told as a dream sequence. Make sure the characters you create have the desire and ability to participate in the story you want to tell.

Some characters are tragic, and a downward-spiraling arc will indicate this most effectively. Other characters are comedic in nature, often because their behavior indicates that they are not aware of their flaws. Buzz Lightyear is funny because he believes himself to be something more than just a toy and he behaves accordingly. Dan Bransfield's Fishman is humorous because he actually thinks he's a pretty good superhero. If the arc of a flawed character brings about an awareness of his dysfunction, it will no longer be an amusing element of his personality. If Archie Bunker had ever suddenly realized the folly of his bigotry, he would've become hesitant or introspective, and the flaw would no longer have been humorous. If handled properly, such a drastic personality change can make for a rather interesting character arc or plot progression.

Dominant Character Traits

Most story characters tend to have a singular, dominant trait and the majority of their actions will be consistent with this personality detail (see Figure 3.59). Recall the fable of the scorpion who hitched a ride on the back of a tortoise to cross a river, but stung the tortoise before reaching the other side, drowning them both, because he couldn't escape his true nature. Sometimes it can be interesting for a character to behave outside of his true nature; however, a good reason must exist for this occurrence or your audience will lose their connection with your character.

Gender and Age Specifics

When you are creating aliens, monsters, and otherwise abstract or inanimate story characters, it is generally not necessary to indicate gender and age. However, when you are creating humans or familiar animals it is often a good idea to do so, either through design or through behavior.

Figure 3.59
Most characters will behave in ways that are consistent with their true nature.

Through Design

In terms of design, it usually helps to exaggerate the otherwise subtle and stereotypical differences that exist between males, females, children, and adults to sufficiently sell the identity of your characters. With regard to human beings, females tend to have rounder edges, thinner necks and noses, larger eyes with longer lashes, fuller lips, longer hair, wider hips, smaller ribcages, longer legs, and smaller feet. Women typically dress and accessorize differently than men. Dangling earrings, heavy makeup, sparkling jewelry, bathing-suit tops, skirts, and high heels do not always necessarily indicate gender, but these accoutrements do imply a certain degree of femininity. Exaggerating physical tendencies is definitely appropriate when designing cartoony humans.

Figure 3.60
Design specifics can easily indicate gender and age.

Animal gender differences are usually indistinguishable to the casual observer. Exceptions include lions and antelopes. You can, however, adorn cartoony animals with typically human attributes or clothing to indicate gender.

Human children tend to have shorter limbs; larger heads; smaller, upturned noses; bigger eyes and ears; and fewer hard edges. Certain grooming styles and articles of clothing, such as large hair bows, pigtails, saddle shoes, oversized short pants, mittens, and absence of facial hair, can also help indicate youth (see Figure 3.60). With regard to animal proportions, youngsters tend to have larger eyes, ears, and feet, with shorter legs and tails. Cartoony animals often wear clothing; therefore, dressing them like human children is often appropriate and effective.

Through Behavior

Indicating an animated character's gender through behavior often requires exaggeration, politically incorrect generalizations, and a bit of stereotyping. For instance, it has been said that men seek to control their emotions with logic, while women often control their logic with their emotions. Men seem to prefer shopping rather methodically, while women seem to enjoy a more casual approach. Men often elect to repair their own cars and program their VCRs on their own, while women will often seek help or read the directions. Women will tend to be calmer in extreme situations, but they freak out if they see a tiny spider. Men will attempt to solve their friends' problems by offering advice or assistance in physical retaliation, while women will provide a good hug instead. Girls play house, while boys like guns. And girls tend to be cleaner and more polite. How might these stereotypical tendencies manifest themselves in the behavior of your story characters?

With regard to the indication of age, children tend to be less subtle, less balanced, and more extreme in their reactions. They often carry toys and will generally respond more physically than their adult counterparts. Children tend to act before they think, while adults strive to do the opposite (although they often fail). Adult dialogue is often more sophisticated and less direct. Children tend to get right to the point even if they can't always find the right words.

Remember that all of these are mere generalizations, but it is very often necessary to exaggerate stereotypical differences to effectively indicate age and gender in animated story characters.

The Sliding Scale

When you are creating a film character who will not be intentionally lifeless or generic, your goal will be to eventually establish a relationship between that character and your audience. The longer your film, the deeper that relationship needs to be to keep your audience engaged. In a feature film, the connection between a viewer and a story character can be considered a long-term relationship. Because of the depth of this relationship, the audience members will ultimately expect to get to know the protagonist rather intimately. To accomplish this effectively, a feature film must present a sufficiently long series of actions, reactions, decisions, explanations, interactions, and conversations. The benefit of the long form is that it allows for a more gradual pace when delivering these behaviors, and this slow, complex delivery results in relatively deep character development. Once a character has been on the screen for several minutes, the audience will start to wonder about his history and goals. Who is this guy? Where did he come from? What is he trying to accomplish? At some point during the course of a feature film, these questions must be addressed to keep the audience engaged.

In a very short film, however, the protagonist will be little more than a passing acquaintance to an audience member. Your viewers won't care so much about the specifics of your character because your film will be over by the time they start asking questions. Therefore, more shallow (but not altogether absent) character development is often perfectly acceptable in a short film. You must still establish an audience-protagonist connection, but you must do so rapidly. This is most effectively accomplished through descriptive design, exaggerated mannerisms, and perhaps introductory text, narration, or dialogue.

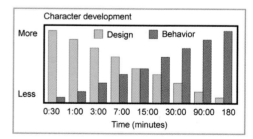

Figure 3.61
The shorter your film, the more you must rely on indicative design for characterization. Behavior is generally a preferred characterization tool in longer films.

Behavior is the most effective and appropriate character development tool in a longer film, while design is especially effective and appropriate in a very short film. The in-betweens will exist on a sliding scale (see Figure 3.61). At one end of the spectrum sits the four-hour epic, in which design is preferably more subtle and a multitude of actions, reactions, conversations, and choices are presented. At the other end of the spectrum is the 30-second gag, in which there is only time for perhaps one or two actions—therefore, design is usually quite descriptive and often much more exaggerated. The longer your film, the more you can rely on gradual development through behavior. The shorter your film, the more you must rely on design and exaggeration.

How Do You Feel about Your Characters?

Once you've at least partially designed your characters and given some thought to their onscreen actions and reactions, it is important to consider how you feel about them. Remember that your relationship with your characters will be significantly longer than that of your audience; therefore, it is especially important for you to like or be interested in your protagonists, antagonists, and supporting players. As the psychologists say, if you don't like yourself nobody else will. The same is true for your story characters. Try to look at your character designs objectively and decide whether they inspire concern, curiosity, neither, or both. If your good guy makes you sneer and your villain makes you feel warm and fuzzy inside, you might indeed require professional help, but more than likely your designs could use a bit of rethinking.

Where to Get Ideas for Characters

Ideas for your characters can come from almost anywhere. For example:

◆ **Think of a person or a pet you know (or knew, or know of) and then vary, exaggerate, twist, or caricature with subtlety or reckless abandon.** For design, try using Photoshop or morphing software such as Elastic Reality to alter a photograph of your chosen victim (see Figure 3.62). For behavior, consider the feelings that come up when you think about this individual, and use that information to drive the choices your story counterpart will make. Exaggerate what you know or remember about this person or animal. If it was your strict grandfather who liked watching films, have him behave like a drill sergeant and regularly quote famous movie lines. If it was your small and gentle pet garter snake, perhaps make him a rather large and ferocious king cobra instead.

◆ **Combine elements from the genre/style matrix (see Figure 3.63).** Put a tiger's head on a robot body, bat wings on a swordfish, or a pair of space antennae on an old man.

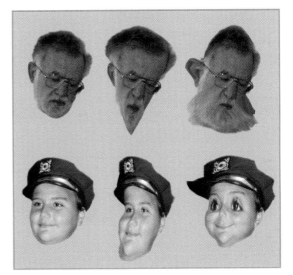

Figure 3.62
Using software to mess around with a drawing or a photo is an excellent method for coming up with a new, caricatured, or severely exaggerated character.

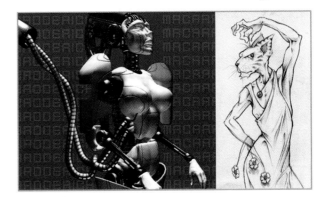

Figure 3.63
Mixing elements from different genres or species can lead to some interesting results.

89

◆ **Anthropomorphize a non-living entity.** You can accomplish this by giving *charac-ter* to a non-character or by adding human elements to an otherwise inanimate object, such as facial features and appendages to a traffic light (see Figure 3.64), or lifelike animation to an office supply (*Luxo Jr.*). Flip through a toy or gadget catalog for ideas. Or take the opposite approach and make an animal, alien, or toy based on a real celebrity or a historical figure (such as Rover Dangerfield).

◆ **Alter, multiply, mix up, or omit anatomical elements.** Give a human six arms or a giant chin. Put someone's eyes on the back of his head. Omit a torso and just have the arms and legs emanate from an oversized head (see Figure 3.65).

◆ **Think of interesting contradictions or juxtapositions.** Examples of this might include a Chihuahua puppy as a guard dog; a six-foot-tall infant; or a typically fero-cious, flying mythological creature who has tiny wings and behaves like a coward (*Run, Dragon, Run!!!*). (See Figure 3.66.)

◆ **Try immersion.** Look at a large number of character images from comic books, action figures, animated films, children's books, and video games. Then close your eyes and let your internal sensory overload combine elements from these various sources in new and interesting ways.

Figure 3.64
Giving character to non-characters or adding limbs to an otherwise inanimate object can be fun.

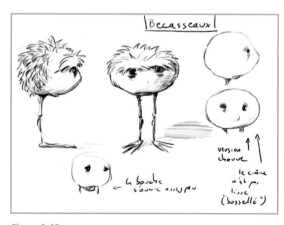

Figure 3.65
Try leaving out major anatomical elements, such as arms, mouths, or in this case, a torso.

Figure 3.66
Contradictions make for interesting characters, such as a cowardly dragon or a fuzzy, floppy-eared warrior.

Figure 3.67
Who might live in one of these places?

◆ **Imagine the world or setting of your story and then consider who might live or operate in such a place.** Who lives in the jungle? What types of mutated insects or reptiles might live near a nuclear power plant with questionable safety standards? Who lingers in dark alleys? (See Figure 3.67.) How has evolution dictated the physical attributes of your alien characters who live on a gravity-free world that is always 400 degrees below zero?

◆ **Consider your plot progression and then think about what kind of characters will be appropriate to your story.** An underdog-beats-the-odds scenario might require an introverted little schoolboy with a pocket protector and thick-rimmed glasses. A natural catastrophe might need a superhero or a particularly tenacious military official to save the day. A futuristic space battle should probably involve a few interesting aliens or robots.

◆ **Consider your character's profession or goal and then give him appropriate physical and mental attributes, a proper uniform, and all the right tools.** A mountain climber will be lean, fit, determined, and adorned with ropes, spikes, and energy bars. A restaurant critic might be overweight and carry a notepad. A junkyard dog will probably be large, ugly, missing one eye, and drool a lot.

◆ **Start with your character's nemesis.** What kind of resourceful hero will rid the city of its giant rat infestation? Who might slay the evil dragon? Who will save the day when Shotgun Sherman escapes from prison and comes to town to exact revenge on the elderly and unsuspecting sheriff? Will it be the deputy, the town drunk, or young Timmy and his trusty slingshot?

◆ **Begin with a name.** What will Shotgun Sherman look like? How about Joey "The Squirrel" Rigatoni or Doctor Henrietta Frankenstein? How might a pitbull named Gandhi behave? What kind of eating habits can we expect from Albert the Anaconda?

◆ **Take a blank sheet of paper and allow your pencil to wander aimlessly around until something interesting or familiar begins to appear.** Then explore and refine until something more concrete develops. Draw some scribbles and random shapes of differing sizes and then add facial features and appendages. Grab a hunk of clay and start pushing and pulling until you see someone you know.

◆ **Work in a similar exploratory fashion with some CG modeling software.** Assemble a pile of primitive shapes and then translate, rotate, scale, connect, and combine them until some interesting and more complex designs begin to materialize (see Figure 3.68). Create a sphere with a large number of vertices and start pulling points and adding deformers until you see something appealing, then run with it.

3. Character Development and Design

91

◆ **Put descriptive words in a hat and pull out a few.** Man, woman, old, young, policeman, stupid, Martian, dog, unicorn, alcoholic, extroverted, overweight.... Put two or three together at random and then try to draw the resulting combination.

◆ **Go people-watching.** Sit in a park or ride the subway and observe clothing, hairstyles, accessories, and behavior. Then go home and invent a story around someone you saw. Combine elements from a number of different individuals into a single unique character. Or do the same with zoo animals.

◆ **Try to think of an animal species that hasn't been used too many times.** Cats, dogs, birds, mice, fish, dragons, rabbits, ducks, ants, and dinosaurs have all gotten more than their fair share of attention from storytellers and character designers. How about a lemur, a tapeworm, or a Portuguese man-of-war instead? Collect reference images from nature books and then try to create caricatured, cartoony, or abstract versions of some of the less popular members of the animal kingdom. If you can't find any new ones, create your own by combining elements from a few different animals.

◆ **When designing creatures, examine animals.** Go zoo-drawing and look at animal documentaries and textbooks, especially those that feature predators, deep-sea animals, or insect close-ups, such as the film *Microcosmos*. As it turns out, Mother Nature is an extremely creative character designer, and many film creatures have been based on existing animal species (see Figure 3.69).

◆ **Look at rocks, clouds, and trees, searching for suggestions of faces and figures (see Figure 3.70).** Sketch your findings and then evolve them into more complex or realistic entities with some appropriate personality traits and perhaps clothing.

◆ **Choose a fundamental emotion and build a character around it.** Psychologists list the six basic emotions as happiness, sadness, anger, disgust, surprise, and fear. Each could very well be the central character trait of a protagonist, a villain, or a sidekick. Use variations of these six as catalysts for a character's physical attributes and behavior.

◆ **Peruse a psychology text or a book on personality types.** One such book is *The Writer's Guide to Character Traits* by Linda N. Edelstein. Select a few character traits (preferably disorders or dysfunctions) and see whether the corresponding descriptions inspire any ideas. Edelstein's book describes physical and mental conditions such as amnesia, insomnia, and hypochondria. Analysis of such disorders and their corresponding causes and manifestations might have been the inspiration for films such as *Memento* and *Hannah and Her Sisters*. Perhaps reading the characteristics of narcolepsy or schizophrenia might generate some ideas.

◆ **Do some blitz drawing.** Rapidly fill a few pages with quick sketches of figures, faces, animals, aliens, clothing styles, and interesting poses. Don't worry about quality, just quantity. See how many different character doodles you can spew out in 30 minutes. Explore and exaggerate with reckless

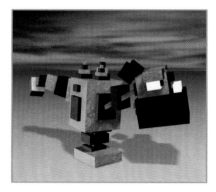

Figure 3.68
Using various shapes and sizes of simple objects as 3D puzzle pieces within a CG software package can be a playful way to invent a new character.

Figure 3.69
Use Mother Nature's imaginative animal design sense as a catalyst for your creatures.

3. Character Development and Design

Figure 3.70
Find interesting faces, figures, and postures in the real world.

abandon, and don't erase. Just keep drawing (see Figure 3.71). Try different styles and species. Close your eyes on occasion and if a character appears before your mind's eye, put him down on paper as quickly as possible.

◆ **Use or alter standard archetypes.** Investigate such sources such as Joseph Campbell's *Hero with a Thousand Faces* and the Italian *Commedia dell'arte* theater for characters, such as mentors, shape shifters, tricksters, harlequins, wealthy misers, and arrogant captains. Consider variations on typical character types from stage and screen, such as the wacky neighbor, the trusted canine companion, the voice of reason, the oppressive boss, the clueless parent, the clown sidekick, the elusive love interest, or any of the seven dwarves.

Figure 3.71
Fill a page with a series of small, quick blitz drawings to find your character's look and personality.

3. Character Development and Design

93

Show Them to Others

Show your character designs to others and note their reactions. Ask your viewer to tell you something about your character based on what they see. Do they like, hate, fear, or feel sympathy for your characters? If their response is not what you planned or expected, you might want to review your design elements.

A Few Examples

Let's take a moment to examine a few unique and interesting CG characters with regard to the concepts discussed in this chapter.

Bart Goldman's Robobird is a hybrid character that combines robotic design elements with those of a wingless bird (see Figure 3.72). His relative size is established by the inclusion of the lampposts in this image. The overall design is elegantly simple, while details such as gears and pistons help to clarify its mechanical nature. This character would be fun to animate, and the limited number of moving parts would make him highly interactive as well. Based on his displayed behavior, Robobird's personality appears curious and instinctive. A couple of details that might further refine this character would be some texture mapping and perhaps a name.

Figure 3.72
Bart Goldman's Robobird

Phil McNally's Vic Vinyl from his short film, *Pump Action,* has a maniacal expression and exhibits sadistic behavior, clearly identifying him as a rather psychotic villain (see Figure 3.73). This character is particularly interesting because one does not normally associate the notion of evil with balloon people. The design elements and behavior that create this contradiction make this character especially unique. Vic's design is fairly simple and was therefore presumably not too difficult to model and rig. Using mitten hands and drawing rather than sculpting his face are a couple of design choices that contribute to Vic's overall simplicity and readability. Other details, such as seam folds, an inflation valve, and a plastic hook on the top of his head, add interest and believability. The alternating colors of his different body parts also help with readability.

Goffer from Francois DeBue's *Sahari* is an amusing space alien, identified as such by his green skin and helmet (see Figure 3.74). According to his bio (http://home.tiscali.be/sahari/char.htm), Goffer is a member of the half-man, half-gherkin race of Agurkans from the planet, Agurk. He is 30 years old, weighs 75 kg, is 1.85 meters tall, and believes himself to be a great leader, despite the fact that he is employed as the mother ship's janitor. This disparity between his self image and his true identity defines most of his onscreen behavior. Much of Goffer's appeal comes from his proportions and facial structure. He has a thick, rounded chest, very thin arms and legs, and large feet. He has no ears or nose, thus focusing attention on his large mouth, goofy eyes, and expressive brows. His two lower fangs add a bit of personality and humor to his expression. Goffer's design is a bit more complex than that of the first two examples; therefore, he was presumably a bit more difficult to model

Figure 3.73
Phil McNally's Vic Vinyl from *Pump Action*

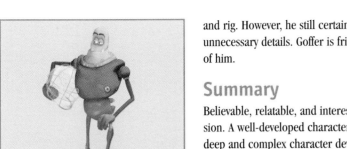

Figure 3.74
Francois DeBue's Goffer from *Sahari*

and rig. However, he still certainly falls under the category of elegant simplicity and does not contain any unnecessary details. Goffer is friendly but perhaps a bit too trusting; his curiosity ultimately gets the best of him.

Summary

Believable, relatable, and interesting characters are equally, if not more, important than strong plot progression. A well-developed character will inspire concern or curiosity from your audience, but keep in mind that deep and complex character development is next to impossible in a very short film; therefore, design and behavior often must be exaggerated to connect your audience to your characters. Character arcs are important elements of storytelling and involve some form of change over time. Whenever possible, apply the concept of elegant simplicity to your characters to help ensure an efficient production cycle. In the next chapter, the subject of art direction and look development will be addressed.

3. Character Development and Design

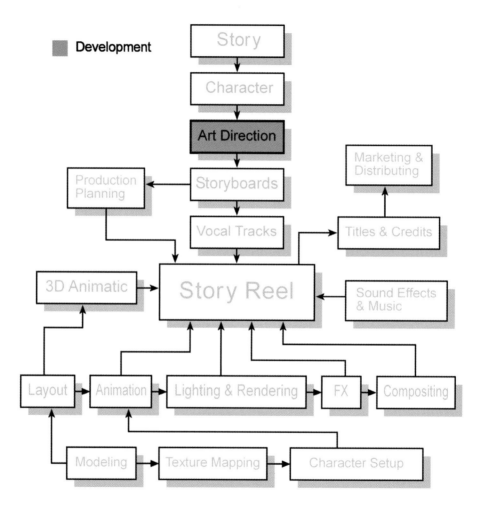

chapter 4
Art Direction

The visual style of your film will undoubtedly evolve and solidify over the course of your production, especially when it comes time to model, texture, light, and render your characters and background elements (see Figure 4.1).However, it is highly recommended that you spend some pre-production time assuming the role of an art director, collecting reference images and videos and creating drawings, paintings, and perhaps sculptures to establish a preliminary standard for style and quality (see Figure 4.2). Will you aim for a simple and fairly abstract, bright, futuristic look or perhaps a dark, claustrophobic, dirty, ominous, realistic,

"Can you paint with all
the colors of the wind?"
Alan Menken and
Stephen Schwartz

4. Art Direction

Figure 4.1
Many CG short-film directors stick very closely to their original art direction plans when creating their final imagery. Your results may vary.

medieval scenario? Ornate and colorful Victorian architecture or a gray and smoggy cityscape made of simple geometric shapes? As you collect and create inspirational material, it is a good idea to hang or place these pictures and objects on the walls or surfaces of your studio and periodically reference them during your production to maintain consistency and motivation, especially if you are working with a team (see Figure 4.3).

Figure 4.2
Preliminary design sketches and paintings will help determine the overall look and feel of your film.

The overall art direction of your film will hopefully provide your audience with a unique visual experience and will also assist you in indicating setting specifics, such as geography, era, size, depth, climate, season, time of day, and perhaps genre.

But most importantly, the look of your film will help to create a mood (see Figure 4.4). A dark and rainy atmosphere with lots of grays and blues might make your audience feel cold, as in the opening shot of *Red's Dream* from Pixar. A bright, sunny landscape with plenty of soft yellows, light greens, and other earth tones will probably make your audience feel warm and comfortable. A bright red and orange sky, cracked surface texture, atmospheric haze, and perhaps one or two cacti should bring out a few portable fans. Clear blue skies, a snow-covered tundra, and a resident penguin will create the opposite effect (see Figure 4.5).

Figure 4.3
Collect plenty of educational and inspirational reference materials and keep them handy.

Figure 4.4
Effective art direction will create a mood.

Connecting Style with Story

Probably the most important issue to consider regarding art direction is the typical necessity of making the visual style of your piece match the intended mood and genre of your story. For instance, wacky comedies tend to work well with colorful, exaggerated, or cartoony characters and settings. Moody or poignant dramas usually feature realistic or semi-realistic characters and dull colors or mere shades of gray (see Figure 4.6). Light parables are usually bright and caricatured. Serious science fiction and monster movies often call for gritty, detailed realism (see Figure 4.7). Mystery, suspense, and horror films work well with dark and dull colors, high contrast, long and dark shadows, mood lighting, fairly realistic characters, and perhaps a bit of inclement weather (see Figure 4.8). Fantasy stories often exhibit unnaturally bold colors with odd, unique, and perhaps rather geometric design elements (see Figure 4.9).

Of course, matching visual style with story genre is not a hard and fast rule. If you want to be especially ironic or catch your audience off guard with a surprise ending or an unexpected punch line, then by all means use a

Figure 4.5
Art direction can also inspire feelings of temperature extremes.

Figure 4.6
Colorful, cartoony imagery goes well with wacky comedies, while shades of gray and semi-realistic imagery will complement a moody drama or a tragedy.

Figure 4.7
Light parables often feature bright colors and caricatured characters, while more serious science fiction stories often call for gritty, detailed realism.

Figure 4.8
Dull colors and a bit of rain will help intensify the mood of a mystery.

bright, cartoony style for your poignant and tragic murder mystery. Just keep in mind that it is usually not a good idea for your story elements to compete against your visuals for indications of genre and mood.

Mood Should Be Suggested Rather Than Forced

It is perfectly appropriate to encourage your audience to feel a certain way with influential visuals; however, it is generally not a good idea to completely dictate their emotional response to

Figure 4.9
Strange and interesting design elements help create a fantasy world.

your story by using too many obvious and overused design clichés. Making teardrop-shaped icicles, frowning snowmen, a crying moon, and processing all of your frames through a blue filter might be overdoing the idea of indicating coldness and sadness. In a cartoon-style comedy, it might be acceptable to exaggerate your mood indicators thusly, but in most films subtlety is more effective and appropriate.

Coming up with a Visual Style

One of the bests way to figure out the overall art direction of your film is to consider the genre of your story, decide on the mood you want to inspire, and then analyze the style and visual elements of existing films that made you feel the way you want your audience to feel. If you plan to create a dark and tragic science fiction tale, study the style and design specifics of films such as *Blade Runner, Alien, f8, Horses on Mars,* and *Dronez.* If you want to warmly deliver a lesson on manners to schoolchildren, consider mimicking the lighting, rendering styles, and caricatured or simplistic character design ideas from films such as *Bert, Kami, Poor Bogo, For the Birds, One by Two, Lunch, Early Bloomer,* or *Geri's Game.* If you want to create a wacky or perhaps fantastical comedy, learn from the artistic choices made in films such as *Ice Age, Polygon Family, AP2000, Baby Changing Station, Alien Song, Fat Cat on a Diet, Fishman, Gas Planet, Pings, Moosin' Around,* or *Run, Dragon, Run!!!* If delivering a poignant metaphor is your goal, review more abstract pieces, such as *Values, Fifty Percent Grey, Le Processus,* or the stop-motion classic, *Balance.* If horror, mystery, or dark fantasy is your pleasure, study the mood-setting visual elements of feature films such as *Seven* and *The Third Man,* as well as shorts like *Puppet, Le Puits, Sally Burton, The House on Dame Street,* and *Silhouette.* If you want to captivate your audience with a unique and fantastical visual experience, take inspiration from the art direction elements of films such as *The Cathedral, El Arquero, Poor Bogo, Sarah, Guernica, Sprout, Occasio, Within an Endless Sky,* and *Garden of the Metal.*

> Exercise: Make a list of a few short and feature films that conjure up specific feelings when you think about them. Then watch these films again and try to identify the art direction elements that contribute to the emotional reactions they inspire.

If you can't find the mood you're searching for by watching short films and features, try browsing through children's books, reading comics, playing video games, and perusing texts and film documentaries on architecture, human and natural history, oceanography, outer space, geology, and world travel.

Direct observation of the real world is also an excellent method of inspiring art direction for your film. Ideas can come from the creepy forest across from your friend's house, the new and modern subway station by the courthouse, the downtown area with all the skyscrapers, the mall, the park, the manmade canals, the filthy bathroom at the train station, the lobby of the city's oldest hotel, or your favorite beach when the sun is setting. On your next vacation, bring a memo pad, a camera (preferably digital), and a sketchbook to record notes and images of the architecture, color schemes, conditions, and design motifs of these places. If visiting such locations is not feasible, flip through travel guides or borrow photos from some of your more worldly friends and relatives (see Figure 4.10).

Figure 4.10
Find interesting visual styles in the real world.

Also think about how elements such as rain, snow, wind, or heat and humidity make you feel. Do falling leaves or lightning bolts conjure up any particular emotions? If appropriate for the intended mood of your piece, consider featuring direct or implied indications of these elements.

Create a variety of pre-production sketches and paintings to work out design ideas and color themes. Digital paint programs, such as Adobe Photoshop or Corel Painter, are especially effective in this experimental stage because you can easily try out alternative color palettes, textures, brush strokes, and artistic filters.

Mood-Inspiring Art Direction Elements

There are four main cinematic tools an art director can use to contribute to the look and feel of an animated film.

◆ Overall style

◆ Quantity, style, design, color, and texture details of environments and props

◆ Weather and other FX

◆ Lighting, rendering, and post-processing filters

Overall Style

The overall style of your film will be dictated by factors such as realism level, color palettes, texture details, and composition.

Realism Level

The first thing to consider with regard to the overall style of your film is the level of realism you want to deliver (see Figure 4.11). This will be indicated by dimension, lighting, texturing, modeling, and exaggeration (or the lack thereof).

Figure 4.11
How realistic should the visual style of your piece be? Almost true to life, cartoony, or abstract?

Highly Realistic

Absolute, true-to-life imagery will immediately connect an audience if it is pulled off successfully, and is especially appropriate for more serious plots and genres, such as mystery, horror, suspense, science fiction, and drama. CG short examples include *The Cathedral*, *f8*, and *Alma*. Keep in mind, however, that a high level of realism is especially difficult to produce, and the indication of mood needs to be created with an appropriate level of subtlety. Radically and inappropriately exaggerating or abstracting the imagery of an otherwise realistic film can easily break its immersive quality.

Semi-Realistic

A nearly real style will give you more room to play with color, texture, and design variations to create your desired mood. Also, a bit more imagination and exaggeration in the design of your characters and backgrounds will feel more appropriate if you stray from absolute realism by a certain degree. Less dimensional and perhaps painterly styles can fall under this category as well, provided the shapes and proportions of your objects and characters remain fairly close to real life. Genres such as fantasy, satire, black comedies, and less serious science fiction are especially appropriate in a semi-real style. Examples include *Respire*, *Eternal Gaze*, *Fifty Percent Grey*, *Insight*, *Passing Moments*, *Geri's Game*, *Rustboy*, and *L'Autre Temps*.

Cartoony

A cartoon look is certainly a very popular way to go. This will give you plenty of artistic license when creating caricatured, exaggerated, or fantastical characters and environments. Cartoony style is generally best suited for comedies and light morality tales. Keep in mind that cartoony doesn't necessarily mean flat. Many cartoon-style films have tremendous depth and even extremely realistic lighting; however, they belong in this category because their characters and backgrounds are significantly caricatured (*Egg Cola*), exaggerated (*Fat Cat on a Diet*), anthropomorphized (*Coffee Love*), or just plain goofy (*The Adventures of Andre & Wally B*).

Abstract or Symbolic

This style of imagery has infinite potential for style variation and is usually most appropriate for fine arts pieces or poignant metaphors. The use of more geometric rather than natural and organic shapes in object design or overall style can help you create fantasy, abstraction, or symbolism. Films with particularly abstracted characters or backgrounds include *Values*, *Framed*, *One By Two*, *Kami*, and *The Dog Who Was a Cat Inside*.

Color Palettes

Another overall style consideration is global color palettes. Consider the effectiveness of different hues and contrast levels (see Figure 4.12).

You might want to create a feeling of warmth or even extreme heat by using appropriate doses of red, orange, and yellow (*La Piedra*). Blues, greens, and whites will often have a cooling effect (*Point 08*). You can mix cool and warm colors so that different areas of the same imagery will have contrasting temperature values.

Realistic story settings generally call for subtler, earthy hues with less extreme value contrasts (see Figure 4.13), while less serious cartoon-style films, especially comedies, will often be brighter and more colorful (*Run, Dragon, Run!!!*).

Gentler pastel colors will tend to imply tranquility (*Respire*), while extreme contrasts between bright and saturated colors will imply energy or confusion, or perhaps indicate a fantasy or alien world (*Sam*).

Glorious black and white is particularly effective for certain genres, such as mysteries, tragedies, and nostalgic comedies (see Figure 4.14).

Figure 4.12
The overall color palette of your piece will help imply temperature and mood.

Figure 4.13
A realistic look will be achieved by using subtle earth tones.

4. Art Direction

103

Figure 4.14
Glorious black and white can help generate a feeling of nostalgia.

Figure 4.15
Adding a brightly colored element to an otherwise primarily black-and-white film can be quite visually dramatic.

Creating a film that is primarily shades of gray but then introducing some colored elements can also be rather captivating and visually dramatic (see Figure 4.15).

Color and contrast can greatly assist you in creating depth. Objects with dull colors and limited contrast will tend to recede, while brighter-colored objects with a lot of contrast will pop into the foreground.

Color can contribute to the differentiation between character personalities (see Figure 4.16). Background color variations can also help intensify mood and attitude. When the slower, gentler, old man is on the screen in Pixar's *Geri's Game*, most of the trees behind him are yellow. In the shots that feature the quicker, more arrogant version of this same man, the trees are mostly red.

> Exercise: Load up your favorite paint program, select some large brushes, and make a series of quick, rough color comps. These paintings don't have to be refined or representational, just colorful. Then consider how different hues and color combinations make you feel. Save these images and use variations on their overall palettes when you create object colors, texture maps, and background paintings for particular shots and scenes that are intended to inspire particular moods.

Figure 4.16
Using different colors for opposing characters can add to the intensity of their conflict.

Texture Themes

Using interesting and consistently themed textures in all of your background objects, props, matte paintings, and even characters is an excellent way to create a strong visual style. Making every texture shiny and metallic might be appropriate for a sterile and futuristic scenario. Different animal patterns throughout can suggest a primitive or natural setting. Painting your textures to match the look of alternative visual mediums is also an especially interesting and fairly popular technique. Supinfocom's *Sarah* simulates the look of a fantastical Japanese video game (see Figure 4.16). *Where is Frank?* from Angela Jedek looks like three-dimensional dry brush paintings, while the objects and characters in Wojtek Waszczyk's *Mouse* look a bit like traditional fabric-covered puppets (see Figure 4.17).

Figure 4.17
Interesting and consistent texture themes can contribute to a strong and memorable visual statement.

Overall Complexity

The level of simplicity or complexity in your character and object models, texture maps, color palettes, and rendering styles will contribute to the overall feel of your short. Simplicity can often assist in visual clarity and is also an appropriate style for light cartoons (*Bert*) and certain abstract metaphors (*Values*). Realistic imagery will often require more complexity in both the style and the number of elements that can be seen in any given shot. A caricatured, cartoon-shaded character might have very simple texture maps painted with large brushes, whereas a realistic character will need more detailed textures with color variation in skin tones and perhaps dirt, freckles, moles, scars, tattoos, hair, stripes, spots, and textile patterns (see Figure 4.18). With regard to backgrounds, simple, open emptiness might create a feeling of freedom or perhaps danger for the lack of cover, depending on the genre and action of your plot. Cluttered scenarios might feel claustrophobic, treacherous, or perhaps safe, because there will be more available hiding places for your frightened protagonist. Then again, there will also be more hiding places for her crafty pursuers!

Composition as Art Direction

The ways in which you compose your shots will also contribute to the overall mood of your film (see Figure 4.19). Using lots of diagonal objects and arrangements will indicate movement, verticals will imply rigidity or stability, and horizontal compositions will often generate feelings of tranquility. Assembling your background objects and

Figure 4.18
The complexity level of your models and textures will impact the overall style of your film.

elements in an organized and symmetrical fashion with relative equality in size and shape will create feelings of balance, stability, passivity, or perhaps obsession. Random distribution and size variation might inspire feelings of discomfort, activity, or casual spontaneity. Try exaggerating or bending the rules of perspective to create abstract surrealism, fantasy, or the indication of extreme depth. Wide-angle camera lenses will give a greater feeling of depth and can help to build suspense, frustration, or a feeling of loneliness and isolation (see Figure 4.20). Low camera angles will help create a feeling of insignificance, modesty, or perhaps paranoia.

4. Art Direction

Figure 4.19
Compositional elements, such as asymmetry and extreme camera angles, can be effective art direction devices.

Quantity, Style, Design, Color, and Texture Details of Environments and Props

Figure 4.20
Composing the elements and camera angles in your shots to favor skewed verticals, diagonals, or obtuse lenses will help with feelings of movement, danger, action, and suspense.

Some animated shorts, such as *Balance, After You,* and *Values,* contain very few (if any) background elements. However, most films incorporate at least a small number of buildings, mountains, clouds, vehicles, and pieces of furniture to help indicate setting details.

Before you begin designing these objects, consider the importance of their existence to your film. Will the non-character elements in your world contribute significantly to your story? Will your protagonist directly or indirectly interact with your background objects and props, or will they simply exist to fill the space or indicate location, era, and other environmental specifics? A snowcapped mountain might look nice way off in the distance as mere eye candy, or it might be the very physical obstacle that your protagonist must conquer to reach his story destination.

Background Mass

Consider the number of background elements you want in your story world (see Figure 4.21). Absence or near absence of background objects will create an abstract, fantastical, or metaphorical scenario. A very small number of background objects might simply contribute to the elegant simplicity of your short or maintain focus on your characters. But it might also create a feeling of loneliness or desolation if your landscapes are vast but somewhat empty (see Figure 4.22). You might want to fill your cityscape with cars, skyscrapers, bus stops, mailboxes, signs, and streetlights or clutter your hero's apartment with furniture, electronics, toys, and boxes. A large number of background objects can effectively add detail and realism to your film, but overdoing it can

Figure 4.21
Lots of background elements, very few, or none at all?

Figure 4.22
Limited background mass in an otherwise vast landscape can contribute to a feeling of desolation.

Exercise: Try to picture your story in your head with no background elements whatsoever. Will it still be effective? Maybe more so. Then try to imagine your story with a huge mess of background objects and props. Will there be any benefit to such complexity? Will you have the time to build and texture all of those models? Will they help tell your character's story or distract from it? Will they serve as obstacles, tools, rest stops, or perhaps hiding places for your protagonist, or will they simply make the landscape more detailed and interesting?

complicate your production, reduce readability, and sometimes even distract from your character development or story elements. Of course, having your background elements become the center of attention is sometimes a necessary story beat, such as when a dam breaks or an asteroid crashes.

Style and Design

Indicative and consistent style in architecture and furniture design can help identify locale and era. Your story might call for decorative, rustic, antique, angular, organic, geometric, or ultramodern background objects. Think about the different buildings, doorways, windows, chairs, and appliances that would exist in a colonial farmhouse, a modern penthouse apartment, a child's room, or a futuristic space station.

Furniture design and style choices can also suggest a few things about a character's gender or personality. A paisley or flower-patterned bedspread might imply a certain degree of femininity. A modern apartment with a black leather sofa, a glass computer desk, sophisticated stereo equipment, and expensive but uncomfortable-looking dining room chairs will probably identify the occupant as a bachelor. The owner of leopard-print curtains might be anyone's guess. An extremely eclectic mix of design and texture in your background elements might imply that your owners or occupants aren't interested in a consistent style, but be wary of creating such variety because it can cause sensory overload.

4. Art Direction

Consider basic design elements, such as lines, shapes, and negative space, when creating and arranging your environments, props, and icons. Straight lines, gentle curves, rectangles, circles, torn edges, and interesting combinations and juxtapositions thereof will help create a variety of different visual styles and contribute to the overall tone of your imagery (see Figure 4.23).

Odd and interesting geometric angles, shapes, and recurring design motifs in your background elements can help your story setting feel unique, fantastical, amusing, or ominous. Designing your buildings and props with acute angles and sharp protrusions might help create a feeling of danger, in which your characters need to maneuver very carefully. Jagged outlines will help create a sense of nervousness or anxiety. Gentle curves will inspire feelings of tranquility. Skewed and imbalanced shapes can create a rather surreal environment, as in the furniture, trees, clouds, and buildings of films such as *The Nightmare Before Christmas*, *Poor Bogo*, *El Arquero*, and *Mouse* (see Figure 4.24).

Figure 4.23
Experiment with different lines and shapes to create interesting negative spaces and visual styles.

Figure 4.24
Odd shapes and skewed angles will help create a surreal or fantastical scenario.

Props and Vehicles

You can use appropriate and identifiable props as shortcuts
to identify era and locale as well as the profession, nationality, religion, heritage, back-story, or favorite hobby of your protagonist (see Figure 4.25). If you fill his bookshelves with trophies and litter his floor with sweatpants, muscle magazines, and dumbbells, he is probably a personal trainer or an athlete of some kind. If his furniture, carpets, books, wall hangings, and bed sheets are all emblazoned with spiritual icons, he probably has a significant amount of faith. A room filled with voodoo masks, witchcraft books, black candles, tarot cards, pentagram carpets, and Ozzy Osbourne posters, on the other hand, will certainly send a significantly different message.

Vehicles are also great indicators of era, geography, wealth, and character profession. Horse-drawn carriages, rickshaws, and personal nuclear-powered jetpacks will tell very different stories about their operators. A large white van with a picture of an oven on the side probably belongs to an electrician or a caterer. A black pickup truck with oversized tires, machine-gun turrets, and a human skull hood ornament will certainly suggest a few things about its owner and the world he occupies.

Exercise: Review some visually memorable films, such as *The City of Lost Children*, *Edward Scissorhands,* or *The Adventures of Baron Munchausen*, and look for specific and recurring design motifs that contribute to the overall tone and feel that is delivered.

Condition

In addition to style and design, the condition of background elements will help imply the personality of your characters, their locale, and the tone of your story (see Figure 4.26). Broken furniture, dirty carpets, and torn curtains might reveal that your protagonist held a raging party last night (or maybe his house always looks like that). An immaculate bathroom might suggest a hospital or the inside of a movie set. Rusty cars with missing fenders, abandoned and condemned buildings, graffiti, bent street signs, and trash filling the streets might indicate poverty or post-war damage. Any of these scenarios might inspire laughter, discomfort, anticipation, or disgust from your audience, depending on the story beats and character behaviors associated with these locales.

Living Backgrounds

Also consider whether your background elements will move or perhaps even have personalities. Rocks and buildings tend to remain static, but not always (*Das Rad*). Most trees will simply sway with the wind, but some will actually talk and throw apples (*The Wizard of Oz*). Suns and moons often have suggested or even definitive facial features. Living background elements can not only contribute to the look, feel, locale, and reality level of your story, but they can also contribute significantly to the flow of your plot and character development.

Matte Paintings

Matte paintings or photographic background plates also make for strong cinematic indicators of depth, locale, and mood (see Chapter 13). A few mountains or buildings with soft contrasts will create a sense of distance.

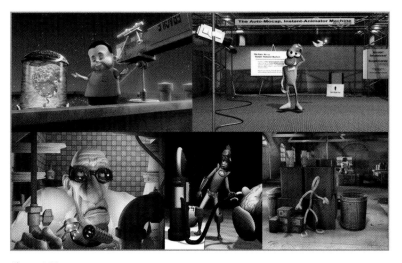

Figure 4.25
Style and attention to detail in props and vehicles will help indicate era and locale as well as biographical information about your characters.

Figure 4.26
The condition of your background elements will add a feeling of history to your settings. Rust, broken tiles, and cracked windows suggest that these places are either desolate or neglected.

Background images of the atmosphere above the clouds will certainly indicate that your characters are floating or flying (see Figure 4.27). A strangely colored sky with three suns and angular clouds will imply an alien world. A background panel with a single hue or perhaps a gentle fade will help make your space and locale less specific and perhaps more metaphorical (*Values*).

4. Art Direction

Weather and Other Effects

Rain; fire; snow; fog; lightning; smoke trails; fast-moving clouds; falling leaves; billowing hair and cloth; sparking high-tension wires; atmospheric haze; flying sawdust; a field of swaying grass; dust puffs when feet hit the ground; and random, underwater, floating particles are just some examples of FX that can contribute to the indication of setting and mood in a CG short film (see Figure 4.28).

It can also be fun to create a surreal, alien, or fantastical world by changing or reversing the normal look or behavior of such effects. If black snow falls or a waterfall flows upward, something or someplace out of the ordinary is definitely on display.

Lighting, Rendering, and Post-Production Filters

Once you've assembled your textured characters, backgrounds, and props on your virtual stage, the ways in which you light and render

Figure 4.27
Matte paintings or background photography can help indicate depth and locale.

your scenes will be the ultimate expression of your intended visual style. For example, you might choose to create a suspenseful, film-noir look by using a single light source with opaque shadows. Amber Rudolph and Tonya Noerr effectively delivered this look in their film *Silhouette*, where the ominous mood is further intensified by dimensional rendering, sharp shadows, and cold, blue lighting (see Figure 4.29).

Figure 4.28
Effects such as smoke trails can contribute to the visual impact of a particular scene.

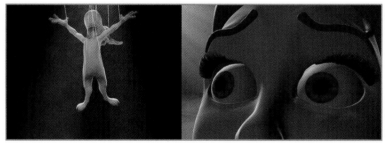

Figure 4.29
Spot lighting in an otherwise black environment creates a feeling of ominous isolation in *Puppet*, while sharp, blue lighting and sculpted rendering helps with the tense mood of *Silhouette*.

Lighting Specifics

The number, placement, and color of your lights will significantly affect the overall mood of a given shot. For instance:

◆ A single overhead yellowish point or parallel light source will create a warm, outdoor, daytime feel.

◆ A low, blue light will create a cold, eerie, ominous tone.

◆ A single bright light source that creates strong white highlights and very dark shadows would be appropriate for an outerspace locale.

◆ An otherwise dark setting with a small, weak light source coming from a candle, a flashlight, a torch, or a lantern will help create a feeling of isolation or suspense.

◆ Lighting a character from behind will create at least a partial silhouette or an ethereal glow, which might be helpful in mysteries or spiritual allegories.

◆ A multitude of different-colored lights, spinning and blinking, might imply that your action is taking place in a dance club or perhaps underneath a landing UFO.

See Chapter 18, "Lighting and Rendering," for more lighting concepts and techniques.

Dimensionality

Your final renders might be fully ray-traced like *Bunny* or flat-shaded like an episode of *South Park*. You might prefer a shallow depth of field to focus attention on your foreground elements or you might omit motion blur to simulate the genre of stop-motion. You could try turning off shadow generation to create depth ambivalence and abstraction.

Simulating Alternative Media

It can be visually compelling to simulate other media, such as traditional oil paintings or video games, through appropriate texturing, rendering, and the application of post-process filters. Realistic photography seems to be the most popular choice, but many software packages can generate other looks such as *toon shading*, in which the characters and objects have edge lines and less sculpted rendering. Short films featuring this technique include *Bert*, *Comics Trip*, *AP2000*, *Bunkie & Booboo*, and *Respire* (see Figure 4.30).

Other films, such as Bill Kroyer's *Technological Threat*, look like traditional cartoons because the animators actually drew on top of rendered 3D frames using pencils and pens.

The characters and props in Supinfocom's *Kami* are modeled and textured like origami sculptures.

Figure 4.30
Simulating the outlined look of traditional animation, but adding the benefit of dimensionality with the use of toon rendering is a popular art direction style for CG shorts.

The films *L'Autre Temps*, *Au Petit Mort*, and *Sarah* achieve the look of bent metal sculpture, moving watercolor paintings, and fantastical role-playing video games with effective use of rendering dimensionality, appropriately painted textures, and background panels (see Figure 4.31).

Figure 4.31
With effective use of texture painting and rendering, the look of alternative art media, such as watercolor painting, metal sculpture, and video games, can be achieved.

Pacific Data Images simulated a hand-painted feel in their shorts *Gas Planet* and *Fishing* with more sophisticated rendering algorithms. If you have the programming skills to do so, then by all means experiment with such technical processes. Otherwise, check your software manuals and search for plug-ins on the Internet that will provide you with such rendering solutions.

One especially captivating example of unique CG visuals simulating another medium is Zbigniew Lenard's *IT*, in which the renders look as if you are viewing the story world through the lens of an electron microscope (see Figure 4.32).

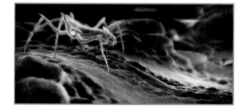

Processing your rendered frames through artistic filters in programs such as Adobe Photoshop or Corel Painter is also an excellent way of simulating the look of traditional (or perhaps not so traditional) visual media and techniques. You can see the continuing tradition of unique art direction from the students of Supinfocom in the utilization of this technique in films such as *Le Deserteur* and *Le Processus* (see Figure 4.33).

Figure 4.32
Zbigniew Lenard achieved a particularly unique visual style by simulating the look of electron microscopy.

Figure 4.33
You can also use post-processing filters to simulate traditional art media such as scratchboard or oil painting.

Exercise: Scan your preliminary drawings, paintings, reference photographs, and test renders into your computer and then experiment with various post-process filters and settings to at least partially predetermine the final look of your film (see Figure 4.34).

Figure 4.34
You might discover a unique and interesting art direction style by scanning a preliminary sketch, painting, reference image, or test render into your computer and then experimenting with various Adobe Photoshop or Corel Painter post-process filters.

Figure 4.35
Simulating the look of a comic book or a video game by using corresponding graphical elements can lead to interesting results.

Graphical Elements and Icons

An interesting method of mimicking certain alternative mediums is to incorporate graphical elements, such as comic book panels or perhaps video game iconography, into your scenes and compositions. This can be an interesting way to create unique and interesting cross-media visual styles, as seen in films such as *Comics Trip*, *Tom the Cat*, and *Polygon Family* (see Figure 4.35).

Creatively displaying or utilizing graphical imagery associated with traditional film production mechanics, such as microphones or frame edges, can assist in "breaking the fourth wall," which should lead to some imaginative visuals. Tex Avery employed this technique in some of his more outlandish cartoons, in which characters would often run outside of a frame, passing over film sprocket holes. A more recent example is Eric Carney's CG short, *Framed*, in which the protagonist wrestles with the very borders of his screen image.

A Few Examples

Let's consider a few particularly mood-inspiring CG short film images and examine their specific art direction elements and the emotional responses they inspire.

Otherworldly color palettes, expansive settings, alien (yet strangely organic) architecture, torch lighting, planets looming dangerously close, red space clouds, strong white sunbeams, complex shadow patterns leaving intricately shaped negative spaces…. These fantastical elements combine to form a desolate and ominous atmosphere that inspires curiosity, wonder, and a bit of dread (see Figure 4.36).

Figure 4.36
Tomek Baginski's *Cathedral*

A bright and clear blue sky with cool, green grass; gentle, pastel-colored clothing; a warm sunset; simple textures; partially dimensional rendering; open, uncluttered, and inviting landscape; limited complexity and details…. The result is a safe, happy, carefree place that generates feelings of warmth, comfort, joy, and tranquility (see Figure 4.37).

Figure 4.37
Respire from André Bessy, Jérôme Combe, and Stéphane Hamache

Textures painted to look like traditional watercolors, gentle earth tones with lots of tans and browns, over-saturation of outdoor lighting, a cute but simple and rather generic character wearing very basic clothing…. This desolate world rendered in a uniquely dimensional watercolor style creates a captivating visual experience with a touch of loneliness and sadness (see Figure 4.38).

Figure 4.38
L'Enfant de la Haute Mer from Laetitia Gabrielli, Pierre Marteel, Mathieu Renoux, and Max Tourret

Singular hue, empty landscape, grainy filter, surreal machinery, wide camera angles, strong lighting with high contrast.... The result is a unique and fantastical scenario that creates feelings of desolation, confusion, and wonder (see Figure 4.39).

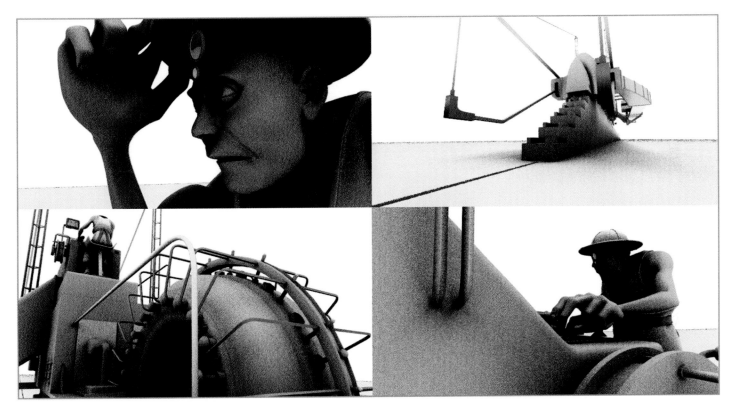

Figure 4.39
Grain.S from Cédric Nicolas and Vincent Meyer

Art Direction Progression

If the mood, climate, and intensity level of your story progresses and evolves over time either gradually or abruptly, it is usually appropriate for the details of your visual elements to change as well.

You can modify art direction from scene to scene to help indicate a change in locale, mood, climate, activity, or perhaps danger level. Your violent fight scene might have crazy camera angles, diagonal and jagged design elements, flying sparks, angular lightning bolts, and bold colors with lots of contrast. The subsequent aftermath might have more traditional camera angles, horizontal design components and arrangements, wispy smoke trails with gentle curves, and more subtle grays or pastel colors.

Figure 4.40
Your plot progression may require modifications to the look of subsequent scenes to match the current mood or locale of your story. However, it is generally good practice to only change details such as color and lighting, while keeping overall style and design consistent.

Keeping design elements consistent but adjusting color and lighting can help indicate a change in season, locale, time of day, or mood. When night falls in Supinfocom's *Kami*, everything becomes different shades of blue. At the end of Mathias Schreck's *Insight*, the scenario dramatically changes from dark shades of gray and brown to bright blues and greens, which not only reveals a new setting, but also creates an entirely different mood. Thelvin Cabezas' *Poor Bogo* changes mood, locale, and temperature to match the progress of the story narration by way of rather extreme but appealing modifications in color and lighting (see Figure 4.40). Despite the significant visual modifications, all of these film examples maintain world consistency because only colors and lights change, while overall style and design remain the same.

Of course, design schemes can change significantly between homes, nations, eras, and dorm rooms. However, if you hope to indicate that your story has moved to a new location or time but stayed within the same world, it is usually a good idea to keep some visual elements unchanged, such as color palettes, overall level of realism, or rendering styles.

Character and Background Connections

Another effective method of determining an appropriate visual style for your short is by thinking about your characters and then deciding where they might live, work, or play. For example:

Figure 4.41
Consistent design themes in characters and background elements

- ◆ A monster with webbed feet might live in a cold, dark swamp with lots of dead trees.

- ◆ A small and paranoid businessman might work in a crowded office area where the ceiling is very low and the gray cubicle walls have skewed angles and sharp edges.

- ◆ Flying creatures probably live in a world where doorways do not need to be on ground level.

- ◆ A cute little bunny might live in a pastoral green meadow where the sun always shines. Alternatively, he could be a stuffed animal who belongs to a little girl who never cleans her room, or he might be caged in a clean yet ominous cosmetics laboratory where everything is white and uncomfortably sterile.

Also consider how closely you want the design and color schemes of your characters to match your backgrounds and props (see Figure 4.41). In most cases your characters should look like they belong in their environments; however, be wary of making their palettes and textures too similar. Unless camouflage or intentional visual obscurity is your plan, it is important that your characters do not get lost in your backgrounds (see Figure 4.42). Of course, when they are in motion, they will often reveal themselves quite effectively.

Figure 4.42
Make sure your characters do not get lost in their backgrounds if you use the exact same color palettes and texture complexity (unless camouflage is your intention).

4. Art Direction

119

For the sake of making your characters stand out from their backgrounds, consider giving them alternative palettes, more extreme color and value contrasts, sharper focus, or different textures. You might even try making the art direction of your characters significantly different than that of your environments. Such disparity between character and background art direction can succeed as a visually cohesive whole as long as some details remain consistent. For instance, the colorful characters and main props in Keith Lango's *Lunch* are especially easy to differentiate from his otherwise black-and-white story world, and the combination works well because the basic design scheme is consistent throughout the short. Other ways of making your characters stand out from their backgrounds include focus and contrast disparity, mild or extreme color variation, dimensionality contrasts, and restricting the use of toon-shaded outlines to characters and foreground elements (see Figure 4.43).

Figure 4.43
There are a number of ways of making your characters stand out from their environments, including focus, color, and outline variation.

A particularly eclectic mix between the styles of characters and background elements without some consistency in at least one specific art direction detail can often look distracting rather than imaginative. An exception would be when these disparate elements are supposed to be from different worlds, as in *Who Framed Roger Rabbit* or the animated short *Grinning Evil Death*, which features two-dimensional, cartoony protagonists battling a giant, shiny, metallic CG space insect (see Figure 4.44). If one character is in color and another is black and white, try to keep their overall designs consistent. If a 2D character is supposed to occupy the same world as a 3D character, make sure some consistency remains in their color palettes or design motifs (see Figure 4.45).

Figure 4.44
Mixing realistic styles between characters and backgrounds is usually only a good idea if those elements are from different worlds.

Figure 4.45
Mixing styles and techniques between characters will result in something of a collage effect, which can be appealing with the right visual style and story tone.

Also consider the story significance of your background elements versus that of your characters. In a typical film, the characters are the driving force of the story so it is usually not a good idea for the environments and props to be so complex and stylish that they steal the audience's attention. In some films, however, this is precisely what the director wants to happen, so it is indeed acceptable to make the visual style of the backgrounds more compelling than that of the characters. In Tomek Baginski's *Cathedral*, for instance, the backgrounds literally overpower the protagonist so it is especially appropriate, if not crucial, for the environments to be significantly more visually stimulating than the main character (refer back to Figure 4.36).

> Typically, variations on the details of an otherwise consistent visual theme is the preferred method of separating characters from environments. Balance is the key. You want to make your characters look like they belong in their settings, but some of their art direction details should be at least slightly different so they read effectively.

Originality

If you have an especially original story, punch line, or character, it is perfectly acceptable for the visual style of your film to be rather ordinary or typical. Remember, it is not necessary for every element of your film to push the limits of cinematic creativity. However, if your story and characters are familiar or generic, it is absolutely critical for your art direction to be interesting and unique—otherwise, there will be nothing original about your film and therefore there will be no reason for anyone to watch or remember it.

If your storyline calls for a highly realistic look, you will have less artistic license when it comes to creating a new visual style. Select unique architecture and design styles and textures and then arrange or rearrange them in new and interesting ways. Or utilize weather effects and creative lighting to add interest and mood to an otherwise typical setting.

When it comes to creating a unique science fiction, fantasy, or cartoony world, the trick is to create a place that does not exist and then make it believable. This is achieved by effectively balancing familiarity with imagination (see Figure 4.46). Start with a familiar setting and then stylize, exaggerate, juxtapose, modernize, or antiquate overall design schemes, color palettes, or individual elements just enough so that a unique visual experience results, but not so far that your imagery loses all connection with reality and you end up with inaccessible abstraction. Make the grass blue, the sky green, and each of the three suns a different shade of red. Use angled clouds and rounded buildings. Create architecture that defies all laws of physics and gravity, with doors in odd places and stairways that lead nowhere. Place a gloomy and ominous medieval castle in the middle of a typical suburban neighborhood.

Figure 4.46
Unique worlds can be created by combining familiarity with imagination.

Of course, if you are creating a completely abstract fine art piece that will not require any story or character relatability, feel free to bend and stretch reality to your heart's content. One idea for visual style originality would be to try to think of a traditional art medium or technique that has not yet been simulated in a CG animated short, such as mosaic sculpture. Similarly, you might try to simulate the style of a particularly unique sculptor or painter, such as Auguste Rodin, Henry Moore, Alexander Calder, or Henri de Toulouse-Lautrec. Marcelo Ricardo Ortiz combined Picasso's abstraction, Dali's surrealism, and Escher's geometric illusions into an interesting visual style combination for his student film, *Guernica* (see Figure 4.47).

Figure 4.47
Perhaps honor your favorite sculptors or painters by simulating their styles and imagery in the art direction of your short.

Look around the real world for an odd and interesting architectural style (Gaudi, perhaps) or a rarely-seen example of Mother Nature's wondrous design sense, such as the inside of a beehive.

You could also combine a couple of radically different design themes between two opposing characters. One could be made of blown glass while the other is made of tiled bricks. Their relationship would likely be rather precarious.

You might choose an alternative setting and color scheme from what is generally considered appropriate for the genre and style of your story—perhaps a sweet love story set in a creepy, medieval torture chamber.

Think Ahead

Think about how your art direction plans will ultimately affect your production pipeline.

◆ Have you designed an extremely rich and complex background scenario that will be difficult and time consuming to build and texture (see Figure 4.48)?

◆ Can you use matte paintings instead of models for background imagery and objects that will be seen only from a distance?

Figure 4.48
A complex setting like this one will be difficult and time consuming to build, texture, light, and render. Make sure the scope of your preliminary creative vision fits within the limits of your available time, budget, and skills.

◆ Consider that realistic models and texture maps take a lot of time to create. You can purchase realistic CG models, but they can be prohibitively expensive. You might also think about using scanned and manipulated photographs for your textures, but doing so will require additional hardware and will often require a bit of work to make your scans map and tile properly.

◆ If you hope to simulate a traditional art medium, such as watercolor paintings, experiment a bit with rendering and post-production 2D image filters to see which method will most effectively and economically generate your desired look.

◆ If you want to create toon-rendered imagery, make sure your software package has this capability and that it works as promised. Often such renders will not be exactly what you expect, and you will have to spend some time adding, erasing, or cleaning up edge lines.

◆ If you plan to intensify the mood of your piece with rain, snow, or fog, consider that procedurally generating such weather effects with a CG program is often quite time consuming and CPU intensive. Consider the idea of adding these elements as 2D post-rendering layers at the compositing stage instead.

Don't force the art director in you to compromise your creative vision because certain imagery might be difficult or time consuming to produce, but do consider how your cinematic, visual ideas will impact your production schedule and budget.

Summary

Effective art direction will create a unique visual experience, indicate setting specifics, and generate a particular tone and mood for your story. Use subtlety to encourage your audience to feel a certain way, rather than trying to tell them how to feel with obvious and clichéd visual cues. Decide on the mood you want to inspire and then reference existing books, films, and real-world locales that conjure up the same types of feelings you want your audience to experience. Strive to be original with your art direction, especially if your plot and characters are familiar or generic. In Chapter 5, we will discuss storyboarding, where you will begin working out the cinematic flow of your story or non-narrative fine arts idea.

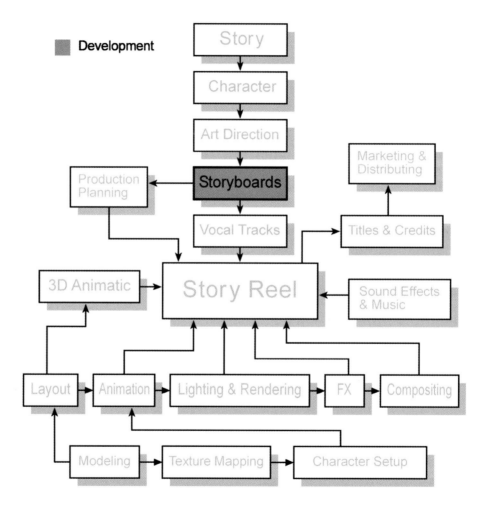

chapter 5
Storyboarding

N
ow that you've come up with a great plot, one or two strong characters, and an idea for your overall art direction, it's time to start figuring out how your storyline is going to flow visually. Your first opportunity to do this is by drawing storyboards. A set of storyboard panels is like a preliminary comic-book version of a film (see Figure 5.1).

Storyboarding is the bridge between a written script and the visual world of cinema. If you wrote out your story in script form, hopefully you imagined how each scene and action would look onscreen. If not, read through your story again and try to picture the best possible way to *stage* each story beat.

> *Staging* refers to the ways in which individual story beats or actions are clearly presented in visual terms. Effective staging comes from a successful combination of camera angles, point of view, composition, and placement of characters and objects.

The first step in realizing your ideas for how your story will translate into cinematic imagery is by getting them down on paper as storyboard panels. Storyboards can be quick and extremely rough little sketches, often referred to as *thumbnails*, or they can be carefully crafted works of art in their own right (see Figure 5.2). The level of refinement of your storyboards will depend on the structure of your team, your drawing skills, and your deadline. If you are working alone, you can make them as rough as you want as long as you understand your own visual shorthand. If you are working with a team, they should be a bit more refined.

A picture is worth a thousand words.

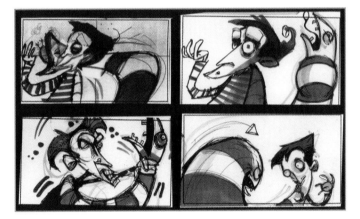

Figure 5.1
Storyboards are like comic book panels describing the events of your plot progression.

5. Storyboarding

125

Although it is tempting to overproduce your storyboard panels into fine works of art that will look impressive when featured in the documentary on the making of your film, don't inadvertently slow down your production by focusing too much attention on what are often considered little more than throwaway templates and staging suggestions. Your storyboard images should be refined enough for you and your teammates to be able to read and interpret them clearly, but rough enough so that your schedule does not suffer unnecessarily.

Also, the style of your drawings should match the overall art direction that you are envisioning for your film. If you are creating a goofball comedy with exaggerated characters, try to draw your boards in a similar fashion. If the visual elements of your film are to be abstract or symbolic, it is neither appropriate nor necessary to draw realistic characters on your boards.

Why Storyboard?

Since you are in the process of creating a film rather than a piece of literature, it is not enough to simply work out the beats of your story on the written page. Cinema is a primarily visual medium; therefore, working out your narrative flow with pictures rather than mere words is often a necessary step in discovering if and how your written or imagined storyline will translate into film. Storyboarding allows you to begin figuring out the best way to express each story beat visually.

Figure 5.2
Storyboards can range from extremely rough to beautifully refined works of art.

In addition to exploring the visual flow of your narrative, storyboarding also provides you with a first opportunity to begin working out the cinematic specifics of your film, including camera angles, composition, point of view, hookups and continuity, object and character motion, cuts, sight gags, posing, facial expressions, and to some degree, pacing.

However, keep in mind that these cinematic issues will mainly be ironed out in the layout, 3D-animatic, and animation stages. You definitely want to start thinking about these details when drawing your storyboards, but realize that you are still in development mode. The main purpose of this step is to continue refining the actual flow and continuity of your storyline with visuals.

Although it is not necessarily required that you storyboard your film, it is certainly highly recommended. Some stories are indeed simply better left in literary form, but most can successfully make the transition into cinematic form if done with an eye toward composition, staging, action, and clarity. Even if you simply create rough thumbnails on notebook paper, the earlier you start working out these cinematic issues and the overall plot progression of your film, the better. Remember that the cost of revisions increases steadily as production continues. It is much easier to fix a structure or pacing problem at the storyboard stage than when you are in the midst of animating and rendering your shots.

Some short film authors actually begin their filmmaking process by storyboarding before (or even instead of) writing out their plot in text form. You might find this to be a preferable method of initially getting your story idea down on paper, especially if you are planning a film with no dialogue. Afterwards, you may or may not find it necessary to express your story in written form as well. The pictures alone might suffice.

Suppose you have actually recorded your story as printed text. Once you begin enhancing your words with pictures, you might discover flaws or pleasant surprises in your plot structure. Some written passages simply will not translate successfully into cinematic form. For instance, you might find that it is inappropriate or even impossible to visually represent all of those cultural and historical setting details that you so eloquently described on the printed page. Perhaps this discovery will indicate that you require some additional dialogue or narration. You might find that your chase scene actually needs a lot more screen time than you originally imagined. You might decide that scene 10 should actually take place *before* scene 9. Your boards might reveal that you had envisioned too many low-angle shots and that they will eventually lose their dramatic impact. Or you might discover that the (hopefully) amusing sight gag you tentatively described in your script will actually work after all, now that you've seen it in picture form.

Keep in mind that the storyboard stage is an exploratory process in which a fair amount of story editing will undoubtedly take place. Your script might have seemed perfectly tight and well paced in its written form, but as you draw your storyboards you will very likely make a few changes—perhaps even some major plot restructuring. Also remember that storyboards should be considered preliminary suggestions of shot staging, not necessarily absolute directives. Don't feel that you need to work out every minute detail of your cinematic vision during the storyboard process. You will undoubtedly discover better ways of staging certain shots once you start seeing and refining them in the animatic, animation, and rendering phases of your production cycle (see Figure 5.3). Maintain an attitude of flexibility and allow yourself to tweak your story on occasion if the current stage of your production compels you to do so. Just make sure that each change is motivated and results in an improvement of your film as a whole.

Another good reason for storyboarding your film is that it will be much easier to pitch your cinematic vision to your boss, your financial backers, your

Figure 5.3
Storyboards should be considered preliminary suggestions and may or may not correspond exactly to the staging of your final renders.

teachers, your mom, or your teammates if you can present your story with images. Many such audience members will not share your ability to visualize your narrative actions in their minds' eyes if you pitch your story with words alone. We all know what a picture is worth, after all.

Principles of Preliminary Shot Construction and Scene Planning

A *story beat* is a narrative term that describes a particular event or action, such as a conversation, a chase, a fight, or a quiet moment of reflection. Every beat of your written, recorded, or imagined storyline will be represented cinematically by a *scene*, which will consist of one or a series of *shots*.

A *scene* is a complete story action that typically takes place in a singular location. An exception would be a chase scene that spans several different locales before reaching its conclusion.

Go through your written or imagined script, separating it into individual scenes and assigning each one a two-word name that effectively describes the story action, the setting, or perhaps both. For example, "wife cooks," "chase Butch," or "cat barbecue." Abbreviations of these scene names will be used when you label your boards and schedule your production, so watch out for duplicates. "Chase Butch" and "cat barbecue" will both become CB, so it would make sense to perhaps change the latter to "backyard barbecue" or BB.

A *shot* is a cinematic term defined as the space between camera cuts, and will typically be identified by a number appended to a scene abbreviation, such as WC01 or CB12. A shot is the presentation of a complete or partial story action from a single, but not necessarily static, point of view. This point of view can drift or zoom as necessary to follow or help tell the story of a given shot. Once the shot cuts, fades, or wipes to a different point of view, a new shot has been initiated. If you stage a quick dialogue exchange between Janice and Larry by showing a close-up of Janice, then cutting to a close-up of Larry, and finally cutting back to Janice, you've created three distinct shots. If you stage this scene from a single, static POV that frames both characters, or you have the camera pan back and forth between these two individuals, the conversation will be contained within a single longer shot (see Figure 5.4).

A one-to-one relationship does not necessarily exist between shots and story beats. For instance, a single story beat might require several shots to be presented effectively and dramatically. In the aforementioned scenario, the story beat is the short conversation between Janice and Larry, which might be delivered with one, three, or perhaps a greater number of individual shots. Conversely, a single shot might contain more than one story beat. A lengthy action sequence that contains several distinct and important plot points

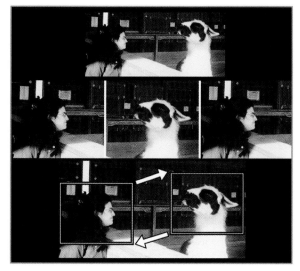

Figure 5.4
A single action, such as a quick dialogue exchange, might be staged with single shot framing both characters, a series of camera cuts that frame one character at a time, or with one longer shot in which the camera pans back and forth between the characters.

Figure 5.5
Some entire short films are contained within the space of a single shot, where the camera either remains static for the duration of the film or drifts and pans to follow the action but never actually cuts.

might conceivably be delivered within the span of a single and particularly lengthy tracking shot. Famous long tracking shots exist in films such as *The Player* and *Goodfellas*. Some short films, such as *Framed*, *Toilet*, *Squaring Off*, *Luxo Jr.*, or *Top Gum*, are in fact entirely contained within the space of a single shot, where the point of view may drift and pan, but the camera never cuts even though several story beats are delivered (see Figure 5.5).

No matter how many shots are required to describe a single story beat, every shot needs to be represented by at least one storyboard panel. Use the least number of panels per shot to effectively describe the action, staging, composition, and point of view. If the purpose of a particular shot is to simply establish a locale, one image should suffice—one shot, one storyboard panel. If an action or a camera move occurs, you might need one storyboard to indicate the beginning composition and story situation of the shot and a second one to indicate the end, or perhaps just one elongated rectangle—one shot, one or two panels. A lengthy chase scene that you'd like to follow with a single extended tracking camera move might require several associated storyboards—one shot, several panels. In general, a single image, a few descriptive notes or arrows, and a secondary frame (if appropriate) will sufficiently describe the action of most shots. The number of shots and corresponding images required to describe the action of an entire story beat will vary considerably.

Every shot in a film is indeed like a miniature story on its own. Most shots will have a beginning that directly relates to the previous shot (unless it is the first shot of a new scene). Each shot will also have a main action, which is the most important piece of information to describe in a storyboard panel. And every shot will have an ending, which will lead into the next shot in the sequence (assuming one exists). This mini story might require any number of storyboard panels to be described effectively. Even the absence of action can be considered a mini story. A story in which Fred sat very still in his chair and did not breathe or blink contains no movement whatsoever, but Fred's stillness is undoubtedly related to something that has happened or is about to happen in an adjacent scene (see Figure 5.6). Perhaps he is reacting with shock to something he just heard on the radio. Maybe he is meditating in preparation for battle. Or perhaps he is sleeping or has passed away.

Establishing shots often don't contain any action, but the message that "you are here" is still a story being delivered, and it must be told effectively with appropriate images, icons, and descriptive text.

There are many kinds of shots—wide shots, medium shots, close-ups, extreme close-ups, bird's-eye views, worm's-eye views, and over-the-shoulder shots, just to name a few (see Figure 5.7). Use the appropriate angle and point of view to most effectively tell the story of any given shot. If your film is about a very small child, a fair amount of low-angle up shots will probably be appropriate. Wide shots are generally used to establish a new locale, while close-ups are often effective for conversations, reaction shots, or inserts (in which the screen is filled with a pertinent object, such as a ringing phone, a bruised and throbbing finger, or the numerical display on a ticking time bomb).

Mix it up. A film made up of only wide shots will not be very dynamic. But don't mix up angles and points of view arbitrarily or repeatedly. Every point-of-view change needs to be motivated by the need to stage a new or existing action more effectively. Cut to a different camera angle only when it feels as if the audience will want to see the current or subsequent action from a more interesting or revealing point of view. An example would be a wide establishing shot that cuts to a close-up of a character in the midst of an action or a conversation (see Figure 5.8).

Figure 5.6
Every necessary shot in a film contains an actual story beat, even if there is little or no actual action taking place.

You must identify and storyboard the main action of each shot. You should only board the previous, subsequent, or secondary actions of that particular shot if they are necessary to tell the mini story that is currently taking place. You often can describe these extra actions just as effectively using text instead.

Figure 5.7
There are many types of shots, including wide, low, over-the-shoulder, medium, down, up, insert, establishing, and close-up.

Figure 5.8
Presenting an establishing shot and then cutting to a close-up is a standard and popular way of introducing a new scene, especially if the locale has changed.

Also, it is often a good idea to hook up individual shots by motivating a camera cut with an action, such as a character looking or pointing in a particular direction, where the object of interest is subsequently revealed after the cut (see Figure 5.9).

Pay attention to a scene's line of action, which is indicated by the direction in which an object or character is facing, traveling, or conversing. Be wary of crossing this invisible line when changing perspective from one shot to the next because it can be particularly confusing to your viewers (see Figure 5.10). Sometimes simply mirroring the offending image from left to right can solve a line-of-action crossing error. Give this a try if you discover such a problem in one of your image sequences.

Watch a few of your favorite films, pausing on each new shot to identify its type. Does the director use a lot of extreme close-ups? When he establishes a scene, does he start with a wide shot and then gradually zoom into the action, or does

> If a change in point of view is timed to the exact moment when the viewer feels the need to see a new or existing action from a different angle or POV, then the cut will seem smooth and appropriate.

Figure 5.9
It is often a good idea to motivate a camera move or cut with a character action, such as a point or a look.

he prefer an actual camera cut? How does his typical shot selection contribute to the overall style and feel of the film?

Apply traditional principles of image composition when staging and boarding your shots. If someone freeze-frames your film at any given point, the resulting image should hold up as a well-composed, static work of art. Balance, depth, overall shape, symmetry, natural randomness, and lines of action are a few of the main composition principles to study. Consider the action of each shot and compose accordingly. For instance, if a struggle is taking place, an off-angle composition will help deliver the feelings of imbalance and uncertainty (see Figure 5.11).

Decide on the central focus of each shot and choose an appropriate camera angle and composition so that the audience does not have to search for the visual story-point messenger. Or, break this rule if you deliberately want your audience to be unsure about where to look, like when staging a shot through the eyes of a pursued victim in a horror film.

Also try to avoid basic design errors, such as edge and object tangents, that create depth ambivalence. Read a few books on drawing, painting, photography, film directing, and shot construction and apply what you learn to the composition of your storyboard images. Review existing films and storyboard drawings to see how the pros compose and stage their shots. If you're not sure whether a particular shot is composed nicely, try blackening the objects and characters of the associated storyboard panel. Creating such silhouette images is often a very effective method of objectively analyzing the overall composition of a shot and quickly revealing balance or tangent problems (see Figure 5.12).

Carefully consider the intended use of camera moves—or more to the point, the *overuse* of camera moves. Only move the camera within a single shot when the action or mood calls for a corresponding and appropriate staging shift. Following a moving object, tracking over to see where your

Figure 5.10
Crossing the line of action is usually considered a cinematic no-no.

Figure 5.11
An off-angle shot will help deliver the message that an intense struggle is taking place.

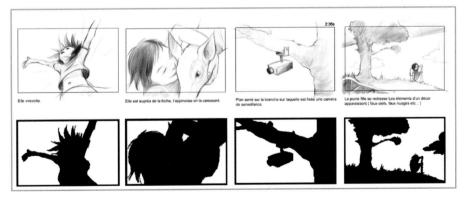

Figure 5.12
Silhouette drawings are helpful for examining overall composition issues, such as balance and negative space.

5. Storyboarding

hero is pointing, panning over to the other conversation participant, pulling out from a close-up to reveal a locale, and zooming in to increase the intensity of a character's facial expression are all good reasons for camera moves. However, the simple fact that it is easy and often tempting to create large, flying camera moves with your CG software is not sufficient reason to do so with reckless abandon. Sometimes large, sweeping camera moves are indeed quite appropriate, such as when you are following a jet fighter chasing a UFO, intentionally creating the feeling of vertigo, or dramatically staging a shot through the eyes of an attacking werewolf. Most of the time, however, camera moves are rather subtle and limited. Watch live action movies carefully—you might be surprised at how rarely cameras actually move. Granted, that is partially due to the fact that real cameras are a lot more cumbersome to move than their digital counterparts, but remember—just because you *can* do something, doesn't always mean you *should*.

When planning camera moves, envision that a real cameraman is filming your action. He will sometimes follow a half-step behind the movement of a character or an object rather than run exactly parallel, especially if the action is swift. If you want to indicate such a camera movement offset, draw your storyboards appropriately with the main action slightly off center (see Figure 5.13). Another example is the idea of the psychic cameraman, who anticipates a destination by revealing the locale before a character gets there (see Figure 5.14).

Figure 5.13
When a quick action is taking place, your camera movements will feel a bit more realistic if they lag behind the motion of your story elements, as if a real person were filming your story and trying to keep up.

Take advantage of the fact that you are creating a 3D film and use depth appropriately and creatively as you stage your shots and scenes. Flat compositions tend to be a bit boring. Use subtle or occasionally extreme angles to increase the feeling of dimensionality. But be careful of overusing extreme camera angles; doing so will make them lose their dramatic impact. Motions should not be restricted to left and right or up and down. Think of each image as a box where your objects and cameras can move in and out.

Also remember that you are creating an animated film in which exaggeration is often necessary, especially when it comes to visuals. Work the necessary amount of exaggeration into the characters and objects of your storyboard panels to convey the desired style and clarity.

Always think in terms of continuity. Each shot is part of a greater whole. Focus on the shot at hand, but think about how it relates to the rest of the scene, and in turn how that scene relates to the overall flow of your entire story. Remember that every action is a step along the pathway toward your story's ultimate conclusion.

Figure 5.14
Sometimes the cameraman will get there first.

From the General to the Specific

When you sit down to begin storyboarding your film, start with very broad strokes and work on the overall structure before focusing on individual story beats. See if you can fit most, if not all, of your story onto a single piece of paper filled with very small, loose, rough thumbnails, each one clearly representing the main action of each plot point (see Figure 5.15).

Consider each story action in your written script. Then close your eyes and try to imagine the clearest and most appropriate way of presenting that action visually. Who's point of view will best deliver the message of the given scene? Should the entire action take place within the space of one continuous point of view, or should it cut to different camera angles as the action continues? If your protagonist is scolding his dog, should you look over the owner's shoulder to see the dog's sullen expression and tucked-in tail, or would it be better to look up from the dog's point of view to see the owner's angry face? Or maybe you should cut back and forth between the two perspectives. If an action occurs where clumsy Clarence falls out of his bed in the middle of the night, you might:

◆ Stage a fairly wide point of view where the viewer can see the entire motion of Clarence's fall from a single perspective.

◆ Zoom in a bit closer on Clarence and then track him or tilt down as he falls.

◆ Center on Clarence and let him fall out of frame. Then cut or pan down to see his inadvertent destination.

◆ Look up from his future destination and let him fall onto the camera lens.

Work with simple shapes and stick figures and don't worry too much about cinematic staging issues just yet. The idea here is to see your entire story as a whole before you focus on the details of any one particular scene or action. Work fast and loose. Cross out, erase, and redraw as much as

Figure 5.15
Your first thumbnail pass should be fast and loose.

needed. You might even find it advantageous to start over from the beginning with a fresh piece of paper a few times. Don't feel you have to get it right the first time; just try to get an overall feel for the flow of your entire storyline in visual terms. And make sure that no matter how rough your sketches are, they are clear enough to effectively describe the corresponding action that is taking place. Explore, have fun, and revisit the ever-popular "why" technique of editing. Apply this questioning word to each story point, making sure that its existence is absolutely necessary for your efficient and economic narrative flow.

Once you can see the flow of your story as a whole, start focusing on the individual actions of your narrative with an eye toward cinematic staging by asking yourself the following four basic questions: (1) What is the action to be presented? (2) From what point-of-view are we seeing this action? (3) What happened before and what will happen after the current action? (4) What is the intended style and mood? Start thinking about the best way to present each story action and draw as many rough images as it takes to describe them effectively. Often a single panel will suffice, but a particularly complex conversation, fight scene, journey, or chase might require quite a few. Use the minimum number of drawings to describe the action sufficiently. Stay fairly loose, and work on several panels on a single page. Review these images objectively, asking yourself whether each drawing or series represents the most effective and dramatic way of expressing the action of the story beat at hand.

Once you're happy with the overall flow of each action in your story, begin refining your boards and focusing a bit more attention on your ideas regarding cinematic specifics, such as composition, object and character placement, point of view, and camera movement.

The Tools and Mechanics of Storyboarding

A storyboard panel is usually a rectangular frame with a designated area for notes, dialogue, or camera direction information (see Figure 5.16). It is not necessary to buy expensive storyboard paper at your local art supply store. In fact, we actually recommend *against* using the traditional white-on-black storyboard panels from art stores and catalogues. The black paper restricts you from drawing or writing outside the borders, which is often a necessary method of working out ideas. Also, your local copy center might charge you extra for making them replace their toner cartridges every time you photocopy your boards.

Usually it is more than sufficient to simply draw a rectangle or two…or four…or more on a piece of paper and leave enough space below and around each one for some written notes or informative scribbles. You might want to cut a rectangular hole in a piece of cardboard as a template so you can draw each panel at a consistent size and shape (see Figure 5.17). This template also comes in handy as an overlay if you want to focus on the composition of a single panel without being distracted by what is outside of its frame.

Also, consider your film's target aspect ratio when you draw your storyboard panels. Standard television frames are 1.33, which means they are 33 percent wider than they are tall. Standard feature film frames are 1.85. An appropriate television panel might be eight inches wide by six inches tall. A film-ratio thumbnail panel might be 2 inches tall by 3.7 inches wide. You don't have to draw your storyboard panels in exact format ratios, but they should at least be fairly close approximations (see Figure 5.18).

Draw with pencils, pens, magic markers, or crayons—whatever medium you're most comfortable using. Just remember that storyboarding is an exploratory process, so try to work fairly fast and loose, at least initially. You might feel the need to tighten them up for clarity's sake in the future. Then again, they might work out just fine as rough sketches. Be sure to keep a good eraser and a lot of extra paper handy.

Keep in mind that you do not have to be a brilliant draftsman to board your film effectively. Often, stick figures and simple shapes will be quite sufficient to describe each shot. The most important element of a storyboard panel is clarity, not draftsmanship. However, if you want fairly refined or realistic storyboards but nobody on your team has the necessary drawing skills, consider the possibility of using photography instead. If your film is about a real

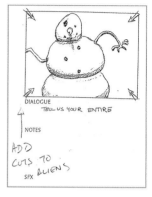

Figure 5.16
A storyboard panel is a rectangular frame, often with a space for notes or dialogue.

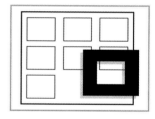

Figure 5.17
Use a cardboard template to draw your frames and focus on single panels.

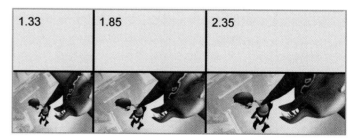

Figure 5.18
Draw your panels in the correct proportions to match your intended final output format.

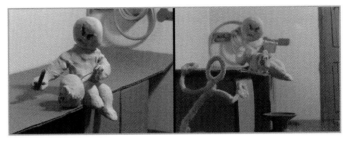

Figure 5.20
If you prefer not to draw, you can also use 3D dioramas.

Figure 5.19
Using live actors and a camera can be an effective alternative to drawn storyboard panels, especially if your characters are humans.

or semi-real human character, use yourself or a friend with some appropriate props, a camera (preferably digital), and a tripod. Then stage your shots as live action photos that can be scanned or digitally transferred into your computer (see Figure 5.19). Another non-drawing option is to create real-world 3D dioramas with action figures, toys, clay sculptures, stuffed animals, and other small objects (see Figure 5.20). Arrange these elements as if you were creating a stop-motion stage and photograph them from appropriate angles. One advantage of this technique is that you can take a variety of different pictures of the same shot from alternative camera angles and then choose the best one later, when you assemble your boards.

You might elect to draw or assemble your boards directly on the computer using your mouse, or preferably a digital pen tablet. Any drawing or painting program will provide you with a suitable canvas on which to draw your boards. There are also a few storyboard software packages available that provide

panel templates and even clip art you can use for the characters and objects in your scene images (see Figure 5.21). Working digitally gives you the advantage of not requiring a scanner to bring your drawings into the computer when you are building your animatics (see Chapter 7, "Production Planning"). Also, digital-drawing programs allow you to easily revise, repeat, rotate, mirror, scale, and color your images while you work. And don't forget about the advantages of the ever-popular Undo button!

There are three main components of a storyboard panel.

◆ Character, object, and background imagery and icons

◆ Movement indicators

◆ Text

Figure 5.21
Consider saving yourself the expense of using a scanner by drawing your storyboards digitally with a piece of storyboard software, such as BoardMaster or The Badham Company's ShotMaster.

Imagery and Icons

The drawings of the characters, objects, backgrounds, cameras, and lights in your storyboard panels need not be masterful works of art. As long as they clearly display all of the necessary information required to tell the story of each shot or story beat, they can be rather loose, rough, abstract, or symbolic. If the proposed art direction of your film is less than realistic, then it will not only save you time, but it will actually be quite appropriate to draw your boards in a similar style. When it comes to drawing your characters, their overall gestures are usually the most important information to describe in a storyboard panel. Head orientation should also be demonstrated clearly, with at least a couple of construction lines and some rough nose and eye shapes. In general, headshots should also indicate facial expressions, even if you merely suggest the mouth and eyebrow angles with a few simple lines

Figure 5.22
Even in very rough storyboards, character drawings should indicate overall gestures, head orientation, and facial expressions (if appropriate).

(see Figure 5.22). Depth should also be described effectively with the proper application of perspective principles, such as horizon lines, overlap, and appropriately diminished object sizes. Depth can also be indicated in a drawing by using thicker lines and darker shadows on foreground elements, thinner lines with lighter shadows for middle-ground objects, and no lines and very limited contrasts on background elements (see Figure 5.23).

Figure 5.23
Depth can be indicated in a storyboard drawing with effective use of line thickness and contrast differences between foreground and background elements.

Figure 5.24
You can effectively indicate perspective and extreme camera angles by using bounding boxes.

Sometimes it is even a good idea to surround more complex objects or simplified figures with lines or bounding boxes drawn in correct perspective to effectively indicate their location and orientation, especially if the current shot calls for a very low camera view or an especially wide-angle lens (see Figure 5.24).

Movement Indicators (Frames and Arrows)

Since a single storyboard is a static panel that represents a portion of a moving picture, it is often necessary to indicate character, object, or camera movement with visual icons, such as secondary frames and arrows.

BASIC CAMERA MOVES

Cut	Instantaneous transition to another point of view.
Pan	Camera rotates to the left or the right from a fixed spot.
Tilt	Camera rotates up or down from a fixed spot.
Track	Camera moves sideways or up/down.
Dolly	Camera moves toward or away from the action.
Zoom	Camera stays in place but the focal lens changes so the image gets larger or smaller.

Figure 5.25
Secondary frames and arrows indicate camera moves, such as pans, tilts, zooms, spirals, and combinations thereof.

Secondary frames will reveal cuts, zooms, tracks, dollies, pans, and tilts. The second rectangle is often drawn inside, overlapping, or next to the main storyboard panel to suggest either the initial or the final framing of a shot if it is to include a composition shift as the result of a camera move. Rotated or slightly offset secondary panels will describe twists and drifts for that handheld feel. To indicate the direction of camera movement, draw small arrows connecting the borders of the main panel to those of the secondary frame. A secondary frame without connecting arrows will indicate an actual camera cut, rather than a move (see Figure 5.25).

Sometimes it might be preferable to use a single elongated frame rather than two separate panels to illustrate a camera pan, tilt, or track (see Figure 5.26). If a shot's camera move is rather complex, it is a good idea to draw a corresponding arrow or path line next to the storyboard panel, representing a top view of the camera's intended trajectory.

Large arrows will indicate the motion of the characters and objects in the scene. Arrows should be drawn three-dimensionally to clearly indicate the specific direction of motion you are planning, especially when depth is involved. It is also usually beneficial to label these arrows with respect to the specific character or object to which they are referring (see Figure 5.27).

Figure 5.26
You can also indicate a camera pan, tilt, or track by a series of connected storyboard frames or a single elongated panel with appropriate arrows to indicate movement specifics.

Text

Words can be used to indicate dialogue or narration, which might be written in a separate panel beneath the main board, in a comic-book-style balloon within the image itself, or simply scrawled between quotation marks wherever there is room on the page. You can also use text for descriptive notes indicating specifics, such as camera motion velocity, and details that are difficult or inefficient to indicate in static drawings, such as sound effects, the flowing movement of a grassy field, necessary historical information, or the number of times your protagonist will snap his fingers. Using text and arrows between the borders of two storyboard panels is also an effective way of describing continuity, wipes, fades, or camera movement details (see Figure 5.28).

Diagram Panels and Numbering

The images we've been describing and illustrating thus far are known as *cinematic storyboards*, which represent the approximate staging, composition, and action that will ultimately be seen from the camera and audience point of view. Another type of storyboard is a *diagram panel*, which shows a particular shot from an alternative point of view, typically from above, with arrows and simple icons representing cameras and objects. These panels are often used adjacent to (or sometimes in place of) cinematic boards to more effectively describe camera, character, or object movement, especially when complex or depth-oriented trajectories are intended (see Figure 5.29).

Also be sure to label each board with its corresponding scene and shot numbers. If a gust of wind or a rambunctious child disturbs the panels you've so carefully laid out on the floor, you'll have a relatively easy time putting them back where they belong if they are labeled appropriately. Number your shots sequentially. If you find it necessary to insert a new shot between CB14 and CB15, you can label it CB14a. It is generally a good idea to write your scene and shot numbers in pencil so you can erase them if you decide to do some major plot restructuring.

Figure 5.27
Larger, three-dimensional, and appropriately labeled arrows are typically used for indicating character or object motion within a shot.

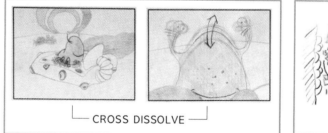

CROSS DISSOLVE

Figure 5.28
You can indicate the specifics of the flow from one shot to another with text and arrows connecting two corresponding storyboard panels.

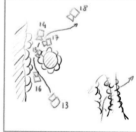

Figure 5.29
Sometimes the best way to describe the action of a particular shot is by using an overhead diagram panel rather than a point-of-view image.

And, as you draw and label your storyboard panels, record a complete shot list on a piece of paper or in a piece of word processing or spreadsheet software. This way, you will have an overall shot list prepared when it comes time to budget and schedule the production of your film.

Exercise: Watch one of your favorite animated shorts. Pause after every shot and draw a quick thumbnail with appropriate movement arrows, frames, and descriptive text. Then analyze your complete set of boards with regard to composition variation, point of view, camera angles and moves. How does the director use different shot types to effectively stage his story actions? Is a particular shot's point of view from an omniscient and objective cameraman, or from an actual member of the story? Does the film have too many of the same types of shots in a row? How much actual camera movement exists? Are extreme angles used, and if so, do they seem appropriate for the dramatic content of the particular scene? Does the camera ever distractingly cross the line of action?

Shuffleboarding and Shot Shaving

You will repeatedly edit your film as it evolves. When you initially wrote or recorded your script, hopefully you went through it with a fine-toothed comb and pruned out or tightened up any pointless or unnecessarily long scenes and actions. The storyboard stage represents yet another excellent opportunity for you to make a story-editing pass.

Lay out all of your boards on a wall or on the floor and review your film as a whole. Previously, you examined the overall flow of your story when you created your first rough thumbnail pages. Now, when your boards are a bit more refined and contain preliminary ideas for cinematic details, such as composition, POV, and camera moves, you will likely find it quite revealing to look at your story again as a complete and continuous visual experience. You might find it necessary to shuffle individual boards or even entire scenes to deliver a particular story point with a bit more effectiveness or dramatic flair (see Figure 5.30). Perhaps the earthquake should happen *while* Larry is proposing to Mary, instead of right after he proposes. Maybe your hero's argument with his mother-in-law will have more dramatic impact if you start with a close-up and then pull wide, rather than the other way around as you had originally planned. Use your objectively critical eye and look for what works and what does not work cinematically.

Figure 5.30
Lay out all of your storyboards on the floor or on a wall and use your objectively critical story sense to determine whether any *shuffleboarding* is necessary to make the structure of your film more logical, effective, and entertaining.

- Are there too many over-the-shoulder shots?
- Do any shot sequences break the line of action inappropriately? If so, can you fix the problem by simply mirroring a particular storyboard panel?
- Are you unnecessarily establishing the same locale with multiple shots from alternative camera angles, where one would be more than sufficient (see Figure 5.31)?

◆ Are there any shots that do not hook up properly with their neighbors?

◆ If a car is traveling left to right in one shot, do you have it moving right to left in a subsequent shot, in which it is supposed to be continuing in the same direction?

◆ Does your camera jump back and forth between wide shots and close-ups too repetitively?

Look at every storyboard panel and ask yourself, "Why is this shot in my film?" Every shot needs to directly contribute to a story beat that subsequently contributes to character development or plot progression. Any shot that does not fit this criteria needs to be cut. Establishing shots are only appropriate if it is necessary to show locale or perhaps set a mood. Sometimes a sequence will work just as well (if not better) when the setting details are vague, abstract, or even entirely absent. If a particular shot was planned for the sole purpose of showing off that beautiful texture map you painted on the bottom of your protagonist's shoe, it should be left out unless it somehow moves the story along. Try to indicate transportation by using shortcuts. Show your characters getting into the car, then perhaps show a single shot of the vehicle heading down the roadway, and then show a shot of the arrival. Only fill in extra shots along the way if you need to indicate that a long distance is being covered or if an important conversation or action takes place during the journey.

> If a shot does not contribute to the narrative flow or character development that ultimately leads to your story's conclusion or punch line, cut it.

When you are happy with this new visual representation of your story, consider holding a pitch meeting with a few select individuals (see Figure 5.32). Walk your viewers through your story by describing the action, dialogue, or narration of each shot and

Figure 5.31
Look for cinematic structure problems, such as redundancies (multiple shots establishing the same setting) and repetition (close-up, wide-shot, close-up, wide-shot, and so on).

Figure 5.32
Consider holding a pitch session with a few select friends or well-respected colleagues.

story beat while flipping through your boards one at a time or pointing to the appropriate one on the wall. Try to elicit some constructive feedback with regard to the structure, composition, pacing, and clarity of your cinematic vision. If anyone is unclear about a certain story point, it may or may not necessarily indicate a story problem. That specific plot point might simply need an alternative or extra storyboard panel in order to be described more effectively. Or perhaps an audience member sneezed during your presentation and missed an important piece of information. Then again, there might indeed be a flaw in your story structure. Discuss the unclear section with the person who mentioned it and see whether you can work together to identify the source of the confusion.

Remember, if you are going to need to make significant changes to the details of your cinematic vision, sooner is always better (and cheaper) than later.

Summary

A storyboard sequence is like a comic-book version of a film. The storyboarding process will allow you to work out the beats of your story visually and begin exploring ideas for cinematic details, such as composition and camera moves. A story beat refers to an action or event in a narrative, while a shot is a cinematic term used to describe the delivery of a story action from a single (but not necessarily static) point of view. A single shot might contain several story beats. Likewise, a single story beat might need several shots to be delivered effectively. Every shot in a film tells a miniature story. The main action of this story must be storyboarded. Many types of shots exist, including close-ups, over-the-shoulders, and bird's-eye views. Point of view changes should take place when it is necessary to show a new or existing action from a more appropriate perspective. Pay attention to traditional composition principles when staging your shots. Always think in terms of continuity when you are working out the visual representation of each shot and story beat. Initial storyboards should be small, rough, and loose, allowing you to experiment with the overall flow of your story before you hone in on the details. The main ingredients of a storyboard panel are character, object, and background imagery; movement indicators, such as secondary frames and arrows; and text used to indicate dialogue, narration, or direction specifics. There are two types of storyboard panels. Cinematic boards represent an action from the camera's point of view. Diagram boards show an action from a non-camera POV, often from above, with simple icons and arrows representing objects, cameras, and their corresponding trajectories. Use the storyboarding process as an opportunity to further edit your narrative flow. Arrange all of your boards on a wall or on the floor and then analyze your story as a whole. Cut and rearrange as necessary to make sure that your story is dramatic and entertaining. Look for story and future cinematic issues and try to work them out in this less expensive pre-production stage. Make sure every shot and story beat directly or indirectly contributes to the flow of your story by analyzing each storyboard panel and asking yourself, "Why is this scene in my movie?" And consider pitching your film to a few select friends by walking them through your storyboards.

6. Case Study 1: Virgil and Maurice

chapter 6
Case Study 1: Virgil and Maurice

Our first case study focuses on a CG short with especially unique character designs and art direction. We'll let the student director, Morgan Kelly, describe the production process of his individual cinematic vision....

The Beginning

As a student at the California Institute of the Arts, I studied character design, 2D and 3D character animation, story, and film theory. The curriculum there stresses the fundamentals of these disciplines while simultaneously encouraging individual style and growth. The Character Animation program requires all students to complete a short animated film each year. The year-end goal at CalArts is for each student to personally develop and implement each aspect of production on the film, from story to design to animation to final editing. After two years of studying traditional animation, I began my first CG short film, *The Terrible Tragedy of Virgil and Maurice*, during the spring semester of my third year (see Figure 6.1). I then returned to it at the end of my fourth year and expanded on the story and animation to complete the four-minute short film in April of 2003.

> **VITAL STATISTICS**
>
> **Title:** *The Terrible Tragedy of Virgil and Maurice*
>
> **Director:** Morgan Kelly
>
> **Team Size:** One
>
> **Total Running Time:** 4 minutes, 4 seconds
>
> **Production Cycle:** About eight months, full-time
>
> **Date of Completion:** April 2003
>
> **Software:** Maya, Adobe Premiere, Adobe After Effects, Photoshop, QuickTime 5, Final Draft
>
> **Total Production Cost:** Two years tuition at the California Institute of the Arts, minus scholarships, plus traditional art supplies and equipment for backups

Story and Design

The story for *The Terrible Tragedy of Virgil and Maurice* involves two characters who are physically conjoined but have entirely different personalities. Virgil is a dramatic, vaudevillian performer and Maurice is a vulgar, narcoleptic serpent who is in place of Virgil's right arm (although I ultimately switched it to the left). And then there is Houdini III, a small bird beloved by Virgil who is tragically swallowed by the serpent. The entire short film was created, from early concepts and ideas to the final rendering, compositing, and output, in eight months.

Figure 6.1
Morgan Kelly's third- and fourth-year film project at CalArts

When it comes to short film production, I believe that story is the most integral, but design is definitely the most fun. I love to draw and I love to design (see Figure 6.2). I wanted to bring the texture, design, and style I could create in a 2D character environment into a 3D film. While preparing to design the short, I took into consideration the strengths and weaknesses of CG, my limitations as a beginning CG artist, and the impending April 26th film deadline. An example of my compromise with these issues began on the concept and design of the main characters. It was important to me to put all my energy into the design, modeling, and animation of only *one* character. With the limited time, I felt that having to model and rig two separate characters would leave me with two characters only half as good as one. So I conceptualized hybrids of two characters with two personalities. In my sketchbook I just played around with ideas of conjoined Siamese twins, conjoined twins with different features and proportions, and identical twins. Another idea was a character with interchangeable heads. The thought was that he could juggle three or four heads and randomly replace one of those with his own—each new head containing a new personality for him to react with (see Figure 6.3). But the simplest idea, design-

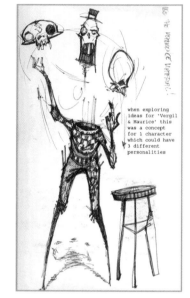

Figure 6.3
An early idea for the main character(s)

wise, was a character with split personalities who would argue with himself. The two characters would be given opposite emotional personalities, which would hopefully set up an interesting scenario where they could argue and disagree, but be unable to distance themselves physically from each other. That situation sounded like hell to me, but would be a lot of fun to animate.

Character Design

My general working method has been to use designs to creatively explore and discover story concepts, as opposed to writing the script and then designing the characters to match the story. The initial design, which gave me the concept for the film, was sketched during a trip to Mexico. Locals would walk along the beach selling fish. I made a sketch of a character with lots of beaded garb and a fish for a hand (see Figure 6.4). I liked the idea of the guy talking to a creature that replaces his hand. But would the man control

Figure 6.2
Story is integral, but I love to draw and design!

his arm or would the creature have control over it? There was definitely more entertainment value in putting the creature in control of the limb. Then I did some sketches where the creature occupied the entire limb but still retained the joints and manipulation of a human arm. The problem was that the creature looked like a puppet and not a separate character. This illustrates how the initial designs and asking these questions contributed to forming the story.

After a few drawings, the fish became a snake. I also decided to use the anatomical movement of the snake instead the human arm. Some of the initial designs had Maurice the size of an average snake, but I enjoy more asymmetry in design. I made Maurice larger so he would offset the balance of Virgil and become more of an obvious burden to him (see Figure 6.5). Since Virgil's persona was the polar opposite of Maurice's, his design had to also reflect that. I made Virgil's face soft and appealing, with large eyes and a fragile physique. Since he only had one normal hand, I made it larger than usual for more communicative gesturing.

Figure 6.4
More early design sketches created while I was vacationing in Mexico

Inspiration

To keep motivated and inspired while moving around, I had a small, plastic-sleeved folder full of paintings, drawings, and illustrations of different artists and some of my film's characters and storyboards. I'd fill it with art that had mood and great color. The folder contained illustrations by such artists as Joe Sorren, Enki Bilal, Eric Pigors, Shaun Tan, Mark Ryden, Laurel Huggins, and Mike Mignola and doodles by Jeremy Bernstein. My most obvious design influence is Tim Burton's *The Nightmare Before Christmas*. I referenced that film to see how the stop-motion modelers sculpted their shapes from 2D designs. I also enjoyed the subtle imperfections and textures in the topology of their characters. And after a tour of the *Oddworld Inhabitants* game studio, I was hooked on their character designs as well, including their application of illustrative textures on non-photo–real character models.

Pre-Production

My production pipeline was very rough and incongruous. It began simply with sketches and notes. I had a sketchbook with me everywhere I went to keep all my ideas intact. Any time an idea popped up that might work for the short, I'd sketch or write it down—for instance, pieces of conversation I'd hear in public. I liked that those would

Figure 6.5
Final character design

come from random sources, which were honest and genuine. I would often make small vignettes with the characters to figure out who they were and write down lines of dialogue to discover how they'd act toward each other. I felt that before I could begin, the two characters had to seem real to me. Then I could drop them into any situation and let the story naturally evolve from how they would react to a problem. Figure 6.6 is an example from my sketchbook showing Virgil, depressed, sitting outside of the vaudevillian theater and talking to a small bird perched on his fingertip. Meanwhile, Maurice is slithering below, eyeing the bird hungrily. This concept was another jumping off point for me—a boy with a snake for an arm. The boy loves his pet bird; the snake wants to eat the bird. That twisted situation still makes me laugh.

To help me solidify the characters' personalities, I wrote character descriptions and back stories for them. Here's a piece that I wrote for the character development of Virgil and Maurice:

Virgil Pettycoat is a 23-year-old, pale, thin, lanky, blue-eyed, male human with a unique condition. He's often quiet, which at times leads others to believe he is dimwitted. But he is of average intelligence, perceptive, and sensitive to the situations of others. When he does speak, his voice ranges from dramatic to melancholy. Our timid Virgil also has a dark side to his person. It is literally attached to him; Maurice—a large, vulgar, antithetical snake—is in place of Virgil's right arm (see Figure 6.7). Maurice loves a stiff Sapphire and tonic, small rodents, back massages, and oil rubdowns. He hates when people joke about him being Virgil's right-hand man and when he is pet against the grain of his scales. Their symbiotic relationship is not without friction. Maurice feels limited by his physical connection to Virgil, and therefore despises him for it. As a result, he constantly criticizes Virgil, curses at him, and belittles him in front of others. Virgil feels constantly on his toes around Maurice. The only time he can be alone is when Maurice passes out. Because Maurice the snake is a narcoleptic, he will suddenly drop limp along Virgil's side in a deep sleep, accompanied by a horrendous snore. It's during these times that Virgil feels the most like himself. He is at ease and enjoys the silence mostly. Virgil is a dreamer while Maurice is a pessimistic realist. Maurice sees Virgil's dreams as naïve, simple, and worthless.

Figure 6.6
The concept sketch that inspired my storyline

Figure 6.7
Early sketches for Virgil and Maurice

Story Reel

I was concurrently creating storyboards from the vignettes and writing the script in Final Draft based on notes I had in my sketchbook (see Figure 6.8). The two simultaneously evolved, helping me to solidify my storyline and keep all the content organized. When I had a sequence of storyboards together, I'd scan them into Premiere for the story reel. As the story reel grew, I'd add some necessary sound effects and music for the mood. The character thumbnail drawings from my sketchbook grew into detailed illustrations. From those I made a schematic front and profile drawing of Virgil and Maurice to be scanned into Maya for the basis of the modeling. As I was modeling/rigging the characters, I was also finishing up the rough story reel. I recorded scratch dialogue of myself and a friend from the script. This was added to the story reel as I further edited the timing. For the final voice actors, I used two talented, artistic, and comedic friends of mine, Eric Malamud and Ron Yavnielli. We did some test readings of the script to get the characters' voices worked out. The recording was done digitally in a sound studio at CalArts, then burned to a CD. I edited the new audio and added it to the story reel, replacing the scratch dialogue. Around this time I had also finished up my rough modeling/rigging. Now I could finally animate!

Modeling

The most daunting obstacle I feared was overcoming the technical aspects involved in creating a short film with computer graphics. I don't consider myself a "technical Mafioso." I can't absorb a program easily by just taking a class and watching demonstrations. I have to jump into it with a problem that needs to be solved and mill around to become familiar with the program. Classes were integral for me when I'd hit a wall and then need direction with a specific problem.

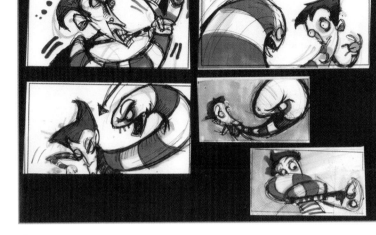

Figure 6.8
A few storyboard panels

Modeling, rigging, texturing, and lighting can be quite complex. But the cliché about "a complicated use of the basics" was the foundation for my CG experience. I didn't feel that I had to have an expert's touch in digital modeling, so when I modeled the character, I used whatever means were necessary to stay true to what made the traditional design appealing to me.

After the schematic drawing was imported to Maya as an image plane, polygons were used to model the head and limbs of Virgil. It's an intuitive method because of the close comparison to clay modeling. I felt comfortable that I could push and pull the CVs around to find nice shapes for the character. Then I sculpted the upper body from a NURBS sphere because it gave a smoother curve when it was deforming. It looked better when I'd bend Virgil's spine and then straighten him out quickly to reverse the curves during animation. Lastly, subdivision surfacing seemed best for Maurice's texture and extreme manipulation for posing. I worked very hard at the shapes and silhouettes of each body part individually, and how they came to form the body shape as a whole. It was important to have smooth lines and arcs to streamline the body of the snake, and to contrast it with some harder edges on Virgil. Even on Virgil, I wanted each body part to cascade nicely into the next limb. At this point I had the rough model made up of the head, torso/neck, arm, hand, pelvis, two legs, and a cylinder for Maurice. The model was made with the arm and snake stretched outward, but the body, head, and legs were laid out in a natural standing pose for Virgil.

Setup

It's easy to get stuck noodling your character models and textures while procrastinating and postponing animation. But storytelling is projected through animation. The last thing I wanted to have was a demo reel with just a fancy character model rotating in space. It felt to me that every day that passed was a day of animation lost! I knew that I was going to use Jeremy Cantor's SimpleGuy skeleton to speed up the rigging process (see Figure 6.9). I re-proportioned it to the scale of Virgil and began to apply the rough pieces of the model to the skeleton. After many tests using an IK chain and clusters for Maurice, I parented him to the skeleton body. Now the animation could be blocked out even though the model had not been completely refined. I began the animation knowing that as long as the model had the correct proportions and size, I could tweak and texture it later, as well as waiting to add details such as the eyes and facial controls. I believe that it made the entire experience much more enjoyable. If I was frustrated with the animation I could parlay my efforts toward refining the face or add some more textures.

Figure 6.9
The pre-built SimpleGuy rig was re-proportioned and then used as the basis for Virgil's internal digital structure.

Both Virgil and Maurice had very simple facial controls. I didn't bother with any blend shapes. Virgil was set up with eyes, eyelids, eyebrows, and a jaw to get his expressions. Maurice had just lids and a large jaw. He initially had pupils like Virgil, but I ended up liking how he looked with all-black eyes. That also sped up the animation process since I didn't have to make his eyes focus on anything. However, there is one shot where Maurice rises up to strike at a small blue bird. I wanted him to seem much more menacing for that moment, so I positioned the cam-

Figure 6.10
Maurice's normally black eyes were turned yellow and red for this intense scene.

era to look up at him—made the gray clouds point in toward him, curved him upward, and changed his eyes to be yellow with red irises (see Figure 6.10). That inconsistency on the eyes didn't bother me because of the more intense effect it had on the shot. The eyebrows on Virgil were free-floating objects parented to his head, with clusters to shape his expression. For their mouths, I ran three joints down their jaws from the head bone. All the lip synchs were done by rotating the joints to roughly get the phonetic shapes. The multiple joints in the jaws also allowed for overlap in the animation. This facial setup satisfied me, especially considering the fact that Kermit the Frog could act out a gamut of emotions with no facial movement except for a hinged jaw!

Texturing

All of the character textures were rendered traditionally. I sketched them out, then rendered them with AD markers or Trias for the base, ink for detail, then opaque soft oil pastels and a white paint pen on top for highlight. This way the backgrounds (also traditionally rendered) and the characters would have a consistent quality (see Figure 6.11).

Animation, Rendering, and Editing

The finished rig and model were pretty light and had fast playback. It helped that my scene environments were very light also. But to minimize some frustrating animation drag, I did create a lower-poly model, which I parented to the skeleton for the animation. I'd just hide the low-poly, and then make the high-poly visible for the render. I began to animate the bodies of the characters according to the story reel and dialogue. As a scene was completed, I'd create a quick test render of it and then replace the scene in the story reel with it. I also began to render out some test shots with textures and lighting.

Figure 6.11
The backgrounds were drawn using traditional materials.

The lighting was entirely global illumination with white lights, then colored spotlights for light sources for the shadows (see Figure 6.12).

Whenever a shot had everything roughly together, I'd render it out for After Effects. Shots were rendered separately in layers of foreground planes, characters, ground plane, props, and background planes. The sky was always added in After Effects. Not many students at CalArts were making CG films, so at night I usually had access to all 14 computers for rendering and working. All of the computers in the CalArts Maya lab were networked together, where each student had been given 8 gigabytes for their work. As my rendered scenes and movies began to grow, I had to request more space for my film. I eventually had 30 gigs of hard-drive space. As the deadline neared, I used multiple computers so I would not have any downtime while waiting for renders. As my Maya-rendered frames would finish (generally rendered from six to eight computers), I'd make uncompressed movies of them in QuickTime. When those were done, I'd import them into my After Effects computer into their appropriate layers. When all the layers were in place, I'd make an uncompressed QuickTime of the compiled layers, which would be dropped into the Premiere story reel on a separate computer. The story reel would be constantly updated with the new renders to view the overall film's progress. If there were no renders finished from Maya, QuickTime, After Effects, or Premiere, I would work more on the animation computer. After the body animation was done for the entire piece, I finished the facial setup and did that animation. This really snapped up the overall emotion of the animation since the previous work was relying on just the body. The story reel became the final film after constantly being

Figure 6.12
A global illumination setup was used for lighting and rendering.

updated with newer work. I was continually showing the evolving story reel to friends and professors to get feedback on the clarity of the story and the pacing of the overall film.

End Result

Partially based on my short film's presence in my demo reel, the summer after graduation I landed a job at Electronic Arts-Maxis as a Maya character animator on *The Sims 2*. Then, in the fall, I started working as an assistant character animator at DreamWorks Feature Animation on *Shrek 2*. I'm currently trying to sneak my way into a visual development position.

Conclusion

I recently attended a panel discussion at the Animation Union in Burbank, California. The evening's topic was about the current overall transition in the animation industry from 2D to 3D. Many of the speakers were involved in a small debate over the pros and cons of creating a short film, and how it related to advancing an artist's skill and aiding their demo reel. A student's 3D animation demo reel was shown to the audience as a successful example of someone recently hired at a feature animation studio. The reel had about five animation sequences, each with a different character. It showed a range of acting and style and portrayed by example that it's not necessary to have an entire short film on your reel to get work. Some argued that when you create a short film, there will inherently be shots that are weaker than others. Some felt that it was better to put your efforts into a couple of scenes to have greater quality. I think if you're in a rush to get work at a studio, then perhaps this route is true. But making a short film is an invaluable microcosm of experience that forces you to become involved in many aspects of filmmaking. At CalArts, many students will begin their demo tapes with a "best of" reel, featuring the strongest shots from their films mixed in with different animation assignments. This shows off their strengths and is followed by their short films in their entirety, displaying their pacing, story, mood, and rhythm on a shot-to-shot basis. Making *The Terrible Tragedy of Virgil and Maurice* broadened my filmmaking perspective and opened up avenues by being showcased in festivals, which pushed it out to a larger audience than the recruiters who merely fast-forward through demo reels. With all that I learned while making this CG short film, I can't wait to begin my next one!

The Terrible Tragedy of Virgil and Maurice is included in the short film collection on the DVD that came with this book.

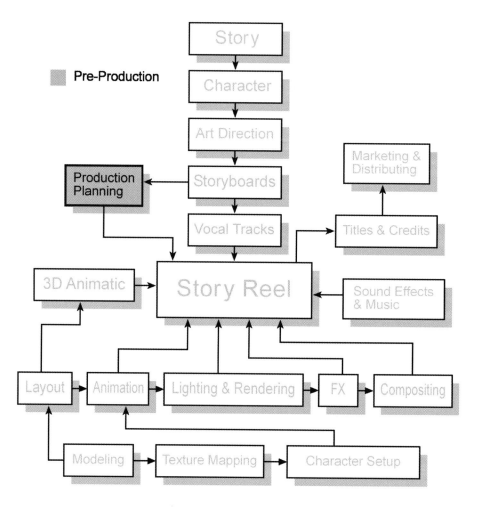

chapter 7
Production Planning

Budgets, schedules, outlines, blueprints, game plans, flowcharts, strategies…. To a cinematic story-teller who is eager to dive into the more creative areas of short film production, such words might inspire dismissive shrugs or all-out fear and loathing. After all, creating a short film is supposed to be a fun and exciting experience, and the idea of spending even a small amount of time planning and organizing (or reading a chapter like this one!) might seem like an unappetizing chore rather than an interesting part of the production process.

However, every short film director we interviewed either wholeheartedly acknowledged the benefits of preplanning or regretted having not done more of it. As the saying goes, "Those who fail to plan, plan to fail."

If you happen to have unlimited time and money, you might be able to get away with just rushing into production without a plan and simply making things up as you go along. Some filmmakers actually prefer to work this way to stay fresh and motivated. However, we assume that you have a budget and an official or self-imposed deadline; therefore, it is extremely important that you assume the role of producer and create at least a semblance of a production plan to organize and streamline your filmmaking process and avoid unexpected complications down the line (see Figure 7.1).

A production plan is like a roadmap and, of course, in order to construct a logical and methodical pathway toward a destination, you must have at least some idea about the specifics of where you are going (see Figure 7.2).

Consider the intended length, style, and complexity of your short film based on the plans and discoveries you made in your development phase.

◆ How long will it be? 30 seconds? Three minutes? Seven minutes? Half an hour?

◆ What is the overall style of your film? Cartoony or perhaps highly realistic?

◆ How many characters? One? Three? Two dozen? Perhaps none at all; just a few abstract shapes?

"It is a bad plan that admits of no modification."
Publius Syrus

Figure 7.1
In this chapter, you will assume the role of producer.

153

◆ Will there be dialogue? Narration? Music? Sound effects?

◆ Will there be rich or limited background elements?

◆ Will your images be ray-traced, hardware-rendered, or toon-shaded?

◆ Will you need procedural effects, such as smoke, water, fire, rain, cloth, or hair?

◆ What will be the final output format of your short? A 320×240 AVI file running at 30 fps for the Internet or perhaps a 24 fps film rendered at 1024×768?

To plan a sensible route toward a particular destination, you also must know some specifics about your starting position.

Figure 7.2
You need to know where you're going before you can figure out how to get there.

◆ Are you a student, hobbyist, or professional?

◆ How much total time and how many hours per week can you devote to this project?

◆ When can you start?

◆ Do you have an official or self-imposed deadline or just a vague idea of when you'd like to be finished?

◆ What necessary equipment do you already own?

◆ How much money can you spend?

◆ What are your skills? Storytelling? Character design? Animation? Lighting? Organization?

◆ Will you need to bring in teammates or do you have sufficient time and skills to go it alone?

Once you have some idea of the details of your origin and destination, you can build an organized, efficient, and cost-effective pathway toward project completion by constructing a production plan made up of the following four elements:

◆ An overall production pipeline

◆ A budget analysis

◆ A schedule

◆ Asset organization and safeguarding

An *overall production pipeline* is the full series of steps needed to complete your film. *Budget analysis* will determine whether and how you will be able to afford the journey, with regard to both money and time. *Scheduling* is the process of placing your production tasks in a logical order and then figuring out the best way to divide and conquer each step. *Asset organization and safeguarding* involves file structures, naming conventions, and backup procedures.

Your Overall Production Pipeline

A complete CG short film production process is typically broken up into four stages.

- **Development.** This is the initial planning phase, in which the elements that will dictate, inspire, and guide production are created, assembled, and organized. These elements include scripts, character designs, reference materials, look-development imagery, and storyboards.

- **Pre-production.** This is the stage in which you create the digital elements that will actually be used in your film. Think of them as the fundamental puzzle pieces of your production. These include vocal tracks, 2D and 3D animatics, CG models, texture maps, and character rigs.

- **Shot production**. In this stage, individual shots of your film are blocked, animated, lit, rendered, and composited. In other words, this is where the gathered puzzle pieces are assembled into a cinematic whole.

- **Post-production.** This is the final tweaking phase that begins after all of your film elements have been created and assembled. The puzzle pieces are all there, but a few of them might need to be touched up, rearranged, deleted, or resized to fit better. Marketing and distributing are also considered post-production steps.

At this point, we are assuming that you have already completed your development phase and you are ready to begin production on your short film. The first step in preparing for this journey is to construct an *overall production pipeline*, which will consist of a global task list including all the steps necessary to fill in the blanks between development and project completion. It is the structure and general order of the steps involved in the official production stages where the elements of your film are created, assembled, ordered, and refined. The remaining chapters of this book represent a fairly standard production pipeline consisting of the following steps:

- Pre-production
    - Vocal Tracks: Writing, Recording, and Processing (Chapter 9)
    - Story Reels and 2D Animatics (Chapter 10)
    - 3D Animatics, Layout, and Camera Direction (Chapter 11)
    - Modeling (Chapter 12)
    - Materials and Textures (Chapter 13)
    - Character Setup (Chapter 14)
- Shot production
    - Animation (Chapter 16)
    - Lighting and Rendering (Chapter 18)
    - Visual Effects (Chapter 19)
    - Compositing (Chapter 20)

◆ Post-production

　　◆ Sound Effects & Music (Chapter 21)

　　◆ Titles and Credits (Chapter 22)

　　◆ Marketing and Distributing (Chapter 24)

Not every producer would necessarily group each of these steps in the specific categories we have assembled here. For instance, some might consider texture mapping to be a shot production step and compositing to be a post-production step. How you officially classify your individual production steps is not particularly important as long as they follow a logical order.

For example, you might be creating a film without dialogue or sound effects, in which case your chosen music score will dictate the beats of your story. You might render all of the elements of your shots in single passes, thus removing the necessity of a compositing phase. You might prefer to texture map your models after animating them, rather than before. You might also feel that rigged CG puppets will be necessary in your 3D animatic, so you'll set up your characters beforehand. An appropriate digital pipeline for such a film might look like this:

1. Music
2. 2D animatics and videomatics
3. CG modeling
4. Character setup
5. 3D animatics and layout
6. Animation
7. Texture mapping
8. Lighting and rendering
9. FX

Take a moment to examine the development phases and overall production pipeline scenarios from a few existing short films (see Figure 7.3).

As you can see, a production pipeline can vary quite a bit from project to project depending on the scope and complexity of each film. Some productions will significantly reorder these steps. Some CG shorts require dialogue, while others are mute. Some filmmakers fully render their scenes in single passes, while others create layers and require a fair bit of compositing.

	Squaring Off	Alien Song	Venice Beach	Pump Action	Cane-Toad	Early Bloomer	Chubb Chubbs
Story							
Character Design							
Art Direction							
Story-Boarding							
Vocal Tracks							
2D Animatic				Video-matic			
3D Animatic							
Modeling							
Texturing							
Character Setup							
Animation							
Lighting & Rendering							
Visual Effects							
Compositing							
Sound FX							
Music							
Transitions							
Titles & Credits							
Running Time	1:15	0:43	4:29	4:03	3:56	3:35	5:40
Team Size	One	One	One	One	Two	70ish	100+
Production Time	4 weeks	9 weeks (part time)	about 1 year	14 months	5 months	about 4 months	about 1 year

Figure 7.3
This chart identifies the actual steps that were used in a few example short film productions, but it does not necessarily represent the chronological order of each step.

For example, the production of *Squaring Off* varied rather significantly from a standard pipeline because it began as a simple animation experiment and was not initially intended to become anything resembling a narrative film; therefore, very few official development steps actually took place (see Chapter 19).

Instead of starting with a script, *Alien Song* began with a character and a song. The story idea wasn't invented until after a good portion of the animation had been completed.

Venice Beach used live filmed background plates with CG characters, thus requiring a significant compositing stage (see Figure 7.4).

Figure 7.4
The production of *Venice Beach* included a significant compositing stage.

Pump Action made use of videomatics rather than storyboards or 2D animatics for scene planning (see Figure 7.5).

The authors of *Cane-Toad* elicited a good number of external critiques during the course of their production cycle, thus motivating them to revisit their scripting and layout stages repeatedly.

The production of *Early Bloomer* consisted of all the steps listed except vocal track recording and lip-synching (see Chapter 23, "Case Study 4: Early Bloomer").

The complexity of *The Chubb Chubbs* required a full-scale production cycle that included every conceivable production pipeline step, as well as a very large team.

Although the specifics of these pipelines varied significantly, each was logical and appropriate for the particular needs of the corresponding production cycle.

Figure 7.5
The development stage of Phil McNally's *Pump Action* involved filming videomatics with live actors as well as puppets.

Story Reel

Arguably, the most efficient and logical way to build a short animated film is to establish a software-based editing bay, where you will construct a *story reel* that will act as an evolving template upon which your film will grow (see Figure 7.6). A story reel, also known

Figure 7.6
A story reel begins as a slideshow of held storyboard images with necessary audio, and then evolves gradually into a final film.

7. Production Planning

as a *progression reel*, officially begins with a 2D animatic, where your storyboard images are assembled sequentially with a piece of non-linear editing software (such as Adobe Premiere) and then held for appropriate durations and synched up with any crucial audio files to effectively deliver the story points. As your production continues, you will replace each held storyboard image with evolving 3D imagery until your story reel becomes your finished film. See Chapter 10 for more information on story reels and 2D animatics.

Flowcharts

It is recommended that you draw a flowchart of your planned production pipeline so you have a visual representation of your organizational flow. A flowchart generally consists of boxes representing specific production stages or tasks with connecting arrows indicating how each step will flow into the next (see Figure 7.7). A flowchart will provide you with the ability to see your entire production plan as a whole, which can be very helpful when you are explaining your pipeline to your teammates, managers, teachers, or financial backers. A flowchart version of the production pipeline we are outlining in this book is featured at the beginning of each chapter.

Preplanning Your Journey

Completing each step along your production pipeline will of course cost money and time. Before you dive in headfirst, it is always a good idea to play producer and construct a budget as well as a production schedule to not only organize your plan, but to determine whether you will have enough money and hours to complete your journey. A producer has two main goals in mind—finishing under budget and on time. The creative side of the filmmaker inside you might come to resent these goals during the course of your production, but a bit of tough love from your internal or external producer will often be necessary to ensure that you actually reach your finish line.

Budget Analysis

Before you attempt to schedule your production, determine the feasibility of your cinematic vision by constructing a complete budget analysis consisting of fairly accurate financial and time estimates.

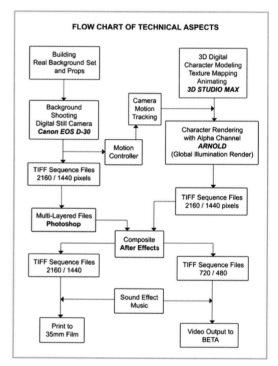

Figure 7.7
Production flowchart from Jung-Ho Kim's *Venice Beach*

If the film you are planning turns out to be too expensive or too time consuming for you to accomplish, it is much better to discover this before you begin than in the middle of production. By crunching the numbers and estimating the hours it will take to produce your film, you will discover whether or not you will need to take preliminary measures to make your production fit within the limits of your available money and time. However, if you choose to skip this important pre-production step and rush right into production without doing any sort of budget analysis, don't say we didn't warn you if you find yourself shelving your film indefinitely because you unexpectedly ran out of money or time halfway through (see Figure 7.8)!

Financial Estimate

To begin estimating how much your particular film is going to cost, consider the different types of production expenses you will potentially incur.

Types of Production Costs

Production costs generally fall under the following eight categories:

Figure 7.8
Don't let this happen to you!

- Computer hardware
- Software
- Office or studio supplies
- Purchased digital assets
- Training
- Personnel
- Marketing and distributing
- Soft costs

Production Cost 1: Computer Hardware

Obviously the most important piece of hardware you will need is a decent computer (see Figure 7.9). A PC or a Macintosh will generally be your best bet. Systems such as SGIs are indeed powerful, but they won't offer the same level of expandability or range of available software. Debates

Figure 7.9
You won't get very far without one of these.

rage between PC lovers and Macintosh aficionados regarding superiority; however, you can effectively and efficiently create a successful short film on either platform. Macintoshes are generally considered to be more user friendly, but the PC world offers a wider selection of CG software choices. If you are looking to purchase a new computer and you can't decide which way to go, try to make your software selections first and then choose the platform accordingly. Also, if the majority of your friends are using one particular platform, it is a good idea to follow in their footsteps because you will have that much more advice and technical assistance available.

The five main elements to consider when purchasing a new computer are

- Processor speed
- Operating system
- Video card
- RAM
- Storage space

Processor or "clock" speed will determine how fast your computer can process data. Higher clock speeds will mean greater interactivity, as well as faster image processing and shorter rendering times. Try to get your hands on the fastest computer you can afford, but be aware that the speed difference between the fastest and the second fastest processors out there will be marginal, while the price difference might be substantial.

RAM (*Random Access Memory*) represents the amount of data that can be processed at any given time. Increased RAM will allow you to run more software simultaneously, multitask more effectively, load heavier scene files into your 3D packages, play back larger video and audio files, work with higher-resolution imagery, and assemble more data into a single scene file or animatic. 512 MB of RAM should be sufficient to create a fairly simple film, but we suggest at least 1 GB or more.

An operating system is the overall software interface of your computer, which includes the desktop and your basic computer management tools. The most recent PCs generally come with Windows XP, while the latest Macintosh operating system is OS X. Many software packages run on either system, but a few will not. Machines with slightly older operating systems, such as Windows 2000 or Mac OS 9, will generally run most recent software, but if you are using a significantly more ancient operating system, upgrading is highly recommended.

Storage space refers to hard drive capacity. You need to make sure you have enough room to store all of your necessary files, which will include installed software, scene files, texture maps, audio files, reference imagery, rendered images and clips, preferences, and so on. If feasible, it is preferable to have two or three smaller hard drives rather than a single huge one. Distributing different types of files between hard drives is advantageous for reasons of organization as well as safety. For instance, if you have three 60-GB hard drives rather than a single 180-GB unit, you can put your operating system and all of your installed software on drive C, your data files on drive D, and your audio and reference files on drive E. This way, if drive C crashes (and hard drives occasionally do), you will indeed have to reinstall your operating system and your software, but your data won't be lost. You can also use your alternative drives as backup stations for one another.

A video card is the piece of hardware that processes your computer's data into the imagery that is displayed on your monitor. Video cards can range in price from around $50 to as much as $3,000. You need a card that is powerful enough to display your graphics and play back your movie files effectively, but like everything else, this does not mean you need the top-of-the-line product. Generally, something in the $300 to $600 range should be sufficient for your needs unless you are planning to create *Finding Nemo* on your desktop. When you purchase a new video card, make sure it supports recent OpenGL and DirectX shading languages because many graphics packages require such technical specifications.

Other Hardware Costs

In addition to these main computer components, there are quite a few other hardware items and supplies you might need for your film production (see Figure 7.10).

Figure 7.10
You might need some of this stuff as well.

Obviously you must have a monitor, and you'll want as much screen real estate as you can afford. We recommend at least a 19-inch screen to work comfortably in CG. A dual monitor setup is very convenient, but of course it will require the expense of a second monitor and an appropriate video card.

A second processor in your PC will allow you to multitask more effectively, which can greatly increase your productivity. It's like having two computers in one. But keep in mind that purchasing a second processor will almost double the price of your machine.

A CD drive is a hardware necessity. Without one, you won't be able to install most software packages. A DVD drive is a good idea for reviewing and capturing reference material. A CD burner is highly recommended, mainly for making backups. A DVD burner is actually preferable, because DVD-ROMs can hold about five times as much data as CD-ROMs. However, DVD burners are more expensive than CD burners, as are the blank discs.

A scanner is a recommended peripheral that you can use to digitize storyboards, reference imagery, or traditional drawings and paintings, which can be used as texture maps or modeling templates. If you don't want to buy a scanner of your own, your local all-night print shop likely offers inexpensive scanning services. But realize that you can purchase a decent scanner for as little as $40 these days, so owning one is a fairly inexpensive convenience.

A printer is also a handy piece of hardware to own. As your project develops, you will likely find yourself needing hard copies of script drafts, schedules, shopping lists, hardware specifications, various production imagery, and cover letters. Of course, you can bring such files to your local print shop on CD-ROM, but decent printers are not prohibitively expensive nowadays so we definitely recommend that you purchase one of your own. There are two basic types of printers—inkjets and laser printers. Inkjets are less expensive, but laser printers deliver better image quality. Remember that printers are not expensive, but ink cartridges are. Look for compatible third-party cartridge stores on the Internet. If you think you will need a scanner as well as a printer, consider an all-in-one unit that will also generally include photocopying functionality. As always, balance your needs against your funds when you make your choice.

Digital pen tablets are nice to have, especially when you are working with drawing or painting software.

Speakers or headphones are necessary when you are working with audio files. Some computers have built-in speakers, but their quality is generally rather poor. You can purchase a decent set of external speakers for as little as $30, so it is generally a worthwhile expense.

A digital microphone will offer you an inexpensive method of bringing vocal tracks and sound effects into your computer.

Digital cameras are great for capturing reference images, and many can now record short movie files you can use for motion studies or even rotoscoping. Keep in mind that movies recorded on digital cameras generally have a maximum resolution of 320×240 and tend to be limited to 30 seconds or so in length. Such specs are generally fine for reference, but if you plan to film longer high-resolution videos, you'll need a camcorder. However, converting small movie files from digital cameras is faster and less expensive than importing from a camcorder. A digital camera can also double as a scanner.

Camcorders are helpful for filming animation reference videos as well as potential rotoscope imagery (see Chapter 16, "Animation") and videomatics (see Chapter 10, "Story Reels and 2D Animatics"). Most digital camcorders have still-picture functionality, but the resolution and quality generally doesn't match that of digital cameras.

Production Cost 2: Software

It goes without saying that you will need a sufficient CG modeling and animation package to create a CG film (see Figure 7.11). There are many choices available, each with individual strengths, weaknesses, quirks, and price tags. Some of the most common are as follows:

◆ Animation:Master from Hash, Inc. $299. Available for both Windows and Macintosh computers.

◆ Carrara Studio 3 from Eovia (formerly Infini-D from MetaCreations). $399. Macintosh only.

◆ Cinema 4D from MAXON. $600. Windows and Macintosh.

◆ Lightwave from NewTek. About $1600 for the full version. Windows and Macintosh.

◆ Discreet's 3ds max. About $3500. Windows only.

Figure 7.11
CG software packages come with a variety of specific features and price tags.

◆ Softimage from Avid. Price can range from about $4,000 to $14,000 depending on the version and the status of Avid's promotional discounts. Available for Windows, Linux, or SGI.

◆ Maya Complete or Maya Unlimited from Alias. $1,999 and $6,999, respectively. Available for Windows, Macintosh, Linux, or SGI systems.

All of these packages offer full functionality in the areas of modeling, animation, lighting, and rendering. Some are better with audio file handling, while others have some degree of compositing capabilities. Depending on the versions, procedural effects such as particles, cloth, and hair are also included in some of these packages. Discounted student versions are available on the more expensive packages.

Before you purchase a piece of CG software, be sure to check its technical requirements to make sure your operating system is compatible and your computer specs are sufficient.

Although it is possible to complete an entire short film using only a CG modeling and animation package, it is very likely that you will need other software solutions for tasks such as non-linear editing, texture-map painting, storyboard drawing, audio processing, and compositing. A few examples include

◆ Adobe Premiere or Final Cut Pro for story reel assembly, editing, and sound synching

◆ Adobe Photoshop or Corel Painter for texture maps, background paintings, photo manipulation, and image filtering

◆ Adobe Illustrator or Macromedia Freehand for drawing images or charts and graphs

◆ Sony's Sound Forge for audio recording, processing, and manipulation

◆ Adobe After Effects for compositing

In addition to programs you will use for creating the digital assets and imagery for your film, you might also need software for other production tasks, such as writing, organizing, and scheduling. These include word-processing programs, such as Microsoft Word or WordPerfect, spreadsheet programs, such as Microsoft Excel, and database software, such as FileMaker Pro. Other handy software utilities might include file renamers, screen grabbers, and virus scanners.

Investigate your software possibilities and choices with regard to functionality and affordability. Visit their Web sites for information. Read reviews and ask around. Download and evaluate trial versions whenever possible. Also consider what your friends or colleagues are using. If your choices are consistent with theirs, you will be able to share information and files much easier.

Production Cost 3: Office and Studio Supplies

A quiet and organized place to work will help to maintain your productivity and sanity (see Figure 7.12).

A desk can be as simple as an old door propped up on a few cinderblocks or as sophisticated as an ergonomic workstation with keyboard drawers and footrests. Either way, make sure your work surface is solid and you have enough room to work comfortably. If you need room for printers and scanners and perhaps a bit of surface space for writing and drawing, you might need to get creative and build extensions or additional shelving on which to place your digital tools. Wide monitor risers are helpful because they allow your keyboard to be pushed underneath and out of the way when you need to use pencil and paper.

Take measures to avoid conditions like repetitive stress injury. You will potentially be spending long uninterrupted hours on your film, so make sure you don't sacrifice your physical health for the sake of your art. If any part of your arm, hand, or back aches or tingles after working for a couple of hours or so, investigate the causes and solutions of these conditions immediately. If the symptoms are ignored for too long, serious and permanent damage can result.

Figure 7.12
A comfortable and efficient work area will help ensure a high level of artistry and productivity.

Get a chair that is comfortable enough to sit in for hours at a time, but not so comfortable that you melt away into blissful slumber in the middle of your work sessions.

Other necessary office equipment might include bookshelves, lights, a mirror for motion study, surge protectors, tripods for your cameras or camcorders, a digital voice recorder, art supplies, and file cabinets. If you need to purchase such items, be sure to include them in your budget estimates.

Production Cost 4: Purchased Digital Assets and Other Computer Expenses

It might be possible and appropriate for you to purchase certain digital assets that you don't have the time, desire, or skills to build yourself. These include the following:

◆ Character, prop, and environment models can be purchased and sometimes even downloaded for free from various Internet sites, such as http://www.digimation.com, http://www.turbosquid.com, http://www.3dcafe.com, and http://www.its-ming.com.

◆ Character puppets are not as easy to find as models, but you can locate a few good ones at Web sites such as Turbosquid and http://www.vfs.com/~m07goosh/freestuff.htm. Software plug-ins, such as The Setup Machine from http://www.anzovin.com, can provide interactive solutions for creating custom character rigs without requiring extensive knowledge in that particular discipline.

◆ Texture maps are also available from sites such as http://www.3dcafe.com, http://www.realworldimagery.com, and http://www.amazing3d.com.

◆ Image filters for programs such as Photoshop are also available for creating a wider variety of styles and effects for your final images.

◆ You can purchase sound effects on CDs at your local music store or download them from a variety of Web sites.

◆ You can purchase royalty-free songs and scores in CD form as well as from various Internet sites. You can also license copyrighted songs. This can sometimes be a formidable expense, but if your film absolutely relies on a specific piece of music, you will need to add corresponding licensing fees into your budget calculations.

◆ You can also find and purchase photographs that might be used as reference material, background imagery, or texture maps from stock photography books. A quick Internet search will also result in a very large number of sites on which you can buy and download photographs and copyright-free illustrations from agencies as well as individuals. http://www.clipart.com for example (a site that was used extensively for this book).

◆ Program scripts and various material shaders and rendering algorithms can also be downloaded from various Web sites, such as http://www.high-end3d.com, to expand the functionality of your software packages.

See Appendix C for more information on where you can acquire some of the above digital assets.

Other computer expenses you might run into include Internet fees, Web site hosting fees, customer support fees, and of course, repairs.

Production Cost 5: Training and Reference Materials

Before or during your production cycle, you might discover that you need to learn a thing or two about a particular discipline or software package. To do so, you might have to purchase textbooks or training videos, take classes, or hire private tutors. See Appendix B and Appendix C for lists of books and Web sites that can help further your education as a digital artist and filmmaker. Surf the Internet for instructional videos and investigate schools in your area to see whether they offer classes that meet your needs.

Production Cost 6: Personnel

You may be fortunate enough to have volunteers or fellow students as your teammates; however, you might actually have to pay for your crew. Keep in mind that in addition to their salaries, you might be required to provide them with equipment as well. Voice actors will also sometimes come with a price. Other personnel expenses you might face include installation and repair technicians, couriers, and technical support providers.

Production Cost 7: Marketing and Distribution

Unfortunately, once your film is complete, you will still have to spend some money to allow your desired audiences to see your work. Such marketing and distribution costs include the following:

◆ Video or film recording fees might be required for transferring your short onto necessary formats for your intended display purposes.

◆ Duplicating your film so you have multiple copies for festival entries and job interviews might also cost you a few bucks (see Figure 7.13).

◆ You will have to purchase blank CDs or DVDs if you plan to distribute your film in digital format.

◆ Postage and envelopes. Unfortunately, Internet connections are not always fast or robust enough for e-mailing or FTPing potentially large movie files to festivals and HR departments.

◆ You might also have to pay entry fees for some contests and festivals.

◆ There are also printing costs for labels, attached resumes, or promotional items, such as posters or business cards.

◆ Internet hosting fees will cost a bit too, if you want to use a personal Web site as your presentation locale.

Figure 7.13
Don't forget to consider distribution costs, such as blank discs, labels, and postage.

Production Cost 8: Soft Costs

In addition to the expenses directly associated with your short film production, there might be a few indirect costs that you don't necessarily need to factor into your budget analysis, but you should at least acknowledge. For example, if you take a sabbatical from your day job or extend your college stay to produce a short film, realize that your existing or potential income might be reduced or perhaps completely eradicated, which may adversely affect your financial situation, health insurance coverage, or credit rating.

But also keep in mind that the creation of a high-quality short film will very likely be worth a bit of financial sacrifice. The potential rewards can often make the risk quite worthwhile.

How Much Does It Cost to Produce a Typical CG Short?

Unfortunately, there is no simple answer to this question because there is really no such thing as a "typical" CG short. The cost will depend on the complexity and length of the film, the size and cost of the team, and the amount of assets needed versus those already available.

For instance, *Squaring Off* was created by a single individual using pre-owned hardware and software. The only asset that was purchased specifically for the film was a piece of copyright-free music downloaded from the Internet for $15. Let's assume, however, that no assets had previously existed for this film. The cost of the equipment used for this production would have been as follows:

◆ $2000 for a computer (1.8 GHz Pentium III, 512 MB of RAM, GeForce3 video card, 60-GB hard drive)

◆ $1100 for a digital camcorder used for sound effects recording

◆ $12 for a camcorder tape

◆ $2000 for Maya 4.0 CG software

◆ $600 for Adobe Premiere used for sound FX synching

◆ $15 for music

The total for all of this comes to $5,727. Of course, if certain assets had not been already available, a certain degree of budget shaving would have taken place. For example, the sound effects could have been recorded using a $10 microphone rather than an expensive camcorder, which was used only because the director already owned one. Adobe Premiere was also a pre-owned luxury item. The sound-synching could have been accomplished within Maya, although the process would have been less efficient.

Many students are given access to all the equipment they need as part of their tuition fees. Therefore, the total cost of films such as *Venice Beach*, *Mickey's Buddy*, *El Arquero*, *Horses on Mars*, and *Run, Dragon, Run!!!* would basically be the price of tuition for the necessary number of semesters at the appropriate schools. For example, Sheridan College in Ontario runs approximately $12,000 per year for their computer animation program. Ringling School of Art and Design in Sarasota, Florida charges around $20,000 per year for tuition. California Institute of the Arts in Valencia costs approximately $29,000 per year. Also keep in mind that these numbers do not include fees and housing.

Films such as *The Chubb Chubbs*, *Bunny*, and *Geri's Game* were created by large teams of salaried professionals with state-of-the-art equipment and substantial marketing campaigns. The costs for films of such scope and complexity can easily run into the six- or even seven-figure ranges!

Let's assume you have a decent computer but no extra money whatsoever to spend on software. You might be surprised to learn that you can potentially create a CG short by *legally* gathering every piece of CG and filmmaking software you might need without spending a penny! If you are using a Windows operating system, try http://www.blender.org for a piece of fully-functional CG software you can download absolutely free. Windows users can also download GIMP from http://www.gimp.org, which can be used for background and texture painting. And Windows XP users can use the bundled Movie Maker package as a surprisingly robust non-linear editing software solution. Some software packages are available in trial form, meaning they will expire after 30 days or so. If your production cycle is short enough, you might be able to get sufficient use out of such promotions. An example of a fairly substantial CG short that was created almost exclusively using free software is Eddy Moussa's 15-minute science fiction tale, *Out of Memory* (see Figure 7.14). For more information on his production process, peruse his Web site at http://membres.lycos.fr/garbager.

Figure 7.14
Eddie Moussa managed to complete a 15-minute CG film using only free software.

How Much Will Your Film Cost?

When a studio is asked to bid on a project, they will examine and sum up the costs of each production step and then provide their prospective client with a fairly accurate total estimate on how much they will charge for their services. Then, of course, the client can accept the bid, negotiate, or simply turn it down. Similarly, you can examine the potential cost of each step along your planned production pipeline and then bid this estimate to yourself (see Figure 7.15). Once you've seen this preliminary dollar figure, you can tell yourself, "Okay, that sounds good. Let's get started." Or maybe, "Hmm…that's a bit pricey. Let's see where we can nip and tuck." Or perhaps, "Are you insane? I can't afford that!"

Unless money is no object, which is rarely the case, it is important that you come up with a fairly accurate initial cost estimate for your production pipeline so you can make any necessary cost-reducing adjustments to the scope of your intended film before production begins. Examine each step along your digital pipeline and figure out which of the six previously listed production costs will apply and how. Then sum it all up, add a bit of padding, and see where you stand.

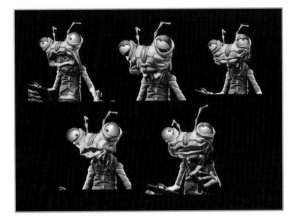

Figure 7.15
Once you have completed a preliminary cost estimate, you can bid your proposed production budget to yourself and then respond accordingly.

Let's assume you will follow our overall pipeline proposal and you've already completed your early development phase. Analyze how you will accomplish each production task to determine cost.

- ◆ **Dialogue.** Can you get away without it? Where will your voice actors come from? Are they free? What hardware do you need for recording purposes? What software will you need to process your audio files? Does your CG package handle sounds sufficiently so you won't need any additional editing software?
- ◆ **2D animatic.** If you drew your storyboards on paper or photographed them, you'll need a scanner or a digital camera to bring them into your computer. What software will you use to assemble your animatic? Something inexpensive, such as QuickTime Pro ($30), or will you need the additional functionality of a package, such as Premiere ($600) or Final Cut Pro ($1,000)?
- ◆ **3D animatic.** What software will you use? Will you need fully rigged characters or simple stand-in models that you will refine later?
- ◆ **Modeling.** Do you have the necessary digital sculpting skills? If not, should you buy a book on the subject and educate yourself, or will you have to hire someone to build your models? Can you purchase suitable models instead?
- ◆ **Character setup.** Do you have the necessary skills to set up your characters effectively and efficiently? If not, will you purchase textbooks or training DVDs, take a class, or hire someone to do the work for you? Can you purchase a pre-built character rig or construction system that will work with your models?
- ◆ **Animation.** Will you do it all yourself or build a team? Will your teammates charge you for their services? Do you need to buy animation books or training videos? Will you need to create or purchase reference books or videos of humans or animals in motion?

◆ **Texture mapping.** How will you create your texture maps? Will you simply use the procedural textures included in your CG package? If you paint them digitally, you will need appropriate software, such as Photoshop or Painter. If you paint them traditionally, you will need to buy, borrow, or rent a scanner or a digital camera to get them into your computer. Can you purchase appropriate textures? How much will they cost?

◆ **Lighting and rendering.** Will you use the rendering tools of your modeling/animation software, or will you need a separate package, such as RenderMan, or perhaps an external plug-in that you might purchase or download? How much hard drive space will you need to hold all of your rendered images? A film-resolution TIFF frame might be as much as 10 MB. Internet-appropriate JPG images might be around 50 K. Do some quick math to figure out how much storage space you'll need. For instance, a five-minute film running at 30 frames per second will contain approximately 9,000 frames. If your intended resolution is 720×486 (TV), each frame will be about 1 MB; therefore, you'll need approximately 9 GB just to hold your rendered images. Keep in mind that you'll also need space to store earlier render versions and other digital assets, such as software packages, scene files, texture maps, scanned storyboards, and sound FX files.

◆ **Sound effects and music.** Will your film require either of these audio assets? You can record your sound FX yourself using a camcorder or a microphone. Or you can buy sound FX CDs or purchase them from various Web sites. You can also find many free sound effects on the Internet. Just make sure they are not sampled from existing sources without permission; otherwise, you can get into copyright infringement trouble. If you want to use a modern recording of an existing song, you will have to pay for permissions if you ever hope to see your film in a public forum. Copyright-free recordings of folk songs and classical pieces are available at your local CD store as well as on the Internet. There are a number of Web sites from which original music can be purchased "for a song." Writing and performing your own music is an excellent option, assuming you are a decent songwriter and you have the necessary hardware and software, which can be costly.

◆ **FX.** Will you want your film to include effects, such as rain, snow, fire, or smoke? If so, how do you plan to create such assets? In 3D or 2D? Many CG software packages have built-in particle systems you can use quite effectively, or you can create 2D effects as separate layers with the right software and then composite them into your rendered images.

◆ **Compositing.** In many cases you can create your final imagery completely within your CG modeling/animation software in single rendering passes. However, it is sometimes more effective and efficient to composite separate image layers to create your final frames. Such layers might include background plates, effects passes, and separate character and background renders. Compositing these layers together will require additional software, hard drive space, and perhaps training materials or teammates.

◆ **Text.** How will you create the titles and credit lists for your film? Will they be simple 2D lines of text or complex flying 3D objects? Will you use your modeling/animation CG software to create such text, or will you need a separate package?

◆ **Duplicating, marketing, and distributing.** How do you plan to get your film out into the public eye? You could post it on a Web page, which of course will cost you a monthly hosting fee. If you plan to enter contests and festivals, realize than many have entry fees and you will usually have to pay for postage. Burning your film onto CD-ROMs or DVD-ROMs will cost you the price of a burner and the appropriate number of blank discs. Getting your film out to video tape will require additional hardware. Dumping your short out to film will probably require a professional service, which can be quite costly.

Hopefully, you already own most of what you need to complete your production. At the very least, you'll need unlimited access to a computer and a piece of CG software. You can probably borrow or rent other items that you will use rarely, such as scanners. One advantage to renting is that you generally won't have to bear the costs of repairs or upgrades.

Go through each step of your proposed digital pipeline and do a preliminary analysis of what you will need to complete each production phase.

Now, based on this analysis, make a final list of all the assets you will need to complete your production and then figure out the method and cost of acquiring each item. Consider what you already have versus what you need to purchase, as well as what you can borrow, rent, or create. Then, to be on the safe side, add 20-percent padding to cover unexpected expenses that might arise.

Create a chart like the one shown in Figure 7.16, preferably with a spreadsheet program that will sum the cost column for you.

Now add up the individual costs of your preliminary budget analysis to determine just how much your production is going to set you back.

The important question you'll need to ask now is, "Can I afford this?" Hopefully, the answer is yes, but sometimes the answer turns out to be, "Uh oh, I'm in trouble!"

What To Do if Your Financial Bid Is Too High

If you run the numbers and your cost estimate is beyond what you can afford, don't throw in the towel just yet. There are several possible solutions to the problem of an over-inflated production budget.

◆ Raise more cash
◆ Simplify your intended cinematic vision
◆ Take more time
◆ Lower your production costs

Raise More Cash

Is it possible to increase the amount of money you can spend on your production? If you are a hobbyist working at home, perhaps a friend or relative might be willing to make a donation. Consider a part-time job. Take out a personal loan or borrow from a credit card. See whether any software or hardware companies might be willing to sponsor a filmmaker who is using one of their products. Such scenarios are rare, but they are possible. If your production costs fall under the category of art/film school tuition, can you get scholarships, financial aid, or student loans?

Simplify Your Intended Cinematic Vision

As we've mentioned many times, simplicity in design and execution are worthwhile goals for a CG short. Minimizing the complexity of your proposed film idea can significantly lower your production costs by allowing you to reduce your team size, use less powerful (and less expensive) software and hardware,

Item	Plan	Method	Cost
Computer	I have one but I'll need a bigger hard drive.	Purchase	$80
Scanner	I'll use the one at the local 24-hour print shop. $1 per scan times 50 storyboard images.	Rent	$50
CG Software	I found an older version of Softimage on eBay.	Purchase	$300
Editorial Software	I want the latest and greatest version of Adobe Premiere.	Purchase	$600
Voice Actor	My friend from the drama club volunteered.	Borrow	$0
Character Models	I'm a lousy character sculptor but I found a good model for sale on the Internet.	Purchase	$60
Character Rig	I'll do it myself, but I need to buy a good book on the subject.	Purchase and Build	$40
Teammates	One free. The other wants $500.	Purchase	$500
Sound FX	I'll record my own with the microphone that came with my PC.	Build	$0
Music	I'll buy a CD of copyright-free classical music and find a suitable piece.	Purchase	$20
Making Portable Copies of My Film	I'll make DVD dubs. Need to buy a DVD burner.	Purchase	$300
Distributing	I'll be sending my short to 12 festivals. Need to buy blank DVDs and pay for entry fees and postage.	Purchase	$100
Subtotal			$2050
20% Padding			$410
Total			$2460

Figure 7.16
A hypothetical cost analysis chart

delete unnecessary production steps, and even do without certain equipment that you had previously thought you would need. Simplifying your film idea will also shorten your production cycle, which will mean less money spent on potential teammate salaries, upgrades, repairs, and technical support fees. If you are working on your short as a full-time endeavor between jobs, the shorter your production cycle, the sooner you can go back to work and replenish your savings account.

If you plan to use dialogue, carefully consider whether you can possibly tell your story silently instead. Doing so will save you money and time because you will no longer have to find or hire voice actors, schedule recording sessions, utilize audio equipment and software, model phoneme face shapes, and perform lip-synch animation. If your story absolutely needs words, perhaps you could use narration instead of actual dialogue. This option will still require voice actors and audio equipment, but phoneme face-shape creation and lip-synching will not be necessary. Or, if appropriate for your story genre, consider silent-film-style dialogue cards or even comic-book-inspired word balloons.

Can you reduce the length of your story? Delete unnecessary scenes and make sure all existing story points are told efficiently. The shorter your film, the shorter your production cycle.

Can you tell your story using fewer characters? Each character in your film needs to be modeled, rigged, and animated. Are you absolutely certain that you need to show every single animal species in your Noah's Ark story? Surely you can leave out a few dozen or so.

Will you be able to render all of your scene elements in single passes, thereby removing the need for a compositing stage?

Can you simplify your characters and background elements so they take less time to build, animate, and render? Perhaps your goofy cartoon alien works just as well with three fingers instead of five. Maybe you don't need to actually model every single tree. Look into instancing or using 2D cards or background plates instead (see Chapters 13 and 20).

Take More Time

Although lengthening your production cycle might very well end up costing you more, giving yourself more time might actually save you some money. You might be able to get away with half as many teammates if you give yourself twice as much time to complete your film. Also consider that rendering times can eat up a substantial portion of your schedule. Although you can indeed decrease these times with RAM and CPU upgrades, doing so can be costly. On the other hand, if your schedule is long enough to accommodate slower rendering times, you might be able to get away with weaker and less expensive equipment. Giving yourself an extended deadline might also mean that you can spend fewer hours per day on your short, thus allowing you to simultaneously work a full- or part-time job to offset your production expenses.

Lower Your Production Costs

Don't buy more computer than you really need. A 3.0-GHz CPU is certainly faster than a 2.8. However, the speed difference will probably be barely perceptible, while the cost difference might be a bit more painful. It is certainly tempting to assemble the finest workstation money can buy, but even a package deal at a local chain store will be sufficient for most production needs these days. Do you absolutely need an $1,800, 23-inch flat screen LCD monitor, or will a 19-inch CRT for $300 do the trick? Look for secondhand equipment in classified ads and on eBay, as well as returned or discontinued and heavily discounted store items.

Carefully consider your software choices. Prices can range from free to several thousand dollars. In many cases, you do indeed get what you pay for; however, just because a particular piece of software costs 10 times as much as its competitor, it doesn't necessarily mean that it is 10 times as powerful. This holds true for sophisticated 3D CG packages, paint programs, and editing software, as well as simple databases and renamers.

Also keep in mind that you can very likely get away with older versions of your chosen software packages. Often the absolute latest version of a particular program only has a few extra bells and whistles compared to last year's version, which you should be able to find for a significantly lower price.

Borrow or rent as much as possible, especially when it comes to seldom-used items. If you are only going to need a scanner once to convert your storyboard drawings into digital files, go to a local print shop rather than buying a scanner. See whether you can occasionally use such items at work or school if feasible and permitted.

Try to get multiple uses out of single items. A camcorder can double as a microphone, and a digital camera can double as a scanner.

Use talented friends and relatives instead of professional actors for dialogue/narration recording. If your teammates will be charging you by the hour, see whether you can possibly do a bit more of the work yourself and hire a smaller team.

Time Estimate

Now that you've analyzed the financial feasibility of your production, the next step is to create an approximate overall time estimate, which will not only determine whether your deadline is reasonable, but will also act as a preliminary production schedule.

To do this, you will need to determine how much time it will take to complete each of the three phases of your project cycle—pre-production, shot production, and post-production. You can accomplish this by analyzing each individual production step within each phase.

If you don't feel that you have sufficient experience to generate fairly accurate time estimates for any of the individual tasks, seek advice from friends, colleagues, fellow students, or books.

For bidding and budgeting purposes, a producer at a professional studio will need to make his estimate extremely accurate and will often crunch the numbers down to the hour. For your purposes it is probably not crucial for your estimate to be quite so precise, so think in terms of days rather than hours. When you are making these estimates, consider the concept of a *man-day*. We define a man-day as an eight- to ten-hour block of time. A man-day might differ from your actual workday, depending on how many hours per day you will be able to spend on your film. If you will be working on your film part-time, say four hours per day, then it will take you two workdays to fulfill one man-day. So if you estimate that it will take five man-days to complete a specified task, realize that it will actually take you ten part-time days to finish, not five. Same total hours, but different end dates.

Similarly, if you want to think in terms of weeks, consider what a week means to you. If you're working full time but taking weekends off, then a week would be five days. If you are a bona fide workaholic, then a week to you is probably seven days. If you estimate that a certain production task will take 35 man-days to complete and a workweek for you is Monday through Friday, then your estimate in weeks would be seven. If you plan to work seven-day weeks, then this task will take five weeks. Remember, the ultimate goal for your overall time estimate is to determine your completion date. The actual hours spent getting there are of secondary importance at this stage.

Once you have estimated the total amount of days that each production phase will take, you will need to divide these tallies by the number of members on your team and adjust for the actual contributions that each teammate will deliver. Also factor in any periods during which you might not be working at full capacity, such as holidays or vacations.

Pre-Production Time Estimate

We have defined pre-production as the stage in which the digital building blocks of your film are initially created and organized. Make a list of these assets and then try to roughly estimate how long it will take to create each one.

◆ **Vocal tracks and other necessary audio files.** If your film will require dialogue, consider that you will need to find appropriate actors, stage recording sessions, and process your audio files. This can take anywhere from a few hours to a few weeks depending on the number of lines being spoken per character. If sound effects or a music track will dictate the action of your film, it will be necessary to locate or create such audio files at the pre-production stage. Writing and performing original music will obviously take a lot more time than licensing an existing song or purchasing a piece of copyright-free music on a CD or from an Internet store.

◆ **CG character models.** Obviously, the time it will take to create these assets will depend on the number of characters in your film and their overall complexity. A simple character model might take a day or two, while a complicated model might take a few weeks. Also consider that depending on your facial animation process and the possible existence of vocal tracks in your film, you might need to sculpt expressions and phoneme shapes for your characters.

◆ **CG backgrounds and props.** In general, background and prop models should take less time to build than character models. However, this does not mean that they are trivial. Like everything else, a time estimate for such assets will depend on their quantity and complexity.

◆ **Texture maps.** Using procedural texture maps within your CG package will certainly take less time than painting your own original textures; however, a fair amount of trial and error will be required to determine the right parameter settings. Try to come up with a list of all the texture maps you will need and then estimate how long it will take to paint each one. Using photographed maps might save you some time, but cleaning them up and making them tile properly (if necessary) will also take a bit of work.

◆ **Background paintings.** If your shots will require such assets, make a list of how many you will need and then how long it will take to paint (or perhaps photograph) each one.

◆ **Character setups.** Rigging even the simplest of characters can be rather time consuming depending on your software of choice and your skill level. A very simple character with disjointed geometry pieces might take a few days to set up effectively, while a complex character with organic forms, multiple limbs, hair, and clothing will probably take several weeks.

Go through the above categories and jot down an appropriate time estimate for each one, based on the needs of your film. Then sum up the total to come up with your own pre-production time estimate.

To initiate a running example, let's say you came up with an estimate of 50 man-days. Suppose you'll be working full time, meaning one man-day equals one workday, but you'll be taking weekends off. Your pre-production phase will therefore reach its finish line in 10 weeks.

Shot Production Estimate

Before diving into actual shot production, we recommend that you create a 3D animatic of your entire film. If you plan to take this step, you will need to make a rough estimate of how long it will take to produce your 3D animatic. The time estimate will depend on the number of shots in your film, the size of your team, and the speed of each contributor. A rough but fairly standard estimate would be approximately two shots per man-day. So if your film has 60 shots and you have two teammates of equal speed, creating a 3D animatic should take 15 days. That would be three weeks if you are taking weekends off, or two weeks plus one day if you are working seven-day weeks.

Now that you have your rough estimates for pre-production and 3D animatic creation, it's time to look at actual shot production.

Draw a chart with nine columns, like the one in Figure 7.17. Use a spreadsheet package if you have one available, so the software can sum up the totals for you. Otherwise, use pen and graph paper or a dry-erase board and do the math yourself.

These columns represent the level of completion of each shot and follow a typical digital pipeline of the steps required for individual shot production, described as follows:

◆ **Blocking.** This is where the basic animations of your characters and objects are established. Blocking involves providing just enough animation refinement so the story of each shot is clear, but without any details.

◆ **Animation.** This is where you refine your blocking passes and add details until your characters and objects are moving convincingly. Don't forget to include sufficient days for any facial animation and lip-synching that might be required.

◆ **Lighting.** This is obviously where you place lights appropriately in each shot so your stories will be told with the intended clarity and mood.

◆ **Rendering.** This is where your software creates a series of snapshot images of each frame of the current shot based on the placement, materials, and textures of your characters and objects, as well as the placement, setting, and movements of your lights and cameras.

◆ **FX.** This is where you add any appropriate secondary or particle effects, such as cloth, hair, feathers, snow, rain, smoke, fire, or water.

◆ **Compositing.** This is where, if applicable, you assemble the separate image layers of your shots into final collages. If you render all of the elements of each scene in a single pass, then compositing is not necessary.

◆ **Audio.** This is where any shot-specific sound effects or music are synched up to your rendered imagery.

Now, fill in a man-day estimate for every step of each shot, based on your individual experience and advice from your friends, colleagues, teachers, or teammates. Consider that rendering may or may not require any man-days. If you set up your shots and then render them overnight or while you are away, then this step will not cost you any actual man-days.

Keep in mind that not all shots are the same. Some will be very short and simple, while others will be very long and complex. Some will require particle and audio FX, while others will not. Analyze each shot based on its length and complexity and try to come up with an appropriate number for each step.

Figure 7.17 represents an example chart for a very short eight-shot production, assuming a 3D animatic was already created and renders will run while the team sleeps.

Now add up all the columns and rows to get a total shot production estimate. In our example, the total number of man-days is 100. Working half time at five days per week, that would translate to about 40 weeks. In a full-time, five-day-week scenario, we'd be looking at about 20 weeks. A seven-day-per-week workaholic would finish in about 14 weeks, assuming he didn't burn out halfway through.

The addition of a second team member may or may not cut these numbers exactly in half, depending on his speed and the actual skills he will bring to the table. If you and your teammate are both generalists and can handle all stages of each shot, then you should each be able to do four shots in their entirety, and the time estimate can be approximately halved. However, if you will concentrate on animation while your teammate focuses on lighting, FX, and compositing, it will be a bit more complicated to come up with an accurate estimate because your teammate will finish shot number 2 and then have to sit idle while you spend your eight days on shot 3. He might be able to start lighting after your second animation day, but then a lot of overlapping will take place, and you'll need a much more detailed schedule to come up with

Shot	Frame Count	Notes	Block -ing	Anim	Light -ing	Render -ing	FX	Compos -iting
1	20	Simple	1	5	1	0	1	1
2	40	Complex	2	9	3	0	0	0
3	50	Complex	2	8	3	0	0	2
4	15	Simple	1	5	1	0	2	1
5	30	Medium	1	7	1	0	1	0
6	80	Complex	2	8	2	0	1	1
7	25	Simple	1	5	1	0	0	0
8	100	Complex	3	10	4	0	3	1
Total Man Days	100		13	57	16	0	8	6

Figure 7.17
A hypothetical shot production estimate chart for a simple production

an accurate time estimate for shot production. Regrettably, if your team is made up of artists with different skill sets, you'll have to simply make an educated guess. In the described scenario where one teammate animates while the other does the rest of the work, you can probably cut the total number by about a third.

Post-Production Estimate

For our running example, with a lone filmmaker working five full-time days per week, we are looking at 10 weeks of pre-production, plus three weeks for the 3D animatic, plus 20 weeks of shot production, equaling 33 weeks so far. Post-production tasks need to be factored in as well. These might include final editing, film grain filters, color correction, post-camera moves, titles, and credits. Hopefully this will be the shortest of the three stages. Approximate the time it will take to add all of the finishing touches to your film. For our example, let's say 12 days for final edits, three days for a flying 3D title and some simple text credits, and then two weeks to burn copies and send out festival entries. That's another five weeks, so adding it all up so far, you have 38 weeks.

Consider, however, that many things can go wrong in the midst of a production. Computers can crash, files can get overwritten, and teammates can quit. Because of such possible mishaps, we recommend padding your initial estimate by 20 percent, just to be safe. So with padding, now you're looking at 46 weeks—just under 11 months.

What was your total number? Was it more than you expected? If so, is your deadline somewhat flexible, so you're still in good shape and ready to begin production? Or does the disparity between your time estimate and your fixed deadline represent a major problem?

Another method of discovering the timeframe feasibility of your production is by working backwards from your deadline. If you have a deadline that you must respect, make a quick task table that extends from today until the date of your finish line. Then start filling in appropriate time blocks in reverse chronological order from your deadline. If you finish before you reach today, you're in good shape.

What To Do if Your Time Estimate Doesn't Jibe with Your Deadline

If you are expecting to create a successful and memorable CG short in a matter of weeks, you're probably going to be rather shocked when you schedule out your tasks and discover just how long it is going to take to realize your cinematic vision. Quality takes time. Jason Wen's lush and ambitions *f8* took three-and-a-half years to complete. Kevin and Moon's *Henry's Garden* took two-and-a-half years. Moonsung Lee's elegantly "simple" *Bert* required a 13-month production cycle (see Figure 7.18). Victor Navone's 43-second *Alien Song* took approximately nine months to produce (working part time).

If you do have a deadline and your preliminary estimate suggests that you will not be able to finish on time, don't give up on your film or lower your quality standards just yet. There are several ways you can effectively shorten your production cycle to fit within your timeframe.

◆ Extend your deadline

◆ Spend more money

◆ Simplify your intended cinematic vision

◆ Bring in more teammates

Figure 7.18
Quality takes time. For these films that goal required production cycles of 45, 30, and 13 months, respectively.

Extend Your Deadline

The most obvious yet potentially least feasible option is to change your deadline to a later date. If you are working alone and your deadline is merely self-imposed, then you will need to consider the ramifications of taking this step. Will extending your deadline adversely affect your life by forcing you to postpone other plans or projects? Will your finances drop to zero if you work on your film longer than you had planned? Or do you think you will simply burn out or lose interest if your finish line is pushed out farther? If you are working with a team, the idea of extending your deadline will need to be discussed and will be less likely to occur. If your deadline is externally imposed by a client, a boss, a publisher, or a semester end-date, this option might be extremely difficult or perhaps even impossible to implement.

Spend More Money

Consider a faster computer with more RAM. Greater computing power will mean higher interactivity and faster rendering times. More powerful (and expensive) software will often be more efficient and allow you to generate more assets in less time.

Buy instead of build. If you think it will take you a month to digitally sculpt your characters, think about purchasing models from friends or Web sites instead. You can also purchase assets, such as character rigs, texture maps, and software scripts/plug-ins, rather than constructing them. Buying digital elements almost always takes less time than building them yourself. (See Appendix C for a list of digital asset resources.)

Simplify Your Vision

As we discussed in the budgeting section, the simpler your film, the less expensive and less time-consuming it will be to produce. Examine your intended cinematic vision and make sure it is as economical and efficient as possible. See what you can do without, such as dialogue, particle effects, multiple characters, complex backgrounds, and so on. If you can eliminate or simplify any of these elements without compromising your quality standards or the clarity and flow of your story, you should be able to produce a successful film in a reasonable amount of time.

Bring in More Teammates

Introducing additional members to your team can significantly shorten your production cycle. One artist can be modeling while another is painting textures and another is testing rendering styles. The more animators you have working concurrently, the more footage you will get per week. Of course, you need to choose your teammates wisely. Make sure that everybody on your team is sufficiently skilled and can work well with others. An animator who needs too much supervision or works too slowly might actually have a negative effect on your production schedule. Similarly, a teammate with a bad attitude or an unreliable work ethic can also be a hindrance rather than a benefit. Consider the law of diminishing returns. A larger team does not always translate into more footage per hour. Each new team member will indeed contribute to your production, but realize that the more people on your team, the more complicated your production organization will become. You might find yourself spending too much time supervising, solving technical problems, breaking up arguments, or rearranging schedules and not enough time working on your film. Balance the contributions that each new teammate will make with the amount of time they will take away from your own ability to contribute to your production.

Balancing Money Versus Time

There is a common principle in the business world suggesting that only two of the following three elements are possible with regard to a typical production cycle.

- Fast
- Cheap
- Good

If a client wants his production to be fast and cheap, it won't be good. If he wants the product fast and good, it won't be cheap. If he wants it cheap and good, it won't be fast.

The business world states that a client must pick two of these elements, but cannot have all three. When it comes to creating your CG short, however, *good* must be assumed. If you are embarking on this journey with anything less than the goal of creating cinematic excellence, then please don't bother. But of course quality is presumably your goal, so according to this business mandate, you must pick one of the two remaining elements—fast or cheap, but not both. Cost and time are very often at odds with one another (see Figure 7.19). If you purchase character models you will save time but lose money. If you

Figure 7.19
Money and time expenditures are often inversely proportional.

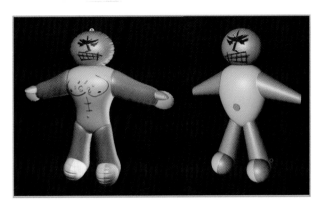

Figure 7.20
Simplify whenever possible!

use less powerful tools, you will save money but lose time. In general, a fast production cycle will be more expensive, while an inexpensive production cycle will take more time.

So following this business principle and assuming that quality is a given, your production cycle will either be fast, *expensive*, and good or *slow*, cheap, and good. However, despite what the MBAs will tell you, when it comes to creating a CG short, it *is* indeed possible to have all three elements. The trick to accomplishing this feat is to keep your cinematic vision relatively simple and search for ways to reduce your budget without damaging your schedule and vice versa (see Figure 7.20).

Decreasing the complexity of your film will save you both money and time. Searching for secondhand tools, slightly-less-than-state-of-the-art hardware, next-to-latest versions of software packages, and rent-instead-of-purchase opportunities will save you money without compromising much in the way of productivity. Also, finding volunteers rather than paid employees will benefit your schedule without adversely affecting your wallet.

If you strive for elegant simplicity and plan your production carefully and efficiently, you can prove the business world wrong and create an inexpensive, high-quality product in a relatively short period of time. Just be realistic about how you define "relatively short."

Staffing

To accurately create a schedule for your production cycle, you'll need to have an idea of your staffing plans. The first and most obvious question is whether to work alone or with a team. Both scenarios have their advantages and disadvantages (see Figure 7.21). In some cases you might not have a choice. Perhaps you're the only person in town who has

	Working Alone	Working With a Team
Pros	Singular vision. You don't need approval from anybody else for your decisions.	Potentially less work for you, therefore a shorter production cycle.
	It's all yours. You don't have to share the credit or the rewards.	Wider skill sets available to you, so greater potential for all tasks to be done well.
	Easier to schedule and organize your production.	Opportunities for other "eyes" on the work, for wider varieties of input and better objectivity.
	You can set your own hours.	If you or a member of your team is sick or absent, others can possibly fill in so that production does not have to stop completely.
		Opportunity to learn from others.
		Opportunity to practice supervisory skills.
Cons	Only one contributor, so your film will potentially take longer to produce.	Scheduling, organizing, and task management will be more complex.
	All technical and creative problems are yours to solve.	Potential for too many cooks stirring the pot and inability to reach a consensus on certain decisions.
	You take all the blame and responsibility for any missed deadlines, negative reviews, or neglected copyright issues, etc.	You must put your trust in others and learn to delegate specific tasks that you might prefer to do yourself.
	You might not be skilled in all disciplines, but you'll have to handle them anyway. Your weaknesses will show, unless you can successfully hide them.	You might end up spending too much time supervising, babysitting, and organizing, rather than actually working.
	Hard to maintain objectivity.	Your credit and rewards will have to be shared.
	If you get sick or too busy to work on your short, production will come to a dead stop.	

Figure 7.21
Advantages and disadvantages of working alone versus working with a team

sufficient skill or desire to create a short film. On the other hand, you might be creating your film as part of a school assignment where your instructor is requiring you to work with teammates. You might be lacking in certain skill sets and will therefore need to bring in a few specialists to help out in those areas. Or your deadline might be too tight for you to reach on your own, thus requiring you to collaborate. Analyze the size and complexity of your production versus your available time, money, and skills, and then try to build an appropriately-sized team based on your needs.

If you will be working on a team, the next obvious question is, what size? In general, the more teammates you have, the more work that can be accomplished simultaneously, and therefore, the shorter your production cycle. However, keep in mind that this is not always the case. If your team is too large, you might spend too much time organizing, delegating, and perhaps supervising, rather than actually producing content for your film. If appropriate and feasible, interview your potential teammates and perhaps even check references so you can be confident of everyone's skills and work ethics before entering production. Also consider that crewmembers can call in sick, take vacations, or abandon your project for a full-time job opportunity in the middle of your production. Be sure to speak with your teammates in advance about the possibility of such interruptions, and then schedule accordingly and try to line up potential replacement artists just in case. Try to build a team that is large enough to benefit your schedule but small enough to manage effectively.

Another consideration when working in teams is the actual contributions that each crewmember will provide to your production. If everyone is a generalist with equal skills in storyboarding, modeling, rigging, animation, lighting, rendering, and compositing, scheduling your production will be a bit easier because each team member will be able to produce complete shots in tandem. However, having a full team of equally skilled generalists is rarely the case. In most scenarios you will have different artists with different skill sets. Such a scenario might be a bit more difficult to schedule efficiently because certain tasks and their corresponding contributors will often have to be "on hold" while they wait for their turn on a specific shot.

A few tips when working with teams:

◆ Assign a single person to be your asset manager. This individual will be responsible for organizing and managing your digital assets as well as making regular backups. More than one individual contributing in this capacity is generally not recommended because overlap, confusion, redundancies, and inadvertently overwritten data can result.

◆ Conduct regular meetings where all team members can review the current cut in order to maintain consistency and motivation.

◆ If feasible, try to allow your teammates to learn and grow during your production by giving them challenging work, rather than simply giving all the hard stuff to your stars and keeping your juniors at that status for the duration of your production.

Scheduling Your Production

Now that you've determined the size of your intended team and made any necessary adjustments to the complexity of your cinematic vision to ensure that your production cycle will fit within the limits of your available timeframe and finances, it's time to organize the steps along your pathway toward film completion by creating a schedule for each of the three phases of your project cycle—pre-production, shot production, and post-production.

There are many ways to schedule a short animated film production, depending on the complexity of your film, the steps included in your overall digital pipeline, the size of your team, and your available hours and assets. Before you begin, you need to answer a couple of important questions about your overall production plan.

- Will you be working alone or with teammates?
- Where will music fit into your pipeline?

If you work alone, your schedule will be rather linear. Although you might bounce back and forth between different tasks, you will basically be doing one thing at a time. If you work with a team, obviously you can accomplish certain tasks simultaneously.

If music will dictate the action of your story beats, you will need to schedule creation and recording time into your pre-production phase. If music will be used as a final enhancement to your storyline, then it can be composed or acquired much later and then scaled, offset, or edited to fit with your visuals.

Pre-Production Scheduling

Start by making a list of all assets that will be required for shot production. These include

- Vocal and/or music tracks
- A 2D animatic
- A 3D animatic
- Character models
- Texture maps
- Character setups
- Background models and props
- Background paintings or photos

← October 27	← November 3	← November 10	← November 17	← November 24	← December 1

October 27					November 3					November 10					November 17					November 24					December 1				
M	T	W	T	F	M	T	W	T	F	M	T	W	T	F	M	T	W	T	F	M	T	W	T	F	M	T	W	T	F

Figure 7.22
Create daily or weekly columns depending on the expected length of each task.

You should have determined the quantity, complexity, and build times of these elements when you created your time estimate. Here in the scheduling stage, you simply need to organize a sequential plan for creating each of these assets. The order you choose for the creation of these elements is not particularly important as long as you get them all ready for shot production at an appropriate level of completion.

Lone Filmmaker Pre-Production Scheduling

If you are working alone, then obviously you will be creating all of these assets yourself. This might not necessarily be the most efficient way to accomplish such a task, but it will indeed make for the simplest schedule.

Start by building a task table, where each column represents either a day or a week depending on how long you expect the creation of each asset to take. If most of your assets will take at least a week to build, then use one column per week, titling these columns with the start date of each workweek. If you expect to work much faster, then break up each week's column into sub-columns representing the number of days in a typical workweek (see Figure 7.22).

Then simply fill in the necessary time blocks for each task you will accomplish. Figure 7.23 might represent a typical pre-production schedule for a lone CG artist creating assets for a film with two characters and a bit of dialogue.

← Oct 20	← Oct 27	← Nov 3	← Nov 10	← Nov 17	← Nov 24	← Dec 1	← Dec 8
Dialogue	2D Animatic		Char Model 1	Char Model 2	Texture Maps	Char Setup	Prop Models

Figure 7.23
Pre-production task table for one filmmaker creating two characters and a small amount of dialogue

Pre-Production Schedules for Teams

Building a task list becomes a bit more complicated when additional teammates are included in the mix. Each team member will have his or her own row and corresponding task blocks. Determining who does what and when will depend on the specific contributions that each teammate will make. Regardless of the size of your team, if you are the sole director or the project lead, it will probably make sense for you to assemble your animatic alone and perhaps elicit occasional feedback from your crew. If more than one person will hold the title of director, then this task should be collaborative. If each team member is a generalist who can model, texture, and rig characters, it might make sense to give each artist his or her own character to build concurrently. If you have a team of specialists, however, you might prefer to structure your pre-production more like an assembly line, where the individual tasks follow a sequential order and are placed on the appropriate artists' rows. Figures 7.24 and 7.25 represent a couple of example scenarios.

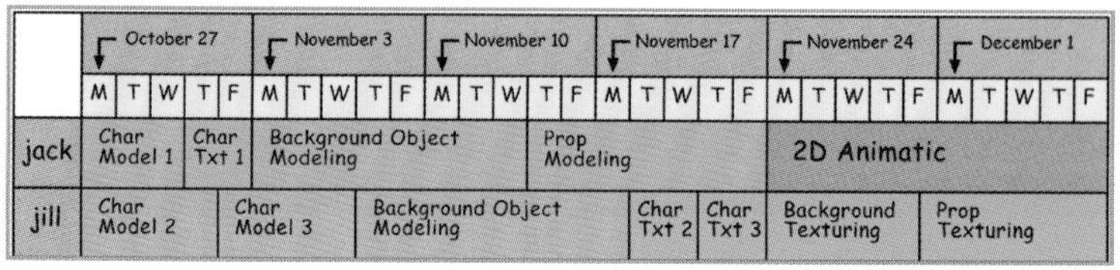

Figure 7.24
No dialogue, music to be added in post, three characters, a fair amount of background elements and props, a two-person team, both generalists, and one director

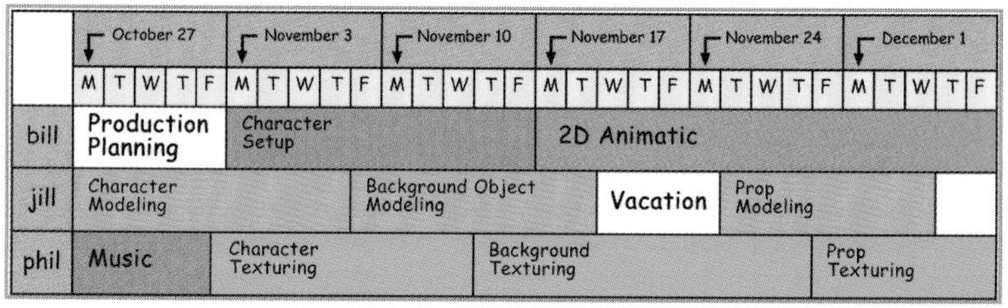

Figure 7.25
No dialogue, but music will dictate the action; two characters; a three-person team, one director who is also the character rigger, one modeler, and one musician who also paints textures

Shot Production Scheduling

A final shot will be a video clip or a series of image frames rendered from virtual stages containing background objects, props, character puppets, texture maps, lights, animations, and particle effects. All of these elements need to be created or acquired and then assembled, rendered, and possibly composited during your shot production stage. To sufficiently organize, schedule, and track the production of your shots, it is a good idea to create two charts.

- A global shot schedule
- A shot progress chart

> When you are scheduling time blocks for modeling and rigging, consider whether you will need detailed and functional character puppets just yet or whether you would prefer to use rough stand-in models for your 3D animatic and layout phases, and then refine and rig them just before your blocking and animation stages begin.

A *global shot schedule* will represent your overall plan of attack, while the *shot progress chart* will be used to track the completion level of each individual shot from blocking through final imagery. With these two charts working hand in hand, you will be simultaneously monitoring your entire forest as well as your individual trees (see Figure 7.26).

Global Shot Schedule

Start with a chart similar to the one you constructed for your pre-production schedule, with week (or day) columns and a row for each shot-producing team member. The number of columns in your chart will be determined by your initial time estimate. In our running example, we had estimated 100 man-days for shot production. If our hypothetical filmmaker will be working alone at five days per week, we would need 20 (week) columns. If our filmmaker brings in a partner, then we would need 10 (week) columns. Four team members? Five columns. You get the idea.

As you fill in your schedule with shot-production tasks, you might find that you need additional columns, so make sure you leave a bit of extra room on your paper just in case.

Once you have this chart laid out, insert the necessary time blocks for each shot, factoring in the amount of time each one will take to produce based on your initial time estimates. In some productions, each shot will be completed from start to finish in a single uninterrupted block of time. In other productions, different stages of each shot will be handled in different time periods and perhaps by different teammates. For instance, you might block a particular shot but then move on to blocking a few others before you return to the first for final animation, lighting, and rendering. One team member might block and animate certain shots, while others will handle the lighting, rendering, compositing, and other finishing touches. The way you organize your shot production schedule will depend on how many teammates you have, as well as their availability, skill sets, and working speed (see Figures 7.27 through 7.29).

Global Shot Schedule

	October 27	November 3	November 10	November 17	November 24	December 1
	M T W T F	M T W T F	M T W T F	M T W T F	M T W T F	M T W T F
bill						
jill						
phil						

Shot Progress Chart

Shot	Frame Count	Notes	Block-ing	Anim	Light-ing	Render-ing	FX	Compos-iting
1								
2								
3								
4								
5								
6								
7								
8								

Figure 7.26
To organize and track your shot production, you will need a global schedule as well as a shot progress chart.

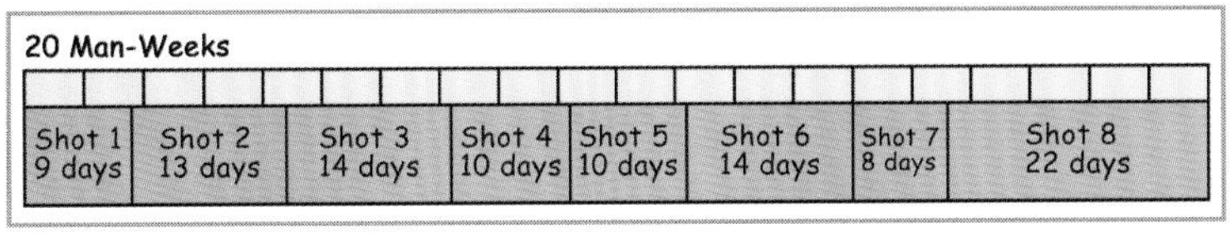

Figure 7.27
Possible global shot schedule for a lone filmmaker attacking each shot from start to finish sequentially

> When you insert task blocks into your schedule,
> don't forget to factor in vacations and holidays.

As you fill in these time blocks, try to be efficient with your scheduling so that none of your teammates are sitting idle, waiting for their turn on a particular shot (see Figure 7.30). This is not always a simple task, so be patient and spend the necessary time to assemble your schedule in the most efficient manner possible.

Keep in mind that your actual production will very likely stray a bit from what you've laid out on your shot-production schedule. Certain shots will take longer than you thought; others will go more quickly. Some shots will have to be revisited at a later date. Team members might be unexpectedly absent. Shots might need to be reassigned in mid-production. Because variables such as these exist, it is important for you to create your shot-production chart in a format that is easy to edit and update. A dry-erase board is a very popular medium on which to create this chart. Just make sure that it is kept in a safe place where your kids or your cat are unable to inadvertently erase your entries. A large piece of paper can also work just fine when you draw your row and column lines with an indelible marker and you fill in your time blocks in pencil so you can erase and redraw them as necessary. Using appropriate computer software has obvious advantages in this capacity because of the ease in which data can be inserted, duplicated, erased, and edited. Also, it is very easy to add columns and rows to digital charts.

As your shot-production cycle continues, you will need to mark your time blocks somehow to indicate the completion level of each shot. There are a number of ways you can accomplish this. You might want to use different colors to indicate different stages of each shot. You might use no color for a shot that has not yet begun, yellow for a shot that has been animated, green for a shot that has been lit and rendered, and blue for a shot that has been completed or finalled. Some producers like to use removable stickers on a dry-erase board,

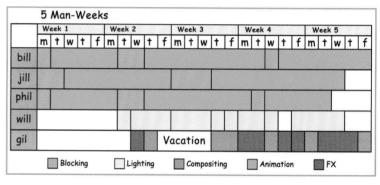

Figure 7.28
Possible global shot schedule for a team of three filmmakers, each one a generalist who can take a single shot from blocking through compositing

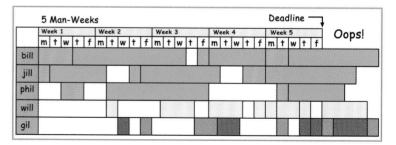

Figure 7.29
Possible global shot schedule for a team of five specialists

Figure 7.30
A poorly planned production schedule will have task holes and will unnecessarily extend your deadline.

with different shapes, colors, or markings indicating the completion level of each shot (see Figure 7.31). Any of these methods will work as long as the one you choose allows you to glance at your schedule and quickly understand the status of each shot, as well as step back so you can see the overall progress of your entire production.

Shot Progress Chart

In addition to your global shot schedule that will indicate the start and end dates of each stage of each shot, you will also need an individual shot progress chart that will represent the completion level of each shot. You will fill in the cells in this chart as each shot develops from blocking through final tweaks (If your production pipeline is rather simple and the color coding on your global shot schedule is sufficiently descriptive, you may be able to do without a separate shot progress chart).

Build a chart like the one you constructed for your shot production time estimate, with columns representing each shot stage and a row for each shot (see Figures 7.33 through 7.36).

As your shot production cycle progresses, simply fill in each appropriate cell with an X or a checkmark as each shot stage is completed. When all of the cells on this chart have been filled in, your shot production is basically complete (see Figure 7.32).

Shot Ordering

There are three basic ways in which you might order the process of completing each shot in your production. Borrowing a bit from terms normally associated with the animation process (see Chapter 16), we have listed these three scheduling options as follows.

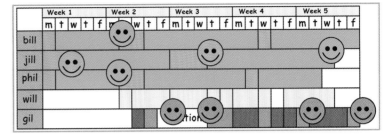

Figure 7.31
Indicate your progress by color-coding your task blocks or using stickers to indicate completion levels.

While it is always preferable to label every shot as "FINALLED" before you move on, sometimes for the sake of momentum, deadline demands, or burnout avoidance you might need to temporarily abandon a particular shot before it is satisfactorily completed, with the idea that you will return to it at a later date if time permits. Such shots are generally given the label "CBB," which stands for "Could Be Better." A CBB label on your progress chart might indeed stick out like a sore thumb, but allowing yourself one or two might mean the difference between finishing your film and allowing a single particularly frustrating shot to put you so far behind schedule that you might never recover.

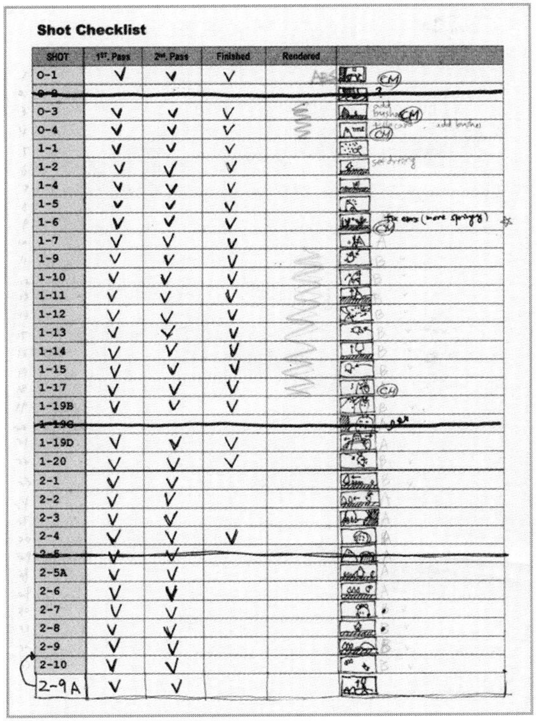

Figure 7.32
Shot progress chart in mid-production for Moonsung Lee's *Bert*, indicating the completion level of each shot.

- Straight ahead
- Hero shots
- Layering

Working through your shots in a *straight ahead* fashion means completing them sequentially. Shot 1 is taken from blocking through final tweaks before you move on to a full completion cycle on shot 2. Then shot 3, then shot 4, and so on (see Figure 7.33).

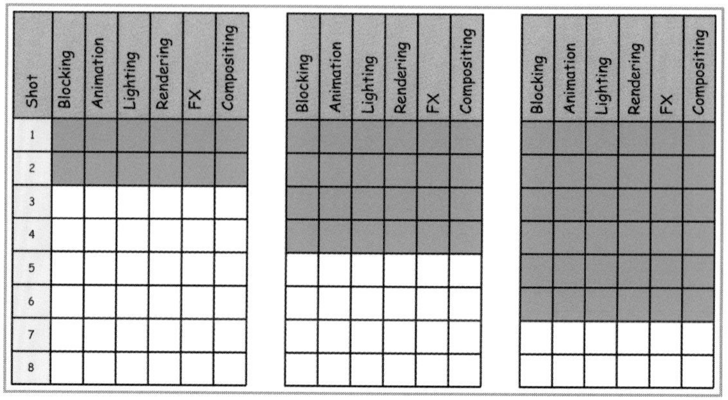

The *hero shot* method involves selecting certain crucial shots and completing each one before you fill in the blanks between them. (This can be compared to the pose-to-pose method of animating; see Chapter 16.) If your film has eight shots, perhaps you've selected shots 1, 5, and 8 as your hero shots. These will be completed first, and then the remaining shots will be completed in whatever order seems appropriate (see Figure 7.34). The main advantage of the hero shot method is that long before you complete your production, you will have a few finished shots that can serve as examples of your quality and style goal for your future shots. As production continues, you can point to a completed and particularly successful hero shot and say, "Our next shot will be finished when it looks like this one." Another advantage to this method is that you might be able to use your first few completed hero shots to assemble an early teaser trailer, which you can post on your personal Web site or on any number of Internet forums and online film festivals to generate early buzz for your CG short.

Layering means completing all of your shots in overall stages. First you will block all of your shots; then you will go back and finalize the animation on all shots; then the lighting, rendering, compositing, and so on. This way your entire film evolves as a whole, rather than as individually completed parts (see Figure 7.35).

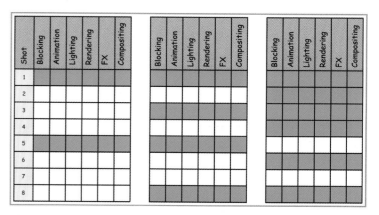

Figure 7.33
Project completion levels at 25 percent, 50 percent, and 75 percent using the straight ahead method

Figure 7.34
Project completion levels at 25 percent, 50 percent, and 75 percent using the hero shot method

The particular shot ordering method you choose will of course affect the organization of your overall production chart. If you choose to work in a straight ahead or hero shot fashion, each of your time blocks will represent an entire production cycle for an individual shot. If you work in a layering capacity, you will need to insert separate time blocks for individual shot stages (see Figure 7.36).

Post-Production Scheduling

In the pre-production and shot-production phases, all of the elements of your film are created, assembled, animated, and lit. Rendered image sequences are then created and possibly composited into nearly final collages, which are used in place of your held storyboards or your 3D animatic renders in your story reel, with appropriately synched sound effects and music.

Once you reach that point of your production cycle, your film is all there. There are no new assets or shots to be created. However, you must still add finishing touches before you can truly call your film complete. These final details might include sound effects and music, film grain filters, post-camera moves, color correction, wipes and fades, titles, and credits. And just like the pre- and shot-production phases, this post-production stage should also be scheduled.

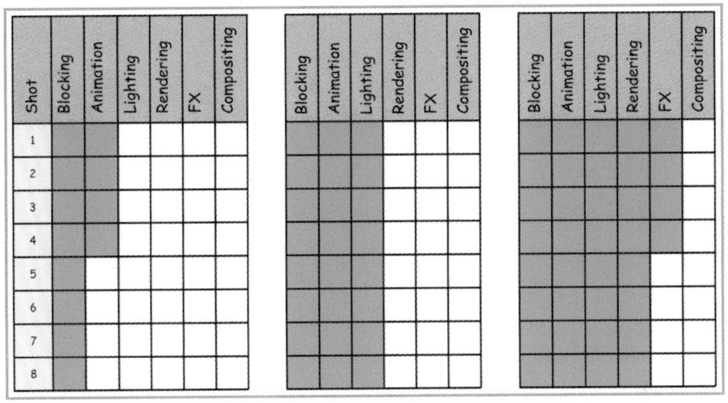

Add necessary columns and task bars to your overall shot-production schedule and your shot progression chart to represent shot-specific post-production tasks, such as post-camera moves and color correction (see Figure 7.37). Then create a final chart like your shot-production chart, with dates across the top row, and insert time blocks to represent the time it will take to complete each global post-production task, such as titles and credits.

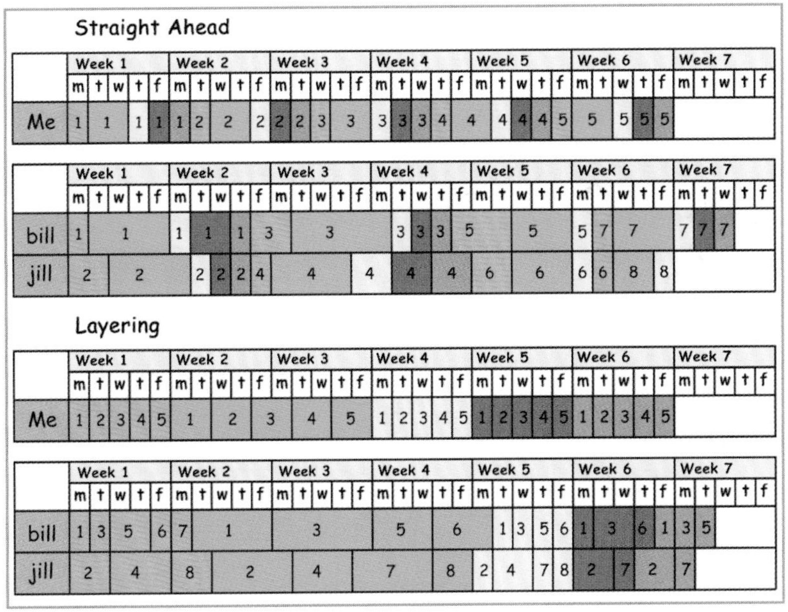

Milestones

Another important scheduling element is the notion of *milestones*. A milestone is an intermediate deadline that helps you gauge progress. As you lay out your schedules for the three production phases, mark a few points to be regarded as milestones and indicate target dates so you can see how efficiently you're heading toward your finish line. One such milestone might be the completion of your storyboards. Another might be the point at which you finalize the animation on 50 percent of your shots. It is much better to potentially discover that you're falling behind while you're still in the midst of production than to

Figure 7.35
Project completion levels at 25 percent, 50 percent, and 75 percent using the layering method

Figure 7.36
The structure of your overall shot-production chart will differ depending on which method you choose to attack each individual shot task.

make such a realization only after you've failed to meet your final deadline. You might be able to apply corrective measures during the course of your production, but once you've finished, it will be too late.

What If Your Official Schedule Doesn't Fit with Your Deadline?

Despite the fact that you made every attempt to accurately determine the timeframe feasibility of your production when you created your initial estimates, you might be unpleasantly surprised to find that your official production schedules tell a different story. If this is the case, do not simply ignore your findings and forge ahead, blindly hoping that things will somehow work out anyway. Take the time now to apply the previously described suggestions for how to adjust your production specifics to make the length of your project cycle conform to your available timeframe. A few extra hours here in the planning stage can save you many headaches down the road and will help eradicate the possibility of having to lower your quality standards—or worse yet, abandon your project before you reach your finish line.

									Shot-Specific Post-Production Tasks			
Shot	Frame Count	Notes	Block -ing	Anim	Light -ing	Render -ing	FX	Compos -iting	Wipes & Fades	Post Cam Move	Color Correct
1											
2											
3											
4											

Figure 7.37
You can add shot-specific post-production tasks to your shot progression chart.

Asset Organization

Another important aspect of production planning is the management and organization of your digital assets. Being able to easily access, share, and sufficiently safeguard your files is essential to a smooth and successful production cycle.

Directory Structures

Try to organize your directories as logically as possible so it is easy to locate your files. A pyramid structure typically makes sense, where you have a top-level directory for your entire short and then more specific levels as you work your way down into subdirectories where different types of files are stored, including CG scenes, audio recordings, reference images, background plates, texture paintings, test renders, and final imagery (see Figure 7.38).

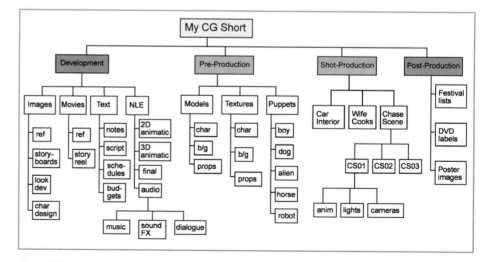

Figure 7.38
Pyramid directory structures generally make the most sense.

A disorganized directory structure is like a disorganized office. The result is a lot of wasted time spent searching for and putting away your tools and materials. A disorganized directory structure also increases the possibility of file redundancy, overwriting, and lost work. Figure 7.39 represents a rather inefficient directory structure, while Figure 7.40 shows two examples that are much more organized.

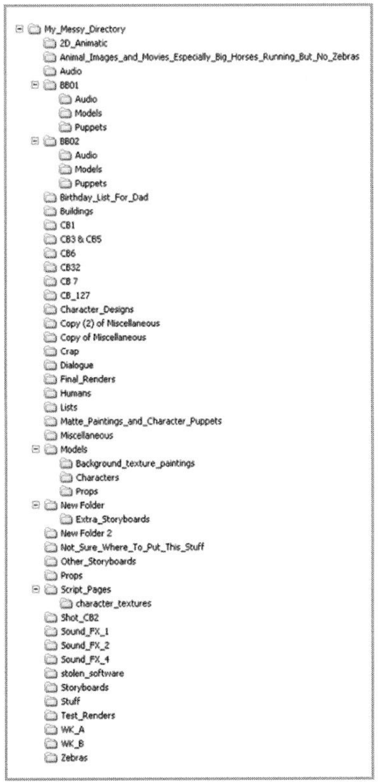

Naming Conventions

Assigning logical names for your data files and your CG scene elements is another important aspect of asset organization.

Figure 7.39
A disorganized directory structure like this one results in a lot of wasted time searching for files and creates the risk of asset redundancy.

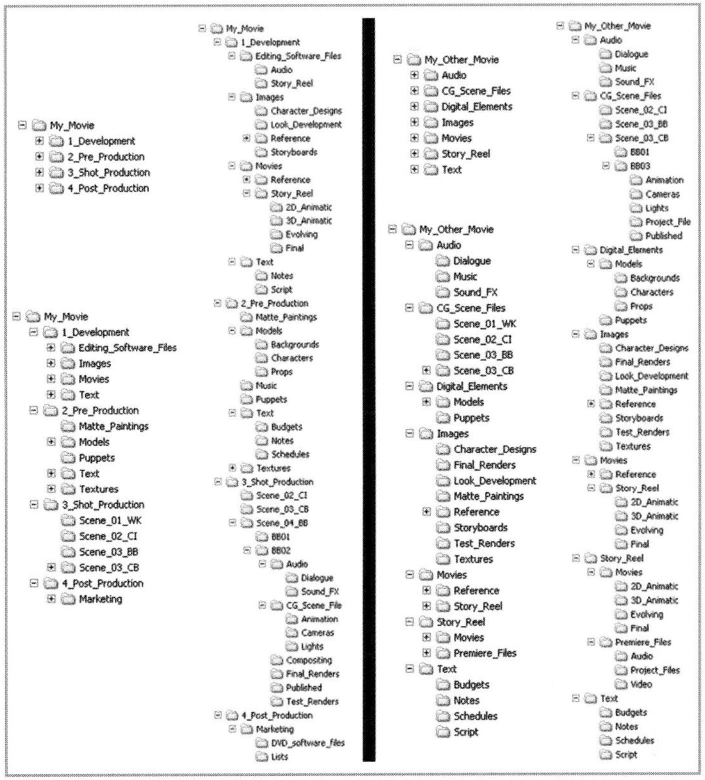

Figure 7.40
A well-organized directory structure like one of these will make it easy and efficient for you to store and locate your files.

Data Files

File names should contain separate fields indicating pieces of information that help to identify the contents of the file at a mere glance, such as file type, shot name, creator, and version number. Individual field names should be long enough to be descriptive, but short enough so that your file names remain manageable and easy to type. Two or three letters for each field is typically sufficient.

◆ **Too long:** scene01_animation_blocking_Alexander_version12.mb

◆ **Too short:** s01_a_b_a_12.mb

◆ **Just right:** sc01_anim_bl_al_v12.mb

The number of individual fields in a given file name will vary depending on the type of file, the size of your team, and how you have chosen to break up your story into individual scenes and/or shots. For instance, the file name for a reference image of a horse skeleton could be rather simple, containing only fields for file type and content description, such as ref_horseSkel.jpg.

If you have several images of horse skeletons, you could differentiate them by making the content name more descriptive or by including an additional number field, such as ref_horseSkelRearLeg.jpg or ref_horseSkel_2.jpg.

You may or may not find it necessary to include a field that identifies the file as an image or a movie clip. Such information can generally be found in the file name extension; however, if you have your folder options set to hide extensions, then an extra field might be in order, such as ref_horseWalk_mov.

The file name for a CG model or a character rig should have fields for the character or object name, the type of file, necessary information about the file, and the version number, such as elmer_model_lorez_v1.mb or unicorn_rig_noFacial_v3.mb.

If your film is extremely short, it might exist in its entirety as a single CG scene file; otherwise, you will very likely break up your production into separate shots. If your film is rather long, you might further organize your production by grouping your shots into separate scenes or sequences. Sequences are typically identified by descriptive abbreviations, while shots are generally given numbers. A CG project file from your 3D animation package could be called CS05_anim_v12, where "CS" might stand for "Chase Scene" or "Charlie Sings."

Scene CS05 at the compositing stage might be identified as CS05_comp_v3.af.

If you have more than one animator generating shots, an associated field should also be included, such as CS05_anim_al_v7, CS05_anim_ana_v12, or CS05_comp_ben_v3.

A shot that has been finalled might be called CS05_anim_final_al_v27.

CG Scene Elements

When you are working in your 3D software packages, you will typically have a scene file containing several different types of digital elements, including character rigs, object models, deformers, particle emitters, lights, and cameras. Logical and descriptive names for these items will be very important for quick identification as well as scriptwriting, if the need arises (see Figure 7.41).

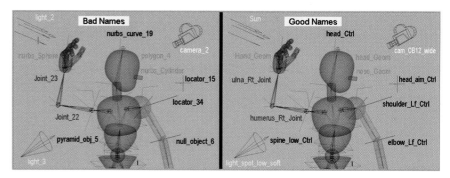

Figure 7.41
Give the elements of your virtual CG scene stages logical names so they are easy to identify.

If your virtual stage contains a lot of furniture, include a sufficient number of naming fields to differentiate one object from the next, such as chair_dining_01, chair_tvRoom_brown, and chair_tvRoom_red.

Names for cameras and lights should contain information about their type, such as cam_persp_main, cam_top, cam_face_lock, light_spot_1, and light_ambient_blue.

Character rigs will potentially have deep hierarchies containing geometry, skeletons, and animation control objects. The top node can simply be the name of the character or a descriptive word, such as jimmy, blueUnicorn, or alien_infantry_small.

Objects within character hierarchies should have very descriptive names, such as dragon_torso_geom_hi, dragon_neck_joint_3, or dragon_foot_IK_ctrl_left.

See Chapter 14 for more detailed information on naming conventions for character rigs.

Versioning and Publishing

While you are working on the digital files of your short film, it is crucial that you save often. Few situations are more frustrating than when your computer locks up or crashes and you realize that you haven't saved your work in several hours. Some software packages have an auto-save feature, where a temporary version of an active file is saved at regular intervals. However, if you prefer to save your files manually, doing so every 10 minutes or so is not a bad idea. Also, every time you make a significant change or update to a digital file, it is highly recommended that you "version up" at your next save. If you're tweaking the animation on cs05_anim_ken_v09, and after a lot of pain and effort you finally manage to get that tail motion exactly the way you want it, immediately save the file as cs05_anim_ken_v10. Multiple versions of a single file will certainly use up a lot of hard drive space, but additional storage is typically less expensive than lost work. Keep perhaps the last three to five versions of any given file readily available in case you decide that your latest tweak made things worse and you want to go back to a previous version. Older versions should be zipped and perhaps backed up to save hard drive space, but they should still be accessible just in case. Do not permanently delete any files until your project is complete—and even then you'll probably want to keep most of them accessible for sequels, job applications, magazine articles, or future experiments.

It is always a good idea to have an official "published" directory for your finished files. This will be the directory where you and your teammates place files that have been finalled and are ready to be carried over into the next stage of your digital pipeline. Each team member should have his or her own working directories with associated permissions so others cannot inadvertently overwrite their active files. Keep all previous versions of a given file in the appropriate working directory, and keep the latest and greatest in the published directory, where it can be accessed (but not overwritten) by the rest of your team.

Safeguards and Backup Plans

As you are working on your film, treat your digital files as precious commodities. Take every possible precaution to safeguard them from harm. If you are working on a team, try to make sure that your files have permission protection so they can only be overwritten by their owners. Also, protect your files by safeguarding the equipment that houses them. Purchase surge protectors, keep your warranty paperwork handy, and make sure you have sufficient technical support available for your computer and your peripherals.

In addition to safeguarding your files, it is imperative that you back them up on a regular basis (see Figure 7.42). And just in case you weren't paying attention, we'll say it again: *It is imperative that you back up your files on a regular basis*!!

If something goes horribly wrong with your computer, your schedule might indeed be set back a few days while the repairman does his job. But if you failed to back up your files regularly, and all of your digital scenes, audio tracks, reference photos, and rendered images were sitting on your computer's single hard drive with the broken vacuum seal, you'll lose an awful lot more than a few days.

Save your files often and back them up in a variety of locations. You should make daily backups of your most recent files or updates to devices such as secondary or external hard drives, CD-ROMs or DVD-ROMs, Zip drives, or USB flash drives. You should also place weekly backups on removable media, such as CDs, DVDs, or Zip disks, and then store them away from your computer, preferably at a different location altogether. If you are making your film at home, store your weekly backups at the office, in your school locker, at your Mom's house, or if you really want to feel secure, in a safety deposit box. Also take advantage of the Internet for additional backup storage solutions. Sites such as http://www.xdrive.com offer online hard drives where you can upload, download, and share files. Consider a Web site where you can store your backups, and perhaps attach important files to e-mails and then send them to a friend or to your school or office computer.

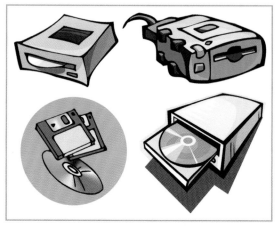

Figure 7.42
Back up your files regularly!

Some filmmakers might feel that daily backups are overkill and that once a month is sufficient; others will make quick backups every hour. Schedule your backups at whatever intervals will make you feel comfortable and secure. The most important time to make a backup is whenever you've made significant progress on a particular scene or image, where the work you've accomplished was especially difficult and you'd really be in trouble if you had to do it over again.

Murphy's Law

Murphy's Law suggests that everything that *can* go wrong *will* go wrong. We prefer to be a bit less pessimistic and merely state that everything that *can* go wrong *might* go wrong. Computers break and people make mistakes. Hard drives crash occasionally, and files sometimes get deleted and overwritten. Equipment can get stolen. Your dog might eat your storyboards. Your son could spill milk inside your PC. However, such problems will not be showstoppers if you protect your digital assets by locking your office door, photocopying and scanning your paperwork, setting file permissions, and scheduling regular backup sessions.

In addition to applying such safeguards to protect your digital assets, you must also protect your budget and schedule by taking precautions against other kinds of problems that might arise during your production cycle. For instance, consider the following scenarios and solutions.

- **You discover that your initial time and financial estimates were way off.** Make sure you pad your estimates and your schedules by 20 to 30 percent. It is much better to guess high and come in under budget or ahead of schedule than to find yourself in the opposite situation.

- **The Internet is down and you can't communicate with your offsite partners.** Set up secondary methods of file sharing, such as regular meetings or snail mail.

- **It's Saturday morning, you have a fixed milestone on Monday, your computer won't boot up, and tech support is not open on weekends.** Call your more technically savvy friends or co-workers to see whether they can help. If your recent files are backed up on removable media, bring them to another computer—perhaps the one at your office or your brother's house. If necessary, rent a machine for the weekend. Then, when tech support opens on Monday morning, find out whether they offer weekend support for an additional fee and consider making the investment.

- **Your fastest animator gets a "real" job in the middle of your production and needs to quit. He takes his computer with him.** Plan for this possibility by padding your schedule and having a few replacement artists in mind or on deck. Make sure that your exiting animator doesn't take any necessary files with him before you've had a chance to make copies.

- **No matter how hard he tries, one of your animators just cannot seem to get a particular shot to look right, and he rejects any attempts you make to help him or reassign the shot to someone else.** Be patient and remind him that you're all in this together and that there's no shame in seeking help. Burning out by stressing over a single shot can adversely affect your entire production. Before it completely destroys his motivation and your schedule, convince him to leave this one as a CBB and promise to let him try to fix it another time.

- **The FBI catches you using pirated software.** One word: Don't!

Many things can and probably will go wrong during the creation of your film. Realize this going in and take every possible precaution to ensure a smooth and successful production cycle.

Backup and Restore Yourself Too

Safeguard yourself and your teammates from harm as well. Safe and secure digital assets won't mean much if you burn yourself out or develop carpal tunnel syndrome halfway through your production. Take regular breaks (see Figure 7.43). Try to eat right, exercise, and get a good night's sleep as often as possible. Investigate the proper ways to set up your equipment and furniture to avoid muscle strain and nerve damage. If possible, invest in ergonomic chairs, forearm rests, or wrist braces. Some digital artists find it helpful to push the monitor and keyboard toward the back of their desk, allowing them to rest their elbows on the front of the desk, thus reducing wrist strain that can result from a posture where their elbows float in space.

Your film might indeed end up being a major milestone of your career, and you should of course give it the attention and effort required to turn your story idea into cinematic excellence.

Figure 7.43
Taking regular breaks to safeguard your health and motivation is equally as important as safeguarding your digital assets.

Just make sure that achieving this goal does not result in any permanent damage to your health, your lifestyle, or your love of filmmaking. Keep things in perspective and live to animate another day.

Study Others

Look at books and Web sites of shorts that are similar to yours in length and complexity. If the information is available, investigate how these films were organized, scheduled, and budgeted. Explore the Web sites listed in Appendix A for some good examples. Also, send e-mails to some of your favorite filmmakers if you want information on their software choices, team structures, efficiency tricks, production durations, and solutions to any problems they might have encountered along the way. As we've discovered during the creation of this book, most filmmakers are very happy to answer questions about their productions, especially when you preface your questions with a few compliments. Learn from the successes as well as the mistakes of others.

Share Your Progress with Others

During your production cycle, it is often helpful to share your progress with others for feedback and motivation. Ask a few select friends or colleagues to drop by your studio every once in a while to see whether they have any inspirational comments or meaningful suggestions.

You might also want to consider making a Web page that charts your progress. This is a good way to keep yourself organized and motivated, as well as an opportunity to build up anticipation in your future viewers. A Web page featuring information and imagery from your film can serve as a recruiting tool as well as a demo reel supplement. Some example Web sites that have generated a great deal of anticipation for their featured film productions by posting their progress regularly include:

- Brian Taylor's *Rustboy*: http://www.rustboy.com
- Josh Staub's *The Mantis Parable*: http://www.themantisparable.com

Summary

Unless you have unlimited money and a completely open-ended deadline, it is very important to create at least a basic production plan consisting of an overall pipeline, a budget analysis, a schedule, and an asset organization plan. The cost and time expenditures required to complete a CG short will vary considerably depending upon its complexity and length, your equipment choices, and the size and skills of your team. Consider that time and money are often somewhat inversely proportional. Saving on one generally requires spending more of the other. Strive for elegant simplicity, and create a logical and efficient schedule so you can complete a high-quality film within a reasonable budget and timeframe. And be sure to organize and protect your assets sufficiently. The next chapter will present our second case study, and Chapter 9 will cover the creation and recording of vocal tracks.

chapter 8
Case Study 2: Silhouette

Our second case study features the stylish and moody *Silhouette*, created by Amber Rudolph and Tonya Noerr as a collaborative senior thesis project at Ringling School of Art and Design. Tonya has agreed to tell the story of *Silhouette's* production cycle....

The Beginning

We started our process by searching for a piece of music that would help achieve our animation goals. After hearing Beethoven's Sixth Symphony in Allegro, we knew it was a perfect fit for our piece. The music was very emotional and powerful. We sat and listened to the music for several hours and brainstormed ideas and visuals that we associated with the music (see Figure 8.1). We both drew from our own thoughts and experiences, and from a great collaborative effort, we came up with our narrative.

Coming up with the idea of the narrative was the easy part. Figuring out the choreography of the ballet was a greater challenge. By using reference books and videos, having help from the Sarasota Ballet Company, and drawing from Amber's past ballet experiences, we were able to come up with the dance steps and timing necessary to make our piece.

VITAL STATISTICS

Title: *Silhouette*

Directors: Amber Rudolph and Tonya Noerr

Team Size: Two

Total Running Time: 2 minutes, 10 seconds

Production Cycle: About a year and a half

Date of Completion: March 2001

Software: Alias Maya, Right Hemisphere Deep Paint, Nothing Real Shake, Adobe Photoshop, Adobe Premiere, Sony Media Software ACID

Total Production Cost: Approximately three semesters tuition at Ringling School of Art and Design

Silhouette took about a year and a half to complete. A third of the time was spent in the story development and storyboarding process. We did about 20 different story reels during our process to iron out the ballet choreography (see Figure 8.2).

Figure 8.1
Design sketches inspired by the music

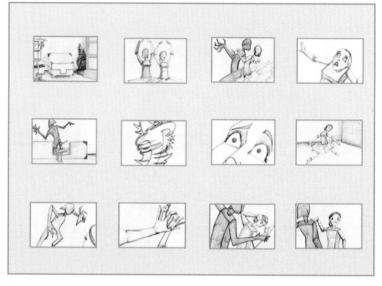

Figure 8.2
Storyboards

Story

Our thesis, which was told through the art of computer animation, tells the story of a toy ballerina. The story takes place at night. There is a music box on top of a dresser in a young woman's room. As the music box opens, the tune of Beethoven's Sixth Symphony in Allegro is heard. The ballerina comes to life and dances to the music. As the music intensifies, her shadow on the wall begins to take on its own personality (see Figure 8.3). The shadow continues to grow larger and more frightening until it finally pops out of the wall and takes on a three-dimensional form. The ballerina backs up in fear, but the shadow continues to go toward her in a similar style of movement. When the ballerina finally reaches the point of being trapped by her shadow, she realizes that the shadow is not really attacking her, but mimicking her movement. At this point of realization, she begins moving toward the shadow and overcoming her fear by taking control. As she takes control of the shadow, the shadow begins to shrink and eventually fades away, and her fear is conquered.

Evolution

After blocking in the motion, we found areas in our piece that needed to be strengthened. The two most critical parts that needed help were also the most important. The pivotal moment was not climatic. After much revision, Amber and I decided to have the shadow strangle the ballerina and bring her to a near-death experience emotionally and physically. The other part was the ending. We investigated several endings until we finally came up with the one that is in our final piece. Amber and I decided that we wanted the ballerina to defeat her fear and have the shadow go back to normal.

Figure 8.3
Is it real or just a figment?

Looking back now at the piece, several years later, I have to admit that we're still not happy with the pivotal moment and the ending. Amber and I both feel that during the process we got away from our original idea and concept. In some of our original storyboards the ballerina doesn't get strangled. Instead, she is cornered against the jewelry box and hiding her face in fear. As she peeks through her fingers she sees that the shadow is no longer aggressing toward her. At this point she figures out that he is not attacking her, but just mimicking her movement. As she starts to move, the shadow follows her. Then we come to our original ending. At this point, the music turns lighter and softer. For those of you familiar with Beethoven's Pastoral, you'd realize that we cut the music here in our final piece and used another section from the music. Originally, though, we wanted to keep the brighter music and refrain from chopping it up. The shadow and she would have then done a dance together, and as they danced the shadow would have slowly shrunk and ended up going back to his place on the floor. Now that I've spent some time away from the piece, I wish we would have stayed closer to our intended story. It's hard when you are doing these productions in college because you get so influenced by the faculty and your peers, and the piece becomes less of what you set out to do.

Figure 8.4
The protagonist and her seemingly harmless shadow

Characters

The ballerina is a toy who lives inside a music box. She has a little bit of stage fright, which causes her imagination to run wild. Her lack of self-confidence causes her to become weak and intimidated. When she finally realizes that she can overcome her fear, she gains confidence and becomes stronger. She's the star of the show and captures the viewer with her grace and beauty.

She is small in size, and she is wearing a warm-toned costume that is trimmed in red ribbon. Her tights and shoes are pink, and her tutu is white. Her hair is pulled back into a bun that is held by a barrette (see Figure 8.4).

Is it real or just a figment of the imagination (see Figure 8.5)? That is a question that the ballerina has to ask herself. The shadow takes on its own personality and form as the ballerina struggles with her inner fears. The shadow is confident, cocky, and determined, which are the same characteristics that the ballerina wants to have. When the ballerina finally gains her confidence, the shadow becomes subservient and eventually diminishes.

Figure 8.5
The villain!

The shadow character is two-dimensional at the beginning of the piece and then evolves into 3D. The 3D shadow is black and semi-transparent, and its final look is achieved in post-production. We rendered the shadow out separately from the ballerina and background and did a simple composite in Shake to create his final semi-transparent look.

Music

The music in our piece was very important because it set the timing for the animation. We choreographed the ballet and acting to go with Beethoven's Sixth Symphony in F Major in Allegro. The piece was very powerful so we knew it would be perfect. The only problem we had with the music was that it was too long for our animation. The only way that we could use the parts of the music that we needed was to cut it up and put it back together using ACID. I recomposed the sound the best that I could to fit our needs. After I had the music edited to our satisfaction, I added the rest of the sound effects to complete the piece.

We did our storyboards and started production with a version of Beethoven's Sixth from a different symphony, which caused problems. We were unable to get the rights to that particular version. When we finally found a version that we could have the rights to, we found that the music was different in a lot of places. This caused us to lose a lot of valuable time because we had to go back and revisit the storyboard stage for a bit. I would advise anyone who is doing a short film that depends on sound and/or music to make sure he or she secures the rights to it before moving ahead with the production. It causes fewer headaches further down the road.

Beethoven, often called the Son of Enlightenment, was known for his beauty of sound, balance, and symmetry of structure. His music was a reflection of his experiences and his own inner life. Beethoven's Sixth Symphony, the Pastoral, is a representation of a thunderstorm and a brook. The piece was meant to stir up emotion. The spirit of the music is remote from external conflict. It floats high in a mysterious realm of its own and it involves a series of unprecedented inventions in the domain of musical structure.

Teamwork

From working together previously and being friends, Amber and I decided to collaborate on our thesis. We knew we would be able to work well together and draw from each other's strengths. It was amazing how it all fell into place. We split up the animation into shots so that we both worked on each character. The day we sat down to assign shots, we were amazed at how smoothly it went. The scenes I was most interested in doing, Amber wasn't, and vice versa.

Working with a partner can also be challenging because it is like having two directors on one production. Things were challenging at the beginning because we were spending so much time together in a small space. Once we learned to balance our friendship time with our work time, things began to gel together. When you're working with your best friend, you must make time for coffee and shopping, or it puts a strain on your friendship if you only focus on work. Through the process of making this piece, we found that learning to communicate with one another and reaching compromises was just as important as learning the technical side of animation.

Modeling

Amber did a lot of character sketches in pre-production to arrive at our final characters. She modeled the ballerina from one of the character sketches that we both liked. Amber modeled the ballerina in Maya using NURBS, except for the hands, which were done in polygons (see Figure 8.6). Amber also modeled all of the ballerina and the body shapes for the shadow. The shadow was modeled in polygons. Amber often asked my opinion on what I thought about the models and the different blend shapes, which helped the characters meet both of our visions.

Figure 8.6
Character modeling

While Amber was working on the modeling, I focused on character setup. During pre-production we purposely designed the ballerina with ball joints. Because she is a toy, it worked well with her character design. This allowed us a lot of freedom when setting up our ballerina because we could get the poses we desired without experiencing deformation problems. We used a simple skeleton for her body and the tutu. I used a lattice and rigid-bound her to the skeleton. This allowed her body to flex in a lot of extreme poses without getting bad deformations. I also used the same technique on her feet for her ballet shoes because we needed several extreme poses with her ankle and foot when she danced. For the tutu, we bound the cloth geometry to several joints and animated the joints to create the secondary motion (see Figure 8.7).

The shadow's setup was fairly easy; we just smooth-bound him to his skeleton. Because he was a shadow, we were just concerned with his skeleton affecting the correct areas of his body. If we had a few normally undesirable deformations, it didn't matter in this case because they added to his character.

The story takes place on top of a young woman's dresser. Amber and I took personal objects from our own rooms and compiled them to help make our environment (see Figure 8.8). This added a level of personal touch to our piece because all the items were dear to us. Also, the little heart tag on the teddy bear has our initials in it.

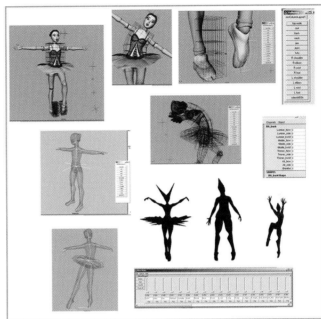

Figure 8.7
Character setup featuring lattice-controlled deformations

Figure 8.8
Various objects and props

8. Case Study 2: Silhouette

We wanted the music box to be special, so we did a lot of research to design the perfect one for our ballerina. Amber and I visited several antique stores and thrift shops. I used the pictures I gathered from the stores with some of the images I found in books to design our music box.

The jewelry box design was based on my own jewelry box that my grandma gave me. The butterfly, candles, teddy bear, perfume bottle, and incense burner were based on our own objects as well.

Amber and I also decided that we wanted to keep the environment in a cooler palette; that way, the ballerina's warm costume would make her stand out from her surroundings.

Texturing

Amber textured the ballerina and I did most of the environment. I started off texturing some of the objects the way they appeared in real life, and I quickly discovered that they wouldn't fit into our environment that way.

We used Deep Paint and Photoshop to do most of the texturing work. From scanning in cloth from a fabric store, to drawing my own designs for the textures, we were able to create the world in which the story took place.

Animation

One of the biggest challenges for us was to keep a consistency in the movement of both characters. Amber and I wanted it to look like one person animated the piece. In order to accomplish this, we had to work closely together to make sure our walks, jumps, and other characteristics matched.

The ballerina was a personal challenge for me. I didn't know much about ballet before this project, so I had to do a lot of research on ballet movement before starting this piece. Amber, on the other hand, has a dance background, which came in very handy (see Figure 8.9).

Lighting

Amber and I decided that we wanted the main light source, the key light, to come from a window on the opposite corner of the room. The window is never seen, but the light beam suggests it (see Figure 8.10). Fill and bounce lights were placed around the scene to light the areas that needed more

Figure 8.9
Character animation

Figure 8.10
Lighting that sets a definite mood

light. We also used the light linking method in Maya to achieve the overall look of the environment. A duplicate of the main key light was also used to create the 2D shadow by assigning the light to the shadow character and turning off its geometry.

When the ballerina defeats the shadow at the end of the piece, the lighting changes. I animated the intensities of all the lights in the scene to dim, and I turned on a spotlight to create a theatrical effect.

End Result

Because this was our senior thesis at Ringling School of Art and Design, we had to abide by the school's time constraints. Once the final submission day came, we were no longer allowed to work on the piece. A long year and a half of focusing on nothing else had just come to an abrupt end.

When we completed our piece, we had no idea what was going to happen next. Then the whirlwind hit as we started receiving phone calls. *Silhouette* was a finalist in the Student Academy Awards, and it was shown at SIGGRAPH, New York's Digital Salon, and the Florida Film Festival. The success of our piece helped us both get our first jobs out of college. I went to Industrial Light & Magic, where my first project was animating on *Star Wars Episode 2: Attack of the Clones*. Amber accepted a job at Big Idea Productions, where she worked on her first feature film, *Jonah*. Although we chose different paths after college, we still remain close friends. For me, the best part of this entire experience was the strong friendship that grew between Amber and I as a result of this journey we took together.

At the time of this writing, Tonya Noerr had recently completed her animation duties on *The Lord of the Rings: The Return of the King* in New Zealand. She is currently lending her skills to Sam Raimi's *Spiderman II* at Sony Imageworks in Los Angeles.

Amber Rudolph is currently in New York, animating on Blue Sky Studios' upcoming CG feature, *Robots*.

Silhouette can be seen in its entirety on the DVD that came with this book. More information about Ringling School of Art and Design can be found in Chapter 15, "An Interview with Jim McCampbell."

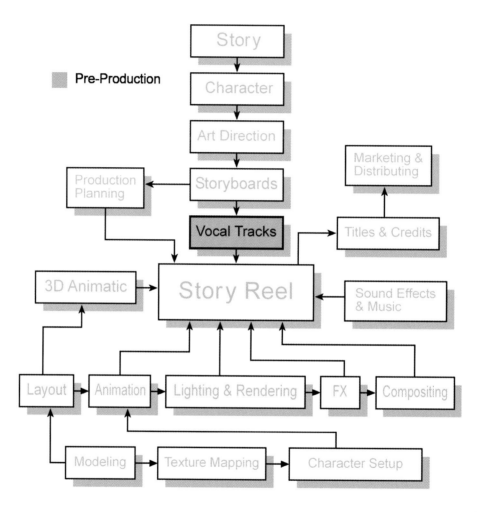

Pre-Production

Story

Character

Art Direction

Storyboards

Production Planning

Vocal Tracks

Marketing & Distributing

Titles & Credits

3D Animatic

Story Reel

Sound Effects & Music

Layout

Animation

Lighting & Rendering

FX

Compositing

Modeling

Texture Mapping

Character Setup

chapter 9
Vocal Tracks

Some of the most successful and memorable animated shorts of all time contain no words at all. Examples include *For the Birds, Bunny, Balance, Bert, f8, The Cathedral, Early Bloomer, Eternal Gaze, Gas Planet, Geri's Game, Knick Knack, Lunch, Passing Moments, Puppet, Technological Threat, Values, Sprout,* and *Tin Toy.*

Film is, after all, a primarily visual medium, so it is almost always preferable to *show* rather than to *tell.* And for the sake of budget limitations, time constraints, and more universal appeal, we highly recommend that, if possible, you consider the option of a mute film—one that has sound effects and/or music, but no actual spoken words.

On the other hand, vocal tracks will sometimes be absolutely crucial to a story's effectiveness and entertainment value. There are indeed a number of memorable animated shorts that actually depend on vocal tracks for their humor, style, poignancy, and mood. Such word-dependent films include *Creature Comforts, Alien Song, Harvie Krumpet, The Big Snit, Das Rad, The Great Cognito, Poor Bogo,* and *The Deadline* (see Figure 9.1).

There are three types of vocal tracks you might use in a film.

1. Narration
2. Monologues and soliloquies
3. Dialogue

Narration refers to explanatory spoken words coming from an off-camera, typically omniscient orator or from the inner thoughts of a particular character, usually the protagonist. Feature films that make great use of narration include *Apocalypse Now, Deep Cover, Raising Arizona,* and *Blade Runner* (although some fans prefer the non-narrated, director's cut version). CG shorts that utilize narration include

> "Talk is cheap," but "cheap is always more expensive."

Figure 9.1
Many shorts, such as *Early Bloomer,* work especially well without words; however, films such as *The Deadline* rely on vocal tracks for humor and effective storytelling.

Horses on Mars, *Jabberwocky*, *The Hare as Interpreter*, and the classic *Tony de Peltrie*. A *monologue* is a speech delivered by a single character, usually aimed at an internal or external audience, while a *soliloquy* is a monologue in which the speaker addresses himself. The CG short *Cane-Toad* contains a lengthy monologue, while many Shakespeare plays contain eloquent soliloquies (see Figure 9.2). *Dialogue*, of course, refers to words exchanged between two or more characters.

Figure 9.2
Perhaps because he has no mouth, the protagonist in *Horses on Mars* tells his tale through narration, while the storyteller in *Cane-Toad* delivers a lengthy monologue that doubles as narration when he is off screen.

Although we recommend creating a mute film if feasible, we also understand that there are a number of good reasons to use vocal tracks in your CG short (see Figure 9.3).

If you're unsure whether your film will require vocal tracks, flip through your storyboard panels or show them to a friend and see whether your story makes sense without words. You might discover that with careful staging and effective animation, you won't need vocal tracks at all. Or you might find that simply including a bit of narration will be more than sufficient to introduce, explain, or punctuate your entire story action.

	Using Vocal Tracks	Doing without Vocal Tracks
Pros	Helpful in delivering information on abstract concepts, back-story, and motivation, which are a bit harder to indicate through silent behavior and body language alone. An opportunity to practice and learn about audio recording and processing, which might come in handy someday on the job.	Reduced production complexity due to fewer steps and avoidance of the time-consuming and difficult task of lip-synching. Greater universal appeal. Language can sometimes be limiting and restrictive. Remember that actions generally speak louder than words. You won't need to waste your time reading the rest of this chapter!
Cons	Use of dialogue will increase the complexity of your production. You'll need to write good dialogue; find decent voice actors; stage a recording session, which requires time and extra equipment; get the audio into your computer; manipulate and improve it as necessary; link it up to your story reel; construct a method of modeling appropriate phoneme shapes for your characters; and suffer through the often difficult animation task of lip-synching. Dialogue creates less universal and international appeal. Words are less powerful than actions when expressing emotion. If you get the wrong voice actor, it can blow the whole cinematic experience for your viewers.	Abstract concepts, goals, motivations, complex emotions, and character histories are more difficult to express with body language and visuals alone. More pressure on your ability to model and animate effectively by using facial expressions and body language to deliver messages that might otherwise be told more easily with words.

Figure 9.3
To speak or not to speak, that is the question....

9. Vocal Tracks

Only Vocalize When It's Absolutely Necessary

Words must always have a purpose. They should only be used when they help move the story along or explain something that cannot be done sufficiently with visuals. Only use vocal tracks when they are absolutely necessary.

Most messages can be delivered at least as effectively, if not more so, using body language, action, or clear imagery alone. For example, it would be preferable to feature a scene with a setting sun instead of having a narrator say, "The day became night." Animate a character clutching his stomach with a pained look on his face instead of having him announce, "I don't feel so good" (see Figure 9.4). In the feature film *What's Eating Gilbert Grape*, there is a scene in which Gilbert watches from a distance while his retarded brother plays with a new friend. The look on Gilbert's face effectively reveals feelings of pleasure as well as a tinge of jealousy. It was not necessary for the filmmakers to introduce a subsequent scene in which Gilbert vocalizes his feelings to a friend; his facial expression was much more telling than mere words could ever be. Audience members generally appreciate such subtlety.

Figure 9.4
It is not necessary for this character to announce that he feels sick. His body language and facial expression deliver this message quite clearly.

Also, never use dialogue to *explain* a current situation unless there is necessary back-story information to be delivered, the action occurs off screen, or the recipient of the explanation cannot see the action occurring. Having a character describe a situation to himself or to the audience while that situation is occurring is either completely redundant or an indication that you did not stage the scene effectively. For instance, if you present a shot in which someone climbs into bed, there is no reason for the character to inform the audience of his action by saying, "I'm going to bed now." However, this line is perfectly appropriate if he is announcing his intentions to someone in the other room or if the line is heard from somewhere off camera, where the action is not visible (see Figure 9.5). Having Clumsy Clarence yell, "Holy crud! I'm falling down the steps," from off screen will certainly inform the audience of the situation; however, cinematically, such a story might be better told with appropriate sound effects and a few loud grunts.

While you generally should not use dialogue to describe a current situation, you can use it effectively to expand upon the story being told if doing so will add necessary information, impact, emotion, or back-story to the scene. However, it is almost an absolute rule that dialogue should never be completely redundant to a concurrent action. When we see Clumsy Clarence falling down a flight of stairs, he might very well complement the action by screaming, "Help!" or yelling out a few curse words; however, it would be cinematically redundant for him to say, "My goodness, I seem to be falling down a flight of stairs."

Figure 9.5
Using spoken words to describe a current situation or story action is only appropriate if the occurrence is not visible to the recipient of the message

Just as dialogue should not be redundant to a story action, it should also almost never be completely redundant to body language. Sometimes a character will use vocals to express his thoughts, emotions, or reactions and other times he will use body language, but it is rarely considered good cinematic form to use both to tell the same story (see Figure 9.6). The form of communication a character decides to use will often depend on his age or personality. Frederick might respond to a plate of lima beans by crossing his arms and politely saying, "No thanks. I do not care for such vegetables," while little Freddie might send the same message by grasping his throat and pretending to vomit. Neither one of them, however, needs to do both. Only vocalize a character's thoughts when it is not possible to demonstrate them through action or body language or if his personality lends itself to oration. Body language is often more expressive and is always less expensive to produce.

The only time it is acceptable to repeat the same message simultaneously with spoken words and body language is when a particular phrase needs extra impact. If Dad yells at Junior to "SIT DOWN!" the message will be quite clear. But if you want to emphasize the fact that Dad is really, really angry, you might also want him to grit his teeth and point forcefully at a nearby chair. Dad's words alone *or* just his gesture will effectively deliver the message; however, combining the two will give it significantly more emphasis (see Figure 9.7). An excellent example of this exists in Disney's original *Peter Pan* when Captain Hook commands to Mr. Smee, "You will go ashore, pick up Tinkerbell, and bring her to me." In addition to speaking these words, he simultaneously points and gestures a sign-language version of the same statement with his hand. Without the additional hand motions, the message certainly would have been clear; however, it definitely had more impact as a result of the intentional and effective sign-language redundancy.

Go through your script and your storyboards and look for scenes where actions might speak louder than words. Are there any scenes in which the dialogue you've written seems redundant or unnecessary?

Exercise: Watch a vocal-track–inclusive animated film with the sound turned off. How well can you follow the story without hearing the vocal tracks? If a scene makes complete sense when it is viewed silently, watch the scene again with the volume back on and consider whether the accompanying vocal tracks add anything to the story being told or whether they are simply redundant.

Figure 9.6
Obviously the baboon with the sunglasses is telling the other monkey to back off. A line of dialogue such as, "Not this time, my friend; you got the last one," would be acceptable because it would reveal a bit of history that the body language does not show. However, a line such as, "Back off!" or "It's mine!" would be unnecessarily redundant. That message is clear without words.

"Come on up, Buddy... Come on."

Figure 9.7
Usually dialogue or body language alone will be sufficient to effectively deliver a message, but combining the two will give the statement extra emphasis.

Writing Vocal Tracks

Dialogue is one of the most effective tools available for characterization. How a person talks and the things he or she says will help define personality, style, nationality, age, intelligence, motivations, goals, relationships, and mood. In Chapter 3, we discussed how it is often necessary to exaggerate certain physical and behavioral traits to effectively define a character in the limited timespan of a short film; the same holds true for dialogue. Consider exaggerating certain stereotypical tendencies when you write vocal tracks for the characters in your story. For instance:

◆ Young children will tend to use short words and sometimes lisp or use "f" in place of "th." "Gueth what? My birf-day ith tomorrow!"

◆ A stereotypical modern teenager will say "like," "ya know," and "I'm all" quite a bit. "I was like, 'No way!' and then she's all, 'Fine, don't believe me!'"

◆ An elderly person will avoid slang and perhaps intersperse his thoughts with health complaints or reminders of his age. "When I was a young boy like you, I'd walk three miles to school every day. Of course, today, with my arthritis, I'm lucky if I can walk three blocks!"

◆ A famous and eloquent college professor will rarely pause or lose his train of thought because his words have been carefully chosen and are well rehearsed. Years of repeating the same material might also make him sound dry and monotonous.

◆ A true intellectual will generally have an impressive vocabulary.

◆ A pseudo-intellectual will use (and often misuse) plenty of million-dollar words.

◆ A sophisticated character will avoid contractions and will use words such as "shall," "moreover," and "certainly."

◆ An insecure or nervous person will pause or stutter frequently and often say "umm" and "uhh."

◆ A wealthy and arrogant individual will take every opportunity to remind others of his success and will often refer to his material possessions by their brand names. "My Jaguar was fine while I was at Harvard, but after I made my first million, I wouldn't be caught dead in anything less than a Ferrari!"

◆ Many languages other than English do not use articles (a, an, and the), so a character will sound stereotypically foreign if you omit them from his dialogue. "When I was young boy, I would ride to store on bike." Of course, this assumes you are making an English-language film in the first place.

◆ Robots and aliens sound non-human when they use multi-syllabic synonyms and avoid slang and contractions. "Be assured that any attempts at thwarting our occupation of your feeble planet with your primitive weaponry will be most futile."

Of course, all of these are mere tendencies and storytelling conventions. Not every teenager uses slang, and not every professor is especially articulate. Many foreigners speak English perfectly, and some robots don't sound robotic at all. Feel free to defy stereotypes and invent any style of speech you desire for your film characters, but realize that using stereotypes can often be an extremely effective form of exaggeration.

Think about the design, history, personality, goals, and physical traits of your characters. Then provide them with fitting vocal styles and word choices.

◆ Your teenage surfer might call his girlfriend "dude" and get "totally bummed" when the weather is "gnarly."

◆ Your crooked politician might refer to himself in the third person and answer direct questions with clichés and rhetoric. "Irving Lincoln is not the kind of man who puts the cart before the horse!"

◆ Your fantastical elf might speak in rhyme. "Please forgive my verbal curse, but I must always speak in verse."

◆ Your sweet old grandmother might speak slowly and often use outdated words such as "icebox" and "seltzer."

Or you can create unique and amusing characters with vocal styling that deliberately contradicts their physicality (see Figure 9.8). Imagine:

"To thine own self be true; and it must follow, as the night the day, thou can'st not then be false to any man"

◆ A bodybuilder with a lisp

◆ A beautiful princess who curses all the time

◆ A drill sergeant with the vocabulary of a sophisticated Shakespearean actor

In your daily travels, listen to the conversations that occur around you and pay attention to the way people talk. Carry a notebook and jot down interesting or character-defining lines of dialogue coming from the chatting customers in the supermarket checkout line; the hosts, guests, and callers of your favorite talk-radio station; your boring chemistry teacher; the exuberant evangelist on late-night TV; the dishonest politicians debating against each another; the regulars at the local pool hall before and after a few drinks; the teenagers at the mall; the irate customer in line at the post office; the kid in the toy store pleading with his mother; and the strange man who stands outside the subway station talking to himself. Try to notice tendencies, consistencies, or perhaps even memorable sentences you might want to use verbatim in your story.

Figure 9.8
Characters with vocabularies that contradict their design can be interesting.

When you are analyzing and writing monologues and conversations, keep in mind that real human dialogue is rarely perfect. Vocal tracks should not sound rehearsed; most conversations are basically ad-libbed. People often pause, stutter, repeat themselves, start over, cough, grunt, interrupt themselves and each other, use gibberish, curse, lose their train of thought, and answer questions indirectly or with irony. It is often tempting to write beautifully articulate dialogue to make yourself or your characters seem clever (and doing so is indeed sometimes appropriate), but realize that believability is generally more important and effective than eloquence.

For example, this exchange sounds rehearsed, contrived, and totally unnatural.

John: "Say, Fred, are you aware that Steven is hosting a party this evening? Do you plan on attending?"

Fred: "No, John, I do not think I shall attend. I actually do not care for Steven very much."

John: "But Fred, have you neglected to consider the fact that Steven is my uncle's adopted son?"

Fred: "Yes, John, I realize that he is your relative, and while you are indeed my friend and I do not wish to insult your family, I must repeat that I simply do not enjoy Steven's company."

The following version sounds a lot more believable.

John: "Hey, uh, you goin' to Steve's party tonight?"

Fred: "And hang out with that loser? Are you crazy?"

John: "Yeah but—"

Fred (interrupting): "Blah, blah, blah! I know he's your damned cousin or whatever, but he's still a jackass."

As you are writing dialogue, think about and jot down how you ultimately want your words to sound. Consider that the same line of dialogue will have several different meanings depending on its context, delivery, inflections, associated body language, and the tone and style of the vocal performance. If your story contains a scene in which John shows Fred a picture of himself standing in front of the Eiffel Tower, and John responds, "That's very interesting," you'll want to give some thought to the delivery of that particular line to make sure it carries the intended message. If John gives a slight emphasis to the word "interesting," he might indeed be impressed by the photo. If he emphasizes and elongates the word "very," however, he might be implying that something is not quite right about the image. If he emphasizes "very" and "interesting" while rolling his eyes, he obviously thinks the photo is somewhat less than interesting. If he uses a long pause after the word "very," he might actually think the picture stinks but perhaps he doesn't want to insult the photographer (see Figure 9.9).

Even a single word can carry several different meanings depending on context and inflection. Think about how many ways you might say the word "no". It can be a simple answer, a command, a plea, an invitation for another guess, or a sarcastic synonym for, "I already knew that."

Be especially wary of creating soliloquies. People do sometimes talk to themselves when trying to make difficult decisions ("If I go to the party, I'll have to see that loser, Steve, but if I stay home I'll be the loser!") or while sitting in traffic ("Why did I get on the freeway at five o'clock? Stupid, stupid, stupid!"). However, it often sounds somewhat unnatural for a character to carry on a lengthy conversation with himself unless he is rehearsing for a performance or is perhaps mildly schizophrenic. Narration is often a preferred method for vocalizing a character's inner thoughts. Of course, you should try to deliver the message with a combination of fewer words and more body language.

In general, strive to keep your dialogue natural, believable, and succinct.

Figure 9.9
Depending on context and delivery, a simple line of dialogue might imply sincerity, jealousy, or perhaps sarcasm.

Tip: Be sure to read your written dialogue out loud to make sure it sounds natural and does not contain any inadvertent tongue twisters, distracting rhymes, or unwanted alliterations.

Performing and Recording Vocal Tracks

Once you have created effective and believable dialogue for your characters, you'll need to record useful and convincing performances of your written words. In a typical production pipeline, vocal tracks are recorded in the pre-production stage, and they directly or indirectly influence your future animations and shot staging. Sometimes *scratch tracks* are recorded at this stage, where placeholder dialogue readings are performed by anyone available (often the director) before the official voice actors are brought in. These scratch tracks will generally be sufficient for synching up dialogue with imagery in your 2D and 3D animatics, but before you actually animate your shots, you will need your official voice actor deliveries. Narration can certainly be recorded after your shots are in the can, but dialogue is almost always recorded beforehand.

To turn your written words into recorded vocal tracks, you will need two things—equipment and talent. Equipment is the easy part; there are a number of viable choices at your disposal (see Figure 9.10).

Figure 9.10
There are a number of equipment choices available for recording vocal tracks.

◆ Connect a microphone to your computer and record directly into digital format. Basic PC microphones are extremely inexpensive and are generally sufficient. In a pinch, you can use a set of headphones as a microphone.

◆ Try a digital voice recorder, but make sure you set it to low speed/high quality. Most voice recorders allow you to transfer your recordings directly into your computer as digital audio files in standard .aiff or .wav format via a USB cable.

◆ Use a camcorder and transfer the taped sessions into your computer with a FireWire cable, then extract the audio tracks using appropriate software, such as Adobe Premiere or QuickTime Pro.

◆ Use a digital camera with movie mode in the same manner.

◆ Rent a session at a professional sound stage. This option will give you the best recording quality; however, it will likely be the most expensive.

Whichever method you choose, make sure you have a quiet place to conduct your recording sessions. Background noise is something you might want to add later, not something you should have to spend time removing.

You can, of course, lift vocal tracks from existing films, television shows, speech recordings, comedy routines, and songs. However, you should only use such pre-recorded vocals for experiments, school assignments, or demo reel pieces. These recordings are generally copyrighted and you will not be able to use them in a film that will be displayed publicly unless you get the necessary permissions and often pay licensing fees. Sometimes a short film will need to use an existing voice recording or song for its poignancy or punch line (*Alien Song*), but in general, it is preferable (and potentially less expensive) to record your own audio tracks.

Voice Actors and Style

When utilizing voice talent, we cannot stress enough that you must find good actors. A weak or unappealing vocal performance can ruin an otherwise successful CG short. If you can afford it, try to find professionals (or at least folks with some experience). If you are in a school that has a drama department, try to find some talented acting students who might be willing to help out for nominal fees, credit, experience, potential exposure, or just for the fun of it.

Also, use appropriate actors whenever possible. If your film will feature a five-year-old girl, try to find a five-year-old girl to play the part. A thirty-year-old pretending to be a five-year-old will usually sound like an obvious and ineffective imitation.

Often the right actors can mimic animal sounds quite well, or you can purchase them on royalty-free CDs or download them from Internet stores.

When it comes to inventing a voice for a cartoon character, monster, demon, alien, fairy, or other such creature, work with your actors and strive to invent something appealing and truly unique. This can sometimes prove to be deceptively difficult. Strange voices often sound comical when they are meant to be scary. An adult pretending to be a cute and talkative little space alien can easily sound downright annoying if it is forced or overdone. The voice belonging to a fantastical creature or a cute cartoon character should be something more interesting than the result of an actor merely raising the pitch of his own voice or adding a lisp. Aim for some originality by giving it a bit more thought than that. Try something subtle or understated—or perhaps an exaggerated and seemingly mismatched accent, which often works well for cartoon characters (think of Pepe le Pew or Foghorn Leghorn).

Consider the following speech elements when inventing voices for your characters and appropriately modifying them for particular emotional states and story situations.

◆ **Overall style.** Does your character use a lot of contractions? Does he pause often between words or sentences? Does he stutter? Does he punctuate every sentence with a swear word? Do words flow from his lips like gentle rain or pop out in sputters like a machine gun?

◆ **Tone and pitch.** These will help indicate personality, mood, age, condition, and gender. A small child will usually have a higher-pitched voice than an adult. A young teenage boy going through puberty will have a voice that abruptly and unexpectedly switches between low and high pitches. A large monster will often have an appropriately low-pitched voice. A witch might have a high-pitched squeal, especially when she is laughing. An excited person's pitch might rise uncontrollably, while a tired or sick person will often speak slowly and perhaps more deeply than usual.

◆ **Volume.** This can imply tiredness, anger, confidence, the location of the person being addressed, and the specifics of the given situation. The volume of an angry person's voice will tend to be at one extreme or the other—very quiet or very loud. A cat burglar will whisper to his teammates during a heist, while a lecturer will often need to raise his voice to reach the back rows of his classroom.

◆ **Speed.** An impatient, excited, or nervous person will generally speak rather quickly. An intense or angry person will tend to speak slowly unless the situation is urgent, in which case he might speak faster than usual. Someone who is tired or bored will speak slowly.

◆ **Vocabulary.** This will suggest a character's age, intelligence, culture, and nationality, as well as the era of your story. A small child will tend to use simple words; an intellectual will use big words. A pseudo-intellectual will misuse those same big words. Certain regional words, such as pram or loo, will imply a character's homeland. If your characters exist in an ancient era, they might use archaic words such as thy, yonder, or begat.

◆ **Pronunciation.** This might suggest a character's intelligence, age, nationality, or region of origin. Is it "toe-MAY-toe" or "toe-MAH-toe?" If someone says "nucular" or "foilage," they might sound less educated. People from certain areas of England often use "f" instead of "th."

◆ **Articulation.** This will help imply mood, context, tiredness, species, or perhaps level of sobriety. An angry mother scolding her son might over-articulate her messages so they cannot be misunderstood. Someone giving an important speech might also give extra emphasis to careful articulation. Robots and aliens are stereotypically quite articulate as well. If a character mumbles or slurs his speech rather incomprehensibly, he might be tired, inebriated, or perhaps just talking with his mouth full.

◆ **Accents.** These will indicate a character's homeland, be it Australia, Scotland, Texas, or perhaps Jupiter. Depending on who is listening, certain accents can also carry connotations based on associated history and cultural stereotypes. Will British, German, or Southern accents conjure up any preconceived notions about a particular character?

◆ **Language.** If a character speaks in a foreign tongue, he might be from another country or another planet, or he might be a member of an alternative species. A pair of teenage friends might make up a new language just to keep secrets. You might want to invent a strange and unique tongue for your fantastical centaurs or your cartoon spiders.

◆ **Inflections and emphasis.** This will help indicate mood or personality. The phrase "yeah, sure," can reveal whether the speaker is friendly and accommodating or downright sarcastic, depending on the word or syllable that is stressed.

Effective combinations of these speech elements mixed with the actual word choice will help define personality, history, nationality, intelligence, species, physical or emotional state, irony, connotations, and subtext. A robot might speak in a monotone with a metallic echo. A crafty villain might talk slowly and quietly. An injured soldier might slur his words and punctuate them with grunts and sighs. Think about a simple line of dialogue such as, "Come here." If someone yells this line from another room in a fairly average tone of voice, it might simply imply that something interesting is on TV. If such words are delivered slowly in a calm and soothing voice, it might sound like someone enticing a shy cat. If this line comes from a sultry and feminine voice with a French accent, it will likely sound rather alluring. If these same words are delivered loud and fast through obviously pursed lips and with a tinge of anger, we can probably expect some punishment to follow. If your villain says the words slowly and softly, your protagonist might want to consider backing away carefully.

Examine your character design sketches or test renders and try to imagine suitable voices that will fit nicely (see Figure 9.11). Sometimes this means making fairly obvious choices, such as a deep, raspy voice for a monster; a high-pitched lisp for a cartoon bunny; or a loud, articulate, Southern-accent for a drill sergeant. But try to create voices that are at least somewhat original. However, this does not necessarily mean

Figure 9.11
What kinds of voices might you invent for characters such as these?

you should try to achieve originality by simply creating voices that contradict a character's design or personality. Making a meowing dog, a cartoon bunny with a deep, raspy voice, or a drill sergeant with high-pitched lisp will indeed be out of the ordinary, but such extreme mismatches are generally only appropriate in comedies (see Figure 9.12). Doing this in a more serious, subtle, or poignant film is only a good idea if it has some relevance to your storyline or you offer a reasonable explanation, such as an injury or an illness that had caused the uncharacteristic vocal style or tone.

If your film has multiple characters and they are not meant to be identical, give each of them a distinctive voice. Your audience should always be able to identify and differentiate your characters by the way they speak. If possible, try to use a different actor for each of your characters. If this is not feasible, make sure your voice actors can invent sufficiently distinct voices for each of the characters they will play.

Figure 9.12
A pot-bellied gremlin with a strangely mismatched voice can be rather amusing.

When conducting your dialogue recording sessions, keep in mind that the ways in which your actors deliver their lines might inspire you to go back and make a few changes to your character designs so they fit better. Be open to this possibility because vocal style is a significant element of character design, and it should be allowed to influence physicality when appropriate.

Just as you paid attention to real-world characters when you were doing research for your written words, listen carefully to the conversations of people around you for inspiration when coming up with style, tone, and accents for your film characters.

- How do children sound?
- How do elderly people sound?
- How do tired people sound? Busy people? Lazy people?
- How does someone adjust his tone and speech patterns when scolding a child? Buttering up his boss for a raise? Trying to sell a car? Asking a girl out on a date?

Watch films with especially stylistic vocal tracks that you can potentially borrow and alter for your own characters. Try David Mamet's *Glengarry Glenn Ross* or Woody Allen's *Hannah and Her Sisters* for interesting examples of style and tempo. Also watch (and listen to) very old movies, period pieces, foreign films, and standup comedy routines to study different accents, vocabularies, styles, and pronunciations.

Sometimes, while writing lines of dialogue, you will have a very specific delivery in mind, and it will be necessary to find the right actors and direct them effectively so they give you exactly what you want. However, realize that dictating every detail of an actor's vocal performance will often result in dialogue that sounds rehearsed, forced, or unnatural. It is often a good idea to allow your voice actors some degree of creative freedom during your recording sessions. Give them enough direction so you get what you need, but not so much that you stifle their ability to deliver believable performances.

Occasionally, allowing complete creative freedom is the best way to go. Give your actors their lines, but let them deliver their words naturally in their own voices—perhaps even allow them to ad lib and change, subtract, or add a few words here and there. You might be pleasantly surprised at the results.

Always get multiple takes. Ask your actors to deliver each line in a few different ways so you have several versions to choose from when it comes time to assemble your vocal tracks and create your animations. Get alternative recordings of the same lines delivered at different speeds, tones, moods, and levels of articulation. Also, have your actors provide you with a few non-verbal sounds, such as grunts, coughs, sighs, and laughs. Even if you do not initially plan to use such sounds, once you start animating your shots, you might discover that you need a few of them after all. It is always better to have something and not need it than to need something and not have it.

Remember that a line of dialogue is generally said just once in a film. When reading a book, you can always go back and reread a sentence you missed or misunderstood. You can also rewind a videotape or a DVD for the same reason. However, your audience may not have pause and rewind controls when viewing your film; therefore, it is very important that your dialogue recordings are succinct and clear. Make sure your actors enunciate appropriately so your audience will be able to hear and understand what is being said. You don't want a screening of your film to be disrupted by someone constantly leaning over to his friend and asking, "What'd he say?" Discourage such behavior by writing believable and succinct dialogue and recording clear and understandable vocal tracks.

Visual Accompaniment

Think about the body language that will ultimately accompany or emphasize the words coming out of your characters' mouths (see Figure 9.13). If you know exactly how you'll want a character to pose and move while delivering a particular line of dialogue, note it in your script and direct your actors accordingly because it will help them create fitting vocal performances. If you don't have anything specific in mind, pay attention to the posture and movements of your actors while they deliver their lines and either film them or make some quick sketches you can reference later at the animation stage.

Figure 9.13
Posing and body language are often used to complement or clarify a line of dialogue.

In fact, it is always a good idea to film your actors during your recording sessions. In addition to giving you body language reference, doing so will provide you with indispensable guidelines for your future modeling and setup phases when you prepare your digital sculptures for lip-synching. Have your actors deliver secondary performances of a few lines of dialogue while they deliberately over-enunciate each word. Remember that when animating, it will often be necessary to exaggerate movement extremes for the sake of clarity, so take this opportunity to gather potentially useful information about such visual magnifications. In addition to filming your dialogue sessions, take a series of still photographs of your actors making facial expressions and phoneme shapes. Give them specific directions such as "Smile," "Give me an angry face like you want to rip my head off," or "Say 'oh' and 'eff'"

Figure 9.14
As long as your voice actors are available, film or photograph them for future reference.

(see Figure 9.14). When you ask them to create these face shapes, be sure to get subtle and exaggerated versions of each. Also, give them more interpretive directions and let them come up with a few natural and perhaps unexpected faces on their own: "You just drank some spoiled milk!" or "How does an oak tree speak?" When collecting these photographs, make sure you get images of every conceivable facial pose you might need for your film. If you are creating a sinister demon creature, it might not be necessary to snap a photograph of his voice actor crying or expressing remorse, but you'll very likely need a number of sneers and snarls and perhaps an evil smirk or a maniacal laugh.

Phonemes

To create effective lip-synch performances for your animated characters, you will need to pose and shape their mouths to match the sounds of each spoken word and syllable. This can be accomplished in one of two ways.

◆ Create blend shapes for each appropriate mouth shape (see Chapter 12, "Modeling").

◆ Place necessary bones and deformers in and on your characters' faces so you can pull and twist them into the desired shapes (see Chapter 14, "Character Setup").

(Note that you will use these same methods to create various facial expressions.)

The set of distinctive mouth shapes that combine to visually enunciate syllable sounds are known as *phonemes*. Not every distinct letter or syllable sound needs its own phoneme shape; you can usually use the same shape for several different sounds. The standard set of phoneme shapes that is generally sufficient for most animated characters is detailed in Table 9.1.

Absolutely realistic enunciation might require a wider range of shapes because there are subtle differences between many of the phonemes that are grouped together in Table 9.1. For most animated character lip-synching, however, these eight should suffice (see Figure 9.15). If you are making a fairly stylized or cartoony film, you might be able to get away with even fewer by assembling the first and third into a single group or combining the fourth and fifth.

Photograph the faces of your voice actors mouthing each phoneme shape. Get a subtle version as well as an exaggerated version of each. Also, get images of every phoneme shape combined with a variety of different attitudes. You'll want a full set of happy, sad, angry, scared, and surprised phoneme shapes (see Figure 9.16). These photographs will be extremely helpful when it comes time to model, set up, and animate your speaking characters.

Obviously, if the vocal tracks for your film will be restricted to narration, such photographs will not be necessary; however, you should still capture a handful of facial expressions as long as you have your voice actors available. After all, there is no such thing as having too much reference material.

We will discuss phoneme shapes further in the modeling, setup, and animation chapters of this book.

Table 9.1 Standard Phoneme Shapes for Animated Characters

Phoneme	Shape
C, K, G, Y, Z	Often a rather neutral shape
AH, I (EYE)	Mouth open fairly wide
EE, N, S	Wide mouth shape
U, OOH, W, CH, SH, D	Small round shape
OH	Open, round shape
B, M, P	Lips closed and pulled in a bit
F, V	Overbite shape—lower lip under top front teeth
L, TH	Tongue showing between teeth

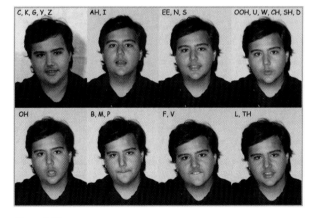

Figure 9.15
The eight basic phoneme shapes

213

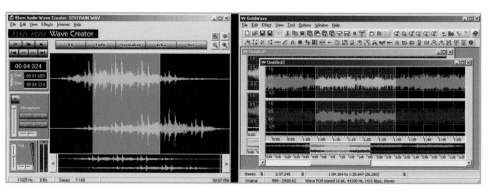

Figure 9.17
There are a number of software packages available for audio editing, including Blaze Audio's Wave Creator and GoldWave Digital Audio Editor.

Figure 9.16
To assist in your lip-synch modeling, setup, and animation, photograph your voice actors mouthing various versions of each phoneme shape.

Processing Vocal Tracks

Once you have your vocal tracks transferred into your computer as digital (.wav or .aiff) files, many of them will need to be cleaned up and perhaps manipulated a bit before you can use them effectively. There are a number of audio software packages you can use to change various details of your vocal recordings so they will suit your needs more precisely (see Figure 9.17). Some of the manipulations you may want to apply to your recorded vocal tracks include:

◆ Background noise cleanup so your character voices are decipherable and your recordings sound professional.

◆ Separations, where individual voices are extracted from conversations or from noisy recordings.

◆ Speed changes to make your vocal tracks fit with the style and pacing of your storyline. For instance, you might need to speed up a particular line of dialogue to make it sound more urgent. Keep in mind that changing the speed of an audio track will alter its pitch as well.

◆ Pitch and tone adjustments to compensate for a speed change or to create a new character or voice that differs from that of your original actor. Such adjustments can also affect the implied emotional state of a speaking character. For instance, lowering the pitch of a recorded statement might make the speaker sound tired.

◆ Volume changes to suit the needs of a particular story point. Increasing volume might help indicate anger or urgency; decreasing volume might help imply distance or mood. Changing the volume of individual words or syllables from a vocal recording can also alter the tone and meaning of the original statement, such as "THIS is my car!" versus "This is MY car!"

◆ Effects and filters, such as echoes, which you can add to make someone sound as if he or she is far away or trapped in a cave. You can apply metallic effects for a robotic sound or scratches and skips to create a nostalgic feel. You can even play a vocal track backward for a surreal effect or to match a small bit of time travel in your storyline.

◆ Cutting and pasting to create entire conversations out of individual statements or new sentences from pieces of others.

Experiment with the tools your audio software packages offer and try to come up with interesting variations on existing recordings. You might be able to create the voice for a monster, alien, robot, or cartoon character by simply taking a natural human vocal track and manipulating it with filters, speed changes, and pitch variations.

To String or Not to String

Depending on your organizational preferences and the software you will use for synching up your vocal tracks with your visuals, you might need to assemble or cut up your audio recordings in different ways. You might want them broken up into individual lines of dialogue, assembled into conversation chunks, or perhaps strung together into one large audio file (see Figure 9.18).

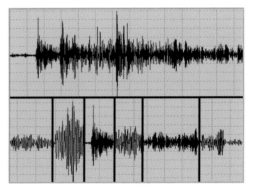

It is generally recommended that you use a piece of digital editing software, such as Adobe Premiere or Final Cut Pro, to synch up your vocal tracks to your imagery for the various stages of your story reel (see Chapter 10, "Story Reels and 2D Animatics"). These programs allow you to insert small or large sections of dialogue into your story reel and then synch them up interactively. Using individual lines of dialogue or conversation chunks as separate audio files will provide you with a great deal of flexibility and fine control over your audio synching; however, it will mean more files to organize.

Figure 9.18
You can assemble vocal tracks into large chunks or break them up into small pieces, depending on your organizational plans and software requirements.

Many CG software packages have extremely limited audio capabilities; they lack even the most rudimentary tools for layering or appending tracks. Any shots or scenes that will be synched with vocals within such packages will require full audio tracks containing all of the necessary dialogue for the shot at hand. This might require you to use a piece of audio software to string together a series of vocal recordings into a single file.

If you recorded individual lines of dialogue, you might find it necessary to assemble them into conversations before inserting and synching them into your story reel. If you recorded entire conversations, you might need to cut them up into individual sound bites for more control and flexibility when inserting and synching them with your editing software.

You might even go so far as to assemble all of your vocal tracks into a single large audio file containing all of the dialogue for your entire film. Doing so will obviously mean you will have to do all of your synching by manipulating your imagery rather than by shifting individual dialogue lines or conversations separately. This is generally not the most ideal way to handle vocal tracks, but it will certainly make for a less complicated file structure. This might also be a necessary step if you are creating a very short film in which all of your shots are contained in a single scene file within your CG software package, and you need one long audio file for the entire story.

Exposure Sheets

Once your dialogue tracks are recorded and processed, you might find it helpful to write them out on *exposure sheets* that you will use to synch up phoneme shapes in your animation stage (see Chapter 16, "Animation"). An exposure sheet typically has one column for frame numbers, another for storyboard drawings and film direction notes, and a third column for dialogue. Recorded dialogue or narration is reviewed carefully and then written vertically down this third column, where individual syllables are separated to indicate how many frames it will take to deliver each one (see Figure 9.19). Transferring dialogue onto exposure sheets can be a long and tedious process, and while doing so is generally a necessary step in traditional animation pipelines, most digital animators find that exposure sheets are unnecessary because it is so easy to make timing adjustments at the actual lip-synch stage, where the necessary dialogue tracks can be viewed as waveforms that are visually synched to the timeline in your CG software package. Exposure sheets might indeed make your lip-synching process more efficient, but hold off on creating them until you reach the animation stage, and try getting by without them first.

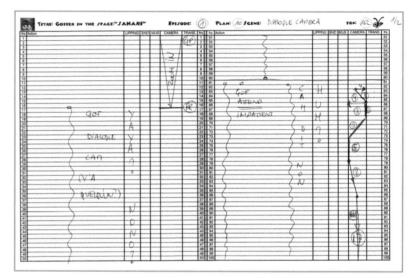

Figure 9.19
An exposure sheet is used to time out dialogue on a frame-accurate basis.

Alternative Techniques

If you have determined that you cannot effectively tell your story using visuals and body language alone, but you really don't think you'll be able to handle the expense and extra work of recording dialogue tracks, building necessary blend shapes or deformers, and creating lip-synch animation, there are a few alternative techniques you might consider. These will allow you to use words without suffering through such complications (see Figure 9.20).

Figure 9.20
If your film absolutely needs words but you cannot logistically use recorded vocal tracks, consider alternative techniques such as dialogue cards, word balloons, or subtitles.

◆ **Dialogue cards.** As seen in the silent films of the early twentieth century, dialogue cards can be interspersed between shots as necessary. This can be an especially useful technique if you are going for a particularly nostalgic style. Don Hertzfeldt made effective and humorous use of this technique in his 2D short, *Rejected*.

◆ **Subtitles.** These are generally only appropriate when a character is speaking in a foreign or made-up alien tongue and it is necessary to reveal what the character is saying. However, it is generally not a good idea to simply use subtitles instead of recorded dialogue because they will probably be more distracting than informative.

◆ **Word balloons.** These can be used in place of audio tracks and are especially appropriate if you are trying to simulate the look of a comic book.

Keep in mind that some critics will view these solutions as copouts when actual recorded dialogue would have been preferred. If you truly won't have the budget or time to create dialogue tracks and lip-synch your characters accordingly, it is usually a better idea to try and modify your story so it does not need dialogue at all—or tell a simpler story this time and create your word-dependent film at a later date, when you have the necessary assets available. If words are absolutely necessary for your film, try to use vocal tracks instead of these solutions if at all possible, unless you are certain that the style of your film would truly be better served by one of these alternative techniques.

Summary

Many popular and successful animated shorts are mute, while others rely on vocal tracks to help deliver their story points. There are three types of vocal tracks you might use in a short film—narration, monologues and soliloquies, and dialogue. A mute film will generally be easier to produce and will have greater potential for universal appeal; however, vocal tracks are sometimes necessary for describing abstract concepts, historical information, character goals, and complex emotions. Film is a primarily visual medium, so it is generally better to *show* rather than to *tell* whenever possible. Body language is more economical and often more informative than vocal tracks. You should not use dialogue to simply describe a clearly visible situation as it is occurring, and dialogue should almost never be redundant to a story action. Dialogue should only be redundant to body language when a particular statement requires extra emphasis. Listen to real-world conversations and study how people actually talk. Realize that natural human speech rarely sounds perfectly articulate or rehearsed. Find strong vocal talent and use appropriate actors for your character voices whenever possible. Character voices and variations based on mood and story situation can be described by details such as style, pitch, volume, vocabulary, articulation, accents, and inflections. Remember that a simple line of dialogue or even a simple word can take on a variety of different meanings depending on its context and delivery. Work with your actors to find the right balance between direction and ad-libbing to get the most effective and natural vocal recordings possible. Write succinct and believable vocal tracks and strive to capture clear and understandable recordings. Film or photograph your actors as they deliver their lines and form phoneme shapes to get inspiration for accompanying body language as well as reference for facial expressions and lip-synching. After you have transferred your vocal recordings into your computer, you may need to erase background noise, change speed, adjust volume, cut, append, or add effects to better suit the needs of your story. The next chapter will describe the process of initiating the construction of your actual film with the creation of a *story reel*.

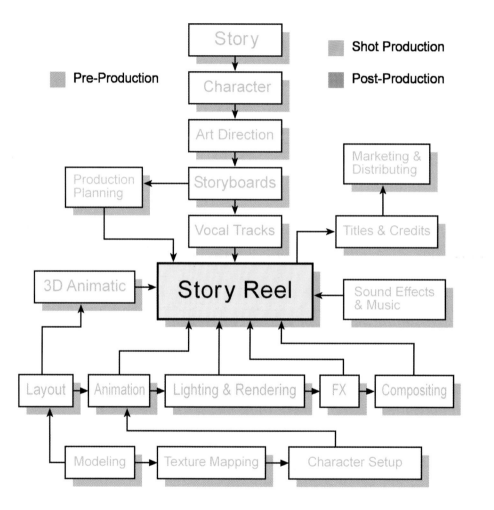

Story

Character

Art Direction

Storyboards

Vocal Tracks

Pre-Production

Shot Production

Post-Production

Production Planning

Marketing & Distributing

Titles & Credits

3D Animatic

Story Reel

Sound Effects & Music

Layout

Animation

Lighting & Rendering

FX

Compositing

Modeling

Texture Mapping

Character Setup

chapter 10
Story Reels and 2D Animatics

A t the storyboard stage, you began the process of converting your narrative tale or fine-arts concept into visual form. Storyboarding provided you with your first opportunity to experiment with shot staging, continuity, and basic editing. The next logical and recommended step in the process of realizing your story idea in cinematic terms is to use a piece of non-linear editing (NLE) software to build the first stage of your *story reel*, which will act as a template upon which your film will grow. The software package containing your evolving story reel will serve as the central *editing bay* for the remainder of your production cycle, where the visual and audio elements of your film will be assembled, continuously refined, and frequently edited until your cinematic masterpiece is complete.

A story reel begins as a *2D animatic*, which is a digital slideshow of sequential storyboard images displayed for appropriate durations and synched up to any audio files that are crucial to story point delivery (see Figure 10.1). When you reach the 3D animatic stage (see Chapter 11, "3D Animatics, Layout, and Camera Direction"), you will replace the held storyboards in your story reel with 3D layout images, which will add dimensionality and indicate basic camera direction as well as the placement of your scene elements in 3D space. Then, as your shots progress from blocking through animation, lighting, rendering, and compositing, you will continuously replace each visual block of your story reel with more and more finished versions until all of your shots are finalized and your story reel has evolved into a nearly completed film. You will still need to add final edits and last-minute additions such as titles, credits, and perhaps sound effects and music, but all of your actual shots will officially be in the can.

Depending on how you structure your production, your story reel might build up in a global, linear, or perhaps sporadic fashion. You might wait until all of your held storyboards have been replaced with 3D layouts before you create any fully animated versions of your shots, and then render all of your shots only after they have all been classified as *animation finals* so your film evolves as a whole. (Refer back to Figure 7.35 in Chapter 7, "Production Planning.") Or it might grow more sporadically, where at any given stage of your production, your story reel will be a mixture of shots at varying levels of completion. Some will still be held storyboard drawings or photos, while others will be 3D layout images, hardware-rendered blocking passes, full-color renders, or final composites (see Figure 10.2). No matter how your story reel ultimately develops, it begins here with a 2D animatic.

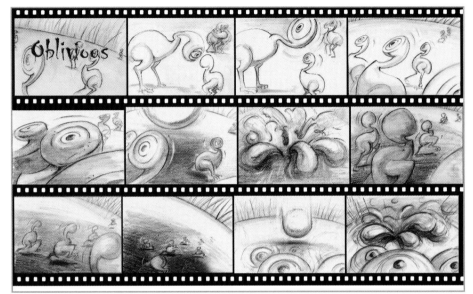

Figure 10.1
A 2D animatic is a movie file of sequential storyboard panels, where each one is held for an appropriate duration to effectively deliver its story point and synch up properly with any necessary audio files.

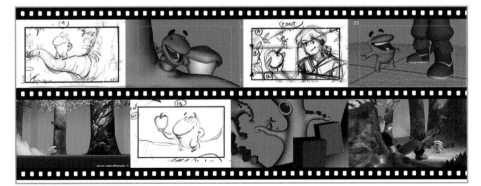

Figure 10.2
Your story reel might build sporadically, where at any given point in your production cycle, the level of completion of your individual shots may be quite mixed.

Creating a 2D Animatic

A *2D animatic* can be defined as storyboards plus timing and necessary audio. The best way to describe a 2D animatic is by example, so take a moment to view the two samples included on this book's DVD.

Recall that the main purpose of storyboarding was to analyze the structure and flow of your written, recorded, or imagined story idea in picture form based on individual drawings or photographs. The main purpose of a 2D animatic is to analyze your story idea in *moving* picture form. The focus of a 2D animatic is still primarily on story issues such as structure and pacing. This is not the time to concern yourself too much with cinematic details such as camera movement and 3D object placement just yet. You will address those aspects of film thoroughly in the 3D animatic stage. You certainly want to think ahead about such cinematic elements as you assemble and edit your 2D animatic, but remember that in this stage you still mainly reside in story land, not so much in film land just yet.

As you enter this initial stage of story reel construction, remember to maintain an attitude of flexibility, keeping in mind that you will probably be editing your film continuously from now on. Strive to create a 2D animatic that is effectively structured and well paced, but realize that all of your cinematic questions will probably not be answered fully here. As your individual shots evolve, you will likely make changes to their staging and frame counts, which might force you to make adjustments to your overall story reel construction as well as your audio synching. Such continuous editing is to be expected in a production cycle, so be prepared for the fact that the structure, pacing, and staging details of your final film will probably differ from your 2D animatic by some degree.

To create a 2D animatic, you will need:

◆ Your storyboards

◆ Any necessary audio tracks, which might include temporary or final dialogue, narration, music, or sound effects

◆ A method for bringing your storyboard drawings or photos into your computer

◆ A piece of non-linear editing software that will allow you to assemble your storyboards, hold them for story-appropriate durations, and synch them up to your audio tracks

The DVD that is included with this book contains 2D animatics from the films *Pom Pom* and *Sahari*. Watch them and notice the structure, pacing, and staging differences between these early animatics and the final versions of the films they ultimately became, which are also included on the disc. It is very likely that your film will undergo a similar amount of change between your 2D animatic stage and your final version.

Presumably, you have already created the first two items. Chapter 6 covered storyboarding, and Chapter 9 described how to write, record, and process vocal tracks. If your film will have dialogue or narration, you will need these vocal tracks for your 2D animatic. If you are creating a mute film, then vocal tracks obviously don't exist. However, many films that do not have dialogue or narration use music as the driving force for story pacing. If this is the case with your film, you might want to jump ahead to Chapter 21, "Sound Effects and Music," and then return to this chapter once you have your music tracks available. Similarly, if you feel that certain sound effects will be essential at this early cinematic stage, then you need to prepare them as well.

Scanning

To assemble your storyboards into a story reel, you first need to bring them into your computer. Before you do so, think about the size and palette you will want for your scanned images. It is generally a good idea to scan the images at a large resolution and in full color so you have the highest-quality digital versions possible. For the sake of file size, clarity, and personal preference, you can always reduce them after the fact.

There are three basic tools you can use to transfer storyboard panels into your computer (see Figure 10.3).

◆ A flatbed scanner

◆ A digital camera

◆ A digital camcorder

Figure 10.3
The three most popular tools for digitizing storyboard panels are flatbed scanners, digital cameras, and camcorders.

Decent flatbed scanners are fairly inexpensive these days, and they offer extremely high resolution and quality. Most scanners come with software that allows you to adjust details such as brightness and contrast during or after the scanning process. You could go to a local print shop that offers scanning services, but the convenience of having a scanner of your own is generally worth the price.

You can use a digital camera to photograph your storyboard drawings and then transfer them into your computer through a USB connection or a data card reader. Setting up your camera on a tripod will help with image consistency. Digital cameras do not offer the same level of resolution choices and image-processing functionality as scanners, but remember that your digital storyboard images will basically act as placeholders in your story reel, so absolutely perfect picture quality is generally not a major issue at this stage.

Most digital camcorders have still-image functionality, so you can use one to capture digital photos in addition to videos. In general, the resolution and image quality of a photo taken with a camcorder will not be as high as one taken with a digital camera, but again, even medium-quality images may suffice at this stage. Most camcorders come bundled with digitizing software, and most editing software packages have frame- and video-capture functionality as well. A potential advantage of using a camcorder (or a digital camera with movie-mode functionality) is that you can film and digitize your storyboard images as video clips rather than still images, which might allow you to do a bit of preliminary timing during your capture sessions. Instead of scanning or photographing your storyboard images as individual frames that will need to be held for specific durations, you could record video clips of each storyboard panel with hold times that approximate your intended shot pacing.

Using a camcorder also allows you to create video clips that zoom in on secondary frames or pan across elongated panels to simulate the actual camera moves that certain storyboards merely suggest with descriptive graphics and icons. Using video clips of storyboard panels with preliminary camera moves will make your 2D animatic that much more cinematic. (See the *Sahari* animatic on the DVD.) Of course, if you capture your boards as still images, you will still be able to add zooms and pans using the right piece of editing software, but if you add such camera moves during your capture session, you might save yourself a few steps down the line.

Whichever tool you use for capturing your storyboards, it is always a good idea to be consistent with the placement and angle of each board when it is scanned or photographed. Doing so will make it easier to edit the digital versions efficiently and will allow you to run scripts to make the same adjustments or enhancements on all of your images as an entire batch. If you use a scanner, place each board at the same corner of the bed and orient them all consistently, or if the accessory is available for your scanner and your budget will allow it, consider purchasing an auto document feeder for high-volume scanning sessions. If you use a digital camera or camcorder, use a tripod and construct a simple cardboard frame so you can place each story-board panel in exactly the same spot when it is being photographed or filmed (see Figure 10.4). Another option is to draw your boards on pre-punched animation paper and then lay them on a pegboard for position and angle consistency.

Figure 10.4
For the sake of consistency, use a tripod and a card-board frame when using a camera or camcorder to digitize your storyboards.

If you drew your storyboards directly on the computer using a piece of appropriate software, then obviously you won't need to scan them. If you chose to use photographed actors and sets as your storyboards and you captured such scenes with a digital camera, then your storyboard photos are already in the proper digital format; you simply need to transfer them into your computer using the proper USB cable or card reader.

Once you have all of your storyboards digitized as individual images, you will probably want to bring them into a program such as DeBabelizer or Photoshop to adjust resolution, contrast, brightness, size, orientation, and perhaps image format to suit your needs. If all of your storyboard panels were digitized at a consistent size, angle, and placement, you should be able to batch process them in one fell swoop, rather than manually performing every necessary manipulation on each image individually.

If you captured your storyboards as videos, you can either extract individual images or keep them as movie clips, depending on how you plan to process and assemble them. Fortunately, most editing software packages can handle both still images and video clips. Of course, if you established preliminary timing or created rough camera moves during your videotape session, it will probably be more efficient to keep such shots as movie clips.

Audio or Images First?

Before you assemble your scanned storyboard images or video clips with your editing software to begin creation of your story reel, it is important to consider whether your audio will be dictating your visuals or vice versa.

If your film will be primarily visual with perhaps only a few lines of dialogue, a handful of sound effects that will be timed to your animations, and a music track that will be composed or selected after all of your shots have been rendered, then you'll want to insert your storyboard images or clips into your editing software first, working out the hold times for each shot to satisfy your intended cinematic structure and timing. Then, once you're happy with the visual flow of your 2D animatic, it will be time to add your dialogue tracks and any sound effects you need to effectively deliver your story in this rough form. Music may or may not be necessary at this stage.

If the flow of your story action will be dictated by a piece of prerecorded music, then you'll want to insert your music track into your editing software before you work out the hold times of your storyboard images.

If your film will have a significant amount of dialogue, you will probably want to work with your visuals and audio tracks somewhat simultaneously. A lot of back and forth will undoubtedly occur. For dialogue-driven scenes, you'll time your visuals to match your audio. In scenes without dialogue, obviously, you'll merely time your shots based on visual flow (see Figure 10.5).

Sound effects are usually added after visual timing has been established, but if your film will feature any sounds that will be absolutely crucial to initial story timing, such as a ticking time bomb and a subsequent explosion, you might need to synch your 2D animatic visuals to such audio tracks, rather than vice versa.

Sometimes, if a filmmaker has yet to choose his voice actors or they are currently unavailable, preliminary placeholder dialogue recordings known

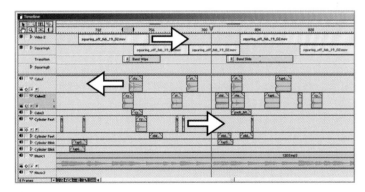

Figure 10.5
Depending on which is primarily dictating your story actions, visuals or audio, you will mainly shift and trim one of these element types to synch up with the other. However, a significant amount of back and forth will likely be necessary as your editing passes continue.

as *scratch tracks* can be recorded by someone who is readily available, often the director himself. Such rough recordings are usually quite sufficient for the initial timing passes that are established during the 2D animatic stage. However, keep in mind that before you create your final animations and lip-synchs, you will need your official dialogue tracks recorded by your chosen actors.

Assembling Your Shots

Now that you have your storyboard images, video clips, and necessary audio tracks ready to go, you can assemble them into a filmstrip of your entire story as a project file within your chosen piece of editing software.

To create effective story point delivery and appropriate audio synching, you will need to hold each storyboard image for a specific duration. You might need to trim or retime video clips as well. Different software packages provide various methods and levels of interactivity for such shot editing.

Remember that each shot in your film will be represented by at least one storyboard image. An establishing shot will probably only take a single image held for perhaps a couple of seconds. A shot that follows a speeding car might require a movie clip that pans across the length of a single elongated frame. An action shot might require several boards to effectively deliver all of its essential story points.

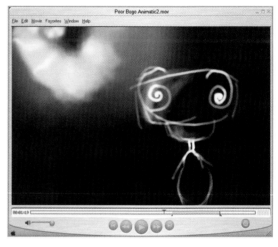

Figure 10.6
Although not as fully functional as the more expensive options, at $30 QuickTime Pro is a very cost-effective software solution for story reel assembly.

One of the simplest and potentially least expensive software packages you can use to create your 2D animatic is QuickTime Pro from Apple. This software allows you to assemble still images into video clips, and then combine these clips into a single large movie file containing all of your held storyboards and moving-camera clips. You can hold storyboard panels by copying a single image, and then pasting it sequentially enough times to create the desired hold time. For instance, if you are running your film at 24 frames per second, you can copy a single image and then paste it 23 times to create a one-second hold. You can create these holds as separate movie files with or without attached audio files, and then assemble them as an entire movie file. You can also cut, copy, and paste after you have assembled the shots. QuickTime Pro also allows you to insert, append, and layer audio tracks into an existing movie file. For a mere $30, this package offers a fair amount of editing capabilities and might serve your needs quite well, especially if your film is fairly short and simple (see Figure 10.6).

If your film will be rather long or you feel you will need to do a lot of fine adjustments to your shot timing and audio synching, you will probably want to invest in a more sophisticated piece of editing software such as Ulead VideoStudio ($100), Adobe Premiere ($400–700), Final Cut Pro ($999), or Avid Xpress Pro ($1,695) (see Figure 10.7). These packages allow you to drag and drop your images, clips, and audio tracks into a timeline to see a visual representation of your film as an assemblage of individual element blocks on single or multiple tracks. Having this visual chart of the puzzle pieces that will make up your entire animatic makes it easy and efficient to experiment with shot timing and audio synching. You can interactively shift, retime, trim, and layer individual frames, shots, lines of dialogue, or sound effects independently or in groups. You can also make global timing adjustments rather easily in

most of these packages. In addition to interactive editing functionality, several of these programs also allow you to create a variety of transition effects, including all manner of wipes and fades, as well as simple compositing effects, basic camera moves, and text overlays. Another advantage to most of these more sophisticated packages is that they give you the ability to change the pitch, tone, and length, as well as add dynamic volume curves and various effects to individual or groups of audio tracks. Most of these packages also allow you to record voiceovers while your clips actually play. With the more expensive packages, you can also create zooms and pans to simulate simple camera moves.

Those of you who are working with a Windows XP operating system might be happy to discover that a fairly substantial piece of NLE software, Windows Movie Maker, is already available to you for the low, low price of absolutely free (see Figure 10.8)! This package was likely included in the installation of your operating system, but if not, you can download it from Microsoft's Web site (http://www.microsoft.com).

Figure 10.7
More sophisticated non-linear editing packages, such as Adobe Premiere, offer additional functionality such as interactive clip adjustment, audio manipulation, simple compositing, and text overlays.

Movie Maker is an extremely intuitive piece of software that contains many of the features found in the more sophisticated and expensive NLE packages. You can insert, trim, split, combine, and assemble images or video clips on a time-line and then synch them up to sequential audio or music tracks. Wipes, fades, and basic video effects such as double time, film grain, and mirroring are also included, as well as the ability to capture videos directly from a camcorder. Although Movie Maker does not have the same level of advanced functionality as packages such as Premiere or Final Cut Pro, it is an extremely viable solution and if your operating system supports it, you certainly can't beat the price.

Visit the Web pages associated with the aforementioned products for more information, as well as opportunities to download demo videos and trial versions to determine which piece of software will suit your needs the best.

Figure 10.8
The Windows XP operating system includes its own very functional NLE package called Movie Maker.

Timing Adjustments and Sound Synching

As mentioned before, the 2D animatic stage is still in the realm of story land, so most of your attention should be focused on making sure your story is being told well in visual terms, rather than thinking too much about the details of shot staging or camera direction just yet.

Your main concern at this stage is to create a well-paced and efficiently structured whole. When it eventually comes time to layout, block, and animate your scenes, you will focus on the timing details of each shot independently, and then drop them into your evolving story reel to continue editing the overall structure of your entire film.

Once your held storyboards, video clips, and necessary dialogue, sound, or music tracks are assembled in your editing package, it is a simple matter of interactively shifting these puzzle pieces around and manipulating their lengths until your audio tracks are synched up effectively and this new moving-picture version of your story flows with effective and entertaining cinematic pacing.

If the flow of your story action is dictated by a piece of prerecorded music or a conversation that is already timed perfectly, then your audio synching will consist of shifting and scaling your visuals accordingly. If your visuals and your audio tracks will go hand in hand, expect to be bouncing back and forth quite a bit.

Assuming you are building your story reel with a piece of NLE software that offers interactive editing capabilities, play around with different timings and cuts until you are satisfied with the overall structure and pacing of your 2D animatic. Apply the same critical eye you used when you assembled your original storyboards on a large desk, wall, or floor space to analyze your entire story in visual terms. Look for continuity problems, line-of-action crossing, multiple shots that redundantly deliver the same story point, too many close-ups in a row, too much back and forth between wide shots and close-ups, and any other structure or flow issues that seem to stick out like sore thumbs. Make sure you focus on individual scenes as well as your entire animatic. Add, delete, erase, redraw, replace, trim, copy, paste, rescan, and retime your storyboard images and clips as necessary while it is still simple and inexpensive to do so, but watch out for new continuity issues that might come up as a result of adding or subtracting storyboard panels.

Experiment with as much reckless abandon as your creative juices will allow. To repeat one of our recurring mantras, the cost of revisions steadily increases as production continues, so do plenty of story structure and pacing experimentation at this stage, while it is still relatively simple and economical to change and perhaps replace your imagery and audio files. Once you enter the animation, lighting, rendering, and compositing stages of shot construction, it will no longer be quite so economical to make such changes, so make sure you are completely happy with the overall flow of your story reel before you move beyond the 2D animatic stage.

Again, maintain an attitude of flexibility and be willing to go back a few steps and change your storyboard drawings (or perhaps your actual script) if your analysis of your early story reel dictates that such measures are necessary to help you reach cinematic storytelling excellence. Don't let a plot hole or a structure problem remain just because you don't want to go back and rework your script. Fix such problems today; tomorrow it might be too late or too expensive to do so.

Also, if you are creating a film with dialogue or narration, take another pass at investigating the necessity of your vocal tracks at this initial stage of your story reel. Once you have assembled your 2D animatic, watch it several times without sound to see whether any shots (or for that matter, your entire film) will work as effectively with visuals alone. Perhaps a few extra boards or some clearer staging will make some of your intended dialogue tracks redundant and unnecessary. Although it might sound as if we are anti-dialogue, we prefer to think of ourselves as merely pro-simplicity. Dialogue might indeed be crucial to your story point delivery, but for the sake of economy and simplicity, take this opportunity to make sure all of your vocal tracks are absolutely necessary. Don't cut out a line of dialogue just because we are constantly recommending simplicity, but do consider carefully the necessity of each one.

Simulating Camera Moves

Using secondary frames and appropriate arrows, you can indicate future camera moves such as zooms, pans, and twists on your storyboard panels. A held storyboard image with such iconography will generally be sufficient in a 2D animatic; however, with a video camera or the right editing software, you can simulate rough versions of your intended camera moves, which will help you create a more cinematic early story reel. At this stage, the more cinematic information you can deliver rather than merely describe, the better (see Figure 10.9).

Figure 10.9
Zooming and panning with a camcorder or utilizing such features within certain editing packages will allow you to simulate basic camera moves in your animatic.

You can create such camera moves at the capture stage by using a camcorder or a digital still camera with movie mode. Arrange your camera-move–inclusive storyboard panel and adjust your camcorder lens so the initial image composition is framed properly. Then, while filming, zoom, twist, or pan toward the secondary frame or along the elongated panel until you reach the final shot composition indicated by the arrows on your storyboard. These moving storyboard panels will be added to your story reel as video clips and will provide rough approximations of your intended final camera direction.

If you are using sophisticated editing software such as Premiere, Final Cut Pro, or Avid Xpress Pro, you can include simple zooms and pans to held storyboard images so they become camera-move–inclusive video clips. StageTools also offers a package called Moving Picture ($199–268) with an extremely simple and intuitive interface for creating movie clips of animated zooms, pans, and twists layered on top of still images. Moving Picture is available as a standalone tool or as a plug-in for most NLE packages.

Videomatics

As an alternative to a 2D animatic made out of held storyboard drawings, some filmmakers prefer to initiate their story reels with videomatics. A *videomatic* is a rough, filmed version of a future animated short, in which live actors are videotaped performing most or all of the scenes and actions pertinent to the story (see Figure 10.10). You can also use pets, toys, puppets, or other props in place of or in addition to live actors. For instance, if a shot requires a character to fall from the top of a ladder, it would certainly be safer to use a dummy of some sort, rather than a real person.

Figure 10.10
An alternative to a 2D animatic made from storyboard drawings is a filmed animatic, especially if your sets are simple and your characters are human.

Videomatics are helpful for filmmakers who lack the means or desire to actually draw their storyboard panels. Videomatics can also work as future reference clips for animation, especially when the subject matter is realistic humans, which are very difficult to animate convincingly from one's imagination alone.

You can assemble the individual takes of a videomatic with your editing software in the same manner as you did storyboard images or clips. If you managed to videotape your entire story in a single take, you might find it beneficial to break it up into smaller clips so you can edit and audio synch them individually. Also, if you used a microphone during your tape sessions and you plan to use any dialogue or sound effects that were recorded, you will probably want to extract your audio track from your video, and then break it up into smaller bits. This way, it will be easier to shift, trim, clean up, replace, or otherwise manipulate the bits individually during the future editing passes of your story reel. Most NLE software packages allow you to extract audio tracks from filmed videos.

Show It to Someone

Unless your intention is to keep your film production a closely guarded secret, now is another excellent time to get some feedback on your progress. Without offering any explanations, historical information, or disclaimers (other than simply defining it as a rough cut), show your 2D animatic to a few select individuals and ask for their objective impressions of your film thus far. The main issues at this stage are structure, pacing, and continuity. Ask your viewers if the story flowed nicely and whether they were engaged and entertained. Were they bored or confused at any point? Did they notice any glaring plot holes? Was the ending too predictable or perhaps anticlimactic? Review their responses and consider initiating a subsequent editing pass to address any issues that might have come up. Just make sure you successfully balance the desire to please your audience with the need to maintain your own individual artistic vision.

Summary

A 2D animatic, which represents the initial stage of your evolving story reel, can be defined as storyboards plus timing and necessary audio. Consider cinematic details while creating a 2D animatic, but realize that this stage is still mainly focused on story elements. To create a 2D animatic, you will need your storyboards, any audio tracks that are crucial to initial story point delivery, a method of digitizing your boards, and a piece of editing software where your story reel will take flight. Whether your audio tracks will be dictating your story beats or simply enhancing your visuals will influence how you assemble and synch the individual elements of your 2D animatic. The elements that make up your story reel at this stage are simple and easy to alter or replace, so before you move on, take advantage of this early and interactive opportunity to experiment with the structure and pacing of your 2D animatic until you are certain that your story flow is clear and entertaining.

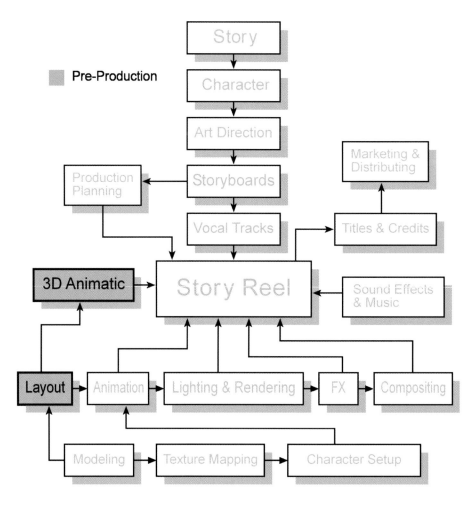

Pre-Production

Story

Character

Art Direction

Storyboards

Production Planning

Vocal Tracks

Marketing & Distributing

Titles & Credits

Story Reel

3D Animatic

Sound Effects & Music

Layout

Animation

Lighting & Rendering

FX

Compositing

Modeling

Texture Mapping

Character Setup

11. 3D Animatics, Layout, and Camera Direction

chapter 11
3D Animatics, Layout, and Camera Direction

Your story reel was initiated in the 2D animatic stage, where you mainly focused on story pacing and the discovery of how well your written or imagined script would work in visual terms. Now it's time to *extrude* your story reel into a 3D animatic, where you will add dimensionality and begin working out staging and camera direction issues.

"All the world's a stage."
William Shakespeare

Building a 3D Animatic

Stage one of your evolving story reel is your existing 2D animatic, which is a slideshow of 2D images held for story-appropriate durations and synched to necessary audio tracks. Stage two of your story reel's evolution involves replacing your 2D imagery with 3D versions that describe the overall placement and movement of your characters, props, and background elements, as well as camera posi-

Storyboards = Story + static imagery

2D animatic = Storyboards + timing + necessary audio

3D animatic = 2D animatic + spatial depth, staging, and camera direction

tioning and motion. These rough, three-dimensional, yet sometimes static versions of your shots are known as *layouts*. Once you have replaced all of the 2D storyboard images and video clips of your story reel with these individual shot layouts, you will have a completed 3D animatic of your entire film, where you can work out overall spatial flow and continuity. (See the 3D animatic from *El Arquero* on this book's DVD.)

As you traverse the dimensionality bridge from flat storyboard imagery to 3D shot layouts, you will likely discover that the initial frame counts you planned out in your 2D animatic might need to be tweaked a bit. Since you painstakingly worked out the continuity and timing issues of each shot in your 2D animatic stage until you arrived at effective and entertaining story pacing, you will certainly want to make every attempt to keep your initial frame counts unchanged in your 3D layouts. However, realize that with the dimensionality upgrade, new cinematic information will be revealed which might require you to shorten or lengthen a few shots to make them work successfully in 3D space. If you are building your story reel using a decent piece of NLE software, this should not be a major issue because it is very easy to shift video and audio tracks around to accommodate new shot lengths. Remember that CG film production typically involves some degree of constant editing, so be prepared to nip and tuck your story reel now and again as your individual shots evolve. However, if the structure and pacing of your film are being dictated by a pre-recorded music track or a perfectly timed dialogue sequence, then you obviously need to stick with the shot lengths defined in your 2D animatic.

Keep in mind that in the 3D animatic stage, you should not concern yourself with performance or lighting issues just yet. Shot staging and camera direction are the priority, while animation and lighting are very basic. If a bit of detail in either of these areas is crucial to story point delivery at this early stage, then you will need to do a bit of refining where necessary, but for the most part, default lighting and simple global character positioning and trajectories should suffice.

With the addition of dimensionality, scene staging, and actual camera direction, your 3D animatic will bring you that much closer to your final film. But when it comes time to fully animate your characters and objects, you might find yourself making changes to the staging and camera work that you set down here at the 3D animatic stage. Be confident about the cinematic decisions you make at this stage, but don't be surprised if your film turns out a bit differently in the end (see Figure 11.1).

Layout refers to the initial stage of an actual CG shot, where the position and basic trajectories of your objects, characters, and cameras are initially worked out on a virtual stage. A *3D animatic* is the second phase of your evolving story reel, consisting of sequential shot layouts synched to necessary audio.

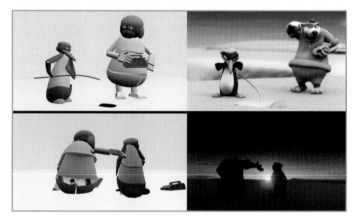

Figure 11.1
The staging and camera direction of your initial shot layouts may or may not exactly match that of your final renders.

Creating Individual Shot Layouts

A *shot layout* is a very rough three-dimensional representation of the staging and camera direction of a particular story action, in which the scene elements are typically made up of simple placeholder models. After a shot passes the layout stage, the simple, animatic versions of your digital scene elements will be replaced with your actual background objects, props, and character puppets, which will then be fully animated. A shot layout will display the minimum amount of information necessary to indicate the intended placement and rough movement of your objects, characters, and cameras. The initial layout version of a given shot will contain two basic elements:

◆ Placement and overall trajectories of scene objects and characters

◆ Placement and movement of the camera

Stage Setup

Before you decide on camera placement, there must be something for your digital lens to focus on. Using your chosen CG package, create preliminary virtual stages where the action of each scene will take place.

You only need to include those scene elements that are crucial to preliminary shot staging. Objects that can be classified as fine details are generally left out. Typically, the digital elements that exist in this stage are simple, low-resolution, placeholder versions of your final object models and character puppets. Often, basic primitive models or simple combinations will be sufficient. A house could be a cube, a car could be represented by an elongated cube for the body with two horizontal cylinders for the wheels, and a character could be a tall, rectangular cube with a sphere on top (see Figure 11.2).

Figure 11.2
Low-resolution, placeholder versions of scene objects and characters are typically sufficient for shot layouts.

However, you might find it difficult to work out your staging issues unless you use more refined versions of your objects and character models. If this is the case, then jump ahead to the modeling chapter before returning here to set up your virtual scene stages. Similarly, you might feel that it is crucial to be able to pose your characters to initially stage your shots effectively. If so, then you need to set up your character models as digital puppets before you assemble your shot layouts (see Chapter 14, "Character Setup").

Within your CG package, assemble and place your layout-appropriate background objects, props, and characters based on the preliminary staging you envisioned and described during your storyboarding stage. If you were happy with the overall look of your 2D animatic, then you'll obviously want to try to recreate the staging and composition indicated by your initial drawings, but don't be surprised if you find you need to assemble slightly or significantly different scene layouts here, now that the element of dimensionality has been added to the mix. Make sure that the digital elements of your virtual stages are assembled so you can choose a camera angle that will most effectively tell the story of each shot. For instance, don't hide the focal point of a shot behind less important objects unless obscurity is your intent (see Figure 11.3).

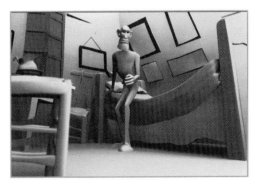

Figure 11.3
Assemble your scene elements logically so you can place your cameras effectively.

Basic Object and Character Movement

Once you have your simple, digital elements placed in their story-appropriate positions on your virtual stages, some of them might need to traverse or rotate over the course of a given shot to effectively deliver its story point.

The first step will be to establish a shot length. Set your timeline appropriately in your CG scene file, based on the timing indicated in your story reel. If the 2D animatic image representing your current shot was held for two seconds, then assuming you are working at 24 frames per second, you will need 48 frames in your timeline.

Once you start working out the basic movements of your scene elements, you might find that your previously established frame counts are not sufficient for the action that will take place in a given shot. For instance, you might have a shot where your villain falls off a cliff, and you estimated that it would take one second for him to hit the ground so you held your storyboard image for 24 frames. However, when you actually assemble this shot as a 3D layout and drop your simple CG villain model from atop your virtual cliff, you might discover that one second seems too fast and that two seconds looks a lot better.

After you establish an appropriate frame count for a given shot based on the preliminary movements of your scene elements, it is always a good idea to give yourself a bit of margin-of-error padding by adding *frame handles* to your timeline. Handles are a few extra frames at the beginning and end of a shot that will give it some room to grow if the need arises. When you drop a layout shot into your story reel to replace a held storyboard image, you might find it necessary to shorten or lengthen the shot by a few frames for the sake of pacing and continuity. Obviously shortening is always an option, but having a few extra frames at both ends of a shot will give you an opportunity to experiment with slightly shifted or elongated shot lengths and different cut points during your subsequent editing sessions. Four or eight frame handles are typical.

When it comes to indicating the basic trajectories of your placeholder scene elements, keep things as simple as possible. It will typically be sufficient to establish and keyframe (see Chapter 16, "Animation") the initial location and orientation of an object or character at the first frame of a shot, then place and keyframe a new position at the end frame and let the computer generate the trajectory in between. If the movement of a scene element is a bit more complex than simply translating from here to there, you might need a few additional key frames in the middle of your shot to describe the trajectory sufficiently (see Figure 11.4). But don't get carried away with details at this stage. The most important pieces of information are the position and orientation of your moving scene elements at the start and end of each shot. The details in between should only be described if they are necessary for you to effectively define the staging and camera direction of the shot.

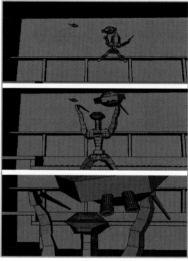

Figure 11.4
Keep your object and character trajectories as simple as possible at this stage.

Which Comes First—the Animation "Chicken" or the Camera "Egg"?

When you are adding a CG element to a previously filmed live-action background clip, as is the case in most visual effects pipelines, the director and his team will typically establish the cameras angle and movement before the digital animator gets involved. Then, to maintain consistency with the staging of the background plates and to make sure that the added CG elements look spatially correct, the animator is generally forbidden to touch the digital camera that was manipulated and keyframed to exactly match the position and movement of its live-action counterpart. If after adding a digital element and establishing its preliminary movement it is discovered that the shot needs to be shortened or lengthened a bit, the animator can attempt to request such a change and, if the director approves it and any necessary handle frames exist, the editor can apply the timing adjustment. However, in a visual effects scenario, changing the angle or movement of the camera based on the needs of the animator almost never happens.

Here in the world of CG short film production, however, your objects and characters (as well as your cameras) exist in the digital realm—and after all, you are both director and animation supervisor. Therefore, you can achieve effective shot staging by jumping back and forth between camera direction and scene element movement.

But which should come first—object and character trajectories or camera positioning and movement (see Figure 11.5)? Well, sometimes one and sometimes the other. It basically depends on the specifics of the shot at hand and how you choose to work. For a shot that follows the movement of a flying dragon, it will probably be appropriate to establish the creature's trajectory first, and then figure out how the camera should track it. In a shot where it is important to show the boundaries of a room, it might make sense to choose an appropriate camera angle that stages the room effectively, and then move your characters around as needed.

It typically makes sense for most shots to proceed in the following order:

1. Establish the positions and trajectories of scene elements with placeholder objects and characters here in the layout stage.

2. Choose an appropriate camera angle that effectively stages the beginning of the shot. Then, as the shot progresses and the scene elements move around, either leave the camera in place, reposition, or animate it as necessary to maintain effective staging.

3. Refine the movement of your characters and objects in the animation stage.

4. Make necessary final adjustments to camera angles and movements based on any staging differences that might have resulted from your animation refinements.

When you reach the animation stage and refine the basic posing and movements of your characters and scene objects, try to stick with the staging you established here in the layout stage. Because you are the director, you typically don't need anyone else's permission to change the length of a shot or adjust a camera angle or move, but make sure you have a good editing- or staging-based reason to do so. While you do have the option of jumping back and forth between camera direction and character movement as many times as needed, at some point you should try to lock down one or the other so you don't find yourself in an endless loop.

If your film will involve combining filmed background plates with digital characters and objects, be sure to take down as much information as possible from your live action sets because you will need to build virtual versions of your stages and cameras within your CG package so the perspectives match. Measure the height of the camera from the ground as well as its distance from various scene objects. Also record camera lens information, as well as the dimensions and relative distances of any and all physical scene objects. Then, when you create your CG scene files, you will accurately build and position the camera and any necessary digital objects so your character movements and their cast shadows will work visually and spatially with your filmed background images that will be projected behind them. This process is known as *matchmoving*.

Figure 11.5
Should animation lead or follow camera direction?

Once you are happy with the position and movement of the camera in a given shot, *lock* its attributes so you don't inadvertently "bump" it while animating your characters and scene objects.

11. 3D Animatics, Layout, and Camera Direction

Instead of working out object movement and camera direction on an individual shot-by-shot basis, sometimes it makes more sense to work out the action of an entire story beat or sequence, and then break it up into different shots. An example of this might be a complicated chase scene where a policeman pursues an escaped convict as he quickly maneuvers through a suburban neighborhood, jumping fences, entering and exiting houses, and crossing busy streets. You might want to figure out the basic trajectories of the two characters for the entire chase scene, and then cut it up into various shots—some from the policeman's point of view, some from the convict's point of view, some wide shots where both characters can be seen, some close-ups to reveal the determination on each opponent's face, and perhaps a low shot as the runners leap over a sleeping dog.

Camera Direction

After you have assembled your scene elements and established their basic trajectories, the next step is to place your digital camera and move it appropriately to deliver the story beat of the current shot as clearly and effectively as possible with appropriate cinematic style.

There are two basic types of camera setups.

- ◆ Lock-offs
- ◆ Moves

A *lock-off* is the simplest form of camera setup, where the position and angle remain fixed for the duration of a single shot. A *camera move*, of course, involves rotating, translating, and/or zooming the camera while the shot progresses. The necessary staging and your particular cinematic style will dictate the type of camera action you will choose for any given shot. In general, it is a good idea to mix things up a bit. A film consisting of only lock-off shots might feel a bit dull. A film where the camera never stops moving can sometimes feel a bit unnatural and perhaps somewhat unsettling.

Try not to get too carried away with camera moves. It is tempting to create big, crazy, sweeping camera moves simply because it is very easy to do so in CG, but remember that just because you can do something doesn't necessarily mean you should. If your camera needs to follow a jet-fighter chasing an elusive spacecraft or you want to create the feeling of imbalance or nausea, then by all means set your camera at odd angles and fly it all around to your heart's content; however, most of the time camera moves should be rather subtle. Watch live-action films to see how little the camera generally moves. Of course, this is partially due to the fact that a real camera is a lot heavier and more cumbersome to move around than its digital counterpart, but just make sure that if you do add exaggerated camera moves, you are doing so to support or add necessary mood to a given story point, not simply because you can.

Figure 11.6
Try the same shot from various camera angles.

After you establish the basic positioning and trajectories of your scene elements, take advantage of the fact that you are working on a digital stage (rather than a real-world movie set) by experimenting with various camera angles and moves until you find one that delivers the given shot with clear and entertaining effectiveness (see Figure 11.6). Try the same shot from a low angle as well as a high angle. Try a static camera and a moving camera. Try subtle as well as exaggerated camera moves.

If you are not sure what will ultimately be the best staging for a particular shot, assemble and render multiple *takes* of the same action with slightly or significantly different camera positions and movements. That way, you will have several choices so you can pick just the right one that hooks up properly with its neighbors during your next editing pass. Another advantage of having multiple takes of a given shot is that it will allow you to create overlaps, where an action is repeated from one shot to the next, if your cinematic style requires this type of continuity. If you do create more than one take of a particular shot, make sure you give your scene files and renders descriptive names so you know which one is which. For instance, you might name them LM02_anim_lowerPOV_v6 and LM02_anim_higherPOV_v7.

Point of View

Point of view is the first thing to decide when you are placing a camera. From whose perspective is the shot playing out? Typically, the point of view will come from one of three places:

◆ A participant
◆ A witness
◆ An objective observer

A *participant* is someone who is directly involved in the story action. The point of view would either be through his eyes or over his shoulder. Looking through the eyes of a story character is a technique often used in horror films to increase audience empathy. Over-the-shoulder shots are common during conversations.

A *witness* perspective comes from someone who is, or could possibly be, physically present in the scene but is not actually participating in the story action. For example, a witness perspective might be the point of view from an audience member watching a tennis match or a cameraman trying to keep up with someone running down a crowded city sidewalk.

An *objective observer* is not a member of the story action and can therefore be placed anywhere in space to stage the shot with the utmost clarity and entertainment value. Examples might be the view from above a room that ignores the existence of a ceiling, an omniscient cameraman who frames in on the final destination of a moving object before it actually arrives, or a physically impossible camera move that follows a flying bumblebee.

Focal Point, Framing, and Composition

Once you have decided on the identity of the camera's "eye," then think about where this subjective or objective observer might be sitting, standing, floating, or flying.

Consider the focal point of the shot. Typically, you would want to stage a shot so that the focal point is clearly visible. Exceptions might be during a chase scene, when it may feel more natural to lose the focal point on occasion, or when you are looking through the eyes of a frightened victim who is looking around a forest to find the source of that horrible sound, when the viewer should feel lost and confused.

Imagine you are at a baseball game and you have the ability to place and move your point of view wherever you please to follow the action clearly and improve the overall entertainment value of your experience. During a pitch, you might choose to stand behind the catcher and see the ball coming right at you. Or you might want to follow the ball as it leaves the pitcher's hand and flies toward the batter. After a good hit, you might want to pull back to see the whole diamond and all the runners at the same time. After a homerun is hit, you might want to zoom in on the batter's face to see his reaction, and then cut over to the bleachers to see a fan catch the ball and then wrestle with his neighbors over its possession.

Apply the same thought process to the shots in your film. Think of a particular story action or shot, and then close your eyes to envision it playing out before you, imagining the best point of view to follow the action clearly and with effective style. If you have a shot in which a father is scolding his child, you might look over Dad's shoulder to see Junior's reaction, look empathetically through Junior's eyes to deliver a first-person account of Dad's anger, or pull out a bit wider to see both characters at the same time from the side or from above.

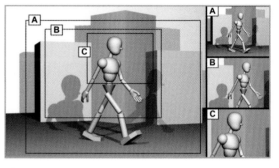

Figure 11.7
How much of a given virtual stage should be framed?

Framing involves deciding just how much of a given scene should visually fit within the rectangular frame of the screen (see Figure 11.7). A shot's framing might simply include a character's head or an entire crowd scene. After you have assembled your scene elements, experiment with different framings to decide just how much visual information you want to deliver.

Be sure to consider other basic concepts of composition when you are laying out your scene elements and choosing your camera perspective and angles. A few examples include

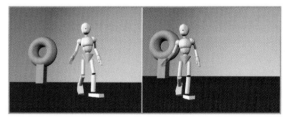

Figure 11.8
Consider negative and positive space when composing your shots.

◆ **Negative space.** Balance the filled and empty spaces of your compositions for clarity and simplicity (see Figure 11.8).

◆ **Silhouette.** Even if you create color, lighting, style, or blur differences between your foreground and background elements, your film might ultimately get shown in a wide variety of venues with different exposure levels and print qualities where your subtle separation techniques might be less effective. Paying attention to a scene's silhouette will ensure that your story actions will read clearly in all display formats (see Figure 11.9).

◆ **Dimensionality.** Embrace the fact that you are working in a three-dimensional realm by utilizing overlap and perspective to create depth in your scenes. Flat compositions are typically less interesting and feel less natural than those with a bit of angle and depth (see Figure 11.10).

◆ **Rule of thirds.** A common but not necessarily hard-and-fast rule of composition states that dividing a screen into thirds and then placing important subjects at the line intersections will result in well-balanced compositions (see Figure 11.11). Consider this "rule," but like everything else, don't apply it blindly.

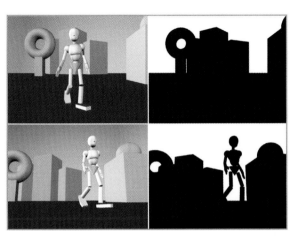

Figure 11.9
Turn off all the lights in your scene file to analyze the clarity of a given shot's silhouette.

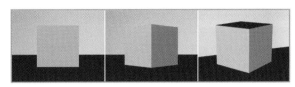

Figure 11.10
Avoid flat compositions. Use slight or significant angles to increase dimensionality.

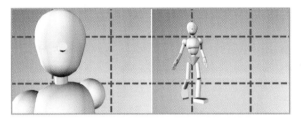

Figure 11.11
The rule of thirds

Shot Types

As we briefly described with flat storyboard images in Chapter 5, there are a number of standard shot types to choose from with regard to position, zoom level, and camera angle. A few examples include

◆ **Close-ups.** These shots hone in on a focal point. A standard close-up might display a character's face, while an extreme close-up might fill the frame with just his eyes (see Figure 11.12).

◆ **Medium shots.** These shots might frame one or two actors from the waist up (see Figure 11.13).

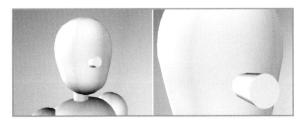

Figure 11.12
Close-ups and extreme close-ups

Figure 11.13
Medium, long, and extreme long shots

11. 3D Animatics, Layout, and Camera Direction

239

◆ **Long shots.** These shots show an entire figure and a good portion of the background. An extreme long shot would show a landscape or a cityscape (see Figure 11.13).

◆ **Point-of-view shots.** These shots see the world through the eyes of a character (see Figure 11.14).

◆ **Over-the-shoulder shots.** These shots are self-explanatory (see Figure 11.14).

◆ **Bird's eye shots.** These shots look down upon a story action (see Figure 11.15).

◆ **Worm's eye shots.** These shots look up from a very low point of view (see Figure 11.15).

◆ **Wide shots.** These shots simulate a wide-angle camera lens, where the viewer is closer to the action than in a long shot, but more of the scene is visible because of the exaggerated perspective (see Figure 11.16).

◆ **Skewed shots.** These shots have an angled point of view, as if the viewer has tilted his head to one side (see Figure 11.17).

Of course, point of view, composition, zoom level, or lens angle can change while a shot plays out, which brings us to….

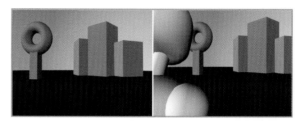

Figure 11.14
Point-of-view and over-the-shoulder shots

Figure 11.15
Bird's eye and worm's eye shots

Figure 11.16
Wide-angle shots

Figure 11.17
Skewed shots

Camera Moves

Camera moves can be separated into four basic classifications.

◆ Fixed rotations ◆ Zooms

◆ Translations ◆ Combinations

Fixed rotation shots involve the camera rotating but not moving.

◆ A *pan* is where the camera rotates horizontally about its Y(up)-axis. A pan is often used to reveal the full expanse of a wide landscape (see Figure 11.18).

◆ A *tilt* is where the camera pivots up or down by rotating about its X-axis—for instance, looking through a character's eyes as he stands in one place and gradually looks up toward the top of a skyscraper (see Figure 11.18). Pans and tilts are often used when the subject matter of a scene will not fit within the framing of your camera lens, so it would be necessary to look left and right or up and down to reveal more of the setting to your audience. Also, be wary of panning and tilting too fast because this will cause a strobing effect, which may or may not be desirable.

◆ A *roll* is a rotation around the Z-axis, often used in action-based, point-of-view shots to increase the feeling of vertigo (see Figure 11.19).

Translations are where the camera actually moves from one position to another.

◆ A *track* is where a camera moves perpendicular to the camera lens axis, either side to side or up and down (see Figure 11.20). If a character is walking down the street, you can follow his movement by tracking alongside him or by fixing the camera in one spot and panning at the right speed to keep him in frame.

◆ A *dolly* is where the camera physically moves forward or backward, toward or away from a target. Dolly moves are often used with point-of-view or follow perspectives in which a character is walking, running, driving, or flying (see Figure 11.21).

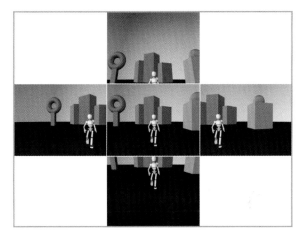

Figure 11.18
Pans and tilts

Figure 11.19
Rolls

Figure 11.20
Tracks

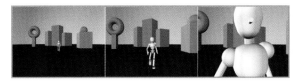

Figure 11.21
Dollies

A *zoom* is where the camera changes focal length to hone in on a detail or to reveal more of the scene (see Figure 11.22). A zoom is similar to a dolly, but in a zoom, the lens angle changes from wide to close-up or vice versa while the camera stays in place, whereas in a dolly, the camera actually moves.

Figure 11.22
Zooms

Combinations utilize more than one of these classifications in the same camera move. For example:

◆ A *dolly-pan* involves the camera moving forward or backward while rotating about its vertical axis. An example might be a point-of-view shot of a character walking while turning his head to look behind him.

◆ A *crane shot* involves any combination of translating and rotating, where the camera levitates or flies around as necessary to follow an action or dynamically change perspective for the sake of style. An example might be swinging from a worm's eye POV to a bird's eye POV (see Figure 11.23).

◆ A *dolly-zoom* is where the camera translates forward while simultaneously zooming out or vice versa. This effect is often used in horror films to create a surreal visual, where a character's framing remains the same while the perspective angle changes (see Figure 11.24).

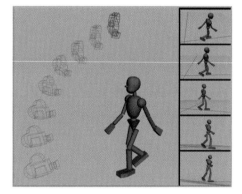

Figure 11.23
Crane shots

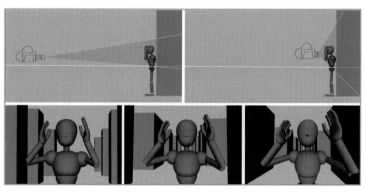

Figure 11.24
Dolly-zooms

Setting Up and Animating a Digital Camera

To effectively frame and follow the action of your virtual stage layouts, you will need digital cameras that can be translated, rotated, and zoomed with ease and precision. A default CG camera will typically be a single object that can be translated and rotated, with additional attributes for details such as focal length (see Figure 11.25).

Such cameras are typically sufficient for most shots, but sometimes it might be necessary to improve upon their setup and functionality in order to control them effectively and efficiently. For instance, if you want a camera to remain fixed on a particular subject while either element moves around in space, a two-node camera is a good idea, where a target exists and the camera is aim-constrained to always point in its direction.

A third, up-vector node is sometimes added to this camera-and-target setup so the twist and roll of the camera can be controlled (see Figure 11.26).

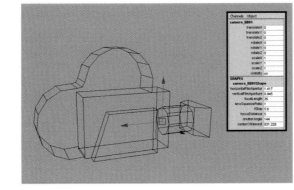

Figure 11.25
A typical one-node camera

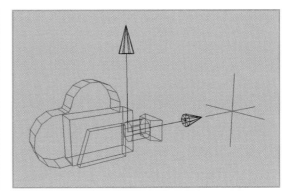

Figure 11.26
A camera with an aim-constraint target and an up-vector control

Digital camera setups might require a more complicated hierarchy of nodes and constraints depending on the needs of a given shot. For instance, imagine you are animating a witch on a broomstick and you want the camera to spin around her while she flies. You could create a master node that will be attached to the witch, and then make the camera a child of this object. You could also aim-constrain the camera to its parent so that when you spin this master node around, the camera will fly in a circle around the witch while keeping her in frame (see Figure 11.27). You could also simultaneously move the camera up and down to make the scene a bit more dynamic.

In scenes that require lip-synching, it is a good idea to create a face camera that will be attached to a character's head via parenting or appropriate constraints. That way, you will always have a framed view of your character's face available in a secondary window, no matter how complicated the action of the scene might be.

As you move your digital camera around, it is sometimes a good idea to imagine that a real cameraman is staging and following your story action. Because real cameras are typically somewhat heavy, it often feels more natural for them to ease out, slow in, and perhaps settle a bit, rather than starting and stopping effortlessly on a dime. You might also want to simulate a handheld feel by adding a bit of randomness and shake to your camera while it

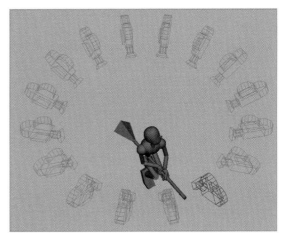

Figure 11.27
More complex camera hierarchies might be necessary for certain shots.

tracks and dollies. However, keep in mind that adding high-frequency shakes and jitters to your CG camera might make it difficult for you to focus on character movement and performance. Therefore, it is often preferable to apply *2D post-camera moves* to your rendered frames instead. (See Chapter 20, "Compositing.")

11. 3D Animatics, Layout, and Camera Direction

Also imagine that your simulated real-world camera operator will invariably suffer from human error. He might follow just behind the action on occasion or sometimes actually anticipate it. Overshooting will occur once in a while as well—this is when a tracked, moving object stops abruptly but the camera keeps traveling in the same direction for a beat before suddenly realizing that the subject of the shot has been left behind, and thus the action must be reframed by moving the camera back or by cutting to a new shot. Adding such real-world imperfections can help to make your shots feel more natural.

Also remember that you are working in a 3D realm, so whenever appropriate, take advantage of this fact by moving your camera in and out, rather than simply up and down and side to side. Of course, don't overdo it by arbitrarily creating big, sweeping crane shots just for the heck of it. Honor the "rules" of picture composition and cinematography, which include subtlety and simplicity, but try to deliver an appropriately three-dimensional experience to your audience.

Layout Rendering

Once you have a virtual stage layout assembled with your scene elements, characters, and cameras positioned and moving around properly, you will need to create 3D renders that you can use as clips in your evolving story reel.

Generally, you will not need to set up any lights for your layout scenes unless it is absolutely crucial to do so at this stage. For instance, if it is important for a preliminary shot layout to look ominous in order for you to decide on prop and character placement, you might want to add a low light source to help send that message. Images and video clips of your shot layouts will typically be hardware-rendered with default lighting (see Chapter 18, "Lighting and Rendering") for the sake of speed and simplicity.

A rendered shot will either be a series of individual frames or a movie clip. Most NLE software packages are able to import either format, but it is typically a bit more efficient to create movie clips because you will have fewer individual files to organize and track.

Depending on how you proportion your working camera view window while laying out and animating your scenes within your CG package, the height and width of your frame may or may not correspond to that of your chosen render format. For instance, your CG modeling window might be a perfect square, while you plan on rendering wide-screen images. As a working guideline, it is helpful to create an appropriately sized and pro-portioned rectangular line object, known as a *reticle*, which will be connected to your camera (see Figure 11.28). Also check to see whether your CG software package features *film-gate* or *safe-area* displays that will indicate the parts of your screen imagery that will be guaranteed to fit onscreen. That way, you can compose your virtual stages accurately so you don't inadvertently cut off the display of any important scene elements when you render your shots at their final aspect ratios.

You might, however, choose to render full-frame images, and then crop them down to the desired sizes and proportions after the fact, using a program such as DeBabelizer

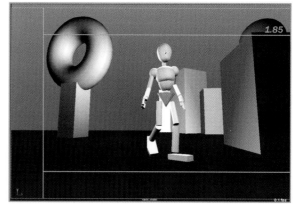

Figure 11.28
Build a reticle object and attach it to your camera to describe the actual aspect ratio of the final framing that you will ultimately deliver.

11. 3D Animatics, Layout, and Camera Direction

or Photoshop. An advantage of rendering expanded, full-frame images is that you will have the opportunity to recompose or add any necessary post-camera drifts or shakes to your final imagery (see Chapter 22).

Editing

As previously mentioned, during the course of your production you will repeatedly return to your software-based editing bay to refine the assembly of your individual shots into an effectively structured and well-paced cinematic whole.

When you initiated your story reel as a 2D animatic, your priority was story elements rather than cinematic details, mainly because you were working with flat drawings that merely suggested your plans for scene assembly, camera direction, and animation. There was simply not enough visual information for you to focus on actual cinematic details just yet. Here at the 3D animatic stage of your story reel's evolution, you use actual 3D scene layouts that describe basic object, character, and camera positioning and movement, so cinematic details, such as staging and continuity, become the priority.

To arrive at effective cinematic flow, you must consider the forest as well as the trees. This is done by jumping back and forth between your software-based editing bay and your individual shot layouts. As you work out the positions and movements of your scene elements in your individual shot layouts, it is important to think about how each one will cut together with its neighbors. Then, in your editing bay, watch your shots in sequence and adjust shot lengths and cut points on your evolving story reel or, if necessary, go back to your CG software to tweak the staging and camera direction details of individual shots before you re-render and cut them back in.

Each time you re-edit your story reel and play it back, try to watch it as if you were seeing it for the first time in order to analyze it with as much objectivity as possible. Editing can be thought of as the art of shot assembly, and it involves the following fundamental elements:

◆ Rhythm and timing   ◆ Continuity   ◆ Cuts and transitions

Rhythm and Timing

Like a piece of music, the rhythm and timing of your shot assembly will dictate the overall dramatic pacing and style of your sequences, as well as your entire film. If you are creating a dynamic, high-energy action film or sequence, you will probably want to cut from shot to shot rapidly and only hold on individual shots for long periods of time if the camera is tracking a moving object or character. That way, the audience's perspective will continuously (and often abruptly) change, so they will need to pay close attention to keep up with the action. If tranquility is your intention, you will probably linger on individual shots much longer, moving the camera slowly and gently if at all (see Figure 11.29).

Figure 11.29
Fast action films will typically cut quickly and abruptly between shots with dynamic camera moves, while more tranquil films will have longer shots with gentle camera moves.

You should hold an individual shot long enough to deliver the story point, but short enough to keep the story moving with appropriate pacing. Hold a shot for a long time if you want to give your viewers time to think or scan all of the details of the setting. Use short hold times for action sequences in which you want to keep your audience members of the edges of their seats. Realize that any shot that is less than a quarter of a second or so in length will pretty much only read subliminally, so only use such rapid-fire hold times when there is a good reason to disorient or confuse your audience.

Also be wary of metronomic timing. If every shot in your film holds for exactly three seconds, it might feel a bit dull. Give your film more interesting overall rhythm by breaking up your shot lengths—a few quick shots, then a slower one to give your audience a moment to catch up.

Continuity

In terms of visual flow, continuity is the notion that individual shots in a sequence should connect logically with regard to the position and trajectory of scene elements. Perfect continuity will link shots in such a way that the viewer will not be conscious of the cuts and the movement of your camera and scene elements will appear seamless.

The placement and orientation of your scene elements should make sense between shots. If a character is holding a coffee mug with his right hand in one shot, he shouldn't be holding it with his left hand in the next shot (unless you've indicated the switch somehow).

When an object or character is moving, the action should feel like it continues logically from one shot to the next. If a character is pushing open a door to enter a room, and then you cut to the room's interior, facing the character as he enters, he should not be pulling the door open. If Bill and Jill are facing each other and Bill decides to exit the scene by walking off to his right, and then you then cut to a shot where Jill watches Bill leave, it would not make sense for her head to turn to her right because this motion would not follow Bill spatially (see Figure 11.30).

Figure 11.30
Be wary of continuity errors like this one, where the second character turns his head in the wrong direction.

Also pay attention to the 180-degree rule. In most shots, an invisible line will exist between characters or along a character or object's gaze direction or actual trajectory. If your virtual camera abruptly moves from one side of the line to the other between shots, confusing discontinuity may result. If a character is flying from screen left to screen right in one shot, don't reverse his travel direction in the subsequent shot if he is meant to be continuing along the same path. If the character does indeed reverse directions, it would make sense to see the turn at the end of the first shot, at the beginning of the second shot, or in a new shot that sits between the two (see Figure 11.31).

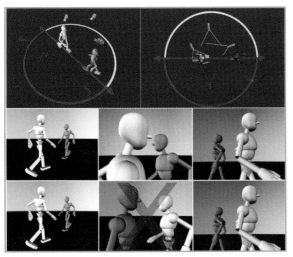

Figure 11.31
Crossing the line of action from shot to shot can be confusing.

Figure 11.32
Feature the scene element that best reveals the story action in each shot.

Cuts and Transitions

When and where to cut from one shot to the next is crucial for effective visual flow. Cutting to a new shot is appropriate when you need to improve the current staging of a story action, change the ownership of the current point of view, take the audience's attention to another place or event, alter the mood of the scene, or deliberately disorient your viewers. The action of one shot might also motivate a cut, such as when a character points to something off screen.

Consider the most revealing element at any given moment in a story action (see Figure 11.32). If Skippy throws a rock at Old Man Potter's living room window, it might not be very interesting to simply present the entire action from a single, wide shot with Skippy on one side of frame and Potter's house on the other. It would probably be more cinematic to start from a shot that shows Skippy throwing the rock, perhaps from an over-the-shoulder point of view; then cut to a side or tracking shot of the rock flying through space; and then perhaps frame the window, waiting for the rock to crash through it. Then you might cut to Old Man Potter's face as he looks up in surprise from his dinner. Whichever element best reveals the story action at any given point should typically be the focal point of the current shot, be it Skippy, the rock, the window, or Mr. Potter.

The general rule is to try to cut to a new shot at the exact moment when you think your audience will feel the need to see the action from an alternative point of view. If for no apparent reason Mr. Potter suddenly looks toward the next room because he heard a loud crash, the audience will probably want to know why. Then you can decide whether to show the source of the noise or keep the audience in the dark a bit longer while Mr. Potter hides under the table and calls 911.

In an action sequence, you should cut to a new shot when it is no longer possible to stage the action effectively from the current point of view, no matter how much you rotate or translate the camera. If a character runs out of frame, you will probably want to cut to a new perspective rather soon unless there is some good reason to linger on the scene he left behind.

To keep up the pace of an action sequence, it is often a good idea to cut in the middle of a character or object's movement. If Bill is falling down a flight of stairs and you stage a side view shot in which he tumbles from upper screen left to lower screen right, it will typically be more dynamic to cut to the next shot just as Bill begins to break frame, rather than waiting for him to fully exit, which may cause a break in continuity.

Overlapping an action can be effective when you want to emphasize a particular story point. If Bill recovers from his tumble at the last second by performing a flawless midair somersault, but then slips on the oriental rug at the bottom of the stairs as he makes his would-be-perfect landing and crashes into the glass coffee table, it might be fun to show the table crash two or three times from various angles to emphasize the severity of the impact. However, overlapping should be utilized sparingly; as with every extreme cinematic technique, overuse will diminish its effectiveness.

Types of Cuts

There are a number of standard cut types that filmmakers use regularly. A few examples include

◆ **Cut in.** This is a quick shot that cuts away from the main action to provide a close-up of an object that is somehow related to the story point of the sequence.

◆ **Cutaway.** This type of shot is often used to suggest the passage of time, where the director cuts away from the main action and then returns.

◆ **Cross cutting.** This is a series of cutaways and cutbacks in which alternating views of different actions are mixed together sequentially, describing two different situations that are somehow related. This technique creates the feeling of being in two places at one time and also works to build suspense. You might also use cross cutting to alternate between different views of the same action to reveal how multiple characters might witness the scene.

◆ **Match cut.** This type of shot shows the continuity of action by showing its start in one shot and its follow-through in the next shot. For example, imagine a close-up of a hand pulling on the interior handle of a car door in one shot, and then a wider, outside shot of the door slamming shut.

◆ **Shot-reverse-reaction.** This is a sequence of three shots. The first shot is a person's face, the second shot is what that person is looking at, and the final shot is another look at the person's face to reveal how he or she feels about or reacts to the scene revealed in the second shot (see Figure 11.33).

Figure 11.33
A shot-reverse-reaction sequence

◆ **Establishing.** This is a general wide shot used to describe where a story action is going to take place so that when the staging cuts to a close-up, the audience is aware of the setting.

◆ **Jump cut.** This type of shot occurs when two shots are mismatched in space or time and the transition between the two shots feels abrupt or awkward. The audience must pause a moment to figure out what happened between shots 1 and 2. Many directors feel that jump cuts are to be avoided, but others incorporate them as stylistic devices.

Types of Transitions

In addition to deciding when to cut from one shot to another, it is important to decide how to make the transition. Should you use an immediate cut or something a bit more dynamic? An immediate cut is certainly the simplest and most common, but implementation of other transitions such as dissolves, wipes, or fades (either here or in the compositing stage) may add to the style of your film and can also help to imply the passage of time or a change in locale.

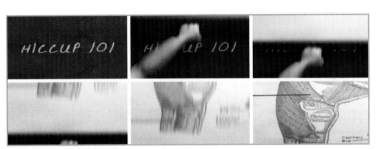

Figure 11.34
An example of a wipe

Sound can also play a part in such transitions. For instance, toward the end of shot A, the music that corresponds to shot B might begin to fade in to help link the two shots more smoothly.

The three most common types of non-immediate shot transitions are

◆ **Wipe.** This is a gradual spatial transition from one image to another, in which one image is replaced by another by means of a moving edge or shape that reveals the new shot, such as an overlapping horizontal, vertical, or diagonal translation, the expansion of a circle, or the turning of a page (see Figure 11.34). Using wipes is often considered a stylistic choice, which inherently makes the audience more aware that they are watching a film. The *Star Wars* films make regular use of this technique.

◆ **Fade.** This refers to the gradual disappearance or emergence of an image, typically to or from solid black.

◆ **Dissolve.** This is a soft, gradual transition from one shot to the next, in which the preceding shot fades away as the following image simultaneously fades in (see Figure 11.35).

Figure 11.35
A cross-dissolve is a popular type of shot transition.

Economy

Remember that you are creating a short film, not a full-length feature; therefore, economy must always be your goal. When you are staging a story action, it is generally a good idea to cut to the chase quickly and deliver the given story point with as few individual shots as possible.

11. 3D Animatics, Layout, and Camera Direction

Also, don't make any shots last longer than necessary. For instance, a lengthy, meandering tracking shot through a house that finally reveals a kid sleeping in his bed is only appropriate if important information is being revealed during the tour. Otherwise, just start the sequence in the bedroom. Get the story point told and move on.

Always ask yourself what the story is that needs to be told, and then decide on the action and the staging that will deliver the story point as efficiently as possible. For instance, if Junior is heading off to college, it would be more efficient to have him engage in a group hug with his whole family than to have him embrace each parent and sibling individually.

Summary

A 3D animatic represents stage two of your evolving story reel, where rough layout versions of your shots replace the held storyboard images that were assembled during the 2D animatic stage. The focus of a 3D animatic is basic positioning and movement of scene objects, characters, and cameras. Creating a basic shot layout involves assembling your scene elements on a virtual stage and establishing the correct number of frames on your timeline, and then adding camera positioning and potential movement. It is always a good idea to add a few extra handle frames to each shot to give yourself some margin of error in your future editing passes. Keep the movements of your scene objects as simple as possible at this stage so you can work out the overall pacing and trajectories of your film as a whole. Refining the animation on individual shots will come a bit later. Camera actions are either lock-offs or moves. Camera moves include pans, tilts, tracks, zooms, and combinations thereof. Try not to go crazy with big, sweeping camera moves unless doing so is particularly appropriate for the style and action of your film. If you are not entirely sure of what will ultimately be the perfect staging for a particular shot, create multiple takes with different camera directions so you can experiment with a few choices in your next editing pass. When you are establishing your camera direction, consider the point of view, focal point, framing, and overall composition of each shot. Also imagine that your camera is being operated by a real person. Adding appropriate imperfections can make the visual flow of your film feel a bit more natural. With the benefit of dimensionality and actual camera direction, here at the 3D animatic stage you can begin to edit your story reel with a higher degree of precision, focusing on rhythm, continuity, and cutting issues. The next chapter will discuss the subject of CG modeling.

chapter 12
Modeling

Before you started your 3D animatic, you very likely created basic digital objects as representative placeholders for the actual characters, props, and background elements that would ultimately be used in your shots (see Chapter 11). Now it's time for the real deal.

When modeling in 3D, you assume the role of a digital sculptor (see Figure 12.1). As it is for a traditional sculptor, it is important that you study the human figure and the rest of the world around you to develop a strong understanding of reality, even if you are creating an abstract or cartoony film. You must also choose the appropriate tools and materials that are best suited to crafting your vision, build your CG objects in a style that closely follows or perhaps grossly exaggerates natural reality, and examine your models and their silhouettes from every possible angle to make sure their shapes and dimensions will be clear and appealing from all perspectives.

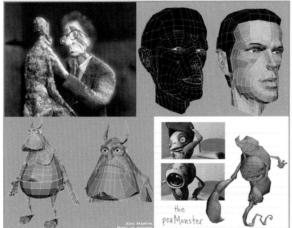

Figure 12.1
CG modeling can be described as digital sculpture.

> "The sculptor must learn to reproduce the surface, which means all that vibrates on the surface, soul, love, passion, life... Sculpture is thus the art of hollows and mounds, not of smoothness, or even polished planes."
> August Rodin

Many of the tasks involved in CG short film production have their roots in traditional art media. A successfully staged shot is like a well-composed photograph. Believable animation can be compared to a convincing acting performance. Effective lighting and texturing will result in an aesthetic experience similar to that of a painting on a canvas. And a quality CG model is like a fine work of sculpture, where a design idea or character sketch is shaped into a dimensional form.

Modeling is the first in a series of steps involved in the creation of the digital elements that will be assembled and animated in your shots. The aesthetic and technical choices you make here will have a profound effect on the challenges you will face in your future production stages with regard to the size of your files, the length of your render times, the complexity of your character rigs, the detail level of your texture maps, and the efficiency of your animation process. So, like all other stages of CG short film production, strive for economy and efficiency whenever possible.

◆ Avoid unnecessary details, especially in objects that will only be seen from a distance.

◆ Consider the type of visual experience you plan to deliver or the specific skill you want to demonstrate, and then model your digital elements accordingly. For instance, if you want to deliver visually spectacular imagery that will be appropriate for IMAX theaters, then you will probably need richly detailed object models. However, if the primary goal of your CG short is to demonstrate your character animation skills, then use simple and efficient models to keep your scene files light and interactive so you can focus on performance issues. Remember that less is very often more (see Figure 12.2).

◆ Prioritize your models and focus most of your attention and detail on those objects and characters that are most important to the delivery of your story.

◆ Consider the use of texture maps as an alternative to sculpting every little detail of your digital models.

Figure 12.2
If demonstrating your animation skills is the central focus of your short, use simple and efficient character models.

Modeling and Production Workflow

A typical modeling pipeline would include the following steps:

1. Determine what you need to build.
2. Collect reference material.
3. Draw sketches and/or create physical sculptures.
4. Scan 2D imagery to use as background templates.
5. Experiment with tools and techniques to produce your model effectively.
6. Assemble a logical directory structure and name your models sensibly.
7. Create alternative resolutions.
8. Create blend shapes if necessary.

In this book, we are assuming that you already understand the basic principles of 3D computer graphics and possess a working knowledge of an appropriate modeling and animation software package. If you need a primer on CG fundamentals, see Appendix B, "Suggested Reading," for a few suggestions on books that sufficiently cover the basics.

The above list represents a fairly conventional modeling production pipeline. Your particular pathway might vary, of course, depending on the individual needs of your film as well as your preferred working methods. For instance, you might not require any reference material, or your final models might be simple enough that you don't need low-resolution versions to work with them efficiently.

Keep in mind that modeling is not necessarily an isolated task. As you begin to assemble your virtual stages, texture and rig your characters, and begin to animate, you might discover that you need to make changes or additions to your existing models. Perhaps you will need more vertices to rig a character's

12. Modeling

shoulder effectively. Or maybe you will find that you didn't create enough facial blend shapes to perform your lip-synching successfully. Build your models as accurately and efficiently as possible, but accept the possibility that you might have to revisit some of them on occasion.

Step 1: Determine Your Needs

Look through your storyboards and animatics and make a list of the models you will need to complete your film, analyzing their number and complexity based on:

◆ Style   ◆ Category   ◆ Type

Style

The style of your film will significantly impact the creation of your digital models. A highly realistic piece will probably require rather detailed models, perhaps including clothing and a large number of blend shapes for effective facial animation. A cartoony film will likely call for simpler objects and characters. An abstract piece might only require basic, primitive shapes (see Figure 12.3).

Cartoon-style films often work best in two dimensions, where exaggeration, line quality, silhouettes, and lines of action can easily be emphasized. The challenge of recreating such a typically flat style in 3D is to make the characters and objects look good from any given point of view. An excellent example is Avi Goodman's character from Figure 12.4, which is extreme in its design, with a lot of emphasis given to its head and very pronounced mouth. Cartoon characters have a very specific and identifiable look, so you should draw model sheets showing various angles to better understand the character's design and nature in order to achieve a good translation of a cartoon figure.

Conversely, if you are planning to develop photo-realistic models, then it is necessary to do research and find as much reference material as possible (see Figure 12.5). Anatomy books are essential if you are going to model a realistic human form. It is important to understand the muscle system and the skeletal structure if you are going to model a body that will bend and deform correctly when it is rigged and animated. In addition, knowledge of anatomy provides you with a good understanding of important matters such as volume changes and the way muscles behave under the skin, which are

Figure 12.3
Cartoony and abstract characters and objects are typically rather simple.

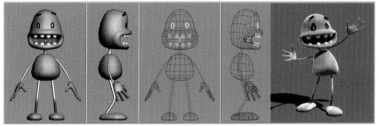

Figure 12.4
This simple and appealing character will look good from all angles.

Figure 12.5
Collect and study reference material before you build detailed and realistic models.

useful when you are generating facial expressions and mouth shapes through the use of skin deformations and blend shapes.

Even when you are modeling realistic fantasy creatures, such as werewolves or dragons, you must reference the anatomy of real animals to add the element of believability to the particular characteristics that distinguish such creatures of legend (see Figure 12.6).

Figure 12.6
Fantasy creatures are more believable if they are based on real-world animals.

Categories of Models

The models you will build for your short film can be separated into the following three categories, differentiated by their purpose and functionality:

◆ Characters   ◆ Props   ◆ Background elements

Characters

Characters exist to deliver the actions and emotional impact of the events in your short film. They possess the unique quality of personality; therefore, these models must be developed with the potential for movement and performance.

For the purpose of your film, a character model can be as simple as a rubber ball or it can be as complex as an eight-legged alien spider with tentacles, hair, jewelry, and clothing. The important thing is that your character models must be able to convey unique personality traits.

When you are modeling organic characters, it is important to choose default poses that will allow you to rig and bind them effectively and efficiently (see Chapter 14, "Character Setup"). For bipeds, the two most standard poses are the da Vinci pose and the relaxed bind pose (see Figure 12.7). In the da Vinci pose, where the extremities of the character are fully extended, texture maps will be easier to apply due to the fact that the surfaces are stretched. However, the da Vinci pose will typically present a few difficulties during the setup and binding phases because elbows and knees will need to bend by large degrees to reach their flexed position, making it harder to avoid unwanted folds and intersections. The relaxed bind pose, on the other hand, starts with such joints pre-bent in a single plane at about 45 degrees, so they won't need to rotate as far to reach their extremes, thus making their surface deformations a bit easier to control.

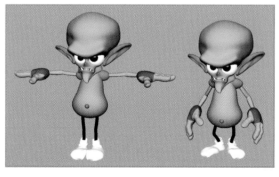

Figure 12.7
The da Vinci and relaxed bind poses

It is also important to plan the distribution and flow of the geometry on the model, using more vertices in areas that will need to bend and deform, such as shoulders and knees (see Figure 12.8).

Consider the role that a specific model will play within the context of your short film. For instance, when modeling your protagonist, keep in mind that the entire story will revolve around this particular character; therefore, a great deal of care and detail should go into his construction. On the other hand, if you are creating background characters that are going to be placed far away from the cameras, then you can probably get away with building them as much lighter models. In addition, it is crucial that you make a careful assessment of the details that must be modeled and the ones that are going to be supplemented by the use of textures; otherwise, you could experience unnecessary complications during later stages of your production pipeline due to inefficient models with too many unnecessary vertices.

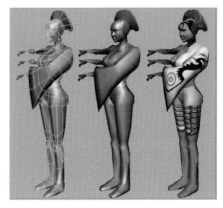

Figure 12.8
Use more vertices in areas where a character or object will need to bend.

Props

Props typically refer to objects that are used by (or interact somehow with) your characters, such as chairs, books, doors, computer keyboards, pencils, baseball bats, and cars (see Figure 12.9).

By definition, props are inert unless they are set into motion by an external force, such as a character or a gust of wind. A prop that can move around of its own accord would be considered a character.

Background Elements

Background elements are structures and objects that make up the spatial settings where the events of your film take place, such as buildings, mountains, telephone poles, and asteroids. Foreground objects that round out the details of a scene but are not actually manipulated by your characters also fall into this category. Examples include carpets, tables, framed pictures, trees, and parked cars.

Figure 12.9
Props are objects with which your characters will directly interact.

Based on your needs, the level of complexity involved in the development of your background elements could vary dramatically. A background setting can be as simple as two large, primitive objects. Such an approach was used in the short films *Values* and *After You*, where the sets were made up of a pair of planes for the former and a ground plane with a sky sphere for the latter (see Figure 12.10). This is a simple yet effective course of action if you are under a deadline and you plan to dedicate most of your modeling time to your characters.

On the other hand, the style of your film might demand that you build a much more complex environment, like that of *Rascagnes* or *Theme Planet*, in which more detailed backgrounds play an essential role in setting the mood of the film (see Figure 12.11). In such circumstances, it is crucial that you optimize geometry wherever possible and rely on the use of texture maps to make up for the absence of the finer details in your environment elements. It is also wise to plan out the execution of your shots before you begin modeling because you should only model the sections of the environment that are actually going to be seen on the screen.

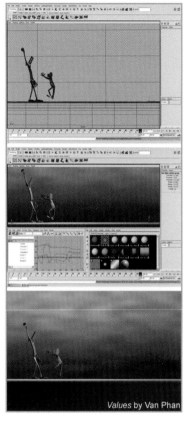

12. Modeling

Figure 12.11
More complex backgrounds might be necessary for the style of your short.

Object Types

It will be important to consider what kinds of objects your film will require, as well as the type of geometry you will use to build them.

Organic versus Hard-Surface Models

By taking a look at the world around you, you can identify diverse objects and structures due to the nature of their origin. Objects derived from the natural world are often characterized by an organic or somewhat irregular appearance. Examples include plants, animals, clouds, rocks, and trees. Hard-surface objects and assembled goods are typically manmade and have a tendency to be more geometric and symmetrical in shape, such as cars, bookcases, guns, houses, and robots (see Figure 12.12).

Figure 12.10
A pair of primitive objects with appropriate texture maps can sometimes be sufficient for a simple background setting.

Values by Van Phan

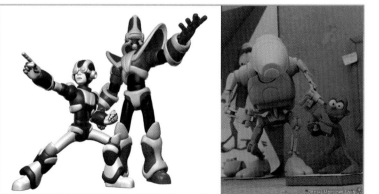

Figure 12.12
Organic and hard-surface models.

Organic objects tend to be more difficult to replicate in a digital form than rigid objects and structures because of the complexity of the surfaces that need to be created. A photo-realistic human arm is much more challenging to create than a simplified robotic version of the same limb.

Geometry Types

The three main types of geometry that are utilized in the modeling process are polygons, NURBS, and subdivision surfaces (see Figure 12.13). Each geometry type presents particular advantages and disadvantages, and they all require different sets of modeling techniques. However, your ultimate choice of geometry does not really matter as long as the models you create meet the requirements of your overall workflow and maintain the integrity of your initial designs.

Figure 12.13
Polygons, NURBS, and subdivision surfaces.

Polygons

A *polygon* is defined by the existence of a minimum of three vertices connected by edges. When multiple polygons are joined together, a *polygonal mesh* is generated. Polygons are versatile and intuitive to work with, and they are a perfect choice for modeling objects that contain corners and sharp edges because individual edge lines are always straight lines. Also, polygon meshes render quickly and because every 3D package in the industry supports them, they can be easily imported and exported between different software packages.

One potential disadvantage of polygon models is that they have a tendency to look faceted, so to create curved and smooth surfaces you need to increase the surface's resolution by using a large number of vertices. This added resolution of course results in a heavier model that will most likely impact you in the character setup and rendering stages (see Figure 12.14).

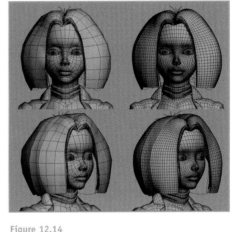

Figure 12.14
A large number of polygons is required to describe curved surfaces.

NURBS

The term *NURBS* (*Non-Uniform Rational B-Splines*) refers to a type of geometry that results from mathematical calculations between the weights of control points that are connected by a typically invisible hull encasing the actual surface of a model. NURBS surfaces possess a perfectly smooth visual quality and present a high degree of malleability when their control points are used to influence significant areas of a surface. This type of geometry is often preferable when you are modeling organic forms because it takes fewer control points than polygon vertices to describe curved surfaces. Also, its inherent UV system facilitates the application of textures, and due to their topology, NURBS files can be very small in data size.

One downside of working with NURBS surfaces is that they must often be divided into smaller patches, and the resulting process of stitching them together while trying to preserve an appropriate flow of the geometry can become a time-consuming and nerve-wracking task.

Subdivision Surfaces

Subdivision surfaces are a kind of topology that can be described as a fusion between polygons and NURBS. Subdivision surfaces have the versatility of polygonal meshes combined with the smooth appearance of NURBS surfaces.

Because this type of geometry lacks inherent UV parameterization, subdivision surfaces are harder to texture than NURBS surfaces. Also, subdivision surfaces are particular to the 3D software package that features them; therefore, they can only be rendered within the same program and typically cannot be exported into other packages.

Choosing an Appropriate Geometry Type

When you are deciding between polygons, NURBS, or subdivision surfaces for your models, consider the following factors:

◆ Which type of geometry are you most proficient and comfortable working with?

◆ How much time can you invest in experimenting with a type of geometry with which you are not familiar?

◆ Which type of geometry would best fulfill the needs and requirements of a given model? Hard surfaces with sharp edges typically work best with polygons, but it is generally more efficient to use NURBS or subdivision surfaces for organic objects. Also, think about the advantages and disadvantages that each type of geometry has to offer. And realize that not all of the models in your film necessarily need to be modeled with the same geometry type.

◆ Consider the possibility of combining geometry types on a single object or character. For example, you could use subdivision surfaces for a character's hands and NURBS patches for her shirt, with overlapping wrist sleeves to hide the intersections. Perhaps polygons might work best for her geometric jewelry.

Step 2: Gather Reference Material

Before you start the modeling process, it is wise to gather as much reference material as possible, especially when you are creating realistic characters and objects or detailed models that are based on the real world. Remember that all artists use reference to some degree or another, and it is not considered cheating to do so. Any process that helps to increase the believability and appeal of your models will improve the overall visual quality of your film. Bookstores, libraries, and the Internet are excellent places to search for sources of reference. When you are searching for images of a particular subject in a library, try looking in the children's section, where the books will tend to have more images than the books in the regular sections. If your collection of reference imagery exists in digital form, be sure to organize your picture logically inside appropriately named directories.

Step 3: Start with Drawings or Sculptures

Hopefully, most (if not all) of the visual elements of your short film were sufficiently designed with consistent and appealing art direction in the pre-production stage. Still, it is highly recommended that you do preliminary sketches before you start the process of building a model to help you foresee and eliminate many possible complications before the actual modeling process begins.

Sculpting your models in the real world before building them in the computer is also a great way to start; this will help you verify the proportions and the style of your future models and will allow you to make more concrete decisions up front, before you enter the digital realm. Physical sculptures can describe the forms and details that 2D sketches only hint at (see Figure 12.15).

Step 4: Scan

In addition to helping you work out the design and detail specifics of your future models, your sketches and sculptures can be used as actual background templates within your CG software to help with modeling accuracy.

If you are starting with sketches, draw your soon-to-be-modeled character or object from various orthographic perspectives (front, right, left, top, and so on), scan these images into your computer, and project them onto image planes in their respective views within your CG package. If you created physical sculptures, photograph them from appropriate angles, preferably with a digital camera. Then import (or scan if necessary) your photographs into your computer and use them in the same manner as background plates in your modeling windows.

Then, using these background images as guides, trace the drawn or sculpted forms and outlines when you are constructing your models. This procedure ensures that the proportions and appearance of the 3D model will be consistent with the original design (see Figure 12.16).

Step 5: Experiment and Choose the Right Tools and Techniques

If time allows, experiment with the modeling tools your CG software package offers. Try using different techniques with simple geometry to determine which methods will provide the fastest, most effective, and highest-quality results for your particular purposes.

Modeling Techniques

Every 3D software package provides a wide variety of tools and techniques you can use to model your characters, props, and background elements. Some packages emphasize polygon modeling tools, while others focus on NURBS or other geometry types. Examine your software manuals thoroughly so you don't miss any especially powerful or timesaving tools that may be offered, and use whatever techniques are the most logical and familiar to you to ensure an effective and efficient modeling process. A few of the more common methods are as follows.

© Renato dos Anjos

Figure 12.15
A physical sculpture will allow you to visualize a future digital model and will help you work out its proportions and details.

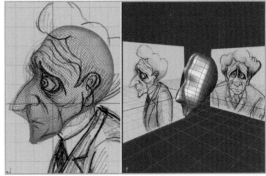

Figure 12.16
Using scanned drawings as templates will help you build models that accurately represent your designs.

12. Modeling

261

Working with Primitives

Primitive CG objects are basic geometric structures, such as cubes, spheres, cylinders, cones, or planes, and every 3D software package will allow you to create such objects with ease.

You can assemble primitive objects to create more complex structures. You can build a snowman from a series of spheres, with a cone for his nose and a couple of cylinders for his hat. You can even build somewhat abstract characters by assembling primitive objects creatively (see Figure 12.17).

You can also use primitive assemblies as inner templates for creating complex structures. Simple objects are combined to describe the basic structure and proportions, and then an outer skin is modeled around these primitives.

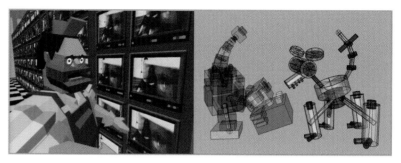

Figure 12.17
You can assemble primitive objects to create interesting and abstract characters.

Free-Form Modeling

You can develop a model using the basic transformation functions of translation, rotation, and scaling on individual or groups of vertices of any type of geometry. Whether you are working with NURBS, polygons, or subdivision surfaces, you can create a complex shape by starting with an appropriate primitive object and then manipulating its points effectively and adding vertices as needed. For example, you could start with a simple sphere and then push and pull individual and groups of vertices until a stylized or even complex and realistic human head results (see Figure 12.18).

Surfaces from Curves

Depending on your software, you might use spline, Bezier, or NURBS curves as the starting point for generating 3D surfaces.

The three most common modeling procedures that begin with curves are

◆ **Extrusion.** In this procedure, a curve that represents the cross-section of an object is projected along a specific axis or an assigned path. An example would be to project a circle along a lengthy curve to create a garden hose. Most CG software packages will allow the cross-section curve to scale as it extrudes to form tapering shapes, such as tentacles or a sheep's horns.

Exercise: Look at a few fairly simple and rather geometric objects around you, such as a lamp, a chair, a computer, a door, or a plastic toy, and analyze them to see how you might build reasonable representations of them inside the computer using only primitive objects. Then try the same analysis with more complex objects, such as cars, action figures, or shoes.

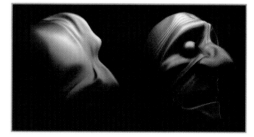

Figure 12.18
You can construct complex forms by manipulating the points and adding details as needed on a formerly simple object.

262

◆ **Revolving.** This is an efficient way of generating a three-dimensional form by means of revolving (or *lathing*) an edge curve around a given axis. You can quickly create objects such as wineglasses or vases using this method. Typically, CG software packages will provide the option for you to further refine the shape of the resulting surface by interactively adjusting the control points of the original curve. You can then manipulate the final structure for more detail and complexity, expanding upon its initial symmetrical form (see Figure 12.19).

◆ **Lofting.** A surface can be formed by sweeping or *lofting* across a path that has been framed by a succession of cross-section curves that define the boundaries of the anticipated object (see Figure 12.19).

Using Deformers as Modeling Tools

Deformers can be extremely powerful modeling tools, especially when large groups of control points or vertices need to be manipulated all at once due to a high resolution level in a particular surface. After the modifications to the geometry have been finalized, the deforming object typically can be removed, and the changes will be preserved if your deletion options are set accordingly. A few of the most common deformers are listed below:

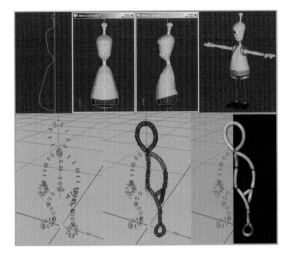

Figure 12.19
Revolving and lofting are popular methods for constructing 3D surfaces from basic curves.

◆ **Clusters.** You can group control points of a surface under the influence of a cluster. As a result, you can select all of the affected points and manipulate them simultaneously by simply moving, rotating, or scaling their corresponding cluster.

◆ **Lattices.** A *lattice* is like a cage that can surround an entire object or portions thereof. As a modeling tool, a lattice enables you to alter large areas of a surface by manipulating the lattice's control points, which will then influence the geometry encased within the boundary of the lattice. The more vertices the lattice boundary contains, the more detailed influence you will be able to apply to the deforming geometry (see Figure 12.20).

◆ **Wrap deformers.** You can generate this type of deformer with a low-resolution piece of geometry that wraps around the high-resolution surface of a model. This deformer is comparable to a lattice in terms of its functionality. The wrap deformer is developed in such a manner that it shares a similar topological configuration with the surface of the model, so the resulting modifications on the high-resolution geometry will be more accurate and predictable.

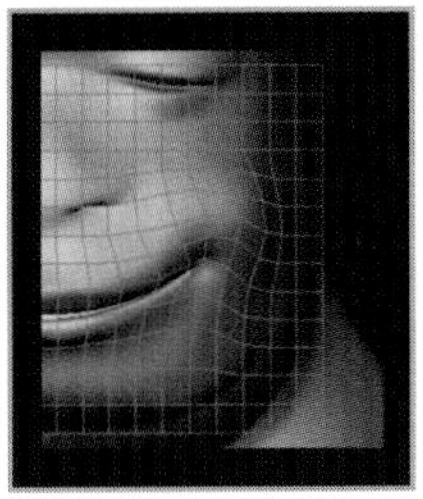

Figure 12.20
A lattice is a deformation cage that you can use to deform the geometry it surrounds.

Check your software manual for other types of deformers that might be available for use as modeling tools, such as twister and skew manipulators or wire deformers.

Booleans

You can use intersecting models to cut holes and chunks out of one another or to create new objects from their unions and intersections (see Figure 12.21). This process of using Booleans is available in virtually all CG modeling packages.

12. Modeling

Procedural Modeling

Some CG software packages offer procedural techniques you can use to build complex objects, such as landscapes or trees and nerve endings that you can import into your 3D scenes. Such procedural solutions offer a somewhat randomized approach to modeling that can provide you with some interesting results, especially for abstract and organic forms (see Figure 12.22).

Plug-ins and stand-alone software packages with robust procedural modeling capabilities are also available. Examples include

◆ TREE STORM and BAMBOO from Onyx Computing
(http://www.onyxtree.com)

◆ Xfrog from Greenworks Organic Software (http://www.xfrog.com)

◆ NatFX from Bionatics (http://www.bionatics.com)

◆ SpeedTree from IDV (http://www.idvinc.com)

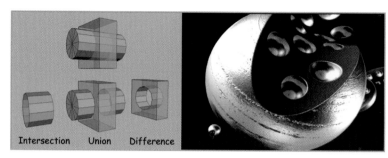

Figure 12.21
You can use Booleans as sculpting tools.

Exercise: Examine a few objects around you and try to imagine which modeling techniques you might use to create digital versions of them. For instance, you could easily build a pencil by revolving an edge curve, while a car would require a combination of much more labor-intensive processes.

Figure 12.22
Procedural modeling is a convenient way of creating complex organic shapes.

Alternative Modeling Techniques

A number of alternative techniques are also available that can be used to streamline, enhance, or actually replace manual modeling procedures.

Displacements

Displacements are particularly useful when you need to create small or subtle surface details on a model, such as the pimples on a golf ball, skin wrinkles, or tree bark (see Figure 12.23). Using conventional modeling tools and techniques to create such fine details would be extremely time-consuming and would result in extremely heavy and inefficient models. Displacements can be done using bump maps or textures with appropriate properties that will modify the geometry of a particular surface without requiring any actual modeling. The resulting effect of such displacement maps will not be directly visible on the surface of the model until it has been rendered, so a bit of trial and error is generally necessary to achieve the intended result. Also keep in mind that models with displacement maps might result in lengthy rendering times because of the surface calculations required and the fact that the underlying geometry will typically need a high degree of resolution to deform properly.

Displacement maps can also be expression-driven to increase or decrease their influence when a particular motion occurs. For instance, you can set displacement-based eye wrinkles to automatically intensify when a character blinks or squints.

Cards, Tiles, or Billboards

You can map a 2D picture or a painted texture onto the surface of a simple object, such as a plane, and then use it as an extremely low-resolution stand-in for an actual 3D model. Such *cards* or *tiles* are typically used for background objects when the camera perspective does not change enough to give away the lack of dimensionality of these shortcuts. Cards and tiles are typically aim-constrained to always face the camera so the flat surface does not reveal itself if the perspective shifts.

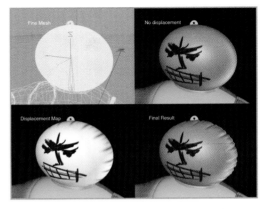

Figure 12.23
For fine details, you can use displacement maps instead of actual modeling.

Similarly, you might project an image of a landscape or cityscape onto a large plane or the inside of a huge sphere to create a background setting, rather than actually modeling all of the individual buildings, trees, rocks, hills, or clouds of a particular scene (see Figure 12.24).

If you have a particularly complex scene with a large number of background objects, you might be able to reduce your rendering times and increase your interactivity by rendering your setting and then using the resulting image as a background plate in your scene (instead of using the actual geometry pieces). This shortcut is especially effective for distant objects.

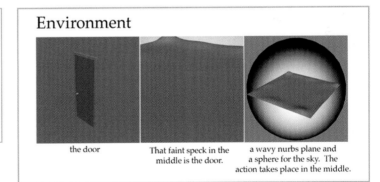

Environment

the door

That faint speck in the middle is the door.

a wavy nurbs plane and a sphere for the sky. The action takes place in the middle.

Figure 12.24
A painting projected on the inside of a large sphere surrounding your virtual set will typically be more efficient than modeling a complex background.

Instead of projecting a background image inside your CG software and rendering your 3D and 2D scene elements as a whole, you can build and photograph a setting made of real-world objects or sculptures and then composite it behind your digital characters and objects after the fact (see Figure 12.25 and Chapter 20, "Compositing").

3D Scans

If you have an actual sculpture of a particular character or object and you are lucky (or wealthy) enough to have access to a 3D scanner, you can create an accurate and detailed digital version of your physical model (see Figure 12.26). However, this method can be rather time-consuming because you will probably need to sculpt the physical form of the object to be scanned and then clean up the digitized geometry, make file conversions, do some grouping, and add UV coordinates to the surface of the model so your texture maps will apply properly.

Buy or Borrow Instead of Build

Sometimes the process of developing compelling models might not be your main priority, and based on your deadline constraints, you might prefer to spend your available time on other aspects of your short film, such as scriptwriting, animation, or lighting. If so, a viable option for procuring models for your project could be to purchase or download them from Internet sites and model libraries. Such third-party digital objects can range in price rather significantly. Some downloadable digital characters will also include internal skeleton rigs, allowing you to skip the character setup process as well as the modeling stage for a particular character. Web sites that contain models for purchase or download include:

Figure 12.25
You can create, photograph, and then composite physical sculptures behind your digital models.

◆ http://www.daniel3d.com/pepe-school-land/gotomisc.htm

◆ http://www.turbosquid.com

◆ http://www.its-ming.com

Step 6: Naming Conventions

When you are naming the models in your scenes, you should assign a prefix and suffix that clearly describe the nature of your objects. A naming convention that is intuitive and easy to understand will make life easier for you and your teammates. The first part of the name should identify the model or its owner, so choose abbreviations that will be easy to recognize. For example, use "cap" for captain, "whl" for wheel, or "sea" for sea.

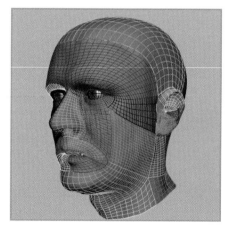

Figure 12.26
Digitizing a real human head will allow you to acquire a detailed and accurate virtual model without requiring as much actual sculpting time.

You can use other abbreviations to describe the level of resolution (lo, mid, or hi), the spatial location (right-center-left, up-down, or front-back), the nature of the object (spl for spline, pch for patch, nbs for nurbs, or poly for polygonal), or a detailed explanation (upper_left_molar). The idea is to

12. Modeling

convey a sufficient amount of information about an object with as few letters as possible. For example, you might use cap_lores_hat for a captain's low-resolution hat or cap_lf_hires_eye_poly for a captain's high-resolution, polygonal left eye.

You can also use appropriately placed capital letters to differentiate objects, such as capLf_eye, capRt_eye, or capToe_pinkyRt.

Step 7: Create Alternative Resolutions

For future use, it is typically important to generate one or two alternative versions of each of your models with different geometry resolutions. One set will be your high-resolution models, which include the detailed geometry that will be used for your final renders. The other set of models will be low-resolution versions that you will use for your layout and animation stages, where a high degree of interactivity is necessary (see Figure 12.27).

One way to generate low-resolution versions of your models is by replacing your high-resolution models with assemblies of simple geometry pieces, such as cylinders and spheres, which you can then sculpt to better match the outlines of your real surfaces. For characters, you can simply parent such primitive objects to the joints of your skeleton rigs, providing you with highly interactive models as a result of the absence of deformations and point weighting (see Chapter 14, "Character Setup").

Another method of creating lighter versions is to decrease the resolution of your actual high-resolution models. You can do this manually, by carefully deleting points or by using software that allows you to de-res your objects automatically. The key in this step is to create low-resolution versions that are close approximations of their corresponding high-resolution models so that you have consistent edge lines when you switch between them. If there is too much disparity between your low-resolution and high-resolution versions, you will end up having to place and pose many of your objects and characters at least twice to avoid intersections and accurately establish your spatial relationships.

Figure 12.27
It is typically a good idea to create lower-resolution versions of your characters for increased interactivity when you are animating.

It is also worth mentioning that NURBS and subdivision surfaces have properties that allow you to quickly increase and decrease the level of detail that is displayed on the geometry so you can choose between interactivity or exacting accuracy at any given moment.

Step 8: Create Necessary Blend Shapes

Once you have a finalized model, you can duplicate and alter it through the use of deformers or direct control-point manipulations to create variations of the original form with the same topology and vertex count. By repeating this process several times, you can build a library of blend shapes that you can use as morph targets for things like muscle deformations and facial animation. For example, using expressions or other channel connection procedures, you could set a bicep to bulge whenever the elbow bends. As for facial animation, you can duplicate a master neutral shape once for each required facial shape and then alter it to resemble a specific expression or phoneme (see Figure 12.28). You can then connect the set of target shapes to the master or base model using some form of software-specific blend-shape tool. Such a tool allows you to morph your original shape toward a single target shape or a combined influence from several shapes to form a new facial expression. If you are going for a realistic style, you should spend some time researching the way muscle systems work on a face and pay attention to how such muscles change in volume as they stretch and contract to create different expressions. If facial expressions are a very important aspect of your short film, you might want to develop a more complex, layered blend shape system that simulates human anatomy, where muscles and skin work together to create realistic facial expressions. This same principle can also apply to thinking or talking animals and cartoon characters that need to express complex human emotions.

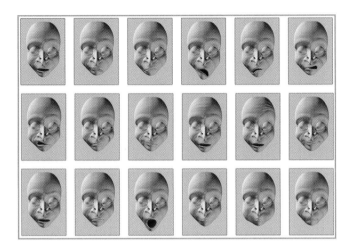

Figure 12.28
Facial animation is typically accomplished by building a series of morph targets representing various expressions and phoneme shapes.

Tips

Here are a few tips that can help to ensure a smooth and efficient modeling pipeline.

◆ It is usually a good idea to approach the development of a model as a whole rather than in separate parts. Instead of putting a lot of work and detail into one area and then moving on to the next, work out the overall shapes and proportions and then refine the model as a whole, as if you are gradually using smaller and smaller sculpting tools.

◆ Occasionally create 360-degree turntable renders for the purpose of scrutinizing your model from different angles. Look for consistency in the volumes and interesting silhouettes.

◆ If appropriate, utilize your CG software's mirroring tools, which allow you to model only half of an object and then mirror it along the proper axis to create the finished form. Many objects in nature, such as human torsos, are symmetrical and can therefore be modeled this way. Some CG software packages have persistent mirroring tools that will automatically build the opposite half of an object while you focus on a single side. Check your manual for details.

◆ Merge or group smaller objects into single models, especially for insignificant or distant elements. A cityscape, for instance, would typically be easier to manage as a single object with many parts, rather than as a pile of individual skyscraper models.

◆ If possible, don't model parts of objects that will not be seen from the camera view (see Figure 12.29). This technique can save memory and rendering time, but keep in mind that you might not be able to get away with this shortcut if the other side of an object might be seen in a reflection or if the object's cast shadow reveals the absent surfaces.

Figure 12.29
Save time and memory by not modeling parts of objects that will be obscured.

◆ Reuse assets whenever possible. If you've built a rather complex model of a house, you might be able to assemble an entire neighborhood by copying the first model and then changing a few colors or making some minor proportion changes on the duplicates, rather than starting from scratch for each of them.

◆ If you need multiple and identical copies of a single object, consider creating instances rather than actual copies (see Figure 12.30). The difference between a copy and an instance lies in the fact that a copy is a new and separate object, while an instance is a phantom model of the original that only utilizes a very small amount of memory. The disadvantage of this technique is that you cannot reshape individual instances unless you convert them to actual copies first. However, you can typically translate, rotate and scale, instances individually.

Figure 12.30
Instancing saves memory.

◆ Apply shaders and checkerboard textures to your models. A gray Blinn shader will cast specular highlights, allowing you to easily detect small errors and irregularities on the surfaces of your models. Applying a checkered texture on a model will give you a better idea of the way your future texture maps will be applied to the surface. Also, checkered textures will help when modeling morph targets because they will allow you to better scrutinize how the surfaces behave when transferring from one shape to another.

◆ Be sure to use the same unit of measure, such as centimeters, in all of your scenes and models to maintain scale consistency.

◆ When your scene is getting overloaded with geometry and you begin to lose interactivity, create visibility buttons or display layers to hide and unhide objects (or parts of objects) that get in the way of your productivity. Such switches will also be helpful when you animate your shots.

Summary

In this chapter, we described a recommended process for building your digital models, which begins with identifying your needs and then collecting reference material, scanning design sketches to use as templates, choosing the most appropriate geometry types and techniques, organizing your assets, and building any necessary lower-resolution versions of blend shapes. Your CG models can include characters, props, and background objects and you can choose a realistic, cartoony, or abstract style. Various geometry types, such as polygons and NURBS, are available, as well as a host of modeling techniques including primitive object assembly, point-pulling, curve extrusions, Booleans, deformations, and "tracing" scanned drawings. If CG sculpture is not your forte, consider purchasing or downloading your models instead. And be sure to analyze your storyboards and vocal tracks to determine what blend shapes you might need to create for body deformations and facial animation.

In Chapter 13, "Materials and Textures," we will discuss the process of creating and applying materials and textures to your digital objects to give them greater visual detail, interest, and appeal.

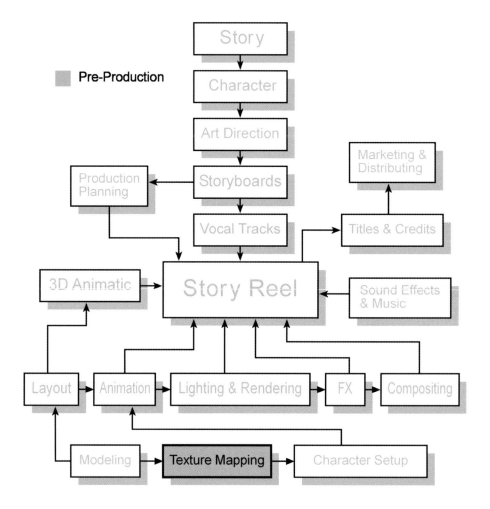

Pre-Production

Story

Character

Art Direction

Storyboards

Production Planning

Vocal Tracks

Marketing & Distributing

Titles & Credits

3D Animatic

Story Reel

Sound Effects & Music

Layout

Animation

Lighting & Rendering

FX

Compositing

Modeling

Texture Mapping

Character Setup

chapter 13
Materials and Textures

I magine if you could somehow have an artist like Salvador Dali art direct your CG short. He would probably choose a sur-realistic color scheme with lifelike textures. Andy Warhol would very likely use primary and secondary color palettes with a flat textural quality, while Picasso would no doubt make a stylistic choice following his mood *du jour*, which might range from subtle realism to colorful abstraction. So, like the great artists of the past and present, it is important for you to come up with a unique (or at least appealing) visual style for your cinematic work of art, selecting materials and textures that will be consistent with your vision.

Beauty is only
skin deep.

Through the use of materials and textures, you provide your audience with an extra layer of visual interest and add depth to the elements that are displayed onscreen (see Figure 13.1). A film containing only default, gray-shaded objects without color or texture will result in a visual experience that is far from interesting, unique, or exciting.

To construct a believable digital reality, patience and meticulous observation are key. Use your critical eye to study objects in the real world to determine how color, surface detail, patterns, and texture combine to form natural and appealing visual quality (see Figure 13.2).

For instance, imagine that you intend to replicate a photo-realistic wooden surface. The first step would be to determine the nature of the object you are trying to portray. It could be a manufactured form, such as plywood or particleboard, or it could be a natural object, untouched by human hands. If the

Figure 13.1
Materials and textures add extra layers of visual interest to digital objects and scenes.

13. Materials and Textures

271

choice is the latter, a new set of options would arise. Should the wooden surface have the appearance of oak, maple, walnut, or perhaps mahogany? Each of these would display unique physical attributes, so you would need to decide on the best way to recreate their visual characteristics effectively. You would have to assign a base material with appropriate color and surface qualities. One texture layer might convey the fibrous quality of the raw wood, while a second layer might describe the waving flow of the surface grain. You should also consider additional factors, such as the age and condition of the wood, for added realism and detail. Perhaps the object is old, wet, moldy, rotten, weathered, and cracked. Or it might be polished and varnished, so its appearance would be more sleek and reflective.

Figure 13.2
Realistic and detailed surface imagery will result in a believable visual experience.

Of course, if you are going for an abstract or cartoony look, you would likely simplify or exaggerate the natural color and textural qualities of your wooden objects.

Not too long ago, computer-generated images were restricted to a synthetic visual quality in which everything resembled plastic, metal, or glass. However, technology has evolved and simplified to the point that nowadays we have a wide variety of looks available to us. You can not only accurately recreate what you see in the real world through the use of lifelike texture maps, but you can also experiment with alternative graphic styles. For example, you could use a toon-shader to create a cartoon look, or you could use appropriate materials and texture maps to simulate the look of watercolors, pastels, or clay (see Figure 13.3).

Creating the visual surface quality of a digital model requires three basic steps.

1. Assigning materials
2. Creating textures
3. Applying textures

Step 1 involves choosing the fundamental surface characteristics of an object. Step 2 is the process of painting or acquiring 2D or 3D texture maps, and Step 3 involves attaching those textures to their appropriate surfaces.

Figure 13.3
Using today's tools and technology, you can create a wide variety of unique CG imagery, well beyond the computerized, synthetic looks of the past.

Assigning Materials

Materials establish the underlying surface characteristics of digital objects and dictate how they will be displayed when they are lit and rendered (see Figure 13.4). The basic attributes to consider when you are assigning a material to a specific object are as follows:

Figure 13.4
Material attributes, such as color, diffusion, and translucency, will establish how digital objects react to light.

◆ **Color.** This attribute results from the combination of hue, value, and saturation. In the real world, color is not a property inherent to objects, but a property of light. When you look at a red ball, you perceive that specific color not because the ball itself is red, but because the surface of that specific ball has a quality that reflects the red portion of light, which bounces back into your eyes, while the surface of the ball absorbs the rest of the color spectrum. However, in the world of CG, color is calculated from a system that interpolates primary hues (red, blue, and green) combined with variants of value and saturation. For example, white would come from the full application of red, blue, and green, while aqua would be a combination of only blue and green with an appropriate value setting.

◆ **Ambient color.** This attribute can be described as the effect of a light source that is inherent to the material itself. For example, if you were to create a polygonal sphere and you set the ambient color to the highest value, then the surface of the object would be illuminated almost evenly when rendered, regardless of the influence of any external light sources (or lack thereof). On the other hand, if you were to set this attribute to a lower value, the shading of the object's surface would be more affected by the influence of an external light source.

◆ **Diffusion.** This attribute determines the way light spreads and gets distributed over a given surface.

◆ **Specularity.** This attribute measures the degree in which certain materials can reflect light in the form of a bright and highly concentrated highlight (see Figure 13.5). In other words, it determines how shiny a surface will appear. This characteristic can typically be seen on sleek, finely polished, or wet surfaces. The color of a specular kick is also a consideration. A black bowling ball will look especially shiny if its specular highlight is white, while a darker gray highlight might indicate that the ball needs to be cleaned.

◆ **Transparency.** This attribute regulates how much can be seen through the surface of an object (or the parts thereof), and can range from absolute opacity to complete invisibility.

◆ **Translucence.** This property determines the way light can filter and gets diffused through the surface of an object. You can see real-life examples of this effect on plant leaves, human skin, and sheets of paper.

◆ **Reflectivity.** This is a mirror-like property intrinsic to certain types of materials, which allows the surface of an object to cast reflections of its surrounding environment.

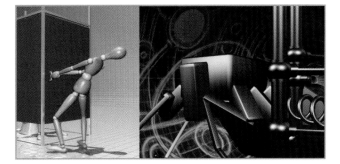

Figure 13.5
Specular highlights exist on polished or shiny objects.

◆ **Refraction.** This refers to a phenomenon that occurs in the real world when a ray of light makes a trajectory at a slanted angle from one medium (such as air) into another medium of a different density (such as water). Refraction produces the distortion of an image when it is viewed through a medium such as water or glass. Conditions such as concavity and convexity on a transparent medium will also produce the effect of refraction.

◆ **Incandescence.** This attribute makes a material appear as if light is emanating from it. However, this attribute does not generate light that could affect other physical elements of its surrounding environment. Rather, it merely makes the incandescent object appear to glow, especially at night.

Material Types

If you attentively observe the world around you, you will notice that everything has a material composition of very particular properties. You might see objects made out of metal, wood, plastic, glass, cloth, latex, or leather, just to name a few.

Even though every material in the real world has its own unique qualities and peculiarities, in CG you can classify materials into a few basic types, known as *shaders*, that are present in every high-end 3D software package. The criteria used for this classification are based on the material's behavior under the exposure of light. Three of the most common basic shaders are

◆ **Lambert.** This is the best choice when your intent is to convey dry, unpolished, or matte surfaces. This type of material is capable of diffusion; however, it is completely devoid of specular quality. Real-life examples of surfaces that display the properties of the Lambert material are chalk, paper, and raw wood.

◆ **Phong.** This type of shading is the typical choice of material when the purpose is to depict sleek and extremely well-polished surfaces that reflect light in the form of highlights that are bright, sharp, and highly concentrated. This material type is especially appropriate for glossy surfaces, such as plastic or varnished wood.

◆ **Blinn.** This type of shading casts specular highlights that can be diffused by adjusting the attributes of eccentricity and specular roll-off. The Blinn shader works well for emulating metallic surfaces that require somewhat diffused highlights, such as brass, aluminum, and gold.

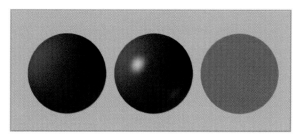

Figure 13.6
Most CG packages offer standard material types, such as Lambert, Phong, and solid color shaders.

Most CG packages contain other materials as well, including solid color shaders that are not affected by light, which would be appropriate for objects such as black holes or LED displays (see Figure 13.6).

Textures

Once your surfaces have been assigned the properties that determine the ways in which they will react to the lighting of your scenes, you can use textures to dress up their geometry to further improve their aesthetic value and believability. Textures take over where materials leave off, adding extra layers of depth and definition to objects and providing you with an additional opportunity to add a personal and unique visual touch to your work (see Figure 13.7).

Most surfaces in the real world display imperfections and irregularities, which can also be simulated with texture maps (see Figure 13.8). In the case of a brick wall, for example, you could certainly model all of its details brick by brick, including its surface characteristics. However, such an approach would be very time-consuming and would result in

Figure 13.7
Creative use of texture mapping will give your film a unique and personal touch.

a heavy object that would take a long time to model and render. Instead, you could apply appropriate texture maps to a flat surface to more efficiently simulate the visual characteristics of a brick wall.

Creating Textures

Following your own personal preferences and art direction, you can now begin the process of generating or obtaining your textures. Your options range from creating and scanning traditional paintings to the most synthetic approach that utilizes procedural algorithms. The means you follow to generate your texture maps will aid in the fulfillment of your vision, from the most realistic to the most whimsical or abstract of styles.

Figure 13.8
Using texture maps is often much more efficient than actually modeling all of the surface details of a particular object.

Before you create your textures, it is a good idea to decide on their resolutions based on the texture's purpose and on the type of final output that is intended for your short film.

If the resolution of a texture image is set too low and the textured object is placed close to the camera, errors, artifacts, and enlarged pixels might be seen (see Figure 13.9). On the other hand, if too many high-resolution textures exist in a scene, especially on distant objects, your render times might be unnecessarily high. It is important to find a sense of balance, and the best policy is to always test your textures at different resolutions to see how they render.

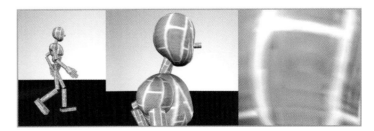

Figure 13.9
If the resolution of a texture is too low, it will become pixelized when seen close up.

Parameters exist to help in this respect. If a texture is intended for an object that is located far away from the camera, a size of 128×128 pixels might be sufficient. However, if the texture is for an object that will be very close to the camera, then a higher resolution (such as 720×720) would

13. Materials and Textures

be more appropriate. Also, if your intended display format will be film, the resolution of your texture images should be particularly high, such as 1024×1024 (1K), or perhaps even larger. Fortunately, you can utilize programs such as Photoshop or DeBabelizer to easily resize a texture file to the desired resolution.

Sometimes it makes sense to have two or perhaps three different versions of a single texture image at varying resolutions. You would use the highest-resolution image in shots where the given object is very close to camera and the lowest-resolution image for more distant placements.

Making Your Own Textures

Texture images can be created manually, generated procedurally, or acquired from existing sources. If you are going to create your own texture images and you want them to be at least loosely based on reality, it is a good idea to gather and analyze as much reference material as possible (see Figure 13.10). Bookstores, public libraries, the Internet, and of course, real-world objects are great sources for texture map reference. If you have a digital camera, keep it handy

Figure 13.10
Gather reference, especially when you are creating realistic textures.

when you are out and about because you never know when you might see a particularly interesting pattern of rocks or tree bark that you might want to reference for a future texture map image. And a camcorder is obviously an excellent tool for capturing animated textures, such as flowing water or moving clouds.

Starting with Traditional Media

Using traditional media, such as acrylics, watercolors, pastels, and airbrushes, you can produce an immeasurable variety of textures that you can scan or photograph later. Then, with the aid of Photoshop or any other similar software package, you can apply further details or modifications to the image. This process is strongly recommended for projects in which the artistic direction is driven by a unique and personal style. For instance, Doug Aberle's animated short, *Fluffy,* was one of the first CG films to use this technique of painting textures with traditional media before translating them onto digital models (see Figure 13.11).

Figure 13.11
Fluffy was one of the first CG films to feature hand-painted textures.

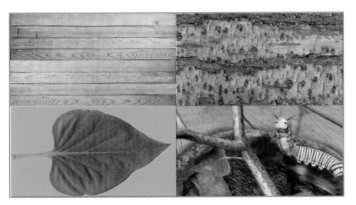

Figure 13.12
You can scan and map photographs of real-world objects onto your digital objects.

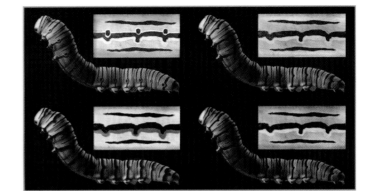

Figure 13.13
Creating textures with digital paint programs is a very popular method.

Digitized, Real-World Textures

The world around us is a boundlessly rich source of reference materials, and you can use such natural imagery directly, by importing photographs of real-world textures and patterns into the computer using a scanner or digital camera (see Figure 13.12). Seek out and photograph materials and surfaces that are suitable to your needs, such as dry leaves, human skin, animal fur, rock formations, brick walls, and so on. A digital paint program can be an invaluable tool for adjusting, modifying, merging layers, creating tiles, or adding some final touches to your imported real-world texture images.

Painting 2D Digital Textures

Another viable way to generate textures is to paint them using digital tools rather than traditional media, thus removing the need for scanning or importing. Software such as Corel Painter, Adobe Photoshop, or the freeware application, GIMP, provide a wide range of tools and utilities which should satisfy even the most detail-oriented texture painter (see Figure 13.13). These packages also offer the ability to further modify your texture paintings with a substantial variety of filters and image-processing tools you can use for purposes such as blurring, darkening, colorizing, simulating a large number of traditional media, and creating completely unique and surreal imagery.

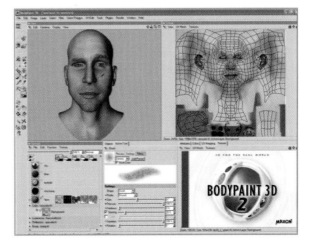

3D Painted Textures

You can also use 3D paint programs, such as Right Hemisphere's Deep Paint and Maxon's BodyPaint 3D for texture creation, in which colors and patterns are applied directly onto a 3D object (see Figure 13.14). You can also use this process as a starting

Figure 13.14
You can use programs such as Maxon's BodyPaint 3D to paint textures directly onto CG objects.

point for creating templates that can be used as guides for the creation of a final texture. You can even unwrap these templates and later export them to your favorite 2D paint program, where you can then trace or modify them to create more refined texture images. A 3D program is also helpful when you are adding finishing touches to a surface that has already been textured by other methods.

Procedural Textures

Instead of creating textures by painting them manually using traditional or digital tools, you can generate them procedurally. Procedural texturing utilizes numerical algorithms to simulate natural patterns, such as marble, wood grain, cloudy skies, rock formations, textiles, and certain animal skins (see Figure 13.15). Adjusting numerical parameters will result in an infinite variety of patterns and color combinations, so a fair amount of trial and error will typically be necessary to arrive at the exact look you desire. One advantage of this technique is that the textures do not have a fixed resolution limit, so the camera is free to zoom in without compromising detail. There are two types of procedural textures: 2D and 3D. Two-dimensional procedural textures are applied on the surface of a model in a similar fashion to manually created texture maps, whereas a 3D procedural texture influences the geometry that is positioned within its spatial boundaries. If you use a Boolean procedure to cut into an object that has a 3D texture, the pattern will show up on the surface of the resulting hole.

Due to the potentially time-consuming nature of effectively adjusting the parameters associated with procedural textures, many 3D software packages come with a default library of predefined patterns, which might be suitable for your particular artistic vision. However, if you want a custom-made procedural texture with a specific behavior, be prepared to do a good deal of experimentation.

Figure 13.15
Procedural texturing creates colors and patterns based on mathematical algorithms.

Acquiring Existing Textures

In addition to creating textures manually or procedurally, you can acquire a wide variety of texture maps from Web pages and CD-ROM libraries, and every 3D software package comes with a set of default textures that might satisfy your needs. The contents of these data banks, however, are usually of a generic nature, and you might have to customize them to meet the needs of your art direction plans.

> Regardless of the techniques you use to create or acquire your texture maps, be sure to give them logical filenames and organize them sensibly in your directory structure so you can find and identify them efficiently.

Texture Mapping

Texture mapping allows you to add significant detail to even simple objects without increasing geometry complexity. For the creation of a digital human head, for instance, you could model a relatively simple mesh and then implement texture maps for details, such as pupils and irises, skin color and imperfections, wrinkles, and any number of additional physical characteristics you might want to add, including tattoos, pimples, or a five o'clock shadow.

Textures and Geometry

Except in the case of procedural generation, once you have created or acquired your texture maps, you must apply them properly to your digital objects.

Like virtual labels or decals, texture images are attached to the geometry of CG models through the influence of a coordinate system. While a 2D image file is based on an XY coordinate system, textures are applied to digital models based on U (horizontal) and V (vertical) coordinates, which span the surface of the object (see Figure 13.16). The way you apply a texture map varies depending on the nature of the surface. The topology of a NURBS surface has an implicit UV coordinate structure, so the texture can be fitted to the geometry based on the parameterization of the surface. On the other hand, polygons and subdivision surfaces require the actual creation of a UV coordinate system for their surfaces.

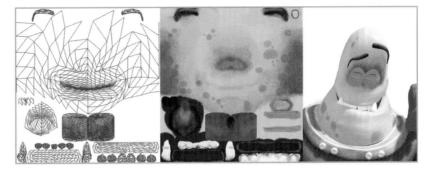

Figure 13.16
Textures are mapped onto digital objects via UV coordinates.

Mapping and Projections

When a texture map is applied to a 3D surface, the results will vary depending on the projection method that is used. Be sure to test all of the mapping systems available in your CG package to ensure that your textures are placed on your objects at the correct position and orientation.

The most standard projection mapping methods are planar, cylindrical, spherical, and cubic.

◆ **Planar.** The planar method operates by a direct projection of a texture image from a particular point of view in 3D space (see Figure 13.17). This is a common method used to project texture maps over flat objects, such as books, floors, or walls.

◆ **Cylindrical.** Cylindrical projection works by casting a texture image around the geometry of a model, much the same way as a label gets wrapped around a tin can (see Figure 13.17). This approach is obviously appropriate for cylindrical objects, such as pencils, columns, or even simple faces.

◆ **Spherical.** Spherical projection behaves similarly to cylindrical projection; however, it closes on the top and the bottom of the projection, sometimes distorting the image in the process. Often it is necessary to hide the distorted seam with a secondary object of some kind, like a hat. This is a good option for texturing objects such as faces, globes, basketballs, and planets (see Figure 13.17).

◆ **Cubic.** The cubic method projects an image onto a piece of geometry from six different directions, each one corresponding to a different axis plane. This procedure is ideal for objects such as buildings, boxes, and rectangular room interiors.

Figure 13.17
Planar, spherical, and cylindrical mapping

Layering

Often it is difficult to create the desired look of an object surface using a single texture image. Creating texture layers can be helpful because they allow you to focus on individual details independently (see Figure 13.18). For instance, consider an old piece of metal that was found on the street. You could assign its metallic quality as the base material, then add one texture layer that represents the unpolished characteristic of its surface, another for the rust, a third for scratches, and a fourth for dirt and dust. Another benefit of this method is that you can combine individual texture layers in different ways to form an endless variety of surface imagery.

Tiling

To apply a repeating pattern over a surface, it is often more efficient to make a small image and then *tile* it, rather than painting a large texture map to cover the entire surface (see Figure 13.19). Patterns such as checkerboard squares and bricks are ideal candidates for tiling. The important consideration when tiling is to make sure that the edges connect properly and often seamlessly. Many digital paint programs allow you to work in a tiled fashion so you can see a number of individual tiles assembled together, and all are affected when you edit a single tile. Without such functionality, making sure that your tiles visually connect seamlessly can be a rather arduous task.

Complementing Materials with Textures

In addition to adding detail, patterns, and imagery to the surfaces of digital models, texture maps can also be used to build upon the material attributes that have been assigned to alter or complement their existing visual qualities. A few of these material-enhancing texture types include:

◆ **Color mapping.** This combines or replaces the RGB material attributes applied to an object with the use of a colored texture. For example, if a Caucasian human face has an appropriately beige base material, you could use an additional color map for different tanning levels.

◆ **Specular mapping.** This controls the intensity of an object's specular highlights. You can use a specular map to intensify the wetness of lips or the gleaming quality of eyes.

◆ **Transparency maps.** These determine the locations of transparent areas on an object, which you can use to create holes in surfaces.

◆ **Reflection maps.** Instead of assigning actual reflective attributes to surfaces, you can use reflection maps to speed up render times. For an object to reflect its surroundings by way of rendering, you must employ ray tracing (see Chapter 18), where light rays are virtually bounced around a scene to

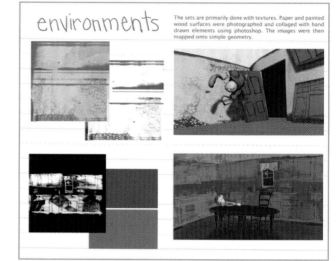

Figure 13.18
You can use layered textures to create unique and painterly imagery.

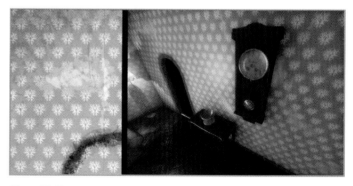

Figure 13.19
Tiling a small image can be an efficient method of texturing a larger surface.

determine where shadows fall and reflections land. Rendering scenes using this process can be very time-consuming; therefore, it is often preferable to render an image of a background setting, and then project it in a mirrored fashion onto a surface to create a fake reflection (see Figure 13.20). This method is typically most successful for backgrounds that do not contain moving elements.

◆ **Bump mapping.** You can use bump mapping to produce the illusion of surface relief, such as the pimples on a golf ball. A bump map consists of an image composed of values and tints, where the darkest areas represent concavities and the lightest tints represent convexity. Bump mapping is a quick, simple, and efficient way of giving a flat surface the appearance of bumps and irregularities after it is rendered (see Figure 13.20).

◆ **Displacement maps.** These are similar to bump maps; however, in this procedure, the geometry of the surface mesh is actually affected by the texture to form a truly three-dimensional relief. This particular type of mapping is fairly costly in terms of render time because the computer needs to calculate the displacement of the geometry; however, the savings in actual modeling time might be a satisfactory tradeoff. Keep in mind that for this type of map to work properly, the surface of the object being displaced must have a sufficiently high number of vertices.

Applying Textures to Cameras and Lights

You can also use texture images in conjunction with cameras and lights in the same manner in which a slide projector is operated, where the view or the light beam is masked or otherwise altered by the existence of an image that it passes through (see Figure 13.21).

This technique is especially useful when you want a light to shine a complex pattern of colors, as if passing through a stained glass window, or when you want a pattern of light and dark to be projected onto an object, such as the shadows of prison bars on an inmate's face.

Background Plates

Thanks to the power of most computers and software packages these days, you can model and render every object that might exist in your digital scenes; however, it is often preferable to use background plates and matte paintings to reduce man hours and rendering times.

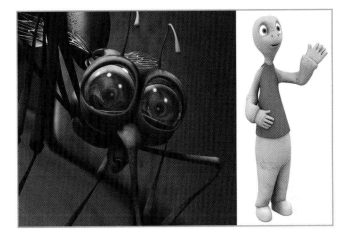

Figure 13.20
Reflection and bump mapping

Figure 13.21
You can apply textures to lights.

13. Materials and Textures

A background plate is typically a plane that is connected to a camera and sits in the distance behind the foreground elements of a particular scene. A matte painting, photograph, or movie file is then projected onto the background plate to expand the visual depth and complexity of a setting (see Figure 13.22).

Background plate images are most useful for distant elements that would otherwise be difficult or inefficient to build as geometry, such as clouds, cityscapes, constellations, or complex settings with large numbers of objects. Matte paintings are also especially useful for fantasy settings or when you want your distant background to have a very specific and perhaps abstract look.

The main advantage to matte paintings and other imagery projected onto background plates is that they do not significantly increase file sizes or rendering times as would actual 3D background objects. And of course, they can save you a significant amount of modeling work. Imagine if your film contained a scene that took place in a library, where there was a wall with hundreds of shelves and thousands of books. Creating digital objects for each of those books would be extremely time-consuming from a modeling, texturing, and rendering point of view. Painting or photographing such an image and then projecting it behind your main objects, characters, and actions would potentially be faster and more efficient.

The Hare as Interpreter by Red Goat Animation Studio

Figure 13.22
You can project an image on a flat or curved background plane to inexpensively expand the depth and detail of a digital scene.

One of the downsides of using background plate imagery is that camera moves can often break the perspective illusion. The more distant the background plate, the more freedom you will have to move the camera around before you reveal the shortcut. Another disadvantage is that obviously you will not be able to manipulate individual elements from a background plate as you can with an actual 3D object.

Therefore, it is sometimes necessary to combine 3D elements with projected 2D background imagery. If a character needs to run to the back of the library and pull a book from the shelf, you will need to have an actual 3D model of that object placed appropriately in the scene so it looks like it is a part of the 2D wall image. This would be a case in which you would need to be very careful with camera moves because the perspective of the single 3D book would subsequently change, but the other 2D books would not.

Sometimes you can assemble multiple pictures adjacent to one another on a single background plate (or several independent background plates) to create a more complete background image. This technique is known as *pan and tile*, and can be used to create a very wide or curving background setting out of connected smaller images, offset at slight angles at their edges to form something like the inside of a cylinder (or a portion thereof). This way, a camera inside the setting could pan right or left while keeping the continuous background in view (see Figure 13.23).

If you have actually built all of your distant objects as 3D models but you find that the scene is taking way too long to render, you might be able to simply render the distant elements once, and then use the resulting image on a background plate in place of the actual geometry pieces. Consider this technique when you are using the same background setting for multiple scenes, and especially for shots that use locked-off cameras.

In addition to static imagery, you can project movie files or image sequences onto background plates in most CG packages. You could use such imagery for a scrolling background behind a racing bicyclist or for a skyline with moving clouds.

Figure 13.23
The pan and tile technique

Carefully balance the timesaving advantages of using background plate imagery against the potential staging restrictions it might impose upon your camera direction style.

Summary

Materials and textures can add an extra layer of detail, definition, and visual interest to your digital scene elements. Combining the application of material attributes, such as color, specularity, reflectance, and translucency, with painted, photographed, or procedurally applied texture maps, you can create an endless variety of aesthetic styles based on your own personal art direction preferences. Textures can be mapped onto CG objects using various projection methods, and they can also be used to enhance material attributes and mask or alter the effects of your scene lights. You can also use 2D imagery as background plates to increase scene depth and save time in the modeling and rendering stages. The next chapter will describe character setup—the process of turning your CG character models into "animatable" digital puppets.

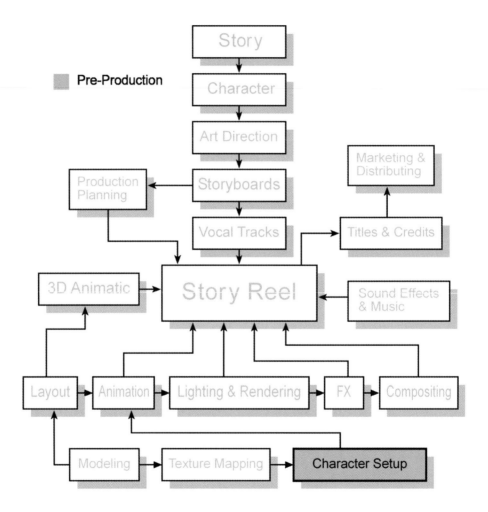

Pre-Production

Story

Character

Art Direction

Storyboards

Vocal Tracks

Production Planning

Marketing & Distributing

Titles & Credits

3D Animatic

Story Reel

Sound Effects & Music

Layout

Animation

Lighting & Rendering

FX

Compositing

Modeling

Texture Mapping

Character Setup

chapter 14
Character Setup

Although it might be possible to animate some of your simpler character models by merely translating, rotating, scaling, or reshaping their overall forms or individual parts, you generally need to turn most of your character models into digital "puppets" that can be posed and animated more efficiently.

A typical digital puppet is an animator-ready character model with an internal skeletal structure and a set of control objects. The process of assembling your character models into animatable digital puppets is known as *character setup*.

It is not necessarily imperative that you set up your characters before you build your 3D animatic or shot layouts. Simple, unarticulated character models might indeed be sufficient at those stages; however, you will definitely need workable puppets before you actually animate your characters during shot production.

Character setup can be one of the most difficult, tedious, and technically challenging aspects of short film production. A good character puppet can mean the difference between animating your shots efficiently and suffering through them with great pain. Many students and hobbyists have found themselves spinning their wheels at this stage much longer than expected, only to find insufficient time remaining in their schedules to animate their shots effectively. If you are relatively new to this skill, we highly recommend you get a comprehensive book on the subject, take a class, watch an instructional video, or bring in a teammate with sufficient experience to create workable and efficient character puppets within a reasonable timeframe.

Because of the technical nature of character setup, it would be impossible for us to go into any great detail on this particular subject in a single chapter. Furthermore, any truly detailed explanations would quickly become rather software-specific, which would also be inappropriate for this book. Therefore, we will merely cover the basic definitions, strategies, and techniques involved in this discipline. For more detailed information about the specifics of setting up characters with your chosen CG software package, consult a manual or other appropriate source.

What Is Character Setup?

Character setup is the process of turning your character models into digital puppets so you can pose and keyframe them effectively and efficiently. Imagine a typical stop-motion animation puppet, where a clay model or latex skin is sculpted as the outer geometry of a character. For an animator to pose such

> "Science may set limits to knowledge, but it should not set limits to imagination."
> Bertrand Russell

external geometry, the skin is usually built around a metal armature or a set of bendable wires. Digital character setup is similar—a set of joints is typically assembled inside a character model such that when this inner skeleton is posed, the outer geometry bends and twists appropriately (see Figure 14.1).

Unlike stop-motion puppetry, digital character setup allows you to add special features and shortcuts, such as scaling functions, constraints, pose memory, foot lockdowns, persistent head orientation, eye targets, automated muscle bulging, and visibility toggles.

There are two parts to building a digital puppet.

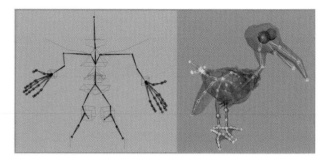

Figure 14.1
Digital puppets

- Rigging   - Binding

Rigging involves creating a character's internal skeleton and any necessary movement controllers and special functions. *Binding*, also known as *skinning* or *enveloping*, is the process of connecting a character's geometry to its skeleton so it bends and twists properly and without any unwanted tearing or intersecting.

Rigging

Rigging generally begins with the assembly of an internal skeleton hierarchy and then the creation of any desired control objects and extra bells and whistles. Occasionally, the creation of a character will actually begin with an internal skeleton, and then its external geometry is built around the joints. But most of the time, a character model is initially sculpted in a default position, and then its skeleton hierarchy is assembled inside (see Figure 14.2). When it comes to setting up biped character puppets, professional riggers tend to prefer starting with models that have been sculpted in either a da Vinci pose or a relaxed bind pose. A character in a *da Vinci pose* has his feet together, legs straight, and arms extended horizontally. In a *relaxed bind pose*, the knees and elbows are slightly bent and the arms are dropped closer to the character's sides (refer back to Chapter 12, Figure 12.7). It is typically easier to model and texture map a character in a da Vinci, but the binding process of character setup is often a bit more successful with a relaxed bind pose because the geometry does not deform as much when the joints bend to their extremes. When you reach the binding stage, you will dis-

Figure 14.2
A skeleton is typically built inside a character model that has been sculpted in a default pose.

cover that it is easier to control the reshaping of a bound geometry piece when it is stretching rather than when it is compressing, so it is generally better to start with a character model whose appendages are not fully extended. The same goes for animals—a dog model should have his leg joints slightly bent. A pair of bat wings should be halfway between fully open and fully closed.

Joints

In virtually every piece of CG software, you can assemble individual pieces of geometry into hierarchies, where one object is the parent of a single or several children. When a parent moves, the kids follow. Digital children can typically only have a single parent, but they can have an unlimited number of children, grandchildren, great-grandchildren, and so on (see Figure 14.3).

A digital skeleton is typically made up of a hierarchy of bones and joints. *Bones* are the individual skeleton pieces with *joints* on each end. One joint is generally the base, and the other is the end. The base joint of one bone can be the child of another parent bone, while an end joint can be the parent of one or several child bones or can simply exist as the last joint in a particular hierarchy chain, like the tip of a finger (see Figure 14.4).

Most digital bones have ball joints by default, meaning they can rotate in all three axes, as in shoulders, necks, and ankles. If the rotation of two axes is disabled or locked, the joint will only be able to rotate along a single axis, thus turning it into a hinge joint (such as a knee) or a twist joint (see Figure 14.5). All fully functional CG software packages also allow you to limit the rotations of a particular joint—for instance, if you don't want a knee to be able to bend the wrong way.

The first step in building a skeleton hierarchy for a digital character is to find its functional center and then place a top-level root joint at that spot. In general, a character's root joint should be located at its center of gravity, which may or may not correspond to its anatomical root. In a biped character, such as a human being, the functional center typically exists at the anatomical root where

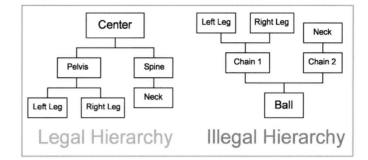

Figure 14.3
In a typical CG hierarchy, an object can have multiple children but not multiple parents.

Figure 14.4
Joint hierarchies can be simple chains or complex systems.

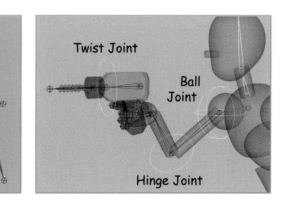

Figure 14.5
CG joints are typically ball, hinge, or twist joints.

It is generally a bad idea to impose rotation limits on ball joints. Leaving limitless rotation possibilities on such joints will allow an animator to potentially bend an appendage into an illegal pose; however, technical difficulties such as unwanted elbow flipping and the inability to reach certain desired poses might occur when limits are imposed on ball joints. Leave your ball joints open and avoid illegal poses visually, rather than digitally.

the spine meets the pelvis. When building a quadruped skeleton, however, it is often desirable to cheat anatomy and place the root joint in the middle of the back rather than where the spine connects to the pelvis, closer to the rear hips. The anatomical root of a fish is right behind its head; however, it is generally advantageous to place the main joint of a digital fish a bit further back. The immediate child of a character's root joint is often placed at the anatomical root, thus giving the animator the option of making global translations or rotations from either the center of gravity or the anatomical root (see Figure 14.6).

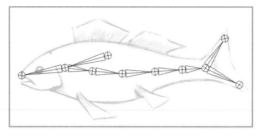

Figure 14.6
The top root joint of an internal skeleton hierarchy is often placed at the character's center of gravity, and its immediate child is placed at the anatomical root.

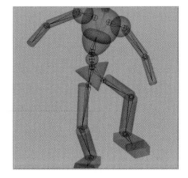

Figure 14.7
On a biped puppet, it is always a good idea to allow the pelvis to rotate independently from the rest of the torso.

When building a skeleton hierarchy for a biped or other similar creature for which the main root joint is typically placed at the base of the torso, it is important to give this joint two separate children, one for the pelvis and the other for the first joint of the spine, so each can be rotated without affecting the other. A pelvis joint that can be rotated independently is sometimes referred to as the "Elvis" joint, for obvious reasons (see Figure14.7).

For a biped or quadruped character, spines typically extend up to a character's collarbone, where the skeleton hierarchy then splits three ways, toward the neck and the arms (or front legs). Of course, if your character has more than two arms or more than one head, additional branches will be required. Arms will generally have a collarbone joint, a shoulder joint, an elbow joint, a wrist joint, and an appropriate number of finger joints. Be sure you give both arms their own collarbone joints so your character can shrug each shoulder independently (see Figure 14.8).

Some character riggers find it helpful to have an extra joint in the middle of the lower arm for better wrist-twisting functionality and to enhance the deformations in this area (see Figure 14.9).

Biped characters typically do not need individual hip rotators because unlike collarbones, the pelvis rotates as a single unit. The legs of a biped character will generally have hip joints, knee joints, ankle joints, ball-of-the-foot joints, and one or more joints for the toes.

Skeleton hierarchies for multi-legged creatures, such as turtles, insects, spiders, and certain space aliens, differ from that of normal bipeds in obvious ways. A single pelvis joint might branch off into

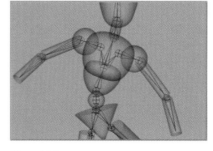

Figure 14.8
The top of the spine usually branches off toward the neck and separate collarbones.

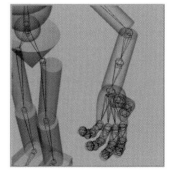

Figure 14.9
Adding a twistable joint in the middle of the forearm can sometimes help during the binding process.

four, six, eight, or perhaps more leg hierarchies. A centipede might have several leg hierarchies branching off from each spine joint (see Figure 14.10).

A fish skeleton is basically a skull connected to a spine. You can place the main top-node joint at the center of gravity. The anatomical root joint is typically placed behind the head and then branches off to a skull joint in one direction and a series of spine joints in the other direction. You can connect additional joints to appropriate places along the spine to control the fins (refer to Figure 14.6).

Study human and animal anatomy books for more information on skeletal systems in various types of creatures. The more you know about real-world anatomy, the better you'll be able to invent skeletal structures for fantasy creatures and then rig such puppets accordingly.

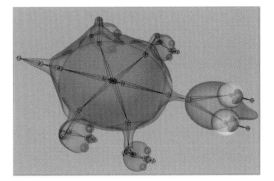

Figure 14.10
Multiple legs can branch off from a single pelvis or from different spine joints.

Basically, you want to make sure you have a joint at every location on your character that needs to bend. However, when it comes to spines, tails, and tongues, you can typically get away with significantly fewer digital joints than exist in anatomical reality. If you bind the geometry effectively, a small number of joints can actually create better and more efficient deformations on your surface (see Figure 14.11).

Simplicity is especially crucial during the character setup phase because an overly complex digital puppet can mean larger file sizes, longer load times, restricted interactivity, and an inefficient animation process. Use the fewest number of joints necessary to allow you to pose your characters successfully. Does every finger need all three knuckles, or might two suffice? Can you get away with as few as four, or perhaps only two, spine joints?

Forward Kinematics versus Inverse Kinematics

Characters with rigid skeletons are typically posed by simply rotating most of their joints. Top-level root joints are generally translated and rotated for global positioning and orientation, but the actual pose of the body is reached by rotating each of the remaining joints. Posing skeleton chains and hierarchies by rotating joints is known as *forward kinematics* or simply *FK* (see Figure 14.12). For instance, bending an arm with forward kinematics typically involves rotating the shoulder and elbow joints independently to reach the desired pose. This is a simple method for posing appendages, and it simulates anatomical reality.

An alternative method of posing joint structures is by using *inverse kinematics* or *IK*, in which the end joint of a skeleton chain is translated to a desired location and the individual joints in the hierarchy bend automatically to compensate. The end joint that gets translated is sometimes known as an *end effector* or *goal* and is typically controlled by an *IK handle* (refer to Figure 14.12).

Some CG software packages automatically create end effectors and IK handles whenever a joint chain is built, while others require you to identify the root and handle of an IK controller manually.

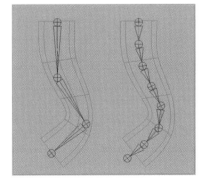

Figure 14.11
With proper binding, three joints can do the job of seven and will certainly be easier to animate.

Most CG animators tend to prefer IK for legs; however, using FK or IK with arms is often based on personal preference. Some animators always use IK for arms; other try to always use FK. Many prefer FK arms in some cases and IK arms in others, depending on the needs of the performance at hand.

The main advantage of an IK handle is that it allows for independent positioning of an end effector. In a typical skeleton hierarchy, when one joint translates or rotates, all of its children will follow. However, if an IK handle is created on an appendage, a wrist or a foot can remain in place while the torso translates, the shoulder shrugs, the spine bends, or the pelvis twists (see Figure 14.13). For instance, if you have a standing biped, you would generally want to be able to shift the hips around while the feet stay planted on the ground. With IK you can place the feet at specific locations by simply translating the ankle or heel rather than rotating the hip and knee joints as you would have to do with FK.

IK controls are preferred when the actual location of an end joint is important or when an end joint needs to stay in a specified spot such that the movement of the rest of the skeleton hierarchy will not affect its position. FK manipulation is preferred when you need the ability to control the rotations of the in-between joints. For instance, if you want to place a character's hand on a doorknob, it is much easier to accomplish this by translating an end effector than by trying to bend the shoulder and elbow joints until the wrist lands at the desired location in 3D space. However, if you want to rotate an elbow joint by itself while keeping the shoulder locked, FK posing would be more efficient.

IK controllers tend to work most predictably on two-joint chains, for instance, where the root of the IK controller is at the shoulder and the handle is at the wrist with only an elbow joint in between. Using an IK handle to pose a longer chain, such as a six-jointed tail, might lead to unpredictable rotations of the middle joints. Chains such as tails and tongues are typically easier to animate using FK unless the end of the chain needs to land in a specific location.

Some CG packages allow you to switch back and forth between FK and IK controls on a particular joint chain. This way, you can use FK for swinging the arms during a normal walk cycle and then switch to a wrist IK mode when the character decides to walk on his hands.

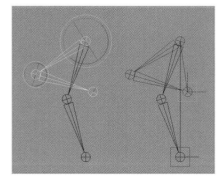

Figure 14.12
FK joint rotations versus IK translations

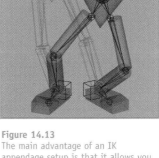

Figure 14.13
The main advantage of an IK appendage setup is that it allows you to move your character's body around without affecting the placement of an end effector.

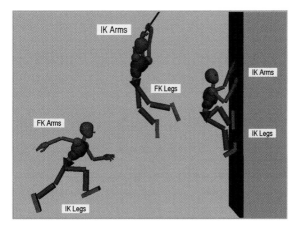

Figure 14.14
Varying FK and IK settings might be appropriate for different types of character actions.

Table 14.1 Pros and Cons of FK and IK Control

	Forward Kinematics	Inverse Kinematics
Pros	You can control and perhaps isolate the rotation of an in-between joint. Easy to add delayed, overlapping motion to subsequent joints. You get naturalistic "arcs" by default. No unexpected elbow/knee flipping.	You only need to move a single object, rather than rotating two or more to reach a desired pose. Easy to place an end effector in a specific location in 3D space. An end effector, such as a wrist or ankle, can be locked down so that it stays in place when the rest of the body movies.
Cons	To reach a desired pose, you must rotate two or more joints, rather than just moving an effector. Very difficult to place an end joint in a desired location in 3D space by rotating its parent joints. An end joint will always move with its parents and will have to be tediously counter-animated on a frame-by-frame basis if you want it to stay in place while moving other body parts.	Difficult to control or isolate the rotation of the in-between joints. Naturalistic overlap is hard to achieve. Often need to watch out for unexpected elbow/knee flipping as a result of programmatic IK "solutions."

Imagine animating Spiderman running, jumping, wall crawling, and swinging. For the running and jumping sections, you'd probably want to use IK legs and perhaps FK arms. When he crawls up the side of a building, you'd probably want IK controls for the feet and hands so they can stick to the wall. When he swings, you'd probably want IK arms attached to his web vines and perhaps FK legs so you could rotate the joints independently to create realistic, overlapping leg movement arcs (see Figure 14.14). Take a look at Table 14.1 for some of the pros and cons of FK and IK control.

Control Objects

Instead of using direct joint manipulation to pose a character's skeleton, many setup technicians prefer to create control objects that will drive joint positions and orientations by way of constraints or expressions.

A *constraint* is like a digital magnet, where the position, orientation, scale, or aim of one object is "glued" to that of another. You can use constraints for many purposes, such as attaching a hand to a steering wheel or aiming a pair of eyes at a particular spot.

An *expression* is a piece of digital code that can perform a wide variety of single or multiple functions, such as programmatically connecting certain attributes of one object to those of another. For instance, if you had a pair of connected gears, you could use an expression to tell the second gear to automatically rotate in the opposite direction whenever the first one is turned.

Control objects are often created out of nulls, primitive objects, or simple curves that are shaped to resemble crosshairs, boxes, or perhaps text letters indicating their function or corresponding joint (see Figure 14.15). If you want a control object in the shape of a cube, it is generally advantageous to use a set of linear curves in a cubical shape rather than an actual primitive object because the curve object will not inadvertently show up in your renders since it has no actual faces or form. You can constrain joints and IK handles to control objects so the animator can pose and animate a skeleton hierarchy by moving the controls rather than the joints.

There are several potential advantages to adding control objects to your character setups.

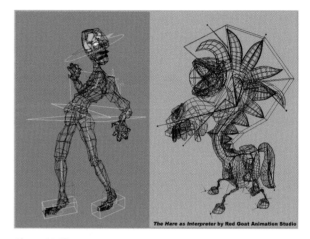

The Hare as Interpreter by Red Goat Animation Studio

Figure 14.15
You can form control objects into less obtrusive and potentially more intuitive shapes.

◆ Joints can be visually distracting. Control objects can be smaller or made out of less obtrusive objects, such as nulls.

◆ You can shape control objects into more intuitive forms, such as arrows or letters.

◆ You can use control objects for more advanced functions, such as eye-aim targeting.

◆ You can assemble control objects in their own separate hierarchy, which can be easier to troubleshoot, hide, and re-structure if necessary.

◆ Because all of your animation data will exist on your control objects rather than your joints, it might be easier to make any necessary hierarchy changes to a skeleton structure without losing or messing up parts of an existing performance. Using a set of control objects might also make it easier to transfer animation between puppets that have slightly different skeletal structures.

IK handles are very often constrained to control objects. An advantage to this is that it allows you to place such constraining objects anywhere in your hierarchy of joints or controls. For instance, if you want the location of a character's foot to be completely independent of its torso, you can place the foot IK controller at the same hierarchy level as the torso joints or controls, where it will not be affected by body movement. If you want to pose the arms with IK handles rather than with joint rotations but you don't want your wrists to get left behind when you move your character's center or torso, you might want to make your wrist IK controllers children of their respective shoulders.

A *pole vector constraint* is another control object that can sometimes prove useful in conjunction with an IK chain. When you are moving the IK end effector of a simple joint chain, such as an arm or a leg, the elbow or knee will sometimes twist into an undesirable position. Constraining the IK handle's plane of influence toward a simple object sitting out in space somewhere will allow you to control the twist of an elbow or knee by translating the constraint object appropriately. Check your manual for specific details on the creation and usage of pole vector constraints in your chosen piece of CG software.

Advanced Rigging Techniques

A character setup containing only a skeleton hierarchy, a few IK handles, and perhaps a set of control objects will often be more than adequate for efficient character posing and animation. However, you might find it helpful to add a few bells and whistles to your puppets to expand their functionality and provide you with some potential workflow shortcuts.

One common special feature is a head-rotation-lock mechanism. In a typical character skeleton hierarchy, the neck and head joints are children of the torso. If you are animating a stalking creature whose torso bends and twists with each footstep, you would have to counter-animate the skull joint every time the spine rotated in order to keep the head vertical. However, if you constrained your skull joint to a control object above or outside of the hierarchy of the torso so it is not affected by spine rotation, the head's orientation would be independent of the torso. This way, the head can remain vertical (or perhaps locked onto a target) while the rest of the character bends and twists.

Another feature you might want to add to a character puppet is squash and stretch functionality for more cartoony performances. Often you can accomplish this by simply scaling your characters' joints, in addition to simply rotating or translating them.

Most CG packages allow you to write short or even long and complex scripts or expressions you can use to add all manner of additional functions and shortcuts to your puppets. For instance, you could write an expression to automatically make a joint thinner whenever you make it longer, so that any geometry being squashed and stretched by way of joint scaling would maintain its volume and therefore look more natural. A pair of simple expressions for such functionality might look something like this:

```
ArmJoint.scaleX = sqrt (1 / ArmJoint.scaleY);
ArmJoint.scaleZ = sqrt (1 / ArmJoint.scaleY);
```

You can also use an expression to make a biped character's hips automatically stay centered between the feet. You could accomplish this by making the X position of the hips equal to the average of that of the two feet, and then doing the same for Z. Typically, you would leave Y translation alone. A two-line expression for a feature such as this might look like:

```
Hips.translateX = ( leftFoot.translateX + rightFoot.translateX ) / 2;
Hips.translateZ = ( leftFoot.translateZ + rightFoot.translateZ ) / 2;
```

Other expression-driven functions you might want to consider using include:

◆ **Automatic muscle bulging.** For instance, you can set the shape or size of a bicep object or cluster to expand or change whenever its corresponding elbow joint rotates.

◆ **A lower eyelid rotating halfway upward whenever the upper lid is rotated down.** This would be a simple matter of an expression such as `lowLid.rotX = (- 0.5) * upLid.rotX`.

If you create automated controls in your character setups, such as a persistent hip-centering expression, it is very important to include the ability to override and disable such functionality. Keeping a character's hips automatically centered between its two feet might be appropriate for certain mechanical creatures, but creating believable character movement almost always requires a proper indication of weight. Often you achieve this primarily through careful and deliberate hip placement and movement controlled by an actual human being with aesthetic sensibilities rather than a computer script that knows nothing about animation.

14. Character Setup

293

◆ **Automated tail follow-through.** Suppose you have a tail made out of a three-joint chain. You could use a set of expressions that would make the second joint follow the rotation of the first with a small delay, and then the third joint could programmatically follow the rotation of the second with a similar delay. With such a setup, you could animate simple tail movements by rotating the first joint, and then a natural-looking follow-through would happen automatically on the other two joints. You could create an additional expression that would allow you to adjust the time delay so slow tail movements would have a longer delay than quick motions. Consult the scripting section of your software manual for the exact syntax for how you might create a function such as this.

◆ **FK/IK dials.** Sometimes it is advantageous to have the ability to switch an appendage from being FK-controlled to IK-controlled. Most software packages allow you to make this switch over a single frame, but you might want the ability to do this gradually over the course of several frames. If your software does not have a "dial" functionality, you might be able to create this feature using expressions. The trick is to create three versions of an appendage. One would be, for instance, the real arm, where the geometry would attach. Then a second identical FK arm would exist, where you could rotate the shoulder and elbow joints independently. An identical third arm would contain an IK controller rooted at the shoulder and ending at the wrist. The rotation of the real arm would be constrained to both the FK arm and the IK arm. Then you could write an expression in which sliding a new "dial" node would cause the constraint weight of the FK arm to go down while that of the IK arm would go up, and vice versa (see Figure 14.16).

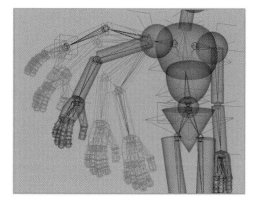

Figure 14.16
An FK/IK dial allows you to switch controller modes over the course of several frames, which might help with transitions between free and locked appendage movement.

Creating a fully functional biped foot setup is another advanced rigging scenario that can be tricky depending on the specifics of your software package. Often, a global foot controller is placed at the heel, which can be used to rotate and translate the foot from that spot. Then, custom attributes are typically added to the controller that allow the animator to perform functions such as independent knee twisting, toe curling, and raising the heel so the foot is perched on its ball. Another method is the popular *reverse foot setup*, which involves building a backward joint hierarchy starting from the heel, extending through the toes and the ball of the foot, and ending at the ankle, which serves as a constraining object for the leg IK handle (see Figure 14.17).

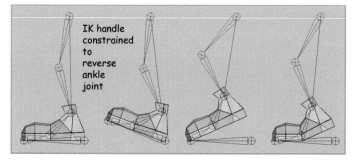

IK handle constrained to reverse ankle joint

Figure 14.17
The "reverse" foot is a common setup that allows for toe and ball-of-the-foot pivoting.

Although it is tempting to add all manner of special features to your character puppets, be wary of arbitrarily adding extra controls and expressions just to impress your teammates. Character puppets can quickly become complex and heavy, leading to troubleshooting difficulties, slower load times, and diminished interactivity as a result of too many bells and whistles. When you are deciding whether to add a special feature, carefully consider whether you will ever actually use it. Demonstrate the full extent of your technical prowess on your demo reel, not on your elegantly simple short film character puppets.

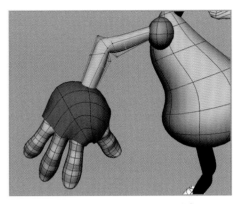

Figure 14.18
Vertices near the shoulder and wrist belong exclusively to the first and last joints, respectively, while those near the middle have multiple influences.

Binding

The second part of character setup is typically known as *binding*, *skinning*, *deforming*, or *enveloping*, and it refers to the process of connecting a puppet's outer geometry to its skeleton structure so it bends and twists nicely when the internal hierarchy is posed and animated.

Characters such as robots, toys, mannequins, and certain insects that are built out of separate rigid body parts can often be bound to an internal skeleton by simply parenting these geometry pieces to appropriate joints.

However, connecting a smooth and malleable piece of skin geometry to an internal skeleton is generally a bit more complicated. Think of a piece of digital geometry as a center axis with a collection of connected vertices. Parenting such an object to a joint involves hierarchically connecting the entire object to the joint. Binding, on the other hand, can be thought of as parenting individual or groups of vertices (rather than entire objects) to joints. When you simply parent an object to an individual joint, the movement of the object is dictated only by that one joint. With binding, however, vertices can be influenced by multiple joints with adjustable levels of intensity or weight. For instance, consider an arm model made out of a vertical cylinder object with several spans. If this arm is bound to a two-joint chain, the vertices at the top should be influenced by the upper-arm joint alone, while the lower vertices should be influenced by only the lower-arm joint. Those in the middle should be influenced by both joints to create a smooth bend (see Figure 14.18).

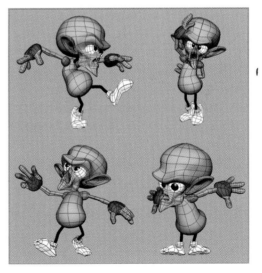

Figure 14.19
Be sure to bend and twist your characters into extreme poses when testing the integrity of your skin binding and vertex weighting.

When you initially bind a piece of geometry to a skeleton chain, a typical CG package will programmatically assign influence values to all of the vertices on the object. Usually, such automated *vertex weighting* will not immediately result in nice outer skin deformations until you go in and adjust some of the influence values manually. You'll want to experiment with different weight values and then test your puppet for unwanted tearing and overlapping by creating "calisthenics" performances in which your character is bent into extreme poses (see Figure 14.19). This manual weighting process can be rather tedious, especially if your character model has a lot of vertices. Look for helpful tools such as vertex weight mirroring to help streamline your binding process. As an added feature, some packages will also allow you to actually *paint* vertex weights on geometry pieces, which is certainly faster and more intuitive than typing in numbers, but even this process can take quite some time.

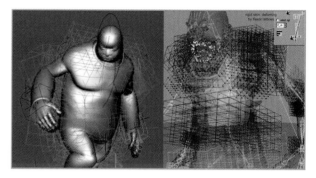

Figure 14.20
Beyond simple vertex weighting, you can shape outer skins using deformers such as lattices.

Fortunately, most packages offer more advanced tools for making your outer skins behave properly, including:

◆ **Lattices.** These are like cages you can construct around existing geometry. Lattices create an influence field over the objects within them. When the lattices are scaled, bent, rotated, or reshaped, the geometry inside is similarly altered (see Figure 14.20). The main advantage of a lattice is that it can typically have a significantly lower resolution than that of the geometry that it is influencing; therefore, it can be bound to a skeleton and controlled with increased interactivity. You can also carefully sculpt lattices into body cages that surround an entire character and closely resemble his form, like a thick, faceted body glove. You can bind these cages, rather than your actual character skin, to a skeleton and use them to deform the more complex geometry inside. An advantage of having such a low-resolution, skinned outer body shape is that you can use it as a stand-in puppet for more complex body geometry so the animation process can be more interactive and efficient. Then you can import the real geometry or simply make it visible for fine-tuning.

◆ **Clusters.** These are collections of vertices you can group into sets. This allows a setup technician to work with groups of vertices (rather than individual ones), which is often more efficient.

◆ **Blend shape deformers.** These are duplicates of existing geometry pieces that have been reshaped and can be used as deformation targets. When a joint moves to a certain angle, the original geometry can be programmatically set to ease toward the form of a blend shape. With these deformers, you can form skinned geometry into very specific shapes whenever appropriate manipulations are applied to specific control hierarchies.

◆ **Wire deformers.** These are simple curves that typically contain a small number of points you can use to bend and shape more complex pieces of attached geometry.

◆ **Bulge/sculpt objects.** These can sit under a character's skin and be programmed to expand or contract with the rotation of a particular joint. Bulge/sculpt objects are particularly useful for simulating muscle flexing.

Most CG packages contain some variation of all of the deformers listed. Consult your software manual for more information.

If you have a character that is geometrically dense and becomes non-interactive when rigged and skinned, build a set of low-resolution stand-in body parts that closely approximate the shape of the final version. Then create a lighter puppet by simply parenting these stand-in models to appropriate joints on your internal skeleton. You can accomplish most of your animation work with this interactive low-resolution version. Then you can copy your animation data over to your official heavy version for your final tweaks. A middle-resolution, skinned version is sometimes helpful as well, in which a copy of your body geometry is created with significantly fewer points and then bound to your skeleton (see Figure 14.21).

Figure 14.21
If a character is particularly vertex-heavy, it is often advantageous to have two or perhaps three different resolution puppets for varying degrees of interactivity.

Other Setup Tools

In addition to creating skeletons, controls, scripts, and binding solutions for your digital puppets, another part of character setup is creating external control mechanisms, such as shelf buttons, pop-up windows, and script plug-ins.

Most CG packages allow you to create custom buttons that can act as shortcuts for single or multiple commands, such as selecting objects, recording or applying a saved pose, keyframing all or selected objects, toggling the visibility of appendages, or swapping out the display of different resolution-level geometry.

You can write more complex scripts to expand the functionality of most CG packages and streamline your workflow. Some popular plug-in examples include random motion generators, object renamers, graph-editor display filters, vertex weight copiers, and pop-up windows with character imagery you can use as highly interactive tools for selecting animation controls (see Figure 14.22).

Consult your software manual for information on creating custom buttons and plug-ins, and explore Web pages such as http://www.highend3d.com, from which you can download, test, and perhaps utilize such tools in your production.

Facial Systems

Setting up a character's face for expression-shaping and lip-synching is also a very important part of character setup, unless of course your characters are faceless or designed so that their expressions will remain static.

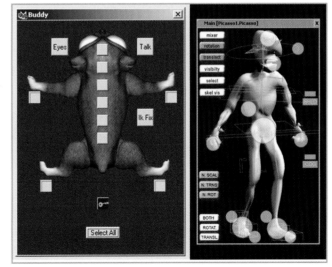

Figure 14.22
A graphical interface for selecting animation controls can be extremely intuitive.

The two most common methods of setting up facial expression and phoneme controls are

◆ Morph targets
◆ Skeleton- or deformer-driven manipulation

Morph Targets

The morph target method of facial animation setup involves the use of blend shapes. Typically in the modeling stage, you sculpt multiple copies of a character's face into desired shapes based on the facial expressions and phoneme shapes you want your character to be able to hit. Target shapes are often created by merely altering the shape of one specific area of a face, such as the left eyebrow or the right side of the mouth.

Once you have targeted these alternative face shapes by way of your CG software's specific methodology, a list is typically generated in which you can morph your original face toward a particular expression or phoneme shape using a slider bar or some similar interface. You can create new facial expressions by mixing morph target influences from two or more distinct face shapes. You might want the eyebrow pose from your "surprised" target shape, the left mouth shape from your "sneer" target, and the right cheek bulge from your "chipmunk" target.

During the character setup phase, it is sometimes advantageous to construct a custom plug-in for manipulating morph target sliders. Doing so will potentially allow you to create facial expressions and lip-synch performances with greater control and efficiency (see Figure 14.23).

The main advantage of this method is that you have predefined face shapes you can target, which is helpful when you want to pose a face into a specific phoneme shape every time your character mouths a particular syllable sound.

The main disadvantage of the morph target method is that your shape possibilities will be somewhat finite. If you want to manipulate a character's face into a shape that cannot be reached with your current set of morph targets, you will have to sculpt and target new face shapes or add a layer of deformation controls on top of this system.

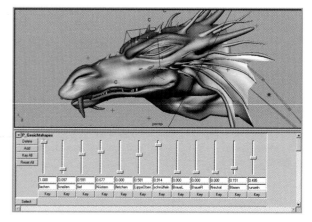

Figure 14.23
You can create new face shapes from a small number of morph targets by mixing their influences over the original geometry.

Skeleton- or Deformer-Driven Manipulation

The second common method of facial animation control is to set up a character's face the same way you would typically assemble the rest of the body—adding joints, control objects, and deformers you can use to pull and twist the face into any shape you can imagine.

Place joints or deformers in all of the areas you might want to shape, including eyebrows, cheeks, and various spots around the mouth. Then bind appropriately and animate your facial expressions and phonemes by translating, rotating, scaling, reshaping, and keyframing these controllers (see Figure 14.24).

A third method professional animation studios and effects houses commonly use is a muscle-driven setup in which many of the actual muscles that exist inside a real character's face are created underneath the skin, so they can be flexed and twisted to sculpt the outer geometry into shapes that are often convincingly realistic because of their anatomical accuracy and influences. The character technicians responsible for the facial controls in the *Shrek* films utilized this type of system. Keep in mind, however, that muscle-driven facial setups are typically quite complex and can result in very heavy and potentially non-interactive character puppets. Therefore, we do not recommend this methodology unless you have sufficient time, skills, and the CPU power to properly and efficiently handle such complexity.

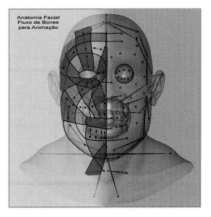

Figure 14.24
Placing skinned joints inside a character face is another common facial animation system.

The main advantage of this method is that you can pose a character's face into an unlimited number of distinct shapes, which is especially useful for cartoon characters that require a great deal of exaggeration.

The main disadvantage is that you do not by default have specific target shapes readily available that correspond to certain exact phoneme or facial expressions you might need to reach. However, you can create such targets by manipulating your face controllers until you reach a desired shape and then recording the pose information from each controller so you can reapply it at a later time if you want to repeat the exact same face shape.

Setting Up Non-Characters and Secondary Objects

Sometimes you also need to set up non-character objects and secondary geometry pieces so you can animate them more efficiently. For instance, a piece of complex machinery with rotating sections, spinning gears, and moving pistons might be easier to animate if you place a skeleton inside. Even something as simple as a swinging chain, rope, or vine will be more animator-friendly if you add necessary joints and control objects. Similarly, secondary objects, such as ponytails, tassels, loose clothing, and hanging jewelry, will be much easier to animate if you place an appropriately shaped skeleton chain inside (see Figure 14.25).

Figure 14.25
Your ability to pose and animate non-characters and secondary objects will benefit from a few carefully placed joints and controls.

Expressions and scripts can also help with non-character rigs that need to move in predictable ways. For instance, you could write an expression to make the wheels of a car spin at the proper speed whenever the chassis is translated. A complex set of different-sized gears could be expression-driven to rotate appropriately whenever a single gear is turned. However, when it comes to secondary character appendages, clothing, and accessories, it is typically preferable to animate such objects by hand or with the help of procedural FX algorithms.

Puppet Testing

After you build your character puppets, it is extremely important to test them out before you enter the shot production stage. Bend every joint, press every button, and try a few extreme poses to ensure that nothing unexpected occurs. If an IK chain is going to flip around uncontrollably or a piece of bound geometry is going to bunch up, tear, or overlap another object, it is better to discover such puppet problems while you are still in the pre-production stage. A few unexpected problems will undoubtedly come up during shot production, but do your best to work out as many kinks as possible by sufficiently testing out your character rigs at this stage. And be sure to test your rigs with poses and movements that will actually occur in your film. If your dog character will spend most of his screen time napping, don't test his rig with just a simple walk cycle. Make sure that he will also behave properly when posed lying down

Naming Conventions

It is always a good idea to give logical names to the hierarchy elements of your character and object puppets in your CG project files so you can easily identify them. There are four main types of objects that might exist in a digital puppet.

- Geometry pieces
- Skeleton joints
- Control objects
- Deformers

Name the very top node of a puppet with one field indicating the identity of the character or object, and perhaps a second field for a version number or additional descriptive information.

- Dog
- Butch_v3
- Bumblebee_3
- White_dragon
- House_brick_5

Some character riggers like to differentiate between certain object types by naming geometry pieces based on basic body-part names (thigh or shin) and skeleton joints based on anatomical terminology (femur or tibia). However, mainly because control objects and deformers also need to be named, it is generally preferable to use a separate field to indicate object type.

- Thigh_geom
- Thigh_joint
- Thigh_ctrl

A third field is generally added to indicate details such as left, right, top, bottom, front, rear, or perhaps numbers in the case of a series of jointed objects, such as a tail hierarchy.

- Thigh_geom_Lf
- Leg_Front_Lf_ctrl
- Antenna_joint_top
- Tail_def_3

An advantage to using separate fields is that it makes it easier to use wildcards to select groups or write scripts.

- Select Tail_ctrl_*
- Duplicate Leg_Front_*_joint

Buy Instead of Build

If you plan to set up your own character puppets, consult a software manual, third-party textbook, Web page tutorial, colleague, or teacher for more detailed and software-specific information on basic and advanced rigging and binding techniques.

However, you should realize that character setup can be a difficult and time-consuming task. The potential length and complexity of this stage might be more than your schedule or sanity can handle. If you feel that this is the case, consider buying or downloading a pre-built rig or a semi-automated character setup plug-in system you can apply to your own character models.

One such pre-built rig is "Simpleguy," which you can purchase from http://www.turbosquid.com. (Search for "simpleguy.") This rig is a fully functional, Maya-compatible, biped character that you can use as is, or you can toss his geometry pieces and then re-proportion his skeleton and controls to fit inside an alternative character model (see Figure 14.26).

Another option is the Setup Machine from http://www.anzovin.com, which is a systematic tool for constructing a puppet rig inside a pre-built biped or multi-legged character model. The Setup Machine also contains FK/IK switches as well as tail additions; it is available for Maya, Animation Master, and Lightwave.

As luck would have it, some generous CG artists, including Andrew Silke and Javier Goosh Solsona, actually have free puppet rigs available for downloading. See Appendix C for these and other character setup options, where you can learn or borrow from the pros.

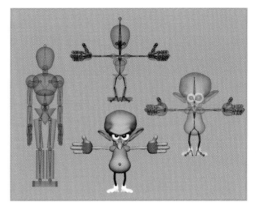

Figure 14.26
You can re-proportion some pre-built digital puppets, such as Simpleguy, to fit inside an alternative character model.

Summary

Character setup is the potentially difficult and time-consuming process of turning a character model into a digital puppet you can pose and animate efficiently with joints, control objects, and deformers. A digital puppet resembles a typical stop-motion puppet, where an outer skin is built around an inner hierarchy of armature parts or wires. However, the digital version can contain a wide variety of additional features and shortcuts. Character setup is broken up into two disciplines—*rigging*, which is the assembly of the joints and controls, and *binding*, which is the process of connecting the outer geometry to the inner hierarchy so it bends and twists appropriately when the controlling skeleton is posed. The first step in creating a character's inner skeleton is to find its functional center joint. Typically, its immediate child would be the anatomical center, which will usually branch off separately toward the spine and the pelvis. Simplicity is a very important goal in your character setup phase. Use the fewest number of joints and controls possible to keep your puppets interactive and easy to troubleshoot. *Forward kinematics* is the process of rotating individual joints. *Inverse kinematics* involves translating an *end effector* so the in-between joints bend appropriately to compensate. IK controls are preferred when the location of a chain's end joint is important. FK controls are preferred when you need to control the rotations of the joints within the chain. It is often advantageous to build control objects that drive your joints by way of constraints and expressions. Binding is like parenting individual vertices or groups of vertices to joints, where their influence can be shared. After a piece of geometry is skinned, you generally need to tweak the *vertex weighting* so the skin behaves properly. Using lattices and deformers can often make this process a bit less tedious. If your character's geometry is fairly heavy, consider building a low-resolution version with which you can do most of your animating with a high level of interactivity, and then transferring over to the full version for your final tweaks. The two most common facial animation systems are *morph targets*, in which default face geometry can ease toward specific blend shapes, and *skeleton and deformer manipulation*, in which a face is bound to an internal hierarchy structure and posed from within. Chapter 16, "Animation," will explore the subject of character animation.

Figure 15.1
Jim McCampbell

chapter 15
An Interview with Jim McCampbell

The computer animation students at Florida's Ringling School of Art and Design (http://www.rsad.edu) have produced an impressive collection of CG shorts over the past several years, including an unparalleled number of accepted SIGGRAPH Electronic Theater entries. The consistent artistic and technical excellence of these films can be attributed, at least partially, to the philosophies and quality standards set down by Jim McCampbell, Ringling's Computer Animation Department Head. We had the opportunity to ask Jim a few questions to find out the secrets to the continuing success of his students.

Q: *First of all, tell us a little bit about your background.*

A: My first experience with computer animation was in 1980. As a Graphic Design major at the University of Tennessee, I took what must have been one of the first computer animation courses for artists. This was literally before the mouse was around. We used a variant of UNIX called Felix, and everything was typed in as code to get an image. It was a tough course…but it was enough to really get me hooked.

After graduation, I worked for a number of advertising agencies, working my way up to Senior Art Director. One day, in 1986, the president of the agency I was working for at the time called me to his office. Of course, I thought I was fired. Instead, he explained that they had a large number of broadcast animation clients, and wondered [whether], if they were to purchase a Silicon Graphics computer, would I be interested in learning how to use it. I was more shocked than if I *had* been fired.

They had decided to purchase Wavefront software, and [they] sent me to Santa Barbara for a week of training. Those who remember the old days know what I mean when I say it was a lot to learn. The toolset was not very artist-friendly. I worked hard that week and crammed every bit of knowledge I could into my head…. Remember, there was no Web to get help from back then. You were on your own. When I returned, I was informed that there had been a change…. They had decided to buy Alias software instead, and I was to go to Toronto the next week for their training. I completed that one as well, and my first version of the software was Alias 2.4. I spent years working on projects for a lot of different clients. I was considered unusual at the time because I had an art background. It was mostly programmers making the animation back then.

Later, I began working for film and video companies because I could do a wider range of more complex work in that environment. When I made that move, they were using software from Thomson Digital Image (TDI), much of which was to become Maya almost 10 years later. I started to do half broadcast work and half character animation. I worked 14-hour days at least six days a week up until 1995…. I was getting burned out in production, and began looking for something different.

Animation was really beginning to take off at that point, and it became obvious to me that everything was going to explode soon. Up until then, animators were like magicians. We were all very secretive about how we did what we did. Not many wanted to share their secrets because knowing those things was how we made our money. When I saw an advertisement for a faculty position at Ringling School of Art and Design, I made the decision to buck tradition and go tell everyone everything I had learned over the years. I started there in the summer of 1995 and became Department Head in 2000.

Q: *Can you describe some of your responsibilities as Department Head?*

A: I'm responsible for guiding the curriculum toward the support of the department's vision and mission. That is done in collaboration with departmental faculty and staff, whom I am responsible for supervising. I'm also in charge of guiding the technological development of the department toward support of the departmental curriculum. I maintain the departmental budget, coordinate with the admissions office, determine teaching assignments, coordinate departmental outreach efforts, visiting artists, etc. On top of all that, I still teach two-thirds of the senior-level courses personally.

Q: *Describe a typical Jim McCampbell workday (or work week, if that makes more sense).*

A: If I tell you that I teach two days a week and have summers off, you will (as most students do) think, "Wow! What a cake job!" Appearances can be deceiving. On the days of the week when I don't teach classes, I am always working up lessons for those upcoming classes and attending to the endless administrative duties that run the department.

On teaching days, it goes like this: Class from 8:30 to 11:15. Lunch (usually a meeting here). Class from 12:30 to 3:15. Then more meetings. Eat dinner, and then answer student e-mails late into the night. Ringling's Computer Animation faculty give up a lot of their personal time meeting with students both in person and electronically to give them feedback on their projects. Not because they are required to…but because they really care about the students' success and the quality of the work.

Summers are usually spent doing professional work so that the students will have instruction by faculty with current professional experience.

Q: *During the school year, do you still do studio work or does the school job take up all of your professional time?*

A: Ringling requires its faculty to stay professionally active. I do numerous animation projects during the course of the year through my freelance company, Peculiar Pictures. I use mostly Ringling faculty, graduates, and sometimes even students to help on the larger ones. Recently, we completed a 30-minute character animation for children using the voice talents of Tim Conway and Don Knotts. Doing professional work keeps full-time faculty current and confident in the classroom.

Q: *What do you bring from your professional experience to your current job?*

A: I believe that I teach my students strong practical skills and a superior work ethic. Having spent years in production, I understand the demands and constraints that are in place. I have always felt that I could teach them to be creative while working inside those parameters. I have a lot of hands-on experience in both animation and education at this point.

Q: *In what other ways do you stay connected with the industry?*

A: On top of the freelance work that I do, we have on average about 38 animation studios and computer gaming companies that come to campus to recruit the students each year. This allows me the opportunity to discuss industry changes and trends with them, and then fold that information back into the curriculum. I have a large number of personal contacts in the industry that act as a sounding board, too. Also, Ringling's entire Computer Animation faculty attends SIGGRAPH each year and other animation conferences as well. We also have a number of visiting artists from the industry that come to campus and do presentations.

Q: *Describe your curriculum. How long is the program?*

A: Ringling's Computer Animation major is quite unique in several different ways. First, unlike most other institutions, ours is truly a four-year BFA program in Computer Animation. Although many other schools may claim that they have a Computer Animation major, the reality is that most only have a few individual courses on the subject. This is simply not enough for someone who aspires to be a professional animator in today's competitive world.

Next, the structure of our curriculum is most unusual. We have worked very hard to create a balance between the conceptual and the technical. In parallel with learning the technology, our students learn all of the important aspects of concept development and story development as well. Ours is a philosophy of communication through movement, so it is very important to have a great idea to communicate. Our student work is highly successful and universally well received because it is not only technically sound, but because of the unique designs and interesting stories as well. Our students think.

Our department prides itself on the fact that its curriculum is deep, not wide. Many other schools adopt an approach of having you sample a broad spectrum of tools and techniques that are used in a wide range of computer graphics applications. Instead, Ringling students delve deeply into animation as an art form. With our concentrated focus, we are able to address the subtle nuances that distinguish movement from true animation.

It is also noteworthy that the department is somewhat exclusive. We only accept 45 new students per year.

Q: *What are the entrance requirements for your program?*

A: You'll need a solid academic background and a history of taking as many studio art and art history courses as possible in a college-prep program. We really do care about your academic training. Liberal arts preparation is an important part of a Ringling education—and it makes you a better artist, too.

What we do not require: SAT and ACT scores. But they do help us identify the most appropriate classes for you. We strongly recommend that you take one or both of [the tests].

The Computer Animation department prefers an indication of ability in traditional art skills in its admissions portfolios. We don't want to see how much you think you already know about animation; we want to see that you can draw and have a sensitivity to color and composition. Gesture drawing showing weight, form, and balance are great.

Q: *What are the qualifications of your teachers?*

A: We have an eclectic group of faculty in the Computer Animation department. Some are former Disney and Blue Sky character animators, some have a film school background, some are technical directors, and some have worked with studios doing LBE. We even have one who has done a considerable amount of gallery work. The thing that all of us appreciate most about each other is our highly collaborative nature. It's the glue that bonds all of the craziness together. We all share the same philosophy, and our diverse backgrounds allow us to approach the curriculum from multiple viewpoints. All of the perspectives of those diverse backgrounds are channeled toward the success of the department and its students.

15. An Interview with Jim McCampbell

Q: *If a student just wants to become an animator and doesn't want to "waste" time doing modeling, lighting, character setup, etc., can the student just do animation exercises or is he/she required to complete an entire film as his/her thesis in order to graduate?*

A: I can see where the "animation exercise only" philosophy might work for a large studio hiring artists to do nothing but animate characters that have been modeled, rigged, textured, and lit by someone else, but I believe it is unfair to the average student. Unless you are working in that type of large-studio "sheltered" environment, you are going to have to have a much larger set of responsibilities in order to gain employment. With so many animators in the marketplace now, far fewer students get hired straight out of school to do only character work. It still happens…but I need to prepare them for the possibility that their job may be more all-inclusive than that. That means learning modeling, lighting, rigging, texturing, etc., too. So, all students in the Computer Animation department do a senior thesis project, and all of them learn multiple aspects of the production process. We are still very character-heavy, but we do manage to graduate students who are well rounded.

Q: *Do the students ever work in teams or just as solo filmmakers? Do you encourage group projects?*

A: We encourage them to collaborate on group projects if they so desire, and [we] have had some very successful ones in the past. However, the vast majority of students seem to prefer working solo on their senior project. I think it mostly has to do with the satisfaction of determining one's own fate. Students who work on group projects are allowed to do longer-format projects since they are combining their resources.

Q: *Do you encourage their films to be politically correct and G-rated?*

A: No. In fact, we have had some that were real jaw-droppers. For some reason, they don't seem to get as much festival play as those that are targeted to a broader audience, though, and the students have noticed this. We frequently remind them that they are making the film for the audience and not for themselves. Beyond that, if they want to do something that is way out there, we allow it…as long as it fulfills the department's requirements of a senior project. They just have to understand that everyone might not appreciate their sense of humor or perspective and that it can possibly impair their success when looking for a job.

Q: *Does your curriculum stress fundamental art skills, such as drawing, painting, and sculpture?*

Figure 15.2
Fundamental art skills are stressed as entrance requirements as well as curriculum electives.

A: Yes. Drawing is the main skill that will get you admitted to our program, and it is held in high regard institutionally. Painting and sculpture classes are available as electives through other departments. We consider drawing to be a fundamental component to the animation process.

Q: *Does Ringling offer a 2D animation program as well? If not, are there traditional animation classes available, and if so, are they required classes or are they electives?*

A: We don't offer a 2D animation degree, but Computer Animation majors take a year of 2D traditional animation as part of the curriculum here. They are required classes.

Q: *Do the Computer Animation students get a well-rounded education with liberal arts classes and such, or is the program focused completely on art and CG studies?*

A: The education is very well rounded. Ringling School of Art and Design is accredited by both the Commission on Colleges of the Southern Association of Colleges and Schools (SACS) and the National Association of Schools of Art and Design (NASAD) to award the Bachelor of Fine Arts degree. Liberal arts are a very important part of the curriculum. How can one be a complete artist without understanding the world around them? How can you function successfully in today's society without being multifaceted?

Artists and designers play a significant role in society. Visual arts professionals must understand diverse aspects of past and present cultures and develop their capacity for creative expression and effective communication. Our goal is to have our students become discerning visual thinkers and ethical practitioners in their chosen area of art and design. In order to accomplish this, a complete education is mandatory.

Q: *If a student gets a job offer before he or she graduates, is the student encouraged to try to finish school first, or do you feel that it is more important for the student to get out into the workplace as soon as possible?*

A: We feel it is extremely important for them to complete their degrees. When job offers come, they may be for only a film or two. A college degree is something that you will use for your entire life. Besides, if you are valuable enough to get that offer now—before finishing school—how much more valuable will you be with the knowledge gained after completing the degree?

Q: *What equipment is available to the students? What is the accessibility?*

A: As of this writing, we have three teaching labs in our major, each with 16 2.8-GHz dual-processor workstations in them. We also have a separate render farm with 80 more machines, and [we] are preparing to add to that. We replace the equipment every other year with the highest end available, so the students are always working with the most recent technology. We have a very large and talented Institutional Technology staff that takes care of the hardware and software for us.

For video, we have five non-linear editing stations exporting to DigitalBeta tape decks. (Although any of the workstations can be used for editing, these are directly connected to the decks.) We have digital audio and digital routers, too, and of course we are able to record to DVD for demos. We also have a separate traditional animation lab and sound room.

We use Pixar's Alfred render-scheduling software on our render farm. It's wonderful. Students can submit and monitor projects from the Web. Their jobs go into a queue and get rendered based on a formula we have for a fair distribution of resources. The farm renders 24/7. Any time a machine is not in use in the lab, Alfred finds it and starts rendering a job. There is never a lost CPU cycle. Our labs are open until midnight each night, and from midnight until 8:30 all 128 machines come alive to render the day's jobs.

15. An Interview with Jim McCampbell

Q: *Where do the students get their music, sound effects, and voice actors?*

A: We have an extensive library which we have the rights to, and we add to it each year. We also have a sound room in which students can generate their own music and effects using a keyboard and Proteus synthesizers. Voice talent comes in the form of our close relationship with Florida Studio Theater or from friends and faculty. My children's voices have been in Electronic Theater several times.

Q: *What are some of the students' biggest challenges when working on their shorts?*

A: Keeping them short! They have the tendency to try and make a feature film, and the production timetable simply won't allow it. The senior project spans almost two semesters, but it goes by a lot faster than you might think. Students tend to overextend themselves in this way. They don't have a feel yet for how much can be accomplished in this short period. Coming out the other side, we always have the seniors talk to the juniors about their experiences so that [the juniors] might learn how to pace themselves and scale their projects appropriately.

Another challenge is sorting through all of the information and possible directions they get from critique. Often there is conflicting information there, and they have to work at learning how to understand the root of why a specific comment was made. They don't have to use the possible solution that was suggested, but they do have to address the problem.

Q: *Do you recall any films that had particularly problematic production cycles? If so, can you recall the specifics of their problems and solutions?*

A: The production cycle is the same for all of the projects. We have very strict deadlines, which helps prepare [students] for their future in the industry. Every project will have its share of problems…this is why problem-solving skills are so carefully cultivated. Learning how to logically dissect the problem and solve it is a very valuable experience.

Q: *In researching and collecting example material for this book, we looked at student work from all over the world. The volume of quality student shorts coming out of Ringling in the past few years has been quite impressive, both technically and conceptually, including a rather unprecedented number of SIGGRAPH ET and CAF acceptances. What's your secret?*

A: That's probably the question I am asked most often. There are three qualities that a SIGGRAPH-worthy animation possesses. They're conceptually unique, they are technically well executed, and they're short. That's it. If your work is all three of those things, you have a great chance of getting in. If you are missing even one of those three, you have a real challenge on your hands.

Q: *Is it a disadvantage being so far away from the Meccas of the film, TV, and games industries, like Los Angeles, San Francisco, and New York?*

A: No, not really. In a way it is less distracting. We don't have the access to part-time faculty like some other schools do, but in reality that might be a positive. When part-time faculty come in from their work and teach a single class, it can be difficult to have a truly cohesive program. Having mostly full-time faculty here allows us to dedicate ourselves fully to the department, its curriculum, and its students.

Q: *Do you have career counseling and job placement?*

A: Yes. A major benefit of attending Ringling is the access to our Career Services center to help with job placement. We have established solid relationships with all types of companies in the animation industry. Recruiters from these companies make regular visits to campus to interview students for open positions. They frequently bring back Ringling alumni with them to talk to the students about their job experience.

Q: *Do you have any favorite student films from the past few years that really stand out in your memory?*

A: I really felt like the projects we've had in Electronic Theater the last few years were very solid. I've seen some work from the graduate program at Supinfocom in France that was really impressive, too.

Q: *Any final words of advice for the budding digital filmmakers out there?*

A: Sure. Just remember that your goal in life is to be happy. It's that simple. In the animation business, it's too easy to let your work *become* your life. Be careful to stay balanced in your commitment to work and family.

Q: *Thank you very much for your time, and congratulations on doing such a great job.*

A: Thank you!

Figure 15.3
A few Ringling shorts from recent SIGGRAPH Electronic Theater shows

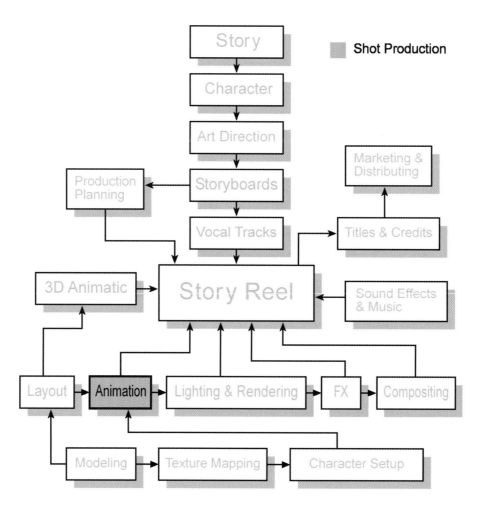

Shot Production

chapter 16
Animation

The focus of storyboarding was to translate your script into visual terms. The focus of your 2D animatic was to work out basic story pacing and continuity issues. The focus of your 3D animatic was overall scene staging and camera direction. Now, it's time to focus on performance—the very heart of character-based storytelling.

"He's alive! He's alive!"
Dr. Frankenstein

In the 3D animatic stage, you created rough layout versions of your shots with basic object and character positioning and trajectories, possibly using simple stand-in models. Here at the animation stage, you will upgrade to your final models and character rigs and refine their movements to more effectively deliver your story points with dynamic clarity or subtle inference.

As you animate your shots, you will create quick hardware renders and then drop the resulting image sequences or video clips into your story reel as replacements for the layout versions created in your 3D animatic stage. Then, with each refinement pass, you will continuously replace each shot in your story reel with more finished versions until all of your shots can be classified as *animation finals*. You will still need to light and render them, but the movements and performances of the scene objects will be more or less finalized.

Just as the creation of your layout versions might have inspired you to make adjustments to the length of certain shots that you initially planned out in your 2D animatic, fully animated versions of your shots might similarly require timing changes to your story reel. Refining the posing and animation of your characters and scene objects might also necessitate adjustments to your existing camera placement and movements.

What Is Animation?

According to most dictionary definitions, to *animate* something means to bring it to life. However, film animation often involves the creation of convincing and believable movements for non-living objects, such as falling rocks, cameras, ceiling fans, assembly-line robots, or wind-blown leaves. Therefore, we prefer to simply define animation as the art of movement. Bringing an otherwise inanimate object to apparent life is a subcategory known as *character animation*.

As a process, animation can be defined as the creation or manipulation of individual images or objects, such that when these images or manipulations are displayed in succession, the illusion of movement results.

311

Traditional animation typically involves individual drawings played in succession, while stop-motion animation typically involves the sequential manipulation and filming of existing physical objects and puppets. Three-dimensional CG animation has similarities to both types of animation and to many filmmakers, it represents the best of both worlds.

CG animation is somewhat similar to stop-motion animation in that the process involves the manipulation of virtual objects and puppets rather than the creation of individual drawings. However, in stop-motion such manipulation needs to occur on a frame-by-frame basis. The CG animator, on the other hand, can work like a senior traditional animator, keyframing object positions and character poses on selected frames representing movement extremes, and then let the computer act as an assistant animator, creating the motion in between these extremes. But always remember, for CG animation to turn out well, the computer—sometimes known as the world's dumbest in-betweener—must be supervised; otherwise, the motion of your objects and characters will tend to look unnaturally stiff, robotic, or watery (see Figure 16.1). "Supervising" the computer means creating a sufficient number of intermediate keyframes or shaping your function curves carefully so the movements in between your extreme poses are under your control, rather than being mathematically interpolated.

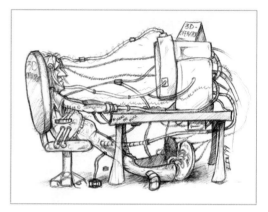

The greatest strength of CG animation is its seemingly limitless editorial capabilities. Unlike in stop-motion and traditional animation, in CG it is very easy to go back into an existing animation and make small or global changes. If you want to make the first half of a performance faster, it is often a simple matter of scaling down the corresponding set of keyframes in a function curve editor or a digital dope sheet. If you want to redo the animation of a character's left arm while leaving the rest of the performance alone, you can delete the appropriate keyframes and then reanimate that particular limb independently. If you want to make a character jump a bit higher, it might be as simple as adjusting a single vertical translation keyframe. Going back and making such changes in a traditionally animated performance would require a great deal of erasing and redrawing. Such corrective editing in stop-motion is all but impossible; typically, you would need to reanimate a shot from the beginning if you needed to insert even a very minor adjustment.

Another great advantage of CG is the ability to try something and then reverse time by simply hitting an undo button or reloading a previous version of a scene file. In CG it is also easy to reuse elements. Often you can copy the animation from one character or appendage to another and then quickly tweak it to add some movement variation.

Keep in mind, however, that the infinite editing capabilities available to a CG animator are not only a blessing; they can also be something of a curse. Because it is so easy to go back and make tiny adjustments, sometimes it's hard to know when to stop. An endless loop of trial and error can result. Fortunately, your external or internal producer will eventually remind you of a looming deadline, and at some point you will simply have to move on.

Character Animation

CG animation involves creating the illusion of movement on otherwise motionless digital objects, including cars, spaceships, falling snowflakes, swinging curtains, ocean waves, shrapnel, clouds, cameras, lights, and of course characters. *Character animation* distinguishes itself because it involves breathing life, rather than mere movement, into humans, animals, creatures, and other living or non-living things. Adding the illusion of life to an otherwise inanimate object or creature involves giving it personality, emotion, motivation, and reactions.

The movement of a non-character typically comes from external forces alone. The specifics of character movement, on the other hand, come from a combination of internal and external forces. A falling rock needs to rotate properly and follow a believable trajectory, while a falling human also needs to react appropriately depending on his physical and mental state before, during, and after the fall.

Keep in mind that character animation does not necessarily have to be restricted to actual characters. Any inanimate object can have character as long as its movements look like they are motivated from within (see Figure 16.2). A bouncing ball that pauses each time it hits the ground and then anticipates before it pops back up will look like it has some degree of internally generated motivation. Camera motion that simulates the movements of a live operator or the point of view of a story character might need a bit of implied personality or attitude.

Figure 16.2
Even non-living objects can have character when they are animated appropriately.

Styles

Character animation generally ranges between two style extremes—realistic and cartoony. Convincingly realistic animation involves exacting attention to detail and subtlety. Cartoony animation allows for more artistic license. In cartoony animation, the focus is mainly on definitive poses, whereas realistic animation is often more concerned with the natural movement in between the poses. Posing is certainly important in both styles, but the story being delivered by a cartoony character performance absolutely depends on definitive poses—the space in between is generally of secondary importance. Realistic character movement, on the other hand, tends to flow through poses with more timing differences between separate body parts.

Realistic animation follows natural rules of gravity and physics. Subtlety and naturalistic imperfections are often the emphasis. The smallest timing error can ruin the believability of an otherwise realistic performance; therefore, realistic animation is generally considered to be more difficult and more time consuming.

In cartoony animation, there is a greater margin of error with regard to exacting attention to realistic motion. Exaggeration is often the key; anticipations are bigger; poses are more over the top; squash and stretch is more extreme; and joints often bend the wrong way during in-between poses to create more "snap" (see Figure 16.3). Characters can stop on a dime and freeze completely. Gravity can often be temporarily defied. Also, in cartoony animation there is a greater opportunity for a diverse range of animated styles. For instance, *limited* animation is a style in which details are kept to a minimum and characters tend to pop from pose to pose without a lot of attention paid to what happens in between.

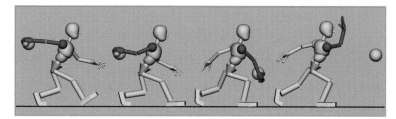

Figure 16.3
A greater illusion of "snap" sometimes requires breaking joints in the midst of an action.

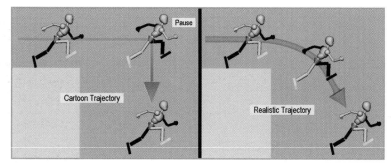

Figure 16.4
Realistic and cartoony animation styles are often differentiated by trajectory specifics.

Figure 16.5
What would be the appropriate animation style for each of these characters?

Cartoon trajectories also tend to be quite different from their realistic counterparts. If a cartoon character runs off a cliff, he will tend to continue horizontally for a bit, pause, and then drop straight down. A realistic character, on the other hand, will be pulled downward by the force of gravity as soon as he clears the cliff's edge, and his trajectory will be an arc that steadily becomes more vertical as the drop continues (see Figure 16.4).

Of course, a lot of animation falls somewhere in between absolute realism and snappy, cartoon-style motion. Fantastical creatures and aliens are often animated based on fairly realistic gravity and physics, perhaps with a bit of exaggeration thrown into the mix.

Typically, the design of a character will dictate his animation style. Consistency is generally appropriate. A toon-shaded kitten with a tiny body, impossibly skinny legs, big feet, and an enormous head with huge, round eyes will probably beg for a snappy, cartoony-style of animation. If you design a perfectly proportioned digital human with detailed texture maps and realistic hair, your audience will probably expect him to follow the laws of gravity and physics to a tee (see Figure 16.5).

Examples of realistic animation in CG include the feature film *Final Fantasy* and the shorts *f8* and *Geri's Game*. You can see snappy, cartoon-style animation in features such as *Jimmy Neutron* and in many CG shorts, including *Lunch* and *Polygon Family*. But keep in mind that we are only categorizing the style of these pieces based on the actual movement of their objects and characters. Many CG films effectively combine one style of animation with an alternative style applied to other digital components, such as lighting, rendering, and effects. For example, the feature film *Ice Age* uses extremely snappy, cartoon-style animation with fairly realistic lighting, rendering, and fur motion, while the short *Respire* applies subtle, realistic character motion on top of toon-rendered imagery.

Blocking

During the 3D animatic phase, you initiated the CG production of your individual shots by creating very rough layout versions in which you established the overall placement and trajectories of all crucial scene elements. The next step in the evolution of a shot is known as blocking.

Blocking can be defined as the basic posing, timing, and trajectories of a performance without any extraneous details. It represents the minimum amount of posing and keyframing in which the story of the performance is being delivered clearly and effectively. Depending on the action of a particular shot, the specifics of what would qualify the shot as successfully blocked can differ significantly. If a shot needs to tell the simple story that Joe is walking from point A to point B, a single walking pose that merely slides from the starting point to the final position will probably be sufficient for a successful blocking pass. However, if the purpose of the shot is to show that Joe is not only walking from here to there, but he is also injured, you will probably need a few extra poses to tell that particular story. If a shot needs to tell the story of a dozen giant spiders climbing over a wall, the most important element will be their trajectories, rather than their individual poses. It might even be sufficient to hide the legs and simply float the spider torsos along their intended paths (see Figure 16.6). If part of the story of this spider shot involves one of them pausing on top of the wall to rear up in anger, that particular member of the ensemble will need legs and a definitive pose, while the others may not. Only add details to a blocking stage if they are absolutely necessary to deliver the story point.

Figure 16.6
When you are initially blocking a swarm of creatures, it might be sufficient to hide their appendages and simply create trajectories for their torsos.

Recall that the cost of revisions will steadily increase as production continues. This is especially true in animation, where the more complexity and higher number of keyframes that exist in a performance, the more difficult and time consuming it will be to troubleshoot or make global changes. This is the main reason for a blocking pass. If you can tell the story of a shot with a very small number of keyframes, it will allow you to experiment with different timings and trajectories quickly and easily. However, if you animate every finger joint and add a significant amount of overlapping action and keyframe delays right off the bat, it will take a lot more time to make any necessary global changes to the performance. Stay in the blocking stage until you are sure you are happy with your overall timing and trajectories before you add any details.

As you begin to animate your shots, you might decide to bring each sequence or perhaps your entire film to a blocking level before you go back and refine each shot individually. The advantage of this is that you can get the basic story of a sequence or entire film worked out before you add the details. Continuity is a fundamental element of filmmaking, so it is always a good idea to make sure the overall actions of your shots hook up properly before you go in and refine them.

16. Animation

315

The Magic

During the blocking stage, a character's movements will typically look like a series of poses applied to an otherwise inanimate puppet or a character in a fixed pose merely floating from here to there along an appropriate trajectory. A blocking pass graduates to the classification of animation only after enough details have been added to make the character appear as if it has a life of his own. As long as the viewer can see the animator behind the puppet, true animation has not yet been achieved, and your character is still simply moving. When a performance actually crosses the line where the movements appear to be coming from within (rather than from without), the animator all of the sudden goes away and the puppet officially comes to life. This is the magic of animation—the Dr. Frankenstein moment, if you will.

Not all animations will necessary reach this level, but when they do, the desire to experience that magic once again on a future shot is often the very thing that keeps a filmmaker motivated.

Study and practice the concepts of character animation to present your audience with convincingly dynamic characters who successfully channel the flow and emotional content of your story. Digital puppets that merely move from pose to pose without any sense of internal motivation or personality might indeed tell your story, but it won't be told well.

The Fundamental Principles of Animation

In the early days of filmmaking, the senior animators at the Disney Animation Studio began analyzing what constitutes the illusion of life. At that time, their existing film characters looked like moving drawings. Although the drawings themselves were quite expressive, their movements were repetitive and unnatural. Therefore, audiences saw their characters as cute drawings moving about, rather than accepting them as living beings. If Disney was ever going to be able to make a successful full-length animated feature (like the upcoming *Snow White*), audiences would need to establish a connection with their onscreen characters, and this could only be accomplished if their movements successfully indicated weight, personality, motivation, and emotion. Through extensive observation and analysis, the Disney animators eventually came up with 12 fundamental principles of animation which, when applied appropriately to a character performance, would result in the illusion of life.

Although most scholars would agree that the original list of 12 entries is quite complete and needs no elaboration, we have actually broken tradition and doubled its size. So, with apologies to Frank Thompson, Ollie Johnston, and all the other early masters, we hereby present the original 12, plus 12 additional fundamental principles of character animation.

Principle 1: Squash and Stretch

Organic objects tend to have some degree of malleability. When forces act upon them, they will deform appropriately depending on the nature, direction, and degree of those forces mixed with the physical properties of the objects themselves. If you step on a tennis ball, it will squash vertically and stretch horizontally. When you apply squash and stretch in your animations, it is important to remember that if volume is not maintained, your object will appear to be expanding or contracting. If you squash a digital tennis ball vertically but neglect to simultaneously stretch it horizontally, it will seem to be shrinking.

You can also apply squash and stretch to rigid, articulated structures, such as skeletons and Luxo lamps. When such a structure compresses downward, certain joints will rotate forward or sideways to accommodate it. When you drop from a standing position into a squat, your hips move down while your knees move forward. Your legs can be said to be squashing and stretching, even though the individual joints are neither compressing nor expanding (see Figure 16.7).

Principle 2: Anticipation

This is the setup before the main action. It lets the audience know that something is about to happen and gathers the necessary energy (see Figure 16.8). For instance, think about reaching behind you with a tennis racquet before you strike the ball. When a boxer throws a jab, he avoids anticipation because he specifically does not want to inform his opponent of his intentions. In animation, however, a viewer's eye tends to lag behind by a few frames, so it is often necessary to announce that something is about to happen so your audience doesn't miss it.

Anticipations are often physical movements in the opposite direction of the intended motion, but they can take on other forms as well—for instance, a growl before an attack or a deep breath before a bold statement.

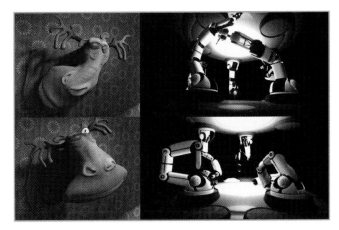

Figure 16.7
You can apply squash and stretch to malleable organic objects as well as rigid, jointed assemblies.

Principle 3: Staging and Composition

Animation is communication. Successful staging will result in the clear presentation of an idea. Identify the story being told and choose the best scene layouts and camera angles to deliver that story with appropriate style and mood. If a scene has a singular focus, you need to decide

Figure 16.8
Anticipation is the announcement that an action is about to occur.

whether it should it be centered or perhaps off to the side a bit. Maybe the best staging for a particular shot would be to put its main focus off the screen and reveal the action with sound or dialogue. Also, the visual flow of a scene's focus should guide the viewers' eyes as intended.

An arbitrary freeze frame should result in a well-composed work of art (see Figure 16.9). Poses should be strong, and elements of your scene should work well together visually. Typically, you should not hide important scene elements behind less important elements.

16. Animation

317

Principle 4: Straight Ahead versus Pose to Pose

These are two traditional methods of animating. *Straight ahead* involves stepping through the individual frames of your scene and manipulating them sequentially. *Pose to pose* involves defining the extremes and then filling in the spaces in between. Straight ahead generally requires more pre-planning. You can only perform stop-motion by animating straight ahead; you can animate traditionally either way. CG animation is often accomplished with some variation of pose-to-pose methodology. Straight ahead is indeed possible in CG, but it is not especially practical unless you are trying to simulate the feel of a stop-motion film.

Principle 5: Follow-Through and Overlapping Action

Anticipation is the setup before a main action; *follow-through* is the extension—for instance, the continuation of a tennis stroke after the ball contact (see Figure 16.10). Follow-through is also evident when a secondary appendage, such as a tail or an antenna, is indirectly driven by the primary motion of the body. Secondary follow-through will generally occur later than the main action because the force dictating the main action takes longer to reach the appendages. When an object in motion changes direction, stops accelerating, or stops completely, secondary parts of that object will continue in the original direction after the change in the main force—for instance, a woman's dress fluffing forward after she stops walking or a ponytail bouncing in an "S" motion when someone jumps up and down. Follow-through is often reduced if an appendage has and uses its own muscles. When a cat runs, the muscles of its tail often tighten to reduce follow-through and maintain balance.

Overlap is the concept that not all moving parts of a body will start and end at exactly the same time. If you turn your head and point, your arm movement might begin before your head finishes turning. Overlap is nonexistent if the head and arm start and stop on the same frame or if the arm waits to move until the head has completed its motion. Such non-overlapped motions tend to look robotic.

Figure 16.9
Pausing at any given frame in your film should result in the display of a well-composed, static work of art.

Figure 16.10
Follow-through is the logical extension of an action.

Principle 6: Slow In/Slow Out

Organic motion tends to accelerate and decelerate into and out of actions except when met with a force that causes an abrupt stop or direction change, such as a wall or a floor. The movement of an object will look mechanical if you don't apply this principle.

Principle 7: Arcs

The individual parts of an articulated skeleton move as a result of joint rotations. When a wrist travels from point A to point B, it typically does so as the result of elbow and shoulder rotations. Therefore, the motion of the wrist will tend to describe an arc. Of course, it is possible to move one's wrist in a straight line; however, continuous compensatory adjustments in the rest of the arm are required to achieve this motion, and such movements tend to look less organic (or at least more deliberate), such as a straight jab. To make the motion of a body part move along a desired arc, you often need to insert a breakdown pose between the extremes to help define the specifics of the body part's trajectory (see Figure 16.11).

If you want a character's movements to look robotic, defy the concepts of arcs, overlap, and slow in/slow out.

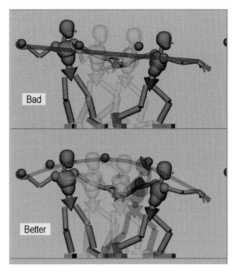

Figure 16.11
Arcs typically look more natural and sometimes require an intermediate breakdown pose to effectively describe the desired trajectory.

Principle 8: Secondary Action

This is any motion that is secondary to the main action—for instance, drumming your fingers on your knee while talking. Secondary actions often reveal emotional subtleties or hidden thoughts. If the secondary action pulls the viewer's attention away from the main action, however, it becomes the main action.

Principle 9: Timing

Varying the speed of a particular motion can indicate different weights, forces, and attitudes. A slow head turn might indicate a careful or casual search, while a quick head turn can indicate surprise (see Figure 16.12). Fast walks can imply determination; slow walks can imply depression.

Metronomic character timing is usually undesirable. It generally looks more natural to break things up a bit. Certain parts of an individual performance should typically be faster or slower than other parts. In a yawn, typically the mouth will open slowly and then close much faster. If these two movements had the exact same frame count, it might not read as a yawn.

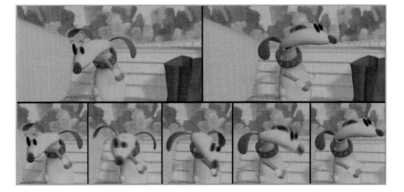

Figure 16.12
A different story will be told depending on the speed of a particular motion.

Timing differences will also help define animation style. Cartoony movements tend to be snappy, while realistic movements are often a bit slower and more organic.

Principle 10: Exaggeration

Exaggeration is used to increase the readability of emotions and actions. Animation mediums don't deliver all of the same information that exists in real life. A CG film image will be virtually 3D, but not truly dimensional; sound typically comes from a single source; and depth perception is non-interactive. Because of such limited information being delivered, it is often necessary to exaggerate to effectively tell the story of a particular performance (see Figure 16.13). Effective exaggeration isn't always a matter of making a motion larger, though. Significantly *decreasing* an action is also a type of exaggeration (accentuating the subtleties, that is.) For instance, completely stopping a character's motion for an unnaturally long period of time can demonstrate a particular emotion, such as shock or disgust. Exaggeration is, of course, especially appropriate in cartoon-style animation.

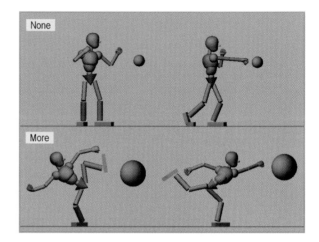

Figure 16.13
For the sake of clarity, exaggeration is often a necessary component of animation.

Principle 11: Solid Drawing

In traditional animation, each individual drawing should be a work of art on its own. This adds to the appeal and readability of a performance. It is also important to stay on model. Each drawing should look like the character being presented. It is distracting when, for instance, the size of a character's head is inconsistent during the course of an animation. In CG, a solidly modeled character will similarly contribute to the appeal and clarity of its movements.

Principle 12: Appeal

Appeal is the most subjective of all the principles. Ask yourself whether the presentation of your idea is pleasant to look at, or perhaps unpleasant if that is your intention. Apply fundamental aesthetic principles to your shots. Keep in mind, however, that appeal does not necessarily mean attractive. In the context of animation, appeal simply means that a character or its performance is visually interesting.

Principle 13: Simplicity and Readability

Try not to unnecessarily complicate a scene, character, or performance. Do just enough to tell the story. Too much secondary action or too many details can sometimes confuse the issue and make the idea being presented unclear. Successful character animation delivers clarity through extrapolation, simplification, and exaggeration.

Principle 14: Posing

Body language is typically the most powerful tool in an animator's arsenal, and strong poses are the building blocks of body language. Interesting and clear poses are extremely important for effective and natural-looking animation and clear story-point delivery.

Pay attention to center-of-gravity issues. Does your character look as if he is about to fall down when he is supposed to be standing comfortably?

It is usually a good idea to avoid too much symmetry in your poses. One hip is often a little higher than the other. Weight is rarely distributed evenly over both feet (see Figure 16.14).

Turn off all of the lights in your CG scene or temporarily color all of a character's geometry solid black to analyze whether the silhouette reads effectively (see Figure 16.14).

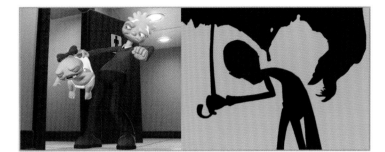

Figure 16.14
Weight distribution and silhouette are two important elements of effective posing.

An important component of posing is the concept of extremes. An extreme pose typically exists at the point where a particular motion begins, ends, reaches its climax, or reverses direction. In cartoon-style animation, entire bodies often reach extreme poses together, while in realistic movement, different body parts tend to reach their extremes at different times.

Every pose has a value associated with the message or story point it is intended to deliver. Ask yourself the importance of each pose, and then, based on that level of importance, consider how long that pose should be held to tell its story effectively. If you merely blend through an important pose, it won't have much of an opportunity to deliver its message. Some poses should be held for very short periods of time, others for much longer. A thoughtful gaze typically should be held longer than a frightened glance before a frantic flight. This combination of posing and timing based on hold lengths is typically the very essence of basic storytelling through body language.

Principle 15: Forces

An object moves when forces are applied to it. Consider where these forces are coming from. Are they being generated from internal sources, such as desire, intention, and muscle movement, or from external influences, such as gravity, the wind, or a push from another character? The origin, magnitude, direction, and duration of these forces will dictate how your characters move. Consider how these forces will affect your character. Does your character resist them or does he go with the flow? Do multiple forces cancel each other out? Understand a force's attack and decay. How powerful is the initial hit of the force? How long does an object continue reacting to the force? What is the material of the object? A rubber ball will continue bouncing much longer than a bowling ball.

The most important force to consider is gravity, which in most scenarios exists as a constant and must be acknowledged and applied appropriately to your characters for their performances to look believable.

Principle 16: Weight

Demonstrating the implied mass of a character is perhaps the most important principle to consider when you are attempting to create believable animations, especially when realism is the intent. The indication of weight is a function of the proper application of forces, squash and stretch, anticipation, follow-through, overlap, posing, timing, exaggeration, and slow in/slow out. Whether a character looks especially heavy or especially light when he gets up from a chair depends upon how these principles are applied. An obese man will probably move rather slowly and require a lot of anticipation or utilize a rigid leverage point and a good push, whereas a very skinny young boy will bounce up without requiring nearly as much energy. Heavier objects require more force to initiate, slow, stop, or reverse the direction of their movements. Consider the different amount of force required to move or stop a balloon as opposed to a bowling ball.

Placement of a character's center of gravity is also an important aspect of weight. Physics rules indicate that a static object's center of gravity (COG) must be directly above or below the average of its point(s) of suspension. For instance, when you stand on one foot, your COG needs to be directly above your supporting foot; otherwise, you will begin to fall. Of course, this all changes if you are in motion, leaning on something, or if other external forces are present, such as wind (see Figure 16.15).

Figure 16.15
In a static pose, the center of gravity will be vertically in line with the average of the points of suspension; however, movement or external forces will alter the application of this generalized physics rule.

Think about pivot and leverage points as well. When a character that is reclining on the floor wants to stand up, he needs to establish one or perhaps a series of leverage points for his hands, knees, or feet to push himself off the ground (see Figure 16.16). When performing a jump, the legs push away from the ground and need to fully extend before the feet go airborne.

Also watch out for isolated body part movements. Even the simplest arm move often involves contributing motion from the shoulder and torso. Keeping your individual body parts appropriately working together is another helpful method of weight indication.

Pay particular attention to this principle because if you don't apply it effectively, your character motions will be less than believable no matter how well you apply all of the other principles.

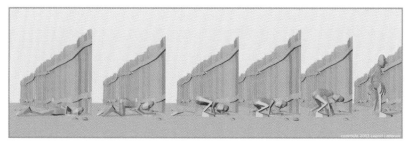

Figure 16.16
Displaying weight is often a matter of establishing and using leverage points to push one's body into a new position.

Principle 17: Twinning and Texture

To maintain natural-looking performances, it is usually desirable to break up the motion of individual body parts so they are not doing the exact same thing at the same time. For instance, when a character slaps his hands down on a table, you might want his left hand to hit a frame or two before the right. If you try to save time by copying animation from one appendage to another, it is usually a good idea to go in and at least slightly vary the motion afterwards. Keep in mind, however, that sometimes it *is* indeed appropriate to twin the movement of a character's individual body parts (see Figure 16.17). For instance, when a gymnast finishes her dismount from the balance beam and throws her hands up in the air to announce the completion of her performance, her arms should actually reach their extremes on the exact same frame; otherwise, the judges will take a few points away from her score.

A variation of the twinning concept is when members of a swarm or flock exactly mimic one another. Pay attention to the overall texture when you animate groups of objects or characters. Consider a flock of birds or a field of grass reacting to the wind. What is the overall feel of the group? Is there enough variety in the poses and trajectories of the individual elements? Is every bird flapping its wings at the exact same frequency? Is the wind affecting every blade of grass in exactly the same manner at exactly the same time? Are the individual elements supposed to be working together? If so, are you using an appropriate amount of variation between these individuals? Are your synchronized swimmers or dancers exactly in synch? If so, is this intentional? Even when individual members of a group try to copy one another exactly, minor variations often occur. Break it up, but not so much that unintentional chaos results.

Figure 16.17
Although appendage twinning typically looks unnatural, for some motions it is perfectly appropriate.

Principle 18: Details

Sometimes the difference between a good animation and a great animation comes from effective attention to detail. You never know where a viewer's eyes might be wandering. Just because the main focus of a shot is on your character's face, don't forget to animate the toes. Details such as thigh muscles jiggling when a foot hits the ground add to the naturalism of a performance and can help tell the story and effectively indicate weight and anatomical realism.

Introducing naturalistic imperfections will also add to the believability of your shot. Movement is rarely perfect. When a running dog decides to make a sharp turn, his feet might slip and slide a bit. In Pixar's *Geri's Game*, there is a great moment when the old man reaches out to grab the back of his chair, but misses the first time. This small movement detail adds to the realism and believability of the animation, as well as helping to define the old man's diminished physical dexterity.

Keep in mind, however, that it is usually not desirable to confuse an action with too many arbitrary details (see principle 13). Remember that every movement must happen for a reason. Details can indeed round out and solidify a performance, but more is not necessarily always better. And don't try to hide animation errors behind overly detailed modeling, lighting, texture maps, and particle effects. This is an undesirable variation of the attention to detail concept.

When you are animating a character performance, make sure you look at it from all angles to make sure that all necessary axes are being animated so you don't end up with two-dimensional movements that only look good from one side. Although an animation typically only needs to look good from the given shot's actual camera angle, at some point you might decide to change the point of view or perhaps borrow the animation in another shot, so don't forget to analyze it from alternative angles.

Frozen holds are typically a no-no in CG animation. Unless it is particularly appropriate to your animation style or to a specific story point, it is generally a good idea to keep at least some part of a character's body moving when he holds still. Small details, such as breathing, blinking, or subtle swaying, will keep a character from looking unnaturally frozen in place.

Also, watch out for technical glitches, such as geometry intersections and IK pops.

Material integrity is also an important detail to consider. Is it appropriate to squash and stretch a rigid object, such as a stone? Some animators will do this as an aesthetic choice. Others prefer to follow realistic rules of physics.

Principle 19: Planning Ahead

Because of the extensive editorial capabilities of CG, it can be tempting to simply animate by trial and error, throwing down a few arbitrary poses at random time intervals, with the idea that you can just move things around until it looks right. This method of working can certainly add to the spontaneity of a performance, but it is usually not the most efficient way of working. In most cases, it is a good idea to plan out a performance before you start, especially if you have deadlines to meet. Act out the intended motion in front of a mirror with a stopwatch and take down some numbers. Make some preliminary drawings. Study reference material, especially if you are attempting to animate a specific person or species convincingly. As the carpenters say: Measure twice, cut once.

Principle 20: Hookups and Continuity

To maintain flow and readability, each shot needs to cut properly with the next one. Make sure the spatial relationships between your characters are consistent from one shot to the next.

An object's trajectory should generally look like it continues sensibly after a camera cut. Try to stage subsequent shots so the new camera position does not confuse the clarity of the action (see Figure 16.18).

If you cut away from a particular action and then return later, the changes in the scene should make sense with the length of the time lapse unless you are intentionally breaking the rules of reality for reasons of fantasy or humor.

Sometimes actions should overlap for emphasis, but be careful of overdoing this effect.

Figure 16.18
The implied trajectory of a moving object should visually hook up logically from shot to shot.

Many cinematic fight scenes are littered with continuity problems. In one shot, Buster is kneeling on top of Sluggo, and then in the next shot they are both standing up and exchanging punches. Such continuity lapses break the flow of the action.

Principle 21: Acting

Character animation is acting. Always keep this in mind (see Figure 16.19). A character performance needs to tell a story. A basic story, such as Wanda walks across the street or Fred falls off a cliff, will be told by posing and timing, but when these characters act rather than just move, the stories become

Figure 16.19
Character animation is all about acting.

complete. Is Walking Wanda in a good mood? Is she late for work? Is she annoyed by the crowds around her? Is Falling Fred screaming in horror, or is he excitedly waiting for the bungee tied to his ankle to catch him in midair? Such additional information personalizes the performance, makes it real, and connects it to the audience.

Consider a character's personality, motivation, and emotional state before bringing him to life. Who is he? What is he trying to accomplish by this performance? How is he feeling? What are the circumstances surrounding his action? Such preliminary information will dictate how your character will move. Arbitrarily making Wanda look around while she is walking across the street will not improve the performance unless there is some purpose for this action. Every movement must exist for a reason. Don't simply add details for the sake of completion unless you know the source of each addi-

tional movement, and always ask why. Why is Wanda looking around while she is crossing the street? Is she new to the city and merely taking it all in? Is she worried that the cars will start moving before she makes it to the other side? Does she think someone is chasing her? Knowing the purpose of this simple action will help you to know when you've animated it convincingly.

Keep in mind that even though every movement needs a purpose, that purpose doesn't necessarily need to be especially profound. If Wanda scratches her head while she's walking, there might in fact be a significant story point attached to this movement. Perhaps Wanda is a sorceress and she can stop time by scratching her forehead. On the other hand, this action might simply represent a nervous tic that helps define her obsessive personality. Or maybe she just had an itch. Whether or not an action has a deep or almost insignificant meaning, make sure you are adding it for a reason.

Giving a character a recognizable mannerism can help round out his personality and separate him from the other members of your cast. Think about a limp, a habit of constantly adjusting his hat, a tendency to fidget with the point of his tail, or a unique way of holding his cigarette with thumb and pinky.

Study character performances in existing live-action and animated films. Who are your favorite actors? Why are they your favorite actors? Probably because they have the ability to transform themselves into believable, interesting, and memorable characters. As an animator, you must possess this ability as well, and similarly deliver believability and interest through the movements of your digital actors. Again, to connect your audience to your characters, the characters must display personality, motivation, attitude, and emotion through effective body language, facial expressions, and dialogue. By *acting*, that is.

16. Animation

325

Watch films with the sound turned off to analyze how actors use body language to define or complement a story action. Take notes and make sketches. Also study yourself in front of a mirror performing the same action in a variety of ways, depending on the physical or emotional state you want to imply. How would you wake up and get out of bed if you had too much to drink the night before? How would you perform this action if you suddenly realized you were late for school?

Principle 22: Layering

A third method of animating is known as *layering* (as opposed to straight ahead or pose to pose). This method, very often utilized in CG, is accomplished by starting globally and then gradually honing in on the details. The process typically involves initially establishing the overall posing, timing, and trajectories of your character as a blocking phase, where sometimes appendages are hidden and a torso merely floats from here to there along an intended path. Details are then added after these global issues are refined and approved (see Figure 16.20). Layering can sometimes be thought of as animating from the inside out. First you focus on the global position and orientation changes of the main axis of your character; then perhaps the spine and the pelvis; then the head, the legs, the arms, the feet, the hands, the fingers, and the toes. Last, you address the fine details, such as ponytails, earrings, and eye blinks.

Figure 16.20
Layering is a popular CG animation technique in which global posing, timing, and trajectories are established and then details are added in subsequent refinement passes.

Animation layering can be compared to the academically preferred method of painting, where the overall composition and colors are established rather abstractly with large brushes at first, and then the image slowly comes together as a whole as the details are refined with smaller and smaller brushes (as opposed to completely finishing one corner of the painting before moving on to another). The layering method is especially desirable in CG so global timing can be refined before there are a large number of keyframes to tweak.

Layering is typically the preferred method of animating when a character's position and orientation are the most crucial pieces of information in a given shot, rather than his individual poses. For example, in a shot that displays the motion of an ant crawling up a wall, the trajectory and overall timing will probably be more important than the leg poses so layering would be an appropriate approach. Pose to pose, on the other hand, typically makes more sense in shots that involve body language and acting, when the poses mainly tell the story rather than the character's position in space. Most CG animators end up developing some hybrid method between pose to pose and layering, and then lean a bit toward one or the other depending on the specifics of the given shot.

Recall that blocking is achieved when the fundamental story of the shot is told effectively, minus the details. In a layered shot, this point is reached when the characters are in the correct places at the right times and enough layers have been added to tell the story effectively. In pose to pose, on the other hand, successful blocking is reached when there are just enough poses so the meaning of the performance is clear.

Principle 23: Understanding the Principles

It is not enough to simply be able to recite these principles from memory. To animate effectively, you must truly understand them. You need to apply these principles appropriately, and sometimes you need to leave out certain ones entirely. Blind implementation of the fundamental principles of animation can result in all sorts of inappropriate motion. For example, if you apply non-twinning to the motion of a bird's wings, the poor beast will appear to be injured or perhaps inebriated. Typically you don't need to apply anticipation to a cat before it jumps because default feline posture is already an anticipatory crouch (see Figure 16.21). A standing human, on the other hand, must bend his knees before attempting to go airborne. It is certainly okay to squash and stretch a bowling ball; however, bending the laws of physics thusly should be the result of an aesthetic choice rather than blind implementation of the squash-and-stretch principle. If you are asked to make a character look heavier, you can only accomplish this if you truly understand which principles need to be applied and how. Rules are made to be broken, but you must truly understand a rule before you can break it creatively and appealingly.

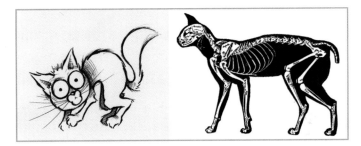

Figure 16.21
Truly understand the principles so you don't apply them blindly, such as adding too much anticipation before a small cat jump. A feline's default posture is already an anticipatory crouch.

Principle 24: Forget the Rules

After you've studied and understood the fundamental principles of animation, strive to use them instinctively rather than methodically. Try not to get too caught up in the idea of applying them academically at every turn. Often it's better to turn off the analytical side of your brain and follow your gut instead. Your best weapon as an animator is your ability to self-critique objectively and effectively—especially in CG, where trial and error is such a viable technique. When you review your own work, don't ask yourself which of the fundamental principles are being applied properly; rather, simply ask yourself whether your animation feels right. If it does not, then use the vocabulary of these principles to identify the source of the problem and try to figure out which ones are not being applied appropriately. The ability to use the vocabulary of these principles is also important when you are teaching or supervising; however, never forget that your instincts as well as your innate and objective sense of style and appeal are much more powerful animation tools than any available list of rules or principles.

Learning to animate successfully is indeed all about observation and analysis, but too much knowledge can sometimes get in the way of aesthetic appeal. If it looks right, it is right.

Of the 24 fundamental principles, which are the most important? Of course all of them deserve adequate attention, and you should understand and apply them appropriately. But the ones that are most important for effective story-point delivery through body language are posing, timing, and staging, while weight seems to be the one that goes wrong most often. Effective implementation of these four principles will result in convincing performances in which your characters will be acting rather than simply moving.

CG Animation Basics

In CG, manipulating objects and posing characters is typically accomplished by translating, rotating, and scaling entire hierarchies, groups, or individual body parts. Each of these object attributes will carry a value in 3D space, indicated by numerical units in the x, y, and z axes. A box at the center of your CG software's world typically will have translation values of 0 units in x, 0 units in y, and 0 units in z. Assuming your CG package considers vertical movements as y translations, repositioning the box directly upward by 10 units would result in a translation value set of {0, 10, 0}, in which 10 may refer to inches, centimeters, or perhaps miles, depending on your software settings. Default scaling values are typically {1,1,1}. If you squash and stretch an object, its resulting {x, y, z} value set might be something like {1.414, 0.5, 1.414}.

From a technical point of view, CG animation simply involves changing the values of these attributes over time while recording their start, end, and any necessary intermediate values as keyframes. Creating a ball that pops up and then falls down might simply involve changing its y translation value from 0 to perhaps +10, and then back down to 0 over time. The motion of a swinging pendulum on a grandfather clock might be indicated by its z rotation changing repeatedly from perhaps −30 degrees to +30 degrees (see Figure 16.22).

Animating a CG character typically involves translating his center and IK handles, as well as rotating and perhaps scaling his joints to achieve desired poses, and then keyframing the movements of each body part at appropriate time intervals.

In an early pose-to-pose blocking pass, you might record keyframe values for the position, orientation, and scale of every body part as a whole, and then experiment with different frame positions for each keyframe set until you arrive at the desired initial timing of your intended performance. Then you would typically add in-betweens and shift individual keyframes around to create timing variations and delays on separate body parts.

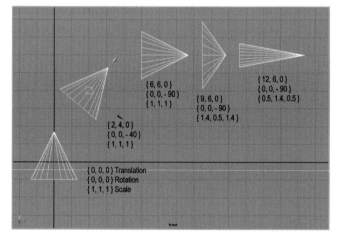

Figure 16.22
CG animation is basically the process of changing and keyframing an object or hierarchy's basic attribute values over time.

In a layered blocking pass, you might begin by simply animating your character's center-of-gravity node (or perhaps the entire character) along a specific trajectory with enough keyframes to achieve the desired overall timing. Appendages might simply follow along in their static poses, or they might be kept hidden until you get the overall timing and trajectory of the torso to look almost right. If you are using IK legs, they might get temporarily left behind on your initial blocking pass of the singular COG node. Then the leg movements can be keyed to catch up with the action of the torso in your second layer of gradual animation refinement. Or you might move the COG and the feet together as a group in the first stage of your blocking pass.

If your character has a master node, it is generally a bad idea to animate it over time. Rather, the main purposes of the master node are global positioning and orientation. You might finish the animation on a particular shot, only to realize that the entire performance needs to be shifted a few feet to the left.

Assuming you only animated the nodes below the master, you could simply move the master node to the left, which would change the start, end, and intermediate positions of the performance without changing the specifics of the animation itself. If you try to create a traversing walk by animating the master node, a large number of keys will be required to get either foot to stay in one place for longer than a single frame. The movement of the feet will be continuously overridden by that of the master; to keep them from sliding, you would have to counter-animate against the master on a frame by frame basis, which is extremely inefficient. Try not to dictate the movement of a single object or node from multiple sources.

Remember to keep your animations as simple as possible for as long as possible. Only add refinement keyframes after you are happy with the overall posing, timing, and trajectories of a character performance. The more keyframes you have, the more difficult they are to pinpoint and adjust.

> If you are animating with a character puppet that has a large number of deformers and expressions controlling geometry pieces that are extremely vertex-heavy, you might find yourself suffering from a significant lack of interactivity. If so, it would be wise to go back to the character setup stage and create an alternative puppet with the same inner hierarchy and animation controls, but with lower-resolution bound geometry or perhaps simple, faceted geometry pieces parented to individual skeleton joints. You can use this more interactive stand-in puppet for most of your performance work, and then copy your animation data to the full-resolution version for final details. Some CG software packages allow you to create multi-resolution puppets in which you can toggle the display of heavy and light geometry pieces depending on whether you are prioritizing high interactivity or fine details. Consult your software manual for more information on multi-resolution character rigs as well as copying and pasting animation data between puppets.

Another attribute that can usually be animated is an object's visibility. Animating the visibility of an object on and off can create surreal strobing effects and can also be helpful when a character needs to pick up or drop something. Typically, when a character is holding an object in his hand, it will be parented to his palm geometry or his wrist joint. Because many CG software packages do not allow you to change the parenting of an object over time, it is sometimes a technical challenge for a character to drop what he is holding. A common CG trick is to have two identical objects—one parented to the hand and the other completely independent of the character. When your character is holding the object, have the parented one visible and the independent one invisible. At the exact frame where he lets go, reverse the visibility of both objects, making sure they are in the same location at the swap frame, and then drop the non-parented one to the ground. The parented object still exists in his hand, but no one will be the wiser because it is not visible (see Figure 16.23).

Figure 16.23
You can have a CG character drop an object by having one parented object and a second independent copy, and then keyframing their visibility attributes at the moment of release.

16. Animation

Function Curves

All fully-functional CG software packages allow you to view and manipulate the animation of individual or groups of moving objects by displaying a set of function curves representing attribute changes over time. Once you have keyframed the translation, rotation, scale, and other changeable attributes on an object or character hierarchy, you can launch a graph editor window containing function curves that can be moved or reshaped to adjust and control your animations with exacting detail.

A typical CG function curve is a linear, spline, or Bezier curve whose shape is dictated by at least two keyframes—one at the start and one at the end. Additional in-between keys may also be present to help create the desired curve shape. Each keyframe on a function curve will indicate the exact value of the given object attribute at a particular point in time, while the curve connecting these keyframe dots will describe the complete range of the changing values of that attribute over time. If you keyframe the position of a rocket flying straight up starting at the ground and ending 1000 yards above the Earth one second later, an associated y-translation function curve will exist with a ground-value key on frame 1 and a second key further to the right and 1000 yard-units higher than the first one (see Figure 16.24).

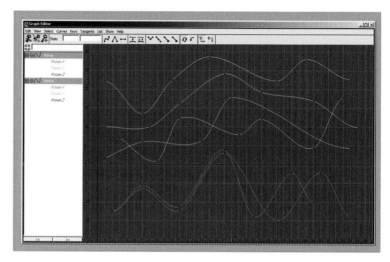

Figure 16.24
A moving object's changing attribute values can be viewed and manipulated as function curves in a graph editor window.

You can also adjust the in and out tangents of each keyframe to sharpen or smooth the shape of the curve as it passes through the current keyframe. Different keyframe tangents will result in the associated attribute value changing abruptly, smoothly, or even pausing for a beat (see Figure 16.25). Most CG software packages allow you to define a default tangent type so that new keyframes will be recorded as desired. Of course, regardless of the default setting, you can always go into the graph editor after recording a keyframe and adjust its tangents to suit your needs.

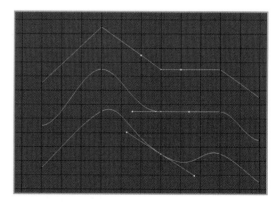

Figure 16.25
Different tangent types, such as linear, flat, or smooth splines, will translate to abrupt or smooth value changes, as well as pauses and direction reversals.

Typically, you will want to use a mixture of flat, spline, sharp, and smooth keyframes in your animations, depending on which type is appropriate for the specific movement at hand. Using only linear keyframes will result in a robotic or mechanical feel, while using only smooth splines will make your motions look watery or rubbery. If any of these movement styles is your intention, then stick with a singular keyframe type; otherwise, break them up appropriately and never simply let them remain in whatever default state your CG package initially records them.

Linear keys are appropriate for immediate direction changes or abrupt stops. Flat keys are generally appropriate for gradual direction changes and pause plateaus. Spline interpolation keys are typically appropriate for in-betweens. When you start to block a shot, it is often a good idea to set your default keyframe type to flat because you will initially be recording extreme poses and positions, which typically exist at pauses and direction changes. Then, change your default setting to smooth splines for your in-betweens so you don't create unwanted pauses in the middle of your actions. You will certainly have to go in and make adjustments after your keyframes are recorded, but setting your default tangent types logically should save you a few steps.

A fourth type of keyframe tangent is typically known as *stepped*. A function curve with stepped keys will hold each keyframe value constant until the next keyframe. Then, with each successive new keyframe, the curve will pop to the new value over a single frame (see Figure 16.26). Stepped keys allow an animator to create pose-test blocking passes, in which each character pose is held for a specific duration before popping into the next one. The stepped blocking method emphasizes individual poses but does not display timing or trajectory specifics between them, and is therefore most appropriate for performances that involve body language and acting. Such animations rely on individual poses to deliver their shot information effectively, as opposed to action- or swarm-based shots in which the characters' overall positions and movements in space have more initial importance than their actual poses. Therefore, using linear, spline, or Bezier curves for the early blocking phases of such shots typically would be more appropriate.

It is very important to realize that the motion of an object is described by the shape of its associated function curves and not necessarily by the locations of the individual keyframes. Depending on the tangents, a keyframe in the middle of a U-shaped function curve may or may not actually correspond to the lowest point of that curve (see Figure 16.27).

Try to use as few keyframes as possible to create your intended curve shape. If a curve has a single, linear keyframe at the beginning and another at the end, it will be a straight line. If, however, you want the curve to arc upward in the middle, you can accomplish this by adding an in-between key somewhere along the curve. However, it might be more efficient in the long run to achieve the same curve shape by merely adjusting the tangents on the extreme keys (see Figure 16.28).

Figure 16.26
Some animators prefer to block their animations by using stepped keyframes that will result in poses that will be held for specific durations and then popped into new ones over single frames.

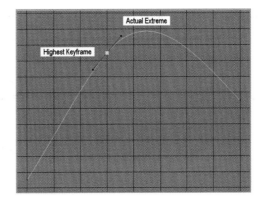

Figure 16.27
It is extremely important to understand that the movement of a CG object is dictated by the shape of a function curve and not necessarily by the actual location of the individual keyframes, which may or may not represent actual motion extremes.

Consider a ball dropping from a particular height and then bouncing three times. If you keyframed its position at the extremes and had your software preference set to create linear tangents by default, the associated y-translation function curve would look like the first example in Figure 16.29. Such linear motion would not display any slow in/slow out, where the ball continues at the exact same velocity throughout the length of its motions despite the direction changes. Such motion often looks rather unnatural or mechanical. To adjust this motion behavior, you could simply change the keyframe tangents to flat spline interpolation so the ball slows into and out of each direction change, as in the second example in Figure 16.29. This type of motion would look as if the ball had been tied to a pair of rubber bands, one above it and one below, resulting in a gentle direction change at each extreme. However, if you wanted the ball to look like it was bouncing on a rigid surface, the curve should look like the third example in Figure 16.29, where gravity is acknowledged, causing the ball to slow down at its peak and then accelerate downward until it abruptly changes direction at each ground contact.

If you want the bouncing momentum to diminish over time, each successive curve peak will need to be lower in height than the last, and each bounce will need to last for a progressively shorter duration. If the curve is to be associated with a golf ball bouncing on a hard surface, the bounce heights will drop gradually, as opposed to the motion of a bowling ball, which would lose kinetic energy much more abruptly (see Figure 16.30).

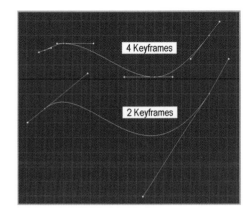

Figure 16.28
Creating a desired curve shape might require intermediate keyframes or just careful manipulation of the tangents on the extremes.

Keep in mind that the shape of a function curve in a graph editor is not a visual representation of an actual trajectory; rather, it describes a changing attribute value over time. This can sometimes be a bit confusing the first time you look at a function curve because a flat graph editor window will typically look similar to an orthographic window in your CG software package. But remember, an orthographic window represents space, whereas a graph editor window represents space and time.

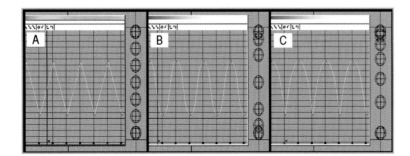

Figure 16.29
Depending on how you set your keyframe tangents, the up and down movement of a bouncing ball might look unnaturally mechanical, rubbery, or appropriately respectful of gravity.

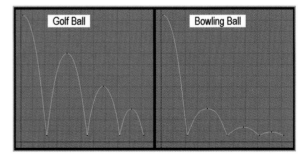

Figure 16.30
A bouncing golf ball will maintain its kinetic energy longer than a bowling ball.

16. Animation

Even though the y-translation curves in Figures 16.29 and 16.30 look something like the trajectory of a ball bouncing down a hallway, no amount of manipulation to these curves will actually result in the ball moving horizontally. To achieve such motion, a second curve describing x or z motion would need to be present. By having one curve describing the ball's vertical motion and another describing its horizontal motion, you can adjust each component of the ball's trajectory individually. If you wanted the ball to maintain its bounce height but travel further down the hallway, you could simply move the final z- or x-translation keyframe upward. If you wanted the horizontal trajectory to continue after the last bounce, you could move that same last z keyframe to the right so the ball stops bouncing before it stops traversing (see Figure 16.31).

With each new keyframed attribute, another curve will appear; before you know it, a graph editor displaying the animation of a particular object or hierarchy will resemble a plate of multi-colored spaghetti, which will make it difficult to make adjustments or troubleshoot motion problems. Fortunately, you will probably not have to spend too much time dealing with all of your curves at once unless you are making global changes. Most of the time, you will only have a few displayed at a time. But even a seemingly simple character performance will have a rather large number of curves and keyframes associated with its motion so, again, be as efficient as possible when setting keyframes.

You can accomplish global timing or spacing changes in the graph editor by selecting and translating or scaling large groups of keyframes or entire curves. You can make an entire animation happen at a later point in time by sliding all of the existing function curves to the right until the initial keys are at the desired start frame. You can slow down or speed up sections of a performance by horizontally scaling the keyframes that occupy the timeframe in question (see Figure 16.32). Making a section wider will slow the action, while making a section thinner will speed it up. Scaling curves vertically will typically make an action larger or more extreme.

As you can see, the ability to manipulate the position and tangents of single or groups of keyframes as well as the position and scale of curves will provide you with precise control over every aspect of the motion of an object or character. The trick is to learn how adjustments to function-curve shapes translate into actual movement alterations. To better understand this relationship, create some simple movements on a single object and then experiment by shifting your keyframes around vertically and horizontally to analyze how one affects the other. Also, with graph editor open, move your object around and record new keyframes to see how they affect the shapes of your curves. Even the most seasoned CG animator will find himself doing a bit of trial and error on

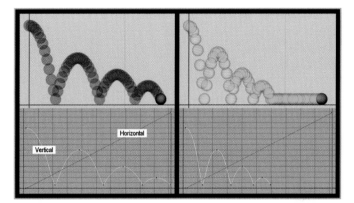

Figure 16.31
A bouncing ball that is also traversing down a hallway will require two function curves—one for vertical movement and another for horizontal.

Tip: To focus on a particular movement channel, look at your object or character action from an appropriate orthographic view. If you've animated a ball bouncing down the street and you just want to analyze the up-and-down motion, look at it from a side orthographic view where the ball is coming toward you. Because an object's apparent size does not change with depth in an orthographic view, you will be able to focus on the specifics of its vertical movement by eliminating your ability to see its horizontal traversal.

16. Animation

333

occasion, shifting keys from here to there until the desired object motion results, but the more you practice, the more you will be able to predict how your curve manipulations will affect the motion of your objects and characters.

Perhaps because of the potentially daunting technical nature of function-curve editing, some CG animators almost never open the graph editor; they prefer to work in a traditional animation mode, setting keyframes on entire character hierarchies for extreme poses and then creating more full-pose in-betweens until the performance is complete. This is certainly a respectable way to work, and many animators, especially those who are transitioning from traditional tools to CG, find such an approach to be the most direct and sensible way to work. However, next to an undo button, the graph editor is easily the most powerful tool a CG software package has to offer, so at least experiment with it for a while before you decide to avoid it completely. Working sensibly with the graph editor will allow you to be more efficient with your keyframes. For example, if you are animating an out-of-control ice skater you might need quite a few keyframes to describe the motion of his flailing arms, but perhaps only start and end keyframes for the trajectory of his body. The fewer the keyframes, the easier time you will have trouble-shooting and making adjustments to your animations. With a bit of practice, learning how to manipulate function curves and accurately predict the results will make you an extremely efficient animator.

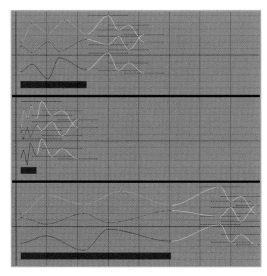

Figure 16.32
You can scale curve sections horizontally to increase or decrease time durations.

Don't fear the power of the technology sitting before you; rather, embrace it and understand its strengths and limitations. Remember that the computer is not a magical device. It cannot think or animate; it only runs programs. It cannot do anything a person cannot do; it simply performs mathematical tasks much faster. Once you learn how to speak the language of your hardware and software, you will be master of the tool, not the other way around.

Cycles

An animation cycle is a movement that loops when played back multiple times, such as the motion of the hands on a clock. You can use cycles as shortcuts for movements that repeat over time (see Figure 16.33). When you are animating film characters, however, be wary of cycling actions because motions that repeat themselves without any variation at all can look unnatural. If you are animating a

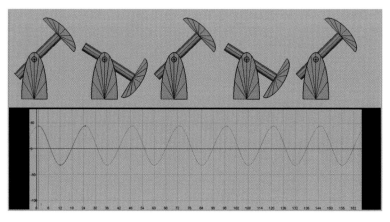

Figure 16.33
You can cycle object motion that exactly repeats itself over and over.

character taking a walk by looping a basic two-step cycle, consider adding a bit of variation here and there or perhaps a bit of secondary motion, such as head turns or breaths, to keep the overall performance from looking too mechanical. Of course, cycles are typically quite appropriate when mechanical motion is the intent, as in oil well rigs, pistons, or assembly line robots.

Gimbal Lock

Depending on your software, on occasion you might encounter the annoying phenomenon known as *gimbal lock* when you are rotating objects in your CG scenes. 3D computer graphics assemble objects as hierarchies, where one is always the parent of another. Rotation axes typically work the same way, where x, y, and z are ordered such that each has an assigned priority. Imagine a foot for which the y-axis is up, the x-axis is horizontal and perpendicular to the foot's length, and the z-axis extends from heel to toe. If y was the priority, then rotating the foot in that axis would take x and z along for the ride so that both of these non-primary axes would maintain their exact functionality. However, if z had the highest priority and y was number two, then rotating the foot

90 degrees in y would take x along with it but leave z behind, thus making x and z the same axis (see Figure 16.34). You would no longer have a single axis by which to rotate the foot axially because z rotations would be identical to x. You could still rotate the foot as necessary, but the resulting motion would be more complex than simply a single axis rotation, and undesirable interpolations between keyframes might result. Examine your function curves as proof.

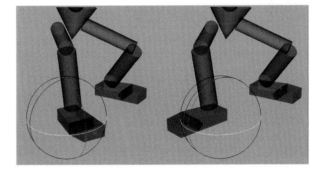

Unfortunately, this gimbal lock scenario is somewhat unavoidable in CG packages that allow individual control over all three rotation axes. Creating an actual hierarchy of rotators, one for each axis, will sometimes make the problem a bit easier to trouble-shoot, but it won't be cured completely. If your software package allows you to set rotation orders on your objects, experiment to find the order that allows you to animate efficiently. Feet seem to work best in most situations when y has the highest priority, x is secondary, and z is last.

Figure 16.34
The unfortunate CG phenomenon known as gimbal lock occurs when two rotation axes become identical.

Troubleshooting

In addition to providing you with precise control over your animated objects and characters, the graph editor also serves as an extremely effective trouble-shooting device. Whenever something strange or unexpected occurs in the motion of an object or character, the answer can almost always be found by analyzing the associated function curves. If a character is supposed to be slamming his foot down on a spider but the motion looks slow and gentle, it is probably easing in rather than accelerating toward the floor. You can probably fix this by simply adjusting a single keyframe tangent on the foot's y-translation curve to make it sharper. If an unwanted pause occurs during the linear trajectory of a rolling bowling ball, there might be an extraneous flat keyframe in the middle of the x or z translation curve that should either be changed to a smooth spline key or simply deleted. If a particular movement is rather jittery, there might be several extraneous keyframes at odd positions, creating a curve that is jagged rather than smooth. If a foot is supposed to stay in place for a few frames during a walk cycle but it drifts, you might have smooth Bezier keys at either end of the pause, making the connecting curve segment a shallow sine curve rather than a proper horizontal line (see Figure 16.35).

Dope Sheets

Another animation tool that exists in many software packages is typically known as a *dope sheet*. This tool describes object and character motions as time blocks on a spreadsheet-like interface (see Figure 16.36). Digital dope sheets are extremely intuitive tools that allow you to quickly and easily make timing adjustments to your animations. You might find that digital dope sheets are easier to understand and manipulate than piles of function curves, but they do not offer the same degree of precise control as a graph editor. You can make timing adjustments in both dope sheets and graph editors, but graph editors provide additional control over keyframe values and tangents.

Walks, Runs, and Other Basic Motion Tests

After you've created a character puppet but before you've actually animated your shots, it is always a good idea to create a few locomotion cycles and basic motion tests to not only test out the functionality and reliability of your rig, but also to practice the art of digital keyframing—and most importantly, to begin developing your character's motion style.

Walk cycles are an excellent place to start. Creating a basic walk cycle will help characterize a digital actor with regard to his body language dynamics. How high does he lift his feet when he takes a step? Does his torso stay rigid or sway back and forth as he walks? Does he slump or stand straight? Do his arms swing casually by his sides or does he keep them bent up tight to his chest?

A walk cycle can also help establish a character's mass. A heavier character will tend to move a bit slower and not lift his feet very high or keep them airborne very long. A lighter character might bounce a bit more, lift his feet higher, and not require as much help from the movement of his pelvis to get his feet off the ground at each step.

Once you have a basic walk figured out, create a few more walks displaying different physical and mental states. How does your character's overall posture and motion specifics change when he is angry, depressed, in a hurry, tired, injured, or inebriated (see Figure 16.37)?

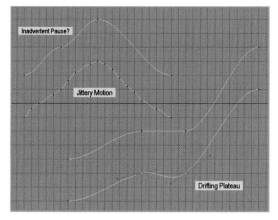

Figure 16.35
You can usually identify problems, such as inadvertent pauses, jittery motion, and drifting pauses, by simply looking for inappropriate tangent types or extraneous keyframes on corresponding function curves.

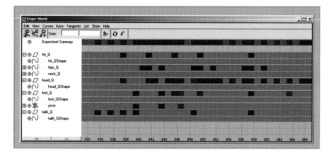

Figure 16.36
While function curve editors offer a higher level of precise control, digital dope sheets represent another powerful device for manipulating and troubleshooting CG animation timing.

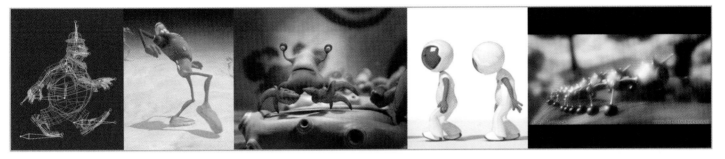

Figure 16.37
Test out your character rigs and begin to define personality and motion dynamics by creating a variety of walk cycles displaying different physical and emotional states.

Here are a few details to keep in mind when creating typical walk cycles:

◆ Don't forget to rotate the pelvis. Twist it toward the foot that is kicking out in front. And drop one side as its corresponding foot comes off the ground (unless the character is very heavy or injured, in which case you should try doing the opposite).

◆ Counter-rotate the upper torso to oppose the motion of the pelvis.

◆ Keep the supporting leg straight while the torso passes over it (see Figure 16.38). However, in certain walk variations, such as a sneak, the supporting leg would stay bent.

◆ Let each foot kick out fully extended for a beat before dropping to the ground, rather than straightening on the exact same frame as when the heel hits.

Of course, like every set of apparent rules in this book, these are mere tendencies. Feel free to bend, break, or ignore them to suit your own particular animation style.

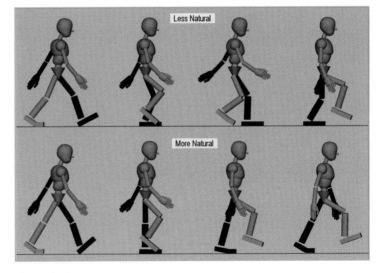

Figure 16.38
In a normal biped walk cycle, remember that the supporting leg typically does not bend while the hips pass over it.

If time permits and it seems appropriate to do so, consider trying a run cycle as well. But keep in mind that a run is not just a walk in fast motion. A walk is a series of controlled "falls" toward and over a supporting foot, while a run is a more like a series of alternating one-legged jumps. The fundamental difference is that in a walk at least one foot is always on the ground, whereas in a run there are points at which both feet are airborne (see Figure 16.39).

16. Animation

337

Although there are definite benefits to creating initial walk and run cycles for your characters, don't linger too long on these basic motions. Get your characters up and acting as soon as possible. If there is time in your schedule to do so, give yourself a few story-appropriate animation assignments that will help you learn your way around your character puppets and further define their motion dynamics and style. A few typical character tests that will help you practice indicating life, weight, personality, and attitude include the following:

◆ Pick up a heavy object (see Figure 16.40).

◆ Push or pull on a stubborn door that won't budge (see Figure 16.40).

◆ Climb over a wall or up a tree (see Figure 16.40).

◆ Perform numerous types of jumps.

◆ Fall down on the ground and then get up to a standing pose.

◆ React to some surprising news.

◆ Wrestle with another character.

◆ Make Junior eat peas, despite the fact that he hates peas.

After you've created a few walk cycles and motion tests, you might discover a problem or two with your character rig. Perhaps one of your character's knees bends the wrong way when you lift his foot. Maybe you need a couple more bones in the tail to get the curve shapes you need. Perhaps you need an eye-aim-constraint control after all. Although it is always regrettable to have to go back to an earlier step and make adjustments or improvements, it is much better to discover that such changes need to be made before you begin animating your shots, rather than halfway through production.

Figure 16.39
The fundamental difference between a run and a walk is that in a run there are moments when both feet are off the ground at the same time.

Figure 16.40
Performing basic motion tests such as pulling on stuck doors, lifting heavy objects, and climbing walls will help you define the mass and motion dynamics of your characters.

Animating with Forward Kinematics and Inverse Kinematics

In Chapter 14, we described how appendages and other joint chains can be set up and animated by way of forward kinematic rotations on individual joints or with the use of IK handles for translating end effectors, such as wrists and ankles.

Review your storyboards to get ideas for motion tests. The additional benefit to creating directly story-appropriate animation tests is that you might be able to use them as templates or perhaps even actual performances in finished shots.

In most cases, you will probably want to animate your legs with IK handles so they can be treated as separate objects from the rest of the body. This way, they will stay in place when appropriate and can be repositioned without affecting other body parts. Using FK legs instead would be rather inefficient for motions that involve standing, walking, running, or jumping on surfaces because it would be difficult to place your character's feet in their desired locations by rotations alone. And, after setting a large number of keyframes to try to keep your character's feet in place, every time you decide to make even the smallest adjustment to the motion of the torso or pelvis, you would have to recreate all of those FK keys. IK legs are clearly the way to go for most surface-based animations. If, however, your chimpanzee character is swinging from a vine and you want to get some nice overlap in the knee joints, FK rotations might make more sense.

When it comes to arms, some animators prefer IK all the time, while others like having direct control over the shoulder and elbow joints and therefore prefer FK. In general, it all depends on the situation. If the important issues are elbow overlap, arcs, and the pose of the arm relative to the torso, then FK rotations would typically be the way to go. If, on the other hand, the actual location of the wrist is very important or it needs to stay in one place while the torso moves about, then IK would definitely be the preferred methodology. Just be wary of the dreaded marionette look when translating wrists with IK handles. Be sure to use a sufficient number of in-between keyframes so the trajectory describes an arc when appropriate (refer to Figure 16.11).

Sometimes it makes sense to switch modes during the course of a character performance. You might want to use FK arms to get some nice, natural overlap in the elbows while your character is walking normally, but then switch to IK arms if he suddenly decides to walk on his hands. Switching between FK and IK in the middle of a shot is sometimes the most efficient way to go, but more often than not it is best to pick one method and stick with it for the duration of the shot. Switching modes will create additional keyframed attributes that must also be given attention and adjusted appropriately whenever timing or motion changes need to be made to an animation. Since the arms could be animated using either method during the normal walking portion of the shot but IK arms would be crucial during the walking-on-hands section, it would be simplest to use IK arms for the whole shot. The first part might require a few extra keyframes to get the overlap motion, but your graph editor will contain at least two fewer function curves, and your animation will therefore be that much easier to troubleshoot and tweak.

Facial Animation

Body language is typically the very heart of a character performance, but assuming your digital actors actually have faces, it will usually be necessary to breathe life into that portion of their anatomy as well. There are two basic types of facial animation you might encounter during your short film production:

◆ Facial expressions
◆ Lip-synching

Depending on the story being told by a given character performance and the role that expressions and dialogue enunciation play in the shot, you can create facial animation before, after, or in tandem with body movement.

When you are creating facial animation for non-abstract characters, remember that a face is not a collection of independently moving elements, but a complex assembly of muscles and tendons that work together to form expressions and phoneme shapes. When a character smiles, it is not a simple matter of only lifting the mouth edges. The cheeks will also bulge somewhat, and the eyes will tend to squint (see Figure 16.41). Watch yourself in a mirror to see how your mouth, eyes, cheeks, jaw, eyebrows, forehead, and even ears contribute simultaneously to your face shape.

Also, make aesthetic use of asymmetry when you create your facial expressions and phoneme shapes. Doing this on occasion will add to the naturalism of your characters and their performances (see Figure 16.42).

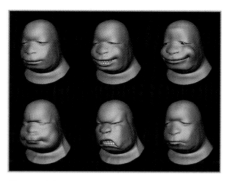

Figure 16.41
Remember that most facial animation involves more detail than simply reshaping a character's mouth.

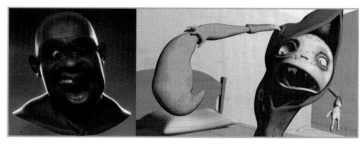

Figure 16.42
A bit of asymmetry is often rather expressive.

When you are applying facial animation to a cartoon character, it is often desirable to exaggerate and include a bit of squash and stretch at the extremes. Don't worry about pushing it too far in the beginning. You can always go in and tone it down after the fact.

Facial Expressions

Regardless of whether your film has dialogue, if your character puppets have faces, they will generally need to display emotion and attitude to help deliver the intended message of a given performance.

The most expressive parts of the face are the eyebrows and the mouth (see Figure 16.43). Most basic expressions can be described by these two elements alone; however, don't forget to add necessary details to the rest of the face for the sake of naturalism.

Experiment with different combinations of eyebrow and mouth shapes along with various levels of eye and jaw openness until you arrive at the desired facial expression. Then, when you are happy with a particular facial expression, record the appropriate attribute settings in case you want to use them again later.

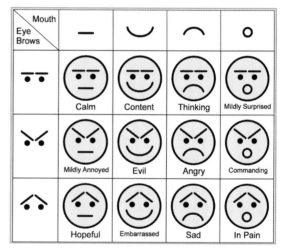

Figure 16.43
Basic facial expressions are mainly described by eyebrow and mouth shapes.

Eyes

When animating eyes, remember that they typically move together rather than independently, except in the case of certain reptiles and perhaps robots or aliens.

The closer the object being focused upon is, the more the eyes will cross. If you are animating a character reading a book, cross his eyes a bit; otherwise, he will appear to be focusing beyond the location of the text (see Figure 16.44).

Also consider that eyes tend to dart and stick rather than move around slowly, and their movement is often somewhat independent from that of the head. If a character turns to look to his side, his head might move slowly and smoothly, but his eyes will typically snap to the side at some point and stay focused until the head catches up (refer to Figure 16.44).

And don't forget to blink the eyes every so often. A normal unconscious blink typically takes about two frames to drop, holds for one or two frames, and then takes three to five frames to open again. A purposeful blink will tend to stay closed a bit longer.

Lip-Synching

Lip-synching is the process of animating a face to match the timing of a vocal track, and is typically accomplished by morphing toward appropriate phoneme shapes in synch with dialogue. (Refer to Chapter 9 for information on phoneme shapes.)

The first step is to bring the digital dialogue file into your CG software as a vocal track. Most CG packages allow you to see the waveforms of a vocal track in the timeline so you have visual and audio cues by which to synch up your phoneme shapes (see Figure 16.45).

The next step is to form appropriate phoneme shapes with your character face at the right times so the movement of the face looks like it is delivering the dialogue line convincingly. When it comes to abstract or extremely simplified cartoon characters, simply opening and closing the jaw at appropriate times might be sufficient, but more complex or realistic characters will require more detail (see Figure 16.46).

If you created a series of phoneme target shapes in your modeling and character setup stages, you would simply dial in the proper shapes and rotate the jaw accordingly when those syllable sounds come up in the vocal track. If you are using a joint- or muscle-based system, you will need to create appropriate phoneme shapes by moving, rotating, and scaling your control objects.

Figure 16.44
Eyes will cross when focusing on a near object and typically will move somewhat independently from the motion of the head.

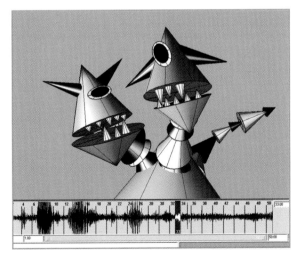

Figure 16.45
The first step in lip-synching is to load a dialogue track into your CG software package so it can be viewed as a waveform.

Here are a few things to keep in mind when you are creating lip-synch animations:

◆ Consider the personality and mood of the person delivering a particular line of dialogue. If a character is very angry, he might keep his jaw shut tight, and his phoneme shapes might need to have a bit of lip pursing layered on top. Overlay a bit of variation on top of your phoneme shapes for increased naturalism, but don't add so much that the readability of the particular shape gets lost (see Figure 16.47).

◆ Don't over-enunciate when you are creating realistic lip-synching. Watch yourself in a mirror delivering your lines of dialogue, and you will see that you typically do not form a new phoneme shape for every syllable. Sounds blend into one another, and some will not require much movement at all from one syllable to the next. For instance, when you lip-synch the word "require," you can typically get away with skipping the "q" phoneme shape and flow directly from the "e" to the "i." Children tend to enunciate with a bit more exaggeration than adults, but always be wary of overdoing it.

◆ Closed-mouth phoneme shapes, such as "m" and "f," should be held for at least a couple of frames so they read. Open-mouth shapes, such as "ah" and "oh," typically should not be static if held for more than a few frames. Let the mouth reshape itself a bit as the sound is held.

◆ Don't forget to pose and animate the tongue appropriately, especially when you are creating "th" and "l" phonemes.

◆ Imagine or simultaneously create body language that will work appropriately with your lip-synch performances. Remember that body language and dialogue typically should complement one another and, except when a word or a line of dialogue requires extra emphasis, they should never be redundant. Only combine opposite meanings between dialogue lines and body language when irony is the intention, such as when a character says, "I'm very shy," while striking an overly confident pose. In a close-up, body language will be less relevant, of course, but don't forget to animate the head to help deliver the intended attitude of the vocal performance.

Exposure Sheets

Some digital animators find it beneficial to create exposure sheets to help with dialogue animation. An *exposure sheet*, or *X sheet*, breaks down dialogue vertically into a series of rows, listing what letter or syllable is delivered on what frame (see Figure 16.48). X sheets are very helpful in traditional animation processes—especially stop-motion, where pre-planning is absolutely essential. However, because of the ability to adjust keyframes on the fly and quickly create test animations in most CG packages, many digital

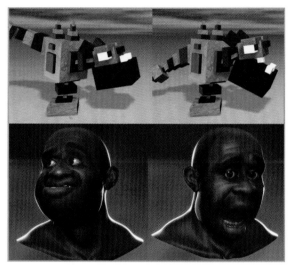

Figure 16.46
Lip-synching for abstract or extremely simple cartoon characters might be a simple matter of opening and closing the mouth at appropriate times, but more realistic or expressive characters will require increased detail.

Figure 16.47
Mixing phoneme and facial expression shapes is often necessary to visually deliver a line of dialogue with the appropriate indication of attitude.

animators find that a waveform display of a dialogue track lined up with their software timeline is more than sufficient, and that X sheets are not necessary. Typical X sheets might also contain film direction notes. Try one if you have the time. And if it helps to make your animation process more efficient, then by all means use them.

Using Reference

Some believe that the difference between a great animator and a mediocre animator is that a great animator never needs to use reference. But in fact the great animator is the one who recognizes when and how to use reference. Working from reference material is especially helpful when you are animating realistic human characters because the margin of error is so small. If your film will contain human characters and you hope to animate them convincingly, take the time to study yourself in a mirror, analyze existing film clips, or videotape yourself and some friends performing the motions that will exist in your short. Then use these reference pieces either directly or indirectly when you create your animations to ensure that you will deliver convincingly realistic performances.

The most indirect method of working from reference is to work from a live source. If you have a large mirror handy, watch yourself performing story-appropriate actions and use a stopwatch to get timing estimates. Pay attention to individual body parts as you act out your scenes. How do your hips shift to keep your balance when you lift one foot? How do you anticipate or create an appropriate leverage point to push from when getting up from a chair? When you turn your head, is it a completely isolated movement or does your spine rotate as well?

Search for videos, DVDs, or digital movie files that contain helpful character movements and study them by taking notes or making sketches. If feasible, videotape yourself, your actors, your pets, or the animals at the zoo performing directly or potentially story-relevant actions. The

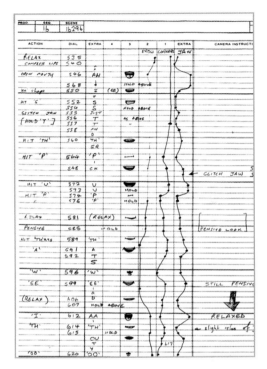

Figure 16.48
Exposure sheets are typically considered overkill for CG animation, but if you think they might increase your efficiency and productivity, give one a try.

advantage of using recorded sources is that you can carefully study the same movement over and over by pausing, replaying, and stepping through frame by frame. Look for extremes on individual body parts. In general, analyze the hips and feet first. Jot down frame counts for the amount of time the left foot takes to complete a step or how many frames it takes for a particular head turn to finish. Sketch every fourth, eighth, or perhaps sixteenth frame, or look for poses that might qualify as extremes, and then sketch those and any in-between poses that will help describe timing and trajectories. Then review your notes and sketches when it comes time to animate your shots.

Direct usage of reference material involves bringing video clips into your CG package as background imagery and then animating your digital characters side by side or directly on top of your filmed humans or animals (see Figure 16.49). Posing and animating a character on top of a filmed background plate is sometimes known as *rotomating*, and is a fairly popular CG method for capturing realistic performances onto a digital puppet without having to deal with the expense and complication of using motion-capture technology. Motion-capture will certainly provide you with more accurate data, especially in the fine details and natural imperfections of realistic motion; however, rotomating will allow you to more easily interpret and perhaps exaggerate the recorded performances to suit the needs of a given shot. Furthermore, motion-capture technology is generally prohibitively expensive for the purposes of a CG short unless you happen to have access to such equipment at your workplace.

Figure 16.49
Copying or tracing motion from a live source can be helpful for indicating subtle nuances in realistic performances.

Remember, working from reference is no more cheating than when a portrait or caricature artist works from a photograph or a live model to successfully capture someone's likeness. Copying someone else's animation, however, is not only cheating, but also plagiarism. A recognizable performance in a CG short can cause a lot of trouble for the director. Only borrow from someone else's animations for personal study, but never for public display (unless you are creating a satire).

Tips for Animating Animals

When you set out to animate animals, there is no substitute for solid research. Go to the zoo, examine nature books and videos, surf the Web for clips, watch your cat for a while, and take notes or record a few sketches. Understanding the specifics of how particular animals move will not only help you deliver convincing performances of whatever species happens to be in your film, but it will also assist you in creating believable movements for fantasy and science fiction creatures. If your film will feature a few otherworldly creatures or monsters, look for members of the animal kingdom that resemble your designs to help you invent the details of their motion dynamics.

As we mentioned previously, the secret to successful animation is observation and analysis. Apply this process as much as possible for the real animals or invented creatures of your film. Meanwhile, here are a few general tips to help you get started:

◆ Animals are arguably less intelligent than humans; therefore, their movements are often dictated by instinct rather than conscious thought. When a cat hears a sound in another room, he will quickly snap his head in the direction of the sound, whereas a human might consider whether he'd left the washing machine running before turning to look. Human concern level is variable, while animal concern level is typically high; therefore, animals tend to move first and think later. Humans at least attempt to do the opposite whenever possible.

◆ Many animals (especially insects) tend to move erratically, running and then pausing, rather than smoothly and calmly meandering from here to there.

◆ Many quadrupeds tend to walk utilizing a delayed-diagonal foot pattern, where equal intervals pass between each footfall. The left-front foot takes a step, followed by the right-rear, then the right-front, and finally the left-rear (see Figure 16.50). In a trot, the diagonals move almost exactly in tandem.

◆ A run is not a fast walk; rather, it is a different foot pattern altogether. The front and rear legs push off like syncopated jumps. However, in a typical quadruped run cycle, the two front feet do not hit the ground or push off at the same time, and the same goes for the rear feet. Rather, they come together in midair, but then separate before hitting the ground. This way, the animal takes full advantage of the fact that he has four legs by performing four individual pushes at each cycle, rather than two, which would be the case if the feet did not separate (see Figure 16.51).

Figure 16.50
Quadruped walk cycles typically utilize some variation of a delayed-diagonal foot pattern.

Figure 16.51
When quadrupeds run their legs come down separately, rather than in exact pairs, so that all four feet independently kick the ground in each cycle to maximize speed.

◆ Cat legs are somewhat bent in their default positions. This way they can jump without necessarily having to anticipate and can immediately begin walking or running after landing. If a human or a dog jumps down from a wall, his legs will compress and then straighten before he can comfortably begin walking or running. A cat only needs to compress and can therefore hit the ground running. Cats also have enormous play in their shoulder blades, which contributes to the smoothness of their movements. This helps them as predators because they can keep their body and head in a perfectly straight line while stalking because the shoulders absorb and compensate for all of the leg motion.

◆ Cat spines are quite elastic, which allows them to twist in midair as well as bend and extend radically to help them run faster.

◆ Horse and dog spines are much more rigid and only bend a small amount while walking and running (see Figure 16.52).

◆ The hind legs of most quadrupeds create a Z shape, where the upper mid-joint is the knee, the lower mid-joint is the extended ankle, and the ball of the foot is the support point. In normal animal motion, the first and third leg joints typically remain parallel. They can in fact rotate independently, but this typically only happens as the result of an external force.

◆ Small animals, especially birds, make very quick movements. Head turns can often be as fast as a single frame.

◆ Wing flapping is all about catching and pushing up on air pockets. In a flight cycle, a bird wing opens wide on the downward movement to push against the air, and then tucks in while lifting so as not to push itself downward as well (see Figure 16.53). This lift between pushes typically must happen rather quickly or the bird will begin to fall.

Figure 16.52
Cat spines are extremely elastic, while horse torsos are more rigid.

16. Animation

345

◆ Sharks are fish. Whales and dolphins are mammals. The most obvious anatomical difference is the orientation of the tail fin, which is vertical in fish and horizontal in mammals. Therefore, fish swim by swinging their tail fins left and right, while mammals swim by moving their tails up and down. Also, fish spines do not typically bend up and down, only side to side. When a fish pitches downward or upward, the spine does not arc; rather, the whole body stiffly rotates as a whole (see Figure 16.54). However, axial rotation allows for some degree of twisting, as often seen in photographs of salmon attempting to jump upstream.

◆ Snakes and worms dynamically create arbitrary leverage points wherever necessary to facilitate pushing their bodies to create forward motion.

Animating Non-Characters and Secondary Objects

In addition to animating humans, animals, and other living creatures, you might need to create believable movements for non-living creatures or secondary objects, such as cars, cameras, falling rocks, earrings, ponytails, loose clothing, swinging chains, billowing curtains, or windblown leaves. Occasionally, you can use procedural animation techniques to create such movements but often it is more efficient to simply animate such objects by hand.

To animate falling snowflakes or a small avalanche, you can usually get away with simply creating a set of appropriate trajectories for a half dozen or so individual flakes or rocks. Then copy these animations to the other objects and make subtle timing and value adjustments to their f-curves to create overall randomness.

Path animation is an alternative method that is often used for simple object trajectories. This method involves drawing a curve in 3D space and then attaching an object so the curve acts as a motion path. Path animation is especially helpful if you want an object's trajectory to be a very specific shape, such as a perfect circle. Paths can be recursive as well. If you are creating our solar system, you might create an elliptical path for the moon's orbit around the Earth, and then another much larger path for the Earth's orbit around the sun. Sometimes you might find it helpful to animate a character's center or an IK handle along a path as well. For instance, if you have a character riding an invisible bicycle, it might make sense to attach his feet to a pair of vertical circles where the pedal motion would occur, and then offset one foot by a half cycle (see Figure 16.55).

You can animate more complex objects, such as chains, clothing, curtains, or tablecloths, by inserting a sufficient number of joint chains inside and then rotating appropriately. Or you can create clusters to control the points of a surface and then animate them with timing offsets to create naturalistic secondary motions.

Figure 16.53
Wing movement involves pushing down at full extension and then folding in for lifting up.

Figure 16.54
Fish spines do not typically bend forward; rather, their entire bodies will stiffly rotate when pitching forward.

A popular CG trick you can use for simple chain and cloth movement, as well as tails, fish spines, and antennae, involves simply rotating all of the joints in a single chain to their extreme positions, setting keyframes, and then delaying the motion of each successive joint by a few frames to create nice, smooth overlapping movement (see Figure 16.56). The length of the delay will depend on the speed of the swing motion. When you apply this shortcut, make sure that your function curves are set to cycle before and after their keyed frame ranges; otherwise, the joints will pop at their extremes.

Playing to the Camera

As we discussed in Chapter 11, object and character animation will be codependent with camera direction. Typically, the staging of a shot will begin with basic placement and trajectories of the digital scene elements; then the camera will be positioned and moved to follow the action effectively. However, as you refine your object movements and character performances, you might have to go back and make adjustments to your camera direction to maintain effective shot staging. At some point, typically at the blocking milestone, you should be able to lock your camera positioning and movement, and then just focus on animation details.

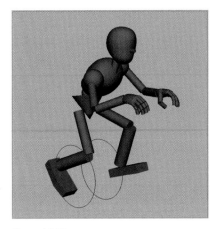

In an interactive 3D video game, an animation needs to look good from all possible angles because the user controls the point of view. In filmmaking, however, the director chooses the viewer's camera angle. Sometimes, to most effectively compose the image in your camera perspective view, you might need to cheat a pose or a trajectory in such a way that the character would look off balance or positioned incorrectly when viewed from an alternative modeling window (see Figure 16.57). This is known as *playing to the camera*. While you are working on your objects and character animations, definitely bounce around between different orthographic and perspective views, but remember that the camera view is the only one that ultimately counts. In filmmaking, an animation doesn't have to be right; it just has to look right. This is yet another reason why it is important to lock down the camera direction as early as possible. Playing to the camera is much more difficult when you are chasing a moving target!

Also, don't waste time animating objects or body parts that will be out of frame, such as a character's toes in a shot that stages him from the waist up. However, keep in mind that out-of-frame objects might be seen in reflections or cast shadows, so animate accordingly.

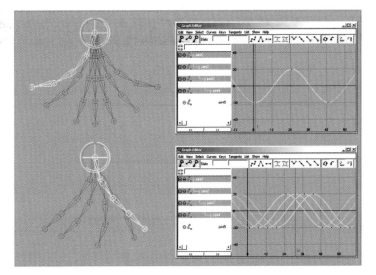

Figure 16.56
A simple trick for creating overlap on simple swinging chain motions is to rotate and keyframe all of the joints at their extremes and then shift the function curves of each successive joint forward in time by a few frames.

When you are animating a particularly explosive action, it often helps to pretend that the camera's operator or tripod is actually in the scene. Have it react to the force of the animation. For instance, if you stage a low close-up shot of a giant ogre's foot slamming down on the ground, you might want the camera to shake a bit immediately afterward. Adding such detail to the movement of a CG camera, however, will make it a bit more difficult to evaluate the animation while the shot is progressing. Therefore, such camera reactions are often added as two-dimensional post-camera moves after the shot has been rendered (see Chapter 20, "Compositing")

Objective Self-Criticism

Objective self-criticism is your most powerful tool in CG filmmaking. When something doesn't look quite right, you can take advantage of the computer's undo and redo buttons until a particular performance looks exactly the way you intended. Preplanning is highly recommended, but you will rarely set down your keyframes perfectly the first time so be prepared to do a fair amount of curve shifting and test rendering as you create your character performances.

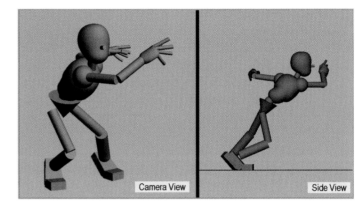

Figure 16.57
For effective staging, it is sometimes necessary to cheat a pose or a motion so it looks correct in the camera window, even though the character might look strange or imbalanced if seen from an alternative point of view.

Use your innate sense of what looks correct and/or appealing. Whether or not you realize it, you are a subconscious expert on real-world motion, especially when it comes to humans. It indeed takes years to learn how to recreate realistic and convincing movement successfully, but even a child can tell whether a CG character in a film looks like he is being properly affected by physics or gravity. So assume the role of that child when you are viewing and analyzing your animations and test renders.

Viewing your work objectively is sometimes more difficult than it sounds. You might be unnecessarily hard on yourself sometimes, while other times you might be so sick of a particular shot that your desire to move on will taint your ability to identify problems. Sometimes, after you work on a shot for a very long time, it is simply too difficult to detach yourself and judge it objectively. Fortunately, there are a few approaches you can take to help increase your objectivity when you are reviewing your animations.

◆ Watch your shots (or at least individual performances) in silhouette. This will allow you to better analyze the overall motion of your animations without being distracted by the details (see Figure 16.58).

◆ Watch your shots mirrored. Some playback tools allow you to do this by simply hitting a single button. If necessary, use the batch-processing functionality of packages such as DeBabelizer or Photoshop to perform a horizontal flip on all of your rendered images, and then reassemble them as video clips (see Figure 16.58).

◆ If something doesn't look quite right in a character performance, apply the process of elimination method by hiding appendages until you discover the source of the problem. Or hide them all, and if the torso seems to be moving properly, redisplay each appendage one at a time until the offending motion appears.

◆ Watch your shots in sequence. Sometimes watching an isolated shot repeatedly will not tell you the real story of how it works in your film. After all, your audience will be seeing your shot in sequence, so put yourself in their shoes as often as possible.

◆ Watch a shot backwards and realize that if an animation looks perfectly okay in reverse, then the timing and physics are probably off.

◆ Draw directly on your screen with dry erase markers or use acetate overlays to analyze trajectories and incremental differences between object positions and character poses.

◆ Always respond to your first impression each time you watch a new version of a performance. The more you watch a given shot, the more you can consciously or subconsciously convince yourself that it looks okay. If you thought you saw a problem during the first playback loop but it gradually faded away, definitely go back and address your initial impression. Your audience typically will see a given shot only one time and will not have the same opportunity to watch it over and over until the glitch fades away. Again, imagine yourself as an audience member and respond to your first impression the same way your viewers will.

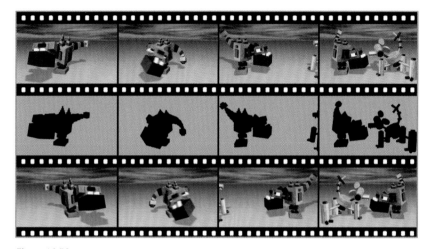

Figure 16.58
There are many ways to attain objective self-criticism when you view your animations, including viewing your shots in silhouette and mirroring your playbacks.

Summary

Animation can be thought of as the art of movement, and the keys to animating effectively are observation and analysis. CG animation involves the manipulation and sequential display of moving digital objects and performing character puppets, and it offers an unparalleled level of editorial capabilities, which are often a blessing but can sometimes be a curse. Character animation is the art of adding the illusion of life, rather than mere movement, to otherwise inanimate objects and characters, resulting in the display of personality, motivation, and emotion. The two basic style extremes in character animation are realistic, in which natural rules of motion and physics are obeyed, and cartoony, in which simplification, exaggeration, and definitive poses are emphasized. Learn and truly understand the fundamental principles of animation, such as timing, anticipation, squash and stretch, and staging, so you can deliver character performances with believable indications of weight, personality, and attitude. But always remember that your instincts are more powerful than any set of rules. After a rough layout phase or 3D animatic, the next milestone of an evolving shot animation is blocking, which can be defined as just enough attention to basic posing, timing, and trajectories so the message of the performance is delivered, but without any details. The details are then added in subsequent refinement passes. Strive to learn how the manipulation of curves and keyframes in the graph editor translates to actual object and character motion so you can become an extremely efficient digital animator. Use reference as necessary and study animal anatomy and motion specifics to help the believability of your real or invented creatures, robots, and space aliens. And remember that your strongest filmmaking tool is objective self-criticism, so try to put yourself in the shoes of your viewers when analyzing your animations.

chapter 17
Case Study 3: Squaring Off

Moving right along from the animation chapter, our third case study features a very simple short that focuses almost exclusively on that specific production component.

The Beginning

Squaring Off began as a self-imposed animation exercise, so there was no script, no storyboards, no production plan, and no story reel.

I had been spending far too much time at the office supervising, rather than actually animating shots, but I was about to embark on a project where I was going to be expected to do both. Concerned about the rustiness of my keyframing skills, I grabbed one of the digital puppets from the upcoming project and tried a few animation tests. Unfortunately, my sense of timing had atrophied a bit from lack of practice. The first day of production was only a few weeks away, and the complex and non-interactive puppets I was practicing with were hardly ideal for getting me back up to speed in time.

VITAL STATISTICS

Title: *Squaring Off*

Director: Jeremy Cantor

Team Size: One

Total Running Time: 1 minute, 15 seconds

Production Cycle: About four weeks, part time

Software: Maya, Adobe Premiere, QuickTime Pro, Ulead VideoStudio 4, Cosmigo Pro Motion

Total Production Cost: $15 for the music; all other assets were pre-owned

Realizing that the only way I would be able to sufficiently get all the rust off my fingers was to generate a large amount of animation in a rather short period of time, I knew I was going to need some extremely light and interactive practice puppets. So I stayed late at the office for a few nights and put together the simplest character puppets I could imagine. I decided to use only primitive objects and simply parent them to skeleton joints, figuring that non-skinned puppets would allow me to scrub my timeline interactively so I could focus all my attention on timing issues.

Character Design

As long as I was creating new characters, I decided to at least put a small amount of creativity into the process, so I gave myself a few restrictions and guidelines that I thought might make my upcoming self-imposed animation assignments a bit more interesting. I'd build four creatures, each with a different number of legs—one, two, three, and four. That way, each character would provide me with a unique challenge when it came time to invent their locomotion cycles. I also decided to only allow the characters to blink and perhaps open and close their mouths. No actual face shapes could be created, so any acting and emotion I would attempt to deliver would need to come from body language alone.

Now that I had significantly increased the difficulty level of my task (for reasons that still elude me), it was time to design my creatures. I decided to give each character a singular design element. The first character would be made out of cubes, another from spheres, the third from cylinders, and the fourth from cones. I vaguely recall having some idea that maybe I'd use them all someday for a short I would call *Primitive Culture*, but as of yet I haven't been able to come up with a storyline worthy of such an obvious and corny title pun. Maybe someday....

I did a few quick idea sketches for the cube character, but nothing interesting developed (see Figure 17.1). So I decided to use my CG software as a virtual Lego playground and I simply created a pile of primitive cubes and experimented with various assemblies of different-sized objects until I eventually arrived at a combination that appealed to me (see Figure 17.2). The original cube character (nicknamed "Cubicle") had two legs, but I thought perhaps I should start off with something a bit more challenging so I amputated one of them (see Figure 17.3). I showed him to a few select friends for some feedback. One person decided he was a dog; another said he was a dinosaur. I didn't much care either way. To me, he was just an opportunity to scrub my timeline interactively.

Figure 17.2
Using a CG package as a virtual playground for assembling simple objects is a fun way to design characters.

Figure 17.3
Before and after the surgery

Figure 17.1
Character sketches...but nothing successful

Character Setup and Animation Testing

Before I created the other three characters, I decided I should do a couple of test animations with Mr. Cubicle. After all, I was supposed to be practicing keyframing, not character design! Turning Cubicle's assembly of primitive objects into a digital puppet was a fairly straightforward process. I split his leg into three pieces and put in a single bone with an IK handle point-constrained to the foot. This way I could move the foot around and the leg would stretch and compress while remaining connected at the ankle. I constrained his knee object to both the foot and the torso so it would always remain halfway between and it would hide the separation of the two leg pieces when they stretched (see Figure 17.4). Then I added a movable pin at the bottom of the foot so I could pivot it from any side or corner (see Figure 17.5). I built the neck in the same manner as the leg so I could move and rotate the head independently from the rest of the body. I added a simple hinge joint for the jaw and a pair of ball joints for the ears. For blinking, I allowed the eyelids to scale vertically until they covered the pupils (see Figure 17.6). The pistons on Cubicle's back were expression-driven to compress and expand by manipulating three custom channels on the torso control.

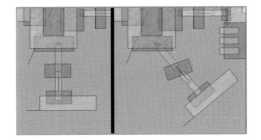

Figure 17.4
The knee object was constrained equally to the torso and the foot so it would always sit halfway between the two.

As long as I was playing character rigger, I figured I'd practice my scripting skills by creating a semi-automated tail control that might work as an effective shortcut for simple movements. I created six tail joints, each with its own control locators. Then I created an expression that would allow me to turn on an auto-delay, so any rotations I performed on the first tail joint would be copied to the remaining joints with a steadily increasing time delay. This way, I could create simple overlapping tail swings by only animating a single node (see Figure 17.7). I also gave myself a keyframable multiplier so I could make the delay very short for fast tail moves and longer for slow tail moves. Of course, I created an off switch in case I wanted more exacting control over the tail poses. I wasn't sure whether I would ever actually use the auto-delay, but it was worth a try.

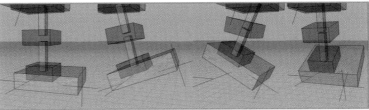

Figure 17.5
A movable pivot for the foot would come in handy.

Once Cubicle was fully rigged, it was time to try a few animation tests. First I had to answer the question, "How does a one-legged creature walk?" Well, obviously he would need to hop. That was my first official animation assignment—make Cubicle hop from here to there. Before starting to animate, however, I needed to answer a second question: "How big is he?" Such information

Figure 17.6
I scaled the lid objects so the eyes could blink vertically.

would significantly affect the specifics of his movement. I ultimately decided that he should be the size of a child's toy—about six inches tall to the top of his back pistons. It took a few tries to get just the right amount of anticipation and follow through into each jump, but I eventually came up with a locomotion cycle that seemed fairly convincing based on his intended size. Surprisingly enough, the tail auto-delay function worked like a charm (at least on this basic movement).

However, the problem with the locomotion cycle was that a hopping creature couldn't move slowly. Even covering the smallest distance required a reasonable amount of energy expenditure. I suddenly realized why Mother Nature didn't invent any one-legged creatures. They would make terrible predators because their prey would always hear them coming. Maybe a one-legged herbivore? Anyway, back to animation. The clock was ticking. Since Cubicle had such a big foot, I had to come up with an alternative motion cycle in which he could sidestep by pivoting back and forth between his heel and toe. Not a very efficient motion, but it would probably look okay for short distances.

With Cubicle rigged and moving around, it was time to get back to the other characters. Number two was "Spheroid," who ended up looking somewhat birdlike (see Figure 17.8). For his feet, I ultimately had to cheat a bit, loosening my spheres-only restriction and allowing myself to use a couple of half-spheres. Sometimes it's okay to cheat a little bit.

I wasn't too fond of Spheroid so I rigged him quickly, made a simple biped walk cycle, and moved on.

"Coney" was next—a three-legged creature made out of cones. I was having trouble deciding between two different head designs, so I decided to just use both (see Figure 17.9). Rigging was easy, but a three-legged walk cycle was a bit of a challenge. A run was simple—just make a quadruped run cycle and pretend the two front feet are tied together. But there didn't seem to be any way to create a walk cycle that didn't look strange and inefficient. It was hard to decide how to shift the hips in a sensible and repeatable pattern. Again, there is no three-legged creature that occurs naturally in the wild, and I was beginning to see why.

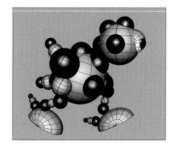

```
$td = tailA_Q.delay;
$tad = tailA_Q.auto_delay;

tailB_Q_auto.rotateX = ( `getAttr -t (frame - $td*1) tailA_Q.rx` ) * $tad;
tailC_Q_auto.rotateX = ( `getAttr -t (frame - $td*2) tailA_Q.rx` ) * $tad;
tailD_Q_auto.rotateX = ( `getAttr -t (frame - $td*3) tailA_Q.rx` ) * $tad;
tailE_Q_auto.rotateX = ( `getAttr -t (frame - $td*4) tailA_Q.rx` ) * $tad;
tailF_Q_auto.rotateX = ( `getAttr -t (frame - $td*5) tailA_Q.rx` ) * $tad;

tailB_Q_auto.rotateY = ( `getAttr -t (frame - $td*1) tailA_Q.ry` ) * $tad;
tailC_Q_auto.rotateY = ( `getAttr -t (frame - $td*2) tailA_Q.ry` ) * $tad;
tailD_Q_auto.rotateY = ( `getAttr -t (frame - $td*3) tailA_Q.ry` ) * $tad;
tailE_Q_auto.rotateY = ( `getAttr -t (frame - $td*4) tailA_Q.ry` ) * $tad;
tailF_Q_auto.rotateY = ( `getAttr -t (frame - $td*5) tailA_Q.ry` ) * $tad;

tailB_Q_auto.rotateZ = ( `getAttr -t (frame - $td*1) tailA_Q.rz` ) * $tad;
tailC_Q_auto.rotateZ = ( `getAttr -t (frame - $td*2) tailA_Q.rz` ) * $tad;
tailD_Q_auto.rotateZ = ( `getAttr -t (frame - $td*3) tailA_Q.rz` ) * $tad;
tailE_Q_auto.rotateZ = ( `getAttr -t (frame - $td*4) tailA_Q.rz` ) * $tad;
tailF_Q_auto.rotateZ = ( `getAttr -t (frame - $td*5) tailA_Q.rz` ) * $tad;
```

Figure 17.7
The tail auto-delay cheat. But would it work?

Figure 17.8
Spheroid

Figure 17.9
Can't decide which head looks better? Use both.

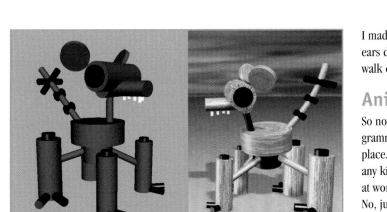

Figure 17.10
Mr. Cylinder

I made the final four-legged beast out of cylinders. It had no mouth, but the ears doubled as eyelids (see Figure 17.10). The rigging was simple, and his walk cycle was rather straightforward.

Animation

So now what? I was having so much fun playing character designer and programmer that I almost forgot why I had started down this road in the first place. Okay, time to get serious about animation. I had no intention of telling any kind of story with these creatures. A major production was about to begin at work, so now was not the time to embark upon the creation of a CG short. No, just a few seconds of animation to get myself back up to speed, and then I could call my experiment a success.

With no real ideas in mind, I grabbed my favorite of the four characters, Cubicle, and literally dropped him into frame. I was unpleasantly surprised by how long it took me to make his initial fall and bounce look okay with respect to timing and weight, but eventually it appeared passable so I moved on. A couple of hops brought Cubicle close to camera; I then decided to make him stretch and shake as I'd seen my cat do every morning while waiting for her breakfast. And remarkably, the tail auto-delay was working out so far. Satisfied that I could now move this one character around with relative ease and ever-increasing speed, I decided I'd stick with the experiment for another day or two and bring in a second character. I wasn't happy with Spheroid and Coney was too complicated, so I chose Mr. Cylinder, vowing to give him a name at some point. He's still waiting, by the way.

My assignment was turning out to be a lot of fun and before I knew it, I had well over 1,000 frames of completed stream-of-consciousness animation. The rust was officially off my fingers. Mission accomplished!

Story

I was ready to abandon the exercise, but I was enjoying it too much so I figured I'd keep going for another day or two. However, I didn't want to just continue making things up as I went along, so I decided I'd try throwing in a quick punch line, mainly to give myself a reason to stop. The punch line was admittedly stolen from Juliet Stroud's *Snookles*, but I figured she wouldn't mind because this was just a personal experiment and nobody would ever see it anyway.

After a few more days, I had 1,800 frames and a mere semblance of an ending, so I could finally stop. On a whim, I decided to show the piece to a few friends and, much to my surprise, my stolen punch line actually got a few laughs. So I figured, what the heck, why not refine the piece a bit and maybe use it as a future demo reel addition?

Textures and Lighting

Since I didn't want to go back and adjust any of the animation that had been staged to a single camera perspective, I decided against doing any camera cuts or moves. Just some simple textures, a ground plane for cast shadows, and maybe some sound effects. The textures were simple, procedurally generated Maya 3D fractal patterns (see Figure 17.11).

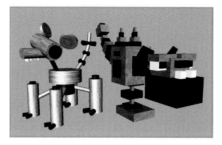

Figure 17.11
Basic 3D fractal textures seemed sufficient for such a simple film.

For the background image, I scanned a photograph I had taken of a sunset in Maui,
adjusted the color to make it a bit more surreal, mapped it onto an image plane, and animated it moving horizontally very slowly over the course of the film (see Figure 17.12).

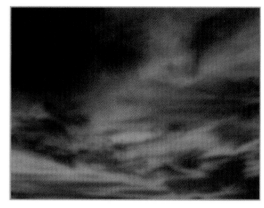

Figure 17.12
I used a color-adjusted photograph of a Maui skyline as the background image.

Two simple point lights, a bit of motion blur, ray-traced renders, and the visuals were complete (see Figure 17.13).

Sound FX

I'd recently purchased a digital camcorder, so I walked around the house recording myself hitting, scraping, and dropping various objects until I had a sufficiently large collection of taps, swishes, and crunches. I then imported the video file using Ulead's VideoStudio, which came packaged with the camcorder, and extracted the audio track using Adobe Premiere. Then, using QuickTime Pro, I separated the large audio track into individual sound bites, giving each of them descriptive names such as footstep_1 and slide_long_2. Then, using QuickTime again, I assembled all of my rendered frames into three separate video files of 600 frames each. I dropped the three video clips back into Adobe Premiere sequentially, and then started inserting my sound effects to synch up with the character's various moves, while manipulating the volume here and there to try to add a bit of auditory depth.

Figure 17.13
The final product

Music

Because my little film had no real story, I figured it should at least have a soundtrack. I purchased a collection of royalty-free classical recordings from a local record store and dropped a few pieces on top of my visuals to see whether anything would fit. Nothing seemed to match the intended tone of the piece, so I decided to see what I could find on the Internet. I eventually stumbled upon http://www.pbtm.com, an online library of original, royalty-free recordings by a composer named Michael Brewer. After listening to several dozen sound clips, I purchased two pieces at $15 each and downloaded them immediately. The livelier of the two pieces, called *The Clown*, had just the tone and tempo I had in mind, but to use it effectively I would probably need to fade in and out and actually slow down the piece for the aftermath section of my film. I wrote to Mr. Brewer, and fortunately he said I could cut, paste, and change the speed of his piece to my heart's content, just as long as the melody stayed intact. Audio and video were now complete. Just one last step….

Titles, Credits, and Transitions

Because the central action of the film involved the two characters engaging in a brief dexterity contest, and the main character was made out of cubes, I decided that *Squaring Off* would be an appropriate pun to use as the title.

Then, using a 2D animation program called Promotion, I made a simple title card for the end and a growing-circle transition to open and close the film (see Figure 17.14). *Squaring Off* was now officially in the can.

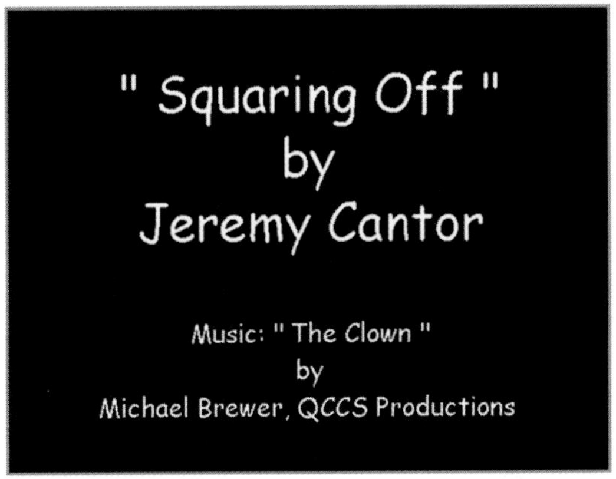

End Result

In Chapter 1, we discussed several possible reasons for making a short film. The initial reason for creating *Squaring Off* was to simply get in a bit of much-needed animation practice. But after the piece was complete, I sent it off to a handful of festivals, and it was actually accepted into a few of them, including Prix Ars Electronica 2002 and Bitfilm Festival Hamburg, 2003.

Figure 17.14
Title card

I also posted the short on a couple of online animation forums and even received two job offers as a result. Additionally, the Cubicle character was licensed by Funny Productions, Inc. for use in a future PBS children's show called *Cory the Clown*, and the film was selected for the DVD collection, "North America's Best Independent Animated Shorts," from Raider Productions (http://www.nabias.com).

So even though this piece started as nothing more than a basic animation exercise, it ultimately graduated to actual short film status (refer to Figure 17.14), resulting in a small amount of exposure as well as some possible financial gain.

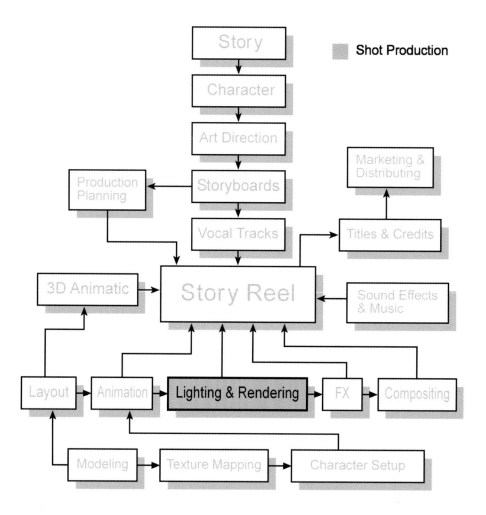

Shot Production

chapter 18
Lighting and Rendering

Lighting can be one of the most enjoyable aspects of short film production because it allows for a significant amount of creativity. The process of lighting a scene through the use of a 3D program requires virtually the same principles as are used in more traditional media, such as painting, theater, photography, and film. By observing the work of master painters, such as Caravaggio, Goya, Rembrandt, Vermeer, Turner, and de La Tour, you can draw inspiration from the exceptional utilization of lights that is evident in their paintings (see Figure 18.1). Similarly, by witnessing a good theater play, you can get a better understanding of the role that lighting plays on a stage and how it works in conjunction with the elements of time and performance. And by examining books that have samples of professional photographs or by studying the execution of lighting in film, you can acquire a better understanding of the fundamental principles and techniques of this particular task.

In the past, the process of generating realistic images through the use of 3D computer applications had been limiting and challenging for the CG artist because only wire-frame images could be generated. However, new techniques, such as global illumination and final gathering, now facilitate the creation of 3D computer-generated images that display remarkably photorealistic quality. And with the ability to experiment with many types of lights, material properties, and textures, you can achieve an endless variety of unique and captivating surreal, abstract, or cartoony digital imagery.

As in every step of the production pipeline, lighting can prove to be an incredibly time-consuming task. Lighting is directly tied to the story of a film in the sense that it defines the mood for every scene. With this in mind, it is important to look at visual references of lighting that correspond to the guidelines that were established during

"Just as our eyes need light in order to see, our minds need ideas in order to create."

Nicole Malebranche

Figure 18.1
Study traditional paintings for examples of stylish and effective lighting.

the art direction stage. Of course, it is also necessary to strive for simplicity and efficiency with regard to the complexity of your lighting setups so you don't create scenes that take too long to render.

The first step in the lighting process is to decide how you want the lighting of your scenes to influence your story point delivery and enhance the visual richness of your film. Typically, lighting is an extremely significant contributor to story delivery and will require a fair amount of work to achieve effective results, but if your goal is to simply demonstrate animation skills, then simplicity will obviously be the key.

What Is Lighting?

In the context of CG, *lighting* is the process of illuminating digital scenes in an artistic and technical manner so the audience can perceive what the director intends to display on the screen with the appropriate clarity and mood. The lighting process requires artistic sensibilities because it involves aspects such as color, composition, and design, and it also requires technical knowledge because of the number of parameters that are involved in even the most basic lighting setups.

The most fundamental purpose of lighting is to make the visual elements of a particular scene visible. But perhaps its most significant purpose is to indicate depth and mood. With the proper implementation of lighting, a sense of unity between characters and environment can be achieved. Other information that lighting can potentially help to deliver includes the spatial relationships between scene elements, the timeframe in which current events are taking place, and the emphasis of the aesthetic characteristics that are particular to the genre of the films. But always keep in mind that lights must be placed carefully so that the appropriate visual information will be delivered to the audience.

Lighting Fundamentals

Before you choose and place lights for your scenes, consider the following fundamental properties of this cinematic element:

◆ **Mood.** The implementation of lighting instills a sense of atmosphere and dramatic mood into a scene, thus adding believability and audience immersion. Proper application of lighting can help to make a story or scene feel warm, comfortable, cold, or ominous (see Figure 18.2).

◆ **Depth.** Lighting helps to portray a three-dimensional world on a two-dimensional screen by creating the illusion of depth by using illumination and shadow casting. Without effective lighting, spatial relationships can sometimes be ambiguous.

◆ **Time.** Lighting can also help to transmit information to the audience regarding the hour of the day and the season of the year (see Figure 18.3).

Figure 18.2
Proper attention to lighting specifics will help establish mood.

- **Position.** The position of lights in a scene is critical for effective clarity, mood, and other scene information. The same light placed in different positions will affect the overall perception of the resulting image. Lights from above tend to look more natural, but a light from below can be creepy.

- **Form and composition.** Through the use of lighting, characters, props, and environments reveal their forms, textural qualities, and spatial relationships. Lighting also creates positive and negative spaces, which aid in the overall composition of a scene.

- **Economy.** Be sure to optimize of the number of lights that are used in a given scene. It is important to always use just the right number of lights placed in the most appropriate positions to create the intended effect. Using more lights does not necessarily lead to better results; rather, it often leads to exactly the opposite effect and can considerably increase rendering time.

Figure 18.3
Lighting can help indicate daytime or nighttime.

Attributes of Lights

You can create an enormous variety of effects with lights, and depending on what kind of software you choose to work with, the set of attributes of the available lights might vary. You might need to adjust these attributes to create specific lighting effects or moods; therefore, it is important to understand the tools that are available to help improve the visual interest of your images.

- **Intensity.** This refers to the brightness of a given light source. High intensity would mean turning the dimmer switch all the way up. A low-intensity situation would be a dim room, perhaps lit by candles.

- **Falloff.** This indicates how a light's intensity decreases as it travels through space. Consider the strength of the light source and the objects you want to illuminate. The light given off by a match will fall off rather quickly, while sunlight will seem to extend indefinitely.

- **Color.** Lights do not have to be white or yellow. For example, if the intended setting is a cold atmosphere such as the North Pole, it would make sense to use blue lights, whereas reddish colors would be more suitable in a violent or intense setting (see Figure 18.4).

Figure 18.4
Colored lights will intensify the mood of a particular scene.

◆ **Linking.** By linking lights to objects, you can select the objects that will be illuminated by a specific light.

◆ **Light effects.** You can use effects, such as glow and lens flare, to increase the quality of an image and its cinematic feel (see Figure 18.5). These effects consume more time during the rendering stage, but such details can add to the overall realism of a scene.

Lighting Styles

The concept of lighting style is intimately related to the particular context and art direction of your short films, but unfortunately, there are no foolproof formulas to the process of lighting a scene. There are, however, three basic categories of lighting styles:

◆ High-key

◆ Low-key

◆ Tonal

Figure 18.5
Effects such as star fields, glow, and sparkles will increase a scene's cinematic qualities.

High-Key or Hard-Key Lighting

High-key or *hard-key* lighting involves the utilization of greatly intense and vibrant lights, which concentrate the illumination into certain sections of a scene, resulting in a high degree of contrast between light and shadow. This style of lighting is perfect when you want to create a dramatic atmosphere. Because large sections of the screen might fall under the veil of obscurity, this approach helps direct the audience's attention toward a particular focal point on the screen (see Figure 18.6).

Low-Key or Soft-Key Lighting

Low-key or *soft-key* lighting provides an even distribution of illumination in a scene, producing an image that has less contrast and fewer shadows. The resulting image is very clear and all of the visual elements on the screen are perfectly evident to the eyes of the audience (see Figure 18.7). Clarity, rather than ominous obscurity, is the typical result.

Figure 18.6
High-key lighting can create a dramatic atmosphere.

©Suruchi Pahwa and Hardeep Kharbanda
Figure 18.7
Low-key lighting results in a high degree of overall visual clarity.

Tonal Lighting

This style of lighting can be described as the midpoint between the two previous extremes, and it generally feels the most natural. Tonal lighting is typically used in more subtle film genres.

Types of Lights

To define the different types of lights available to the CG artist, there are two general areas of concern:

◆ The source and propogation
◆ The role of the light in the scene

Source and Propagation

Lights can originate from an extensive variety of sources, such as the sun, a spotlight, a fluorescent light bulb, or a candle. The CG artist can choose from several types of lights depending on the intended origin and propagation. The nature and size of the space or objects intended for illumination will guide that choice.

The lighting tools that are present in today's CG software have been created with the intention of emulating real-world lighting. The most common of these are

◆ **Point light.** This type emits light in all directions from a single point, like a miniature sun. This is the perfect solution when you are lighting large areas (see Figure 18.8).

◆ **Spotlight.** This type of light originates from a given point in space and its rays expand in a radial manner based on the aperture of the spot. Spotlights have the characteristic of concentrating the light within a "spot" so that it encompasses a specific area. Spotlights are perfect for dramatic moments because they generate hard shadows and create a high degree of contrast on the surfaces of objects (see Figure 18.9). You can also use this type of light to simulate a flashlight beam in a dark room, a searchlight during a prison break, or a stage spotlight when a performer is delivering a monologue.

◆ **Directional light.** The source of this light comes from one direction in the form of multiple parallel rays. Directional lights are mainly used to simulate sunlight or moonlight (see Figure 18.10).

Figure 18.8
Point lights emanate in all directions from a single point in space.

Figure 18.9
A spotlight can focus light on a character, creating a dramatic mood.

◆ **Ambient light.** Normally, this is the first light that is created in a scene. It is a type of light that provides an overall and even distribution of illumination that fills in the space of an environment without emanating from any specific position or direction. It is important to keep in mind that the use of the ambient light will alter the effects of other lights in a scene.

◆ **Area light.** The source of this type of light is shaped like a plane, and the direction of its propagation is perpendicular to the source. This type of light is useful for situations in which a large area needs to be illuminated and a single point source of light is not enough to accomplish the task. Examples of the implementation of this type of light include light that is coming in through a window, from a fluorescent bulb, or from above a waterline, where the surface creates a plane of diffused light that illuminates the scene below (see Figure 18.11).

The Role of Light in the Scene

In addition to deciding on the type of light to use in a particular scene, you must consider its role—whether it is the only source of light, the main source of light, or something more secondary.

Following are examples of light types that you can use individually or in conjunction with other types to achieve a desired effect. Keep in mind, however, that you will not find these classifications in the pull-down menus of your CG software package; rather, they are defined and distinguished by their intended usage and can apply to any kind of digital light.

◆ **Key light.** This is the primary or predominant source of light in a scene (see Figure 18.12). A key light is usually placed in front of the objects it will illuminate, and its placement height will depend on the mood you want to convey. Normally, it is placed at a 30- to 45-degree angle, either to the right or left of the camera, but if you want to indicate high noon, then it would be placed directly above the scene.

◆ **Fill light.** This type of light is used to reduce or "fill" the shadows and areas of high contrast that are produced by the influence of the key light. To achieve such an effect, the light should typically be at about 90 degrees from the position of

Figure 18.10
Directional lights are best for simulating outdoor sunlight.

Figure 18.11
An area light is appropriate for illuminating an underwater scene.

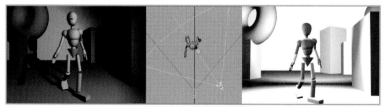

Figure 18.12
Key light example (effect shown in red)

the key light when viewed from above, assuming the focal point is at the center. For example, if the key light is at six o'clock, it would make sense to place the fill light at three o'clock or nine o'clock (see Figure 18.13). The fill light's intensity should be set at around half that of the key light.

◆ **Back light.** Sometimes called *hair light* or *rim light*, this type of light helps separate an object from the background by accentuating its outline, which also adds a sense of depth. The back light is typically placed in a position that is directly opposite from the camera (see Figure 18.14).

◆ **Bounce light.** Bounce light originates from the reflection of light from other objects. When light hits a diffuse surface, some of that light is absorbed while the rest is scattered and will potentially land on other surfaces (see Figure 18.15). In CG, it is often desirable to simulate this real-world effect by placing lights on certain surfaces, rather than allowing the computer to make the necessary bounce calculations, which can be time consuming.

◆ **Kicker light.** This kind of light is useful when you need to add highlights to dark areas or soften specific areas of your object. The placement of a kicker light is normally behind the object and to one side of it. This light works well when it is coming from a low angle (see Figure 18.16).

◆ **Background light.** This light makes the background a relevant element of a scene by creating a new layer of depth beyond the foreground layer. In some cases, a directional light will be enough to illuminate the background area, and normally the background light proceeds from the same direction as the key light (see Figure 18.17).

◆ **Side light.** This type of light is placed to the side of the subject. The use of side lights can provide some illumination to the sides of the subjects if such areas become too dark (see Figure 18.18).

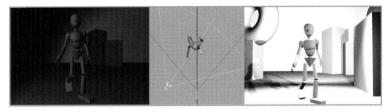

Figure 18.13
Fill light example (effect shown in red)

Figure 18.14
Back light example (effect shown in red)

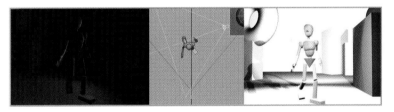

Figure 18.15
Bounce light example (effect shown in red)

Figure 18.16
Kicker light example (effect shown in red)

18. Lighting and Rendering

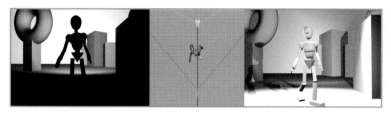

Figure 18.17
Background light example (effect shown in red)

Figure 18.18
Side light example (effect shown in red)

Appropriate combinations of these light types will result in an illuminated digital scene that looks natural and delivers the intended amount of clarity and mood (see Figure 18.19).

Figure 18.19
Combining lights such as keys, fills, bounces, and kickers will help deliver naturalism and readability.

Natural versus Artificial Light

Natural light refer to the light produced by sources that are present in nature, such as the sun, the moon, fire, lightning, and other elements that emit a degree of luminance, such as lava, fireflies, or fluorescent moss. When you are setting up a natural light source such as the sun, you must consider factors beyond mere placement, including color and intensity based on time of day, season, air quality, climate, and perhaps proximity if the given scene exists on a planet other than our Earth (see Figure 18.20).

Figure 18.20
Natural light sources

Artificial lights are created directly or indirectly by humans and include lamp bulbs, flashlights, car headlights, disco balls, traffic lights, laser pointers, and electrical arcs (see Figure 18.21). Typically, these kinds of lights have a cooler quality than their natural counterparts due to their color temperature.

Shadows

Shadows add a great deal of visual information to a scene with regard to depth, spatial relationships between objects, and the indication of light source positions and characteristics. The appropriate implementation of shadows within the context of a lighting setup can help generate a variety of moods in a scene, from tranquil to dramatic (see Figure 18.22).

In the real world, every light source generates shadows; however, the CG artist can control which lights project shadows and which ones do not. Also, most software packages allow you to exclude certain objects from casting shadows. Shadows are often generated from the key light alone; however, it is often more natural for several lights to cast shadows.

In the land of filmmaking, you can even turn shadows into characters, such as in *Peter Pan* or the CG short *Silhouette* (see Chapter 8).

Figure 18.21
Artificial light sources

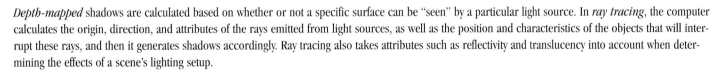

Figure 18.22
Cast shadows will contribute to clarity, dimensionality, spatial relationships, and mood.

Shadow Types

In CG, there are two basic types of shadow generation:

◆ Depth maps   ◆ Ray tracing

Depth-mapped shadows are calculated based on whether or not a specific surface can be "seen" by a particular light source. In *ray tracing*, the computer calculates the origin, direction, and attributes of the rays emitted from light sources, as well as the position and characteristics of the objects that will interrupt these rays, and then it generates shadows accordingly. Ray tracing also takes attributes such as reflectivity and translucency into account when determining the effects of a scene's lighting setup.

Depth mapping is a faster method of generating rendered shadows; however, the effects of ray tracing are typically more realistic.

18. Lighting and Rendering

367

Shadow Attributes

The two main attributes to consider and assign when you are casting CG shadows are

◆ Edge hardness

◆ Opacity

Hard-edged shadows would typically exist in a scene with a single light source, while softer-edged shadows should be used when fills or other secondary lights are present (see Figure 18.23).

Shadow opacity can range from very faint to absolute black. This attribute is also somewhat dependent on the number of lights in a given scene, as well as your specific art direction style (see Figure 18.23).

Lighting Techniques

Although you can study and apply common lighting techniques, every scene will have specific issues that need to be addressed. Unfortunately, there is no such thing as a magic formula you can

Figure 18.23
Shadows can be hard or soft edged and opaque or translucent.

use to quickly calculate the appropriate lighting setup for every situation. The best approach for achieving effective lighting is to consider the appropriate types of lights to be used in a scene, optimize their quantity, and choose their locations and attributes carefully. Always be ready for a significant amount of experimentation. Before you place lights in a scene, identify the primary area where the actions take place, as well as the secondary areas and the background, to decide on an appropriate distribution of lights over the space that needs to be illuminated.

Ask yourself the following questions to help identify the lighting needs of a particular scene:

◆ What are the setting details that will determine an appropriate lighting setup with regard to time of day, climate, locale, and so on (see Figure 18.24).

◆ Is the light coming from natural or artificial sources?

◆ Should the lighting be hard, balanced, or soft?

◆ Should I use a high-key or a low-key lighting setup?

◆ How many light sources exist?

Figure 18.24
Consider important setting details, such as time of day and locale.

◆ What are the positions of the primary and secondary lights?

◆ How should the lighting setup contribute to the intended mood of the current story action?

◆ What scene elements and characters need to be clearly visible, partially obscured, or completely in the dark?

◆ Should the shadows be opaque, translucent, hard, or soft?

◆ Does the lighting of the current scene need to match that of a previous or subsequent scene for the sake of continuity?

The following is a list of typical situations you might encounter during the process of lighting a given scene, with a few corresponding guidelines.

◆ **Default lighting.** This is the standard set of lights that your software adds by default to make the objects of a given scene clearly visible, often originating from the camera itself. Using the default set of lights for a scene is the simplest option available; however, the results are likely to be less than desirable because you will have very little (if any) control over the illumination with regard to attributes such as color, placement, and shadow generation. A 3D animatic or a film that is only being used to demonstrate a singular skill, such as animation, would perhaps be the only scenario in which using a default light setup would be appropriate.

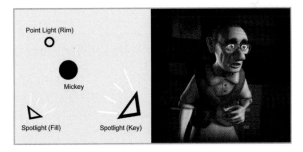

Figure 18.25
The standard, single-subject lighting setup

◆ **Lighting a single subject.** Also known as the *triangle lighting technique*, this is one of the most popular techniques used in live-action films, and it translates easily to the process of digital lighting due to the simplicity and effectiveness of its setup. This is accomplished by arranging a set of three lights in a scene—a key light to serve as the main source of illumination, which will be the only light to produce shadows; a fill light to soften shadows; and a back light to accentuate depth and dimensionality (see Figure 18.25).

◆ **Lighting multiple subjects.** This case typically involves illuminating a larger area that encompasses more elements than just a single subject in front of the camera. The idea here is to apply the same technique that is used for lighting a single subject; however, in this case it is done by repeating the procedure for each one of the given subjects. You need to place enough lights to cover the entire area and make adjustments as needed, since lights will ultimately add up and overlap each other.

◆ **Lighting the foreground.** Sometimes the purpose of a scene might dictate that the elements of the foreground must capture the audience's undivided attention at all times. In such a case, only highlight the foreground section, while making the background area recede into shadow, dim light, or absolute darkness (see Figure 18.26). This way, the subjects in the foreground will be emphasized.

Figure 18.26
Foreground lighting

◆ **Lighting in silhouette.** This technique can be seen as the opposite of foreground lighting. In this case, the illumination is concentrated in the background so that the overlaying elements of the foreground are perceived as silhouettes; for this purpose, background and back lights are necessary. This approach to lighting can create a romantic or mysterious atmosphere depending on the context of the scene (see Figure 18.27).

◆ **Low lighting.** Placing your main light sources underneath your characters can create an eerie or ominous feel, especially if there are no other lights in the scene.

◆ **Soft lighting.** This approach creates a flat, diffused lighting effect, and its setup consists of filling the space with a "dome" of lights. The intensity of every light must be adjusted to be low and even to prevent overexposure of the image. The effect of this method is typically photorealistic, and it simulates the look of a popular and recent technique known as *global illumination* (see Figure 18.28).

Rendering

Rendering is the process by which your CG software calculates every single pixel of a final image, using potentially complex algorithms that consider all necessary scene information, such as geometry location and details, the position and parameters of your lights, shadow attributes, surface reflectance, texture information, and camera specifics. Rendering can be compared to taking a photograph of a theater stage from an appropriate angle after all of the characters, props, clothing, set decorations, backdrops, and lights have been set up. Depending on your preferred editing methods, your rendered imagery from a single shot might be a series of still frames or a movie file.

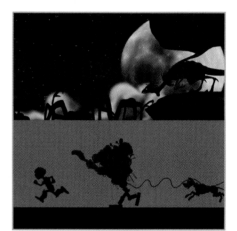

Figure 18.27
Silhouette lighting

The major details to consider when setting up a render are

◆ Quality
◆ Optimization
◆ Resolution
◆ Image format

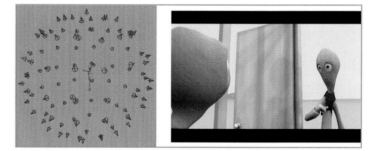

Figure 18.28
A dome of low-intensity lights will help create a soft and photoreal look.

Quality

You can select different rendering methods and attributes that will affect the quality of your images, such as anti-aliasing levels, motion blur, ray tracing, and so on. Anti-aliasing will determine the sharpness of your object edges. Motion blur will generate a degree of blurring on moving objects to simulate the look of a filmed sequence. Turning on ray tracing will initiate a more complex set of algorithms, which will result in longer rendering times but potentially better results. Ray tracing accurately simulates the actual physics of light propagation in the real world according to the principles of geometric optics and the details of the given scene. Ray tracing is especially appropriate in scenes that require sharp shadows, reflective surfaces, bounce lighting, and refraction.

Another advanced rendering method is *radiosity*, in which the inter-reflection of light between diffuse objects and bounce light from the ground or walls is calculated to create a highly realistic look. With radiosity, every object becomes a kind of area light source, producing pleasant, soft shadows that are not possible with normal ray tracing. However, radiosity is not particularly good at handling specular surfaces and it typically requires a lot of memory, especially when it comes to rendering complex scenes.

Almost all fully functional CG packages offer ray tracing capabilities and a few also include some of the more advanced techniques just mentioned. Check your software manual and tutorials for details. Specific rendering plug-ins that can create a visual style beyond that of the more common built-in rendering solutions are also available. One such plug-in is the popular Arnold Global Illumination Renderer, which can be seen in action in Figure 18.29 and on Web pages such as http://www.pepeland.com/ and http://www.boring3d.com.

Of course, absolute photorealism might not be your cup of tea. Perhaps you are going for a surreal, abstract, or cartoony look. Fortunately, by experimenting with the parameters of your material, lights, and cameras, you can generate an infinite number of visual styles. Try various parameter settings and try out techniques such as toon renderers to find the final look that satisfies your particular art-direction plans.

Figure 18.29
The popular Arnold renderer creates imagery that looks extremely photoreal.

Optimization

Rendering time is always an important factor to consider. Obviously, the higher a scene's complexity and your image-quality settings, the longer it will take to render each frame. Rendering complex scenes at high quality and resolution settings can potentially take a lot longer than you might have previously imagined. Therefore, it is crucial that you optimize your scene complexity and rendering settings so you don't find yourself unnecessarily exceeding your deadline while waiting for your frames to be generated.

Use the fewest number of lights possible. Carefully consider the necessity of ray-traced shadows versus the less expensive depth-mapped type. Try lower motion blur and sampling rate settings. Consider the feasibility of rendering a single frame of your distant scene elements and then using the resulting image as a background plate for rendering subsequent frames.

Most importantly, experiment with test renders until you find just the right balance between image quality and render time, realizing that you may have to sacrifice a bit of one for the sake of the other.

Resolution

Resolution refers to the dimensions of your final imagery and is described by a pair of numbers representing width and height based on pixels. For instance, 720 pixels wide by 486 pixels tall is a typical NTSC (*National Television Systems Committee*) television format.

The final resolution of your rendered frames will be determined by the intended display format and viewing forum of your short. If your film will be displayed on IMAX screens, you will obviously need extremely high-resolution imagery. If you plan to allow your audience to download your CG short from your Web site, you will probably use a much smaller final resolution, such as 320×240, to accommodate the fact that not all surfers necessarily have high-speed Internet connections.

When you are selecting the resolution of your final imagery, pay attention to the storage requirements that must be met as your rendered frames pile up. On average, a video-resolution image that supports alpha channels (see Chapter 20, "Compositing") will be approximately 1 MB per image. To determine the exact resolution of an image, multiply the pixel height and width and the number of bytes per pixel. Then multiply this value by the total number of frames of your film to determine how much storage is required to hold all of your rendered images.

Also consider that you might need to make post-camera adjustments, such as shakes or twists, after your frames have been rendered. If so, be sure to render your frames larger than their intended final resolutions so you will have some room to work. If you ultimately decide not to add post-camera moves, you can easily crop to the desired size using the batch-processing capabilities of programs such as Photoshop or DeBabelizer. Remember that it is always better to have a bit too much acreage than not enough. You can always crop out unwanted parts later, but adding imagery beyond your rendered borders to facilitate reframing will not be so easy.

The three main display formats to consider are

◆ Digital media

◆ Video

◆ Film

Digital Media: CD-ROMs, DVD-ROMs, and Web Files

Digital formats are those that will be displayed on computer monitors. For digital files that will be on CD-ROM or DVD-ROM, use a resolution that is not unnecessarily large to ensure that all of your potential viewers will have enough RAM to watch your film. In fact, it is always a good idea to include several versions at different sizes to accommodate as many viewers as possible.

For Internet distribution, consider the bandwidth that is available to your potential audience members and choose a resolution that will result in relatively small file sizes and download durations. Consider the length of your film when you are making this determination as well. Obviously, the more frames that exist, the smaller you will need to make your image resolution to maintain a reasonable file size. Compressing your files is also an excellent way of making the download process more efficient.

Some of the advantages of delivering your film in a digital format are as follows:

◆ Assuming that your viewers have high-speed connections, it is typically faster to deliver your film via the Internet rather than relying on snail mail.

◆ Digital format is cleaner and more economical than video and film.

◆ Many short film festivals are including digital output as a valid entry format, which will save you postage and repeated trips to the post office.

◆ You can use codecs and other compressors to reduce file sizes without compromising quality.

Video and DVD

Video is still one of the favored forms of output for the purpose of submitting films to contests, festivals, and studio recruiters around the world. The possible choices range from the classic VHS to the more sophisticated Betacam SP or even D1, which offers the highest quality of video format. If you do not have the appropriate hardware for video dubbing or you don't want to deal with the problems associated with frame rates, interlaced fields, and non-square pixels, you should take your short film on DVD-ROM or CD-ROM to a dubbing service to get it transferred to video. If you go this route, place a color bar image in front of your short so the editor at the video studio can adjust his color settings if the need arises. For outputting to DVDs that will be displayed on televisions, consider purchasing your own DVD burner and using the authoring software that will likely come bundled with the package or purchase a piece of third-party software, such as the inexpensive DVD MovieFactory 2 from Ulead (see Figure 18.30). For the purposes of video or DVD format, it is ideal to render your images at 30 frames per second and at a resolution of 720×486 with a pixel ratio of 0.9 for NTSC, and 720×576 with a pixel ratio of 1.067 for PAL (*Phase Alternating Line*).

Film

If film is to be your output format, realize that exporting to this medium will require lots of time and money and the use of external resources and services. However, film will still offer the

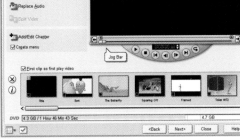

Figure 18.30
DVD-authoring software does not have to be expensive.

highest possible image quality. There are two main basic formats for film imagery—the standard screen, which has a width of 1.33 times its height, or wide-screen formats (also known by trade names such as Cinemascope, Panavision, or Vistavision), which typically have height-to-width ratios of 1:1.85 or 1:2.35. If you are in film school, hopefully a film recorder is available to you; otherwise, you will need to deliver a DVD-ROM or CD-ROM of your short to a film-out service, which might be prohibitively expensive.

Image Format

The type of format you choose will depend on whether your short film is intended for digital media, video, or film and if you are generating sequences of individual images or movie files. Image formats will be indicated by filename extensions, such as .jpg, .tif, .tga, or .bmp for static imagery and .avi, .mov, .qt, .mpg, or .wmf for movie files. Each format has its particular advantages and shortcomings.

The most common formats are as follows:

- ◆ Static image files
  - ◆ **GIF (*Graphic Interchange Formula*).** GIF format is typically used for the Web. GIF files sizes are small so they download fast; however, GIFs sacrifice a lot of image information, such as color resolution. You can use this format for either an image or a sequence of images; however, it is not recommended for high-resolution imagery.
  - ◆ **JPEG (*Joint Photographic Experts Group*).** In JPEG format, the image is compressed but maintains a high level of quality depending on the compression value, which can typically be adjusted either at render time or after the fact in a program such as DeBabelizer. JPEG images are very efficient and fast to download, but the format does not support alpha channels.
  - ◆ **TIFF (*Tagged Image File Format*).** TIFF is probably the most frequently used CG image format. It has alpha channel information and can handle different color depths (up to 48-bit color with a 16-bit alpha channel).
  - ◆ **TARGA.** TARGA is one of the best image-quality formats, but the files are very large.
- ◆ Movie files
  - ◆ **MOV.** MOV (or QT) format is used for Apple and Windows platforms and requires QuickTime Player to view the files.
  - ◆ **AVI.** AVI is used for Windows platforms and requires Windows Media Player to view the files.
  - ◆ **MPEG (*Moving Picture Experts Group*) and WMF (*Windows Media Format*).** These formats are also quite common. MPEG files have the advantage of being rather small because of the sophistication of their compression algorithms, while WMF files have the disadvantage of not being compatible with many common display tools.

When you are generating movie files, try out different compression schemes, such as Cinepak, Sorenson, and DivX, but realize that not all viewers will necessarily have the capability to handle such codecs.

Rendering for Compositing

When you are working with scenes that are not particularly complex, it is easy and efficient to render them in a single pass. Alternatively, complex scenes can be split up and rendered as groups of separate rendering passes. These passes create separate layers of images that you can assemble like digital collages. This process of combining image layers is known as *compositing* (see Figure 18.31 and Chapter 20).

When you render in passes or layers, different scene elements are rendered with different attribute settings. The advantage of rendering in layers is that it provides you with precise control over the

Figure 18.31
You can render scene elements in separate layers and then later assemble them like digital collages using an appropriate piece of compositing software.

color of specific objects and the shadows that fall on them. Another advantage is that it might be easier and more efficient to fine-tune a scene by simply adjusting the parameters and re-rendering subset layers rather than entire scenes. The disadvantages are that you will need a compositing stage and additional work might be required to ensure that all of your layers are effectively assembled to form a consistent whole where separate scene elements visually associate with one another properly. If the separate layers are not combined effectively with regard to shadow interaction and visual consistency, your final images will look like collages and your individual scene elements might not appear as if they exist in the same world. Of course, a collage look might indeed be your intended visual style, in which case visual disparities between your individual layers will be appropriate.

When you are rendering in separate passes, it is important to consider the scene elements that should be included in each layer. Distant background elements are typically rendered separately from foreground objects and characters. Global effects, such as snow or rain, are also good candidates for separate layers. Scene elements that interact with one another, either physically or via shadow casting, are typically rendered in the same layer because rebuilding such interaction in the compositing stage can be especially difficult.

Obviously compositing will increase the complexity of your pipeline and might require additional software and personnel. However, it will provide you with the ability to alter separate scene elements individually, which might make it easier to achieve your intended visual result than by rendering everything all at once. Balance the advantages and disadvantages when you are deciding between single- and multiple-pass rendering.

Lighting and Rendering Production Workflow

The recommended series of steps to follow when you are lighting a digital scene is as follows:

1. Determine the intended style and mood.
2. Study appropriate reference materials.
3. Construct a schematic plan.
4. Block and refine.
5. Experiment with test renders.
6. Perform a final render.

Determine Style and Mood

Hopefully, the visual style and mood of your film was well established in your development stage in the form of color sketches based on your imagination and any reference materials you might have gathered. If not, spend some time working out issues, such as color and composition, with traditional tools before you dive into the digital arena.

Study Reference

Pull up any reference imagery you might have collected in your early development stage and keep it handy as you set up your scene lighting. Study how lighting is treated in paintings, photographs, theater, and all other media to educate your eye and attain a true understanding of the principles and effects of this all-important production element (see Figure 18.32).

Schematic Plans

It is a very good idea to print out images of the top, front, and side views of a particular scene and then draw a lighting plan to help to identify the position, direction, and types of lights for the areas and objects that need to be lit (see Figure 18.33). Doing so will help you estimate where shadows will fall and get an overall idea of the number of lights you will need. By drawing lighting schematics, you will be able to visualize the bigger picture instead of being limited to considering lights from the camera's point of view alone.

Block and Refine

After you have identified and established the types and positions of the light sources necessary for a given scene, begin to add them in a logical order. It is often advantageous to start with an ambient light set at a low intensity value and then add the key lights. Next, place any necessary fill, bouncing, or interactive lights, and then finish with the background lights.

Once you are fairly satisfied with your initial selection and placement of the lights, start to play with their colors, intensity levels, and alternative positions, testing the effects of each light one at a time (see Figure 18.34). Then proceed to combine the lights. Perhaps choose two lights and make a render test with both of them, then choose a different pair, and finally test the overall set of lights and make the final adjustments.

Another efficient approach is to test your lights in a scene with simple geometry for the sake of speed. Then, once you are happy with the setup, replace the low-resolution objects with your full-resolution geometry. You can also speed up the testing process by choosing a single object and making the others invisible. Of course, do your best to be as economical as possible with regard to the quantity of lights used in a given scene.

Experiment with Test Renders

Before you generate final renders, test how the material attributes of your objects, the parameters of your lights, and your camera settings work together, experimenting with different settings to achieve your

Figure 18.32
Examine reference imagery that relates to the desired lighting style of your film.

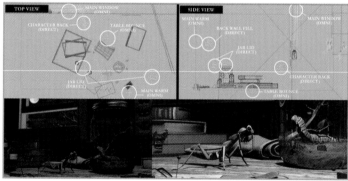

Figure 18.33
Schematic lighting plans can be very helpful.

Figure 18.34
Experiment with different positions, colors, intensities, and the total number of lights in a given scene.

intended visual results and the most efficient rendering times. Try different material diffusion levels and specularity settings against a variety of light colors and intensities as well as different shadow attributes. Also experiment with different depth-of-field settings on your camera. Should all scene elements be

equally sharp, or should there be a main focal point or area that is very clear while other parts of the scene are blurred? Perhaps a rack-focus camera adjustment takes place during the course of the shot, where at the beginning a foreground character is sharp while the background is blurred, but by the end of the shot these details are reversed (see Figure 18.35). Begin by generating extremely low-resolution renders that act as rough color sketches and then steadily increase the resolution as your results become more and more satisfying. Also try rendering small regions before you render the entire scene's image.

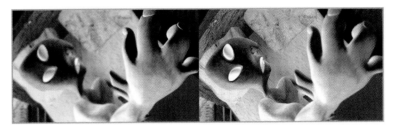

Figure 18.35
In addition to experimenting with material attributes and lighting parameters, test out different depth-of-field settings on your cameras.

Final Render

When you are satisfied with the results of your tests, you can start generating final renders of your digital scenes. If you are fortunate enough to have more than one computer, look into ways to utilize all of them with multi-processor rendering routines.

Summary

The fundamental purpose of lighting is to illuminate the necessary elements of your scene files so they become appropriately visible to your viewers. Lighting is also used to help indicate depth, dimensionality, and spatial relationships. But perhaps most important, lighting is used as an extension of your art direction plans to help generate mood and visual style. The specifics of your lighting setups, including position, color, intensity, shadow casting, and quantity, can suggest moods, such as tranquility, suspense, or high drama.

Rendering is the process by which your CG software creates digital snapshots of each frame of a given scene based on the placements, movements, and attributes of the objects, characters, textures, lights, and cameras existing therein. You can adjust rendering parameters, such as resolution, motion blur, anti-aliasing, and depth-of-field, to generate a wide variety of imagery to suit your needs. However, it is very important to realize that it might take your computer a significantly long time to generate your static images or movie files if your scenes are especially complex and your render parameters are set too high. Be sure to experiment sufficiently to find an appropriate balance between quality and speed so you can simultaneously satisfy your aesthetic sensibilities and your deadline.

Chapter 19, "Visual Effects," will describe a few of the tools and techniques you can use to add visual effects, such as cloth, hair, and visual indications of inclement weather conditions, to your scenes.

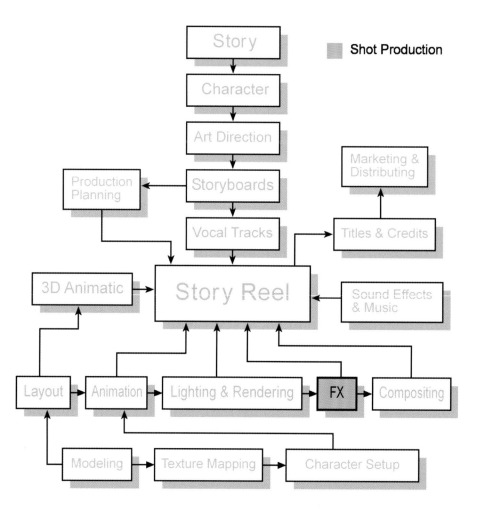

Shot Production

chapter 19
Visual Effects

Animating the trajectory of a flying spaceship or the performance of a digital character typically involves setting and keyframing positions and poses or connecting appropriate objects or hierarchy pieces to motion paths. However, manually animating the natural movement of digital elements such as cloth, hair, smoke, water, snowflakes, or a collection of falling rocks can be significantly more complicated.

You could certainly animate a woman's dress by creating and rotating a sufficient number of internal joints or by attaching a lattice deformer and then manipulating its shape over time (see Figure 19.1). Likewise, you could animate an avalanche by keyframing the trajectory and rotation of each individual rock or by creating a group of associated motion paths. If the dress is made out of very stiff material and the number of rocks in your avalanche is very small, you might be able to get away with using such manual animation techniques. However, if the dress is made of a loose fabric or the avalanche consists of dozens or perhaps hundreds of rocks, keyframing might not be the most efficient method of animating such objects. Also, even in a cartoon-style film, audiences will expect the movement of such elements to be believable; therefore, you will need to simulate the effects of gravity and physics rather convincingly. The dress will need to sway, billow, and wrap around its owner's legs as she moves and perhaps be additionally affected by wind. The rocks will need to bounce, rotate, accelerate, collide, and perhaps break apart as they fall. Such details are extremely difficult and time consuming to accomplish by hand when you are dealing with complicated geometry or large numbers of objects.

Fortunately, most CG packages offer procedural solutions you can use to simulate natural movements of complex geometry or large groups of individual objects (see Figure 19.2).

I wandered lonely as a cloud
That floats on high o'er vales and hills,
When all at once I saw a crowd,
A host, of golden daffodils;
Beside the lake, beneath the trees,
Fluttering and dancing in the breeze.

William Wordsworth

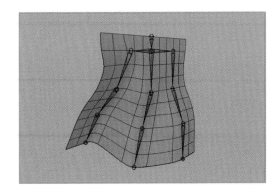

Figure 19.1
You can hand-animate clothing by manipulating an internal skeleton or shaping an external lattice.

Procedural animation is the process of allowing the computer to follow natural rules of physics to create motion on objects or hierarchies based on parameters that have been previously defined for the moving elements. You can define the starting position of a series of rocks atop a hill; then assign mass properties to each rock, as well as the direction and strength of the external forces acting upon them; then initiate the simulation and watch the avalanche occur.

An important consideration to keep in mind when you are creating procedural animation is that the resulting movement and the destination of the moving elements typically will not be controllable. When you are keyframing, you can dictate the location, orientation, and pose of an object or hierarchy at every moment in time. However, when you run a procedural solution, you will operate in a trial-and-error capacity, adjusting your element parameters and re-launching your simulation over and over until the desired movement occurs. Procedural simulations follow real-world physics rules, which have the advantage of resulting in extremely natural object movement but also carry the disadvantages of randomness and unpredictability.

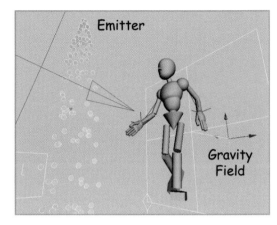

Figure 19.2
Most CG packages offer procedural animation functionality.

For this reason, it is sometimes better to simply animate certain would-be procedural effects by hand, assuming the moving objects are simple and few. For instance, it might be easier to animate a single ponytail by rotating a series of connected joints than by setting up a procedural solution to create the motion. Control is also a factor. If you want each of your avalanche rocks to behave in a very specific manner or pass through a desired location such as a particular car window, you will probably need to animate them by hand. Procedural techniques are appropriate for complex hierarchies or large groups of objects when natural movement is the priority, rather than precise control.

Generally, procedural animation can be broken up into two categories.

◆ Particle effects
◆ Motion dynamics

Particle effects are used to create real-world phenomena, such as rain, fog, smoke, fire, snow, hair, explosions, or fireworks, as well as group movements, such as bubbles, swarms of bees, or schools of fish.

> Setting up and running procedural simulations can be extremely time consuming, especially if you have a rather specific result in mind. Make sure you have carefully considered whether you could efficiently achieve your goal using more direct techniques before you enter the trial-and-error world of procedural animation.

Motion dynamics are used to make objects, such as falling rocks, tumbling dice, jiggling Jell-o, dangling earrings, or loose clothing move based on real-world physics rules and the application of external forces, such as gravity, wind, or the motion of the primary object to which they are attached, like a flagpole for instance.

This chapter will offer very basic information on particle and dynamic effects. Check your manual for specific details on the procedural animation techniques available in your chosen piece of CG software.

Particle Effects

Most CG packages offer particle systems you can use to simulate certain real-world effects. Such systems typically begin with the creation of an emitter object and then the assignment of parameters that will dictate the behavior of the generated particles. Emitters can generate parallel particles for effects such as rain, radial emissions for explosions, or more random trajectories for wind-blown dandelion seeds (see Figure 19.3).

Particles can be points, trails, or simple objects. Points are used for dust, fog, or sparks. Particle trails work for hair, comets, or jellyfish tentacles. And simple objects, such as spheres or planes, can be used to create clouds, bubbles, or confetti (see Figure 19.4).

In addition to defining the type of particles being emitted, other properties, such as size, color, velocity, acceleration, mass, shape, transparency, and lifespan, will contribute to the overall effect being generated. Usually you can assign these attributes to an entire group of particles with varying degrees of randomization or to individual particles for more exacting control. Other factors that will influence the final result include the initial position of the particles, the strength and direction of the forces acting upon them, the existence and influence of any collision objects, and in the case of particle trails, their stiffness and attachment points.

You can also assign particles to paths to create water streams or to goals so they would follow a moving target or attempt to land in predetermined locations.

A campfire could be created by using a particle emitter on the ground that generates a steady upward stream of illuminated red, orange, and yellow points with very short life spans.

Snowflakes would be low-mass particles coming from a very wide emitter, sitting above frame, with an appropriate wind force applied to create wavelike vertical trajectories (see Figure 19.5).

Figure 19.3
Particle emitters are used to generate objects along parallel or radial trajectories for effects such as rain or flying dandelion seeds.

Figure 19.4
You can use different types of particles to create effects such as smoke, dust, clouds, fire, spark trails, or bubbles.

Figure 19.5
Snowflakes are low-mass particles generated from above the frame and affected by wind and gravity.

Fireworks can be simulated by creating a series of emitters up in the sky that generate bursts of multicolored streaks in all directions. These streaks could be affected by gravity and randomly explode into smaller trails with short life spans. You could also add additional forces, such as vortexes, for increased detail and variation.

Fur is typically created by defining an animal's skin as a large single emitter or as a group of smaller emitters that generate persistent and attached particle trails with endless life spans that are set to stop growing at defined but somewhat randomized lengths (see Figure 19.6). In a similar fashion, you could create a grassy field waving in the breeze. Some CG packages separate their fur generation tools into their own category or plug-in, but they are technically classified as particle effects.

Figure 19.6
Hair and fur are specialized and persistent particle trails.

> Like other procedural effects, the creation and animation of hair and fur can be time consuming and CPU intensive. If possible, try to avoid the necessity of using complex hair algorithms by giving your characters hats, crew cuts, bald heads, or simple geometry with realistic texture maps instead (see Figure 19.7).

Figure 19.7
It's no surprise that many CG filmmakers use crew cuts, baldness, hats, or texture maps instead of expensive and time-consuming digital hair procedures.

A trail of airplane smoke can be simulated from an emission of fuzzy, translucent particle spheres that are set to stick to one another while dissipating and floating upward (see Figure 19.8).

An explosion will require an emitter that generates a variety of particle objects in all directions with a significant amount of randomness associated with their shapes, sizes, mass, and spin. Defining how the particles will behave when colliding with the ground, nearby walls, other external objects, and each other will further influence the end result. For effective explosions, it is often a good idea to animate some larger pieces by hand while allowing the simulation to handle the smaller pieces, and then run a second simultaneous emission for the associated smoke.

Figure 19.8
Vapor trails are another common use for particle effects.

Typically, you could create a flock of birds or a school of fish by running a simulation of particles that avoid colliding with one another while following a specified path with some degree of individuality. Then substitute hand-animated motion cycles of individual animals for the particles and randomize or offset their movements so they are not perfectly in synch (see Figure 19.9).

One specialized type of particle object is known as a *sprite*, which is a flat plane with an image or texture mapped upon it with an appropriate negative space alpha channel. Each particle sprite might contain a different image of an object, such as a star, or perhaps a video clip of a flying insect cycle. You then place or move these sprites as particles to create large groups of objects or characters, and then aim-constrain the planes to always face the camera. The advantage of using sprites is that it is significantly less CPU intensive than building all of the necessary geometry for a large number of similar objects or characters (see Figure 19.10).

Another particle system variation is the process of *instancing*, where a single object or character is created and animated, and then a series of duplicates are made that mimic the form and movement of the original geometry. Because instanced objects are not truly independent, they have the advantage of using less memory; however, any changes you make to the source object will be reflected in all of the instances. You can typically change the location, orientation, and scale of individual instances, but their shapes and animations will remain tied to the source object or character. Instancing is a memory-saving technique you can use to create insect swarms or fish schools in which the individual members animate in exactly the same way, but with slightly different trajectories, orientations, and sizes.

As you define and run your particle simulations within your CG package, they will typically be displayed as simple points, lines, or perhaps basic spheres. Once you have experimented with their behavior parameters until you achieve the desired motion results, you will need to render your particle emissions based on their assigned visual attributes, such as color, transparency, and life span. You can render your particle emissions by themselves, using alpha channels for the negative spaces so they can be layered into your final imagery at the compositing stage, or you can render them along with all of your scene objects in a single pass. Working with your particles separately might be advantageous if you have one artist working in that area while another artist is animating your characters. If you are working alone and your scenes are not especially complicated, it might be simpler to keep your particle elements and other scene elements together. But be sure to hide or temporarily deactivate your emitters when you are doing quick renders for animation testing because particle system calculations can significantly increase render times.

Figure 19.9
You can substitute animated motion cycles for particles to create flocks or swarms.

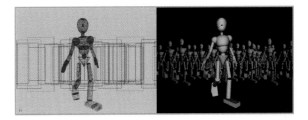

Figure 19.10
Sprites and instances are memory-saving techniques you can use when you require a large number of exact copies.

Motion Dynamics

Elements such as falling rocks, tumbling dice, flowing dresses, or bouncing ponytails can be animated manually by setting position, orientation, and shape key frames on objects, joints, clusters, or lattice points. Alternatively, you can set such objects in motion procedurally in much the same way that you animate particles, by assigning properties, forces, and collision specifics, and then letting the computer create appropriate simulations.

Typically, falling rocks will be assigned mass properties and then given starting positions and a force to set them in motion. You can define the surface upon which they are traveling as a collision object so the rocks traverse, roll, and bounce accordingly when a gravity field pulls them along their downward paths.

A pane of glass can be previously broken up into many smaller chunks, which will be thrown in a specified direction with a certain degree of trajectory and rotation randomization when the appropriate digital force is applied so that an effective shatter occurs when, say, a baseball crashes through it.

Typically, lightning bolts and electrical arcs are made from illuminated curves that are connected at either end to separate objects or locations in space, and then a dynamic simulation is applied that causes them to bend and twist sporadically (see Figure 19.11).

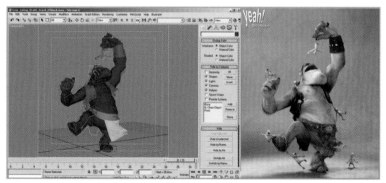

Figure 19.11
You can create electrical bolts effectively using dynamic procedures.

Generally, soft and malleable objects, such as cloth or bodies of water, are either defined as deformable collision objects that are assigned appropriate parameters and forces, or surrounded by lattices which will bend, twist, and reshape based on the properties assigned to their vertex points when forces act upon them. A waving flag or a billowing curtain might have a lattice with rigid anchor points attached at the pole. The remaining vertices will be allowed to flow naturally in the wind while maintaining a consistent distance from one another so the deforming flag within does not stretch like rubber (see Figure 19.12).

Allowing lattice vertices to change their relative distances would be appropriate for a body of water or a jiggling piece of gelatin. Typically, springs are assigned, which will dictate the amount of stretchiness that will exist between points, depending on the intended malleability of the deforming geometry within (see Figure 19.13).

Ponytails, antennae, floppy ears, dangling earrings, or other secondary appendages can be driven by outer lattices or inner curves that are attached at one end to appropriate places on a digital puppet so they swing convincingly when the character moves.

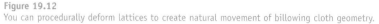

Figure 19.12
You can procedurally deform lattices to create natural movement of billowing cloth geometry.

Remember that not all appendages are necessarily secondary. Cat ears and octopus tentacles have internal muscles that will drive their motions, whereas the ears of a Bassett Hound or the tentacles of a jelly-fish will swing and sway secondarily based on the primary movements of their owner's head and body. Appendages that have internal muscles of their own should be hand-animated, while the motion of truly secondary appendages can be dictated by procedural dynamics. However, it might be considered overkill to set up a dynamic simulation for a single pair of dangling earrings. Key-frame animation will typically be more efficient for such a small quantity of secondary appendages. On the other hand, a character with several dozen hoops hanging from each ear will present a scenario in which a dynamic simulation can come in very handy (see Figure 19.14).

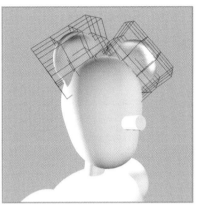

Figure 19.13
Malleable objects can jiggle and deform when you create loose tension values for connected vertex springs on outer lattices.

Figure 19.14
You can efficiently animate a single pair of earrings by hand, but a larger number of such secondary accessories might benefit from the application of dynamic simulations.

Ramping Up

Because of the complexity of the calculations involved, a dynamic simulation typically needs to ramp up over the course of several frames before all of its parameters and forces can be calculated into the simulation effectively. Therefore, it is generally necessary to give at least basic motions to your scene objects as many as 24 to 30 frames before the start of a given shot to give the simulation sufficient time to reach its desired behavior. Without these extra "pre-animation" frames, a simulation will need to quickly calculate these initial frames of a shot, and its initial behavior will often be undesirably subtle or otherwise unexpected.

2D Solutions

Instead of using CG particle systems, certain effects can be created as 2D layers, which can then be composited on top of rendered imagery. For example, you could create rain, snow, or smoke trails in a 2D paint or animation program and then use them as a future composite overlay (see Figure 19.15).

The advantage of using 2D effects layers is that they might be less CPU intensive to create and they can potentially reduce your rendering times by a significant margin.

Figure 19.15
To reduce render times and CG scene complexity, you can create 2D animation layers and then composite them on top of rendered imagery.

Summary

Natural movement of complex geometry pieces or large groups of objects can be especially difficult and time consuming to animate by hand. Fortunately, most CG packages offer procedural animation techniques where object and force parameters are defined, so the computer can generate a simulation that follows precise or potentially altered rules of physics and gravity. Then, the simulations typically need to be rendered based on the visual properties that have been assigned, such as color, transparency, and particle life spans. Procedural animation is accomplished by way of particle systems for effects such as explosions, snow, fire, smoke, and flocks, or with motion dynamics for realistic movement simulations of falling objects, loose clothing, or secondary appendages. The disadvantage of procedural solutions is that their results are not precisely controllable on a frame-by-frame basis, and a significant amount of trial-and-error might be necessary to achieve a desired effect. The advantages, however, are realistic, physics-based movement and the ability to animate large numbers of objects without having to manipulate each one individually. Be sure to consider carefully whether a procedural algorithm is the most efficient method of animating a piece of geometry or a group of objects. Particle systems and dynamic simulations can significantly increase your render times and might require a large amount of experimentation before you achieve the desired result. Only use such solutions after you have determined that you cannot hand-animate with a sufficient degree of efficiency or realism. When you are using motion dynamics, be sure to use a few ramp-up frames before the start of a given shot so the necessary calculations can be performed sufficiently. If you are worried about render times and CG scene complexity, consider the use of animated 2D overlays for effects such as rain or snow.

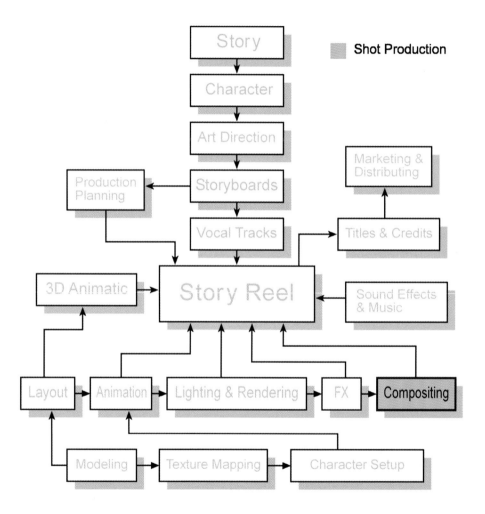

Shot Production

chapter 20
Compositing

Compositing is the last official step of CG shot production, pulling away from the 3D world of modeling, animation, and lighting and working exclusively in the 2D realm of final image assembly and manipulation.

In Chapter 18, we discussed the fact that it is not always necessary or advantageous to render all of the elements of each scene or shot in a single pass. Rather, you can separately render individual or groups of scene elements and then reassemble them as image layers in the compositing stage, where you can achieve exacting control over each layer. Once the separated layers are reassembled and manipulated, the final film image will be complete (see Figure 20.1).

Compositing is similar to editing in that it involves assembling parts into wholes. Editing combines images and sequences horizontally to form an entire film, while compositing combines separate image layers vertically (like a deck of cards) to form completed digital collages (see Figure 20.2).

Pros and Cons of Compositing

Compositing may or may not be a necessary step in your production pipeline. You might indeed be able to generate final imagery directly from your 3D package in single-pass renders, so your rendered frames will not need any post-process assembly or manipulation. Utilizing a compositing step has the obvious disadvantages of increasing the complexity of your pipeline and possibly requiring additional team members, software, and education.

But like all of the other optional steps of CG short film production, such as vocal tracks and texture maps, there are definite advantages to including a compositing step.

> "All parts should go together without forcing. You must remember that the parts you are reassembling were disassembled by you."
> IBM maintenance manual, 1925

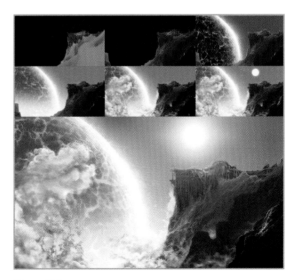

Figure 20.1
Compositing is the process of assembling separate layers to form the final imagery.

389

◆ You can modify the quality of your images or their parts after they have been rendered. For example, you can adjust the colors of a specific character or the shininess of a bowling ball in a particular scene interactively on the rendered imagery, rather than having to go back into the 3D world to re-render the entire shot, which might involve a lot more trial and error.

◆ You can apply 2D effects that might be more difficult or time consuming to produce in the 3D world, such image distortions, lens flares, or camera shakes. Imagine if you have rendered all of the frames of a particularly long and complex shot, only to discover that you are not satisfied with the camera shake. Going back into your CG software to make an appropriate tweak and then re-rendering all of the frames might be extremely time consuming, whereas adjusting the camera shake as a post effect is typically a rather simple matter.

◆ You can combine different media, such as live-action footage, CG imagery, scanned traditional artwork, and 2D animations (see Figure 20.3). You could composite a layer of snow or rain that was created in a 2D paint package on top of your CG imagery, rather than using potentially time-consuming 3D techniques to generate such an effect.

◆ If a particular shot has a static camera and background, you can save on future render times by simply rendering a single frame of the background and then compositing it behind your foreground elements afterward. This is similar to the savings associated with the traditional animation technique of drawing foreground elements on transparent cels and then placing them on top of background paintings to form final imagery, rather than repainting the background for each frame.

◆ You can avoid potential hardware problems. If you have a scene that is too complex for your CPU, RAM, or memory card to handle in a single render pass, you can apply a divide and conquer technique by rendering scene elements in separate layers and then compositing them together after the fact.

◆ When you render for compositing, you have the freedom to modify the aspects of each layer independently, thus giving you exacting control over every small detail, as well as the overall look of each final image.

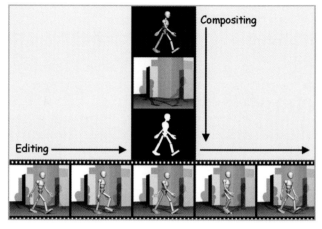

Figure 20.2
Editing can be thought of as a horizontal process, whereas compositing is a vertical (stacking) process.

Figure 20.3
You can use compositing to combine rendered CG layers with imagery from different media, such as live-action background plates or other photographed settings.

The Compositing Process

Compositing reassembles what was previously separated, allowing you a great deal of control over the visual specifics of your final imagery.

Layers and Passes

The concept of *layers* comes from editing terminology and refers to how an image can be divided into separate elements or objects. For example, the main character can be in one layer while everything else can be contained in another. More complex scenarios might have the main character, secondary characters, props, environment, effects, filters, and distortions all in separate layers. To decide how you should group and layer your scene elements, you need to find just the right balance between the added complexity of working with layers and the memory-saving and control advantages of compositing (see Figure 20.4).

The concept of passes comes from the rendering process and refers to the characteristics of the elements that are generated in each rendered layer. For example, if you render your main character separately, that pass might contain all of the visual attributes of that particular digital element, including color information, cast shadows, and highlights. Or a single pass might only include the cast shadows of a particular scene so that you can adjust their translucency interactively in the compositing stage.

Figure 20.4
Compositing works with layers.

Types of Render Passes

Once you have decided which elements should be rendered in each pass, analyze what attributes or details might need to be modified or adjusted while rendering or compositing. For instance, you could modify color on the *beauty pass* and shadow transparency on the *shadow pass*. Some of the common types of rendering passes follow:

◆ **Beauty pass.** This pass will contain only the color information of the included elements. Typically, it will not contain reflections, shadows, or highlights, so when you create a color pass, make sure that other such attributes are turned off in your camera and render parameters. Normally, you use a color pass when you feel you might need to make future changes to the colors of certain scene elements without affecting other visual elements of the final image.

◆ **Specular pass.** This pass will contain information related to the highlights of the included digital elements. With this pass, you can adjust the intensity, color, and softness of object highlights in the compositing stage, thus altering certain material properties to suit the exact specifications of your aesthetic eye. For this pass to work, objects need to be assigned a black material with no diffusion or reflectivity.

◆ **Shadow pass.** This pass will include some (or all) of the cast shadows in a given scene so you can adjust their transparency, color, and softness later. To render only the shadows, you need to turn your objects invisible but leave on their ability to cast shadows (see Figure 20.5).

◆ **Depth-map pass.** This pass will create an image of the scene in black and white, in which objects closest to camera have a white color and those farthest away are black. Objects in the middle will be varying shades of gray. The depth pass is a spatial map of the objects in relation to the camera. You can use this pass to apply effects such as blurring or fog, in which the intensity of the conditions is dictated by camera distance so that, for example, the fog layer will get progressively denser as it recedes.

◆ **Reflection pass.** This pass will contain all the reflections that are displayed on the included objects. Once this pass has been rendered, you can soften, reduce, and change the intensity of these reflections.

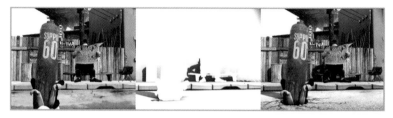

Figure 20.5
A shadow pass

◆ **Lighting pass.** This pass is used to separate each light into its own layer. If you have a typical three-light setup for your scene, then each object in the scene can have three render passes, one for each light. When you are compositing, you can play with the intensity, color, and softness of each light separately as it falls on your scene elements to arrive at just the right balance.

◆ **Other maps.** Depending of the nature of your short, you might find situations in which you require a very specific type of map, such as light beams or a persistent halo effect so that your silhouettes will glow a bit. In every CG film, new ideas for separate render passes will undoubtedly arise (see Figure 20.6).

Compositing Techniques

The fundamental purpose of compositing is to combine, blend, and manipulate image layers, thereby altering and hopefully improving the visual qualities that resulted from rendering alone.

Depending on your software choice, you will find different techniques and tools for applying these manipulations. Arguably, the most common compositing software package is Adobe After Effects, which is available for both Windows and Macintosh platforms and should provide every possible compositing tool you might need (see Figure 20.7).

Figure 20.6
You can use special passes, such as light rays, to increase the overall visual impact of a particular scene.

Within your CG software package you can also create certain effects that are typically added in the compositing stage, such as lens flares and camera shakes, so be sure to consult your manuals and experiment sufficiently to determine whether 2D or 3D solutions will give you the best results in the shortest amount of time.

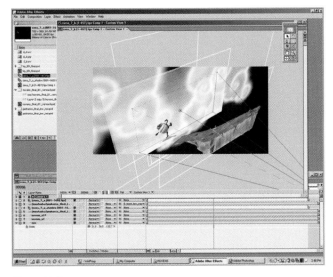

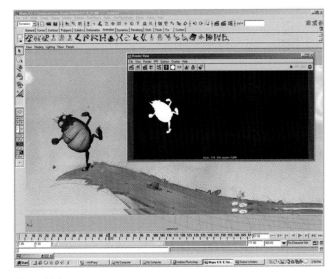

Figure 20.8
Isolating scene elements appropriately is the key to successful compositing passes.

Figure 20.7
Adobe After Effects is a powerful and popular compositing package.

Combining Layers

When you render layers for future compositing, the main goal is to cleanly isolate individual elements from one another so they can be recombined later, like collage pieces (see Figure 20.8). There are several techniques available for isolating and layering your imagery.

Figure 20.9
You can use an alpha channel to isolate characters or objects.

◆ **Alpha channel.** This is one of the most important aspects of a CG image for the purposes of compositing. An *A* or *alpha channel* is an invisible black-and-white layer in your image that is used to separate certain objects from one another (see Figure 20.9). The alpha channel contains information about which areas of the element should be opaque and which should be transparent, assigning them white or black values, respectively. Shades of grayscale determine degrees of transparency.

◆ **Mask.** This is a black-and-white image created separately from the render process, typically in a paint program, such as Photoshop. It is used to mask out areas of scene elements that will need to be transparent. For instance, if you plan to layer a render of a doughnut on top of a background image, you can create a matte for the hole so that the background can be seen through the orifice when the layers are composited together.

◆ **Mattes.** These are images that define transparent areas. A matte is used in place of an alpha channel and can be generated from the color channels of a particular element or from a separate rendering pass.

◆ **Keying.** This process generates the alpha channel for an image by using a specific color, called a *chroma key*, as a transparency generator. In traditional film effects, a pure blue or green background screen is usually used for this technique; however, in CG you can assign any color as a key, so you should a background color that does not exist in the scene elements you want to separate (see Figure 20.10).

Figure 20.10
In live filmmaking, a blue screen is typically used as a background element for subsequently creating alpha channels.

Manipulating Images

In addition to combining layers, you can use the compositing process to modify the visual details of your rendered frames or add extra layers of visual interest, such as lens flares, filters, and post camera moves.

You can also manipulate specific areas of images, such as brightening the head of an individual character, or make more global changes, such as adjusting overall color or adding film grain.

Color Correction

Sometimes there will be situations in which your shots do not maintain a consistent color value or you decide to change the color of certain images to better suit your aesthetic sensibilities. You might also want to make an overall adjustment to values, such as brightness or contrast, to enhance the dramatic nature of a particular sequence or film. By modifying the hue, saturation, and value of your images, you can achieve the exact look you desire (see Figure 20.11).

Figure 20.11
You can make color adjustments to fine-tune your screen imagery.

Adding Effects

Compositing is a very useful and computationally inexpensive method for generating effects, such as lens flares and glows, as well as adding film grain or other treatments to individual frames, sequences, or your entire film.

Distorting

You can also add distortion effects. For example, in an underwater scene, you could use a patterned matte to distort your images, creating a realistic simulation of moving water. Similarly, you can create air displacements from heat or gas sources by using noise distortions.

Camera Adjustments and Shakes

After you have rendered a scene, you can make further adjustments to your camera direction in the compositing stage. For example, you might ultimately decide that a scene could be framed a bit better, so you might want to use a software package such as DeBabelizer or Photoshop to crop and enlarge a certain section of a rendered image to arrive at a more satisfactory composition.

You can also create post-camera moves in the compositing stage with software such as After Effects or Premiere. You might use a simple twist to create the feeling of vertigo, a bit of high-frequency jitter to simulate a handheld feel, or a camera shake to increase the visual impact of a scene involving a giant dinosaur's foot crashing down on an unsuspecting scientist!

To create post camera moves, make sure that you render your frames a bit larger than what will ultimately be shown onscreen so there is extra room to drift and rotate. Otherwise, you will reveal black outside the borders or you will need to zoom in on your frame before you adjust the camera, which might adversely affect your image quality.

Summary

Including a compositing stage in your production cycle will give you the option of rendering subsets of your digital scenes as separate passes that you can combine and further manipulate or complement, which can provide you with more exacting control over your final imagery. You can also apply additional effects, such as camera shakes and film grain filters, in this stage.

Once you have satisfactorily assembled all of your images as final composites, your shot-production stage will be officially complete and you can move on to adding final touches, such as last-minute edits, titles, and credits.

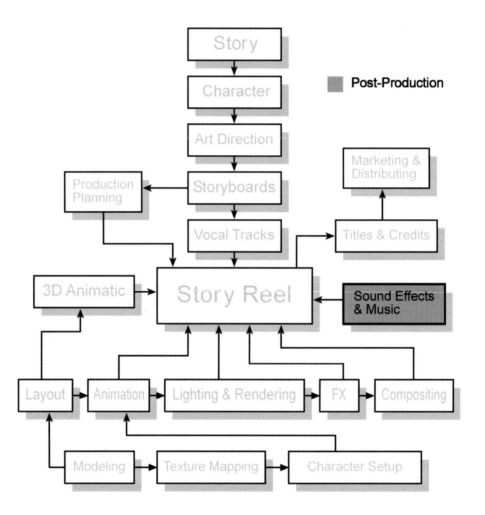

Story

Character

Art Direction

Marketing & Distributing

Production Planning

Storyboards

Vocal Tracks

Titles & Credits

■ Post-Production

3D Animatic

Story Reel

Sound Effects & Music

Layout

Animation

Lighting & Rendering

FX

Compositing

Modeling

Texture Mapping

Character Setup

chapter 21
Sound Effects and Music

Although film is indeed a primarily visual medium, sound effects and music add a layer of refinement to your short's overall cinematic quality by enhancing its mood, realism level, and clarity of story point delivery. Try to imagine a film like *Luxo Jr.* without the creaking sounds of its characters' metal joints and springs or Disney's *Fantasia* without its soundtrack.

Most CG shorts contain both sound effects and music; however, some have one but not the other (see Figure 21.1). *Hiccup 101* and *Instant Animator Machine* have sound effects but no music. *Top Gum* has only sound effects for the duration of the film, but then a bit of music comes in when the credits roll. *Guernica*, *Puppet*, *Values*, and *Repete* have music but no sound effects; however, in these films, certain musical notes, phrases, and percussion hits are intentionally (or perhaps accidentally) timed to specific actions, thereby allowing portions of their music tracks to occasionally act as effective substitutes for actual sound effects.

Sometimes music is used as the very driving force for the story beats and action of a film; therefore, it needs to be created or acquired and then implemented at the initial story reel stage. Certain sound effects are also crucial for initial story point delivery and clarity and will likewise need to be created before (or in the midst of) the animatic or shot production stage. More often than not, however, music and sound effects are added in the post-production stage to complement, rather than actually dictate, visuals; therefore, we have chosen to discuss audio elements here, in the last section of this book.

> "Music expresses that which cannot be put into words and that which cannot remain silent."
> Victor Hugo

Figure 21.1
Some animated shorts have sound effects but no music, while others have music but no sound effects.

Sound Effects

When chosen and implemented appropriately, sound effects can enhance, clarify, exaggerate, or even substitute for visual actions. There are three basic classifications of sound effects.

◆ Visual accompaniments

◆ Visual substitutes

◆ Ambient effects

Figure 21.2
Appropriate sound effects will add impact and realism to scenes such as these.

Sound effects that accompany onscreen actions add clarity, realism, and impact to their visual delivery (see Figure 21.2). A hand slapping a table will certainly read more clearly with an appropriate sound effect. If a character grips his stomach and then opens his mouth, a slightly different story will be told depending on the specifics of the accompanying sound effect, be it a hiccup, a belch, a growl, or a scream.

You can use a sound effect as a substitute for a visual when an action occurs offscreen or is otherwise obscured. If you stage a scene of a walking character from the waist up, the sound of his footsteps will help add realism to the action. A crash might come from another room, causing an appropriate reaction from your onscreen characters (see Figure 21.3). Strange sounds might emanate from inside a box or behind a door.

Figure 21.3
Sound effects can effectively substitute for visuals, especially when you are describing an action that occurs offscreen.

Ambient sound effects are not necessarily tied to a specific location, but serve to round out the mood and details of a certain setting or its conditions. Rain, thunder, chirping crickets, or the sound of a nearby freeway are examples of ambient sound effects.

When you consider the necessary sound effects for a particular scene, remember that it is not always appropriate to link a sound to absolutely every action that occurs on the screen. Too many sound effects can confuse a scene and reduce the clarity of those that are most important to the delivery of the story action. Only create a confusing mess of sound effects when auditory chaos is appropriate for the scene at hand, such as in a prison riot.

Acquiring Sound Effects

You can create, download, or purchase sound effects, depending on your needs, your budget, and the tools you have available.

Making Your Own Sound Effects

Creating your own sound effects involves assuming the role of a Foley artist and using whatever objects, tools, machines, or perhaps pets you have available to generate appropriate noises while capturing them with some type of audio recording device (see Figure 21.4).

Assuming you can create all of your necessary sounds near your workstation, you could simply hook up a microphone to your computer's sound card and capture your audio effects directly in digital format.

A miniature digital recorder is also an excellent option and has the advantage of portability, so you can take the recorder to the source of your needed sound effects. Typically, you can then transfer audio that is recorded with such a device directly into your computer via a USB or FireWire cable.

A camcorder or a digital camera in movie mode can also work as an audio recording device. The minor disadvantage of these tools is that a few extra steps are required to import and extract your necessary audio tracks from their source files.

When you are creating your own audio effects, remember that you don't always need to use authentic source material as long as the captured sound effectively resembles the effect you are hoping to deliver. For instance, you could simulate the sound of horse hooves on a street by tapping a piece of wood on your desktop. A hand clap could probably substitute for the sound of a face slap. The clicking, whirring, rewinding, and ejecting sounds from your VCR might work perfectly for the mechanical noises of your digital robot.

Figure 21.4
Assuming the role of a Foley artist and creating your own sound effects can be a lot of fun.

If you have the appropriate talent, you can sometimes get away with mimicking other sounds using your own mouth. Can you imitate any bird calls? Can you simulate the sound of wind by forcing air through your pursed lips with a slight whistle? Perhaps you could create an effective motorcycle engine sound by sticking out your tongue and blowing a raspberry (see Figure 21.5).

One advantage to creating your own sound effects is that you can make several versions of the same noise and then choose the one that works best later. Turn on your recording device and make a dozen different foot-step sounds by tapping a dozen different objects on a variety of different surfaces. The coffee cup on your desktop might work for your tap dancer's heels, while your finger on the arm of your chair might work for your ballerina's toes.

Figure 21.5
You might be able to effectively mimic certain sound effects.

Purchasing or Downloading Sound Effects

Many audio effects, such as the sound of breaking glass, machine gun fire, a lion's roar, or an avalanche, can be difficult, impossible, or too dangerous to create on your own. Fortunately, you can purchase sound effects like these (as well as many more) on CDs or download them from various Internet sites, such as http://www.sound-ideas.com and http://www.a1freesoundeffects.com. Such purchased assets are typically copyright-free; however, be sure to confirm this before you use them. Taking a piece of audio from a film, song, or other existing source can get you into trouble, and because there are so many other ways to acquire sound effects, stealing or borrowing from copyrighted sources is not worth the risk.

Processing Sound Effects

Once you have acquired your sound effects and transferred them into your computer as .wav or .aiff files, you might need to manipulate them a bit to better serve your needs. Depending on your recording method, your imported audio files might contain background noise or other imperfections. Use a piece of audio processing software, such as Adobe Audition (formerly Cool Edit Pro) or GoldWave Digital Audio Editor to clean up your sound effects so they sound clear and professional.

You might also need to manipulate the pitch, speed, and volume of certain audio files to arrive at the exact sound you are hoping to achieve or to create alternative versions for different uses. Adjusting the attributes of your little brother's dog growl imitation might allow you to use one variation for a Chihuahua and another for a German Shepherd.

If you have recorded or collected a long audio file with a series of sound effects, it is generally a good idea to break the effects up into individual chunks so you can synch them independently.

It is also sometimes helpful to layer sound effects on top of one another to create a more natural or effective noise. For instance, the ambient sound of a busy street scene might require a combination of noises, including car engines, horns, screeches, bells, alarms, walk-sign beeps, footsteps, and various background vocals. Creating a single, layered sound effect has the advantage of reducing the number of files you need to organize; however, it is often preferable to keep your individual sound files separated and then layer them in your piece of NLE software when you synch them to your visuals. That way, you will be able to do a bit more experimentation by varying the volume and synch of each independent layer until you achieve just the right total effect.

Synching Sound Effects

Using your chosen piece of editing software, drop your individual sound effects files into the available audio tracks at appropriate locations to line up with their corresponding visual actions or story points (see Figure 21.6). Some editing packages only offer a single audio track and therefore only allow you to implement sequential sound effects, while more sophisticated packages allow you to create multiple audio tracks so you can create layers and overlaps. If you need layered audio effects but your editing software only allows for a single audio track, you will need to layer your individual sound files separately.

Using your editing software, slide your individual sound effects files back and forth until they synch up properly. In general, sounds that accompany visual actions should be synched up precisely. However, when an action occurs at a great distance, such as a baseball hit seen from the nosebleed section of the bleachers, it will often feel a bit more natural to slightly delay the corresponding audio effect because light travels faster than sound.

Adjust volume accordingly with regard to distance. If a character is walking toward the camera, the sound of his footsteps should get louder as he approaches. Adding such audio depth will increase the overall dimensionality of a shot and enhance the realism of the cinematic experience you are delivering (see Figure 21.7). You can typically make volume adjustments within most NLE packages, but you might need to manipulate your source files directly and then save multiple versions at varying loudness levels. If you do create such variations on a single sound effect, be sure to name your files clearly, such as Footstep_1_loud.aiff and Footstep_1_soft.aiff.

Music

A music track can be the driving force of the action and timing of a short film or it can simply serve as a background soundtrack to enhance its mood. If a piece of music will dictate the timing and story beats of your film, it will obviously be necessary to include it in your initial story reel and then animate your actions and edit your cut points and shot lengths accordingly. If music is to be added as a complement or enhancement to your story, then you can create or acquire it after your film is visually complete.

Acquiring Music

Like sound effects, music can be created, borrowed, or purchased. Regardless of your method of acquiring your music track, try to compose or find something with a style and tempo that fits the genre and pacing of your film. An action piece will typically require something upbeat. A slow, melancholy love story might require something more gentle and melodic. Of course, your film might require a music track that rises and falls in intensity to suit the current story action. Think about the overall mood that you want your film to generate. Should your audience come away feeling happy, sad, or ready to go out dancing? Your choice in music will contribute to your audience's lasting impression of your film, so write, record, or choose carefully and appropriately.

Making Your Own Music

If you have the necessary skills and equipment, creating a music soundtrack for your film can be extremely rewarding and will give you the opportunity to write something that exactly suits your needs and properly synchs up to the highs and

Figure 21.6
Synching up individual sound effects is a simple matter of placing and shifting them appropriately within your software-based editing station.

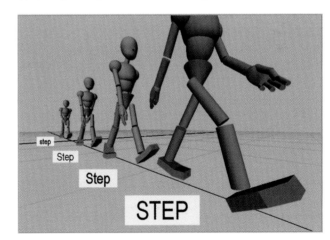

Figure 21.7
Appropriately changing the volume of certain sound effects will help add dimensionality to a visual action.

lows of your story actions and mood progressions. If you don't have the skills yourself, you might try hiring someone to compose and perform a music track for you. If your budget is low, perhaps a piano-playing friend or a student in your school's music department might be willing to lend a free hand for the sake of experience, exposure, or just for the fun of it. If you do hire or borrow someone to write your music track, be sure to wait until you have finalized the visual editing of your film so that your composer will not have to revisit and adjust his soundtrack repeatedly.

If you have a good ear for music but no actual instrument skills or equipment, consider one of the following pieces of digital music creation software:

◆ Apple's GarageBand: http://www.apple.com/ilife/garageband

◆ Cakewalk's Music Creator:
   http://www.cakewalk.com/Products/MusicCreator/default.asp

◆ SmartSound's Sonicfire Pro: http://www.smartsound.com/sonicfire

◆ Sony's ACID PRO 2 (see Figure 21.8):
   http://mediasoftware.sonypictures.com/products/acidfamily.asp

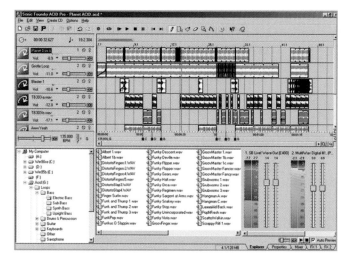

Figure 21.8
Even a non-musician might be able to create an effective soundtrack with the right software and a good ear.

Explore the Web pages listed above for information and free demos so you can quickly evaluate whether one of these music solutions will suit your needs.

Purchasing Music

Before you attempt to use an existing piece of recorded music for a film that will be publicly displayed, it is important to determine the piece's ownership with regard to both composition and performance. A recent pop song will typically belong to a record label. If you hope to use such a recording in your film, you need to contact the label and ask about securing the necessary rights. In rare cases, an artist or record label might allow you to use one of their recordings for a minimal cost (or perhaps even for free) provided you are not expecting to make money from their contribution by selling your film as a music video. However, you should be prepared for the fact that the licensing fee for an existing piece of music will probably be prohibitively high, so make sure your entire production does not depend on securing one particular song (see Figure 21.9).

Figure 21.9
If you create a short that uses copyrighted music recordings as the soundtrack, you need appropriate permissions before you can display it publicly.

There are a number of songs that fall under the category of public domain and can therefore be used without obtaining permission. Depending on the country, songs that were written more than 50 or 75 years ago are typically in the public domain. However, be aware that just because the composition of a piece of music is in the public domain, most recorded performances of the piece will probably be copyrighted. This means you can record your own rendition of *The Star-Spangled Banner* and use it in your film, but you can't use the Jimi Hendrix version without obtaining the necessary permissions. If you plan to create a new performance of a public domain song but your musicians won't be available until a later date, you could use a pre-recorded version as a placeholder during your production cycle to work out your synch points, and then give that version to your new recording artists to use as a reference when they are ready to create your official version.

If you are looking to use an older piece of music but you don't have the means to record your own version, there are many copyright-free performances available on CDs and on the Internet that might provide you with exactly what you need.

If you are looking for an original piece of music, there are a number of Internet sites and CDs that contain original songs you can purchase and use for a nominal fee. Many of these composers will also allow you to partially manipulate their music by adjusting speed or cutting together different portions to make a particular piece fit better with your film (see Figure 21.10). A few such Internet sites are http://www.pdinfo.com/source/TtlRFree.htm, http://www.sound-ideas.com, and http://www.pbtmlive.com/samplelicense.asp.

For more information on music copyrights and public domain songs, check your local library for books on the subject or explore Internet sites, such as http://www.sls.lib.il.us/reference/workshop/suite6.html and http://www.pdinfo.com.

Figure 21.10
Some musicians will allow you to partially adjust the speed and assembly of a composition after you have purchased a royalty-free copy, as long as you credit them appropriately.

Processing Music

Once you have your music created or selected, you will need to bring it into your computer so you can add it to your story reel. If you have downloaded a piece of royalty-free music from the Internet, it will typically already be in the proper digital format (.wav, .aiff, or .mp3). If your music track is coming from a data or audio CD, it should be a simple matter of transferring it into your computer by copying it directly onto your hard drive or converting it to a digital format using software such as MusicMatch Jukebox or Windows Media Player.

If you are recording your own music with digital equipment, a MIDI cord and a piece of appropriate software should suffice. If your music is to be performed on a traditional piano or perhaps an acoustic guitar, you can record directly into your computer with a microphone connected to your sound card or you can use a digital voice recorder; however, the sound quality associated with these methods might not be sufficient for your needs. If this is the case, you will need to invest in a more sophisticated digital recording device or instrument or perhaps rent time at a small professional recording studio.

Just like your sound effects files, you might need to manipulate your music track a bit with regard to quality, speed, volume, pitch, length, fades, or pauses to suit your needs. Again, if you purchased your music from someone else, be sure to get their permission before you change their work in any way.

Synching Music

If your film is simple enough for you to do all of your work within your CG package (and editing software is not a required element of your production), you might be able to simply add your music file to your CG project and then render your film as a video file with the music already attached. However, most CG packages have extremely limited audio capabilities, and you might only have a single channel to work with and therefore would not be able to layer sound effects on top of your music tracks. Even if your entire film exists as a single shot that can be rendered as a whole without needing any visual editing, it is still a good idea to combine your imagery with your audio files using a piece of NLE software, where you will have additional control, functionality, and flexibility.

If your music file dictates the action of your film, you might indeed want to use portions of it within your CG package as you animate your shots so you can time certain actions with certain music beats or phrases. Then you will likely have to slide your shots around during your editing passes to further synch up your entire film.

If your music will be created or purchased and then applied after all of your visuals are complete, be prepared for the fact that you might still need to adjust some shot lengths, cut points, or even animations after the fact. This is yet another good reason to create several handle frames at the beginning and end of each shot, so you will have some flexibility when it comes time to synch your visuals with your music.

Often happy accidents will occur when you are using existing songs on top of your completed imagery, where certain story actions or animation extremes will synch up exactly with an appropriate percussion hit or chord progression. Experiment with this phenomenon by shifting your music track by a few frames in either direction to see what happens. Although it is highly unlikely that every significant story action will synch up with an appropriate portion of your music track, after a small amount of trial and error you should be able to find at least a handful of synch points that will almost seem planned. For any others that are close but not quite exact, you might be able to go back and make a minor adjustment to the length or animation of a particular shot so its action does in fact synch up perfectly.

An example of a music track that occasionally synchs up with the actions and story beats of an existing film is Pink Floyd's "Dark Side of the Moon" CD. When the CD is started immediately after the black-and-white MGM lion roars for the third time at the beginning of *The Wizard of Oz*, a curiously large number of supposedly happy accidents occur. See http://members.cox.net/stegokitty/dsotr_pages/dsotr.htm for a description of the exact setup process and a list of the synch points. Try playing a handful of existing songs or classical music pieces while viewing your film to see whether one of them results in a similarly large number of audio-to-video synch points, and if so, explore the possibility of using that particular piece for your soundtrack.

Summary

Sound effects and music will clarify and enhance the visual actions, realism level, and mood of your film. Sound and music tracks are typically added in the post-production stage unless they dictate the visual flow of your film, in which case they need to be included in your early animatics. Sound effects will accompany and complement an onscreen visual action, substitute for an offscreen or obscured action, or serve as ambient noise to add detail and mood to a setting. When you create your own sound effects, remember that you can often substitute one sound for another when it is dangerous, inconvenient, or impossible to utilize an authentic source, such as for an explosion or a roaring Tyrannosaurus Rex. You can synch sound effects to visuals efficiently and interactively on top of your visuals within your NLE-software-based editing station. When you create or purchase a music track, search for something that fits the style, mood, and pacing of your film. If you plan to use an existing piece of music, remember that there might be two separate copyrights associated with a particular recording—one for the composition and one for the performance. Don't assume that just because the former is in the public domain, you can use the latter without securing the necessary permissions. Even though you might feel that the visual flow of your film is complete, after you add a music track you might find it necessary to go back and adjust the animation or the cut points of certain shots to match your soundtrack more precisely. Before you do so, try sliding your music track forward and backward by a few frames to see how many happy synch accidents occur between your soundtrack and your visuals. Also try this with a few alternative songs to see whether another piece of music might match the visual flow of your film more effectively.

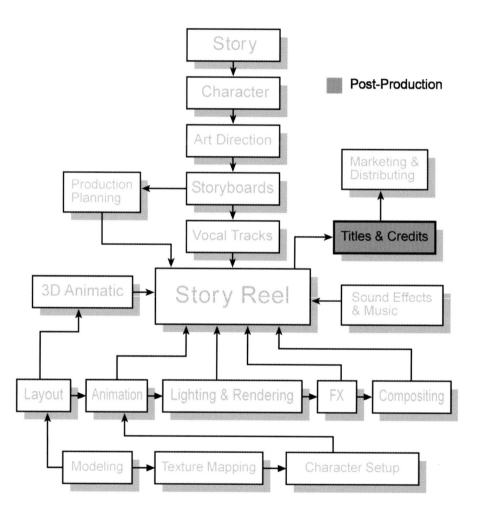

Story

Character

Art Direction

Storyboards

Production Planning

Vocal Tracks

Marketing & Distributing

Titles & Credits

■ Post-Production

3D Animatic

Story Reel

Sound Effects & Music

Layout

Animation

Lighting & Rendering

FX

Compositing

Modeling

Texture Mapping

Character Setup

chapter 22
Titles and Credits

N ow that you have created all of the pictures of your film, it's time to focus some attention on a bit of written text. Text is typically used at the beginning of a film in the form of a title. You might also use more written words in the body of a film as introductions, subtitles, or epilogues. Finally, end credits typically identify those who directly or indirectly contributed to the completion of the film.

Titles

A *title* is a distinctive and unique name, typically appearing at or near the beginning of a short film. It often represents the initial connection to your audience, and it is a first impression of your film that can help indicate the mood, attitude, and style of what is to come.

Be sure to choose a title that is short and concise. See Chapter 2 for a detailed discussion on inventing appropriate titles. Also, your film's title should appear for long enough for your audience members to read it, but not for so long that they grow impatient.

Use clear fonts and colors that work well with the background imagery, and avoid anything too fluorescent. Inventing your own font can be fun, but make sure it is readable and consistent with the visual style of your film (see Figure 22.1).

Think about whether you want your title to be the first thing your audience sees, or if it might be more appropriate to present it after you have displayed a few shots or images. It can also be interesting to include your title as part of an animated opening sequence (see Figure 22.2). Or, you might choose to reveal your title at the end, or perhaps leave it out completely.

Figure 22.1
If your title is something fancier than a simple line of text, its visual style should match that of the rest of your film.

Creating Titles

Titles can be flat, 2D imagery or they can be created out of 3D objects within your CG software package (see Figure 22.3). Choose a dimension based on your art direction preferences and your software comfort level. It can also be interesting to combine 2D and 3D by mapping an image of your title onto a digital object in your opening shot (see Figure 22.4).

Also decide whether you want your title to be static or animated. You can create static titles using any number of painting, drawing, editing, or CG modeling software packages (see Figure 22.5). For animated titles, you might create something using a 2D animation program, such as Flash or Promotion. Most NLE software packages have animated text functionality where your title can fly, fade in, scroll, spin, or execute any number of other acrobatic actions as it enters and exits a frame, as demonstrated in shorts such as *Sahari, Pom Pom*, and *Fishman Unleaded* (see Figure 22.6). For animated 3D titles, create a digital text object and then manipulate your entire title or its individual letters the same way you animated the other elements in your scenes (see *Coffee Love* and *Puppet* on the DVD that came with this book). With animated 3D titles, you have full control over every visual and movement aspect of your text objects, so let your imagination run wild.

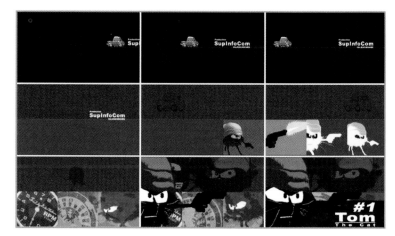

Figure 22.2
A title doesn't necessarily have to be a stand-alone frame preceding your film. It can be combined with moving imagery to create a unique and interesting opening sequence.

Figure 22.3
Titles can be two-dimensional or three-dimensional.

Figure 22.4
Projecting your title onto a digital scene object as a texture map can be interesting.

Figure 22.5
Static titles (Second image © Suruchi Pahwa & Hardeep Kharbanda)

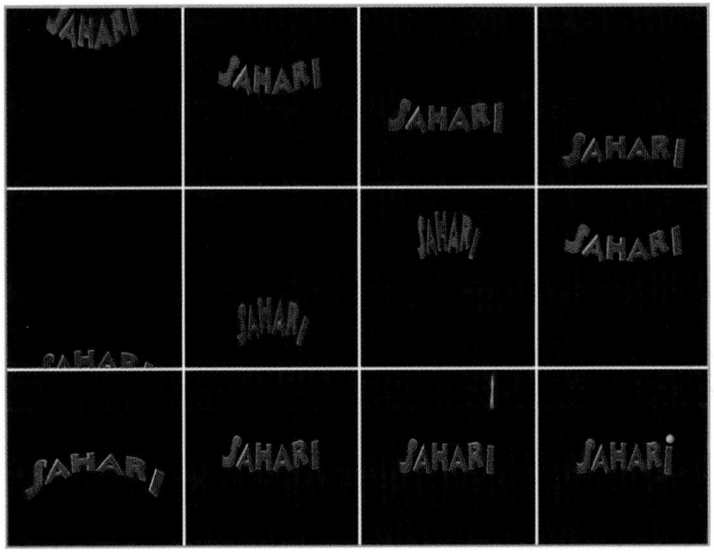

Figure 22.6
An animated title

Introductions, Epilogues, and Subtitles

Sometimes it is necessary to have a bit of text within the body of your film. You might use introductory text to present necessary back-story information to your audience. A famous example of this is in the *Star Wars* films, which open with scrolling text starting with the words, "A long time ago, in a galaxy far, far away...." Sam Chen's CG short, *Eternal Gaze,* also begins with a brief introductory paragraph (see Figure 22.7).

You might also need a bit of text at the end of your film to provide some information regarding significant events that will occur after your story has been told. Typically, such information pertains to the future outcomes of the story characters. For example, "Fred went on to become the leader of his gang and eventually married his high-school sweetheart."

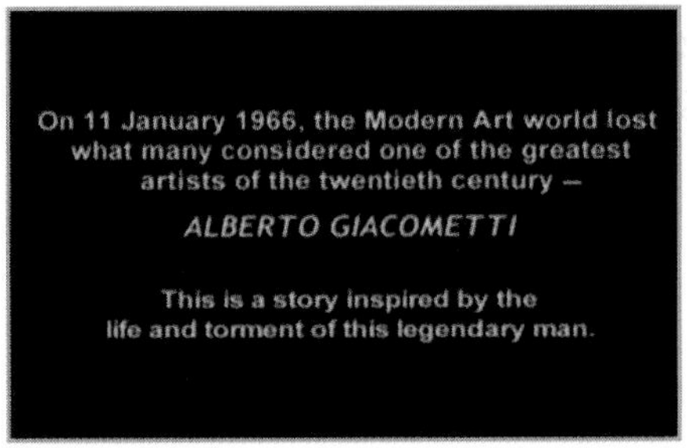

The most common piece of final text you might want to use in your short is a simple, "The End," or perhaps, "To Be Continued...," if you think you might create a sequel someday, or if you just want to end your film on a somewhat existential note.

Subtitles are printed words, statements, or pieces of dialogue that appear onscreen—either between shots as full-screen cards, as seen in early silent films, or during shots, at the bottom of frame, typically for the purpose of translating a foreign or alien language (see Figure 22.8). The general rule for a subtitle or dialogue card is that it should remain onscreen long enough to be read one and a half times at a normal pace. Subtitles at the bottom of a frame should be brightly colored, typically white or yellow, with a black outline so they can be read clearly against any background image. Use standard fonts that are easy to read, such as Times or Helvetica. And don't place your subtitles too close to the bottom of frame; otherwise, they might get cut off on some TV or film screens.

On 11 January 1966, the Modern Art world lost what many considered one of the greatest artists of the twentieth century —

ALBERTO GIACOMETTI

This is a story inspired by the life and torment of this legendary man.

Figure 22.7
You can use text to present important introductory information.

Credits

Credits present an opportunity to recognize by name the persons who contributed to the creation of your short film. Credits are typically displayed at the end of a film, but you might want to list the primary contributors either just before the title, as in "Ringling School of Art and Design presents… a short film by Jessica Sances… *Hiccup 101*," or just after, as in "*PAF Le Moustique*… un film de Jerome Calvet & Jean-François Bourrel."

If you want to credit and thank a large number of people, use a series of pages and separate the contributors logically. Be sure to leave each frame on the screen for long enough for your audience to read everyone's names. However, if your film is going to be delivered in purely digital format, your hold times can be shorter because it is very easy for your viewers to pause as necessary. For a professional touch, consider scrolling your credit list if it doesn't fit on a single screen image.

Make sure not to leave anyone out, and consider thanking those people who indirectly contributed to your film's success, such as the 24-hour pizza delivery guy.

If you plan to use your CG short as a portfolio piece, add your contact information and perhaps a list of the tools you used to complete your film. This could help future employers learn valuable information about your software skills (see Figure 22.9).

If your film is already copyrighted, don't forget to add a © and any corresponding information at the end of your credit list, or as a persistent line of text at the bottom or side of the frame (see Figure 22.10). If there is a Web page associated with your film, be sure to clearly display the URL.

TELL US THE SECRETS TO YOUR ENTIRE PLANETARY DEFENSE SYSTEM.

The Snowman
© 2001 by DUCK

Figure 22.8
Subtitles are used for translating foreign tongues.

Animation By:

Jessica Sances

Produced at the Ringling School of Art and Design Department of Computer Animation

Faculty Advisor
Jim McCampbell

Featuring
Claudia Cumbie-Jones
as Ms. Chokengag

and Illustrations by
Brett Schroeder

Hardware
HP Visualize Series Workstations

Software

Maya 4.0
Shake 2.4
Photoshop 6.0

Special Thanks to:

Brian J. Hall, Billy Kimbrell, Don Phillips Jr.,
Karissa Miller, Phillip Chiocchio, Karen
Sullivan, Mert Balta, Tonya Noerr,
Karen Smith, Deborah Healy, Juan-Carlos
Larrea, Jeff Nilles

And my wonderful and supportive family

© 2002 Jessica Sances

Figure 22.9
If necessary, use multiple credit frames, grouping the contributors and information logically.

If time allows, consider having some animation or imagery accompany your credits as they roll by to keep your audience engaged as you recognize your contributors (see Figure 22.11). This technique appears in feature films, such as *Finding Nemo* and *Ferris Bueller's Day Off*, as well as the CG shorts, *La Piedra* and *Tom the Cat*. For static imagery, you might want to display some character sketches or other development imagery to give your viewers a glimpse at your creative process at work and to present potential employers with a bit more information about your fundamental art skills.

Figure 22.10
Consider having your copyright information as a persistent line of text at the bottom of frame, but make sure it is small enough that it doesn't obscure any of your imagery.

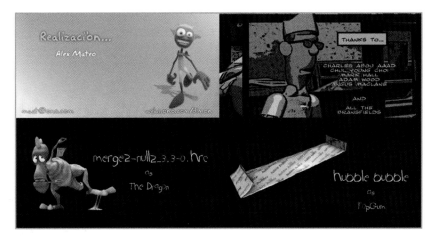

Figure 22.11
Some final animations or static imagery might help keep your audience in their seats while your credits roll.

Bloopers and Outtakes

Bloopers and *outtakes* are clips or scenes that have been removed from a film because they contain mistakes of some kind. For the sake of humor, however, you might want to screen such errors at the end, typically during the credits.

In live-action films, blooper clips generally contain mistakes made by an actor, such as flubbing or forgetting a line of dialogue, tripping over a prop, cursing, or bumping his head on the boom microphone. Recent examples appear in many Jackie Chan movies, in which the audience is presented with outtakes that typically feature stunts that have gone wrong.

Because your digital actors are not autonomous, such mistakes will not actually occur spontaneously; therefore, the only types of actual production errors you might be able to show would be animation problems or technical glitches. However, displaying such blunders is not really recommended because they aren't very interesting to a normal audience member, and potential future employers would not be very excited to see the mistakes made by you or your teammates. Therefore, if you want to show actor mistakes as blooper clips at the end of your film, you will have to invent them. Many recent Pixar films contain such "fake" actor flubs, and you can also see a few invented bloopers on the DVD for *Early Bloomer*.

However, keep in mind that although it can be entertaining to present such invented humorous moments, if you sacrifice other crucial elements or shots from the main body of your film for the sake of these optional addendums, your internal or external producer might not find them particularly amusing!

Summary

In addition to pictorial imagery, you will probably need to add a bit of printed text to your film in the form of titles, subtitles, or credits, and you might want to include some development artwork or a few faked bloopers while your credits roll.

With the addition of these final touches, you can now step back and deem your film a final product! But before you go off and celebrate for too long, you will need to spend a bit of time addressing the subject of Chapter 24—marketing and distributing your short film so that the world (or some subset thereof) can experience your unique cinematic vision.

Figure 23.1
Kevin Johnson
(director) and
Sande Scoredos
(producer)

chapter 23
Case Study 4: Early Bloomer

Our final case study is presented in the form of a pair of interviews with Kevin Johnson and Sande Scoredos (see Figure 23.1), the director and producer, respectively, of an award-winning little parable created in 2003 by a team of artists at Sony Pictures Imageworks who mostly helped out in their spare time. Although this film was indeed created by a fairly large crew of studio professionals, the simplicity of its design elements and the lack of vocal tracks makes it an excellent example of what even a small team or individual could conceivably accomplish within a reasonable budget and timeframe.

Kevin Johnson

Q: *Tell us briefly about your background and your current job position.*

A: I entered this profession 13 years ago as a traditional animator and I worked at several feature divisions, including Warner Bros., Turner, Disney, and Bluth. I've also had an ongoing career instructing animation classes at CalArts for the past 12 years. Over the years I have worked in visual and story development, as well as animation. I began my computer training at Disney and then came to Sony almost four years ago. I am currently in story development at the newly formed Sony Pictures Animation department.

Q: *How did you first get into animation? What initially inspired you to head down that pathway?*

A: I guess it was the *Wonderful World of Disney* on Sunday evenings that first opened my eyes to the world of animation. I was intrigued and amazed by how the pictures seemed so real and full of character. After applying directly to Disney, they pointed me in the direction of CalArts. There I received some training, and that was the beginning.

VITAL STATISTICS

Title: *Early Bloomer*

Director: Kevin Johnson

Team Size: 76 total contributors, mostly part time

Total Running Time: 3 minutes, 35 seconds

Production Cycle: About five months

Date of Completion: April 2003

Software: Maya, Houdini, RenderMan, proprietary compositing software

Total Production Cost: Difficult to estimate because most team members jumped in and out for brief stints whenever their other production commitments would allow.

Q: *Tell us a little bit about your experience as a teacher and the Assistant Director of the Character Animation program at CalArts. What kinds of skills and fundamentals did you stress to your students?*

A: The experience of teaching at CalArts gave me a different perspective than the one I got from the professional world. For one, it is a very rejuvenating experience to keep yourself in the mix of enthusiastic, creative individuals who see no limits with regard to time, money, technology, et cetera. That is a nice contrast to the real work environment. My instruction at CA is really simple. I teach the basic principles of character animation: squash and stretch, working poses, overlapping action, and timing. I feel the students need to have this base to work all their creativity from. At the same time I try to stress the importance of perseverance and taking chances. It is equally important to execute an idea and see it through as it is to have one.

Q: *How did the story for* Early Bloomer *come about?*

A: EB came about through a number of inspirations. The biggest one was my son's frustration at being the shortest kid in his class. I tried to explain that everybody grows differently and one day he will have a growth spurt and then he won't be the shortest. That experience, coupled with a fishing trip where we caught some tadpoles, was the beginning of *Early Bloomer*.

Q: *How did it get started as a production at Imageworks?*

A: It started when several animators that were in a story and performance class I was teaching at Imageworks came to me and asked to use this story as their training project. And from that we pitched this collaboration to Sande Scoredos, who gave us the okay.

Q: *Was this your first short film? Was directing a short something you'd always wanted to do?*

A: Yes. It was the first one where the collaboration was at this level. And yes, this is something I always have wanted to do.

Q: *What was the overall production pipeline for* Early Bloomer?

A: The early development took the most time. It took me many evenings over a four-month period to draw out and cut together a story reel (see Figure 23.2). Once we pitched it to Sande, then things became a little more goal- and time-oriented. There was a two-month period when we built the characters and the pond, making every mistake possible. It took another month and a half to correct those errors and settle on a process that we could use for a final pipeline. Once agreed upon, it made perfect sense. Look development was one area that went smoothly (see Figure 23.3), and that was due to one of our shader writers, Clara Chan, really

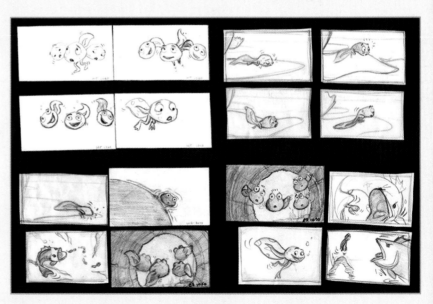

Figure 23.2
Storyboards

hitting the mark nearly every time. It took one month to lay out shots and get them onto an editorial system (see Figure 23.4). Once that happened, we had a real pipeline. That time overlapped with scene setup, which ran for an additional month. Animation itself was relatively short, taking approximately two months. Color and lighting was equally efficient, though at the time it didn't seem so.

Q: *Which production steps do you consider to be the most important?*

A: They all have different levels of importance since without any one of them you would never get an end result, but the one that holds everything together is the story reel. It's the crudest version of the film, and yet it holds all of the important information you need to tell your story.

Q: *Describe your role as director. Did you animate any shots yourself? How often did you meet with your animators and artists?*

A: After I created the story reel, I basically turned into a glorified cheerleader, bringing bits of advice and direction. I didn't animate any shots myself, but I thumbnailed ideas and talked with the animators about what they were thinking. The animators were basically all on the same level, meaning they each had sequences that they were responsible for. There were individuals who took on lead roles in lighting, coloring, and comp, and our Senior Technical Animator, Todd Pilger, helped immensely in getting everything in character animation off the ground. Overall, everyone crossed over to help one another out, which, as a director, I came to realize was very important.

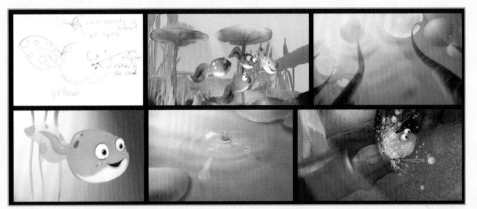

Figure 23.3
Look development

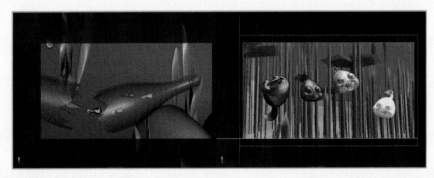

Figure 23.4
Layout

Q: *What are some of the pros and cons associated with doing a group project as opposed to working as a lone filmmaker?*

A: Well, the pros are easy. You can get it done in considerably less time. Also, individuals with different areas of expertise tend to bring you a higher-quality overall product. And more questions can be answered. The cons are: More questions come up, the communication factor becomes a problem that you have to stay on top of, and [there is] the all-encompassing management of a larger group of artists.

Q: *How did you maintain style and quality consistency between all the shots with regard to animation, lighting, and so on?*

A: In the animation department, we have a very open line of communication. This helped to keep myself and all the animators focused on a performance goal and ways to make it better along the way. I delegated the lighting to a pair of amazing leaders, Adrian Iler and Max Bruce, who kept a watch over the consistency in their department.

Q: *What kind of facial animation system was used?*

A: The facial system was a bit of a hybrid that was created by Todd Pilger. Todd and I talked early on and agreed upon a very elastic facial system that would also lend itself to clear, expressive attitudes (see Figure 23.5). It's a combination of blend shapes with a separate set of clusters that you can use in unison.

Q: *What was the biggest challenge in creating this short?*

A: Keeping it going. There were four separate occasions where I almost just gave up. You have to really have passion to create something like this because there are always difficulties that are going to try to derail you.

Q: *Were there any unexpected surprises in the middle of production, either positive or negative?*

A: There was never a dull moment. One of the setup people who was our lifeline to continuing on had an emergency appendectomy. Some animators constantly added frames, which in some cases turned out to be a good thing, and in some cases [was] not such a good thing.

Q: *Do you remember any specific shots that were particularly challenging?*

A: The shot where the main character tries to get away from her legs. I was not sure how it should play out and so it changed for the longest time, right up until the end of the show.

Q: *Do you have a favorite shot from the film?*

A: Visually, I love the shot where the green tadpole passes in and out of the light through the can (see Figure 23.6).

Q: *How did you acquire/create the background music?*

A: I dumped in temporary classical music just to help figure out pacing. There was only one music cue that I really needed, and that was the cancan piece.

Figure 23.5
An intuitive and expressive facial system was crucial.

Figure 23.6
One of Kevin's favorite shots

Q: *Coming from a 2D background, tell us a little about the advantages and/or disadvantages of using digital technology in the filmmaking process.*

A: The advantage of using digital technology is the flexibility it gives you as an artist with regard to camera, color, and lighting. One of the disadvantages you have is the limitation of technology in regard to animation. You must really think ahead on what works for the story and whether or not you will be able to pull it off. Working on shorts in this digital medium allows very little room for mistakes and lack of foresight.

Q: *What did you learn from this experience?*

A: There is never enough planning that can take place, and there is never enough time to do it. Trust and delegate.

Q: *How do you think CG animated short production will change/evolve in the future?*

A: I think that they will expand visually as well as in content. We have just begun to touch on the visual possibilities of this medium, and I think that shorts are the place where that exploration will take place.

Q: *Do you have any advice or tips for our readers? Anything specific about managing a group project?*

A: Plan well and be honest with your limitations. Get individuals that supplement your talents.

Q: *What's next for Kevin Johnson?*

A: More story development and definitely more CG shorts.

Sande Scoredos

Q: *Tell us briefly about your background and current job position.*

A: I am the Executive Director of Technical Training and Artist Development for Sony Pictures Imageworks. We offer over 30 courses, including life drawing, sculpting, acting, and special lectures, as well as specialized task-oriented classes for a wide variety of production disciplines. I came to Imageworks in 1996 to set up the training department, having held a similar post at Rhythm and Hues. As Manager of Worldwide Training for Wavefront Technologies (one of the founders of high-end animation and visualization software), I designed the worldwide training program and curriculum, instructing professionals in the use of 3D computer graphics and animation for broadcast, engineering, gaming, and scientific visualization. I serve on several academic advisory boards and teach at several universities, including MIT and UCLA. I also chaired the SIGGRAPH 2001 Computer Animation Festival in Los Angeles and served on various juries for computer animation festivals and technical conferences.

Q: *As the 2001 SIGGRAPH Computer Animation Festival chairperson, what were the criteria you used when judging the CG short entries?*

A: The judges were instructed not to discriminate or distinguish between students, studios, institutions, and individuals. Each submitter to the CAF was entitled to the same rigor and scrutiny, and to a fair, impartial, and balanced review. Selected pieces were those that demonstrated exceptional accomplishments based on the following criteria:

- Technical excellence
- Innovation
- Artistic achievement
- Content
- Creativity
- Originality
- Narrative quality
- Design
- Entertainment value
- Production values
- Diversity of culture and discipline

Q: *How many films were submitted and how many were chosen for the show?*

A: We received 679 valid submissions. The jury accepted 44 pieces for the Electronic Theater and 74 for the Animation Theater. Thirty-five of the 118 accepted pieces were student films.

Q: *How did you get involved in the production of* Early Bloomer?

A: As part of the Story Development class taught this summer by Kevin Johnson, one of the assignments was to prepare storyboards and present a "pitch" to the class. The students were also asked to propose a personal training project that would challenge them aesthetically and technically and further develop their understanding of how the pipeline works at Imageworks. We also had classes in modeling, sculpting, character setup, effects, and lighting to enable folks to have a better appreciation for what is possible when creating a story. Actually, just about anything is possible in computer graphics, but it is also important for artists and animators to know what happens before and after they have worked on their section of the pipeline.

Q: *What was your role on the project?*

A: I served as the Associate Producer. Kevin Johnson pitched the story, and I thought it was something that would work well for a group training project. The story was charming and the scope of the project was not too big or too small. I had several students interested in developing their creative and supervisory talents, others who needed to update their software skills, and still others who were interested in stylized modeling or animation. In all, everyone who worked on the film was learning new skills. My job was to help Kevin keep the production going and keep the show crewed while making sure that everyone's learning objectives were met.

Q: *Describe your working relationship with Kevin.*

A: Kevin is very talented and creative, and has been a major contributor to our training program at Imageworks. While he was teaching his Story Development series, the animators were also learning some very technical aspects of the pipeline, including modeling, character setup, and lighting. This helped Kevin and his team develop an excellent appreciation for the technical aspects of CG animation. Kevin is great to work with since he is able to balance his creative and aesthetic choices with what is technically feasible. If a story point or effect would be too difficult or take too long to perfect, he would figure out another way to tell it. Kevin is also open to taking suggestions and creative input from his crew, which keeps everyone motivated and involved.

Q: *How did* Early Bloomer *"graduate" from a training exercise to a full-fledged production?*

A: We completed a cut with several elements in place—finalized visual development on several shots; completed the pipeline setup; [wrote] the shaders, rigged the characters, blocked out all the animation, and locked down the look of the characters and the environments. While our President, Tim Sarnoff, and our Head of Feature Production, Jenny Fulle, were well aware of the training project, we screened this cut for them and they were very pleased [with] our efforts, gave their encouragement and support to completing the project, and saw an opportunity for it to be screened theatrically in May. So we basically had from January to April to complete the project.

Q: *Did anything change about the structure or pipeline once it became an official production?*

A: Everything was structured from the very beginning to be a proper production, using the latest facility pipeline tools and all the standards, from modeling to compositing. The crew continued to be pulled from those assigned to training. We also had to complete all the post-production aspects of the project, including sound, music, color timing, film prints, and legal rights.

Q: *Was there an initial schedule and budget for the project?*

A: The cost of the project was incorporated into the regular training budget and the schedule was based on individual training assignments. We had to schedule the modelers to pass the characters and environments on to the setup folks. The biggest chunk of time was spent in the character and environment setup, since these folks had a lengthy series of classes to attend and they were also creating new animation tools and setting up a new and very thorough pipeline. This paid off later since we had so many animators and artists working on the show. Everything that was set up worked well and needed very little support from the setup folks. The music, sound, and film distribution phase required rigid schedules and budgets that we had no problems meeting.

Q: *Were there any new tools or techniques developed specifically for* Early Bloomer?

A: The facial animation system that Todd Pilger wrote for the tadpole characters was terrific and is now part of the facility tools. The muck and the bubble particle systems for the underwater effects developed by Tom Pushpathadam were used again in our other productions (see Figure 23.7). The living, breathing procedural environment that Todd Pilger developed brought the pond to life. Carolyn Oros was able to take the time to write a proper suite of setup tools, scripts, and procedures that have been invaluable to every show since *Early Bloomer.*

Q: *What were the biggest challenges you observed during the production?*

A: The biggest challenge was giving people the amount of time they needed to complete their work. As you know, everyone always wants to make this one little change to make it perfect. Once lighting [was] done, it was not desirable to request a change to the animation, and Kevin and the supes were very careful about making reasonable comments and change requests. We were also very busy with production work in the studio, and it was a challenge to balance the workload. But folks were very dedicated to this project and did everything they could to see it completed.

Figure 23.7
A particle system for the bubbles was developed.

Q: *Did artists and animators stay on the project for the duration, or did they come and go because of other on-the-job commitments?*

A: We had a very small core group of about five people who worked on this project from the beginning to end. Others participated for a shorter time, depending on production assignments and the phase of their training. Everyone who worked on this project was key to its completion and success, and their dedication and creative input was outstanding. We even had two CG supervisors on the show because one had to go onto another assignment. I am very proud of the work they did, and so many of the crewmembers have already advanced their careers due to their participation on the project. Training at Imageworks is an ongoing endeavor, and artists and animators are assigned to training when they first come to the company and then on a regular basis to prepare for their next assignment. As these folks are assigned to training, I develop an individual training plan for each person, which can be to improve and update their current skills or to introduce them to new skill sets. Once initial training classes are completed, there is no better way to demonstrate competencies than to work on a production, so I would assign people to do different tasks according to their training plan and career goals. This gave people an opportunity to demonstrate creative, aesthetic, and technical skills, as well as leadership and management skills. I was able to take the folks in training and match their classroom training experience and past skills with career goals and assign them to various jobs on the show. For example, an animator who only knew realistic animation studied stylized cartoon animation and was assigned character animation, while many of the lighters learned a newer version of rendering techniques we used on the show. Several lead TDs [technical directors] were assigned the role of CG supervisor; a lighter was assigned a shader-writer role. The short allowed a great opportunity for people to work outside their usual area and to take risks and stretch. As long as it was the right fit with talent and training for the task, it all worked well.

Q: *How was* Early Bloomer *marketed and distributed after it was completed?*

A: *Early Bloomer* was screened theatrically in May, 2003, so film prints were distributed. Joe Roth from Revolution Studios screened the film in front of their Eddie Murphy family-fare film *Daddy Day Care*. It was also accepted into the SIGGRAPH 2003 Electronic Theater and screened at the conference in San Diego, and [it] has won many film festival awards. The Marketing department did a wonderful job with posters, press kits, and press releases (see Figure 23.8). They even did a very cute screensaver that can be downloaded from one of the Sony sites. A DVD was created and included a series of gag shots that were also completed by folks in training. These were really pretty funny and gave additional animators and lighters a chance to work on the project.

Q: *Do you have any advice for our readers with regard to short film production?*

A: A lot of talent goes into making a short. I have seen some pretty good shorts done by one person, but they usually fall short in one or two areas, like the lighting is terrific but the animation is stilted, or the animation is great but the story doesn't work. Everyone cannot be great at everything. That's why projects are done by teams—so that the best talent is applied to the right areas. My advice is to build a team, identify talents, have a strong director who knows how to get the best results from people, and have a story that deserves [to be] told. A group project on your demo reel can really showcase your talents and also demonstrate your ability to work with a team and take direction, which is a very, very important aspect of production.

Figure 23.8
Promotional poster image

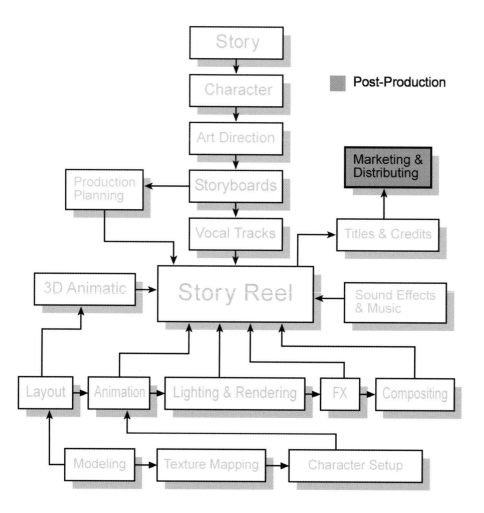

Story

Character

Art Direction

Production Planning

Storyboards

Post-Production

Marketing & Distributing

Vocal Tracks

Titles & Credits

3D Animatic

Story Reel

Sound Effects & Music

Layout

Animation

Lighting & Rendering

FX

Compositing

Modeling

Texture Mapping

Character Setup

chapter 24
Marketing and Distribution

Hitting the Save button for the last time and deeming your film a finished product is an exciting milestone and very likely a huge relief as well. Go out and celebrate your accomplishment, but don't forget that even though your CG short might be finalized, your process as a filmmaker requires a few more steps if you want anybody besides yourself, your teammates, and your friends to see your work.

What was your initial goal when you started your film (see Figure 24.1)?

◆ Was it merely an animation exercise?

◆ Was it a school thesis project created to satisfy your graduation requirements?

◆ Was it a personal project designed to improve your demo reel?

◆ Was it an animated greeting card for your Mom's fiftieth birthday party?

◆ Did you have grand expectations of your film riding the festival circuit and eventually winning an Annie award or perhaps an Oscar?

Figure 24.1
Did you begin your short as an animation exercise, a school assignment, or perhaps a demo reel supplement?

Has your goal changed since you started your production?

◆ Perhaps your piece began as a simple animation exercise but grew bigger than you'd initially planned and has graduated to something more festival-worthy.

> "Now this is not the end. It is not even the beginning of the end. But it is, perhaps, the end of the beginning."
> Sir Winston Churchill

24. Marketing and Distribution

◆ Maybe you initially intended to create a single film for the festival circuit, but you've developed quite a fondness for your characters so now you want to produce a dozen episodes and try to pitch it as a television series.

◆ Maybe you were planning to use your film as a demo reel to show off your animation skills to get a job in the animation department of a particular studio, but halfway through production you discovered that lighting is your real calling, so you're going to submit your reel to a different department instead.

Regardless of your initial (or perhaps revised) plan, we assume your current intention is to get your short film out of your studio and in front of your intended audience. To do so, you will need to effectively market and distribute your film. *Marketing* is the process of informing the outside world of your film's existence. *Distribution* is the process of getting your film to your future viewers, judges, or potential employers.

Before you begin showing your work, it is very important to remember that in most cases, the financial rewards for an animated short will be indirect at best. There are very few opportunities for you to receive direct or immediate financial compensation for your efforts. Some festivals or publishers will offer small royalties or cash rewards. If you are extremely lucky and manage to sell your short as a television series, you will likely get some fairly substantial funding. However, you should probably expect that your rewards will come slowly and gradually in the form of increased exposure and perhaps job offers, rather than immediate cash. But even though the possibility of getting any kind of return on your time and money investments might be limited or perhaps even non-existent, you'll never know until you start putting your film out there for the world to see.

Marketing

Perhaps your CG short is still in progress and you want to generate advance buzz. Or maybe your film is finished and ready for the big or small screen. Either way, there are a number of ways you can alert the world to the existence of your film.

Online

Creating a personal Web page is an excellent place to start. You might create a site dedicated exclusively to your short or make the page a subset of a larger online portfolio that also contains your resume and other examples of your work (see Figure 24.2). It is also a good idea to put production information on such a site, describing certain aspects of your development cycle as well as posting storyboard drawings, character design sketches, lighting experiments, animation tests, and any other imagery that might increase the amount of attention your Web page will potentially receive.

If your film is not finished yet, it is still a good idea to create a Web site as an online production diary where you and others can follow your progress. This is an excellent way to create anticipation

Figure 24.2
A Web page might be exclusively dedicated to your short or it might be a subset of a complete online portfolio.

for your short and has proved to be quite successful for a number of filmmakers (see Figure 24.3).

Free Web-hosting services are available; however, their storage capacity is typically limited and many will include annoying advertisements or pop-up windows on your site. Surf the Internet to find a Web host that offers sufficient storage space, and try to avoid those that have monthly bandwidth restrictions. Once you reach your traffic limit, any new visitors will have to wait until the following month to download your film. If your Web site starts getting popular, this will not be a desirable scenario.

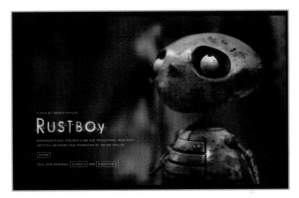

Also be aware that if you put your film on the Web, anybody will be able to download it. In general this is a good thing, and you shouldn't worry too much about plagiarism because nobody can legally do anything with your film without your permission. However, if you are worried about such things, look into using streaming format options with which viewers will be able to watch your film without actually downloading it. Keep in mind, however, that a viewer's ability to view your film as an Internet stream will be dependent upon the speed of their connection and the size of your film, which could limit your audience significantly.

Figure 24.3
You can follow the production of Brian Taylor's *Rustboy* on his regularly updated Web page.

On your Web site, it is a good idea to have a page of links to other relevant and inspirational or educational sites. After you have created this page, contact the owners of the sites to which you are linking and let them know that you have done so. In rare cases, some artists might not want you to link to their site, and others might require that you use a specific image on your links page. But most will be flattered and some will probably offer to return the favor, thus initiating the spread of your Web site's existence through the ever-expanding network of cyberspace.

When you're assembling an online portfolio, try to avoid the temptation to include personal material, such as pictures of your dog or snapshots from your last Halloween party. Such non-portfolio-related imagery belongs on its own Web site. You can certainly offer a link to your personal page from your professional page, but it is generally a good idea to keep the two separate.

You might also look into search engine submission services, which will help to ensure that surfers will find your site when searching for terms such as "CG Short" or "Animation."

Several Web forums dedicated to animation and shorts also exist, including CGCHAR (http://cgchar.toonstruck.com), where you can share your work with a wide variety of hobbyists and professionals for praise, criticism, and advice.

Also, there are a number of online festivals where you can submit your short and potentially receive a large amount of exposure. In fact, many of the images in this book are from films that were found on Internet festivals and contests such as http://www.cgnetworks.com/cgfilms/, http://www.cgfocus.com, http://www.vocanson.fr/, and http://www.10secondclub.org.

And remember that even if your film is not yet finished, you can certainly begin the marketing process by sending still images or small "trailer" clips to online festivals. If viewers respond favorably to your work in progress, your motivation for finishing will certainly increase and you will probably also feel a bit more determined not to keep your fan base waiting too long for your final product.

Networking

Another excellent way to spread the news about your short is by direct networking. Join professional organizations, such as ASIFA and your local SIGGRAPH chapter, if one exists in your area. Attend their screenings and meetings whenever possible to rub elbows with other filmmakers and industry professionals. Often such meetings will offer opportunities for members to show their work, so seize the day whenever it comes around. Try to strike up conversations with other attendees. If you tell people that you are working on or have just completed a short film, they will probably ask you about it and maybe even request an opportunity to see the piece. The more people who see your short, the better—especially if one of those inquiring minds happens to be a festival director, studio employee, magazine editor, professional recruiter, or even just someone who might have a few helpful contacts to any of the above (see Figure 24.4).

Also try to attend the larger conferences, such as the annual SIGGRAPH convention, where you will have many opportunities to see the work of other filmmakers and make contacts.

Have promotional materials or business cards made for yourself, perhaps featuring images or design sketches from your short, and be sure to ask for other people's cards. A collection of business cards can be a great networking tool (see Figure 24.5).

Remember that it is just as important to get yourself noticed as it is to get your film noticed, so be courteous and enthusiastic when you are meeting other members of this closely-knit industry. First impressions can go a long way in both directions.

Print

If you can afford it and you are so inclined, you might consider running an advertisement featuring your short in a periodical, such as *Animation Magazine* or *Computer Graphics World*. Such ads are typically rather expensive, but if your short was a team effort, perhaps everyone would be willing to chip in for a small quarter-page image.

Distribution

Before, during, or after you've spread the word about your short's existence, you will need to get it in front of your intended audience. Opportunities to present your short in person will

Figure 24.4
Getting the attention of magazine editors or writers can result in a great deal of exposure for your film.

Figure 24.5
Business cards and other leave-behinds make excellent networking tools.

be few and far between, so you will typically need to export your film to an appropriate media format and then send or upload it to various festivals and studio human-resource departments.

Exporting

There are five basic formats for distributing your film.

◆ Video

◆ DVD

◆ CD-ROM

◆ Film

◆ Internet

Video is a popular choice, especially for demo reels and many festival submissions. A digital camcorder is probably the best option for exporting your film from your computer to video. Most camcorders come bundled with software that will allow you to record directly from your PC via a FireWire port. NLE packages, such as Adobe Premiere, also provide direct tape export capabilities. Once your film is on a camcorder tape, you can dub it to a VCR as many times as necessary to create your VHS copies. If the original format is digital, the generation loss should be minimal. A decent video card will also allow you to connect the necessary cables directly to a VCR. If you do not have a camcorder or a sufficient video card, you might need a video export device, such as an AVerKey Computer-to-TV Converter (http://www.aver.com). Some festivals will require you to send your submissions (or at least your accepted films) on BetaSP or Digibeta tapes. Check your local phone book for tape-dubbing services or places where you can rent such machines if the need arises.

DVDs are beginning to replace VHS tapes as the preferred format for distributing and submitting short films. The advantage is that the image quality will be higher, but the disadvantage is that you will need to have a DVD burner, which might be beyond your budget, especially when you consider the price of blank discs. If you purchase a burner, it should come with all the software you need to create your DVDs, or you can visit your local computer store to investigate the wide variety of DVD-authoring software that is now available. When you create a DVD, make sure your interface is easy to navigate. A tired recruiter might not bother trying to watch your film if it becomes too difficult or time consuming to find it amongst a complicated hierarchy of flashy intermediate pages.

CD-ROMs are also a convenient option and are more cost effective than DVDs. The main problem will be potential compatibility. You need to make sure your CD will play on Windows-based machines as well as Macintoshes, and your file formats will likewise need to be compatible with the equipment of all your potential viewers. One way to potentially reduce compatibility problems is to add a self-contained video player on your CD-ROM. Some festivals will take submissions on CDs, as will many game company recruiters and HR departments; however, demo reels for film studios and FX houses should be on VHS or DVD.

If you need to export your CG short to film format, you will most definitely need to call upon the services of a local film recording service, which will likely be very expensive. Only export to film when absolutely necessary.

As mentioned earlier, the Internet is also an excellent place for CG short film distribution, either featured in online festivals or displayed on a personal Web site that is sufficiently advertised. When you are preparing your short for the Web, consider that not everyone necessarily has a broadband connection, and if your downloadable film is very large, you might significantly limit your potential audience. Having two or three versions of different sizes is usually a good idea. Also make sure that your file is in a common format that most users will be able to play, such as QuickTime, AVI, or Windows Media. If you use a compression format, such as DIVX, be sure to indicate this on your site and provide a link to a location where users can download such a codec. Of course, before you upload or send your film to online festivals, carefully read their submission guidelines and provide them with the size and format they require.

No matter what format you choose, be sure to label your tapes or discs clearly. A label should have sufficient contact information, typically an e-mail address and a phone number (see Figure 24.6). Use appropriate packaging as well, such as cushioned mailer envelopes or the correct-sized tape boxes purchased from an office supply store or a mailing service. Just be sure that you do not use the kind of envelopes that have fine paper fibers as their cushioning. Recruiters and festival organizers absolutely hate the mess these envelopes can make when they are opened.

Figure 24.6
Make sure you label your tapes or discs clearly with sufficient contact information.

Getting It out There

Who should see your CG short? Festival committees? Judges? Human resource department recruiters? Distribution of your film will typically fall under one of three categories.

◆ Festival and contest entries
◆ Demo reel submissions
◆ Television show pitches

Festivals and Contests

There are a large number of film and animation festivals and contests where you can send your film for exposure and potential prizes. Many are actual film festivals where the accepted entries will be shown at a specific locale or perhaps in a traveling show, while others are online so viewers can visit at their leisure.

It is important to realize that as soon as a work of art is complete, it is automatically protected by copyright law. However, if you want an official US copyright on your film, visit http://www.copyright.gov and follow the instructions on the site. Just remember that an idea cannot be copyrighted—only its execution can. In other words, if you make a film about a child who discovers a TV remote control that works on the real world, you will not be able to file suit against another filmmaker who uses that same idea unless his execution is extremely similar to your own.

When you submit your film to a festival or contest, be sure to read the fine print. Some will have high entry fees that might be outside of your budget. Others might require your short to be submitted on a prohibitively expensive format, such as BetaSP or film. And some might ask you to grant them exclusive rights to show your film, so you would no longer be able to submit or display it anywhere else for a specific period of time. In general, you will probably want to steer clear of any festival that demands exclusive rights, but if it is a forum that will provide you with a large amount of exposure and possibly some financial return, weigh the pros and cons carefully. Many years ago, I (Jeremy Cantor) created a very primitive CG short on my personal Amiga computer. I submitted the film simultaneously to Spike and Mike's touring animation festival and a yearly Amiga short film contest. Spike and Mike accepted the film and a contract was written up, granting them exclusive rights for five years. Because I was young, naïve, and didn't expect anything else to possibly happen with my CG short, I excitedly signed the contract without attempting any negotiations. Days later, I learned that I had also won first place in the Amiga contest and would receive the grand prize of a $5,000 computer system! In addition to the grand prize, my film would also be featured with all of the other top entries on a videotape collection that would be sold in computer stores. Unfortunately, my celebration was cut short when I learned that Spike and Mike would not allow the Amiga folks to display my film on their videotape collection, and the Amiga folks couldn't award the grand prize unless my film could be included on the tape. I had to choose between staying in Spike and Mike's traveling show or opting out of their contract and accepting the Amiga prize instead. A compromise that would allow both was not an option. I ultimately chose Spike and Mike, figuring that the theater exposure would ultimately be more important in the long run than the limited release of the Amiga videotape collection. After sitting on it for several years, Spike and Mike eventually included my film in their touring show, and I learned a valuable lesson that granting exclusivity is typically a bad idea and should be avoided whenever possible.

In addition to Spike and Mike, the largest and arguably most prestigious festivals for animated shorts are the SIGGRAPH Electronic Theater, Annecy International, Cannes, and Sundance. Fortunately, all of these festivals have Web sites where you can obtain their submission requirements. There are few professional experiences more thrilling than seeing your short film displayed on a large screen in a festival such as one of these. At some point in your career, many of you will undoubtedly see (or perhaps you have already seen) your name included in the credits of a feature film, television show, or video game; however, such collaborative exposure typically pales in comparison to seeing your name on the big screen associated with a film that belongs exclusively to you or your team. Check sites such as http://www.awn.com, various animation magazines, and Appendix C of this book for festival listings, and then enter as many of them as possible.

When you are deciding which festivals and contests to enter, try to view and gather information about the films that have been accepted in the past and tailor your submissions accordingly. For instance, SIGGRAPH judges tend to prefer pieces with visually spectacular imagery, while the online 10 Second Club contest focuses exclusively on animation (see Figure 24.7).

The Hare as Interpreter by Red Goat Animation Studio

Figure 24.7
Some festival judges prefer CG shorts with rich and spectacular visual imagery, such as *The Hare as Interpreter* from Red Goat Productions, while others respond to simplicity and clarity in shorts, such as Eric Carney's *Framed*.

An Annie award or a grand prize at SIGGRAPH or Annecy would certainly represent an extremely significant and rewarding feather in any filmmaker's cap. But for many, the Holy Grail of short animated film recognition is an Academy Award nomination or win. If an Oscar is your ultimate goal, make sure you check their recent eligibility requirements at http://www.oscars.org before you send your film to any festivals or post it on the Internet so you don't take yourself out of the running inadvertently. Currently, for an animated short to be eligible, it needs to satisfy one of the following conditions, as stated on the Academy of Motion Picture Arts and Sciences Web site:

◆ The film must have been publicly exhibited for **paid admission** in a commercial motion picture theater in Los Angeles County for a run of at least three consecutive days (no fewer than two screenings a day). Student films cannot qualify in this manner.

◆ The film must have participated in a "recognized" competitive film festival and MUST HAVE WON THE BEST-IN-CATEGORY AWARD. Proof of award must be submitted with the film print. "Recognized" competitive film festivals comprise those established film festivals on the Academy's Short Films Awards Festival List, which may be obtained from the Academy. Television or Internet exhibition does not necessarily disqualify a film, provided such exhibition occurs *after* its Los Angeles theatrical release, or *after* receiving its festival award.

A third rule exists for student films:

◆ A student film may qualify only under II.2.(b) or by winning a Gold Medal Award in the Academy's Annual Student Academy Awards competition of 2003 (excluding the documentary category), provided it meets the length requirement. However, any student filmmaker submitting a film for consideration in the Short Films Awards categories may not subsequently enter the same film in the Student Academy Awards competition.

These rules are indeed strict, but if you manage to follow them and you find yourself nominated someday, doing so certainly will have been worth the effort.

When you submit your film to online festivals and contests, be sure to read and follow their entrance requirements carefully so you don't have to resubmit—or, worse yet, miss a deadline.

In addition to external and online festivals, there are also videotape collections that accept submissions and offer yet another opportunity for exposure and sometimes small royalties. One such distributor is Animation Entertainment, the producers of the *Mind's Eye* series. Their submission details can be found at http://www.animationtrip.com/.

Demo Reel

If you plan to use your film (or excerpts of it) on a demo reel for the purpose of applying for jobs at animation studios, game companies, or visual effects houses, there are a handful of guidelines you should follow.

◆ VHS tapes are still the best format for demo reel submissions. For any studios in the United States, make sure they are NTSC. Some studios will accept DVDs and many game companies are probably fine with CD-ROM demo reels, but always call ahead to find out what formats are preferred.

◆ A demo reel should be rather short. Two to three minutes is a good target length.

◆ Put your best work first. Demo reel reviewers are typically very busy and will often stop watching a tape after 10 seconds or so unless their attention has been sufficiently grabbed.

- One film will probably not be enough for a complete demo reel. Most studios will want to see some variety, so try to include other work, preferably showing some alternative styles and skills. But don't add weak material as filler; only include your best work on your demo reel. Also, if your film is longer than 30 seconds or so, only include snippets in the main body of your reel, and then feature the entire film at the end.

- Tailor your reel based on the specifics of your recipients, and don't send inappropriate work. A large film studio will generally want to see a singular strength, while smaller studios and game companies will want to see a wide variety of skills. A creature shop such as Tippett Studio will not want to see a reel containing spaceships and flying logos, while Nickelodeon will not want to see anything particularly bloody or erotic.

- Label your tape or disc clearly. If you are using VHS, pop your tabs and rewind your reel.

- Include your contact information in the body of the tape as well as on the label.

- Unless every visible pixel is 100 percent yours, include a reel breakdown describing your contributions to each shot on your reel.

- Don't use potentially offensive background music, such as gangsta rap or death metal, unless you are certain that your recipients favor such styles.

More information on demo reel submissions can be found at various locations on the Internet, including http://www.zayatz.com/pages/tips.htm, and a list of animation studios, visual effects houses, and game companies is included in Appendix C of this book.

TV Pitch

If you want to pitch your CG short as a proposal for a television series, you will likely need to create additional episodes. A single short will generally not suffice, although miracles can happen (as with *South Park*).

Investigate the Web pages of the major studios, networks, and distributors, such as Comedy Central and Cartoon Network, to gather the necessary information regarding pitches.

You might have to attend a large television convention, such as NATPE, NAB, or MIPCOM, to have a suitable opportunity to pitch your series idea to a variety of potential buyers. See http://www.natpe.org, http://www.nab.org, and http://www.mipcom.com for more information.

Final Thoughts

In Chapter 2, we discussed the fact that endings are typically more difficult to write than beginnings, and for this book the rule certainly holds true. Trying to summarize and conclude something profound about all that we have covered thus far would be an extremely difficult task; therefore, we will simply call this a mere milestone rather than an actual ending. If you finished reading this entire book before starting on your film, then for you, this milestone can certainly be called a new beginning.

> Accept the fact that you won't win every contest, you won't be accepted into every festival, and you won't land every job. There are many reasons why your film or demo reel might be rejected at any given time, and they don't necessarily reflect on the quality of your work. Realize that the ability to handle rejection on occasion is often the very thing that separates successful creative people from the starving artists of the world. Even J.K. Rowling's manuscript for the first Harry Potter novel was turned down by a handful of publishers before it was finally accepted. Imagine if she had given up after the first one or two rejection letters. Talent and skill are obviously important, but tenacity is also a necessary attribute for a successful CG artist.

If you have been following along and your film production is reaching its finish line as you read this chapter, then it is time to celebrate this milestone and then get busy with marketing and distribution so the world (or at least a few select viewers) can experience the glory of your cinematic excellence.

Wherever you are at this point in your production cycle, we hope that we have provided you with some helpful information and motivation. Good luck, and we hope to see you on the big (or perhaps the small) screen very soon!

appendix A
Shorts List

Alphabetical list of all animated shorts exemplified in this book. Those titles marked with a pair of asterisks can also be found on the included DVD (see Appendix E).

A Close Shave by Nick Park
http://www.aardman.com/people/nick/nick.html
The Incredible Adventures of Wallace and Gromit. Dir. Nick Park. DVD.
Warner Home Video, 2001.

Adam Powers by Richard Taylor, Information International Incorporated
http://www.planetpoint.com/richardtaylor/richardbio.html
Odyssey: The Mind's Eye Presents Computer Animation Classics. DVD. Sony
Wonder. 1999.

After You by Christopher Cordingley
http://www.rsad.edu/~ccording
SIGGRAPH 2003 Electronic Theater Program. DVD. ACM SIGGRAPH Video
Review: Issue 144. 2003.

Alien Song by Victor Navone
http://www.navone.org
SIGGRAPH 2001 Electronic Theater Program. DVD. ACM SIGGRAPH Video
Review: Issue 138. 2001.

Alma by Juan Carlos Larrea
http://www.ringling.edu/
(Portfolio...Computer Animation)
SIGGRAPH 2002 Animation Theater Program Part 2. DVD. ACM SIGGRAPH
Video Review: Issue 143. 2002.

Anniversary by Marc Aubry, Michael Hebert
Computer Animation Festival Volume 1.0. Videocassette. Miramar, 1993.

AP2000 by Loïc Bail & Aurélien Delpoux
http://www.salegosse.com
SIGGRAPH 2001 Animation Theater Program Part 1. DVD. ACM SIGGRAPH
Video Review: Issue 139. 2001.

** *Au Petite Mort* by Jerry van de Beek
http://www.littlefluffyclouds.com
SIGGRAPH 2003 Animation Theater Program Part 2. DVD. ACM SIGGRAPH
Video Review: Issue 146. 2003.

** *Baby Changing Station* by Keith Osborn
http://www.ringling.edu/
(Portfolio…Computer Animation)
SIGGRAPH 2003 Animation Theater Program Part 1. DVD. ACM SIGGRAPH Video Review: Issue 145. 2003.

Balance by Wolfgang Lauenstein, Christoph Lauenstein
The International Tournee of Animation Volume 4. Videocassette. Expanded Entertainment, 1991.

Bambi Meets Godzilla by Marv Newland
Spike & Mike's Festival of Animation Volume 1. Videocassette. Mellow Manor, 1991.

** *Bert* by Moonsung Lee
http://www.moonsunglee.com
SIGGRAPH 2003 Animation Theater Program Part 1. DVD. ACM SIGGRAPH Video Review: Issue 145. 2003.

** *Bios* by Hannes Geiger, Mathis Lex, Tobias Weigand, NLS Engler
http://www.pocketmovies.net/detail_273.html
http://db.swr.de/imkp/contest.out1?p_lw=e&p_kwid=526

Bunkie & Booboo by Terrence Masson
http://portal.acm.org/citation.cfm?id=281388.281824
Little Bytes. DVD. Image Entertainment. 2000.

Bunny by Chris Wedge
http://bunny.blueskystudios.com/bunny_home.html
Ice Age. Dir. Carlos Saldanha and Chris Wedge. 2002. DVD. Fox Home Entertainment, 2003.

** *Cane-Toad* by David Clayton & Andrew Silke
http://www.cane-toad.com
SIGGRAPH 2003 Animation Theater Program Part 1. DVD. ACM SIGGRAPH Video Review: Issue 145. 2003.

Cat Ciao by Sam Chen
http://www.ifilm.com/ifilmdetail/423380
SIGGRAPH 2000 Animation Theater Program Part 2. DVD. ACM SIGGRAPH Video Review: Issue 136. 2000.

Chromosaurus by Don Venhaus
Odyssey: The Mind's Eye Presents Computer Animation Classics. DVD. Sony Wonder. 1999.

** *Coffee Love* by Ty Primosch
SIGGRAPH 2002 Electronic Theater Program. DVD. ACM SIGGRAPH Video Review: Issue 141. 2002.

Comics Trip by Christophe Barnouin, Nathalie Bonnin, Luc Desgardin
SIGGRAPH 2001 Animation Theater Program Part 2. DVD. ACM SIGGRAPH Video Review: Issue 140. 2001.

Creature Comforts by Nick Park
http://www.aardman.com/index.html
Creature Comforts. DVD. Image Entertainment, 2000.

Das Rad (partial CG) by Chris Stenner, Arvid Uibel, Heidi Wittlinger
http://www.dasrad.com

** *Dear Sweet Emma* by Out of Our Minds Images
http://www.outofourmindsstudios.com/

Don't Touch Me by Jeff Kleiser and Diana Walczak
Computer Animation Festival Volume 1.0. Videocassette. Miramar, 1993.

Dragons by Leif Arne Peterson & Alexander Hupperic
http://www.pocketmovies.net/detail_259.html

Dronez by Leif Arne Peterson
http://www.dronez.de/

Early Bloomer by Kevin Johnson
http://www.imageworks.com/films/earlybloomer/index.html
Daddy Day Care (Special Edition). Dir. Steve Carr. 2003. DVD. Columbia Tri-Star, 2004.

** *Eat Your Peas* by Paul Hargrave
http://www.rsad.edu/portfolio/animations/EatYourPeas.html
SIGGRAPH 2003 Electronic Theater Program. DVD. ACM SIGGRAPH Video Review: Issue 144. 2003.

A. Shorts List

Egg Cola (trailer) by Sang Beom Kim
http://www.kewego.com/player/?csig=iLyROoaftYII&sig=iLyROoaftYkR
SIGGRAPH 2002 Electronic Theater Program. DVD. ACM SIGGRAPH Video
Review: Issue 141. 2002.

** *El Arquero* by Raphael Perkins
SIGGRAPH 2003 Animation Theater Program Part 1. DVD. ACM SIGGRAPH
Video Review: Issue 145. 2003.

Eternal Glaze by Sam Chen
http://www.eternalgaze.com
SIGGRAPH 2003 Electronic Theater Program. DVD. ACM SIGGRAPH Video
Review: Issue 144. 2003.

Eurhythmy by Susan Amkraut & Michael Girard
http://accad.osu.edu/~waynec/history/lesson19.html
Odyssey: The Mind's Eye Presents Computer Animation Classics. DVD. Sony
Wonder. 1999.

Evolved Virtual Creatures by Karl Sims
http://www.genarts.com/karl

** *f8* by Jason Wen
http://www.f8movie.com
SIGGRAPH 2001 Animation Theater Program Part 2. DVD. ACM SIGGRAPH
Video Review: Issue 140. 2001.

Fat Cat on a Diet by Ramon Hui
Little Bytes. DVD. Image Entertainment. 2000.

Fifty Percent Grey by Ruairi Robinson
http://www.zanitafilms.com/shorts2.html
http://www.pocketmovies.net/detail_232.html
SIGGRAPH 2002 Animation Theater Program Part 2. DVD. ACM SIGGRAPH
Video Review: Issue 143. 2002.

Fishing by David Gainey
http://pdi-mail-gw.pdi.com/shorts/fishing.htm

Fishman by Dan Bransfield
SIGGRAPH 2002 Animation Theater Program Part 2. DVD. ACM SIGGRAPH
Video Review: Issue 143. 2002.

** *Fishman Unleaded* by Dan Bransfield

Fluffy by Doug Aberle
http://www.aberle.com/
Odyssey: Computer Animation Festival, Vol. 3. DVD. Sony Wonder. 1997.

For the Birds by Ralph Eggleston
http://www.pixar.com/shorts/ftb/index.html
Monsters, Inc. Dir. Peter Docter and David Silverman. 2001. DVD. Walt Disney
Home Video, 2002.

** *Framed* by Eric Carney
http://www.sporksalot.com/animation/framed.html
SIGGRAPH 2002 Animation Theater Program Part 2. DVD. ACM SIGGRAPH
Video Review: Issue 143. 2002.

Funambule by Florent Leibovici
http://www.pocketmovies.net/cat_8_30.html

** *Garden of the Metal* by Hitoshi Akayama
SIGGRAPH 2001 Electronic Theater Program. DVD. ACM SIGGRAPH Video
Review: Issue 138. 2001.

Gas Planet by Eric Darnell
http://pdi-mail-gw.pdi.com/shorts/gasplnt.htm
Computer Animation Festival Volume 2.0. Videocassette. Miramar, 1994.

Geri's Game by Jan Pinkava
http://www.pixar.com/shorts/gg/index.html
A Bug's Life. Dir. John Lasseter and Andrew Stanton. 1998. DVD. Walt Disney
Home Video, 1999.

Getting Started by Richard Condie
http://www.awn.com/condie
Incredible Manitoba Animation. Videocassette. Whole Toon Video, 1990.

** *grain.S* by Cédric Nicolas, Vincent Meyer
http://grain.s.free.fr/#

Greynautz by Sebastian Mayer
http://www.pictoys.com

Grinning Evil Death by Mike McKenna & Bob Sabiston
Computer Animation Festival Volume 1.0. Videocassette. Miramar, 1993.
Wet Shorts: The Best of Liquid Television Vol. 1 & 2. 1991. DVD. Sony Wonder, 1997.

** *Guernica* by Marcelo Ricardo Ortiz
http://www.mrsolo.com/guernica.html

Happy Tree Friends by Mondo Media
http://www.happytreefriends.com
Happy Tree Friends - First Blood (Vol. 1). Mondo Mini Shows. DVD. Ventura Distribution, 2003.

Henry's Garden by Moon Seun and Kevin Geiger
http://www.simplisticpictures.com/
SIGGRAPH 2003 Animation Theater Program Part 2. DVD. ACM SIGGRAPH Video Review: Issue 146. 2003.

Hiccup 101 by Jessica Sances
http://www.i-am-bored.com/bored_link.cfm?link_id=7990
SIGGRAPH 2002 Animation Theater Program Part 2. DVD. ACM SIGGRAPH Video Review: Issue 143. 2002.

Horses on Mars by Eric Anderson
http://www.horsesonmars.com
SIGGRAPH 2001 Animation Theater Program Part 2. DVD. ACM SIGGRAPH Video Review: Issue 140. 2001.

How to Kiss by Bill Plympton
http://www.plymptoons.com
Spike & Mike's Festival of Animation Volume 1. Videocassette. Mellow Manor, 1991.

Hubert's Brain by Phil Robinson
http://www.hubertsbrain.com
SIGGRAPH 2001 Animation Theater Program Part 2. DVD. ACM SIGGRAPH Video Review: Issue 140. 2001.

Iceland by Leif Arne Peterson et al
http://www.pocketmovies.net/detail_222.html

I'm Walking by Elmar Keweloh
http://www.soulcage-department.de

Insight by Mathias Schreck
http://www.insight-the-movie.de
SIGGRAPH 2002 Animation Theater Program Part 2. DVD. ACM SIGGRAPH Video Review: Issue 143. 2002.

It by Zbigniew Lenard
http://www.forum3d.kom-net.pl/f3dftp.php?id=131

It's Alive by Terry Ziegelman, Paul George, Stephen Johnson, Jamie Kirschenbaum
http://www.itsalive3d.com/index2.htm

Jabberwocky by William McCrate
http://www.vfs.com/showcase.php?id=7&category_id=10&page=2

Kami by Lionel Catry, Julien Charles, Nicolas Launay, Olivier Pautot
SIGGRAPH 2001 Animation Theater Program Part 2. DVD. ACM SIGGRAPH Video Review: Issue 140. 2001.

Killer Bean 2 by Jeff Lew
http://www.jefflew.com

Knick Knack by John Lasseter
http://www.pixar.com/shorts/kk/index.html
Finding Nemo. Dir. Andrew Stanton and Lee Unkrich. 2003. DVD. Walt Disney Home Video, 2003.

La Mort de Tau by Jerome Boulbes
http://www.rascagnes.com/Tau/tau.htm
SIGGRAPH 2002 Animation Theater Program Part 1. DVD. ACM SIGGRAPH Video Review: Issue 142. 2002.

La Piedra by Alex Mateo
http://webs.ono.com/usr012/dimon

L'Autre Temps by Thomas Delcloy, Vanessa Lamblet, Celine Lardet
SIGGRAPH 2001 Animation Theater Program Part 1. DVD. ACM SIGGRAPH
Video Review: Issue 139. 2001.

Le Deserteur by Olivier Coulon, Aude Danset, Paolo De Lucia, Ludovic
Savonniere
SIGGRAPH 2002 Electronic Theater Program. DVD. ACM SIGGRAPH Video
Review: Issue 141. 2002.

Le Musicien by Patrick Ermosilla
http://lemusicienlefilm.free.fr

Le Processus by Philippe Grammaticopoulos
SIGGRAPH 2001 Animation Theater Program Part 1. DVD. ACM SIGGRAPH
Video Review: Issue 139. 2001.

Le Puits by Jerome Boulbes
http://www.rascagnes.com/lepuits/lepuits.htm

L'Enfant de la Haute Mer
Laetitia Gabrielli, Pierre Marteel, Mathieu Renoux, Max Tourret
SIGGRAPH 2001 Animation Theater Program Part 1. DVD. ACM SIGGRAPH
Video Review: Issue 139. 2001.

Locomotion by Steve Goldberg
Computer Animation Festival Volume 1.0. Videocassette. Miramar, 1993.

Lots of Robots by Andy Murdock
http://www.lotsofrobots.com

Love Tricycle by Andrew Goode
http://www.lovetricycle.com

Lunch by Keith Lango
http://www.keithlango.com
SIGGRAPH 2001 Animation Theater Program Part 1. DVD. ACM SIGGRAPH
Video Review: Issue 139. 2001.

Luxo Jr. by John Lasseter
http://www.pixar.com/shorts/ljr/index.html
Toy Story 2. Dir. Ash Brannon and John Lasseter. 1999. DVD. Walt Disney Home
Video, 2001.

Major Damage by Chris Bailey
http://www.majordamage.org

Megacycles by John Amanatides & Don Mitchell
Odyssey: The Mind's Eye Presents Computer Animation Classics. DVD. Sony
Wonder. 1999.

** *Mickey's Buddy* by Pete Paquette
http://www.ringling.edu/
(Portfolio...Computer Animation)
SIGGRAPH 2003 Electronic Theater Program. DVD. ACM SIGGRAPH Video
Review: Issue 144. 2003.

Money for Nothing (Dire Straits Video) by Ian Pearson and Steve Barron
http://www.rushes.co.uk

Monkey Pit by Jeff Fowler
http://www.jeff-fowler.com
SIGGRAPH 2002 Animation Theater Program Part 1. DVD. ACM SIGGRAPH
Video Review: Issue 142. 2002.

Moosin' Around by Saul Freed
http://www.subres.com/html/index.htm

Mouse by Wojtek Wawszcyk
http://www.mouse-the-movie.de
SIGGRAPH 2002 Animation Theater Program Part 2. DVD. ACM SIGGRAPH
Video Review: Issue 143. 2002.

O Lobisomem e o Coronel by Krishnamurti Martins Costa
http://www.antropus.com/english/framelobis.htm

** *Oblivious* by Alex Whitney
http://portal.acm.org/citation.cfm?id=945235
SIGGRAPH 2001 Animation Theater Program Part 2. DVD. ACM SIGGRAPH
Video Review: Issue 140. 2001.

Occasio by Maurius Plock
http://www.mp-grafix.de

** *On the Sunny Side of the Street* by Wilhelm Landt, Joachim Bub
SIGGRAPH 2003 Animation Theater Program Part 1. DVD. ACM SIGGRAPH
Video Review: Issue 145. 2003.

One by Two by Hardeep Singh and Suchi Pathwa
http://www.rit.edu/~hsk8182/anim.htm

Out of Memory by Eddy Moussa
http://membres.lycos.fr/garbager/

PAF le Moustique by Jerome Calvet & Jean Fracois Bourrel
http://www.trimaran.fr/paflemoustique
SIGGRAPH 2000 Animation Theater Program Part 2. DVD. ACM SIGGRAPH
Video Review: Issue 136. 2000.

Particle Dreams by Karl Sims
http://www.genarts.com/karl
Computer Animation Festival Volume 1.0. Videocassette. Miramar, 1993.

Passing Moments by Don Phillips, Jr.
http://www.donphillipsjr.com
SIGGRAPH 2002 Electronic Theater Program. DVD. ACM SIGGRAPH Video
Review: Issue 141. 2002.

Pings by Pierre Coffin
http://www.pyercoffin.com/

Plumber by Andy Knight, Richard Rosenman
http://www.redrover.net/plumber.htm
SIGGRAPH 2003 Animation Theater Program Part 1. DVD. ACM SIGGRAPH
Video Review: Issue 145. 2003.

** *Point 08* by Jamie McCarter
http://jamie.ice.org

Polar Bears "Gary's Fall" by Pierre Coffin
http://www.passion-pictures.com
SIGGRAPH 2003 Electronic Theater Program. DVD. ACM SIGGRAPH Video
Review: Issue 144. 2003.

** *Polygon Family* by Hiroshi Chida
http://www.ppi.co.jp
SIGGRAPH 2002 Electronic Theater Program. DVD. ACM SIGGRAPH Video
Review: Issue 141. 2002.

** *Pom Pom* by Laurent Caneiro
http://perso.wanadoo.fr/laurent.caneiro/site_perso.htm

** *Poor Bogo* by Thelvin Cabezas
http://www.thelvin.com/
SIGGRAPH 2003 Electronic Theater Program. DVD. ACM SIGGRAPH Video
Review: Issue 144. 2003.

Pot Belly Pete (as Barry White) by Thad Clevenger
http://www.puzzledust.com/potbellypete.htm

** *Pump Action* by Phil McNally
http://www.captain3d.com/pump/index.htm
SIGGRAPH 2000 Electronic Theater Program. DVD. ACM SIGGRAPH Video
Review: Issue 134. 2000.

** *Puppet* by Raf Anzovin
http://www.anzovin.com/
SIGGRAPH 2001 Animation Theater Program Part 1. DVD. ACM SIGGRAPH
Video Review: Issue 139. 2001.

Puppy Love by Raul Chavez
http://homepage.mac.com/raulchavez/Menu1.html

Quest: A Long Ray's Journey into Light by Michael Sciulli
Odyssey: The Mind's Eye Presents Computer Animation Classics. DVD. Sony
Wonder. 1999.

Rascagnes by Jerome Boulbes
http://jerome.boulbes.free.fr/rascagnes/tau.php

Recycle Bein' by Dominique Boidin, Fabrice Garulli, Fabrice Rabhi, Yann
Tambellini
http://recyclebein.online.fr
SIGGRAPH 2002 Electronic Theater Program. DVD. ACM SIGGRAPH Video
Review: Issue 141. 2002.

Red's Dream by John Lasseter
http://www.pixar.com/shorts/rd/index.html

Rejected by Don Hertzfeldt
http://www.bitterfilms.com

Repete by Fabrige Barbey, Patrice Mille
http://www.protozoaire.com/accueil.html

** *Respire* by Jeromé Combe, Stéphane Hamache, André Bessy
http://portal.acm.org/citation.cfm?id=1006032.1006033
SIGGRAPH 2003 Electronic Theater Program. DVD. ACM SIGGRAPH Video
Review: Issue 144. 2003.

Ritterschlag by Sven Martin
http://home.tiscalinet.de/moviecradle/ritterschlag/index.html
SIGGRAPH 2003 Animation Theater Program Part 1. DVD. ACM SIGGRAPH
Video Review: Issue 145. 2003.

** *Run, Dragon, Run!!!* by Ricardo Biriba
http://www.biriba.net/run.html

Rustboy by Brian Taylor
http://www.rustboy.com

** *Sahari* by François deBue
Francois deBue
http://www.youtube.com/watch?v=dvjFsxxUUDI

Sally Burton by Anna Kubik
http://www.sallyburton.de
SIGGRAPH 2002 Animation Theater Program Part 1. DVD. ACM SIGGRAPH
Video Review: Issue 142. 2002.

Sam by Kyle Winkelman
http://portal.acm.org/citation.cfm?id=1006091.1006099
SIGGRAPH 2003 Animation Theater Program Part 1. DVD. ACM SIGGRAPH
Video Review: Issue 145. 2003.

Sarah by Justine Bonnard, Anthony Malagutti, Ludovic Ramiere, Thomas Renault
SIGGRAPH 2002 Electronic Theater Program. DVD. ACM SIGGRAPH Video
Review: Issue 141. 2002.

Senza Azione by Krishnamurti Martins Costa
http://www.antropus.com/senzaazione

** *Silhouette* by Tonya Noerr & Amber Rudolph
SIGGRAPH 2001 Animation Theater Program Part 1. DVD. ACM SIGGRAPH
Video Review: Issue 139. 2001.

Snookles by Juliet Stroud
The International Tournee of Animation Volume 2. Videocassette. Expanded
Entertainment, 1989.
Spike & Mike's Festival of Animation Volume 1. Videocassette. Mellow Manor,
1991.

SOS by Cameron Miyasaki
http://www.cameronmiyasaki.com
SIGGRAPH 2002 Animation Theater Program Part 2. DVD. ACM SIGGRAPH
Video Review: Issue 143. 2002.

Sprout by Scott Peterson
http://pdi-mail-gw.pdi.com/shorts/sprout.htm
SIGGRAPH 2002 Electronic Theater Program. DVD. ACM SIGGRAPH Video
Review: Issue 141. 2002.

** *Squaring Off* by Jeremy Cantor
http://www.zayatz.com
North America's Best Independent Animated Shorts. DVD. Raider Productions,
2003.

Sr. Trapo by Paco Gisbert
http://www.pasozebra.com

Stanley and Stella in "Breaking the Ice" by Larry Malone
Odyssey: The Mind's Eye Presents Computer Animation Classics. DVD. Sony
Wonder. 1999.

Tango by Zbigniew Rybcynski
Spike & Mike's Festival of Animation Volume 1. Videocassette. Mellow Manor,
1991.

A. Shorts List

439

Technological Threat by Bill Kroyer
http://www.rhythm.com/commercial/animation_directors_bill_bio.shtml
Computer Animation Festival Volume 2.0. Videocassette. Miramar, 1994.

The Adventures of Andre and Wally B by Alvy Ray Smith, John Lasseter
(Lucasfilm Ltd)
http://www.pixar.com/shorts/awb

The Big Snit by Richard Condie
http://www.awn.com/condie
Incredible Manitoba Animation. Videocassette. Whole Toon Video, 1990.

** *The Butterfly* by Leonid Larionov
http://www.leo3d.com

The Cat Came Back by Cordell Barker
http://www.keyframeonline.com/kf.php?op=details&a=218
Incredible Manitoba Animation. Videocassette. Whole Toon Video, 1990.

The Cathedral by Tomek Baginski
http://www.platige.com/index.php?lng=en&tu=27
The Cathedral. Dir. Tomek Baginski. 2002. DVD. Platige Image, 2003.
SIGGRAPH 2002 Electronic Theater Program. DVD. ACM SIGGRAPH Video
Review: Issue 141. 2002.

The Chubbs Chubbs by Eric Armstrong
The Chubb Chubbs. Dir. Eric Armstrong. 2002. DVD. Columbia Tri-Star, 2003.

The Crossing Guard by Joshua West
http://www.m3corp.com/a/gallery/galleryanim02.htm
SIGGRAPH 2001 Electronic Theater Program. DVD. ACM SIGGRAPH Video
Review: Issue 138. 2001.

The Deadline by Stefan Marjoram
http://www.animwatch.com/Spotlight-Deadline.php

The Dog Who Was a Cat Inside by Siri Melchior
http://www.passion-pictures.com
SIGGRAPH 2003 Electronic Theater Program. DVD. ACM SIGGRAPH Video
Review: Issue 144. 2003.

The Freak by Aristomenis Tsirbas
http://www.menithings.com

The Great Cognito by Will Vinton
World's Greatest Animation. Videocassette. Expanded Entertainment, 1994.

The Hare as Interpreter by Istvan Zorkoczy, Andras Liptak
http://www.redgoat.nl

The Instant Animator Machine by Rick May
SIGGRAPH 2001 Electronic Theater Program. DVD. ACM SIGGRAPH Video
Review: Issue 138. 2001.

The Invisible Man in Blind Love by Pascal Vuong
Computer Animation Festival Volume 1.0. Videocassette. Miramar, 1993.

The Mantis Parable by Josh Staub
http://www.themantisparable.com

The Moving Pyramid by Wolf-Rudiger Bloss & Camille Eden
SIGGRAPH 2001 Animation Theater Program Part 1. DVD. ACM SIGGRAPH
Video Review: Issue 139. 2001.

The Sandman by Paul Berry
The International Tournee of Animation Volume 6. Videocassette. Expanded
Entertainment, 1994.

** *The Snowman* by Lane Nakamura
http://www.duckstudios.com
SIGGRAPH 2002 Electronic Theater Program. DVD. ACM SIGGRAPH Video
Review: Issue 141. 2002.

The Sorcerer's Apprentice by Ben Sharpsteen and James Algar
Fantasia (60th Anniversary Special Edition). Dir. Ford Beebe, et al. 1940.
DVD. Disney Studios, 2000.

** *The Terrible Tragedy of Virgil and Maurice* by Morgan Kelly

The Wrong Trousers by Nick Park
http://www.wallaceandgromit.com/
The Incredible Adventures of Wallace and Gromit. Dir. Nick Park. DVD.
Warner Home Video, 2001.

Theme Planet by Michael Sormann
http://www.sormann3d.com/portfolio/TPindex.htm

Tim Tom by Romain Segaud, Christel Pougeoise
SIGGRAPH 2003 Electronic Theater Program. DVD. ACM SIGGRAPH Video
Review: Issue 144. 2003.

Tin Toy by John Lasseter
http://www.pixar.com/shorts/tt/index.html
Toy Story. Dir. John Lasseter. 1995. DVD. Walt Disney Home Video, 2001.

Tinny Tom and the Magic Box by Michiel Krop, Stijn Windig
http://www.tinnytom.com

** *Toilet* by Makoto Koyama

** *Tom the Cat* by Bastien Charrier, Patrick Jean, Lucas Salton, Neila Terrien
http://tomthecat.free.fr

Tony de Peltrie by Pierre Lachapelle, Philippe Bergeron, Pierre Robidoux,
Daniel Langlois
Odyssey: The Mind's Eye Presents Computer Animation Classics. DVD. Sony
Wonder. 1999.

** *Top Gum* by Victor Vinyals
http://kotoc3d.com/victor
SIGGRAPH 2002 Animation Theater Program Part 2. DVD. ACM SIGGRAPH
Video Review: Issue 143. 2002.

Traffic Jam by Ty Primosch
http://www.siggraph.org/artdesign/gallery/S02/onreel/Primosch/1reelpreview.html

** *Values* by Van Phan
SIGGRAPH 2001 Electronic Theater Program. DVD. ACM SIGGRAPH Video
Review: Issue 138. 2001.

** *Venice Beach* by Jung-Ho Kim

When Wolfy Met Holga by Mookie Weisbrod
SIGGRAPH 2001 Animation Theater Program Part 1. DVD. ACM SIGGRAPH
Video Review: Issue 139. 2001.

Where is Frank by Angela Jedek
SIGGRAPH 2001 Electronic Theater Program. DVD. ACM SIGGRAPH Video
Review: Issue 138. 2001.

Within an Endless Sky by Lance Winkel
http://lance.phlinux.com
SIGGRAPH 2002 Animation Theater Program Part 1. DVD. ACM SIGGRAPH
Video Review: Issue 142. 2002.

Yeah! The Movie by Spellcraft Studio
http://www.yeahthemovie.de
SIGGRAPH 2003 Animation Theater Program Part 1. DVD. ACM SIGGRAPH
Video Review: Issue 145. 2003.

appendix B
Suggested Reading

I n keeping with the spirit of *Inspired 3D Short Film Production*, the following list is restricted to books that are not software-specific.

General

Albee, Timothy. *CGI Filmmaking: The Creation of Ghost Warrior*. Plano: Wordware Publishing, Inc., 2004.

Kerlow, Isaac V. *The Art of 3D Computer Animation and Effects, Third Edition*. Hoboken: John Wiley, 2004.

Masson, Terrence. *CG 101: A Computer Graphics Industry Reference*. Indianapolis: New Riders, 1999.

Patmore, Chris. *The Complete Animation Course: The Principles, Practice, and Techniques of Successful Animation*. Hauppauge: Barron's Educational Series, Inc., 2003.

Simon, Mark. *Producing Independent 2D Character Animation: Making and Selling a Short Film*. Burlington, MA: Focal Press, 2003.

Street, Rita. *Computer Animation: A Whole New World*. Gloucester: Rockport Publishers, Inc., 1998.

Subotnick, Steven. *Animation in the Home Digital Studio: Creation to Distribution*. Burlington, MA: Elsevier Science, 2003.

Story and Character Development

Bernays, Anne and Pamela Painter. *What If? Writing Exercises for Fiction Writers*. New York: HarperCollins, 1990.

Blacker, Irwin R. *The Elements of Screenwriting: A Guide for Film and Television Writers*. New York: Macmillan Publishing Company, 1986.

Cleaver, Jerry. *Immediate Fiction: A Complete Writing Course*. New York: St. Martin's Press, 2002.

Edelstein, Linda. *The Writer's Guide to Character Traits*. Cincinnati, Ohio: Writer's Digest Books, 1999.

Egri, Lajos. *The Art of Dramatic Writing*. New York: Touchstone Books, 1972.

Field, Syd. *The Screenwriter's Workbook*. New York: Dell Publishing, 1984.

Hunter, Lew. *Lew Hunter's Screenwriting 434*. New York: Perigee Books, 1993.

Klein, Norman M. *Seven Minutes: The Life and Death of the American Animated Cartoon*. London: Verso, 1993.

Mankoff, Robert. *The Naked Cartoonist: A New Way to Enhance Your Creativity*. New York: Black Dog & Leventhal Pub, 2002.

McKee, Robert. *Story: Substance, Structure, Style, and the Principles of Screenwriting*. New York: HarperCollins, 1997.

Phillips, Kathleen C. *How to Write a Story*. New York: Franklin Watts, 1995.

Rubie, Peter and Gary Provost. *How to Tell a Story: The Secrets of Writing Captivating Tales.* Cincinnati, OH: Writer's Digest Books, 1998.

Smith, James V. Jr. *Fiction Writer's Brainstormer.* Cincinnati: Writer's Digest Books, 2000.

Tierno, Michael. *Aristotle's Poetics for Screenwriters: Storytelling Secrets from the Greatest Mind in Western Civilization.* New York: Hyperion, 2002.

Vogler, Christopher. *The Writer's Journey: Mythic Structure for Storytellers and Screenwriters.* Studio City: Michael Wiese Productions, 1992.

Webber, Marilyn. *Gardner's Guide to Animation Scriptwriting: The Writer's Road Map.* Fairfax: GGC Inc., 2000.

Character Design and Art Direction

Bland, Celia, Jane P. Resnick and Robert Matero. *Creepy Creatures.* New York: Kidsbooks, Inc., 1998.

Canemaker, John. *Before the Animation Begins: The Art and Lives of Disney Inspirational Sketch Artists.* New York: Hyperion, 1996.

Carney, Charles and Allen Helbig. *The Art of Space Jam.* Nashville: Rutledge Hill Press, Inc., 1996.

Carson, Mary Kay. *The Creepiest, Scariest, Weirdest Creatures Ever.* New York: Kidsbooks, Inc., 2002.

Culhane, John. *Disney's Aladdin: The Making of an Animated Film.* New York: Hyperion, 1992.

Dini, Paul and Chip Kidd. *Batman: Animated.* New York: Harper Entertainment, 1998.

Green, Howard E. *The Tarzan Chronicles.* New York: Hyperion, 1999.

Hahn, Don. *Disney's Animation Magic.* New York: Disney Press, 2000.

Hamm, Jack. *Cartooning the Head and Figure.* New York: Perigee, 1986 (Reissue edition).

Hart, Christopher. *Cartooning for the Beginner.* New York: Watson-Guptill Publications, 2000.

Hurter, Albert. *He Drew As He Pleased.* New York: Simon and Schuster, 1948.

Jones, Chuck. *Chuck Redux: Drawing from the Fun Side of Life.* New York: Warner Books, Inc., 1996.

Kent, Steven L. *The Making of Final Fantasy: The Spirits Within.* Indianapolis, IN: Brady Games, 2001.

Kistler, Mark. *Drawing in 3-D.* New York: Fireside, 1998.

Kurtti, Jeff, et al. *Treasure Planet: A Voyage of Discovery.* New York: Welcome Enterprises, 2002.

Kurtti, Jeff. *A Bug's Life: The Art and Making of an Epic of Miniature Proportions.* New York: Hyperion, 1998.

Lasseter, John and Pete Docter. *The Art of Monsters, Inc.* San Francisco: Chronicle Books, 2001.

Lasseter, John and Peter Daly. *Toy Story: The Art and Making of the Animated Film.* New York: Hyperion, 1995.

Lord, Peter and Brian Sibley. *Creating 3-D Animation: The Aardman Book of Filmmaking.* New York: Harry N. Abrams, Inc., 1998.

Rebello, Stephen and Jane Healey. *The Art of Hercules: The Chaos of Creation.* New York: Hyperion, 1997.

Schneider, Steve. *That's All Folks: The Art of Warner Bros. Animation.* New York: Henry Holt and Company, 1988.

Seegmiller, Don. *Digital Character Design and Painting.* Hingham: Charles River Media, Inc., 2003.

Thomas, Frank and Ollie Johnston. *The Disney Villains.* New York: Hyperion, 1993.

Thompson, Frank. *Tim Burton's Nightmare Before Christmas.* New York: Hyperion, 1993.

Thomas, Bob. *Disney's Art of Animation.* New York: Hyperion, 1991.

Vaz, Mark Cotta. *The Art of Finding Nemo.* San Francisco: Chronicle Books, 2003.

Wachowski, Larry. *The Art of the Matrix.* New York: Newmarket Press, 2000.

Wakabayashi, Hiro Clark (Ed). *Lilo & Stitch: Collected Stories from the Film's Creators.* New York: Welcome Enterprises, Inc., 2002.

Weishar, Peter. *Blue Sky: The Art of Computer Animation.* New York: Harry N. Abrams, Inc., 2002.

Withrow, Steven. *Toon Art: The Graphic Art of Digital Cartooning.* New York: Watson-Guptill Publications, 2003.

Storyboarding and Scene Planning

Begleiter, Marcie. *From Word to Image: Storyboarding and the Filmmaking Process*. Studio City: Michael Wiese Productions, 2001.

Block, Bruce. *The Visual Story: Seeing the Structure of Film, TV, and New Media*. Burlington, MA: Focal Press, 2001.

Canemaker, John. *Paper Dreams: The Art and Artists of Disney Storyboards*. New York: Hyperion, 1999.

Katz, Steven D. *Cinematic Motion: A Workshop for Staging Scenes*. Studio City: Michael Wiese Productions, 1992.

Katz, Steven D. *Film Directing, Shot by Shot: Visualizing from Concept to Screen*. Studio City: Michael Wiese Productions, 1991.

Piper, Jim. *Get the Picture: The Movie Lover's Guide to Watching Films*. New York: Allworth Press, 2001.

Sibley, Brian (ed). *Wallace & Gromit, A Close Shave: Storyboard Collection*. London: BBC Children's Publishing, 1997.

Simon, Mark. *Storyboards: Motion in Art*. Burlington, MA: Focal Press, 2000.

Vineyard, Jeremy. *Setting up Your Shots: Great Camera Moves Every Filmmaker Should Know*. Studio City: Michael Wiese Productions, 2000.

Production Planning

Simon, Mark. *Producing Independent 2D Character Animation: Making and Selling a Short Film*. Burlington, MA : Focal Press, 2003.

Subotnick, Steven. *Animation in the Home Digital Studio: Creation to Distribution*. Burlington, MA: Elsevier Science, 2003.

Winder, Catherine and Zahra Dowlatabadi. *Producing Animation*. Burlington, MA: Focal Press, 2001.

Animatics and Film Direction

Goodman, Robert M. and Patrick McGrath. *Editing Digital Video: The Complete Creative and Technical Guide*. London: McGraw-Hill, 2002.

Heffernan, Leo J. *Editing for Better Movies*. Plainville: Kalart Co, 1995.

Katz, Steven D. *Cinematic Motion: A Workshop for Staging Scenes*. Studio City: Michael Wiese Productions, 1992.

Katz, Steven D. *Film Directing, Shot by Shot: Visualizing from Concept to Screen*. Studio City: Michael Wiese Productions, 1991.

Mascelli, Joseph V. *The Five C's of Cinematography: Motion Picture Filming Techniques*. Los Angeles: Silman-James Press, 1998.

Murch, Walter. *In the Blink of an Eye: A Perspective on Film Editing*. Los Angeles: Silman-James Press, 1995.

Piper, Jim. *Get the Picture: The Movie Lover's Guide to Watching Films*. New York: Allworth Press, 2001.

Thompson, Roy. *Grammar of the Edit*. Burlington, MA: Focal Press, 1993.

Thompson, Roy. *Grammar of the Shot*. Burlington, MA: Focal Press, 1998.

Vineyard, Jeremy. *Setting up Your Shots: Great Camera Moves Every Filmmaker Should Know*. Studio City: Michael Wiese Productions, 2000.

Ward, Peter. *Picture Composition for Film and Television, Second Edition*. Burlington, MA: Focal Press, 2003.

Modeling, Texturing, and Character Setup

Calais-Germain, Blandine. *Anatomy of Movement*. Seattle: Eastland Press, 1993.

Capizzi, Tom. *Inspired 3D Modeling and Texture Mapping*. Cincinnati: Premier Press, Inc., 2002.

Demers, Owen. *Digital Texturing & Painting*. Indianapolis: New Riders, 2001.

Ebert, David et al. *Texturing & Modeling: A Procedural Approach, Third Edition*. San Francisco: Morgan Kaufmann, 2002.

Eiseman, Leatrice. *Pantone Guide to Communicating with Color*. Design Books, 2000.

Ford, Michael and Alan Lehman. *Inspired 3D Character Setup.* Cincinnati: Premier Press, Inc., 2002.

Patmore, Chris. *The Complete Animation Course: The Principles, Practice, and Techniques of Successful Animation.* Hauppauge, New York: Barron's Educational Series, Inc., 2003.

Animation

Blair, Preston. *Cartoon Animation (The Collector's Series).* Tustin: Walter Foster Publications, 1995.

Brown, Curtis M. *Dog Locomotion and Gait Analysis.* Wheat Ridge: Hoflin Publishing Ltd., 1986.

Cervone, Tom. *Animating the Looney Tunes Way.* Laguna Hills: Walter Foster Publishing, Inc., 2000.

Clark, Kyle. *Inspired 3D Character Animation.* Cincinnati: Premier Press, Inc., 2002.

Hooks, Ed. *Acting for Animators.* Portsmouth: Heinemann, 2000.

Thomas, Frank and Ollie Johnston. *The Illusion of Life: Disney Animation.* New York: Hyperion, 1995.

Maestri, George. *Digital Character Animation 2, Volume I: Essential Techniques.* Indianapolis: New Riders, 1999.

Morris, Desmond. *Manwatching: A Field Guide to Human Behavior.* New York: Harry N. Abrams, Inc., 1977.

Schatz, Howard. *Athlete.* New York: HarperCollns/Wonderland Press, 2002.

Whitaker, Harold and John Halas. *Timing for Animation.* Oxford: Reed Educational and Professional Publishing Ltd., 1981.

Williams, Richard. *The Animator's Survival Kit.* London: Faber & Faber, 2002.

Lighting, Rendering, and Compositing

Alton, John. *Painting with Light.* Berkeley: University of California Press, 1995.

Birn, Jeremy. *Digital Lighting & Rendering.* Indianapolis: New Riders, 2000.

Brinkman, Ron. *The Art and Science of Digital Compositing.* San Francisco: Morgan Kaufmann, 1999.

Gillette, Michael. *Designing with Light: An Introduction to Stage Lighting.* Palo Alto: Mayfield Publishing Co., 1978.

Kelly, Doug. *Digital Compositing in Depth.* Scottsdale: Coriolis, 2000.

Parrish, David. *Inspired 3D Lighting and Compositing.* Cincinnati: Premier Press, Inc., 2002.

Wright, Steve. *Digital Compositing for Film and Video.* Burlington, MA: Focal Press, 2002.

Post-Production

Goodman, Robert M. and Patrick McGrath. *Editing Digital Video: The Complete Creative and Technical Guide.* London: McGraw-Hill, 2002.

Patmore, Chris. *The Complete Animation Course: The Principles, Practice, and Techniques of Successful Animation.* Hauppauge: Barron's Educational Series, Inc., 2003.

Simon, Mark. *Producing Independent 2D Character Animation: Making and Selling a Short Film.* Burlington, MA: Focal Press, 2003.

Subotnick, Steven. *Animation in the Home Digital Studio: Creation to Distribution.* Burlington, MA: Elsevier Science, 2003.

appendix C
Selected Resources

Schools

Academy of Art University. San Francisco, CA: http://www.academyart.edu

California Institute of the Arts. Valencia, CA: http://www.calarts.edu

Gnomon School of Visual Effects. CA: http://www.gnomon3d.com

The German Film School: http://www.filmschool.de

Ohio State University: http://www.cgrg.ohio-state.edu

Pratt Institute, Brooklyn, NY: http://www.pratt.edu

Ringling School of Art and Design. Sarasota, FL: http://www.ringling.edu

School of Visual Arts. New York, NY: http://www.sva.edu

Sheridan College. Ontario, Canada: http://www.sheridanc.on.ca

Supinfocom. Les Valenccienes, France: http://www.supinfocom.fr

Texas A&M University: http://www-viz.tamu.edu

Vancouver Film School. Canada: http://vfs.com

University of Southern California: http://www.usc.edu/schools/cntv

For a more complete list of schools that offer programs in animation, see http://schools.awn.com.

Festivals, Competitions, and Conferences

Anifest: http://www.anifest.cz

Anima: http://www.awn.com/folioscope

Anima Mundi: http://www.animamundi.com.br

Animex: http://www.animex.org.uk

Annecy: http://www.annecy.org

ARS Electronica: http://www.aec.at/en/index.asp

BIMINI: http://www.bimini.lv

Bradford Animation Festival: http://www.baf.org.uk/2004/home.asp

Bristol International Animation Festival: http://www.animated-encounters.org.uk

Festival de Cannes: http://www.festival-cannes.fr

Filmfest Dresden: http://www.filmfest-dresden.de

Imagina: http://www.imagina.mc

Kalamazoo Animation Festival International: http://kafi.kvcc.edu

Krok: http://www.animator.ru/krok

LA International Short Film Festival: http://www.lashortsfest.com

Melbourne International Animation Festival: http://www.miaf.net

Ottawa International Animation Festival: http://www.awn.com/ottawa

Prix Ars Electronica: http://www.aec.at/festival

SIGGRAPH: http://www.siggraph.org

Sundance Film Festival: http://festival.sundance.org

World's Smallest Film Festival: http://www.bigdigit.com/bigdigit0.htm

Zagreb: http://www.animafest.hr

For a more complete list of festivals and competitions, see http://www.aidb.com/index.php?ltype=list&cat=btype&btype=013.

Magazines

3D World: http://www.3dworldmag.com

Animation Blast: http://www.animationblast.com

Animation Magazine: http://www.animationmagazine.net

Cinefex: http://www.cinefex.com

Computer Arts: http://www.computerarts.co.uk

Computer Graphics World: http://cgw.pennnet.com/home.cfm

Keyframe: http://www.keyframemag.com

Online Festivals and Magazines

3DVF: http://www.3dvf.com

Animation Artist: http://www.animationartist.com

AnimWatch: http://www.animwatch.com

Atom Films: http://atomfilms.shockwave.com/af/home

CG Channel: http://www.cgchannel.com

CG Focus: http://www.cgfocus.com/animations.cfm

CGNetworks CG Films: http://www.cgnetworks.com/cgfilms

ifilm: http://www.ifilm.com

Inside Computer Graphics: http://www.insidecg.com

Pocket Movies: http://www.pocketmovies.net

The 10 Second Club: http://10secondclub.net

VFXWorld: http://vfxworld.com

VOC CG MAG: http://www.vocanson.com

Online Forums and Other Animation and CG Resources

3D Ark: http://www.3dark.com

3D Gate: http://www.3dgate.com

3D Total: http://www.3dtotal.com

Animation Foundation: http://www.animfound.com

Animation Industry Database: http://aidb.com

Animation Meat: http://www.animationmeat.com

Animation World Network: http://www.awn.com

Asifa: http://asifa.net

CG-Char Animation Forum: http://cgchar.toonstruck.com/forum/index.php

CG Focus: http://www.cgfocus.com

CGNetworks: http://www.cgnetworks.com

CGTalk (forum): http://www.cgtalk.com

Death Fall: http://www.deathfall.com

Digital Sculpting Forum: http://cube.phlatt.net/forums/spiraloid/index.php

Highend 3D: http://www.highend3d.com

CG History

CGI Historical Timeline: http://www.accad.ohio-state.edu/~waynec/
history/timeline.html

Historical Timeline: http://www.rit.edu/~dpalyka/702_Timeline.html

Kerlow's Art of 3D Computer Animation, Timelines and Milestones:
http://www.artof3d.com/timelines.htm

Milestones of the Animation Industry in the 20th Century:
http://www.awn.com/mag/issue4.10/4.10pages/cohenmilestones.php3

A Short History of ACCAD: http://www.accad.ohio-state.edu/~waynec/history/
ACCAD-overview/cgrg-history.html

SIGGRAPH: Past and Present: http://www.awn.com/mag/issue2.5/2.5pages/
2.5collinssiggraph.html

A (Spotty) History and Who's Who of Computer Graphics:
http://www.cs.wpi.edu/~matt/courses/cs563/talks/history.html

Story Principles

Professor Henry Jenkins' Genres of Entertainment:
http://web.mit.edu/21fms/www/faculty/henry3/genre.html

Barry Pearson's Links to Internet Articles on Writing Screenplays:
http://www.createyourscreenplay.com/bpIndex.html

Character Design and Art Direction

Action Figures at Kidrobot: http://www.kidrobot.com

Andrew Bell's Collection of Creatures: http://www.creaturesinmyhead.com

Boring3D: http://www.boring3d.com

Brom Gallery: http://www.bromart.com/gallery/index.html

Carlos Baena: http://www.carlosbaena.com

Chip Wass: http://www.worldofwassco.com

Christian Haley Digital Surreal Art Gallery: http://www.christianhaley.com

Christian Senn's Creatures and Monsters: http://www.senntient.com/see

Commedia dell'arte: http://www.geocities.com/commedia_dellarte

Dan Paladin's Wacky Characters: http://www.synj.net

Don Seegmiller: http://seegmillerart.com

Feng Zhu: http://www.artbyfeng.com

Frank Frazetta: http://www.wadhome.org/frazetta

Kirsten Ulve: http://www.kirstenulve.com

Michel Gagne: http://www.gagneint.com

Pixar: http://www.pixar.com

Simon Bisley: http://www.simonbisleyonline.com

Stephan Martiniere: http://www.martiniere.com

The Alphabet of Art: http://www.guidancecom.com/alphabet

Storyboarding

Storyboards, Inc.: http://www.storyboardsinc.com

Famous Frames, Inc: http://www.famousframes.com

Animation and Lip Synching Tips

Animation Meat: http://www.animationmeat.com/index2.html

Keith Lango: http://www.keithlango.com

Michael B. Comet: http://www.comet-cartoons.com/toons/3dhelp.cfm

Flay.com Tutorial Links: http://www.flay.com/LinksByCategory.cfm?CategoryID=6

Facial Animation Papers: http://mambo.ucsc.edu/psl/fan.html

Digital Resources (Models, Rigs, Scripts, Etc.)

3D Café: http://www.3dcafe.com

Andrew Silke's Generi Rig: http://andrewsilke.com/generi_rig/generi_rig.htm

Creature Tools for Maya: http://www.ant-online.co.uk/downloads/CreatureTools.htm

Highend 3D (Scripts, Tips, Tutorials, Etc.): http://www.highend3d.com

Hou Soon Ming's 3d Toon Shop: http://www.its-ming.com

Javier "Goosh" Solsona's "IK-Joe" for Maya: http://www.vfs.com/~m07goosh/freestuff.htm

SimpleGuy for Maya: http://www.turbosquid.com/HTMLClient/FullPreview/FullPreview.cfm/ID/184717/Action/FullPreview

The Setup Machine for Maya/Lightwave/Animation Master: http://www.anzovin.com/setupmachine/index.html

TurboSquid: http://www.turbosquid.com

appendix D
Full Image Credits

Full credits appear in first listings only. Please note: Regardless of whether an actual copyright symbol is included in the corresponding credit found in the list below, all of the images in this book are copyrighted material and may not be reproduced in any form without the expressed written consent of their original creators. Also note, all un-credited images are by the authors.

Front Cover (main image): *Pom Pom* by Laurent Caneiro
Front Cover (film strip): *Squaring Off* by Jeremy Cantor ~ *Cane-Toad* by David Clayton & Andrew Silke ~ *Puppet* © 2001–2004 by Anzovin Studio. All rights reserved. ~ *Bert* by Moonsung Lee
Back Cover: *Run, Dragon, Run!!!* by Ricardo Biriba

I-01: *Technological Threat* © 2004 KFI. Dir: Bill Kroyer **I-02:** *Hiccup 101* © 2002 Jessica Sances ~ *L'Enfant de la Haute Mer* by Laetitia Gabrielli, Pierre Marteel, Mathieu Renoux, Max Tourret © Supinfocom Valenciennes ~ *Pot Bellie Pete* © Thad Clevenger ~ *Naomi Cantor* **01-01:** *Sahari* © Francois De Bue **01-02:** *Framed* by Eric Carney ~ *Bert* ~ *Das Rad* by Chris Stenner, Arvid Uibel, Heidi Wittlinger, Georg Gruber (Producer) ~ *Recycle Bein'* by Dominique Boidin, Fabrice Garulli, Fabrice Rabhi, Yann Tambellini © Supinfocom Valenciennes ~ *Ritterschlag* by Sven Martin (CG) & Ulrich Zeidler (sketches) ~ *Pump Action* by Phil Captain 3D McNally **01-03:** *Adam Powers* by Information International Incorporated. Dir: Richard Taylor **01-04:** *Money for Nothing* (music video) by Ian Pearson & Steve Barron © Rushes Post Production Ltd. **01-05:** *Technological Threat* **01-06:** *Particle Dreams* © 1988 Karl Sims ~ *Eurhythmy* by Susan Amkraut & Michael Girard **01-07:** *Grinning Evil Death* by Mike McKenna & Bob Sabiston © 1990 Massachusetts Institute of Technology **01-08:** *Evolved Virtual Creatures* © 1994 Karl Sims **01-09:** *Tim Tom* by Romain Segaud, Christel Pougeoise © Supinfocom Valenciennes **01-10:** *Point 08* © Jamie McCarter ~ *Mouse* by Wojtek Wawszczyk, Filmakademie Baden-Wuerttembert, The Polish National Film, TV & Theatre School **01-11:** *Respire* © 2003 Virgin. Dir: Jérome Combe, Stéphane Hamache, André Bessy **01-12:** *Passing Moments* by Don Phillips, Jr. ~ *Killer Bean 2* by Jeffrey Lew **01-13:** *Alien Song* © Victor Navone **01-14:** *Rejected* © Bitter Films / Don Hertzfeldt **01-15:** *Bert* ~ *Squaring Off* by Jeremy Cantor ~ *Framed* ~ *Values* by Van Phan, University of Southern California School of Film & Television ~ *Lunch* © 2001 Keith Lango ~ *Toilet* by Makoto Koyama **01-16:** *The Chubb Chubbs* © 2002 Sony Pictures Digital Inc. Dir: Eric Armstrong **01-17:** *The Cathedral* © 2002 Platige Image, Tomek Baginski **01-18:** *The Butterfly* © 2003 Leonid Larionov **02-01:** *Within an Endless Sky* © 2002 Lance S. Winkel **02-02:** *Bert* **02-03:** *Fifty Percent Grey* by Ruairi Robinson **02-04:** © 2004 Jason Taylor ~ *Poor Bogo* by Thelvin Cabezas ~ *Theme Planet* © 2002 Michael Sormann. All rights reserved ~ *Fishman* by Dan Bransfield ~ *The Freak* by Aristomenis Tsirbas ~ *Rustboy* © 2004 Brian Taylor ~ *Run, Dragon, Run!!!* by Ricardo Biriba ~ *Theme Planet* **02-05:** *One by Two* © Hardeep Kharbanda & Suruchi Pahwa **02-06:** *Hubert's Brain* © 2001 Wild Brain, Inc. Dir: Phil Robinson ~ *Occasio* by Marius Plock © MP-GRAFIX Digital Animation ~ *The Terrible Tragedy of Virgil & Maurice* © 2003 Morgan Kelly **02-07:** *Garden of the Metal* by Hitoshi Akayama, Katsuyuki Kamei, Koichi Nishi **02-08:** *Pump Action* ~ *Creature Comforts* © 1989 Aardman Animation Ltd. Dir: Peter Lord **02-09:** *El Arquero* by

Raphael Perkins © Vancouver Film School **02-10:** Jason Taylor **02-11:** *Point 08* **02-12:** *Top Gum* by Victor Vinyals **02-13:** *AP2000* by Loïc Bail & Aurélien Delpoux © Supinfocom Valenciennes **02-14:** *Polygon Family 2* by Hiroshi Chida **02-15:** *Dronez* by Leif Arne Petersen, Manuel Macha, Alex Hupperich **02-16:** *Alien Song* **02-17:** *Values ~ Run, Dragon, Run!!! ~ Fishman ~ Guernica* by Marcelo Ricardo Ortiz © 2002 Vancouver Film School *~ Tom the Cat* by Bastien Charrier, Patrick Jean, Lucas Salton, Neila Terrien © Supinfocom Valenciennes *~ ƒ8* by Jason Wen © Spot of Bother LLC **02-18:** *Comics Trip* by Christophe Barnouin, Nathalie Bonnin, Luc Desgardin © Supinfocom Valenciennes *~ Pom Pom* by Laurent Caneiro *~ Recycle Bein'* **02-20:** *SOS* by Cameron Miyasaki **02-21:** *Oblivious* by Alex Whitney **02-22:** *Snookles* by Juliet Stroud-Duncans **02-23:** *Egg Cola* © Independence, Inc. All rights reserved. **02-24:** *Le Processus* by Philippe Grammaticopoulos © Supinfocom Valenciennes **02-25:** *Silhouette* © Tonya Noerr & Amber Rudolph, Ringling School of Art & Design **02-26:** *Coffee Love* © 2002 Ty Primosch **02-27:** *Le Deserteur* by Olivier Coulon, Aude Danset, Paolo De Lucia, Ludovic Savonniere © Supinfocom Valenciennes **02-28:** *Au Petite Mort* © 2003 Jerry van de Beek & Betsy De Fries **02-29:** *Eat Your Peas* by Paul Hargrave *~ Rascagnes* © Jerome Boulbes/Lardux Films *~ The Dog Who Was a Cat Inside* © Siri Melchior, Passion Pictures, Channel 4 *~ Poor Bogo ~ grain.S* by Vincent Meyer & Cédric Nicolas © 2002 Sapokruteno *~ Repete* by Fabrice Barbey, Protozoaire Production **02-30:** *L'Enfant de la Haute Mer* **02-31:** clipart.com **02-32:** *The Wrong Trousers* © 1993 Aardman / Wallace & Gromit Ltd. Dir: Nick Park **02-33:** Aaron Clement **02-34:** *The Terrible Tragedy of Virgil & Maurice* **02-35:** *Fishman* **02-36:** *On the Sunny Side of the Street* by Joachim Bub & Wilhelm Landt © The Soulcage Department **02-37:** *ƒ8* **03-01:** *Puppet* © 2001-2004 by Anzovin Studio. All rights reserved. *~ Dragons* by Leif Arne Petersen & Alex Hupperich *~ ƒ8* **03-02:** *Theme Planet ~ Love Tricycle* © 2003 Andrew Goode/Pacific Film & Television Commission. Concept art by Cameron Small *~* © Alexander Camargo *~* Bart Goldman **03-03:** Oswald Piras *~ Lunch ~ Polygon Family 2* **03-04:** *Stuart Little* © 1999 Sony Pictures. Dir: Rob Minkoff *~ El Arquero ~ L'Autre Temps* by Thomas Delcloy, Vanessa Lamblet, Celine Lardet © Supinfocom Valenciennes **03-05:** *Ritterschlag ~ Top Gum ~* Jeremy Cantor **03-06:** *Dronez ~ Ratchet & Clank* (video game) developed by Insomniac Games, published by Sony Computer Entertainment America *~ Puppy Love* by Raul Chavez **03-07:** *Das Rad ~ Killer Bean 2 ~ Bert* **03-08:** *Grinning Evil Death ~ Stuart Little* © 1999 Sony Pictures. Dir: Rob Minkoff *~* **03-10:** *ƒ8* **03-11:** *Das Rad* **03-12:** *Eternal Gaze* by Sam Chen *~ Sarah* by Justine Bonnard, Anthony Malagutti, Ludovic Ramiere, Thomas Renault © Supinfocom Valenciennes **03-13:** *Fishman* **03-14:** *Within an Endless Sky* © 2002 Lance S. Winkel **03-15:** *Passing Moments* **03-16:** *Pump Action ~ The Terrible Tragedy of Virgil & Maurice* **03-18:** *Egg Cola* **03-19:** *Hubert's Brain* **03-20:** *Polar Bears: Gary's Fall* © Pierre Coffin, Passion Pictures, Tiger Aspect, BBC *~ Cane-Toad* by David Clayton & Andrew Silke **03-21:** *The Butterfly* **03-23:** *When Wolfy Met Helga* by Mookie Weisbrod, Ringling School of Art & Design *~ Mouse ~ Yeah! The Movie* by Vadim Pietrzynski, Spellcraft Studio *~ On the Sunny Side of the Street* **03-24:** *The Freak ~* Jeremy Cantor *~ On the Sunny Side of the Street ~ Le Processus ~ But No One Cares* © 2002 Glen Thorpe **03-25:** *The Hare as Interpreter* by Istvan Zorkoczy, Red Goat Animation Studio *~ Mickey's Buddy* by Pete Paquette *~ Kami* by Lionel Catry, Julien Charles, Nicolas Launay, Olivier Pautot © Supinfocom Valenciennes *~ Pom Pom ~ O Lobisomem e o Coronel* by Krishnamurti Martins Costa **03-26:** *Values ~ Poor Bogo ~ Repete ~* Laurent Pierlot *~ ƒ8 ~ Eat Your Peas ~ Sahari ~ Moosin' Around* by Saul Freed *~ Iceland* by Leif Arne Petersen, Sascha Roman Robitzki, Lucas "Lotte" Wendler, Ken Tonio Yamamoto *~ L'Autre Temps* **03-27:** *Bert ~ Framed ~ Venice Beach* by Jung-Ho Kim *~ Greynautz* by Sebastian Mayer, pictoys & Annette Brinkmann, KW43 *~ Eternal Gaze ~ Senza Azione* by Krishnamurti Martins Costa *~ The Terrible Tragedy of Virgil & Maurice* **03-28:** *Senza Azione ~ Love Tricycle ~ Fifty Percent Grey* **03-30:** *Mouse ~* Avi Goodman *~ O Lobisomem e o Coronel* **03-31:** *Theme Planet* **03-32:** Jeremy Cantor *~ Values ~ Squaring Off* by Jeremy Cantor *~ Kami ~ Toilet ~ Tom the Cat* **03-33:** *Framed ~ The Instant Animator Machine* © Rick May, Toonstruck Animation *~ Fluffy* © Doug Aberle, Aberle Films **03-34:** Kirill Spiridonov **03-35:** *Lunch* **03-36:** *ƒ8* **03-39:** clipart.com **03-40:** clipart.com (images 2 & 3) **03-42:** Edu Martin (bottom row) **03-45:** Broderick Macaraeg (image 1) **03-46:** © 2004 Jason Taylor *~ La Mort de Tau* © Jerome Boulbes/Lardux Films **03-47:** *Senza Azione ~ The Instant Animator Machine ~ Sr. Trapo* © Pasozebra Producciones, S.L. **03-48:** *Tom the Cat ~ The Hare as Interpreter ~* Edu Martin **03-49:** *Run, Dragon, Run!!! ~ ƒ8* **03-50:** *Run, Dragon, Run!!! ~ Mouse ~ Ratchet & Clank ~* Avi Goodman **03-51:** *Sahari ~ Le Puits* © Jerome Boulbes/Lardux Films **03-52:** *Paf le Moustique* by Jerome Calvet & Jean Fracois Bourrel **03-53:** Edu Martin *~ Mickey's Buddy ~ Dear Sweet Emma* by John Cernak & Loraine Cernak © Out of Our Minds Images *~ Respire ~ The Cathedral* **03-54:** © 2003 Jeff Cooperman **03-55:** *Fishman ~ Iceland ~ Theme Planet* **03-56:** *Passing Moments* **03-58:** *Egg Cola ~ Fishman ~ Pump Action* **03-59:** *O Lobisomem e o Coronel* **03-60:** *Funambule* by Florent Leibovici **03-63:** Broderick Macaraeg (image 1) **03-64:** *But No One Cares ~ Love Tricycle ~ Traffic Jam* © 2002 Ty Primosch & Karen Mathieson **03-65:** *La Mort de Tau* **03-66:** *Run, Dragon, Run!!! ~ Ratchet & Clank* **03-67:** *Run, Dragon, Run!!! ~ Rascagnes* © Jerome Boulbes/Lardux Films *~ Senza Azione* **03-69:** *Polar Bears: Gary's Fall ~* Laurent Pierlot **03-71:**

Eat Your Peas **03-72:** Bart Goldman **03-73:** *Pump Action* **03-74:** *Sahari* **04-01:** *Poor Bogo ~ The Cathedral ~ Au Petite Mort ~ Dragons ~* **04-02:** *Plumber* by Andy Knight & Richard Rosenman (dir) and Randi Yaffa (prod) *~ Run, Dragon, Run!!! ~ The Freak ~ Poor Bogo ~ Love Tricycle* **04-04:** *Le Puits ~* Oswald Piras *~ Recycle Bein' ~ Rustboy* **04-05:** *Respire ~ Poor Bogo ~ La Piedra* by Alex Mateo *~ Iceland* **04-06:** *Baby Changing Station* by Keith Osborn *~ Eternal Gaze* **04-07:** *Early Bloomer* © 2003 Sony Pictures Imageworks. Dir: Kevin Johnson *~ f8* **04-08:** *It's Alive* by Terry Ziegelman & Paul George *~ It's Alive ~ Jabberwocky* by William McCrate © Vancouver Film School *~ Sally Burton* by Anna Kubik. Produced by Georg Gruber. **04-09:** *Sam* by Kyle Winkelman, Joshua Merck, Ginka Kostova, Robin Beauchamp, Raphael Phillips*Rascagnes* © Jerome Boulbes/Lardux Films **04-10:** Edward Ewing (image 2) **04-11:** *Bunny* © 1998 Twentieth Century Fox. All rights reserved. Dir: Chris Wedge *~ The Hare as Interpreter ~ Kami* **04-12:** *Sam ~ Love Tricycle* **04-13:** *Rustboy ~ Alma* by Juan Carlos Larrea **04-14:** *Mickey's Buddy ~ On the Sunny Side of the Street* **04-15:** *Sr. Trapo* **04-16:** *Sarah* **04-17:** *Where is Frank?* © 2001 Angela Jedek *~ Mouse* **04-18:** *Pump Action ~ Respire ~ L'Enfant de la Haute Mer ~ Senza Azione* **04-19:** *f8 ~* Edward Ewing **04-20:** *Coffee Love* **04-21:** *Hubert's Brain ~ After You* © 2004 Chris Cordingly *~ Framed* **04-22:** *Fifty Percent Grey ~ La Mort de Tau* **04-23:** *The Freak ~ Framed ~ The Cathedral ~ O Lobisomem e o Coronel ~ grain.S ~ Run, Dragon, Run!!!* **04-24:** *Le Musicien* by Patrick Ermosilla, Pierre Lasbignes, Cédric Stephan, Julien Ngo-Dit-Gaston *~ El Arquero ~ Le Musicien* **04-25:** *Hubert's Brain ~ The Instant Animator Machine ~ Plumber ~ Fishman Unleaded* by Dan Bransfield *~ Pump Action* **04-26:** *Senza Azione ~ Sr. Trapo* **04-27:** *The Terrible Tragedy of Virgil and Maurice ~ Within an Endless Sky* © 2002 Lance S. Winkel *~ Tom the Cat* **04-28:** *Run, Dragon, Run!!!* **04-29:** *Puppet ~ Silhouette* **04-30:** *AP2000 ~ Respire ~ Bunkie & Booboo* by Terrence Masson **04-31:** *Au Petite Mort ~ L'Autre Temps ~ Sarah* **04-32:** *IT* © 2002 Zbygniew Lenard **04-33:** *Le Processus ~ Le Deserteur* **04-34:** Edward Ewing **04-35:** *Tom the Cat ~ Polygon Family 2* **04-36:** *The Cathedral* **04-37:** *Respire* **04-38:** *L'Enfant de la Haute Mer* **04-39:** *grain.S* **04-40:** *Poor Bogo* **04-41:** *Love Tricycle ~ Bert* **04-43:** *Monkey Pit* by Jeff Fowler *~ Pom Pom ~ Lunch ~ Sr. Trapo ~ Run, Dragon, Run!!! ~ AP2000* **04-44:** *Grinning Evil Death* **04-45:** *O Lobisomem e o Coronel* **04-46:** *Rustboy ~ The Terrible Tragedy of Virgil & Maurice ~ La Mort de Tau* **04-47:** *Guernica* **04-48:** *Theme Planet* **05-01:** *The Terrible Tragedy of Virgil & Maurice* **05-02:** *Coffee Love ~ Le Puits ~ Au Petite Mort ~ Respire* **05-03:** *Bert ~ Run, Dragon, Run!!!* **05-05:** *Toilet ~ Top Gum* **05-06:** clipart.com **05-07:** *Eat Your Peas ~ Monkey Pit ~ Mickey's Buddy ~ Run, Dragon, Run!!! ~ The Terrible Tragedy of Virgil & Maurice ~ Pom Pom ~ Mickey's Buddy ~ Respire ~ Sahari* **05-08:** *Plumber ~ Respire* **05-09:** *Eat Your Peas* **05-10:** clipart.com **05-11:** *The Terrible Tragedy of Virgil & Maurice* **05-12:** *Respire* **05-13:** *Sahari* **05-14:** *Run, Dragon, Run!!!* **05-15:** *Bert* **05-16:** *The Snowman* © 2001 Duck Soup Studios. Dir: Lane Nakamura **05-18:** *The Terrible Tragedy of Virgil & Maurice* **05-19:** *On the Sunny Side of the Street* **05-20:** *Pump Action* **05-22:** *Bert ~ La Mort de Tau ~ La Mort de Tau ~ Sahari ~ On the Sunny Side of the Street* **05-23:** *Le Puits ~ Run Dragon Run!!! ~ Respire* **05-25:** *Sahari* **05-26:** *Sahari* **05-27:** *Sahari ~ Fluffy ~ Pom Pom ~ Run, Dragon, Run!!!* **05-28:** *Venice Beach* **05-29:** *Le Puits* **05-30:** clipart.com **05-31:** clipart.com **05-32:** clipart.com **06-01 through 06-12:** *The Terrible Tragedy of Virgil & Maurice* **07-01:** *Occasio* **07-02:** *Cane-Toad* **07-04:** *Venice Beach* **07-05:** *Pump Action* **07-06:** *Le Musicien* **07-07:** *Venice Beach* **07-08:** *Grinning Evil Death ~ Mouse* **07-09:** clipart.com **07-10:** *grain.S* **07-12:** *f8* **07-13:** *The Cathedral ~ Venice Beach ~ Guernica* **07-14:** *Out of Memory* by Eddy Moussa **07-15:** *Theme Planet* **07-18:** *f8 ~ Henry's Garden*, courtesy Moon Seun & Kevin Geiger *~ Bert* **07-19:** *Lunch ~ Occasio* **07-20:** *Pump Action* **07-32:** *Bert* **07-42:** clipart.com **07-43:** *f8* **08-01 through 08-10:** *Silhouette* **09-01:** *Early Bloomer ~ The Deadline* © 2001 Aardman Animation Ltd. **09-02:** *Horses on Mars* by Eric Anderson *~ Cane-Toad* **09-04:** *Eat Your Peas* **09-05:** *Eat Your Peas* **09-06:** *Monkey Pit* **09-07:** *Mickey's Buddy* **09-10:** clipart.com **09-11:** *Fishman ~ Dronez ~ Run, Dragon, Run!!! ~ Pump Action ~ Venice Beach* **09-12:** *Pot Bellie Pete* **09-13:** *Mickey's Buddy ~ Greynautz* **09-14:** clipart.com **09-19:** *Sahari* **09-20:** *Eat Your Peas ~ The Snowman* **10-01:** *Oblivious* **10-02:** *Pom Pom* **10-03:** clipart.com **10-06:** *Poor Bogo* **10-08:** *Sahari* **10-09:** *Sahari* **10-10:** *On the Sunny Side of the Street* **11-01:** *Iceland* **11-02:** *Cane-Toad* **11-03:** *Guernica* **11-04:** *Dronez* **11-15:** *Plumber ~ Pom Pom* **11-16:** *Bert* **11-17:** *Dronez ~ Baby Changing Station* **11-29:** *Tom the Cat ~ Alma* **11-32:** *Eat Your Peas* **11-33:** *El Arquero* **11-34:** *Hiccup 101* **11-35:** *Bert* **12-01:** *Eternal Gaze ~* Edu Martin *~* Edu Martin *~ Eat Your Peas* **12-02:** *The Butterfly* **12-03:** *Pom Pom ~ Fluffy ~ The Dog Who Was a Cat Inside* **12-04:** Avi Goodman **12-05:** *The Cathedral* **12-06:** *Ritterschlag* **12-08:** Broderick Macaraeg **12-09:** *Pump Action ~ Paf le Moustique ~ Le Musicien* **12-10:** *Values* **12-11:** *Cane-Toad* **12-12:** Hun Chung *~* Daniel Martinez Lara **12-13:** *The Hare as Interpreter ~ Ritterschlag ~ Senza Azione* **12-14:** Oswald Piras **12-15:** Renato dos Anjos **12-16:** *Eternal Gaze* **12-17:** *Money for Nothing ~ Squaring Off* by Jeremy Cantor **12-18:** *Eternal Gaze* **12-19:** *Alien Song ~ Pump Action* **12-20:** *Henry's Garden* **12-21:** *Garden of the Metal* (image 2) **12-22:** *The Cathedral* **12-23:** *Pump Action* **12-24:** *After You* **12-25:** *Venice Beach* **12-27:** *Ritterschlag* **12-28:** *f8* **12-29:** *Rustboy* **12-30:** *Megacycles* by John

Amanatides & Don Mitchell (AT&T Bell Labs) **13-01:** *Rustboy ~ Sr. Trapo* **13-02:** *Senza Azione* **13-03:** *Eat Your Peas ~ L'Enfant de la Haute Mer ~ Kami ~ L'Autre Temps* **13-04:** *Pump Action* **13-05:** *Toilet ~ Grinning Evil Death* **13-07:** *Pops* by David Earl Smith ~ *Where is Frank?* **13-08:** *Sr. Trapo* **13-10:** Edward Ewing (images 3 & 4) **13-11:** *Fluffy* **13-12:** *The Mantis Parable* by Josh Staub **13-13:** *The Mantis Parable* **13-16:** *Sahari* **13-18:** *Eat Your Peas* **13-19:** *Senza Azione* **13-20:** *Paf le Moustique ~ After You* **13-21:** *The Cathedral* **13-22:** *The Hare as Interpreter* **14-01:** *grain.S* (image 2) **14-02:** *Mickey's Buddy* **14-15:** *Guernica ~ The Hare as Interpreter* **14-20:** *Henry's Garden ~ grain.S* **14-21:** *Pom Pom* **14-22:** *Mickey's Buddy ~ Guernica* **14-23:** *Ritterschlag* **14-24:** *Senza Azione* **14-25:** *Sahari* **15-02:** Pete Paquette **15-03:** *After You ~ Poor Bogo ~ Mickey's Buddy ~ Passing Moments ~ Eat Your Peas* **16-01:** Edu Martin **16-02:** *Bunkie & Booboo* **16-05:** *f8 ~ But No One Cares ~ IT* **16-07:** *Moosin' Around ~ BIOS* by Nils Engler, Hannes Geiger, Mathis Lex, Tobias Weigand **16-08:** *El Arquero ~ Eat Your Peas* **16-09:** *Monkey Pit ~ Where is Frank? ~ Sr. Trapo ~ Au Petite Mort* **16-10:** *The Butterfly* **16-12:** *Lunch* **16-14:** *Baby Changing Station ~ The Terrible Tragedy of Virgil & Maurice* **16-15:** *Greynautz ~ Run, Dragon, Run!!! ~ Sahari* **16-16:** *The Butterfly* **16-17:** *Funambule* **16-18:** *Iceland ~ Pump Action* **16-19:** Avi Goodman ~ *Polar Bears: Gary's Fall ~* Avi Goodman ~ *La Piedra ~ Monkey Pit ~ L'Autre Temps* **16-20:** *Guernica* **16-21:** clipart.com **16-37:** *On the Sunny Side of the Street ~ Sahari ~ Venice Beach ~ Greynautz ~ Lots of Robots* by Andy Murdock **16-39:** *I'm Walking* © The Soulcage Department **16-40:** *Toilet ~ Lunch ~ The Butterfly* **16-41:** *Henry's Garden* **16-42:** *Senza Azione ~ Eat Your Peas* **16-44:** *Das Rad ~ Eat Your Peas* **16-46:** *Squaring Off* by Jeremy Cantor ~ *Senza Azione* **16-47:** *Alien Song ~ Moosin' Around* **16-49:** *On the Sunny Side of the Street* **16-50:** *Tom the Cat ~ Ritterschlag* **16-51:** *Puppy Love* **16-52:** clipart.com **16-53:** *Tom the Cat* **18-01:** *El Greco ~* Francisco de Goya **18-02:** *f8 ~ Le Puits ~ O Lobisomem e o Coronel ~ Sally Burton ~ Respire ~ The Cathedral ~ Out of Memory ~ Henry's Garden ~ Rustboy* **18-03:** *Sahari ~ Theme Planet* **18-04:** *Poor Bogo ~ Values* **18-05:** *Horses on Mars ~ Tinny Tom and the Magic Box* by Michiel Krop, Stijn Windig © Lemonade Animation ~ *Polygon Family 2* **18-06:** *BIOS* **18-07:** *One by Two* **18-08:** *Le Puits* **18-09:** *Mouse ~ Puppet ~ It's Alive* **18-10:** *Lots of Robots* **18-11:** *Respire* **18-19:** *f8 ~ I'm Walking* **18-20:** *I'm Walking ~ Dragons* **18-21:** *Bunny ~ It's Alive* **18-22:** *La Mort de Tau ~ Le Musicien ~ Sr. Trapo* **18-23:** *The Hare as Interpreter ~ Greynautz ~ Where is Frank? ~ L'Enfant de la Haute Mer* **18-24:** *I'm Walking ~ Top Gum* **18-25:** *Mickey's Buddy* **18-26:** *Pump Action* **18-27:** *Jabberwocky ~ Puppy Love* **18-28:** *After You* **18-29:** Daniel Martinez Lara **18-31:** *Paf le Moustique* **18-32:** Edward Ewing (images 3 & 4) **18-33:** *The Mantis Parable* **18-34:** *Pump Action* **18-35:** *Guernica* **19-03:** *But No One Cares ~ Respire* **19-04:** *Occasio ~ Dragons ~ Mouse ~ Au Petite Mort* **19-05:** *AP2000* **19-06:** *Eternal Gaze ~ Monkey Pit ~ Yeah! The Movie ~ Polar Bears: Gary's Fall* **19-07:** *Paf le Moustique ~ Le Processus ~ Senza Azione* **19-08:** *Le Musicien* **19-09:** *The Butterfly* **19-11:** *Polygon Family 2* **19-12:** *Yeah! The Movie* **19-14:** clipart.com **19-15:** *Tinny Tom and the Magic Box* **20-01:** *The Cathedral* **20-03:** *Dronez ~* © 2004 Jason Taylor ~ *Venice Beach* **20-04:** *Run, Dragon, Run!!!* **20-05:** *On the Sunny Side of the Street* **20-06:** *The Cathedral* **20-07:** *Run, Dragon, Run!!!* **20-08:** *On the Sunny Side of the Street* **20-09:** *Run, Dragon, Run!!!* **20-10:** *Das Rad* **21-01:** *The Instant Animator Machine ~ Values* **21-02:** *Cane-Toad ~ O Lobisomem e o Coronel ~ Fishman Unleaded ~ Dragons ~ Lots of Robots* **21-03:** *Oblivious* **21-04:** clipart.com **21-05:** Pepe Valencia ~ clipart.com **21-09:** *Guernica ~ Moosin' Around* **22-01:** *I'm Walking ~ La Piedra ~ Grinning Evil Death ~ Dragons ~ Eat Your Peas* **22-02:** *Tom the Cat* **22-03:** *Top Gum ~ Puppy Love ~ Paf le Moustique ~ Puppet* **22-04:** *Silhouette ~ Henry's Garden* **22-05:** *Moosin' Around ~ One by Two* **22-06:** *Sahari* **22-07:** *Eternal Gaze* **22-08:** *The Snowman* **22-09:** *Hiccup 101* **22-10:** *The Butterfly* **22-11:** *La Piedra ~ Fishman Unleaded ~ Top Gum* **23-01 through 23-08** *Early Bloomer* **24-01:** *The Instant Animator Machine ~ Pops ~ The Butterfly* **24-02:** *Cane-Toad ~ Monkey Pit* **24-03:** *Rustboy* © 2004 Brian Taylor **24-04:** *Pump Action* **24-05:** *Pump Action ~ The Freak ~ Greynautz ~ Dear Sweet Emma* **24-06:** *Venice Beach* **24-07:** *The Hare as Interpreter ~ Framed*

appendix E
DVD Contents

Table E.1 Elegant Simplicity

Title	*Creator(s)*	*Time*
Bert	Moonsung Lee	4:29
The Butterfly	©2003 Leonid Larionov	2:31
Squaring Off	Jeremy Cantor	1:21
Framed	Eric Carney, De Anza College	2:30
Toilet	Makoto Koyama	0:22
Values	Van Phan, University of Southern California, School of Film and Television	4:34

Table E.2 Science Fiction and Fantasy

Title	*Creator(s)*	*Time*
f8 (excerpt)	Jason Wen ©2004 Spot of Bother LLC	1:14
Oblivious	Alex Whitney, Ringling School of Art and Design	0:43
El Arquero	Raphael Perkins ©Vancouver Film School	2:07
The Snowman	Lane Nakamura ©2001 Duck Soup Studios	4:44
Eat Your Peas	Paul Hargrave, Ringling School of Art and Design	1:55
The Terrible Tragedy of Virgil and Maurice	©Morgan Kelly, California Institute of the Arts	4:30

Table E.3 Just Plain Fun

Title	*Creator(s)*	*Time*
Tom the Cat	Bastien Charrier, Patrick Jean, Lucas Salton, Neila Terrien ©Supinfocom Valenciennes	5:17
Sahari	©Francois De Bue	2:47
Run, Dragon, Run!!! (excerpt)	Ricardo Biriba, The Academy of Art College, San Francisco	0:50
Polygon Family 2	Hiroshi Chida	3:06
Pom Pom	Laurent Caneiro	1:53
Fishman Unleaded	Dan Bransfield	3:39

Table E.4 Artsy and Surreal

Title	Creator(s)	Time
Au Petite Mort (excerpt)	Jerry van de Beek ©2003 Little Fluffy Clouds, Jerry van de Beek and Betsy De Fries	0:36
Guernica	Marcelo Ricardo Ortiz ©2002 Vancouver Film School, "The Chauffer," written by Le Bon, Rhodes, Taylor, Taylor, and Taylor, performed by Duran Duran	3:44
Poor Bogo	Thelvin Cabezas, Ringling School of Art and Design	1:39
Garden of the Metal	Hitoshi Akayama, Katsuyuki Kamei, Koichi Nishi	2:43
Coffee Love	©2002 Ty Primosch	1:37
grain.S	Cédric Nicolas and Vincent Meyer ©2002 Sapokruteno	6:05

Table E.5 On the Darker Side

Title	Creator(s)	Time
Cane-Toad	David Clayton and Andrew Silke	3:59
Silhouette	©Tonya Noerr and Amber Rudolph, Ringling School of Art and Design	2:06
Puppet	Raf Anzovin ©2001–2004 by Anzovin Studio. All rights reserved.	2:31
Dear Sweet Emma	Loraine Cernak and John Cernak ©Out of Our Minds Animation Studios, Inc.	5:16
Pump Action	Phil (Captain 3D) McNally	4:03
Bios	Nils Engler, Hannes Geiger, Mathis Lex, Tobias Weigand	3:47

Table E.6 On the Lighter Side

Title	Creator(s)	Time
On the Sunny Side of the Street	Wilhelm Landt and Joachim Bub ©The Soulcage Department	4:27
Respire	André Bessy, Jérome Combe, Stéphane Hamache ©2003 Virgin	3:49
Venice Beach (excerpt)	Jung-Ho Kim, California Institute of the Arts	1:39
Mickey's Buddy	Pete Paquette, Ringling School of Art and Design	1:50
Top Gum	Victor Vinyals	2:19
Baby Changing Station	Keith Osborn, Ringling School of Art and Design	1:23

Table E.7 Animatics

Title	Creator(s)	Time
Pom Pom (2D animatic)	Laurent Caneiro	1:30
Sahari (2D animatic; silent)	©Francois De Bue	3:00
El Arquero (3D animatic; silent)	Raphael Perkins ©Vancouver Film School	1:40

E. DVD Contents

456

Index

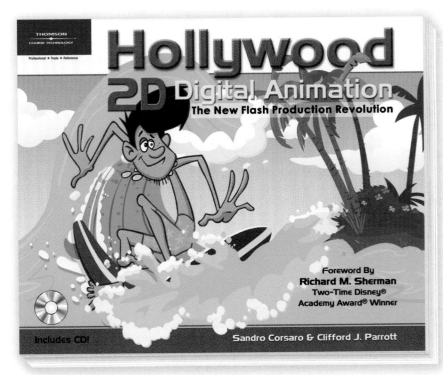

License Agreement/Notice of Limited Warranty

By opening the sealed disc container in this book, you agree to the following terms and conditions. If, upon reading the following license agreement and notice of limited warranty, you cannot agree to the terms and conditions set forth, return the unused book with unopened disc to the place where you purchased it for a refund.

License:

The enclosed software is copyrighted by the copyright holder(s) indicated on the software disc. You are licensed to copy the software onto a single computer for use by a single user and to a backup disc. You may not reproduce, make copies, or distribute copies or rent or lease the software in whole or in part, except with written permission of the copyright holder(s). You may transfer the enclosed disc only together with this license, and only if you destroy all other copies of the software and the transferee agrees to the terms of the license. You may not decompile, reverse assemble, or reverse engineer the software.

Notice of Limited Warranty:

The enclosed disc is warranted by Thomson Course Technology PTR to be free of physical defects in materials and workmanship for a period of sixty (60) days from end user's purchase of the book/disc combination. During the sixty-day term of the limited warranty, Thomson Course Technology PTR will provide a replacement disc upon the return of a defective disc.

Limited Liability:

THE SOLE REMEDY FOR BREACH OF THIS LIMITED WARRANTY SHALL CONSIST ENTIRELY OF REPLACEMENT OF THE DEFECTIVE DISC. IN NO EVENT SHALL THOMSON COURSE TECHNOLOGY PTR OR THE AUTHOR BE LIABLE FOR ANY OTHER DAMAGES, INCLUDING LOSS OR CORRUPTION OF DATA, CHANGES IN THE FUNCTIONAL CHARACTERISTICS OF THE HARDWARE OR OPERATING SYSTEM, DELETERIOUS INTERACTION WITH OTHER SOFTWARE, OR ANY OTHER SPECIAL, INCIDENTAL, OR CONSEQUENTIAL DAMAGES THAT MAY ARISE, EVEN IF THOMSON COURSE TECHNOLOGY PTR AND/OR THE AUTHOR HAS PREVIOUSLY BEEN NOTIFIED THAT THE POSSIBILITY OF SUCH DAMAGES EXISTS.

Disclaimer of Warranties:

THOMSON COURSE TECHNOLOGY PTR AND THE AUTHOR SPECIFICALLY DISCLAIM ANY AND ALL OTHER WARRANTIES, EITHER EXPRESS OR IMPLIED, INCLUDING WARRANTIES OF MERCHANTABILITY, SUITABILITY TO A PARTICULAR TASK OR PURPOSE, OR FREEDOM FROM ERRORS. SOME STATES DO NOT ALLOW FOR EXCLUSION OF IMPLIED WARRANTIES OR LIMITATION OF INCIDENTAL OR CONSEQUENTIAL DAMAGES, SO THESE LIMITATIONS MIGHT NOT APPLY TO YOU.

Other:

This Agreement is governed by the laws of the State of Massachusetts without regard to choice of law principles. The United Convention of Contracts for the International Sale of Goods is specifically disclaimed. This Agreement constitutes the entire agreement between you and Thomson Course Technology PTR regarding use of the software.